The New Image of the Person

Contributions in Philosophy

Kant's Cosmogony: As in His Essay on the Retardation of the Rotation of the Earth and His Natural History and Theory of the Heavens
Immanuel Kant

The Platonic Method: An Interpretation of the Dramatic Philosophic Aspects of the "Meno"
Jerome Eckstein

Language and Value
Charles L. Todd and Russell T. Blackwood, eds.

Inquiries into Medieval Philosophy: A Collection in Honor of Francis P. Clarke
James F. Ross, ed.

The Vitality of Death: Essays in Existential Psychology and Philosophy
Peter Koestenbaum

Dialogues on the Philosophy of Marxism
Society for the Philosophical Study of Dialectical Materialism
John Somerville and Howard L. Parsons, eds.

The Peace Revolution: Ethos and Social Process
John Somerville

Marx and Engels on Ecology
Howard L. Parsons, ed. and comp.

The New Image of the Person

the Person

THE THEORY AND PRACTICE OF CLINICAL PHILOSOPHY

Peter Koestenbaum

Contributions in Philosophy, Number 9

GREENWOOD PRESS

WESTPORT, CONNECTICUT • LONDON, ENGLAND

Library of Congress Cataloging in Publication Data

Koestenbaum, Peter, 1928-
  The new image of the person.

  (Contributions in philosophy ; no. 9 ISSN 0084-926X)
  Bibliography: p.
  Includes index.
  1. Psychiatry—Philosophy. 2. Phenomenology.
3. Existentialism. 4. Anxiety. I. Title.
RC437.5.K63   157'.9   77-84764
ISBN 0-8371-9888-7

Library of Congress Catalog Card Number: 77-84764
ISBN: 0-8371-9888-7
ISSN: 0084-926X

First published in 1978

Greenwood Press, Inc.
51 Riverside Avenue, Westport, Connecticut 06880

Printed in the United States of America

10 9 8 7 6 5 4 3 2 1

ACKNOWLEDGMENTS

The quotations on pages 448-450 are reprinted from Werner M. Mendel, *Supportive Care: Theory and Technique*. Copyright © 1974 by Mara Books, Inc., Santa Monica, California. Used by permission of the publisher.

The excerpts from "Coleman: A Choice Cabinet Choice" and "Conquering the Quiet Killer" on page 165 are reprinted by permission from *Time*, The Weekly Newsmagazine; Copyright Time Inc. 1975.

The article "Time Has Healed Archie Connett" on pages 333-335 is from *San Jose Mercury News*, April 18, 1971. Reprinted by permission of the publisher.

The excerpt on pages 340-341 is from Howard D. McKinney and H. R. Anderson, *Music in History* (San Francisco: American Book Company, 1940), p. 184. Reprinted by permission of the publisher.

The excerpt on page 477 is from Irving Oyle, *The Healing Mind* (Millbrae, CA: Celestial Arts, 1975), pp. 75-76, 77. Reprinted by permission of the publisher.

The quote on page 264 is excerpted with the permission of Farrar, Straus & Giroux, Inc. from *Night* by Elie Wiesel. English translation copyright © 1960 by MacGibbon & Kee. Originally published in French by Les Editions de Minuit, Copyright © 1958.

The excerpt on pages 323-324 is from Jean-Paul Sartre, *Situations III*. Copyright © Editions Gallimard, 1949. Reprinted by permission of the publisher.

Appendix E is from Peter Koestenbaum, *Managing Anxiety: The Power of Knowing Who You Are* (Englewood Cliffs, N.J.: Prentice-Hall, 1974). Reprinted by permission of the publisher.

This book is dedicated to Alice Gutfeld

CONTENTS

PREFACE

The New Image of the Person has many purposes. First, it seeks to help establish clinical philosophy as a bona fide discipline, with both theoretical and practical orientations. It is a textbook for those who wish to practice clinical philosophy.

Clinical philosophy requires solid background in philosophy, especially what are here called the phenomenological model of being and the existential personality theory, and in psychology and psychiatry, especially clinical practice and experience in psychotherapy. Also emphasized are applications of the principles of clinical philosophy to disciplines other than therapy—including the larger issues facing humanity in the second half of the twentieth century.

The growth movement and other new dimensions in psychology, psychiatry, and pyschotherapy are a praxis in search of a theory. Phenomenology and existential philosophy—as serious philosophic undertakings—have developed mostly independently of progress in therapy. These two streams of our culture—phenomenology and existentialism as the theory and the growth movement as the praxis—not knowing each other have, nevertheless, synchronously prepared themselves for each other. The time to wed them is now. Clinical philosophy is thus the ideology of the growth movement.

The view of phenomenology and existentialism presented here is an *updated* version of a philosophic posture some feel is already one generation behind the times. For example, the affinity between phenomenology and Eastern thought has not yet been explored with the emphasis and detail it deserves. Eastern philosophies are full of insights that parallel those of transcendental phenomenology, and the application of these ideas to pyschotherapy has up to this point regrettably been minimal. One of the hopes expressed in this book is to fill this void.

Psychological personality tests and inventories should be based on the most reliable theory of the person available. Clinical philosophy hopes to state fully and systematically the view of human nature that is emerging from the history of ideas in our time. The *evidence* for the accuracy of this evolving image of the person is the cumulative, sensitive, and assumption-free description of the immediate experiences of what it means to exist as a human being in the world. Phenomenology has justified this approach as the one most likely to lead to the truth. Psychometrists can thus begin their work with the outline provided for them in *The New Image of the Person.*

The material in *The New Image of the Person* has been tested for several years in special intensive training seminars in clinical philosophy—an extensive and high-intensity program where therapists, physicians, nurses, teachers, professors, psychologists, graduate students, and others are being grounded and trained in the use of philosophy as a healing art.

Very special thanks are due to the participants in these seminars for their suggestions, examples, commitment, expertise, and their extraordinary integrity, character, and warmth.

Many have helped with the arduous tasks involved in the preparation of the manuscript. Especially high among them is Martha Culley. Thanks are also due to Jean Homan, Emi Nobuhiro, and Myrna Fabbri, and to Joseph Pearson for his work on the bibliography.

Peter Koestenbaum
San Jose, California

BOOK ONE **A Model of Being**

Part I • INTRODUCTION

Chapter 1 • *THE NEED FOR PHILOSOPHY IN PSYCHOTHERAPY*

Technique Is Not Enough

Willard L., M.D., is a psychiatrist specializing in "body work" and Molly P., Ph.D., is a psychologist with a splendid reputation as the area's most effective sex therapist. While to their profession and the public they seem eminently successful, both feel sucked dry by their patients and fear that they will in fact "die" if their anxious unconscious continues to respond as it has to the shadowy unconscious of some of their patients. Dr. L. suffers severely from allergies and has constant problems with skin rashes, whereas Dr. P. experiences depression and has on many occasions seriously contemplated and threatened suicide.

What is their problem? Both therapists appear to confuse technique, psychotherapy, and psychological theories of personality with philosophy. Both are superlatively experienced and competent in the use of many modern, highly imaginative and helpfully powerful growth techniques. But in most cases these techniques operate in a philosophical vacuum. Whatever theory is attached to the technique each happens to be using is minimal and narrow; it encompasses only a small region of being. A comprehensive philosophy, a philosophy of life, or a responsible model of being is neither understood nor considered important in their practice. When the technique has spent itself, when its usefulness is exhausted, there still remains a fragmented, aimless, and foundationless client-therapist relationship. The practitioners themselves have not found their direction, their hope, their meaning, or their security. Technique, especially when used well, nevertheless can lead both patient and practitioner to the very edge of a gaping abyss beyond which they cannot go. It is here that the psychosomatic symptom, the rash, and the psychological symptom, the suicidal depression, appear as defenses against ultimate anxiety. To appreciate and manage this dreadful emptiness, a comprehensive philosophy, a deepened understanding of human existence and of being in general is required.

There is a layer of human nature deeper than psychology. Neither the Oedipus complex nor the archetype, neither the inferiority complex nor the need for safety are the ultimate factors in a human existence. It is not enough to uncover childhood origins of present-day neuroses. Each final psychological cause or ultimate explanation is in turn a symptom, a metaphor, or a symbol for an even deeper, underlying philosophical condition; the symptom is a manifest expression of the less obvious, less picturesque but nevertheless generic malaise, challenge, and hope of what it means, to all of us, to be human.

The solution for the two therapists was a tendency, buttressed by the prevailing and culturally ensconced assumptions of the primacy of technique, to intensify that technique and, if that did not work, to seek alternative techniques. Their response to their own problems—in their practice and in their health—was to prescribe "more of the same." However, when a car does not start because it is out of gas, more pressure on the accelerator and more turning of the starter are of no avail. What is needed is a comprehensive philosophical statement which will place each technique in its proper place and context, a philosophy of life which will determine the purpose of and for the technique. Philosophy exists *in addition to* therapy, not *in lieu of* treatment. Philosophy deepens therapy; it does not replace it.

We must respond to these two friends and those like them—a large population. Technique, although important, fascinating, and spectacular, is not enough to achieve authenticity, self-actualization, meaning, and fulfillment. Technique and depth are not automatically connected. Their relationship is subtle and to implement it requires artistry. A simple way to point out the place of philosophy in therapy is to affirm the following: your symptom (whatever it may be—physical, behavioral, psychological, or social) is an expression of the fact that you are not taking personal and free responsibility for asking life's three basic philosophic questions—Who am I? What is my meaning? What is intimacy? The four relevant factors in this approach are *freedom, self-understanding, meaning,* and *love.*

But there are also those who deride techniques altogether and maintain that love, encounter, and committed relationships are sufficient to bring about desired therapeutic results. That is an untenable position. We *do* need love, care, and commitment from therapist or counselor to patient or client. But we also need a healer who is experienced and competent in the use of technique. Above all, however, we need a comprehensive philosophical grasp and understanding of the patient, his being-in-the-world, and the broader significance of human existence. It is here where philosophy and therapy can join efforts to create the new discipline of clinical philosophy.

Philosophy and Psychology

The philosophical positions of greatest relevance to psychology and psychiatry in general and to humanistic psychology and the growth movement in particular seem to be those of the phenomenological movement. Equally relevant are their applications to the analysis of the human condition carried out by existentialist philosophers, writers, and theologians in a discipline technically known as philosophical anthropology. It can be argued that the phenomenological movement in philosophy (in conjunction perhaps with its offshoot, existential philosophy) is not the prevailing doctrine on the contemporary academic scene. In terms of the philosophy of the establishment—as expressed in journals, meetings, and university departments—this may be quite correct. But in terms of the currents of history—as seen in the general culture and in student interest—this criticism is false or at least exaggerated. The desire to use philosophy to solve human problems has always been high, and the current phenomenological analyses of the human condition provide the most respectable theoretical ground available for a professional and systematic clinical philosophy. Philosophers have long dreamed of calculating rather than intuiting answers to philosophic problems. Symbolic logic was the result—an achievement that superseded two thousand years of Aristotelian logic. Similarly, philosophers have long hoped for a systematic theory of the person with highly specific and testable applications. Phenomenology and existentialism, coupled with the insights of Eastern philosophies, can help us realize this dream.

In short, the history of philosophy is not a mere disorderly accumulation of ideas but a progression to ever more sophisticated views about human nature and its place in the universe. The phenomenological movement, simply because it exists today and because it has a sense of both tradition and precision, is the culmination of the history of ideas. It is therefore reasonable to argue that phenomenology makes clinical philosophy possible.

THE PHENOMENOLOGICAL MODEL OF BEING

There are three expressions which when defined can help illuminate the relationship between philosophy, psychology, psychiatry, humanistic and transpersonal psychologies, and the growth movement in general. The first is the *phenomenological model of being.* This expression refers to the general metaphysical or ontological posture which underlies clinical philosophy. The epistemological language of the phenomenological movement expresses most comfortably the theoretical basis of clinical philosophy. However, the individual and the world are so closely linked that the rather obvious and elementary distinction between a philosophical anthropology (a theory of the person) and a complete metaphysics or ontology (a theory of reality) cannot easily be made.

The specifics of the relationship between a theory of being and a theory of the person are explicated through the concept, borrowed from phenomenology, of *constitution:* From the raw material of being is carved out the phenomenon of individuality and the concept of an ego (in Husserl's words, an egology). The fully integrated understanding of this point makes it possible for a person to take full responsibility for being himself. Thus, the constitution of the individual is the central issue in both the theory and the practice of psychotherapy. Conversely, the relationship between our conception of the uniqueness of the person and the plenitude of being is compressed in the phenomenological concept of *deconstitution:* By eliminating or putting out of action the assumptions implicit in the experience of being an isolated ego, the experience of surrender to the world emerges, and with it arises the sense of oneness with the universe. The psychotherapeutic significance of deconstitution is that it provides the security needed as the absolute beginning for a successful life and the strength required for growth and change to occur in therapy. This point also provides the sense of peace and eternity that may well be the answer to suffering and anxiety about death. Security, which can result from the deconstitution of the individual, [1] is a second central issue in therapy.

If we must make a decision on priorities, we may be inclined to hold that a theory of being precedes a theory of the person. In any choice about metaphysical truth, we might well opt for the primacy of being over the individual. The phenomenological model of being is therefore a specific description of those fundamental characteristics of being that are of unique relevance to the process of applying the insights of philosophy to the problems of meaningful living and, as a derivative, to practicing psychotherapy and in some respects medicine also. In particular, questions of ground or foundation (that is, self-confidence, self-esteem, strength, self-love, and so forth), and the related issue of death (which includes the problem of immortality and reincarnation), as well as the entire spectrum of problems concerning individual identity, can be answered systematically and responsibly in terms of a phenomenological model of being. That model connects the phenomenological movement, which is the current apogee of Western thought, with the inspired and profound collection of world views which make up the tradition of Eastern thought.

The phenomenological model of being and its relation to the healing arts is in great measure the topic of Book One.

THE EXISTENTIAL PERSONALITY THEORY

The second expression which can help define the relationship between philosophy and psychology is the *existential personality theory.* It refers to the philosophical anthropology or theory of man that emerges when we interpret the phenomenon of being human as an act which gathers its meaning and is derived from the above-mentioned general theory of being. The existential personality theory is essentially the subject matter of Book Two.

In many respects the phenomenological model of being and the existential personality theory coalesce and overlap, even though the first is distinctly an ontology and the second an anthropology.

PERSONALIZED EDUCATION IN PHILOSOPHY

The third expression which can clarify the meaning of clinical philosophy is *personalized education in philosophy*. It refers to the clinical, counseling, or therapeutic uses of the phenomenological model of being and the existential personality theory. Whereas personalized education in philosophy may overlap conventional psychotherapy and psychiatry, it contains critical differences. Personalized education in philosophy makes diagnostic suggestions. However, philosophic descriptions in psychopathology will be different from conventional psychological analyses. Furthermore, many patients treated today with conventional therapy or medicine are in truth people who suffer from philosophical conditions, rather than psychological diseases; they suffer from the basic problems of life (such as responsibility, love, and death) and need philosophical insight and help. Diagnostic and treatment suggestions are given special emphasis in Book Three, although many of these are found also in Books One and Two (in the chapters on coping devices).

Each normal and healthy person suffers from conditions that are essential to existence itself and respond only to appropriate philosophic insight. References to unfinished childhood business, unresolved Oedipal conflicts, inferiority complexes, and the like, as well as the techniques of free association, dream analysis, and active listening, useful as these are, are nevertheless of limited value in helping people with their deepest problems. In addition, what is valuable in personalized education in philosophy is the solid perspective on the total human condition made possible by the phenomenological model of being and the existential personality theory.

A therapist must be practiced and experienced. But he must also have sufficient command over the basic structure of human existence to assess any situation accurately and to improvise imaginatively, if necessary. Such control over therapy is made possible by clinical philosophy. Each person is alike in his or her essential philosophical structure. Understanding that insight gives confidence and competence to the therapist. But the pictures in terms of which each person feels and thinks of his or her life are different. Freud and Jung, Adler and Rank, Reich and Sullivan, Horney and Erikson—all these and others have made helpful contributions to the conceptualization of individual differences. But the truly creative therapist will invent a distinct psychology for each of his patients. One may find Freud's visualization helpful; another may respond to Jung's. But the modern therapist need not stop there. Psychological theories of personality can be generated at will, provided the therapist has a flair for creative imagination. The outlines for these imaginative and personalized inventions of psychological theories are garnered by the phenomenological model of being and the ensuing existential personality theory. It is therefore of great importance that responsible therapists understand the philosophic foundations of their practice.

The Role of Metaphor

An important aspect of clinical philosophy is understanding the role of metaphor. "Metaphor," "symbol," "myth," and "symptom" are used interchangeably. Many bona fide psychological and psychiatric problems are best understood as expressions, manifestations, or metaphors for a larger, deeper, and more pervasive existential situation. The same can be said for religion, which might be called a necessary myth to live by, with "myth" used in the old sense of truth rather than its modern meaning of falsehood. Figure 1 illustrates this point. The "literal" truth about being and about persons—abstract and unadorned—is expressed in philosophy as the phenomenological model of being. To manage that truth we need metaphor and symbol, myth and symptom. The philosophic truth is so important that we regress (or progress) to the simplest (and perhaps most effective) forms of picture thinking. Then we can integrate these philosophic insights into our lives in the forms of adaptation, medicine, therapy, and hope. Roughly speaking, when we use the body and its behavior as a symbol for philosophic truth, we get the important and useful mythology of psychology. When, on the other hand, we use spirit as a root-symbol, we get the mytho-

Figure 1

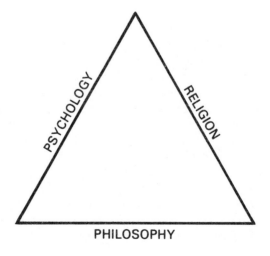

PHILOSOPHY

logy of religion and theology. Psychology and religion—depending on taste, disposition, and upbringing—can serve equally well to manage in metaphoric form the basic questions of philosophy.

For example, a child, whose mother wanted to abort her, is nevertheless born and grows up feeling rejected and worthless. Rollo May describes such a case touchingly when he writes,

This patient, an intelligent woman of twenty-eight, was especially gifted in express-ing what was occurring within her. She had come for psychotherapy because of serious anxiety spells in closed places, severe self-doubts, and eruptions of rage which were sometimes uncontrollable. An illegitimate child, she had been brought up by relatives in a small village in the southwestern part of the country. Her mother, in periods of anger, often reminded her as a child of her origin, recounted how she had tried to abort her, and in times of trouble had shouted at the little girl, "If you hadn't been born, we wouldn't have to go through this!" Other relatives had cried at the child, in family quarrels, "Why didn't you kill yourself?" and "You should have been choked the day you were born!"[2]

In conventional psychotherapy, it may be assumed that the patient's sense of worthlessness and the ensuing symptomatology result directly from the rejection and deprivation she suffered during her childhood. But from the point of view of clinical philosophy the actual situation is quite different: The sense of worth derives ultimately from experiencing one's ontological foundation, *a ground which is always there but is not always perceived.* Mother-love in early childhood *facilitates* this perception and illustrates this universal fact of existence, this philosophic discovery available to everyone at all times. But mother-love does *not* produce, create, or bring about the reality of security. Security is not a psychological feeling but a philosophi-cal fact. It is not an empirical or psychological phenomenon, that is, a real-ity of the world of things and objects, of science, and of political realities, but is what we call a *transcendental* phenomenon, a metaphysical reality related to the structure of our very own consciousness and of the external world, which is always the object of that consciousness. A person is secure, grounded, and at home by virtue of his nature, because of his relationship to his consciousness and to the universe.

Some people are never taught this insight; others never come to this real-ization on their own or are deprived of the opportunity to pursue it. For-tunately, not one but many events in a person's life can teach this truth, ranging from warmly loving parents to a formal program in philosophy, from religion to poetry, from therapy to adversity. Parent-love does not *give* or *make* security. The sense of foundation is not a feeling but a fact, an ontological fact which can be illuminated and brought to life through a loving and supportive environment. However, the reality of our ontological foundation must be not only experienced emotionally but also clarified intellectually. But the reality of that fact is nevertheless independent of and prior to the happenstance of a good childhood.

An extremely important corollary follows from this analysis. If a "good" mother, a security-facilitating mother, is absent, then we can make up for it in later life! There is always hope. If we go one level deeper than psychological approaches permit, we discover a foundation, a home and answers at the core of every human being. This is where philosophic therapy must reach. We can reconstruct our childhood, re-create our early environment, and rewrite our most ancient scripts. The truth and the reality we seek is with us at this very moment. We need but learn to do philosophy—to explore in depth and without bias the structure of here-and-now experience, which in turn is the foundation of all knowledge—to uncover insights that are solutions to agonizing psychological problems. In this way there are answers and solutions for everyone. We need no longer feel harnessed by the circumstances of our childhood and our culture. In other words, every person is *worthy, safe, and secure due to his or her nature and not by virtue of the idiosyncrasies of a particular childhood or environment.* This principle is very important and it should work wherever there is a will or a motivation or each time the decision to cope is freely made. It is an insight which should be made available to children through bedtime stories and early school experiences and to the general population through the media. Health thus rests on an absolute rather than a merely adventitious base. And every person, healthy or sick, can make that discovery for himself.

This is not the place to catalog examples. The principle, however, is of the greatest importance: Psychological explanations of human distress, especially when reference is made to its origin in early childhood, have an air of fatalism about them. It is thought that damage done in early life may well be irreversible. Conventional theories maintain that the adult is produced or caused by the child and we are all limited in our adulthood by the childhood circumstances over which we could exercise no control. The extent to which we can exert control on anything is itself presumed to be the result of very early childhood conditioning and opportunities. Without denying the power of these psychological insights, we must nevertheless also integrate into our thinking the fact that we are at this very moment—as well as always—free to discover our philosophic nature (which means we have access to our foundations) and free, on the basis of this security, to reconstruct our lives.

In contrast to fatalism, an approach based on clinical philosophy, schematized, holds that all persons are the same in that each individual has a uniform and absolute ontological structure. He can either know, experience, perceive, or be aware of that structure, or he can be ignorant of it. A healthy childhood taught him this essential structure; a deprived childhood hid that nature from him. The therapeutically useful principle behind this analysis is that *the philosophic facts about a person's essential human nature can be taught at any time.* The process of facilitating self-disclosure is not one of conditioning, modifying behavior, or introjecting social controls and psychological defenses. It is the act of permitting the discovery within oneself of what one truly is. This philosophy of personality is hope-giving rather than pessimistic, self-determining rather than fatalistic. And herein lies the role of philosophy in psychotherapy.

Another example of how philosophy deepens therapy lies in the interpretation of the Oedipus complex. Freud discovered that he could account for anxiety by organizing a person's life around the root metaphor of the Oedipus myth. Jung generalized Freud's insight—just as Bridgman, in *The Logic of Modern Physics,* generalized Einstein's operational approach to the concept of "simultaneity" found in Relativity Theory into an operationism for all terms used in physics—by showing that anxiety can be understood if we use any one of a very large number of the world's myths.

From the existential point of view it is false to say that a boy's fear of his father or betrayal by his mother is the cause of anxiety. It is false to say that an unresolved Oedipus complex produces anxiety, or that molestation in early childhood produces anxiety in later years. The existential position is that anxiety is always present, that a human being sits on a pool of anxiety the way an Arab sheik sits on a deposit of oil. The phobic has drilled a small hole to the pool; the anxiety neurotic or schizophrenic has fallen into the pool. The Oedipal situation *triggers* anxiety that is always present. It evokes, mobilizes, or reminds the person of anxiety which is pervasive, ubiquitous and at the core of his being. Through the Oedipal situation the child (or the adult in psychoanalysis) discovers the anxiety that is always there. It does not produce the anxiety or give the anxiety to the patient. Furthermore, its resolution does not eliminate the anxiety but serves as a model and metaphor on how one goes about coping with anxiety, defending oneself against it, or translating its experience into the excitement of life and the joy of meaning. Philosophy deepens psychology and psychiatry; it does not supplant it.

It follows from these considerations that a separate profession of clinical philosophy seems desirable. Preparation for it would include not only standard background in psychology, psychiatry, psychopathology, and the like, but also the systematic study of the humanities, with special emphasis on training in philosophy, its history, and the subsidiary fields of epistemology, phenomenology, philosophical anthropology, and existentialism. Hopefully, the program presented in these few pages is carried out in detail, explained with clarity, helpfully illustrated, thoughtfully substantiated, and applied adequately in the chapters that follow.

The Psychological Pyramid

A useful didactic tool to describe and explain the levels of insight achieved by psychology and philosophy is the Psychological Pyramid. The philosophic analysis of the human condition represents, ideally, the most literal (that is, least symbolic or metaphoric) statement possible. Whereas the phenomenological model of being and the existential personality theory may sound abstract and distant from immediate experience, in actuality, the reverse is true. Philosophy purports to describe, with as much accuracy and precision as possible, and devoid of needless adornment or seductive simile, such structures as human freedom, the nature of anxiety, the meaning of guilt, and so forth. These philosophical fundamentals are not ancillary observations; on the contrary, they make up the core and heart of what is anguished and what is hopeful in the human experience. Clinical philosophy, as the phenomenological model of being and the existential personality theory, is therefore the base of the pyramid of psychology. (See Figure 2.)

The management of these underlying philosophical realities is often relegated to metaphor. The direct and literal management of the underlying philosophic issues of life is both possible and useful; the fact remains, nevertheless, that most programs for handling such root philosophic issues as death, loneliness, responsibility, love, and fulfillment are in actual practice carried out through metaphor. These metaphors make up the second level of the Psychological Pyramid. But the "real" problem exists on the level of its exact philosophic formulation. The underlying issue is what is expressed literally in the philosophic statement. And that formulation or statement is in particular the phenomenological model of being as well as the existential personality theory.

Figure 2   The Psychological Pyramid

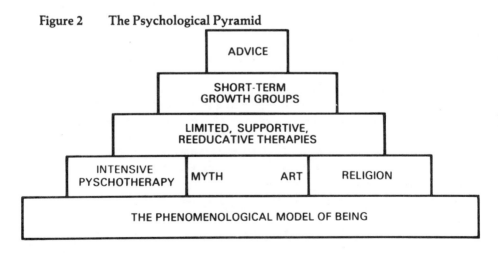

Let us expand on the triangle diagram (Figure 1). There are essentially three types of metaphors for the ultimate philosophic reality of being—the body, nature, and spirit. Each metaphor gives rise to its own characteristic therapeutic approach. When the metaphor is spirit, then the healing theory becomes religion and theology and the healing praxis is ritual and ceremony. This is not to say that religion is fraudulent. On the contrary, the metaphor must be accepted with utmost sincerity before it can function as the surrogate of philosophy.

The situation parallels the enjoyment of music. Perhaps Freud was right and music is the sublimation of sex and aggression. However, music can fulfill its surrogate role only when it is perceived as an intrinsic value and not thought of as merely second-best to the original satisfaction of experiencing sex and expressing aggression. Philosophy may thus be an intrinsic value whereas religion is an instrumental one (that is, instrumental to achieving philosophic insight), just as music may be our instrumental value for the more genuine (that is, intrinsic) experiences of sex and aggression. However, the present contention is that both music and religion, to be effective even as surrogates or instrumental values, must in fact be felt as intrinsic values. This view spells respect for religion without denying the primacy of philosophy.

If the metaphor for the philosophical condition of man is nature, then the healing theory becomes mythology and symbol, and its praxis is art, literature, and poetry. Mythology is therefore real in the same sense as religion and theology. Today one of the few contexts within which we take mythology seriously is in the use of archetypes for dream interpretation and of fairy tales as therapeutic paradigms. However, artistic, musical, and literary forms should be explained as creative and expressive ways of working through basic philosophic issues. The arts therefore exist on the same ontological level as does depth psychotherapy. The logical relation between the arts and philosophy is the same as that between depth or reconstructive psychotherapy and philosophy.

Finally, if the human body should be selected as the root metaphor for the philosophic truth or ground, then the healing process is expressed as intensive psychotherapy, especially in a psychoanalytic or reconstructive mode. We can say that the body is the root metaphor for the psychoanalytic model because some of the key psychoanalytic terms around which the image of human health is constructed involve primitive bodily functions (such as sucking, defecation, coitus), central organs (such as mouth, anus, genitals), and primitive physical relations and perversions (such as the primal scene, Oedipus complex, castration, separation, and incest). Psychoanalysis and other forms of depth psychotherapy are therefore as real as mythology, religion, and the arts. The success of psychoanalysis in working through basic philosophic issues (such as coping with negation and individuation—which is the philosophic equivalent of the Oedipal situation) depends on how seriously and effectively patients or clients can conceptualize themselves in terms of these basic bodily functions. We live in a culture accustomed to bodily, that is, physiological and behavioral, metaphors in psychology. That fact is connected to the general supremacy of the medical profession and the medical approach in our society. What specific metaphor is to be used in psychotherapy is merely a matter of intellectual convenience and pragmatic efficacy. In this matter, let the patient guide the clinician. On the other hand, there can be no harm in redirecting our culture away from metaphor and toward literalness. That would mean an increase in philosophic activity at all levels of society, beginning perhaps with early school instruction in philosophy.

The third tier in the Psychological Pyramid is relatively superficial therapy, examples of which would be supportive and reeducative psychotherapies. Their purpose is limited. They pour oil over troubled waters, but they do not seek to stop the storm. On the next level is even less intensive activity, namely, short-term growth groups, some of which may be no longer than a weekend. At the very top of the pyramid are the most shallow of the healing arts—advice and pep talks, found in many popular self-help books and in inspirational literature. Because the latter are the most visible and are easy to understand, they are also quite popular. Unfortunately, their long-lasting beneficial effects are severely limited.

As we rise in the pyramid, the structure narrows and the healing process increases in superficiality. The final solutions, if they are anywhere to be found, form the base of the pyramid and must be expressed philosophically. We are then in a position to decide what metaphor is best suited to us or, if we are therapists, which is best for each of our patients or clients. It is therefore quite readily possible to diagnose a client philosophically and as a result of that to propose a treatment strategy, a counseling direction, or even a didactic course. However, if we go beyond that philosophic foundation and into the more common types of psychological or therapeutic management, then we must in fact create a special psychology for each client. The goal of the phenomenological model of being and of the existential personality theory is to spell out, in as precise detail as language will permit, the base of this psychological pyramid. In this way we can learn to apply in practice the theory of clinical philosophy.

What, then, in the briefest of terms, is a clinical philosopher? A clinical philosopher invents a unique and different psychology for each one of his patients, clients, or students. He can do that by adding imagination to the fundamental picture of being over which his philosophic training has given him a comfortable overview and a sure command. He needs intelligence, good physical and mental health, devotion, wisdom, information, experience, and a highly developed and creative imagination. He needs strength, courage, and the willingness to be permissive enough to use all aspects of his personality in the authentic service of his clients. To do this, he can devote himself to only a few clients or students at any one time. That spirit is the essence of clinical philosophy.

Historical Diagnosis

Before concluding these introductory comments it is necessary to focus on an attempted simplified diagnosis of the present historical situation in terms of some of the categories of clinical philosophy.

It is tempting but also risky to diagnose our century as if we were future historians with the advantage of two or three centuries of hindsight. What are the primary issues that have shaped and will continue to influence the twentieth century? Those singled out are suggested by central themes derived from existential philosophy and phenomenology: death, freedom for self-definition, futurization or self-transcendence, self-disclosure, and the need to develop an orderly and comprehensive model of being and a philosophic personality theory.

DEATH

The world is facing its death. That is the first major development of long-lasting historical significance in twentieth-century culture. Denying one's death as an individual leads to self-deception and inauthenticity, whereas recognizing, accepting, confronting, and integrating it leads to authenticity, meaning, and courage. These existential insights into the structure of a person's life apply as well to mankind in general. In fact, extrapolated in this sense, their meaning is intensified, since the death-of-myself is conceptualized against a background of the continuation of civilization and of the world, whereas the death-of-the-world has no such reassuring horizon against which hope stands out. Thus, the first fact of the current world situation diagnosed existentially is that the world is dying. "World" in this sense is human life or at least civilized or quasi-civilized existence as we know it.

The fact that the death-of-the-world is a real possibility can be called the *apocalyptic* syndrome. This fearsome perception is based on several rather obvious considerations. One is the ever present threat of nuclear holocaust. Another is the problem of overpopulation, with all its attendant difficulties of famine, anarchy, revolution, and war. There are also the dual threats of technology—exhaustion of natural resources, especially energy, and pollution of the biosphere. Both of these threats in turn are spin-offs from our unwise and dangerous economic self-concept, one which identifies increased consumption with growth and progress.

Each of these dangers alone is sufficient to make the end of the world a real possibility. Our problem is compounded in that we must face their unified assault. In the year A.D. 1000 it was thought the world would end. Thus, the idea is nothing new. However, that apocalyptic syndrome occurred within a religious context—God's plan, which meant salvation and judgment, was the objective. Traditional end-of-the-world philosophies referred to death as a transition, as an inconvenience with a moral message, but never as truly the end. What was distinctly not contemplated was that God and His plan would also perish, as is the case in today's anxiety about the world's death. Fear about the genuine end of the world is an experience unique to the twentieth century. Our one hope lies in the fact that this fear can make mankind resolute to develop mutual love and respect, establish a civilized one-world community and create the will (implementation through new technology would follow almost automatically) to fight this eutrophication of the entire biosphere. In this way the threatened death of civilization can have the same vitalizing effect on the history of mankind as the death of oneself has for giving us the courage to find meaning as individuals.

BIRTH CONTROL AND FREEDOM

Another twentieth-century development which, it would appear, has no precedent in history is the invention and the availability of birth-control methods: We have The Pill and we have legalized abortions.

The fundamental unit of society has always been the family, and the rationale for its existence has been sexual satisfaction and the socialization of children. Historically children and sex have always been connected. It is finally possible, and for the first time in the history of mankind, to ethically separate sex from love on the one hand and to physically separate sex from children, marriage, and family on the other. And birth control is widely used, socially accepted, and often intensively encouraged. As a result, the institution of the family, with all the social, psychological, and religious supports that it enjoys, and with its enormous anthropological significance, is now in danger of becoming obsolete.

Birth control has encouraged the development of the consciousness of freedom, because human beings are now free to define their most intimate relationships. They are no longer tied to biological and social needs and restrictions. Birth control has given support and substance to the previously mostly abstract philosophic freedom for self-definition. History, we can argue, is the development of the consciousness of freedom. History is the increase of consciousness' awareness of itself. With the arrival of the pervasive availability of birth-control methods freedom has scored another triumph in history. In this case it is the freedom for defining heterosexual relationships (that is, separating sex from children, and hence love from marriage) which expands the consciousness of freedom.

That mankind has become conscious of its freedom is also true in a more general sense. Birth control is only one aspect of this comprehensive and expanded awakening. Monolithic states and totalitarian repressions have through their denial of freedom clarified for vast numbers of human beings the preciousness of that freedom. Innumerable liberation movements (political, national, sexual, ethnic, social, and the like) are worldwide manifestations of the increase in the awareness of freedom which characterizes our century.

Freedom inevitably leads to pluralistic societies. Pluralism in politics, standards, ethics, and expectations brings on conflict, confusion, and anxiety. But it also can result in opportunities, consciousness expansion, personal identity and responsibility, and maturity. Freedom also leads to an increase in crime, especially when the free will of the individual becomes legitimately generalized into Constitutional guarantees. Marvin Wolfgang says, "Historically, and cross-culturally, the countries that have greater amounts of individual liberty and freedom have probably experienced a greater amount of social deviance. But that is one of the values we extol— freedom to be different."[3] We must therefore exercise great caution and not destroy freedom in the war against crime.

COMMUNICATION

Another typically twentieth-century phenomenon is the communications explosion. It leads to a one-world self-concept, which is constructive and realistic, but also to oversaturation of input, which is confusing and destructive. We have an excess of objectivity, such as in engineering, with a corresponding decrease in subjective awareness. Today this problem is being commendably counteracted with increased interest in exploring human subjectivity, including emphasis in the research of altered states of consciousness.

SPACE EXPLORATION

A fourth unique development in the twentieth century has been space exploration. We should in all fairness talk about exploring both outer and inner space, because these activities are philosophically related. It is no accident that the phrases "inner space" and "outer space" have the word "space" in common. Their referents have a common characteristic, which is elicited by the important and somewhat mysterious word "space." Outer-space exploration continues the frontier spirit—common to both the United States and Russia—which is an attitude of futurization and hope. The picture of our world from the moon (or at least from outer space), now found in most classrooms, demonstrates both the preciousness of the biosphere and the logic of unity among nations. A human step on the moon suggests that, rather than having exhausted worlds to conquer, we are just beginning. Therefore, space exploration, both inner and outer, means a new frontier has been found. The spirit of hope, first threatened by the apocalypse, can now return to human consciousness.

PHILOSOPHY

The fifth and last development unique to this century is a massive confluence of the two vast rivers of philosophy—Eastern and Western thought —a union which has in recent times given rise to increased interest in the Western world to the exploration of inner space. In addition, the river of Western thought has three tributaries, each coming from widely separated lands—science, theology, and the humanities. It is only recently, by means of the systematic application of phenomenological techniques (to be described in subsequent chapters) that these three disciplines—which in antiquity were strands of one rope but since the Renaissance became specialized and alienated fields of study—are now being recombined. (See Figure 3.)

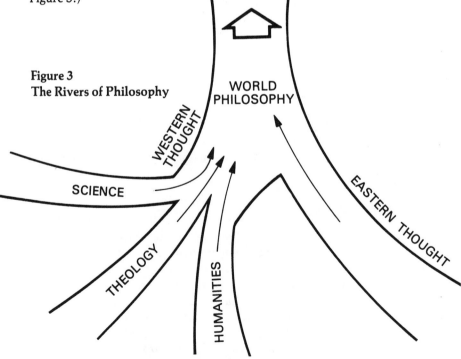

Figure 3
The Rivers of Philosophy

Figure 3   The Rivers of Philosophy

The phenomenological descriptions of subjective states (both conscious-ness itself and certain subjective objects of consciousness, such as feelings) have brought together the objective rigor of the scientific method, the intuitive richness of literature and the arts, and the psychological subtleties of religious insight. This triadic connection is the scientific character of phenomenology. [4] In addition, Oriental philosophy has for millennia anticipated what in the phenomenological movement of Western philoso-phy has come to be known as *transcendental phenomenology* and the study of the transcendental ego. The two significant intellectual developments in the recent history of ideas—the scientific character of philosophy and transcendental analysis—have finally created the conditions which can establish a true and well-grounded world philosophy. This appears to be the last and most promising development of this century. It may well carry within it seeds for the eventual resurrection of the world from its present apocalyptic dangers.

Each of the above unique and unprecedented events of the twentieth century can be comprehensively understood as a manifestation of the fundamental structure of being and the person as conceptualized by a phenomenological model of being and its accompanying existential person-ality theory. These conceptualizations adequately organize the significant events of this century, for this model and personality theory deal with the themes of death, freedom, encounter, futurization, and self-transcendence as well as with self-disclosure. Death in existentialism becomes death in world affairs. Personal freedom becomes social pluralism. Interpersonal encounter and communication lead to the politicalization of birth control and worldwide anxieties. Futurization leads to space exploration and self-disclosure to a world philosophy. Each of these themes derived from an existential personality theory points to a major political and historical event in our day and helps us to understand these events.

Notes

1. Deconstitution, if improperly handled, can also lead to panic.
2. May, Angel, and Ellenberger, Henri F. eds., *Existence: A New Dimension in Psychiatry and Psychology* (New York: Basic Books, 1958), p. 42.
3. *Time*, 30 June 1975, p. 14.
4. This point is discussed at length in Peter Koestenbaum, *The Vitality of Death* (Westport, Conn.: Greenwood, 1971), chaps. 25 and 26.

Part II • PHILOSOPHY AS PHENOMENOLOGY

Chapter 2 • THE PHILOSOPHIC BACKGROUND: PHENOMENOLOGY AND THE THEORY OF KNOWLEDGE

Contemporary psychology and medicine, including humanistic psychology and holistic medicine, will soon be ready to begin the search for their philosophical foundations. These are most likely to be found in the phenomenological movement in philosophy and its adjuncts, existential and humanistic thought in psychology and philosophy; this movement is, up to this date, the culminating episode of the history of philosophy because it encompasses the philosophical advances made thus far in the history of thought. Phenomenology does not deny what preceded it but rather places it all in an advanced and usable context; it is a purification, a filtering, of the history of philosophy. Phenomenology is not a greater movement in philosophy than others have been. Each school of philosophy that has a sense of history will exhibit in its position the integration of tradition with contemporary need. That role is being fulfilled today by phenomenology.

This chapter presents the meaning of phenomenology adapted to fulfill its promise as the ideological foundation and synthesis for philosophies of life and humanistic psychologies. We need to extract from systematic philosophy those basic concepts which are clinically relevant. Therefore, some modification of formal philosophic concepts in epistemology is needed. The following pages outlining contemporary phenomenological ontology will give the reader sufficient information to enable him or her to use philosophy in a clinical setting; and experience in applying phenomenology therapeutically enriches our understanding of basic phenomenological concepts. This analysis is not always a strict and scholarly exegesis of Husserl. Many important advances have been made in phenomenology since his death. The focus here is to establish the theoretical foundations for humanistic psychology and existentialism rather than a mere historical exegesis. Many ideas have been inspired by Husserl, by other phenomenologists, and by existentialist thinkers.

The Fields of Phenomenology

There are three distinct fields which comprise the total phenomenological philosophy: the first is phenomenological methodology or *phenomenology as method*; the second is *descriptive*, psychological, or empirical *phenomenology*, that is, phenomenology as the description of the world. Descriptive phenomenology has two subdivisions: *cosmology* and *anthropology*. The former is comprised of presuppositionless descriptions of the world—nature, science, and the like. The latter consists specifically of phenomenological descriptions of human existence—from feelings to social realities. Since human beings and their worlds are intimately intertwined, it is not always easy to distinguish descriptions of the world from descriptions of persons. In fact, Binswanger's theory of schizophrenia requires that we describe the patient's world in order to understand his inwardness.[1] However, when pheonomenology is used specifically to describe the human condition, we get what is known technically as philosophical anthropology (the philosophical study of man or of the person), also appropriately called existentialism. The expression used here to designate philosophical anthropology is the existential personality theory.

The third field of phenomenology is *transcendental phenomenology*, or phenomenological ontology, which is phenomenology as the description of pure consciousness. Here, phenomenology studies what traditionally has been meant by metaphysics or ontology (the study of reality or of the general characteristics of being). However, it is the analysis of pure consciousness, which represents only one area of being (and a much-neglected one), that is of primary concern to transcendental phenomenology. Thus phenomenology has introduced the study of consciousness into the age of science without resorting to idealistic metaphysics.

THE SCIENTIFIC CHARACTER OF PHENOMENOLOGY

One point often overlooked in most expositions of phenomenology—primary and secondary sources alike—is *the scientific character of phenomenology*. Phenomenology enables us to be both scientific and subjective at the same time and, therefore, come to terms with a long-standing and hitherto unresolved problem. The relationship between phenomenology and science exists on two levels—facts and method.

The differences between science and phenomenology are minor—they focus, for example, on how widely the term "fact" can be applied. For instance, a reading on a thermometer is a scientific fact ("precise" fact) whereas a poetic line about love is a phenomenological fact ("fringe" fact). Both are legitimate descriptions of experience. Fringe descriptions distort precise facts, but it is also true that precise descriptions distort fringe facts. The experience of love cannot be described scientifically, that is, with measurable numerical precision, nor can a temperature reading be usefully described poetically. Furthermore, both science and phenomenology use similar methodologies. The method of science is a *specific* and the method of phenomenology a *general* description of how one in fact garners knowledge. Phenomenology is thus the method of science purified of a few objectivist assumptions, in particular, the presupposition that reality is atomic and that knowledge is inferential.

The discovery of the connection between phenomenology and science is of particular importance since phenomenology now makes possible a genuinely scientific approach to the subjective study of the person. Phenomenology is the much-needed antidote to the reification of the person which results from the uncritical use of the scientific outlook in the study of psychology, psychiatry, and medicine. Nowhere can we see as clearly the failure of a purely objectivist view of reality as we do in the sciences of human beings. If we can now show that the subjective approach (phenomenology) is not the opposite of the objective approach (science) but that both are closely related variants of a single program for acquiring knowledge, then we will have taken a significant step in bridging science with the humanities and Eastern intuition with Western analysis. [2]

The meaning of the scientific character of phenomenology can be compressed into relatively few propositions: (1) Descriptions that are poetic and intuitive, introspective and metaphoric, are of the same logical form as traditional scientific descriptions and measurements. The differences are due to the transformation in subject matter from, let us say, an insect or a nuclear reaction, to a feeling or the sense of selfhood. Furthermore, (2) to observe our acts of observation or our inner consciousness is not different from observing distant galaxies or the behavior of fishes. The focus of the observation has changed and the method of observation must be adjusted so as to avoid distortion. We must be judicious in using microscopes and telescopes. Similarly, we must adjust our focus to outer or inner space as demanded by our subject matter. The method of phenomenology hopes to accomplish that and thus remain strictly in the spirit of science.

Thus, in phenomenology we find for the first time in the history of thought the responsible and successful application of the scientific method to the study of the person. All of these points are of major theoretical importance. Until the beginning of this century—when phenomenology was developed carefully as a methodology, that is, as a method of asking questions and deciding under what conditions these questions were answered, and as an epistemology, a theory of acquiring knowledge—there was no thoroughgoing theoretical justification and method for describing with responsible accuracy the experience of being a person. In other words, phenomenology has made the fundamental, theoretical point that the so-called conventional "scientific" study of the person is shot through with biases, prejudgments, and a priori presuppositions in such a way that the ensuing view of the person is distorted, contrary to the facts of experience, and therefore false and illegitimate. There has not been in existence until recently a critically developed method of inquiry that yields accurate information about human existence. Indeed, phenomenology had been carried on haphazardly and intuitively in the past. But now the method has been systematically developed. The use of physics as a model for the study of the person, which has been the basic program of scientific psychology, is in principle illegitimate. That is a point of major significance which must now be firmly established. Once this is done, the questions we ask about the person will never be the same and the answers will have greater depth.

THREE TYPES OF FACTS

The scientific character of phenomenology can be described with greater precision with the following diagram and analysis:

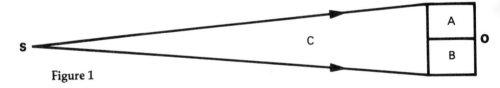

Figure 1

The figure represents the standard model of the phenomenological view of reality. Being is a subject-object or a consciousness-world field that contains three distinct sets of data. Regions A and B represent objects, or, specifically, objects to consciousness. Region C represents consciousness itself. There are two types of objects to consciousness. Region A represents scientific or precise data; B stands for poetic or fringe data.

Scientific data are the experiences of *structure*. The commitment to scientific data is what makes the world appear *discrete*. Scientific data are also what gives us the objects in the world. They are precise and lend themselves to mathematical representation. Precise data are assimilated and managed in the left hemisphere of the brain.[3] Exclusive reliance on scientific or precise data—the conviction that these data are the only bona fide simulacra of reality—dominates contemporary thinking. That precise data have superior reality ascription is a decision (an archetypal decision, as we shall see later) which was made by the pre-Socratic philosophers Leucippus and

Democritus during the fifth century B.C. And that decision at the dawn of our culture—it is not a discovery, as modern physics has pointed out—determined the primary course of Western civilization to the present day which eventually culminated in the technological glory and catastrophe of this century.

Poetic or fringe data are the experiences of *process*. Poetic data make the world appear *continuous* rather than discrete. These data require for their understanding the right hemisphere of the brain. Fringe data are also objects, but they are amorphous, not limited, and unclear. For the study of human experience they transcend the precise data of science. Fringe data are the givens in literature and the arts as well as in the practice of psychotherapy.

Finally, region C consists of transcendental data. These are of an entirely different nature from the scientific (A) and the poetic (B) data. For one, transcendental data are not objects but pure subjectivity. Furthermore, they are not revealed by focusing consciousness on its objects but by performing the transcendental phenomenological reduction and focusing attention on the act of focusing itself. Finally, these transcendental data are unique. We describe only one and we have described the structure of being itself. We do not generalize in the transcendental region as we do in the zone of the objects to consciousness. The uniqueness and singularity of transcendental data have been evident in the rationalistic tradition in philosophy, especially in epistemology. The controversy over whether or not synthetic a priori judgments are possible, which culminated in Kant's *Critique of Pure Reason*, is the problem of transcendental data. These latter include such "events" as freedom, immortality, or eternity, as well as space and time. Our perception of these crucial data, therefore, is *synthetic*—that is, of the world; *a priori*—that is, not derived from observation, and *apodictic* (Kant's word)—which means absolutely certain.

Transcendental data are synthetic inasmuch as the zone of pure consciousness is an important region of the totality of being. They are a priori in that by "observation" usually was meant observed-as-objects. With the introduction of a transcendental reduction (reflexive and self-referential thinking),[4] a new kind of observation (transcendental as opposed to empirical) is possible. But it is not the traditional observation of objects. It is therefore quite proper to say, as has been done in the controversy over innate ideas, that these data are known to be the case without reference to experience.

Finally, these data are apodictic in that generalization, which is the source of uncertainty and probability, is irrelevant to them. There is only one consciousness and therefore there is only one transcendental datum. It is either described accurately or not. There is no room for inductive procedures to cast doubt on the integrity of other and similar data.

Let us now proceed to a systematic presentation of the method of phenomenology.

Phenomenology As Method

The dawning of philosophical activity is to make a decision about method—what general method to use to make any inquiry whatever and, specifically, which to use to make an inquiry about the structure of being and the nature of human existence. Methodology is the first task of any philosophy; nothing is more basic than how to proceed. Before investigating any problem, we must explore the way in which we investigate anything. The activity of investigating investigation, of studying studying, of thinking about thinking, is called methodology. Persons are different, fundamentally, from physical objects, and science, as we know it today and generally speaking, is about physical objects. To study the nature of persons we must take this one methodological factor into consideration. And that is not easy, especially if we wish to work systematically and with precision. Phenomenology is such a method of acquiring knowledge. It is, in addition, a method, perhaps the only one, that is sensitive precisely to those aspects of the person which are different in kind from physical objects. It is also a method that has been developed in detail. [5]

The following discussion and exposition of the philosophic *method* of phenomenology is directed specifically to its use in clinical philosophy. It is the contention here that the method of phenomenology is needed to provide an adequate philosophic foundation for theoretical work in all of the healing arts and sciences. Phenomenology is needed equally to understand and amplify the practical and therapeutic innovations of philosophy for the deepening of clinical work.

The outline of the *method* of phenomenology can be accomplished in four steps: phenomenology as method recognizes first the primacy of the subjective perspective or of first-person experience; phenomenology demands detailed descriptions of experience (Husserl called it "going to the things themselves"), a demand which identifies this movement with the history of empiricism in philosophy; phenomenology expects these descriptions to be presuppositionless, thus implying that the source of error is to be found in the assumptions, deliberate or suppressed, which assign meanings to experience; phenomenology demands the epoche—which involves both bracketing and reduction, and which extends the concept of traditional empiricism to include what we can call a transcendental empiricism or an empiricism of reason as well.

FIRST-PERSON EXPERIENCE

The fact that all knowledge begins with what we have become accustomed to call *first-person experience* is taken seriously by phenomenology and its implications are developed consistently and systematically. We may demand objectivity in knowledge; nevertheless, that objectivity is in the last analysis constructed out of data which are inevitably subjective. The idea of objectivity itself is an invention of subjectivity. The primacy of subjectivity—a phenomenon which Ralph Barton Perry called the egocentric predicament—does not necessarily lead to subjectivistic philosophies or solipsism (the metaphysical position that *only I exist*). But it does show that concepts such as "objectivity" and "the independent existence of an external world" are constructed out of building blocks that have their origin in first-person experience. Moreover, the first-person experience is *mine* and not *someone else's*. Phenomenology is the fearless development of this idea.

DESCRIPTION

Description of that first-person experience as a principal methodological step is the second defining characteristic of the method of phenomenology. The beginning step in any new science is to describe and catalog the range of data which comprise it. Only then are generalizations and theory construction relevant activities. Description as a methodological device does not ignore or distort experience; it respects experience as the foundation of knowledge. Description transfers without "editorializing" into the Book of Knowledge the data as they emanate from the world. Description must carry out this project with a minimum of change or distortion.[6]

To make a commitment to description as a fundamental methodological approach is to operate in the epistemological tradition of empiricism. In fact, phenomenology is the most refined and radical form of contemporary empiricism available. Empiricism is the tradition in the theory of knowledge which developed as a reaction against the dogmatism of rationalistic philosophies and the extravagant and reckless claims of speculative philosophies. The empiricist trend in philosophy branched off eventually into the scientific outlook and its respect for facts; it has also led to the positivistic emphasis on sensations as the source of truth. It has led to the weight that linguistic philosophers, philosophers of ordinary language analysis, and structuralists—all of whom are important in recent contemporary philosophy—give to the examination of our experience of language. In phenomenology, it appears, this reverence for a radical empiricism climaxes, and it does so through the commitment to description (of first-person experience) as our basic access to veridical knowledge.

PRESUPPOSITIONLESSNESS

The description of first-person experience must be *presuppositionless*. Of course, presuppositionlessness is a goal and not an accomplishment.

Phenomenology in its description of reality endeavors to discard all assumptions about the nature of the world that have crept into our constituted experience through science, religion, language, and so forth. Of course, no phenomenologist who is really conscientious will truly ever say, "I make no assumptions." We can say that responsible phenomenology adopts the following view on the project of an assumption-free methodology:

Phenomenology is aware of the problem of the presuppositionless. Truth seems to be connected with the assumption-free. Truth seems to be found whenever we get past assumptions. And that idea itself must be investigated, for it may be just one more assumption. It is important to adopt an assumption-free posture because that is closer to the truth than any view which makes assumptions. It is through assumptions that errors creep into our thought. Therefore, one assumption in the analysis of assumptions is that truth and presuppositionlessness are synonymous.

Strictly speaking, we do not eliminate assumptions but we become aware of them; we identify the assumptions that are made in every cognitive endeavor. Again, it appears that phenomenology has been more successful than preceding philosophic positions in its sharp and sensitive awareness of the presuppositions that hide themselves in our thinking and, consequently, has been more accurate in the recording of authentic facts—facts purified of unexamined and unwarranted assumptions. Furthermore, phenomenology has succeeded in calling attention to assumptions which had hitherto not been recognized as such.

An example of a common assumption, denied by phenomenology to be a prima facie truth, is the Cartesian image or model of the person as a soul, spirit, or mind inserted in a body. That is also the view of the mind-body split. Cartesianism expressed in one's life means to be "out of touch"—out of touch with one's body, with other persons, and with one's feelings, both positive and negative. This severance is an assumption imposed on the field-nature of experience and reality and those who believe it frequently display serious psychological and physical symptoms. The phenomenological redescription of our fundamental human condition—now bereft of assumptions—is one of mind-body and mind-world continuity and is encapsuled in such descriptive phrases as Heidegger's "Man is a being-in-the-world" or in Husserl's idea that "Consciousness is always consciousness of something" (which is the theory of the intentionality of consciousness, to be discussed shortly).

In sum, the ideal of a presuppositionless philosophy reflects the ancient epistemological insight that truth is proportional to that which is the assumption-free and, conversely, that error is related to the presence of suppressed assumptions. If we reach truth through description, if the world shows its face to us through the empirical data it gives us, then assumptions are in fact interferences with the pure transmission of these precious primary, primordial, or originary data. It follows that for a radical empiricism the presuppositionless is also the *true*.

EPOCHE

The last of the four features of phenomenology as method is the *epoche*, the "cognitive yield" of applying the (1) *presuppositionless* (2) *description* of (3) *first-person experience* to the activity of knowledge itself. Phenomenology begins strictly as an epistemology. It is a method (methodology is one of the principal fields of epistemology) which is then applied first to the question of what is knowledge, which is the core problem in epistemology. What does our phenomenological description tell us about the structure of knowledge? Two details emerge—*bracketing* and *reduction*.

To bracket (or to "thematize") is to take a phenomenon out of the stream of experience and examine it in isolation. We study a fish by taking it out of water and performing an autopsy on it. We study a microorganism by paralyzing or killing it—in other words, by removing it from its life-stream or ecosystem—and observing it on a slide under a microscope. We study a streak in a cloud or bubble chamber, which occurs in milliseconds, by bracketing its temporal context through a photograph. To bracket means to cut a phenomenon out of space and excise it out of time in order to examine it with leisure. We study any experience by taking it out of its participation in the practical world; we place it in brackets. We must be conscious of whether or not bracketing affects the phenomenon under study. In the physical or life sciences, from autopsies to the principle of indeterminacy, to study an object is to change it. But phenomenology is closer to photography: the act of phenomenological observation does not affect the phenomenon observed. Reality is left intact. It is only our observation that is added to it. Changes are made only in the mind.

Of particular importance to philosophy is that in bracketing we put out of action the question of the reality of the phenomenon or event. We study an experience as *phenomenon*, as that which is given to us irrespective of its relationship to the rest of experience and regardless of our interpretations of its meaning and its rootedness in reality. When we bracket a phenomenon, and thereby study it as phenomenon, as presentation, we do not make assumptions about its independent existence as an object in the external world. The crucial epistemological problem is shunted aside in the process of bracketing. We do that each time we seek knowledge, and we call that complex process bracketing. In this way we can empathically study a patient's experience and find that it is indeed his experience that we are describing and not our projected theory instead. The therapist, as he sees his patient, must be careful to perceive what is actually there—the feelings of the patient—and not what is also there but merely as projection—his own theories.

The second aspect of epoche is the reduction. The two go together, so that a sharp and unambiguous differentiation is difficult to achieve.

Reduction means to reflect on experience rather than to participate in it. To participate in experience may be to be lost blissfully in the act of making love. To reflect on experience, that is, to have subjected the experience of love to a phenomenological reduction, is to evaluate and report on that experience; it is to think rationally about the meaning of love in a total life. Reflection or reduction is "stepping back" out of involvement in love. Reflection is to observe life rather than be a part of it. The act of reduction introduces abstract thought into human experience. The ability to reflect is a distinctively human capability. In fact, the word *reduction* means in Latin to lead back or to step back.

This concept, sometimes called the transcendental phenomenological reduction, is perhaps the fundamental step in phenomenology, for it is this act which opens up for analysis and description the region of pure consciousness. It is through study of this region (the transcendental region or zone C on the diagram on p. 28) that philosophic innovations can be introduced at the deepest possible level into the understanding of clinical phenomena. Phenomenological psychology is distinguished from empirical psychology at this very point. Empirical psychology is the study of a specific object—the person. And that object can be described analytically as precise data (region A) and intuitively as fringe data (region B). But when we venture into a description of our consciousness of that psychological object and focus on the constitutive or organizing acts of that consciousness of persons rather than on the persons themselves, then we are in an altogether different region of being. We are now studying phenomenological psychology, and we are able to deal with clinical material at one level deeper than traditional depth psychotherapy. This point is discussed further under the later heading, Transcendental Phenomenology.

ADDITIONAL TERMINOLOGY

Central to understanding the notion of epoche and of the two realms of being (transcendental and empirical) are the two contrasting notions of *referential* and *reflexive* thought. Referential thought is consciousness directed outward and away from itself. Consciousness *refers* to objects or points to them in the sense in which a label refers to the contents of a medicine bottle or a word *refers* to its meaning. Referential thought is patterned on the metaphor of light and of vision. It is an arrow or beam that has a point of departure (the transcendental ego) and a destination (an object). Most thinking is of this sort.

Reflexive thinking, on the other hand, is consciousness turned back upon itself. Reflexive thought is uniquely philosophical. It is self-referential; it is not the act of consciousness but of self-consciousness. Reflexive thought is an infinite regress. It is thought thinking about thought. The metaphor for reflexive thought is no longer that of a beam of light but that of a mirror; it is not of an arrow but a coil. Reflexivity in consciousness would be a mystery were it not for the fact that we can always experience it. We can produce it at will. It is a permanent possibility of our human nature. The capacity for reflexive thinking is the key that unlocks the door to transcendental phenomenology.

Imagine a group of people confronting a problem. A small seminar gathers and one person, solicited for the occasion, faints. The group gets anxious, upset, and excited. Immediate action is undertaken. While the group scurries around figuring out what to do, the action is videotaped. After a few minutes the instructor or facilitator calls off the pretense and the "unconscious" participant goes back to his or her seat. Now the videotape is played. The participants observe their concern about their fainted friend. Whereas before they were in a referential mode—the full focus of their attention was on the action at hand—they are now in a reflexive mode, since they now observe and study their reaction to the "experiment." After the discussion is concluded, the instructor points out that their discussion of the videotape was in turn videotaped. In this way they become aware that even their discussion of the fainting episode was itself also partially referential. Now they will see the second tape and will thereby recognize and experience the element of infinite regress which prevails in the reflexive potential of consciousness. The surprise or shock they receive each time they are told they were deceived is typical of the experience of the phenomenological epoche, which changes our thinking from referential to reflexive.

All knowledge is of this dual sort, and the psychotherapeutic intervention is no exception. Psychotherapy elicits additional feelings—which is a referential activity—and then reflects on these feelings, which is reflexive activity. However, reflexivity itself engenders referential feelings. A patient walks into the office angry (referential). The therapist says, "You are angry!" This statement makes the patient reflexive—he now knows that "anger" is the topic for discussion. That distance creates anxiety, which is then a new condition—a deeper one—that must be subjected to therapeutic analysis. Such regression into the transcendental is a philosophic description of what occurs (and why it does) in the therapeutic process.

The participatory act of being involved in or committed to the world is called the *natural* or the engaged *attitude* or *experience simpliciter*. The act of reduction, reflection, or of stepping out of the stream of life and viewing it from the distance of a disinterested observer—which is another central ingredient in the traditional definition of knowledge—is called the *phe-*

nomenological attitude. The natural attitude is the result of referential thinking and the phenomenological attitude is the result of reflexive thinking.

There are many different terms used to designate the two realms of being exposed through the phenomenological reduction. It is important to catalog these terms. Synonyms for the region of pure consciousness, revealed by reflexive thought, are *transcendental dimension, transcendental ego, transcendental consciousness, subjectivity, transcendental subjectivity*, or, sometimes, the *noetic realm* as well as Sartre's *pour soi*. Synonyms for the region of objectivity and world, revealed by referential thought, are the *empirical realm, nature*, the *objective region*, or, occasionally, the *noematic realm* and also Sartre's *en soi*. In the transcendental region resides our freedom and our infinity. In the empirical realm resides the world in which we live and in which our humanity finds its agony and ecstasy.

Phenomenology is the application of the above described method to the description of empirical, psychological, or objective reality. Here phenomenology is the sensitive description of "fringe facts," the kinds of data which are more susceptible to poetic evocation than to strict scientific measurement. Yet these fringe data are at least as important in a total theory of the person as the more clearly measurable ones. This rubric includes much if not most of the body of work carried out by the phenomenological movement[7] and the cumulative knowledge acquired by those thinkers who are usually identified with the humanistic movement in psychology.

Transcendental Phenomenology

The third and perhaps most important field of phenomenology is the exploration of the structure of pure consciousness. That is a philosophical and even religious rather than typically psychological task. Phenomenology as transcendental phenomenology is the exploration of the structure of consciousness as that consciousness is given to us in the "here-and-now."

The only philosophical positions that historically have examined and taken seriously the structure of pure or transcendental consciousness are idealisms. But none have been as systematic, detailed, and cautious about its method as has been phenomenology. Consequently, phenomenology as transcendental phenomenology (for our purpose here, the word *transcendental* in philosophy means consciousness) is the exploration of the structure of consciousness. And that relatively simple point is still frequently and completely misunderstood by theoreticians in the behavioral sciences.

It is a sad truth that so-called conventional psychology and medicine pay little or no attention to the study of the structure of consciousness. In most cases, the notion of the structure of consciousness does not enter, even remotely, into their theoretical or practical considerations. And yet an entirely new range of possibilities for treatment is opened up when we begin to see the implications of transcendental phenomenology.

The growth movement has tried to compensate for this lacuna. Two problems remain, nevertheless. Research in the Third Force in psychology does not always have the requisite rigor and philosophic clarity that such study demands. Also, and more importantly, when states of consciousness are discussed, frequently the topic is in fact an object (that is, a conscious state made into an object) rather than a condition of pure consciousness. The object can be a thought (*eidetic* object), a feeling (*affective* object), a fantasy (*iconic* object), and so forth. We must be careful to remember that in ordinary language thoughts and feelings are states of consciousness, but for phenomenology they are but objects of a different sort. Transcendental phenomenology is the determination to focus attention on reflexivity alone and thus restrict its research to the study of what is truly pure and non-objectified consciousness.

In sum, when the method of phenomenology is used to describe our consciousness, it becomes transcendental phenomenology. But phenomenology has also been used to describe the *objects* of our consciousness, in which case it becomes descriptive, objective, empirical, or psychological phenomenology.

In phenomenology, anything that one can name, talk about, discuss, think about, perceive, or conceive becomes an object to consciousness. We reserve the word *object* for that which is given to consciousness. What is left? Nothing. And, as Sartre has in effect pointed out in his *Being and Nothingness*, "nothingness" then becomes a good descriptive term for pure or transcendental consciousness.

The words *psychology* and *psychiatry* can be interpreted to mean, in terms of their Greek origins, the study of consciousness and the health of consciousness respectively. The study of consciousness as transcendental is not carried out by conventional psychology nor is the question of the health of that consciousness carried out in psychiatry. The meanings of consciousness have become diluted and distorted, so that in their actual practice consciousness becomes an object to itself. The project of examining subjectivity has been abandoned and even such a possibility is often forgotten. One place today where the questions of the existence and structure, of the health and the authenticity of consciousness, are examined responsibly is in the pursuit of transcendental phenomenology. It therefore follows that one discipline in which *genuine* psychology and psychiatry are in fact being done today, according to the intent of these words at the dawn of Western civilization, is in transcendental phenomenology and certainly not in much of what is considered psychology or psychiatry.

As a result, it is crucial for anyone who wishes to be a respectable thera-pist to be in touch with the epistemological considerations that make up the various fields of phenomenology.

Empiricism

An empirical philosophy—which is one of the cornerstones of phenom-enology—is usually associated with the tradition of empiricism in epis-temology. Simply stated, empiricism is the tradition which holds that all knowledge is derived from experience. Empiricism specifically denies the existence of a priori knowledge, that is, knowledge about the world based on rational intuition. Thus, an empiricist would say that mathematics, for example, is a purely formal system which has no inherent contact with reality. Whatever connection does exist, the extent to which mathematics is useful scientifically, is determined experimentally.

The rationalist view, on the other hand, maintains that such a purely intellectual, formal, and thus rational body of knowledge as mathematics is a *bona fide* description of reality despite the fact that its justification does not derive from empirical generalizations. Rationalism implies a continuity of reason and world which empiricism denies. Phenomenology does not only endorse the traditional empiricism of philosophy but extends it to cover the transcendental region which had been heretofore the sole province of the rationalistic tradition in epistemology.[8] We can then describe the structure of pure consciousness, the transcendental region revealed to us through successive applications of the phenomenological reduction. And descriptions of the transcendental zone, which are a radical extension of the traditional conception of empiricism, are given in terms of the rules of reason, of logic, and the like. When we describe that region we are extend-ing, legitimately, the principle of empiricism.

Let us now bring the old tradition of rationalism in philosophy up to date. The reason that descriptions of the transcendental region are logically *certain* (one of the meanings of "a priori") is that they are *descriptions*. All descriptions have the degree of certainty that is given through direct, that is, intuitive, inspection. The certainty of a purely conscious phenomenon (called an axiom)—such as an arithmetic sum—is of the same degree as is the certainty of the existence of and nature of perception (called a sensa-tion). We know a truth about consciousness through the same kind of description that gives us a truth about the world. We know that the *law of the excluded middle* ("every event is either A or not-A") is true by inspecting the meaning of that law. Such inspection may be of meanings or of intui-tions which, traditionally, are analytic or synthetic.

If the law of the excluded middle is analytic, then its subject matter is words and meanings. If the law is synthetic, then it is about the structure of transcendental consciousness and its constitutive decisions. But the distinction between language and experience is neither final nor clear. In either case, the evidence for the truth of the law of the excluded middle is direct inspection, inspection of either meanings or transcendental structures. This type of inspection is observation. It is reflexive observation; it is observation of the zone of transcendental subjectivity. It is an empirical activity where what is observed—through the transcendental phenomenological reduction—is the region of pure consciousness. We must call such activity a *transcendental empiricism.* It is not fundamentally different from traditional empiricism, in which we observe and describe an empirical object, such as a plant, an insect, or the behavior of measuring devices. Nor does it differ in principle from descriptions of poetic data, which are observations requiring not the skills of a scientist but the sensitivity of a poet. But there is one difference. Empirical data (especially scientific but also poetic) lend themselves to and demand generalization. Transcendental data are unique and universal.

The reason that descriptions of the transcendental region are *universal* (which is the second meaning of "a priori") is that there is only *one* transcendental region. Mathematical propositions (which are descriptions of the transcendental zone) describe only *one* event—the one transcendental consciousness that is given in experience, which is also the *only* one that can be given in experience. It is because of this that they appear to be universal (which is what they legitimately are). In addition to their importance for epistemology, transcendental descriptions are the foundations for the psychotherapeutic uses of transcendental phenomenology, an application of phenomenology that has not previously been carried out adequately. Most philosophical applications to therapy have their origin in existentialism as philosophical anthropology and not in transcendental phenomenology. This must be remedied.

Intentionality and the Field of Consciousness

A few words must be said describing the basic ontological reality as seen through the eyes of the phenomenological movement. It is a description of *being,* of the person, of existence, and of reality. This ontology is the basic human situation, the basic world view. It characterizes the phenomenological movement, including existentialism; and it is this description which must serve as the basis for any theory, research, or practice in psychotherapy as well as of the entire realm of ethics and philosophical anthropology.

It is difficult to carry out this description successfully because of obstacles inherent in the task itself. The description tells us that language reflects only part of being. In psychology this thought is expressed through the concept of the unconscious: language handles only part of the person. If we accept the accuracy of that description and take it as a premise, then any attempt to describe the basic metaphysical situation, the basic ontological reality, is bound to fail. This is a preliminary problem of methodology which requires considerable investigation. Here it can only be stated. But let us put this difficulty aside—realizing full well that it cannot be put aside—and examine some salient features of the phenomenological description of the primary structure of being.

The key word in describing the basic ontological situation is *intentionality*, or the expression *the intentionality of consciousness*. The fundamental structure of being is the intentionality of consciousness. We will see later, in Chapter 10, that another dimension can be added to this phenomenological point.

On the basis of the intentional theory of consciousness, being—both small and large, both individual and universal, both particular and total—consists of three continuous but distinguishable elements: subject, object, and the connection between them. The subject-region of the process, flow or stream that is being, is called the *ego*. But it is also referred to as the *transcendental* or the *noetic* region by Husserl. The object-realm of this field is called by him the *cogitatum* (pl., *cogitata*), which in English means "that which is perceived or understood." That region is also called the empirical or psychological realm, as well as the *noematic* region. Finally, the connecting process of action, passivity, perception, understanding, and so forth is called the *cogito* (pl., *cogitationes*). That region can also be designated by such terms as intentionality, self-transcendence, and the noetic-noematic complex.

Thus, the formula *ego-cogito-cogitatum* as the archaic, primordial, or originary description of being itself, is a popular one with phenomenologists. It is useful because it demonstrates phenomenology's connection with as well as the transcendence over the Cartesian philosophy. The latter's description of being is limited to *ego cogito*, which is then, by Descartes and the tradition to which he gave birth, severed from the world of objects. This so-called *Cartesian split* determined the course philosophy was to follow for three hundred years. The Cartesian split became a fundamental rejection of the realism of both the medieval and the ancient periods of philosophy. Realism was the position that subject and object are connected directly and reliably in the act of perception (called "intention"). By recognizing that the *cogitatum* is an integral part of the perceptual process, phenomenology has transcended the subject-object split and made it possible for a person to participate fully in the realities of this world, in both a conceptual and a living way.[9] A diagram consolidating all of these definitions may be helpful. (See Figure 2.)

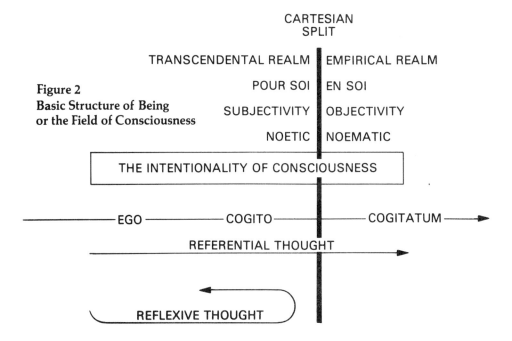

Figure 2
**Basic Structure of Being
or the Field of Consciousness**

A number of metaphors will facilitate the description of this basic onto-logical situation.

The fundamental feature of this description of being is expressed in what is here called the field theory of personality (which is not to be confused with Lewin's field theory). This is a field theory of the person. The field has a particular structure, which can be described by expressions such as an *ego-world, consciousness-world,* or a *consciousness-body* continuum. In a field theory of personality the components of that field are consciousness and bodies or consciousness and things. That is a first approximation to the description of the intentionality of consciousness. [10]

Archetypal Decisions

A concept of importance in clinical philosophy is the idea of archetypal decisions. The world as it appears to us is the constitution imposed by consciousness (Husserl calls the principles of constitution or meaning ascription the *noemata*) upon the raw data of experience. Some constitutions are active, deliberate, and conscious while others are passive, automatic, and unconscious. Since all constitutions are constructions of consciousness and since they all can, at least in theory, be changed, they should be called decisions. By using that word we assign responsibility for them to each person and we concomitantly give that person control and hope. A person who knows he is free is both responsible and hopeful. Constructive change, which means hope, results from the knowledge that our world organization (a concept not unlike the transactional idea of scripts, but more extensive) can be our own personal responsibility.

Careful phenomenological analysis of the transcendental sphere (through reduction) discloses to us these constitutive acts (both conscious and unconscious). It is these acts, which occur in layers and exist concurrently, that bring about the world as we see it. The "presence" of our world is the mirror of the constitutive acts which are operative at this very moment and which are potentially subject to modification. Depth psychotherapy must have access to these persistent, current, and multilevel constitutions.

In other words, my total world perception at this moment consists of an organization by my consciousness of the data given in experience. These constitutions are in theory free; therefore, they can be called decisions. The nature and structure of these constitutions or decisions, all of which must be in existence at this present moment in order for my experience to be what it is, can be uncovered by the activity of transcendental phenomenology or reflexive analysis. Many of these decisions are minor and inconsequential. Some, however, are basic.

The term *archetypal decision* refers to those potentially free constitutions which are the most basic of all. An archetypal decision is the organizational pattern which makes our world what it is. The deepest personal problems in life result from conflicts or contradictions built into these archetypal decisions and then reflected in our world. Taking responsibility for one's life is to understand that it is we who are making these archetypal decisions. Because of the absolute depth at which these archetypal decisions operate, they are rarely questioned. Medicine, psychology, and psychiatry do not reach them. On the contrary, the very existence of these fields depends on the fact that archetypal decisions have been made, are being made, continue to be made, and are not questioned. In fact, questioning becomes a diagnostic tool and triggers an alarm.

Mankind has often been aware of these archetypal decisions. But this awareness does not appear directly with philosophical literalness, but in terms of myths and stories. For example, the idea that a person constitutes his sense of individuality out of a sense of universality, which is discussed in Chapters 10 and 11 in Book One, is one aspect of his immediate, present, and transcendental experience. It is a fact or a decision he is making at this very moment. It is a decision he has made and will continue to make. It is a decision which, if he unmakes it, will demolish his world. As a consequence, the decision is rigidly ensconced. Panic and insanity can be the emotional concomitants of undoing this decision, of deconstituting the sense of individuality. This decision or constitution appears as the mythology that God is in him or that he is part of God. Also, the decision to limit one's universality and choose to organize it in terms of individuals or particulars is symbolized as God creating Man (Old Testament) or God becoming Man (New Testament)—as is the case when a person fantasizes or dreams he has the option, potentially, to identify with the total dream (he experiences himself as a universal possibility) or to identify with one person in that dream (he realizes or actualizes his potential for individuality).

Let us take another example. Transcendental researches reveal that there is freedom in regard to self-concepts. Identities can be chosen and rechosen. A person who, through an altered state of consciousness, meditates or reflects on other possible identities or self-concepts could well experience that philosophic insight about the here-and-now as memory of past lives and as the sense of recollected reincarnations. Thus, when a person in a quasi-trance state sees himself walking barefoot in the streets of ancient Athens, he may think he was Socrates in a previous life, but in phenomenological terms he is but aware of his deep and archetypal freedom to choose and rechoose identities.

Finally, a person in an altered state of consciousness may feel he leaves his body and travels to distant worlds. In fact, he is deconstituting his basic and archetypal decision to experience himself as a body and is identifying himself with the region of his pure and transcendental consciousness alone. After all, inner and outer space are experienced as very similar.

It is possible to compile a list of archetypal decisions. One of the most important of all acts of the conscious constitution of objects is the constitution of the empirical ego. This is the creation of the sense of *my* individuality. It is a passive or unconscious constitution which *can* become active or conscious. The effects of performing this archetypal decision for finitude are a strong sense of alienation, the feeling of being an object, and an intense sense of personal responsibility.

Thus, the primary archetypal decision is *the decision for finitude*. Related archetypal decisions are:

> The decision for personal identity
> The decision for embodiment
> The decision for the scientific outlook
> The decision for life affirmation
> The decision for morality
> The decision for sexual role identification

These presuppositions are rarely questioned. They serve as fundamental assumptions. When we choose to accept them without analysis we also create our specific kind of civilized existence. If these premises should be questioned, we feel threatened and discover the extraordinary and understandable resistances that have amassed against such questioning.

Clinical philosophy leads the patient past his or her psychological foundations straight to these archetypal regions. Psychological and medical problems can often be better understood if their archetypal origins are recognized. Sometimes, by treating the archetypal decisions directly, conventional medical and psychological procedures can be bypassed.

Notes

1. Ludwig Binswanger, *Being-in-the-World*, translated by J. Needleman (New York: Basic Books, 1963).

2. Chapters 25 and 26 in Peter Koestenbaum, *The Vitality of Death* (Westport, Conn.: Greenwood, 1971) try to show the kinds of transformations that are necessary in the positive sciences in order to adjust them to the study of the person. This point, it appears, is of major theoretical importance.

3. See Robert Ornstein, *The Psychology of Consciousness* (San Francisco: W.H. Freeman, 1972).

4. These concepts are introduced beginning on page 00.

5. For some of the most important books discussing phenomenology as a method, the reader should consult the bibliography in the appendix.

6. Ideally, there should be *no* changes and distortions whatever.

7. As recorded in the three comprehensive works of Herbert Spiegelberg: *The Phenomenological Movement*, Volumes 1 and 2 (The Hague: Martinus Nijhoff, 1965), and *Phenomenology in Psychology and Psychiatry* (Evanston, Ill.: North western University Press, 1972).

8. This is a point clarified by the diagram on page 28 about the three types of facts: scientific, poetic, and transcendental.

9. See E. Husserl, *Paris Lectures*, for a discussion of this point (The Hague: Martinus Nijhoff, 1965), p. 12.

10. Chapter 2 of Peter Koestenbaum, *Managing Anxiety* (Englewood Cliffs, N.J.: Prentice-Hall, 1974) discusses a series of metaphors for consciousness.

Chapter 3 • THE PHILOSOPHIC BACKGROUND: PHENOMENOLOGY AND THE THEORY OF KNOWLEDGE (continued)

Historical Background

The historical and philosophical bases for the legitimacy and need for a field theory of being rest on the fact that, traditionally, there have been three disputes about the structure of being. One of these is monism-dualism, or monism-pluralism—which in ancient Greek philosophy was called *the problem of the one and the many.* Another is the idealism-materialism dispute, a conflict which has been a dominant theme throughout the history of philosophy but, particularly, in the time after Descartes. The third confrontation has been rationalism-empiricism, which traces its origins to the Socratic period of ancient Greek philosophy. These three controversies have been the overriding epistemological concerns in one way or another of the history of philosophy since the days, at least in the West, of the pre-Socratic philosopher Thales.

The monism-dualism, or monism-pluralism dispute is the question, which sounds abstract but can become personal, of whether reality is made up of a unity or of a duality, or whether being is one, two, or many, and of whether the root metaphor in terms of which being is to be understood is the number "one" or the number "two" or the concept "many."

This issue has interesting repercussions. One area in which the monism-dualism issue is important is in the analysis of the problem of evil. If you happen to be an encounter group leader or facilitator in a hospital's oncology division for a group of dying cancer patients, then you recognize that the problem of evil is not abstractly theoretical but is of immediate emotional urgency. It is a philosophical problem that needs to be dealt with then and there. It becomes, at this point, a genuine medical emergency.

Specifically, what is the problem of evil? How does philosophical analysis relate to a dying patient?

The philosophical problem of evil is well illustrated by the Manichean heresy, which appeared about the year 200 A.D. and became a major competitor of Christianity. Some believe that Manicheism has its origin in Zoroastrianism, but there is some controversy on this matter. The Manichean heresy, to which Augustine confessed his adherence, is essentially the theory that evil is real. And that is dualism applied to the central issues of human existence. We must have an answer to the question, is Manicheism (or any other kind of dualism or pluralism) a true picture of reality? In Manichean terms, evil is an ultimate reality, and therefore deserves our respect—or forces this respect upon us—because of its power. Furthermore, because it is as real as is good, it cannot be eradicated from the earth. The Manichean heresy, internalized in today's culture as the Jungian archetype of the shadow, has also been fully integrated into the theory of the intentionality of consciousness, that is, the theory of the phenomenological model of being. However, in terms of orthodox Judaism and Christianity, dualism—especially of the Manichean or Zoroastrian variety—is a seriously heretical view. The Judeo-Christian view is not dualistic (that is, good and evil are two poles of a continuum and we must learn to live with this polarity) but is monistic and monotheistic. It holds that there is only one God, and that this God is good. Thus, evil is basically an illusion or, if it is not, it can at least be conquered and is therefore a subsidiary creation of God.

This is an abstract issue, but when we deal with suffering we are forced to make up our minds whether we are to accept it as an ultimate boundary in human existence, a fact which cannot be transcended—which appears to be the view of the Jungian and the existentialist therapies—or whether we will adopt the position that evil can in fact be overcome. The latter view can be associated with some Oriental views, and is above all the Judeo-Christian tradition that the coming of the Messiah and salvation are indeed possibilities for us all.

The problem of evil represents, perhaps in a simplified fashion, the heart of dualism. An example of the application of the monism-dualism dispute in this century can be seen in the different attitudes that our nation has taken toward Hitler as opposed to Stalin. We perceived both Nazi Germany and Stalinist Russia as undiluted evils. The attitude we took towards Nazi Germany was a monistic Judeo-Christian one. Using this world view one deals with evil in terms of unconditional surrender. Evil can and should be totally eliminated from the world, because evil does not possess the solidity and permanence of good. Evil is not as entrenched in the structure of being as is good. The proper attitude, therefore, toward evil is to struggle for its total elimination.

It is because of this philosophy that it made sense for the Allies to demand the unconditional surrender of the Axis powers during World War II. At first we did not succeed, so it appeared, because Japan was still a power. We therefore made one final all-out effort. By exploding two atom bombs we hoped to succeed once and for all in destroying all the evil in the world and usher in the millennium. All we had to do was close our eyes momentarily while the bombs exploded. The horrendous human suffering that resulted was then thought to be a legitimate means to a worthy end.

With Russia and Stalin, on the other hand, we did not adopt that monistic metaphysical attitude, but we followed the dualistic attitude of coexistence. The latter is not an orthodox Judeo-Christian view regarding evil but is instead a humanistic, Jungian, and existential position, in which the ultimate reality is pluralistic, dualistic, or polar rather than monistic.

The phenomenological description of being tries to resolve the epistemological and metaphysical monism-dualism dispute through the theory of the intentionality of consciousness. This theory holds that reality has two poles, that all being and all thinking is polarized. It also says that we are free to focus on either one pole or the other. But we are also able to perceive the total polarized (or dialectical, as it is sometimes called) situation as a unit.

The second basic polar problem in the history of philosophy, the idealism-materialism dispute in metaphysics, questions whether ultimate reality is consciousness or whether it is the object of that consciousness. In more traditional language the issue is whether ultimate reality is mind or matter. [1]

The idealistic view holds that reality is mind or consciousness, and that matter, or the objects of consciousness, is but the illusion of a dream. A dream is said to consist of consciousness, and the material objects in the dream are basically conscious objects. The same analysis applies to the so-called real and waking state. Idealism has been an important view in the history of philosophy, with Plato as its most notable ancient representative and Hegel as its most influential modern one. Its importance is based on the fact that idealism is perhaps the most convenient metaphysics for the preservation of human values. If you feel that human values are crucial, and that you need a metaphysics that makes the preservation of human values central, you may tend toward idealism. You will also tend toward religion, which is often supported by idealistic metaphysics in its theology.

However, if the defining characteristic of reality is found in such words as *objective*, *material*, and *natural*, you may lean toward depersonalized views of the world. You will tend to be scientific and it is likely you will view nature and the impersonal as if it were the ultimate and the real. The real is then the object of consciousness, not consciousness itself. Observations like these are in fact a *phenomenology of materialism*. Philosophers who have maintained, roughly speaking, that matter is the ultimate reality include Aristotle, from ancient times, and Hobbes, the English philosopher.

A third group who tried to solve the idealism-materialism dispute adopted the view that ultimate reality is partially mind and partially matter. Representative philosophers who have maintained this are Descartes, Spinoza, and Locke.

Mind-Matter Interdependency

Phenomenology arose out of this atmosphere of conflict. Our final position on this dispute has severe repercussions on what we believe personality to be, on what we think a human being is, and on what we perceive to be values. Phenomenology has tried to reconcile this dispute by developing a description of being which, rather than taking sides, proposes a synthesis of these various positions. This is achieved through the notion of intentionality, dialectic, or polarity. Rather than ask whether the field is mental or material or whether it is "one" or "two," phenomenology holds that being is mental in one region of its total extent, and is material in another. (We are not talking of persons but of *being*.)

The two characteristics are interfused in a way that is both difficult and important to describe. In meditation we focus on the mental region, the consciousness of that field; in sports we focus on the material region; in hypnosis we focus on the consciousness region; when chiseling a statue out of marble, we focus on the material region. We must realize at all times that although these two regions are in reality intertwined, interpenetrating, and inseparable, they do not coalesce; they do not form one. So it is with us as persons. Part of us is consciousness and part of us is body. We cannot say as does an ultra-mystic that we are really just a consciousness that has an illusory body attached to it or who dreams about a body; nor can we say, as does an ultra-neurophysiologist, that we are just a bundle of nerves with some protoplasmic mass surrounding it, of which the conscious mind is but an illusory epiphenomenon. We must affirm instead that mind and body are two regions of a continuous field. It is incorrect to say that one region is inside the other. Both regions are interdependent; mind creates body and body creates mind.

Given these difficulties, what is mind? How can we define it? The answer is that mind is that which has a body before it. And what is a body? A body is that which is perceived by a mind.

In the first place, *to be* is to be an object; *to be* is to be a piece of matter given to or presented to a subject. We cannot say something exists unless it exists as an object that is offered to a subject or to a consciousness, for an object does not exist in isolation, just as it does not exist without space and space does not exist without time. Furthermore, similarly, and conversely, there can be no subject or no consciousness which exists in isolation. Consciousness exists and is defined only by virtue of its having objects constantly before it. Using a mathematical analogy we can define one as a function of the other. The subject (or consciousness) is defined as the function of an object (body):

$$S = f(O)$$

or mind (M) is defined as a function of matter (m):

$$M = f(m).$$

Conversely, the object is a function of the subject:
$$O = f(S)$$
or matter (m) is defined as a function of mind (M):
$$m = f(M).$$
The meaning of these expressions is that they point to the requirement that we need to define the object before we can define the subject. We need to define matter before the definition of mind makes any sense. And of course the converse is also true. What is a subject? A subject is that kind of event which has before it an object. And how do we define an object? We define an object as a function of a subject. And what is a subject? It is the event that perceives an object. In symbolic form this intentional relationship between subject and object, consciousness and world, mind and matter can be symbolized as $[S = f(O)] \cdot [O = f(S)]$, where "$\cdot$" indicates that both statements are asserted to be true at the same time. We could also symbolize this symmetrical relationship by borrowing a designation from chemistry. Referring now to mind (M) and matter (m) instead of subject and object, our formula looks like this:
$$M \rightleftarrows m.$$

This analysis represents a fundamental structure of existence. It is an irreducible situation, and it is meant to explain a basic meaning of the intentionality of the consciousness-world field. Several terms describe this fundamental interaction of being. In addition to the word *intentionality*, such terms as *polarity, contradiction,* and especially *dialectic* are commonly used.

Some people believe in the development of consciousness out of a history of billions of years of geological and biological evolution. In this connection, the phenomenological model of being is radical. If there were no consciousness there would be no objects; correlatively, if there were no objects there would be no consciousness. These propositions hold true for all time. The ontological argument for the existence of God applies here in an unorthodox way. [2] The field of consciousness-world is a necessary being. The field of consciousness-world cannot not be. The problem of the evolution of consciousness therefore does not arise.

In describing the notions of polarity, dialectic, and the intentional field, we saw that the phenomenological description of the structure of being (and of the person) is an attempt to reconcile fundamental philosophical disputes. The one-many and the mind-matter disputes can be resolved through an intentional theory of consciousness. [3] Phenomenology by means of intentionality describes the relationship between consciousness and its objects; it remains true, at the same time, to the union as well as to the separateness of consciousness and its objects. The name that Western civilization has given to the consciousness pole, to the extreme inward region of consciousness, is God. And the name that has often been given to the extreme objective or worldly pole is Nature.

Constitution and Cathexis

Let us end this consideration of philosophic fundamentals with two related ideas: constitution and cathexis. The former is a conventional concept in phenomenology; the latter, however, is a refinement of phenomenology needed for its clinical application. Whereas the word *cathexis* is borrowed from the terminology of psychoanalysis, its meaning here is modified.

The first concept is the central notion of constitution. There are "grooves" as it were in the intentional consciousness-world field; there exist patterns of organization into which our initially amorphous experience falls. Specifically, in clinical philosophy *constitution* refers to the fact that the *freedom* —sometimes conscious and sometimes unconscious, sometimes active and deliberate and sometimes passive and ̆automatic—which is found in transcendental consciousness has the capacity to organize the material it receives as data from the empirical realm literally into as many combinations as there are mathematical permutations for these data. Certain organizations are common and traditional. For example, sense data which move together—like a running animal or a flying airplane—are usually organized as one object, whereas the background against which they move—the forest and the clouds—becomes a separate object or series of objects. In this manner even an animal appears to develop the idea of an object and a person, the idea of a living thing. For a cat, a bird becomes a real object when it begins to move.

Communication depends on a consensual uniformity of such interpretations. There exists a consensus of basic constitutions based on pragmatic and conventional principles of organization. This consensus forms a system (as that word is used in systems theory). That system of common assumptions and common perceptions makes communication functional and possible. Language is an important "bank," "pool," or reservoir of constitutions.

The rigidity of language is partially responsible for the fact that psychological problems are often the result of constitutions that fail to perform their expected pragmatic task, that is, they are often the result of ineffective constitutions. Psychotherapy hopes to change not necessarily the reality of the patient but the perception of the patient's world. *Reconstitution* is therefore indicated. Before the freedom of transcendental consciousness can effectively reconstitute its world design, *deconstitution* must take place. The latter is the disorganization of the organized world design into its atomic constituents. Insanity may at times be just that kind of anxiety-producing deconstitution. Insanity may therefore be an unexpected opportunity for reconstitution. This view has been espoused by R. D. Laing.

The world is like a puzzle with a near infinity of pieces. But it is a unique puzzle in that there is no right or wrong way to fit the pieces together—just *your* way. A unique world design and a personalized being-in-the-world —perceptions of a specific nature and with a specific meaning—are created each time the puzzle pieces are fitted together to produce a mosaic. That is the process of constitution. To teach children accepted forms of constitution is to socialize them. To deconstitute is to disassemble the pieces. Reconstitution is to create a new order, a new mosaic with the same component pieces. The constitution-deconstitution-reconstitution cycle is an art and not a science. The cycle requires constant attention and fine tuning. Rigidity in constitution means obsession and compulsion. It restricts the possibilities of living. Excessive liberty in the process leads to disorganized and asocial behavior. Somewhere in the middle lies creativity and authenticity.

Cathexis—called also identification or fusion—indicates the attachment or commitment that transcendental consciousness makes to one type of organization (for example, loyalty) and, more importantly, to one region within that constituted organization (loyalty to one's family). This latter region becomes by virtue of the constitution-cathexis sequence the ego or self, the individual identity. A person thus chooses an identity. He or she is not born with an identity, nor is an identity discovered. But before an identity can be chosen it must be constituted as a meaning. Thus, constitution means organization of meanings and cathexis means identification with or attachment to a specific organization of meanings. It is in this context that the expression "ego involved" makes sense. In both constitution and cathexis a central role is played by the freedom of transcendental consciousness. The reality of the constitution-cathexis pair—which is essentially an idea derived from researches in epistemology—means in clinical practice that persons are responsible for their life-styles, their self-image and their world design. Such severe ascription of responsibility is one secret of successful therapeutic work.

The process of establishing an identity and of developing a sense of one's individuality is to perform a cathexis. In that act we identify with something. We appropriate one region of being and say by virtue of that act of appropriation "That is a me" and at the same time we deny another region of being and say through that denial "That is a not-me." We say "yes" to zone A and "no" to zone non-A. And that simple act of saying "yes-no," that simple act of attachment-alienation, of involvement-estrangement, is the act of becoming a person and an individual.

An act of cathexis which is duplicated and illustrated in a living metaphor is the concept of a dream. A person may dream of five individuals but identifies with only one. Theoretically, at least, he is free to identify with any one of the five. The dreamer is free to say, in the dream, "Yes, I am person A" and "No, I am none of the other four persons." That is how dreams exemplify first the act of constitution, which is the creation of the dream, and second the act of cathexis, which is the selection of one person (or other event) with whom the dreaming ego identifies itself. In real life, these same archetypal decisions create us as individuals. From that moment on our human nature as unique and separate persons begins, and it is the dual acts of constitution and cathexis which explain the problems and the joys of the archetypal decision for being finite and thus human. These points will be explained more extensively in later chapters.

Constitutions and cathexes can be either *active* or *passive*. When active we have deliberate and conscious control over them in actuality. That is relatively rare. In clinical philosophy, active constitutions and cathexes (which means also deliberate reconstitution and recathexis) are desiderata under most circumstances, especially when change and growth are required, but such active freedom is also a heavy burden. Passive constitutions and cathexes are habitual and automatic. They are convenient and often necessary. We protect ourselves against anxiety and chaos by invoking these ready-made programs. However, we possess at all times—even at deep levels—the potential for transforming passive constitutions and cathexes into active ones. It is convenient to have many passive programs. A car need not be rebuilt every morning we drive to work. But the potential for rebuilding is always there.

The following hypothesis is a corollary of the active-passive distinction as it concerns constitution and cathexis: The reason we do not remember our earliest childhood experiences is not for any lack of memory power but for the lack of organization of that primitive experience when it occurs. We can recall only experience which is organized in a manner similar to how our experience is organized today, and when we go very far back into our childhood we uncover experiences which are completely disorganized. We interpret that to mean that the child did not know what was going on. For example, will a six-month-old child who has been transported from Vietnam to San Francisco remember in later life what happened to him? He will indeed remember what he once knew. But he did not know that he was being transported from Vietnam to San Francisco. What he experienced during the 1975 "baby lift" is real enough, but it will be very difficult to express it in the language he will have at his disposal twenty years from then. Only art, philosophy, or mysticism will offer symbols equivalent to that experience. The consensual world and its language will not make that possible.

Exercises

We can devise an exercise which helps us to actually experience the structure of the dialectical field of consciousness, especially its capacity for potentially free constitution and reconstitution. It is not enough to theorize and to understand the phenomenological model of being conceptually. Each person must go through the process of discovery by himself, alone. He must retrace for himself the steps of history's great philosophers. The exercise is simple and usually it is effective. Here is a classroom illustration.

The teacher explains to his or her students the epistemological concept of the difference between the *given* and the *interpreted* in experience. The students are informed that knowledge and truth begin and are based on that which is given in experience, namely the data. The given are those phenomena or aspects of phenomena about which we cannot be mistaken. Even though it may be difficult to name the given, it is not difficult to have a sensation of it and to recognize its importance. The field of consciousness functions in the following way: We superimpose on these data our meanings, interpretations, attitudes, and projections. These are our constitutions. We can change the latter—that is where our freedom is efficacious; we cannot, however, affect the structure of the pure data. They are the *Other*; they are determined in their nature by the world outside of our center. To understand this distinction experientially the teacher draws these figures on the blackboard:

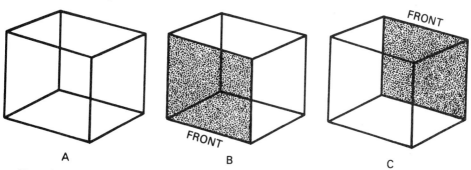

He refers to Figure A and explains that, actually, *given* is a two- and not three-dimensional figure. Given are two triangles, four trapezoids, and a parallelogram. He asks them to try to perceive only that which is given and eschew the obvious perceptual interpretations. That task is difficult because we are thoroughly conditioned to interpret this particular two-dimensional picture in a three-dimensional way.

Then he shows them that there is also a second way to mean or intend a specific cube, a three-dimensional figure, B. It then becomes intuitively apparent that consciousness adds something to the plane figure—the sense of three dimensionality. But now the contention is also that constitution is potentially free. The teacher therefore asks them to shift between the perception of the pure data and the perception of data plus interpretation (A and B). Shifting thus from a two- to a three-dimensional perception is at first difficult and may produce vertigo and nausea, but some practice can lead to relative ease and proficiency. The physical symptoms are the direct experience of our resistance to deconstitution.

Then he shows them that there is also a second way to mean or intend a cube, C. One cube is seen from above pointing toward the left (B) and the other is seen from below pointing to the right (C). He then asks them to develop once more a facility to move back and forth between these two interpretations with the assistance of the cubes with the shaded areas. Then they take some time to reflect on this experience and to familiarize themselves with the experience of the distinction between the given and the interpreted, with their surprising freedom of constitution and their painful resistance to deconstitution. This is an experiential approach to a fundamental epistemological point. It is a point that must be understood thoroughly *both* conceptually *and* experientially.

The denouement of the exercise comes when the students are asked to apply the same reasoning and make the same distinctions in a phenomenon of far greater interest and importance than a mere cube. They should think about human beings, about the concept of the person, and especially about themselves, where, after all, the ultimate evidence for the structure of being and the field of consciousness is to be found. They are asked to divide a piece of paper in half, vertically. On the top of the page and over each column they write the questions, "What am I?" and "Who am I?" In the left column they are to write down descriptions of what is interpreted, conceptual, and learned. That is easy enough. They have done that all their lives. Under the right-hand column they are asked for phenomenological descriptions of their immediate experience, their undiluted givenness. Whereas the column on the left will be well-organized, cogent, and coherent, the one on the right should be spontaneous, impressionistic, associative, and as disorganized as may be necessary to approximate and evoke the uninterpreted primordial sensations.

The next and last step is to experiment with new self-concepts. The students describe identities that are opposite to themselves: if you are timid, experiment with an aggressive self-concept; if you are proud, experiment with a self-effacing self-concept; if you are male, experiment being female, and if you are young, change your self-concept to being old.

In this fashion the students are in touch with their freedom in defining and redefining who they are and with the strong resistances that stand in the way.

This exercise takes time and patience. But it is one in which each individual develops an existential phenomenology out of his own inwardness: He discovers, in his own language, his own terms, and in his own experience, the kind of insight found in Heidegger's *Being and Time*, Sartre's *Being and Nothingness*, and Husserl's *Cartesian Meditations*. The value of the exercise is intensified if it is done repeatedly and if it is alternated with the presentation of straightforward didactic material.

The above two chapters are an outline of the clinically relevant ontology or metaphysics that philosophy has developed after twenty-eight hundred years of Western thought. With that model in mind, the clinical philosopher should be able to derive logically the uniquely individual psychology that each of his or her patients demands. When the therapist is in full command of this fundamental ontology he or she can, with some imagination and much devotion, invent at each moment of therapy the proper psychological system meant only for this unique patient in the office now and not for anyone else.

Some of the value of these epistemological reflections can be found in the following items for further investigation. Primordial being is a consciousness-body-world field. In that field, what Maurice Merleau-Ponty calls the body-qua-mine represents the interface between consciousness and world; it is *my-body* where the relationship between the two is experienced and lived out. Also, the key to philosophic understanding is the act of stepping back, which is called variously reduction, the phenomenological attitude, or the transcendental (or transcendental-phenomenological) reduction. (The reduction needs an amplified discussion, which will follow.)

Furthermore, the archetypal decision for finitude is the constitution of a personality. Its dynamics are principally the constitutions of the concepts (since they are not experiences) of *my-birth* and *my-death*. These are metaphorized as dreams in our consensual world. To fully understand this point—which is discussed in Chapters 12 and 13—is to have acquired the courage for becoming an individual identity and the solace of immortality and reincarnation.

Finally, it is likely that this ontology, that is, the phenomenological model of being, promises to be the theoretical breakthrough needed to produce progress in certain areas of the healing arts where there is at present an impasse. We must look in particular for applications of clinical philosophy to psychosomatic medicine, to parapsychology, and to the concept of life-energy, which is related to the apparently insurmountable lifespan for humans of just under one hundred years.

Notes

1. Bertrand Russell said that before he entered Cambridge University the totality of his philosophical knowledge was this: "What is mind? No matter! What is matter? Never mind!"

2. See Peter Koestenbaum, *Is There An Answer To Death?* (Englewood Cliffs, N.J.: Prentice-Hall, 1976), pp. 176-179.

3. The rationalism-empiricism dispute also can be resolved by phenomenological techniques applied to the intentional field of consciousness. We saw an analysis of that on pages 38-39.

Part III • THE PHENOMENOLOGICAL MODEL OF BEING

Chapter 4 • THE PHENOMENOLOGICAL MODEL OF BEING

To lend depth, accuracy, and professionalism to clinical philosophy, it is necessary for both client and counselor, patient and therapist, or student and teacher to be in possession of a well-grounded and clear phenomenological model of being and existential personality theory. As a result, it is important to find a presentation of these philosophical positions that is didactically effective and philosophically responsible.

Joan B., a woman who is a superb performer and scholar of Baroque music, was asked in a seminar what she wanted to achieve in life. She answered, "I want to understand life fully!" Some, like Joan, do it through music. Others try to achieve the same goal through literature or psychology. Others do it through philosophy. "Understanding life fully" is always a process. But the process wishes to be objectified, to become visible to itself, to create a past and a history for itself. Sartre has given us an inspired description of this process that is the overarching reality of life. In his language, the *pour soi*—Sartre's term for what in the phenomenological model of being is called pure consciousness—always wants to be the *en soi*—his term for what in the intentional theory of consciousness is called the realm of objects. This process or *conatus* goes on forever because it cannot, by the nature of the basic ontological situation, ever be fully consummated. The essence of the process of "understanding life fully" consists not in that the *pour soi* achieves its goal to become the *en soi*, not in that consciousness becomes the objects which it perceives, but to strive in the process of self-transcendence indefinitely. Nevertheless, to understand life fully—as is true of any creative and artistic activity—is to extrude increasing amounts of objectivity the way a spider spins a web. The meaning of the phenomenological model of being lies in precisely that kind of objectification.

A Nonmedical Model of the Person

According to a famous statement by William James, "The classic stages of a theory's career" are three: First it "is attacked as absurd; then it is admitted to be true, but obvious and insignificant; finally it is seen to be so important that its adversaries claim they themselves discovered it."[1] The phenomenological model of being hovers at the present time somewhere between the second and third stages.

The basic outlines of this model can be stated both systematically and simply. It is crucial, however, that this view be taken seriously, accepted in a total, that is, experiential sense, and not be relegated exclusively to the realm of the conceptual. The seriousness with which this view is accepted by the individual, the therapist, by his culture and environment, determines in part its healing powers and therapeutic qualities. That is, the extent to which these ideas are integrated into and reflected by appropriate supportive institutions, by a consensual world view, and by our world-constituting ordinary language is directly proportional to their psychotherapeutic efficacy. In fact, one of the problems in so-called "conventional" therapy is that the latter's research, conception, teaching, and practice are based on a *medical model of the person*[2]—a model which is of course very useful but which is also both narrow and limited. Such a model is ineffective in dealing with the large spectrum of basic questions that arise in anyone's life and are reflected in counseling practice.

Moreover, it is this inaccurate and distorted model of being which, far from being merely the cause of the disease, is the disease itself. The disease of our culture is to accept a view of the person that is contrary to the empirical facts of experience as these are disclosed through the phenomenological reduction and the method of phenomenological description. Thus the self-concept which leads to the pervasive symptoms of meaninglessness, self-denial, and timidity is accepted as "normal" rather than being recognized as dysfunctional, which it is. When the medical model of the person is the conventional one and thereby the standard of normalcy, healing becomes a very limited activity. However, from the perspective of clinical philosophy, this medical model is already a form of cultural psychopathology. The philosophic "cure," as it were, is to overturn the model itself on which the putative cures of conventional therapy have heretofore been based.

Our nonmedical model of the person, that is, the phenomenological model of being, consists of a pair of polarities: the mind-body polarity and the individual-universal polarity. All of being, personal or not, is a polarity rather than a thing; it conforms with the Sartrean view about the *pour soi-en soi* relationship discussed previously. Being is a field rather than an object. Being is dialectical; its existence is a living and changing phenomenon (either as life, which means increasing foci and concentrations of energy through the evolution of species or individuals, or as entropy, which applies to inert matter and means decreasing foci of energy and increased evenness of energy distribution). And life or entropy must be described to occur on the model of a field (such as in a magnet or a capacitor) which includes both stress and oscillation (which characterizes kinetic energy and wave phenomena). In sum, being is process rather than stasis, and the phenomenological model of being tries to take full account of these facts.

These dialectical views of being are expressed by a number of notable modern and contemporary philosophers, including such thinkers of evolution as Bergson, Spencer, and Alexander, and ranging from Darwin to Teilhard de Chardin. In the phenomenological-existential tradition, those philosophers emphasizing the importance of the dialectic in our understanding of being are in particular Hegel and Sartre and to lesser extents but no less significantly Whitehead, Dewey, Husserl, and Heidegger. These philosophers, as well as many others, have sought to capture in their models of being as an evolving process the aliveness of the universe (as life and entropy, as concentrating and diffusing energy). They have tried to preserve in what appears to be a static objectification—a philosophic system which like a high-speed camera tries to capture and fix motion—as well the ingredients of life and subjectivity in the universe. What is typical of these thinkers is their emphasis on the dialectical, process, and field structure of being and their corresponding avoidance of static and reductionistic ontologies. And that is one element which is carefully preserved in the phenomenological model of being. All being is ambiguous, dialectical, and embodies polarities. Being consists of a depth that appears in layers, layers that a phenomenological methodology can gradually uncover.

THE MIND-BODY POLARITY

In the phenomenological model of being, *being* or existence is first a mind-body polarity or field. In fact, we are a consciousness-world field. One part of that continuous field is properly called consciousness, and the other part, body, matter, object, or world. The continuity between these two poles, their permanent interpenetration and interdependence, is expressed in Brentano's and Husserl's use of the word *intentionality* and in Heidegger's emphasis on his descriptive concept of *being-in-the-world*. The medical model of the person, which is no fault of medicine or physiological research, exists in response to the demands of some of the most basic assumptions of our entire culture. And that model—protestations to the contrary notwithstanding—takes seriously only the *bodily, objective,* or *worldly* sense of the person (or of the *we*).

Our culture pays mostly lip service to the mind or consciousness, but it rarely integrates the reality and the nature of consciousness fully and systematically into its theory, research, and application. We must return to primitive cultures—with their animism, mysticism, polytheism, mythology, astrology, magic, and sorcery—to find a world design which makes a genuine effort to integrate the reality of consciousness into the institutions of society and into the healing process. Recent work in holistic medicine is a first step in the direction of implementing the suggestions of this phenom-enological model of being to medicine. Humanistic psychology has endeav-ored to accomplish the same in psychotherapy.

Clearly differentiated life-styles and coping devices follow, respectively, from emphasis on the subjective, conscious pole and from a parallel focus on the objective, bodily, and worldly pole of the field of consciousness that is human existence. The prevailing life-style of the intellectual and scientific establishment is still predominantly body-centered and world-oriented. The basic reason for this nemesis of our culture is the economic support given to expression of an object-centered science and withheld from a consciousness-oriented discipline. We experience today the reverse of the problem that afflicted such great men of science as Galileo and Darwin. These are called *hedonic* life-styles. Slogans such as "get involved" and "make a commit-ment" express the saliency of this orientation. The derivative ethical direc-tion becomes a materialistic happiness and success-oriented value system. And the road to fulfillment is populated with techniques and manipulative devices.

Altogether different life-styles and coping devices follow from a mind- or consciousness-oriented decision regarding the proper focus, emphasis, or favoring along the field of our mind-body polarity. These latter include withdrawn, distanced, and detached modes of being-in-the-world called *ascetic* life-styles. Neither position is right, valuable, proper, or authentic in any absolute sense. Both have their place, and a combination of flexibility and adaptability in this area represents realistic and authentic life-styles. These insights are compressed on the *Master Table.*[3]

THE INDIVIDUAL-UNIVERSAL POLARITY

The second polarity that we are or that being is (which, if we were to plot it, is vertical to the first) is the individual-universal, man-God, or indi-vidual-social set of options afforded us by the structure of the field of consciousness. The resistance against taking seriously the full impact of this polarity is far more severe than is the corresponding opposition to the mind-body polarity. Although it is possible to experience ourselves as either individual or as universal (that is, participating in the universal stream of being that is the world), in actual fact, the medical model of the person—or the ghost-in-a-machine personality theory—rejects the option for uni-versality almost completely. Again, lip service may be paid to the self-concept of universality—as when the notions of meditation and ecosystems are introduced—but our culture does not integrate them adequately enough to be reflected systematically in either research, theory-construction, hypothesis formation, or treatment strategies. The individual-universal polarity is not reducible to the mind-body polarity; each polarity represents a different set of possibilities for self-definition.

The life-styles and coping devices associated with this polarity are, respectively, willpower and surrender (a trust currently called "going with the flow"). Willpower is the way of life of the individual, an approach to life well illustrated in the atheism of Sartre and Camus: we, single-handedly and without precedent or foundation, create or invent our nature, our essence. We define ourselves *ex nihilo*. Our consciousness is an infinite abyss out of which an objective nature, a thing with a past, a concrete reality is nevertheless spontaneously and autonomously (freely) spawned. In short, each person is self-made.

Our Western culture is essentially individualistic and capitalistic, and to that extent it supports in depth only the individualistic option of human reality with its accompanying emphasis on willpower, freedom, and responsibility as coping strategies and ethical desiderata. The relics of the possibility for universality, which are the social, tribal, or communal virtues of religiosity, duty, and patriotism, are receding. But cracks in the structure are becoming visible.

Surrender, faith, and trust as life-styles follow from the universal possibility of our nature. To cope with life from the aspect of universality means "to listen to your inner voices," "to be your body," "to be in touch with your feelings," and "to find and speak with God." It includes the surrender to meditation, which can mean what heretofore has been mostly Oriental and mystical exploration of inner space, as well as Western romantic and artistic love of nature.

No value judgments are intended. Commitment to either the universal or the individual is a legitimate, nonpathological possibility. But a person must be free to make his or her own decision.

Pain

Many exercises can be constructed to provide evidence for the accuracy of the phenomenological model of being. Let us take the example of a strong but bearable pain, such as a toothache, a headache, a burn, a splinter, or an infection. Here are the instructions:

Make a concerted effort to observe the pain in detail and clearly. Describe it. Ascribe to it, if it will help, color, shape, size, and consistency. Ask yourself, for example, "Is it green?" "Is it made of marshmallow?"—whatever questions seem relevant to you. Now reflect on what you are doing. You are establishing a psychic distance between the pain and your center. That is a distinct experience and it should not mystify you; you are simply describing your experience with accuracy. But you must have the courage to reject the commonsense interpretation or reconstruction of this experience, which tells you that the pain is subjective, that it is *in* you, and that you *are* it. In truth, as the meditative experiment discloses, your center and the pain are *separate*—like the two poles of the subject-object magnet.

We continue now by manipulating the objectified pain. We try to change it, enlarge it, throw it away, destroy it, give it to someone else, and so forth. We operate on the pain and with it illustrate the fact that we are also *connected* to it. In this way we illustrate the intentional or field aspect of the subject-object polarity. If it should happen that in addition to the epistemological value of this experience we eliminate the pain (or even intensify it), the healing power of this model is thereby reinforced.

Finally, we can focus (or establish a *here-zone*) on either the observing center (the subject) or the object (pain, in this case) observed. If we are the detached center and accentuate its separateness from the object, the pain, then we exist, by choice, in the ascetic mode. If, on the other hand, we choose to encourage total absorption in the object, which is the pain, then we exist in the hedonic mode. Our ordinary consciousness is ambiguous in this matter and oscillates between these two possibilities. By taking charge of the situation and opting for one of these two alternatives, the nature of the pain and our relation to it also change. The specific change varies from person to person. However, the agony of the pain can change (it will be either heightened or lessened) by this kind of an identification-disidentification exercise.

Another way to approach the realm of subjectivity *and* objectivity experientially is to fantasize watching one's existence being shown on a television screen. As we get into the fantasy and see with ever increasing clarity our life played out, we get a sense of the psychic distance from our center (the transcendental ego) to the most intimate object in the world (our empirical ego). We can experience stepping even further back into transcendental subjectivity by now fantasizing that we are a second party, who enters the room and observes us as we sit watching ourselves on the television screen. This experience of centeredness shows us that our roles are not us but are our objects and that we are free to turn to entirely different sets of options. The fact that these fantasies are indeed possible is phenomenological evidence for the meaningfulness and accuracy of the phenomenological model of being and the person.

A student injured her knees in track. For years she was in agonizing pain. No medication or physical therapy helped. She finally learned to reconstitute her pain. She developed the capacity to perceive the pain as an object before her. She trained herself to sift from that sensory object the given from the interpreted. She learned, through extensive meditation practice, to single out what was presented to her by the Other, by the external, that over which she exercised absolutely no control, from the plethora of interpretations, organizations, assessments, and meanings she ascribed to the pain. She discovered after a week of this analysis that the "painfulness" of the pain was interpreted and not given. Taking advantage of that insight, she reconstituted the meaning of the phenomenon from bad to good, from pain to pleasure. For years afterward she was able to bear the pain through this device.

Philosophy does not necessarily heal or eliminate pain; but the phenomenological model of being can suggest new ways of managing pain and health in general.

Let us now turn from an exercise that illustrates the subject-object polarity of the field of consciousness to a very simple one that demonstrates the individual-universal polarity.

The experience of universality can be had by imagining that inside us is a window or a door. As we open it we notice that it leads to an inner space equally as vast as the external space from which we just came.

The issues introduced have been these: Human reality is a set of possibilities encapsulated in a pair of polarities, both poles of which are valid. We can experience ourselves as a mind—in which case our coping strategies may tend to be *ascetic*—or as a body—in which case we tend to cope *hedonistically*, that is, through commitment, cathexis, identification, or fusion with the objects of consciousness. We can also experience ourselves as individual—we then cope through willpower—or as universal—in which case trust is our coping device. The medical model of the person, which our culture demands and supports, takes seriously only the bodily and individual possibilities of this pair of polarities, and with it denies not only one aspect of our nature but also the reality of the dialectic structure of being.

The above is an outline of the phenomenological model of being. Before we move on, however, to a detailed account and defense of this view and the development of therapeutic and clinical applications, we must consider some metaphysical aspects of phenomenology.

Existential-Phenomenological Metaphysics

The history of thought has given us idealisms, materialism, and dualisms: Idealism—regardless of whether it is called mentalism, spiritualism, subjective, or objective—is the view that the subjective pole of the subject-object field, that is, the subjective dimension of consciousness or being, is the ultimate truth. Conversely, materialism—be it called naturalism, realism, or objectivism—is the view that the only reality is the objective pole of that field of consciousness or being.

Dualism is the position that both consciousness and its objects are real but independent; neither can be explained in terms of the other. The strength of phenomenology as a dialectical philosophy lies in the insight—which has the power to resolve these traditional disputes—that the evidence of unprejudiced and immediate experience discloses the irreducible fundamentum of reality to be a consciousness-object, subject-object, awareness-world continuum. Consciousness and world or mind and matter are thus in direct touch with each other, are part of one field. The problem of mind-matter interaction does not arise, because it is precisely this interaction which is given in the irreducible immediacy of presuppositionless experience.

Furthermore, if we do not begin our philosophy with a model of the world as a space-time container filled with objects but as an intentional field (so that there are not *objects* but that there is a *consciousness of objects* and there is not a *world* but a *consciousness of a world*), then objects need not be concrete, hard, and atomic but can be subtle—such as a concept—with equal ease. The distinction between *given as present* and *given as hidden* is not a mystery. Nor is it puzzling to aver that some, perhaps most, objects shift from being *given* to becoming *hidden*, or the reverse.

Notes

1. William James, *Pragmatism* (New York: Longmans, Green, 1969), p. 198.

2. The general outlines of this model are discussed in Peter Koestenbaum, *Managing Anxiety* (Englewood Cliffs, N.J.: Prentice-Hall, 1974), chap. 2, as the "ghost-in-a-machine theory of man."

3. See Koestenbaum, *Managing Anxiety*, chap. 3. See also Appendix E.

Chapter 5 • *REFLECTION AND THE MIND-BODY POLARITY*

A detailed exposition of the mind-body polarity within the total phenomenological model of being can be compressed into four general statements: definition, reflection (which includes some therapeutic considerations), metaphor, and consequences.

Definition

The mind-body polarity can be *defined* as follows: Unbiased and meticulous description of experience, as given to us directly in the here-and-now, discloses that there exist two clearly *different, connected,* and equally *real* regions of the person and of being. One is consciousness, subjectivity, mind, or awareness (these terms are not meant to have absolutely univocal definitions; their role in description is approximate, evocative, and impressionistic rather than precising).

In phenomenology this first region is often called noetic or the transcendental. These words refer to pure, object-less consciousness.[1] The other region is the body and its environment; it is also nature, matter, object, and world. This region is often called, in phenomenology, the noematic, psychological, or empirical region; it is the *Lebenswelt* (life-world). Its essential feature is that it is the *object* to transcendental consciousness. It is this transcendental region of consciousness which our objectivistic culture refuses to integrate seriously and with commitment into its consensual perceptions, theoretical questions, practical concerns, and fundamental institutions.

The body (that is, *my* body, or technically, the body-qua-mine), as Merleau-Ponty has pointed out, occupies a unique place in the mind-body (or consciousness-world) polarity. It exists exactly between the subjective (conscious) and the objective (worldly) regions. The body-qua-mine can act as both subject and object, as when my hand feels the texture of my cheek. In this illustrative act, my body is the subject as hand and it is the object as cheek. This transitive relation can easily be reversed, since my cheek can feel the texture of my hand. In that case, my cheek acts as subject and my hand, as object. However, careful attention to the structure of our immediate experience discloses that the ultimate region of subjectivity, what we call transcendental consciousness or transcendental subjectivity, *is not necessarily identified with any organ*. Physiology may place it in the brain, and consensual opinion in the eyes or in the heart. In fact, most constitutions of experience place it vaguely in a here-zone located between the eyes, an inch or so inside the skull.

But the direct givenness of experience—which must always be the epistemological foundation of all thought and theory construction—does not make consciousness dependent on any organ or place in the body. Indeed, consciousness need not be located in any particular place in the universe. But if we place it outside of the body-qua-mine, the perspectival characteristics of the world change also. In other words, as long as transcendental consciousness is identified with and is located within the body-qua-mine, the world design or cosmic perspective is the consensual world. If we shift the locus of the here-zone dramatically, such as outside of the body-qua-mine, then the entire world view is transformed also. The consensual world is restructured into a mystical or transpersonal world. The collision of religious or idealistic metaphysics with naturalistic and materialistic ones is witness to this translation or transformation. The shift in perspective which accompanies the relocation of the here-zone can be compared to the transformations which take place in physics when we describe one event (the world as we see it, in this case) from the points of view of two noncongruent systems of coordinates.

Transcendental subjectivity will always in the last analysis perceive the body (or its body) in the modality of the object. To the extent that we experience ourselves as being an ego or a self, that is, an individual, Merleau-Ponty's assessment of the body-qua-mine, as what amounts to the intentional interface between consciousness and world, is quite accurate. But we can go further. To the extent that we are also a larger field, to the degree that the self is not an organ given in experience with unambiguous and consistent boundaries—such as is the case with the brain and the liver—but as protean and amorphous (as can be disclosed by and experienced in meditation), consciousness cannot be objectified. It is therefore not correct to speak of transcendental consciousness as if it were always and unequivocally the body-subject (as Merleau-Ponty has by implication done). My-body—even my-body functioning as subject—will always in addition be an object to transcendental consciousness. We will see later that this observation is important in the management of death and physical pain through clinical philosophy.

Reflection

The mind-body polarity is understood through the unique and epistemologically important phenomenon of *reflection*. We can legitimately ask, what is the evidence for the reality of the mind-body or mind-world distinction? The crucial difference between these two regions, formally designated as the transcendental and the empirical, is made possible and thereby shown to be real through the conscious act of reflection. Reflection, which means not consciousness but *self*-consciousness, not being but reflection on being, is the one act which separates being into its two distinct realms. In phenomenology, the concepts of *epoche, reduction, the phenomenological attitude, thematization,* and *bracketing* have been developed to call attention to the nature and importance of this central human possibility. Phenomenology, rightfully, makes the act of reflection the fulcrum about which pivots the total cognitive enterprise, which of course includes the philosophical description of being in metaphysics.

Therefore, one of the two most general and basic distinctions in being—between mind and matter, consciousness and its objects, or subjectivity and world (the other being the distinction between the individual and the universal)—is brought about by what is probably an exclusively human capability, the capacity to reflect on one's being-in-the-world, the ability to observe one's thinking and perceiving and thus the capacity to be embarrassed, guilty, shamed, and self-conscious. It is to be noted that in the phenomenological movement, and especially in the work of Husserl, the epoche is a central tool. It is derived from epistemological analyses, in which it is shown that knowledge comes about whenever we engage in an epoche. The epoche, which is the act of reflection, also defines the act of knowing.

In other words, I, as a being-in-the-world, as a field of consciousness, or as a subject-object continuum, can reflect on any phenomenon or event whatever (theoretically at least). I can reflect on even the most intense pain, panic, or anxiety, and even on death itself. In fact, anxiety and physical pain are often our experience of the resistances against the act of reflection. Some phenomena are experiences of inordinate attachment. We identify fully with certain persons, objects, and values. When the possibility of detachment is raised, which is usually called loss, we cling tenaciously to the identification. The ensuing struggle is experienced as anxiety and pain.

One example is the fear of flying. A person not used to flying who encounters stormy weather will experience his anxiety as the inability to detach himself from the airplane or even his body in the face of what he perceives as the possibility of death. This experiential truth about the pervasiveness of the possibility of reflection derived from "man's extremity" —which is where philosophy traditionally begins anyway—demonstrates, with a kind of empirical evidence usually applied only in the field of science, that a person is not merely a body, a system of observable behavior patterns, an organism, a machine, or a collection of feelings and emotions, but that a person is in fact also a *consciousness of* that body and *of* all its relations which make up the psychological or empirical ego. This is the phenomenological way to understand the reality and the importance of the consciousness or mind possibility of human existence.

It must be pointed out that reflection (or reduction or epoche) reveals the mind-body polarity only. It does not apply to the individual-universal polarity. The latter is revealed by freedom of constitution and cathexis.

Therapy

Psychotherapy and other forms of counseling can best be understood when we recognize them to be an important illustration of the phenomenological act of reflection. The relationship between being and reflecting on being, between consciousness and self-consciousness, is of the order of the dialectical polarity of being. Therapy is an intensified and exaggerated expression of the tension and the bipolar nature of the field that is human existence. Therapy is a complex activity of first letting the feelings be, then acting out these feelings, reflecting on the meaning, origin, and value of the newly elicited emotions and, finally, contemplating new actions. The therapeutic encounter involves ventilation and challenge or confrontation. Feelings are thereby aroused and acting out becomes possible and often desirable. These feeling phenomena emerge from the patient's being-in-the-world, or from what in phenomenology is called the natural attitude or *experience simpliciter* (Dorion Cairns' expression).

But therapy is also *reflection* on these newly experienced feelings, the buried emotions and the novel actions. In addition, therapy includes reflection on the life that is already in progress and on past life-styles and behavior systems, that is, reflection on self-definition and history. Without reflection (which may or may not include understanding, interpretation, and conceptualization) there is no learning and no control. Thus, psychotherapy is the continual application of the principle of philosophical reflection or of the phenomenological epoche. The material for reflection, which is in the natural attitude, consists of events from the life of the patient, emotions raised by the therapeutic encounter, and possible self-definitions and life-styles. While raising these feelings and issues is part of the function of the psychotherapeutic transaction, an even more significant activity is to reflect on the material it yields. Psychotherapy, like all other forms of knowledge, is reflection on self; it is self-knowledge and self-consciousness.

The act of reflection on oneself is useful abstractly, in that it opens up options, but it is also useful concretely. Although the consistent reflection on those areas of our experience on which we have avoided reflection produces anxiety, it also produces distance. The distance between the patient as sufferer and the patient as observer is the disclosure of the patient's pure or transcendental consciousness to himself or herself. And that region of transcendental consciousness contains the seeds of security, which means ego strength, and freedom, which means possibility for change. As a result of his insight, the patient now achieves growth and authenticity, in short, health.

Excessive focus on technique produces *empirical* material for philosophic analysis. It does not produce the analysis itself. It is incomplete, like sexual teasing without consummation. It has some healing value, even without analysis. But the greater portion of healing occurs after technique. It may have been called assimilation or integration in older forms of therapy. The role of philosophy lies in the reflection on, distance from, and evaluation and assessment of the material developed. That activity moves the patient to understand and use the *transcendental* dimension of his being. To understand and live in the openness of the transcendental dimension of pure consciousness is in itself a fundamentally significant therapeutic experience.

The learning can be abstract or experiential. An example of abstract learning would be exemplified by a man who says, "I behave timidly with women, a behavior pattern of which I was not aware and which stifles my creativity; I can conceptualize it or experience it as fear of my father, who is my stronger competitor in my attraction to my mother. As a result of this understanding I can deliberately, rationally, and consciously develop a program to recondition my habit of being timid with women." Learning can also be experiential, in which case it becomes a working-through. The patient learns through habit to feel comfortable with new and hitherto unexplored regions of his or her emotional makeup. Examples can be drawn from the integration of the shadow area, the demonic, into the patient's being-in-the-world. The demonic can appear perhaps in an image of a crab that clutches the heart, a cancer that must be excised surgically. In this case, the demonic is external to the ego. To experience it, to feel its sting and destruction, eventually helps to make the person whole. That is concrete and experiential learning. To achieve these results, the ability to both *be* and *reflect on being* that defines the person must be utilized consistently. This process we call therapy, and it is but an intensification of an essential cognitive aspect of the structure of existence in general.

Limits

We can reflect on anything, on the most intense pain and on the most glorious joy. We can reflect on sensitive events in our past and on difficult situations in our present. Of greatest interest to the therapist or counselor are the *limits to reflection*. The point where reflection becomes difficult is called the *resistance* in psychotherapy. And the analysis of this resistance is crucial to progress in therapy, as well as of course in religion, philosophy, art, and any other aesthetic or cognitive enterprise. To analyze the resistance is to try to achieve—that is, discover and experience—an intentional field of consciousness. The analysis of the resistance can give the patient an experience in which *both* mind *and* body are clearly discernible, and make that experience available in precisely that area of the personality structure where such intentionality is absent. The patient will then experience that he is not an object such as a self but that he is a field, a consciousness-body field.

Therefore, to resist in psychotherapy means to deny the possibility of dissociating consciousness from its object at one particular point. And it is at that point that the patient experiences his dysphoria. To *overcome* the resistance means success in expanding the field of consciousness and therewith to accrue increased flexibility in the being-in-the-world—reflecting-on-one's-being-in-the-world dichotomy, dialectic or polarity. Specifically, each time a person overcomes resistance to reflection, he has penetrated deeper into the regions of his pure, subjective, or transcendental consciousness. That accomplishment is central to the healing process, or, in a larger context, to growth and living itself.

For example, John has a strain of irresponsibility in his behavior. That character trait can be explained by a father who was irresponsible and by John's identification with his father. John is not aware of his irresponsible behavior. He does not understand or agree with interpretations which call this character defect to his attention. He is resisting. He lives that irresponsibility and he *is* the irresponsibility. The trait is an objective state of affairs and he is fused with that objectivity. If his therapist is now able to introduce an epoche, a state of reflection, into John's experience, then John will be *conscious* of his irresponsibility and he will be *conscious* of his fusion with his father. That is the phenomenological epoche. Once reflection has taken place, John has achieved understanding over his bothersome character trait and is now in a position to exercise rational control over it. The possibility of control is established on certain features of the structure of consciousness: security, which is based on the indestructibility of consciousness, and freedom, which is based on consciousness' power of constitution.

Let us consider three philosophically relevant examples of resistance to reflection—physical pain, an anxiety, and a relationship (especially a transference situation)—with a view to answering the question, Is there a limit to reflection? Is there a point beyond which the attachment to the world or the identification with an object in the world—such as a feeling, self-concept, or person—cannot proceed? Or can reflection (stepping back into the zone of the pure transcendental ego through the transcendental-phenomenological reduction) continue ad infinitum?

This question is related to the issue discussed on p. 55 in connection with Merleau-Ponty's position on the body-subject. The position taken here is that there is a subjectivity which antecedes the body-subject. We must refer to a transcendental consciousness to which the body-subject is an object and which in turn is not a body-subject itself. If there is a limit to detachment, then the position attributed to Merleau-Ponty may well be right. But if such a limit does not exist, then one may well have established with this insight the independence of the transcendental ego, the existence of consciousness without an object.

The history of philosophy, religion, and ethics appears to show that the process of reflection can continue indefinitely. There is no end to the regressive process of reflection because the field of consciousness is experienced to be infinite. Specifically, there is infinity in stepping back. As we move forward, we eventually encounter the object and, of course, always move past the object into the infinite space beyond; however, we can definitely move back into the recesses of our consciousness and encounter more and more primitive levels of subjectivity or inwardness. But there is no attachment (cathexis is the word to use in clinical philosophy) which cannot be withdrawn, no identification which cannot be dislodged. That is an important experience confirmed in the history of ethics and religion in particular. And these are the contentions which the following illustrations should help demonstrate.

There is physical pain about which we can reflect readily such as a headache or toothache. And there is physical pain so intense that reflection seems impossible. Finally, there is physical pain which leads to unconsciousness and even death. With the first type of pain, subjective or transcendental consciousness already feels itself independent of its object, which is the pain. If not totally independent, consciousness can at least experience itself as distant from the pain. Evidence of this is the fact that a person can discuss his toothache with his dentist. The third pain, which leads to unconsciousness, may be interpreted to be the phenomenon, as experienced subjectively, of consciousness having "abandoned" the body; it is the experience of consciousness detaching itself from its cathexis of the body, from its fusion with the empirical ego.[2]

The important pain is the second, the excruciating pain. In the first, consciousness remains in control. In the third, consciousness has detached itself from identification with the pain. But in the second type, struggle and indecision go on between the attached attitude (natural attitude) and the detached attitude (phenomenological attitude, or epoche). The individual is involved with it, committed to it. He writhes and he screams. He cannot detach himself even though he wants to. This experience is the struggle between being and reflection on being, between the natural attitude and the phenomenological attitude. It is the final effort of consciousness to hold on to the body when the temptation is to leave. The pain is the denial of distance, an excessive closeness between body and transcendental ego. It is the resistance to detachment and the last holding on to body fusion. Should the person let go of the identification, he would have a non-aversive experience of the pain. It would be a mystical experience, a peak-experience, the sense of enlightenment.

The morbid condition of the body invites severance and disidentification. To be my-body is to have cathected my-body, to be fused with it. To be in excruciating pain is to be tempted to decathect my-body, to disidentify oneself from it. The pain itself, analyzed phenomenologically and within the context of a phenomenological theory of reductions, is not an irreducible phenomenon. It is instead the experience of a consciousness which with despair and in a final effort maintains this attachment to, cathexis of, and identification with the body. When consciousness finally lets go of the body, when it learns to observe the pain as a receding object, then the act of reflection will have been accomplished and the source of strength, peace, mental health, and conquest over life will have been achieved.

There is always the danger, however, or at least the fear, that this detachment leads to death. It does lead, of course, to transformations in world design. These limits of attachment and identification are then not absolute and final but, strictly speaking, a matter for possible choice and freedom. It is the attachments over which control is difficult to exercise that create the problems of mental health and of life in general. The ancient insight that attachment means vulnerability and suffering—found in Buddhism, Stoicism, and Spinoza, to mention but a few— is accentuated and clarified by this phenomenological analysis. Ascetism suggests we train ourselves over a lifetime to avoid attachments of any kind. Prepared in this fashion, we will have the strength and fortitude to face any and all adversities.

The same situation applies to anxiety. Anxiety arises when we resist the act of reflection in connection with a feeling or a commitment in life. If we know that detachment is always possible and that detachment is essentially a decision—although it may be the decision to give up the body or our life or a dear love—then all ills can be conquered. This detachment will work therapeutically if supported by the culture but is in danger of being inefficacious if we pay only lip service to it. But since the topic of anxiety is discussed at length in Book Two, let us move on to an analysis of transference to illustrate how the central phenomenological concept of reflection has immediate psychotherapeutic applications.

Transference

What Freud has identified as the transference neurosis can effectively serve as a further example of resistance to detachment. The patient who insists on attaching a label borrowed from his childhood to his therapist is, in the act of conscious and compulsive projection, resisting the *self*-conscious insight into the reality of his detached consciousness. The transference neurosis is a resistance against reflecting on the feelings involved (either for the therapist or for the original significant *other* whose surrogate therapist represents). Transference comes about because the patient does not wish to reflect on the feeling but chooses to *be* that feeling. Being the feeling—excessive and thoughtless attachment—is the dysphoria of the symptom. Reflecting on the feeling is the liberation of control over one's life.

As long as the patient loves or hates the therapist (or conversely, as is the case in countertransference), the patient is in the natural or committed attitude. He *is* and does not *reflect* on his being. If the patient is convinced in addition that his feeling about the therapist is "real," "justified," or "deserved"—which it may well be—then he is protected from reflecting on his feeling, or his attachment and dependence on the relationship. He thereby denies his free and secure consciousness. And this denial is the disease. The patient will exhibit transference in those areas of his being-in-the-world where detachment or reflection is most difficult and most painful. The structure of his transference reveals those aspects of his life to which he is uncompromisingly attached. He is prevented (more accurately, he prevents himself) from entering the zone of his conscious subjectivity and from assuming total responsibility for himself. No better excuses than the personality of the therapist and the logically resulting feelings of the patient for the therapist exist for resisting the act of reflection. That is why the analysis of the transference neurosis is one of the most effective methods of psychotherapy.

The relationship between patient and therapist is one of the most sensitive areas for discussion. It is a true threat area—more sensitive than most aspects of the patient's life outside of the therapy hour. This relationship may well be the most rigid and last attachment. If this fusion can be separated, if a transcendental-phenomenological reduction can be performed on the patient-therapist relationship itself, then access to transcendental consciousness is total and complete and authenticity is achieved. This reduction must be lived—that is, not only understood and not even merely experienced; it must also be integrated into the patient's life. That is accomplished through a live witness—the therapist. And that is why when patients can discuss their relationships *to* their therapist *with* the therapist we have the epitome of psychotherapeutic effectiveness.

By extrapolation, we can use the same principles in marriage counseling. A marriage in which the partners can discuss (that is, reflect on being) as well as live (that is, be) their relationship has an excellent chance of success. The same principle applies to parenting and to all other relationships. Resistance against reduction is neurosis.

The patient finds it difficult to relinquish the transference. And each one he gives up is followed by another. The therapist must interpret the entire series of projections as transference until the patient stops all attempts at projection altogether. Then authenticity has been achieved; and it has been accomplished because of the patient's definitive openness to the transcendental dimension. One would not have thought that psychoanalysis is based on the ideas of religious mysticism.

To let go of the transference has similar characteristics to the letting go of the body in excruciating physical pain. The end result is the liberation of the subjective zone of a person's existence. It is the therapist's responsibility continually to point out that the patient's feelings are a matter of transference. The therapist is not the patient's father, mother or brother. The patient does not have his feelings because of the type of person the therapist is but because he projects them on the therapist. If the patient can accept these interpretations, time and again, then he may end up with the capacity to reflect on anything and thereby to distance himself from anything he chooses—for these transference projections are his very last and most rigid resistances. In this manner his consciousness is fully freed in orthodox psychoanalysis.

Freud's explanation of the dynamics is of course quite different. He discovered that the transference neurosis occurred and that its analysis is therapeutic. He did not understand what he had discovered and why his technique worked. The full therapeutic significance of discovering this zone is touched upon in the next chapter, which deals with the individual-universal polarity. It is with this liberation of his pure subjective consciousness that the patient experiences his center and his freedom. We saw earlier that centeredness is the foundation for security or ego strength and freedom is the source of action and change.

Notes

1. The expression "object-less consciousness" may rightfully disturb some readers, since the intentional theory of consciousness maintains that all consciousness is consciousness of something. The expression might, therefore, be changed to "an intentional subject-object field where consideration of the object-pole is temporarily kept in suspension."

2. There are, of course, some theoretical questions here, such as: Why do we say here consciousness is "detached" when other theoreticians would prefer "vanished"? This question is discussed later, and has been discussed in Peter Koestenbaum, *Is There An Answer To Death?* (Englewood Cliffs, N.J.: Prentice-Hall, 1976).

Chapter 6 • TRANSCENDENTAL CONSCIOUSNESS

The Transcendental Reduction

Reflection is another term for the technical concept of the transcendental-phenomenological reduction.

It should be clear by now that understanding pure consciousness, which is an ontological and metaphysical concept, is closely tied to understanding the transcendental reduction, which is an epistemological-methodological concept. To clarify this connection further it is helpful to present in some detail what happens in the reduction. Consciousness is not distanced and separated from its objects all at once. Consciousness and its objects are interfused like land and sea on a stormy shore where, in addition to the cycle of the waves, the tides confuse the precise boundary. When, through the transcendental-phenomenological reduction, we have an experience approximating a pure consciousness, we in fact stand on a beach while the gradually receding sea exposes large land masses. The emergence of consciousness from it objects in the reduction is like a healthy body emerging from a diseased body. The restoration is not sudden, especially in cases in which the disease or injury were severe. Restoration is so gradual, in fact, that one does not quite know when to aver that health has been established.

As we step back out of involvement with objects and allow pure transcendental consciousness to emerge, the following stages can be isolated, each of which has its own distinctive psychotherapeutic significance. Furthermore, the depth of inwardness is proportional to our potential for authenticity, for health, and for control over our destiny. It is therefore desirable—as much for the sake of theory as for practical applications—to learn to carry out the reductions to their fullest extent.

The first level in the process of reduction is prior to reduction, the stage at which reduction does not yet take place. Here there is no experienced distance between consciousness and object; identification and commitment are total and self-consciousness is unknown. At this first level the natural attitude is totally unthematized; we call this condition of consciousness the *animal consciousness*. (See Figure 1.) Some people object to the hypothesis

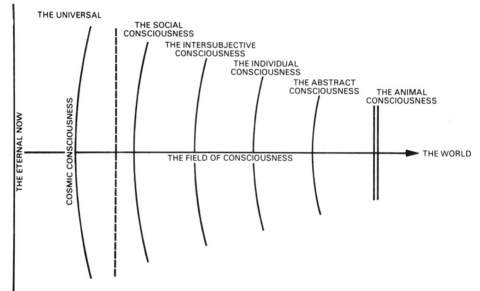

Figure 1   The Transcendental Reductions

that animals differ qualitatively from human beings. Rightly or wrongly, however, we often view animals as instinctive beings, consciousnesses without self-consciousness. We think of animals as pure impulse and no rational reflection. It matters little how this issue is resolved, for our concern is not to understand animals but to elucidate the intimate and subtle structures of our own consciousness as that consciousness reveals itself to us in presuppositionless first-person experience. We need a word to describe consciousness which is totally identified or cathected with its objects, a term more extreme and categorical than Husserl's broader concept of the natural attitude. And that term is animal consciousness.

The act of stepping back from the animal consciousness introduces reduction into human experience; with it begains the exploration of the person as a field of consciousness. That is the fundamental step of reflection. We can now increase the amount of consciousness revealed by making successive reductions. With each new type we enter deeper into consciousness. Increasing the level or the depth of reductions always follows the same principle: The region of consciousness which we enter and thus illuminate by means of one type of reduction, and which is thereby experienced as the region of the subject, becomes the object in the next level of reduction. This process has no end, because it is the very essence of consciousness to be an abyss without bottom, to be an infinite regress, and to lend itself to understanding acts of self-reference.[1] But for practical purposes six reductive steps can be isolated.

The first plateau that is reached in this stepping back is the *eidetic* or *abstract consciousness*. That reduction occurs by making the animal consciousness—which we were before this first reduction took place—into an object. The ability to think—which means mostly to abstract and deal in concepts, to operate with class similarities, and to comprehend relationships—is the phenomenon of distancing, of separating self-consciousness from consciousness. And the first step in thinking is to develop abstract ideas or eidetic objects, as these are called in phenomenology. We take one step back and the whole realm of abstraction, ideas, and essences becomes available to us. Husserl has called this step the eidetic reduction. The analysis of the abstract concepts and essences disclosed by the first reduction is an important field of study in phenomenology. When we explore the eidetic objects of consciousness, we are doing a phenomenology of logic and mathematics, and even, as was the case with Plato, a phenomenology of ethical concepts and ideals.

The second reduction, that is, the plateau we reach when we step one quantum jump back in the process of reflection (or reflexion) is called the *individual consciousness*. This is the basic posture we take in daily life and its full exploration is the first goal of therapy. Here consciousness reveals itself in the structure of being an individual. The object in this act of consciousness is the consciousness which perceives abstract objects, in other words, a self or an empirical ego. At this level consciousness thinks of itself as an individual and isolated self. The consciousness that is the individual self or ego still does not identify itself with other consciousnesses. The ultimate realm of pure consciousness is still experienced as consisting of one region which has been cathected—and is thereby the sense of the individual ego—and another region from which the ego is alienated, a region it has negated. In other words, in the second reduction consciousness experiences itself as single and isolated, different and alienated from other centers of consciousness.

In the third reduction we step back from experiencing ourselves as an individual ego. In that act the subjective sense of being an individual consciousness then becomes the new object of consciousness. That new and deepened level of consciousness is called the *intersubjective* or *intimate consciousness*. The experience of love occurs at this level and it is here where existential therapy takes place. We refer to the fact that this level has been attained in therapy by the terms *therapeutic triangle* or *transcendental relationship*. At this depth, consciousnesses are experienced as connected by a single space-time band or tube. Two people do not feel like two individuals in one bipolar field, where each individual consciousness is an object to the other; they feel like a combined subjective core to which a world of objects is given in common. It is useful for a teacher to point out at the beginning of a course or workshop that the group will develop a single intersubjective field in the classroom and that the common object is the subject matter that is to be learned.

A good metaphor for the transition from individual consciousness to intersubjective consciousness is the docking procedure in outer space. Before docking the spaceships are like two isolated individuals or monads. As they try to connect they make several efforts to match their openings. When they finally lock in to each other, a common door is opened, their space is stretched and expanded, and a larger and communal inner space is created. That is how two people meet. That is how, by performing the third reduction, a person experiences himself or herself no longer as a single conscious ego but as a single consciousness encompassing two egos. A swimmer in a pool is an individual. A second swimmer is also an individual. But with this reduction the new unit becomes the water in the pool, and the two swimmers are merely two focal points within the larger unity. When two persons meet they achieve direct access to each other's center and establish a common conscious field. It is that commonality which we call the intersubjective or the intimate consciousness.

The fourth reduction is the *social* or *communal consciousness.* As reductions increase and the depth we reach in consciousness increases, so does the inner space-time increase. The reductions exhibit a genuine case of consciousness expansion. Social consciousness is thus even more commodious, more spacious, and more extended in time than was the intersubjective consciousness. It is the experience of unity with a large number of conscious centers over a long period of time. The objects to the social consciousness are smaller intersubjective relationships (such as families). Social consciousness is one's sense of history and tradition. It includes one's ethnic memory and collective unconscious.

We in the West have ignored the tribal possibilities of human experience. The Third World movements and the peace movements of the sixties were often expressions of this sense of social unity. The denigration of theory in preference to action (which presupposes a theory nevertheless) has been a result of this deepening reduction. Allowing for theoretical differences is a characteristic of a society based on the individual consciousness. However, the social consciousness often has a common metaphysics which is not subject to question. (This is not to imply the superiority of communist dictatorships over free and individualistic democracies. We cannot consider the former to be genuine expressions of the social consciousness.)

Persons not raised in East Asia or tribal Africa may fail to understand fully the attractiveness of the social consciousness. The Western mind is individualistic, even when it is socialistic. The Eastern mind finds meaning and answers in rigorous regimentation, as persons who have lived in Taiwan and in mainland China can attest. Thinking and world views are prescribed, as are education, marriage, family relations, and occupation; all these are prescribed by an ancient external authority. These ukases are not questioned. The resultant uniformity eliminates anxiety with its attendant mental illness. It makes each person happy with his lot; it curtails ambition but leads to peace of mind. It makes it possible when necessary to accept cheerfully poverty and disease, war and military service, nationalistic or ideological self-sacrifices, and the willingness to close ranks behind a strong leader.

It is pointless to prefer the individual consciousness over the social consciousness. Both represent fundamentally distinct life-styles, world views, and images of the person. Both are represented in different parts of the world; both embody authentic albeit contradictory values. It is important for us in the West to learn to appreciate the identity-providing possibilities of the social consciousness, just as the East can benefit from Western individualistic ideals.

The fifth reduction is *cosmic consciousness.* As we step back even further into the source of our awareness, so far, in fact, that the social consciousness becomes now the object of our consciousness and we observe the stream of history and see it as a game, we reach the impersonal realm in which we realize that we are empty space-time. Inner and outer space are more alike than they are different. They are joined by a common time. When Kant at the beginning of *The Critique of Pure Reason* argues that it is we (that is, the minds) who contribute space and time to all experience, he was in touch with an accurate phenomenological insight: inner and outer space-time are the same. And the properties of space-time are also the properties of consciousness. These include infinity and eternity. When we reach the level of cosmic consciousness in our reductions we contact the religious and mystical possibilities of existence. And the space-time discussed here is not what is derivatively conceptualized in physics, but what the phenomenologist calls *lived* space-time.

With this reduction we have reached the experience of universality, which is one of the polar possibilities of our being. We have therefore reached a major caesura in mapping out the inner recesses of our consciousness. With cosmic consciousness we relinquish the consensual idea of individuals and groups in terms of which social sciences such as history, sociology, and psychology conceptualize human existence and enter the realm of the mystical. With cosmic consciousness the perspective of the individual shifts completely to the metaphysics of the universal. The seesaw has now gone the other way. It has completely left the individual pole of existence and moved to the universal. The basic assumptions about what is real and what is illusion, what is fundamental and what is derivative have now been completely transformed.

The last reduction is the *Eternal Now,* an expression borrowed from Paul Tillich and Alan Watts. The Eternal Now is a state of consciousness one reaches when even space and time become the objects of the intentional stream of consciousness. The subjective core which has succeeded in making an object of cosmic consciousness experiences itself outside of space and time. When we describe this reduction phenomenologically we must use expressions such as *atemporal* and *nonspatial*. These are meaningful concepts, legitimate descriptions of authentic states of being. This aspect of consciousness is present at all times, although we are conscious of it or focused on it only when we have reached the level of reduction in question. The Eternal Now is the final state of mysticism; it is *satori* in Zen, *nirvana* in Buddhism and *samadhi* in yoga. The Eternal Now is an experience in which we are no longer inside space and inside time but have become an observer of space and of time. The posture of the Eternal Now is also needed to understand many of the insights of contemporary physics.

These are some of the results of phenomenological researches in meditation practices and in descriptions of the structure of consciousness. Consciousness is revealed to us through successive transcendental reductions. Consciousness is not a mysterious experience of a few mystics or of some experimental subjects in drug-induced trance states, but the awareness that each of us experiences in the immediate present and in every aspect of our daily lives. We must but learn how to focus on it. Its therapeutic value lies in facilitating the feelings of security, ground, and immortality on which we base our coping strategies and our fulfillment.

A few added thoughts are in order:

1. These reflections point out that sanity and insanity cannot be clearly and unambiguously differentiated. Quite to the contrary, these two modes of human existence may often be but different regions on one and the same continuum. It is frequently merely a matter of convenience and a defense against anxiety to think of an insane mind as a diseased mind totally distinct from a healthy mind. There is a connection between insights about the transcendental reduction and insanity. Cosmic consciousness and the Eternal Now are experiences which can occur under the influence of certain hallucinogenic drugs, especially LSD. But there is a difference: The sane mind has control over these altered states of consciousness and flexibility in moving from one to the other; the insane mind is automatically fixed on one of these states and possesses no flexibility. Finally, these states imply no hierarchy—only choices.

2. The evidence for the truth of this analysis of the transcendental region lies in introspection (using reflexive or non-referential modes of consciousness), phenomenological descriptions of these introspective data, and comparison with other persons about the accuracy of these descriptions. This series of reductions carries out in detail the implications of the phenomenological method. Specifically, the analysis of the reductions develops

the idea of the primacy of consciousness. The here-and-now experience of consciousness is the foundation truth for any theory of being or of the person. We cannot use as our starting point the constituted idea that a brain is "behind" consciousness and brings about thoughts. The brain is not the experienced cause of the centered lucidity and revealing luminosity that is the phenomenon of one's awareness.

3. An existential dream interpretation—which interprets dreams to reflect one's total existence, which believes dreams are as much part of one's existential reality as are any occurrences while one is awake—makes sense and is theoretically justified only because of the primacy of here-and-now awareness. Objections against the primacy of consciousness function as resistances to the responsibility for being ourselves. Without it we choose to perceive ourselves as puppets, not as agents, and as peripheral, not as centered. This truth is steeped in anxiety. Only when we know anxiety is good can we learn to tolerate and integrate truth.

The importance of reflection for philosophy and psychotherapy has thus been introduced. We can now turn to the remaining points in this exposition of the mind-body polarity, one of which is a working metaphor and the other the analysis of consequences.

Note

1. For a discussion of this point, see Peter Koestenbaum, *Is There An Answer To Death?* (Englewood Cliffs, N.J.: Prentice-Hall, 1976), pp. 168-171.

Chapter 7 • METAPHOR FOR THE MIND-BODY POLARITY AND ITS CONSEQUENCES

The mind-body polarity has as its typical metaphor the *magnet* or the *magnetic field*. (The prototypical metaphor for the individual-universal polarity is that of the *bloodstream*—the flow of blood through arteries, capillaries, and veins.)

We must be sensitive to the difficulties inherent in describing matters of such vast generality as "the general structure of being." Language is mostly metaphoric, especially when it tries to name, describe, or clarify abstractions, and in particular when the abstractions refer to transcendental or ubiquitous aspects of being. An abstraction, in this sense, is a word or concept which designates an area of experience that cannot usually be named directly. That area is also one of philosophic significance and is difficult to define ostensively (that is, by pointing). This difficulty rests on the transcendental or reflexive and ubiquitous or universal character of the referents to these abstractions. This applies to the revelations of the transcendental reduction and to the most general categories of experience.

Two examples of abstractions referring to the general characteristics of the transcendental realm are freedom and subjectivity. An abstraction can also be a generality so vast that it is not commonly thought of or named. Examples of ubiquitous analysis are descriptions of being with special reference to its dialectical or polar nature. Metaphors clarify abstract concepts and make them available for the practical purposes of theory construction, research, and clinical use. Metaphors are thus the vehicles through which philosophical abstractions can be understood and implemented. Therefore, the magnet metaphor for the mind-body polarity must also be taken seriously, for it may be our primary way to grasp our nature.

We are a subject-object, mind-body, ego-world field. But we do not know we are such a field. To understand our field nature we must first become *self*-conscious, and that we achieve through the fundamental act of reflection. Becoming self-conscious means to objectify the field that we are, to make the subject-object field itself into an object. Once we have performed this conscious act and achieved a new epistemological posture we describe that field-become-object. And we do that by selecting from our life-world those elements which will facilitate access to being through picture thinking. These then become metaphors, and are often the only access we have to these subtle philosophical investigations.

The Magnetic Field

Briefly stated, being, in its dimension as a mind-body or consciousness-world polarity, is like a magnetic field, where the region of pure, transcendental, or subjective consciousness can be represented by the *negative* pole (to follow Sartre's view that consciousness is *nothingness*) and the region of body, empirical ego, or world can be represented by the *positive* pole (to represent the concretion of being, which follows Sartre's *pour-soi, en-soi* dichotomy). There is no clear caesura between these regions: consciousness gradually "condenses" into matter, just as in a magnetic field the negative pole gradually "positivizes" itself. This field phenomenon describes all beings: from individual physical objects to ideas, persons, the universe, and being itself. The field describes best of all, of course, human existence, but applies also to being as such (as it is studied in ontology) as well as to the universe (which is studied as cosmology). The field also describes all other events, because each "object" (the word is used in the loose or general phenomenological sense of object-to-consciousness) has a stream of consciousness attached to it leading to a transcendental subjectivity.

The illuminating nature and the therapeutic importance of the magnet metaphor to explain and expound the mind-body polarity of being can be elaborated further by exploring some specific consequences of taking this model seriously.

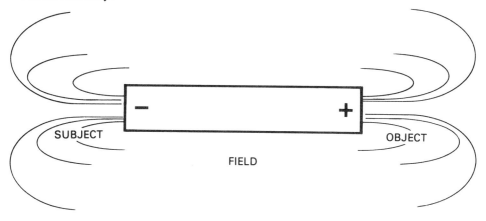

Figure 1   The Subject-Object Polarity

Consciousness has exactly as much reality, existence, truth, weight, importance—or whatever we wish to call it—as does the body and its environing world. Our culture, especially in its academic and research capacities, must be redefined as one which accepts the reality of pure consciousness with the same sense of conviction and assurance as it accepts the reality and the permanence of objects and matter.

Part of the problem lies in the ignorance or confusion about the nature of pure or transcendental consciousness. We must be certain to understand exactly what consciousness is. The body, technically known in phenomenology as one aspect of the psychological or the empirical ego, includes in it feelings as well as thoughts, conscious as well as unconscious material. But a feeling—regardless of how subjective, private, and personal it may be —must not be confused with consciousness itself. An idea—no matter how intimate it may be or how deeply a person may be attached to it—must never be mistaken for awareness proper. This distinction is encapsulated in the phenomenological formula for the intentionality of consciousness: "All consciousness is consciousness of something." Whenever we experience a feeling, have an idea, perceive a physical object, or are conscious of our body, the proper epistemological description of this situation is that there is a *consciousness of* a feeling, a *consciousness of* an idea, a *consciousness of* a perception, and a *consciousness of* our own body image. The consciousness pole in these expressions is the *subjective* pole, whereas the feeling, idea, perception, and body-image pole make up the *objective* pole—even though normally we would call these close and personal phenomena *conscious events*. In phenomenology they become *objects to consciousness*.

In the magnet metaphor it is this kind of nonobjectifiable consciousness, technically known as transcendental consciousness, that is meant. Although pure consciousness always has an object, in itself it can be defined as consciousness without an object. Consciousness is objectless if we bracket it, if we consider it independently of its objects. And it is this kind of consciousness, for which there exists barely a distinctive word in Western languages, that is intended by the negative pole in the magnet metaphor. And not only does this consciousness exist, it is, on this metaphor, equal in reality and importance to its object. Pure consciousness is a continent to be explored. It is a mass as large as any of the globe. Pure consciousness is space as vast as that explored by our spaceships and as deep as that scanned by our biggest telescopes.

We see the importance of this point when we realize that just about all words in any language, including the words *world* and *universe*—almost 100 percent of all being—designate the object pole in this metaphor exclusively. Since no words are left for the negative pole, the temptation of the West has been to deny its reality altogether, and that of the East to over-stress it. The phenomenological model of being seeks to establish an even and healthy balance, according equal respect to both and thus facilitating the mature meeting of East and West.

Thus ordinary language considers feelings and thoughts to be subjective, mental, and conscious events. But in phenomenology, anything that can be named, and that certainly includes abstract concepts, feelings, and ideas, is defined as an object (which therefore can be physical, affective, conceptual, imaginary, and so forth). And it is that kind of pure consciousness, the transcendental dimension, which has the same reality as do all of its objects. Some Eastern philosophies, such as the Hindu systems of Sankhya and Vedanta or some theories of Buddhism, possibly have exaggerated in their monistic metaphysics the predominance of pure consciousness, just as the West has dramatically overstressed the importance or the weight of the reality-mass of the objective zone of being. A phenomenological model of being seeks to present a dialectical balance, which is a living representation rather than a static monolith, of this total existential situation. The magnet metaphor, properly understood, can help us accomplish this philosophical and healing task.

Consciousness and Body Are Different

The second consequence of the magnet metaphor is that consciousness and body—that is, consciousness and world or, technically speaking, the transcendental and the empirical realms—are different in kind from each other and are not interchangeable. Theories about psychosomatic medicine, often maintain, with not much philosophical precision or logical accuracy, that mind and body are either two aspects of one event or that they cannot be readily distinguished. A vague and amorphous monism is substituted for what could be a precise metaphor. However, the dialectic character of the phenomenological model of being requires that the theory make room not only for the connectedness of the subjective and the objective in experience but also for the distinctness, separateness, isolation, and uniqueness of both the subjective and the objective regions of being. Mind and body are distinct.

The positive and negative poles in a magnetic field or of an electrically charged field when conceptualized are imagined to be clearly different from each other. We know which is which; their external relations are determined by their unique essences. The positive pole will repel an external positive pole, but will attract an external negative pole. The type of pole determines the direction of the current. Furthermore, the two poles cannot be collapsed without the concurrent destruction of the magnetic (or electric) field itself. Since each pole can be uniquely identified, it follows that each is clearly different from the other.

We must always keep in mind that this electromagnetic polarity is also the nature of the mind-body and consciousness-world relationship. We cannot treat the mind as if it were part of the body. The mind is not exclusively ruled by medication or glandular secretions. The free consciousness chooses to take or not take the medication. Consciousness can experience the body slipping away and the emotions getting out of control. The mind is a reality in its own right and does not depend on the body as if it were a mere stepchild. Awareness in its purest form is not a bodily function.

The evidence for these assertions does not lie in the analysis of objects. That is a referential activity and requires inductive generalizations. On the contrary, the evidence for the relative independence and absolute equality of consciousness derives from the reflexive examination of the act of examination itself. Such reflexivity yields insights in singular form. And such insights are properly called a priori. Specifically, the evidence for these assertions lies in the fact that the retreat into the realm of pure consciousness is experienced as being without end. Consciousness, because of its potential for self-referentiality, can always observe its states, even the state of observing itself. Retreating into the purity of subjective consciousness, that is, entering into the full openness of transcendental consciousness and into the transcendental realm, is the experience of an infinite regress.

In this way we can show that our innermost consciousness is not a mere function of the body, anymore than the negative pole is entirely a function of the positive pole. The clear and persistent awareness of this separateness of our consciousness is the key to our courage, our security, our integrity, our inner strength, and our inner-directedness. It is also a key to our capacity for self-control and self-discipline as well as to the commitment to rationality in the conduct of our lives. While the separateness of the two poles is only one aspect of the magnet metaphor, full respect must be accorded it.

Thus far the phenomenological model of being has been treated as a clear case of psycho-physical dualism. The phenomenological criticism of Descartes, whose metaphysical position is the modern parent of these mind-matter or mind-body dualisms, lies not at all in the dualistic aspects of Cartesianism. What phenomenology rejects in Descartes is the demand for an unbridgeable split between mind and matter, between the transcendental and the empirical realms. Descartes' position is truly onesided; for him, subject and object are separate and distinct, which is true as far as it goes, but they are not also intentionally related in the continuity of *one* field. In Cartesianism and its successors, the subject-object split is so uncompromising that Descartes must invoke the existence and then the honesty of God, through interesting but convoluted and much-criticized arguments, to guarantee first the existence of the material world (which includes the body) and then our ability to know it.

Descartes was right when he thought of the body as an object. But he was wrong when he separated the body from the sensations of the body. He was also wrong when he identified our perceptions of the body with the mind; he felt that ideas and sensations, including those of our own bodies, exist in the realm of consciousness. On the phenomenological view they exist only as objects *to* and not *in* consciousness. They are not the same as consciousness. Furthermore, Descartes was mistaken when he did not incorporate the consciousness-world continuity, the monistic aspect, in his dualistic system. Finally, Descartes did not make allowances for the concept of the body-subject in his metaphysics.

In short, for the two poles to be different is not enough. The poles of a magnet also represent a unity.

Consciousness and Body Are Continuous

The third lesson this metaphor teaches is that consciousness and body, subject and object, inwardness and world are continuous with one another. Their unity is based on a spatial metaphor, or on a spatialization of the field of consciousness. It is this "spatiality" of the phenomenological model of being—clearly expressed in the word *field*—that permits the existence of opposites within one larger unity. Lived space and lived time (as distinguished from conceptual space and conceptual time) are not just metaphors for consciousness—or one aspect of the metaphor for consciousness— but are also the actual experience of at least one facet of pure transcendental consciousness proper. It is because of this connection that the study of what in philosophy are called the a priori sciences—which include logic, geometry, and mathematics—is not only a reference to space and time (as the intuitionist theories maintain, not, of course, the formalistic ones) but also a description of transcendental consciousness itself. The name assigned to the unique connectedness and living continuity between subject and object is *intentionality*.

Several questions remain. Being or the universe, on this view, is one vast subject-object field, one vast consciousness-world continuum. Our own experience of the center of conscious observation that we are—in short, the ego—participates in this universal subjectivity. Similarly, our personal experience of our bodies and of the world beyond, narrow as it may be within the purview of the vastness of the universe, is also a participation in the larger objectivity of the cosmos. That universal and unifying dialectic is repeated in each individual event; the latter are samples, replicas, or even miniaturized clones of the larger universe. In Leibniz's language, the individuals are monads.

What is suggested here is a way, based on the magnet metaphor, of reconstructing our consensual world view. And that metaphor is in turn based on a phenomenological description of our experience as being-in-the-world. These facts must always be kept in mind when the question of evidence is raised.

The therapeutic significance of this sensitivity to mind-body or subject-object unity lies in the experience of wholeness and integration that it supports and produces. Growth techniques which emphasize the feeling of unity with body and nature are manifestations of the element of unity in this metaphor. Schizophrenia is the subject-object split. Health frequently involves the deliberate effort to reconnect subject and object through the activities of commitment, touch, and participation.

Consciousness Is External to the Body

A fourth consequence of the mind-body polarity which follows from the magnetic field metaphor is that consciousness is literally external to the body and, conversely, the body is literally external to consciousness. Even though the word *external* is spatial, the question of the precise location of this externality is nevertheless difficult to answer. My-consciousness is properly described as a quasi-spatial field stretching out toward an object which is my-body and then through it to the world beyond, which is my-world. But the exact origin of the intentional flow in that field, the so-called here-zone, is difficult to pinpoint. The *here* varies with its objects. When we look into the world with our eyes open, then the *here-zone* appears to be behind the eyes. But if we think or meditate with our eyes closed, then the *here-zone* is strictly nonpositional.

Furthermore, consciousness is experienced to be as much outside the body as inside it. In fact, if we could assign what might be called a *phenomenological mass* to the objects of which we are conscious, it seems obvious that the *contents* of the body occupy a much smaller region among the total objects of the body-image than do *externals* of the body. The body image has more skin than liver, more hair and eyes than gall bladder and aorta, and more mouth than bronchial tubes. Unless one is a surgeon, a hypochondriac, or a narcissist, one is much more aware of the visible or accessible outside of the body than of its invisible or inaccessible interior. The insides of our own bodies are of a conceptual rather than physical nature, at least with regard to our immediate experience. We infer the existence of our inner organs and their structure from the studies of other bodies, mostly cadavers, especially as these researches have been codified in textbooks on physiology and human anatomy.

One might ask, why should we make this subjective experience of one's body, this phenomenology of the body-qua-mine, the root metaphor for the universe? The epistemological truth remains that this experience is in actual fact an inescapable foundation experience from which all theories about the structure of being emerge and on which they are based. The fact that consciousness is external to the body is thus paradigmatic for being in general: All objects have a consciousness external to them.

Finally, out-of-body experiences—to which frequent allusion is made in parapsychology and meditation—must not be either dismissed as hallucinations or exaggerated in the literal belief that a soul leaves its body. The soul is not a thin or diaphanous object that is gingerly inserted in the body at conception or birth, but it is the region of transcendental subjectivity which can be distant from the body and the world (while at the same time it is also continuous with them). If we approach these out-of-body experiences phenomenologically, that is, describe them exactly as they appear and impose no organization or assumptions upon them, then they become merely an exaggeration, a dramatization, or a mythology of what is characteristic in all our experiences, namely the perceptible and variable distances between the subject and any one of its objects whatever.

The effect of integrating these conclusions into psychological and medical theories and praxis is to accord a greater degree of respect and independence to the transcendental region than the medical model permits. In a narrowly practical sense, the result of rectifying in this manner what has been an imbalance of emphasis leads to a better understanding of human freedom, human immortality, and human security—all crucial concerns for a philosophically based psychotherapy. The independent existence of the transcendental region (in the sense that its existence is external to the body) makes both the freedom of consciousness and its indestructibility (two of its cardinal traits) medical and psychological realities rather than mere philosophical and theological speculations.[1]

Interdependency

The last consequence of the magnetic-field metaphor is that consciousness is dependent on and produced by the body and its world (that is, consciousness is a product of nature) in precisely the same way that the body and its world are dependent on and produced by consciousness (which translates "nature is a product of consciousness"). If it were possible to "produce" or create a positive magnetic or electric pole by itself, that pole would instantaneously bring about a negative pole or charge at the other end of the metal bar or at the opposing metal plate of the capacitor. The converse is equally true. A similar situation exists in the field of being, the consciousness-world continuum that we experience as the basic structure of existence. Reciprocal creation is not an actual event as much as a phenomenological and metaphoric description of the support that each regional pole provides for the other. Consciousness is sustained in being by the realm of objects just as the realm of objects is maintained in being by consciousness. Body and consciousness are equally strong, equally potent, equally secure, and equally ancient.

These statements apply as much to the total universe as to an individual person. Therefore, we know that the externality of consciousness should be an integral part of any cosmology. The evidence for this comes directly out of the epistemological analysis of phenomenology, where the intentionality of consciousness is the fundamental result of presuppositionless descriptions of immediate experience. It lies in the primacy of first-person experience. We may see nebulae through our telescopes—we acquire sense data through radio and X-ray telescopes—and we may calculate their ages and their distances. It is nevertheless true that the total operation occurs inescapably within an intentional subject-object field context. Thus first-person experience is primary and must be integrated even into the most abstract and impersonal scientific theories. Even a nebula depends for its being on its contact with a subjectivity. How do we know? We know it the way we know anything—through the meticulous analysis of referential and reflexive acts of consciousness.

The metaphor of a comet (in the comet theory of objects discussed in *Managing Anxiety*) illustrates that an object is by definition a phenomenon which is given *to* consciousness and which is *before* (in the sense of "in front of") consciousness. Correlatively, consciousness is what it is only because an object is given to it or present before it. In other words, consciousness is that which objectifies an object and makes an object possible, the kind of insight traditionally associated with idealistic epistemologies: an object is what it is, or exists, only because some consciousness is aware of it. We cannot define an object without using the concept of consciousness. And this point is not only of passing theoretical interest but is of the greatest therapeutic importance. A patient brings to the counseling hour not only his body, his behavior, and his being-in-the-world, but also his inward consciousness. That consciousness needs attention and understanding. A theory which defends the integrity of pure consciousness also will accord to it the respect and recognition that consciousness deserves.

Questions and Conclusions

This analysis of consciousness and world as interdependent rules out certain questions as meaningless. How, for example, can an empirical, natural, or material event, such as a chemical reaction in the brain cells, cause, produce, or bring about a mental image, a situation which presumably occurs in the act of perception? On the view presented here, where the magnet metaphor is the model and the interdependence of its poles the theme, the coexistence of subjectivity and objectivity, mind and matter, inwardness and world, consciousness and chemistry is coeval, instantaneous, symmetrical, and fully reciprocal. An example of a meaningless theory would be the view that consciousness gradually emerged out of nature as a result of evolution. (The views developed here are closer to Hegel than to Teilhard de Chardin.) Equally meaningless on these premises are the idealistic views, perhaps going as far back in history as Plotinus, that consciousness gradually (in time) condenses into matter, or that consciousness invents material objects, which are then understood to be only projections and inventions and are modeled on the metaphor of the dream (the theory of Maya, for instance).

Needed is a detailed exploration of how these philisophical ideas affect research and practice in psychosomatic medicine. It would appear that research questions as well as therapy strategies will be radically modified if these views are used as working assumptions or basic parameters rather than those of the medical model of being, a model which for all practical purposes ignores the reality of the transcendental dimension.

In Book Three we will examine the concept of participation in the life of the body and the world as an application of this philosophical idea to psychosomatic medicine. And we will see how participation leads to health and healing. Basically, however, this is an area open for future research.

Another intriguing question that follows from the model of a mind-body polarity is its significance for the physical sciences. Fundamental reconceptions of such ideas or parameters as space, time, energy, force, gravitation, and electromagnetism, the relation between microphysics and macrophysics, and so forth, suggest themselves as a result of the phenomenological model of being.

The idea of a polarized field (let us now call it an electromagnetic field) is itself amorphous, vague, and metaphoric. The obvious question arises of which came first, our own personal field experience of being-in-the-world or the theory in physics of an electromagnetic field. It seems rather elementary that the totally general existence of being-in-the-world has ontological priority over the highly specialized and only recently (in the history of mankind, that is) developed concept of an electromagnetic field. It follows that the conceptions and visualizations of the theory of electromagnetism in the form of a field have arisen precisely because the field of consciousness as a basic existential situation was there ready to be used as metaphor long before experimental evidence required the model of an electromagnetic field. In other words, the *literal truth* is the field of consciousness, the consciousness-world field, or the phenomenological model of being. The metaphoric use of that basic truth occurs in physics, where its underlying theory would naturally be expected to pattern itself after the basic structure of human existence.

It is therefore not true that in phenomenology we borrow a concept from physics which we then use metaphorically in philosophy. On the contrary, it is physics which borrows a truth from philosophy and uses it as a metaphor. We can therefore argue that the idea of a polarized electromagnetic field as the fundamental concept in physics has occurred to us because it is the most basic, intimate, universal, and available of all possible metaphors. The theory of the electromagnetic field—on which much of modern physics, and with it most other sciences, is based—is thus a contemporary anthropomorphism. It follows that there may be applications of the phenomenological model of being in other sciences, possibilities which have not yet been explored.

These five consequences of the magnetic field metaphor should contribute to an understanding of the mind-body polarity, which is the first aspect of the phenomenological model of being. The second major theme in the detailed exposition of this model is an examination of the individual-universal polarity.

Note

1. This latter point is developed in detail in Peter Koestenbaum, *Is There An Answer To Death?* (Englewood Cliffs, N.J.: Prentice-Hall, 1976).

Chapter 8 • THE INDIVIDUAL-UNIVERSAL POLARITY

The exposition of the individual-universal polarity parallels that of the mind-body polarity. To develop a mental image, we must envision that this polarity occurs along an axis vertical to the subject-object polarity. It appears that in our culture the resistances to a flexible and total understanding of the individual-universal polarity are even more severe than they are to the mind-body polarity. We are more attached to individualism than we are to materialism. It is easier for us to embrace idealism than universalism.

Our culture's metaphysical resistances to the subjective or mental in the first polarity and to the universal in the second polarity are related to its epistemological resistance to global intuition (contrasted with the analytic intellect) as a mode of being and a mode of understanding. The analytic and discursive modes of consciousness—which are more concerned with self-centeredness and narcissism than with love and compassion—are the dominant world view in our society. The mode of thought of many of our cultural leaders, such as scientists and academicians, is still predominantly materialistic (or objectivistic) and individualistic. The intuitive mode, on the other hand, which is global in its grasp, is more readily associated with the subjective and universal, and is still today a neglected dimension of human existence. The principal reason for this lacuna is the lack of an adequate and respectable theoretical foundation.

The following exposition of the individual-universal polarity consists of a definition, an analysis of a universality, a metaphor, an analysis of individuality, and a discussion of consequences and therapeutic implications.

Definition

There is an individual and a universal aspect to each person. Each of us can possess an individual identity and experience a sense of individual identity. The importance we attribute to this is well expressed by the role the Bill of Rights and the Declaration of Independence play in our society.

Both of these American documents, each of which is supported by a massive history and sociology, are designed to protect the individual from the tyrannical power of society and the state. The self-concept that we are individuals is so dominant in our culture that what is in effect a self-definition, a construct, a constituted entity, an invention, an opinion, and an option is instead blithely confused with incontrovertible fact. The irreducibility of the individual is thought to be a datum of nature. The opposing view is the axiomatization of the universal or the social expressed in mystical and tribal self-concepts. Although an equally valid option, it is not given an adequately serious hearing by the power base of the establishment, except perhaps for some perfunctory lip service.

The fundamental point is that there is also an equally real aspect of us—an authentic possibility for us, a valid self-concept, a true self-image, a legitimate self-definition—which is universal. And our culture does not take that possibility seriously. The universal potentiality of the person makes possible answers to problems of living and therapy that would otherwise remain insoluble. These problems include death, loneliness, and purpose. In discussing this polarity, let us examine first and in some detail our potential to experience ourselves as universal.

Since we and the world together comprise an intentional field between the realm of the subject and the object, universality can be found separately in the realm of pure consciousness and in the realm of nature. It can be found in the transcendental as well as in the empirical realms, since the realm of the subject is infinite, that is, experienced as boundless, as is of course also the case with our experience of the realm of the objective. We can name these transcendental (conscious) universality and empirical (bodily) universality.

Empirical or Bodily Universality

We are, in truth, part of nature. We participate in nature through the dimension of time, inasmuch as we are a part of the total astronomical, geological, biological, and historical stream of evolution. To sever off my-body, my-person, or my-individual-life-history from the totality and continuity of this near infinite evolutionary stream is a decision, a convention, a constitution, and must be lived as such. We cannot deny that this constitution of our individuality and personal history is important. In fact, it may well be the most important constitution ever undertaken. But we can reverse that decision, identify ourselves with the universe—with serious consequences of course—and experience the ego and the body as merely an episode in eons of continuous and unitary evolutionary development.

We can decide to identify ourselves with the geological and even cosmic evolutionary movement rather than with a single insignificant episode alone. The more we learn and the more we know the more effective is this identification. The joy of learning, the love of wisdom, is rooted in this insight. To understand is to be in contact with the universe. The study of biology connects us with all life. The study of geology merges us with the earth, and the study of astronomy identifies us with the universe at large. Herein lie the magnetism of wonder and the attraction of science.

The actual archaeological, geological, biological, and even astronomical explorations and observations can put us in touch *directly* with the stream of evolution in which the universal possibility of our existence is manifested. Reading accounts of explorations, such as those of Darwin, can develop within us vicarious contact with the empirical universal. A sense of connection is established with the actual evolutionary stream. We are not as a result of these scientific explorations in contact with some *outside* or *other* kind of universality. We experience the universaility that we are and have always been.

The study of history has the same effect of connecting us with our possibility for universality. Visiting archaeological sites, reading old manuscripts, inspecting records, and seeing ancient architectures, sculptures, and paintings gives us real contact with the universal possibility that we are. Conversely, we can argue that one reason why people become interested in history and geology is to experience their universal possibility with respect to various types of evolution.

Interest in astronomy touches upon a different dimension of universality —our continuity with space, for we also participate in nature through the dimension of space. We can make the decision—which also has dramatic consequences—no longer to identify ourselves with the spatial individual our consensual world tells us we are and experience ourselves instead as participating now and fully in the spatio-physical realm of nature. We then realize that we are continuous with the biosphere—even with the rest of the universe.

The identification with nature or the empirical realm comprises many stages. It can be total or partial, the latter being easier and thus more common. When we identify with a tribe, a subculture, a tradition, a cause, a family, a nation, a land, a farm, a mountain, a lake, an ocean, a beach, or a house, then our fate and self-development, our sense of meaning and reality are worked out through a life projected onto these empirical realities. With their demise, our reality also vanishes. Much of this identification is experienced in noble emotions. The artist who loves nature, the animist who worships it, the patriot who loves his land and can say *"pulchrum et decorum est pro patria mori,"* the party member who is fiercely loyal, and the homemaker-mother whose identity is in her total devotion to her family—all of these persons have in different degrees and using different symbols manifested and expressed their universal rather than individual potentiality.

Painful and often cruel experiences found in so-called primitive initiation rites also illustrate fulfilling the universal possibility of human existence. Another extreme example would be that of being eaten by a shark—the full horror and pain of which is dramatically demonstrated by the fiercely pointed rows of teeth in its open jaws. The surrender to this engulfment, which is a logical possibility for the deciding or choosing consciousness, is the experience of complete submission to the universality of nature—in this case the shark and the ocean. People who die of exposure in the snow can have a similar experience of physically relinquishing themselves to the world, in which they are as much at home as totalities as they are in their more common mode of alienated, isolated, and lonely individuals.

The feces of wolves in Northern Canada have been examined to discover their diet. Half of the contents are hair and skins of mice; the rest includes caribou bone fragments. And the mice and caribou eat seeds and grasses. We can perceive this process of assimilation and integration as proof of the horror and cruelty of nature. In that case we take the individual perspective as absolute; this is our right, but it is not the only truth available to us. We can also perceive this process as a natural increase in universality—from seed to mouse to wolf. The plants and animals that are eaten suffer only to the extent that they experience themselves as individuals. When they accept their fate, then, as in a primitive initiation rite, the pain itself becomes their experience of being seized by the universality and made one with it. Needless to say, these experiences are not part of everyday life. In fact, they can be such only once! It is no accident that death is involved intimately in the experience of universality. The conflict between the individual and the universal possibility of human existence is as dramatic as it is dangerous. We cannot toy with the extremes of these possibilities, for we are here concerned literally with worlds in collision.

Mrs. N. S., a woman in her seventies, lost her husband—which was tragic and traumatic for her because of their long and devoted love. She had the body of her husband cremated and scattered his ashes over Point Lobos, one of the most romantically beautiful, severe, and powerful promontories on the Pacific Coast. It was in Point Lobos, in the early and unpopulated days of this century, where the romantic foundations for their lifelong love were born. Through the ashes she returned her husband and their love back to the universality from which they came. From the point of view of the phenomenological model of being, she was in touch with a profound truth of existence. It was not a gesture that had meaning only to her; it was not a psychological phenomenon; nor was it a regressive act. It was neither maudlin nor sentimental. It was the witness to a truth, a truth that has answers to life's most pressing problems. Scattering the ashes was a religious exercise in which she experienced her empirical or bodily universality.

This approach that develops our possibility to be a universality invokes our potential for commitment, cathexis, surrender, identification, intentionality, and being-in-the-world. All these modes of being are expressions, instances, and manifestations of what in phenomenology is called the natural attitude.

Transcendental or Conscious Universality

The second approach to understanding our possibility to be a universality is one which moves in the opposite direction—toward pure consciousness, detachment, withdrawal, inwardness, subjectivity; it invokes the important epistemological activity of the transcendental and phenomenological reductions and is represented paradigmatically in the phenomenological as opposed to the natural attitude. The conscious universality is also called cosmic consciousness or higher consciousness as well as transcendental consciousness.

A few preliminary qualifications are in order. The individual body is different from the total mass of empirical being. The individual body is but one item within an enormous mass. The same is true of the relationship between the individual ego and the total mass of universal and cosmic consciousness. We are now discussing, not the individual conscious ego, but the cosmic consciousness within which the former is an insignificant speck. In addition to these considerations, we must recall that the authentic person does not exist exclusively as a body amidst the world or as an ego amidst cosmic consciousness but that he or she exists as an interface between the two.

The theme of the conscious universality and its therapeutic implications is discussed at three levels of depth. The first occurs in Chapter 6, the second is found in this chapter, and the third, which will attempt to explore even greater depths, appears in Chapter 10.

The conscious universality can be made available to us in several ways. These include epistemological analysis, meditation, ascetism, and drugs, to name but a few. The epistemological approach is the formal one and involves analysis of the theory of reductions and the ensuing six modes of consciousness (the abstract, individual, intersubjective, social, cosmic, and Eternal Now). (See Chapter 4.)

Meditation

In essence, meditation techniques are workable, simple, and practical attempts to remove attention away from *objects* of consciousness. This activity releases the subject and the stream of consciousness from its objects and gives us the opportunity to experience our conscious inwardness in its purity. Pure consciousness can reveal its many therapeutically significant attributes.

Meditation techniques are intended to give us the benefits of philosophy, specifically of a transcendental philosophy or a phenomenological model of being, without any intellectual understanding of its meaning and foundation. However, it would appear that meditation without philosophy is of limited value. Meditation may reduce blood pressure and lead to some peace of mind. But the kind of meditation that is of lasting value and can make a profound difference in the life of a person cannot be mechanical or focused solely on technique. Meditation must be used as an experiential and illustrative adjunct to a complete philosophy. Meditation is both the experiential base and the amplifying illustration for a total philosophy. And it is the task of that philosophy to make it possible to live one's life with a *true* picture of reality as the ground on which one feels, thinks, does research, and heals.

In meditation, the individual takes a spectatorial attitude towards all experiences. When a noise intrudes itself upon his consciousness, rather than being disturbed or distracted by it, he now observes with detachment the noise itself. He is then said to meditate on the noise. The quintessence of meditation is to release oneself from the natural attitude—the posture in which the cathecting focus is on the *objects* of consciousness entirely— and in this fashion unfold the pure look of *subjective* consciousness. Meditation must then move beyond the disclosure of the pure ego and deeper into the region of the universality of that ego. Epistemology *teaches us* that this sequence of experiences is possible. Meditation techniques *give us this experience.* A balanced person needs both approaches to the conscious universal.

The following brief definition and description of meditation will show how this collection of ancient and modern techniques can help reveal the possibility of conscious universality.

Meditation practices in the context of religion take three distinguishable forms: identification, detachment, and going-with-the-flow. Identification is the experience of oneness with something other than oneself. When we think we are totally identified with and absorbed in the object of our most intense and devoted concentration, then we have lost the sense of being an ego, of selfhood, individuality and personal identity. We have merely attained a state of holy indifference—the experience of the pure universal consciousness that flows through us and which is the higher self or higher consciousness.

This practice of meditation through identification is illustrated with the Zen *koan.* The koan is a question or statement on which the devotee meditates. It is a directive that is either a paradox ("imagine the sound of one hand clapping") or an apparently pointless observation ("the elbow does not bend outwards"); its answer or interpretation is invariably the nonsense syllable *mu.* Reflection on the "clapping" koan is "solved" when the meditator has achieved total concentration and complete identification with the koan, so that the questioner disappears from awareness and the pure impersonal, universal, timeless, and indifferent observer of all being remains. Identifying through meditative concentration on the "elbow" koan shows that real freedom is total oneness with the nature of the object. Again, the sense of ego-consciousness disappears and an experience of immortal cosmic freedom and indifference prevails.

Detachment, the second type of meditation, consists of ascetic or monastic practices in which each intrusion into consciousness—such as a noise, pain, or desire—is used in turn as an object of meditation. Consciousness detaches itself from each object by saying "I am not that." In *kundalini* yoga, for example, renunciation from the world is achieved by attentive concentration on the experience of energy flowing through the spine.

The final form of meditation is the surrender to the flow of life or being. The indifference of pure and detached consciousness—that is, the experience of conscious universality—is achieved by putting any independent desires out of action. The meditator follows the flow of the body, of a feeling, or of the environment like a leaf floating downstream in a river or a light cork bobbing up and down on the ocean waves. The meditator takes no independent action. In this way individuals can train themselves to become observers rather than participants in life.

These types of meditation open up the transcendental region of experience. And they open the universal possibilities of the subjective region. Meditation is the experience which illustrates the reality of cosmic or higher consciousness as one of the many epistemologically justified regions of being. The existence of this region is denied *twice* by the dominant strands of our culture: first, because it is the subjective and conscious dimension rather than the objective and material; second, because this region of human possibility is universal rather than particular or individual. However, this view of the transcendental deepens our understanding of alternative life-styles.

Ms. D. N., after an outstanding musical career and while still young, joined a strict convent, permanently cutting off all contact with the external world. Some of her friends and relatives were dismayed at what to them was neurotic behavior. Some even cried. "Where have her parents failed?" However, in terms of the phenomenological model of being, her choice can be seen as fully authentic. What she started to accomplish through her music is now being fulfilled by her total submergence in the transcendental dimension, the devotion to the realm of pure and universal consciousness. Joining a convent represents a complete and permanent withdrawal from the world and all its individualistic rewards. Her commitment to this life was the resolve to exist almost exclusively in the realm of conscious universality.

The practice of asceticism is an ancient form of world denial and withdrawal from the realm of objects. We need only mention this vast religious and ethical concern over the entire history of mankind. Asceticism is a life-style organized around the goal of experiencing the reality of consciousness by a constant and deliberate detachment from the things and objects of this world. Asceticism is a value and an ideal not because of masochistic needs but because it is applied epistemology. What in abstract philosophy is the transcendental reduction becomes asceticism when integrated into a total life-style.

Finally, the use of so-called mind-expanding drugs to facilitate these philosophic insights must be mentioned but need not be pursued further. Drugs have the same relation to philosophy as does meditation. In themselves they are of limited value and are of course also damaging and destructive at times. A drug cannot, by itself, lead to the experience of conscious universality. As an adjunct to work in philosophy, however, it can facilitate this understanding by offering experience and serving as illustrative background.

Metaphor

The archetypal metaphors have been carefully selected and are core concepts in this discussion. The paradigmatic metaphor for the mind-body polarity is the magnetic field. The metaphor for the individual-universal polarity is that of the bloodstream. (See Figure 1.) The blood flows from an artery to a vein; in between the blood divides itself into thousands of minuscule capillaries.

This metaphor suggests many ways of achieving the experience of universality. In one, the total bloodstream, from artery to vein, corresponds to the possibility for universality of our existence, since we can identify with

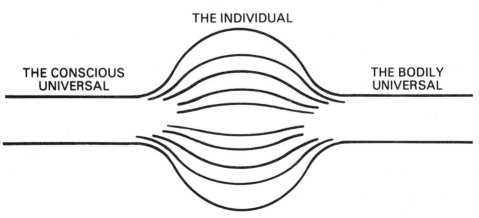

Figure 1   The Individual-Universal Polarity

the total stream of being. We are that bloodstream. Or, if we experience fusion with the bodily or empirical universal, then in our metaphor we identify with the area of the vein. If, however, we experience fusion with the conscious universal, then our experience corresponds to an identification with the artery. If the stream is described as infinite—and it is a fact that no limits to it can be experienced—then identification with its totality as well as fusion with either artery or vein are all experiences of infinity, for half of infinity is still infinite. In other words, the field of consciousness, observed in its totality, is an infinite stream. It is a stream which is perceived as having no beginning and no end. That is our knowledge of infinity. But the same infinity is perceived when we identify ourselves exclusively with only one of the two poles of universality—the subjective or the objective. Cosmic consciousness, even though it is only half of being, is nevertheless infinite. The same is true of the space in physical nature. Space is only half of being, but notwithstanding that it is still infinite.

But we can also identify with one capillary; we can fuse with it, cathect it, become it. We can choose to define one capillary as the ego—or as my-ego —and ipso facto define all other capillaries, as well as artery and vein, as the non-ego. In this case we choose to alienate ourselves—to decathect or defuse—from all aspects of being except the solitary capillary which we call ourselves. We do this by using the mechanism of denial, alienation, or negation. Cathecting one region of being, that is, making that region ours, implies a concurrent alienation from all other regions of being. Alan Watts wrote a book on the illusion of the ego and the primacy of universality. He called it *The Book*. In the Preface he writes, "The prevalent sensation of oneself as a separate ego enclosed in a bag of skin is a hallucination." Although Watts may be right, his wording may be too strong. He assumes that the truth lies in the fusion or cathexis with the universality (or absolute). However, a more tolerant and democratic position is that the choice of being an individual ego rather than a universal consciousness is an equally legitimate decision that can be made by the freedom that is our consciousness.

To summarize, the relationship between the individual and the universal is like that of a capillary vessel to the total bloodstream from artery to vein. We are the possibilities for being *both* the capillary *and* the bloodstream. In addition, we are the possibility for being *either* the universality of the artery *or* the universality of the vein. The importance of these metaphors cannot be overemphasized. The relevance of the individual-universal polarity to the problems of life and to psychotherapy becomes clear when we discuss the applications of the bloodstream metaphor.

Consequences

The first consequence concerns the role of freedom in bringing about one or the other of these polar possibilities, because fundamental to understanding the outcome of this polarity is to recognize the role free will plays. First of all the realization of either of these poles is a free decision. Freedom is an attribute of transcendental consciousness. It means, as we saw in Chapter 3, freedom for constitution, that is, meaning creation, and freedom of cathexis, which is identification, attachment, and fusion. As a result, the self-concept, self-image, identity, world view, or world design of being either individual or universal is not a fact to be discovered but a free decision, a free choice to be made. Life changes if we go through our day equipped with this insight. We can thereby understand what it means to be in control of one's destiny. Whether we experience the world in a mystical or an individual way the world view we make ours is a matter of choosing freely, spontaneously, autonomously, and with full self-determination. (The thoughtful reader must be reminded that the word *ours* already implies an individualistic world view. The English language does not allow for the subject of a sentence in which the choice between individuality and universality has not yet been made.)

The data, that is, the contents of the empirical or objective realm, are given and are not subject to our choosing. We can of course focus or divert our attention. But we cannot modify them. But the meaning, organization, and the location and size of the attachment or detachment imposed upon that realm are matters for free existential choice. And we should glory in the anxiety of that freedom, for this kind of a decision—that is, between being individual or being universal—is an archetypal one. It is a "first" decision, in that it is so primitive that most of the reasons and arguments usually advanced for its desirability and correctness are in actual fact determined already by the very decision they hope to support. The decision for either individuality or universality has already been made when a defense for it is undertaken.

One of many therapeutic consequences of understanding the precise role of free will in the choice between these two polarities is that *we become capable of feeling our responsibility for our existence.* We also understand what it means to be responsible for the specific and unique structure of our existence. Before the cliche that we are responsible for ourselves and for our lives makes any real sense we must understand the transcendental dynamics of this archetypal decision for individuality or finitude. In that decision we identify with one capillary at the same time that we alienate ourselves from the rest of being. Every object, perception, thought, hope, dream, and anxiety—every relationship—is affected. To change it means the complete upheaval of the edifice of our lives. The tendency is always toward homeostasis, and the greater the change contemplated the stronger the resistance against it. It follows that the resistance against archetypal decisions is the maximum resistance possible. It is in this sense that we must understand the existential view that we are fully responsible for what we are. Self-pity and excuses are meaningless because they are unnecessary. Chapter 13 discusses therapeutic techniques for achieving the sense of individual identity which follow from this ontological analysis.

But beyond this observation, it is also true that we can freely identify ourselves with either possibility. We are therefore responsible for our life-style and for coping with existence. A life-style is a free choice to deal with the realities that life presents. We can cope by choosing individuality, and we can cope by choosing universality. We are thus responsible for both our individuality and our universality. If we chose to be individualists, then that must be seen as a deliberate choice. The dynamics of the choice may involve identification with a model, such as an independent and aggressive father. If we choose to be universalists, then that must also be seen as a deliberate choice—this one perhaps using as a model a deeply compassionate mother.

These examples, however, should not lead us to imply that we blindly follow the models of our childhood. We can rechoose them or choose to divorce ourselves from them. The only prerequisite is that we understand the model and our fusion with it, so that we can protect ourselves from the insidious results of nonreflective and thoughtless identification. The authentic sequence is to choose our being-orientation first and then select the appropriate model (individual-father, universal-mother, for example). Unfortunately, in many cases the choice is not authentic, because the sequence is reversed. This is determinism or fatalism. If we understand the ontological order we are also freed from the tyranny of our childhood—but we can endorse the love in our childhood if that is what we had. That again is the hope and control that this philosophical position provides.

Identity

What may well be the two principal psychological problems can be solved by applying these insights. We can argue that the two central problems in life, and therefore in psychotherapy, are the development of a worthwhile sense of *identity* on the one hand and a sense of grounded *security* on the other. The proper understanding and management of the individual-universal polarity can give us the outline for a solution to the dual problems of identity and security, of self-worth and groundedness.

The archetypal decision for being an individual—for being human rather than divine, particular rather than universal, isolated rather than merged or fused, defined rather than amorphous—is the uncompromising integration of death, that is, finitude and limits, into our existence. We must insist that even our death is self-chosen, in that we define ourselves as mortal, dying, alienated, and homeless so as to achieve this sense of particularity. And then, having made that decision, we organize every aspect of the universe to fit this premise.

By understanding these philosophic dynamics of self-creation, the phe-nomenological model of being can help us solve the first major issue in psychotherapy: How to help the client achieve a sense of self-worth, iden-tity, independence, potency, and efficacy as a person. Although we are trained to make these archetypal decisions speedily, it is useful to spell them out in detail for the sake of a more complete theory and more efficient research. We do the same with a complex chemical or nuclear reaction which, although it occurs almost instantaneously, may require hours and pages of exposition to explicate and may have taken years of painstaking and cooperative research to set up.

To choose myself as an individual is to choose the human, the individual, the independent, the sensuous; it is to choose opposition, confrontation, contrast. It is, in short, the choice of the erotic. To make these types of choices—choices which are made intelligible by the bloodstream metaphor and which are the consequences of applying and internalizing that met-aphor—is called in common sense being an aggressive, potent, self-assert-ive, and effective person.

One further way to describe the structure of the archetypal choice in favor of the polarity of individuality, and thus make it available to therapist and client alike, is as follows: We say "yes" to a here-zone, which by virtue of that act becomes concrete. We can also state the matter conversely: It is our saying "yes" to a region of being, our fusing with it, which is the act that makes this region into a here-zone. "Yes"-saying in this sense is made pos-sible by categorically and irrevocably saying "no" to a there-zone. Again, it is the act of "no"-saying, of dissociation, rejection, and alienation which creates the there-zone.

We have already observed that the most concrete form which this con-stitution-cathexis, construction-fusion of the sense of individuality takes (and with it comes the worthiness of one's own identity) is the will to die. Choosing oneself as mortal, accepting death as right (that is, the biological limit of just under one hundred years as certain and a premature death due to disease or accident as uncertain), are the philosophical dynamics of creat-ing a vigorous and effective sense of solid individual identity. To be an indi-vidual and to choose death are synonymous acts. To understand and to live this insight is to have assumed full responsibility for ourselves. That is the secret of self-worth, of inner-directedness, of independence, maturity, and effectiveness as an individual.

Security

How does the individual-universal polarity resolve the second major psychotherapeutic task or problem, the question of ground and home? The decision for universality is the integration of eternity into one's life. Simply stated, the assiduous application of the insight that we can choose ourselves as universal must be seen as an authentic answer to death. We make the decision for universality by reversing the dynamics which lead to the decision for individuality. We identify or fuse with either all of being or with selected regions of being. It is the nature of universality to be permanent. The objective universality (which is outer space and the empirical region) and the subjective universality (which is cosmic consciousness and the transcendental region) are shown to have, upon direct inspection and through the use of the phenomenological sensitivity to transcendental and fringe facts, the characteristic of indestructibility, permanence, support, grounding, and eternity. These are facts accessible to anyone; but it takes their integration into a culture—through myth, religion, tradition, language, ritual, and institutions—before they become a part of one's life-style and one gains the psychological advantages which derive from them. Subsequent chapters discuss some of these issues in detail by developing their clinical implications.

Chapter 9 • A BIPOLAR PERSONALITY THEORY: ITS EXPLANATORY POWER

The discussion thus far has concerned itself with descriptions of personality structures which fall along two vertically intersecting axes: the subject-object axis and the individual-universal axis. The magnet metaphor represents the subject-object axis of our experience and of our possibilities; the bloodstream metaphor points out the individual-universal axis of our existence and potential. We should now present certain implications which follow from mapping being in accordance with this bipolar analysis of the human condition. A bipolar map of being (we may call this activity a topography of being which leads to a topology, ontology, or an ontograph) yields a Tibetan mandala or an American Indian medicine wheel. Jung and others have seen the wisdom of representing our being-in-the-world in these terms, and the structuralists have recently pointed out the pervasiveness of the binary form of thought, experience, projection, and organization.

A bipolar topology has a number of advantages: It is philosophically foundational. It yields a personality profile, which has implications for research, diagnosis, and therapy. As part of that profile, a bipolar personality theory makes possible a variety of testing techniques. Some of these are questions, words and inkblot cards. In addition, a bipolar personality theory can organize a large variety of personality traits. It can also suggest personality traits which, at least hypothetically, are connected. And, it can place into one harmonious context the plethora of healing practices, of medical approaches, of psychologies, personality theories, therapy and growth approaches, so that these need not conflict but may complement each other. We can develop in this way four primary and four secondary personality types or structures.

We can then relate and classify almost any type of psychotherapy. A special attempt to translate Jung's map of the person into terms of these philosophic categories will be made later. We can also incorporate four different and unseful meanings of freedom into this topology. Finally, this profile gives us a chance to define the meanings of health and of normalcy by combining the idea of freedom with the topology of the bipolar personality theory.

A Basic Personality Theory

This theory emerges from the deepest, most basic, and most general philosophic analysis in phenomenology. We can be reasonably confident that with it we have come very close to touching bottom in our "submarine explorations" for foundations. We can develop a personality theory as an outgrowth of an examination of the most fundamental structure of being. We can, furthermore, look for methods of detecting directly the orientation, focus, and constitutions of consciousness. We can endeavor to examine the field of consciousness itself and assess its mode of operation. From these discoveries, different in each person, inferences regarding being-in-the-world, personality structure, life-styles, world design, and indicated treatment programs can be made. The explanatory power of this method—where we begin with an assessment of the archetypal forms, directions, and constitutions of each individual consciousness—is that it permits us to quickly make vast and often accurate generalizations and predictions.

The bipolar personality theory derives from a bipolar theory of being. It is not based on experimental generalizations but results from researches in both descriptive and transcendental phenomenology—that is, the description of being as precise facts (as done in science), fringe facts (as done in art, literature, and clinical work), and finally as transcendental facts, which are descriptions of the unique characteristics of pure consciousness, of "awareness without an object" as it were. Because of its connection with the bipolar theory of being, this personality theory has a right to claim that it is a basic one.

In other words, the parameters by which a bipolar topology organizes all our human potential derive from fundamental epistemological investigations. The two axes in question represent the ultimate analyzable ingredients of our experience—the ne plus ultra of a transcendental fundamental ontology. The axes are not empirical, experimental, statistical, or observational categories. They appear instead in the very structure of consciousness itself, the essential elements of the possibilities of consciousness. And we make these discoveries by a priori descriptions of the transcendental dimension. We describe with these parameters the singular and unique characteristics of the field of intentional consciousness as that field uncovers itself in the activity of a transcendental reduction. This has been the traditional activity of searching for synthetic a priori judgments, the reality of which has been the backbone of the rationalistic movement in the history of epistemology and metaphysics.

Rationalism believes in the infusion of reason—which means the essential acts and patterns of consciousness—into the realm of being. Not only does the world contain the projections and constructions of consciousness, but we can even make further judgments about inaccessible regions of being *because of the continuity of consciousness with the world*. This fact (or premise) makes for synthetic judgments. The a priori nature of these existential (not exclusively logical) judgments consists of descriptions of these governing conscious structures. But the latter are not generalizations—they cannot be—because this is only one field of consciousness. In the transcendental reduction we describe only one phenomenon, a singular structure; that is why a priori knowledge is certain, true, apodictic, as Kant and his rationalistic predecessors held. It describes only one object; probability and induction are meaningless.

The Personality Profile and Test

Consciousness can, among several possibilities, be focused principally on the *objective* region of experience. A person whose field of consciousness exhibits this orientation as its primary mode of constitution is an objective or *outgoing* type. Conversely, consciousness can focus on itself, on the *subjective* region of experience. It is of course important to note that subjectivity and objectivity are always present in all aspects of experience, even though the focus may be on only one. A person who exhibits this latter style as his or her primary mode of constituting consciousness is a subjective or *introspective* type.

It is relatively simple and reliable to elicit information about these fundamental directions and proclivities of consciousness. The following question is one which can have the capacity to assess the extent to which the field of consciousness focuses on the subjective or the objective region respectively; it can measure both intensity and direction:

If you were a university professor and had the necessary ability and time, would you do research in (a) the physical sciences or (b) the nature of consciousness?

(a) ☐   (b) ☐

The subject is forced to make a choice. He is given three points which he can distribute (in whole numbers only) between the two alternatives any way he wishes to indicate preference. If his opinion is emphatic, he can assign all his three points to one answer; if his preference is not very strong, he can assign two points to one choice and one point to the other.

A person who repeatedly responds to questions of this type in the direction of (a) is likely to focus the attention of his field of consciousness in the objective region. That region becomes for him a here-zone for his experience, with all its accompanying implications. The being of this person is tied up with objects and things, with the realm of the Other and of concrete being (the *en soi*, in the language of Sartre). Correlatively, a person whose average responses move in the direction of (b) is likely to be not outgoing and objective but rather an introspective and subjective type. He is the person for whom reality is the inner world; he identifies himself with inward space primarily. (At the end of this section is a list of sample questions, together with an indication of the specific polar axis or axes about which each question makes discriminations.)

Another type of question follows this pattern: The subject is given two relatively common words, such as *here* and *there*. He is told that the universe of discourse is restricted to these two words. His question is either, "Which of these two words do you consider more important?" or, preferably, "Which of these two words do you think you use more often?" The assumption behind these very simple tasks is that a person will choose that word which indicates, discloses, and betrays the general organizational patterns, foci, and cathexes of his field of consciousness. A series of such word-pairs, with the responses analyzed statistically, can give us an indication of whether the subject's consciousness is focused primarily on the *here* (subjectivity) or on the *there* (objectivity). A profile can be developed using either the word check list or the more elaborate questions discussed above. (At the end of this section there is also a sample list of word-pairs).

We can use similar questions to determine the position which a subject occupies on the individual-universal axis. Here is a sample question to make this discrimination (with three points to be divided between the two alternatives):

If you had the choice between two excellent courses in a scholarship program, would you select (a) a course in "Personal Development in an Alienated Society" or (b) a course in "The Connection between Ancient Mysticism and the Most Recent Breakthroughs in Physics and Astronomy?"

The assumption here is that a person reveals the basic organizing principles and structures that his consciousness projects on the world of his experience by his choices between these two alternatives. A person who assigns a value of 3 to option (a) and therefore of 0 to option (b) is then, we assume, one who thinks in terms of individuals and particulars over wholes and unities. He perceives ultimate reality, truth, and value to be the individual, whose existence is constituted through the denial or negation of the rest of existence. We can in this way uncover and analyze the fundamental structures which his particular consciousness projects on the world and which he imposes on all his experience. This is the position of contemporary structuralism.

Conversely, the person whose orientation is toward (b) (he assigns a value of 2 or 3 to that alternative and tends to repeat that pattern in similar questions) will, we can argue, perceive the real, the valuable, and the true as whole, total, or universal. We can then hypothesize a large number of derived personality traits from that insight.

There are names to describe these two orientations on the vertical axis. Although they are unsatisfactory, they do elicit some of the sense of these two poles: the individual orientation represents the *political* person, since the activism and power of the individual is what is emphasized, whereas the universal orientation is the *religious* person, precisely because the element of surrender to a larger universality is implied.

We can likewise assess these orientations or structures of the archetypal constitutions by a word-pair check list, as was suggested previously. Again, we ask the subject to limit the universe of discourse to one pair of words at a time. A sample pair would be *one—all*. The assumption we make is that if a preponderance of *all*-words is checked over *one*-words then the subject has a proclivity for emphasizing unity and totality in his world design and life-style. The converse would hold if the words checked reflect singularity or individuality (such as *one*).

A third type of test involves the use of projective techniques—inkblot cards being but one example. The subject's response to the card content can be explored for subjective, objective, individual, or universal clues. Emphasis on detail, for example, as contrasted with a whole or total response, may indicate a consciousness which has a predilection for perceiving the world in terms of individual or atomic entities, whereas the automatic perception of the card as a whole may indicate that the continuity of a universal totality is perceived as the basic structure of being. References to space and motion, to background and foreground may provide helpful clues in distinguishing between the here-centered subjective perspective of consciousness and the there-centered, object-focused point of view. Again, the contention here is that the implications of these basic structures are major, since these archetypal orientations color one's total world view and life-style. The results can be plotted to produce a profile.

THE SECONDARY ORIENTATIONS

Of considerable interest are the secondary orientations that form part of this profile: the life-styles that result from combining any two adjacent poles. A person whose objective orientation is also individualistic may be called, for lack of a better term, the engineering type or the *engineer*. Reality, truth, value, and knowledge are rooted in the objective world, but the irreducibles, the axiomatic protocols of existence are the atomic individuals. Manipulation as a relational tool and material objects as the source of all value are the core ingredients of the world view prevailing today. This is a result of the power of technology (the engineering orientation) and the consequent influence of the Western hemisphere on world metaphysics.

At the opposite pole of this diagonal axis, we find the mystic life-style. The *mystic* combines two views: ultimate reality is consciousness, that is, *subjective*, and it is *universal* or unitary. The mystic, therefore, identifies his values and his reality with cosmic consciousness.

The *artist* (subjective and individual) and the *naturalist* (objective and universal) are at opposite ends of the other diagonal axis. The artist, in this conception, is the person for whom reality and value are ensconced in his particular and individual subjectivity and consciousness. He is the great individualist, but he is also exceptionally sensitive to inner states of mind, even if these originate outside of him (within society, as in Picasso's *Guernica*, or in nature, as in Beethoven's *Pastoral Symphony*). The naturalist, like a committed environmentalist, identifies with physical nature conceived as whole. His verb is not "to use" (as it would be for the engineer) but "to appreciate." The naturalist can be a nature-lover—a backpacker, a gardener, or a person who imagines himself to be a hermit on a Himalayan peak—or he can be a pure scientist. As the latter he finds in fields such as the physical or life sciences the worship of the world of nature. Science results from wonder and ends in the sense of identity (by virtue of conquest through the mind's knowledge) with the physical universe—very much of an Aristotelian ideal.

In the construction of a test and for purposes of developing a profile it may not be necessary to have questions discriminating along the engineer-mystic and artist-naturalist axes. The profile will fall naturally into one of these areas if we extensively measure a subject's orientation along the primary (I-U, S-O) axes. Nevertheless, it is of value to present some questions that have been used for making these secondary discriminations. We can distinguish—hypothetically at least—between an artistic and a naturalistic orientation by means of this question (with a similar three-point distribution between the choices available):

If you had the money and the interest to buy a valuable painting, would you select (a) a spacious landscape or (b) a sensitive portrait?

The assumption behind this question is that choice (a) indicates a preference for an objective and external as well as universal and unified world view or sense of identity. Choice (b) would then indicate a preference for a subjective, feeling, and individualistic outlook on life.

A question to discriminate along the engineer-mystic axis is the following:

Which do you believe, in the last analysis, has contributed more to the well-being of mankind—(a) meditation or (b) technology?

An (a) answer would directly indicate the mystical orientation, whereas a (b) response tends obviously toward the engineering direction.

It goes without saying that there are problems of ambiguity and interpretation with all of these questions and that many questions are needed. Extensive statistical analyses will help sort out the best questions for test construction. Finally, we can devise questions which force a choice between polarities which are at right angles to each other, such as the engineer and the artist or the introspective and the universalist perspectives. Sample questions are listed on the tables.

Following is a series of sample questions, each indicating the kind of discrimination it intends to make, along with a profile blank, and several profiles. (See Table and Figures 1-6.) The profiles can be constructed on the basis of any questions discriminating along the axes desired. Specifically, these sample profiles are based on the first four questions from the first table.

Table of Sample Questions to Determine Preference Direction and Intensity Along the Basic Axes of Being-Orientation

Discriminations Along a Straight Line.

1. If you were a university professor and had the ability and time, would you do research in (a) the physical sciences or (b) the nature of consciousness?

   (a) ☐   O   (b) ☐   S

2. If you had the money and the interest to buy a valuable painting, would you select (a) a spacious landscape or (b) a sensitive portrait?

   (a) ☐   n   (b) ☐   a

3. Which do you believe, in the last analysis, has contributed more to the well-being of mankind—(a) meditation or (b) technology?

   (a) ☐   m   (b) ☐   e

4. If you had the choice between two excellent courses in a scholarship program, would you select (a) a course in personal analysis and development or (b) a course in current theories of astronomy and cosmology?

   (a) ☐   I   (b) ☐   U

5. If you had the choice between two excellent courses in a scholarship program, would you select (a) a course in "Personal Development in an Alienated Society" or (b) a course in "The Connection Between Ancient Mysticism and the Most Recent Breakthroughs in Physics and Astronomy"?

   (a) ☐   I   (b) ☐   U

6. Which aspects of the study of psychology and sociology do you expect will ultimately prove more important for mankind—(a) the study of personal growth and development or (b) the study of social, political, and economic issues?

(a) ☐ I   (b) ☐ U

7. Given a choice of two books to read, are you more likely to select (a) a book about the inner-space explorations of great artists and philosophers or (b) a book about the beauties of nature or the marvels of science?

(a) ☐ a   (b) ☐ n

8. If you were the head of a foundation, like the Guggenheim or Ford Foundations, that supports worthy and accomplished individuals, would you recommend that its money be spent primarily (a) to support persons who are meditative, reflective, and introspective, such as poets, mystics, and theologians or (b) to support persons who are accomplished in technology and engineering and, like successful administrators or executives, are good at getting things done?

(a) ☐ m   (b) ☐ e

Discrimination Over Right Angles

9. Which has been the more significant contribution to mankind—(a) the advances of Albert Einstein and Enrico Fermi, which can lead to the harnessing of atomic energy for peaceful purposes or (b) Plato's view, which became part of the ethical, religious, and scientific traditions of Western civilization, that there exist universal and eternal truths (the so-called Platonic Ideas)?

(a) ☐ O   (b) ☐ U

10. Which of these two values has contributed most to civilization—(a) the ideals of the scientific method and of scientific objectivity, which have helped mankind control the forces of nature or (b) the ideals of freedom, independence, self-reliance, and individualism, which are incorporated in the Bill of Rights?

(a) ☐ O   (b) ☐ I

11. What type of person do you admire more—(a) an introspective, inward person, who is sensitively aware of the delicate shadings of human emotions or (b) a self-made person who stands alone and is ready to conquer all odds single-handedly?

(a) ☐ S   (b) ☐ I

12. If you should see the following news items with headlines of equal size in your morning paper, which would you read more attentively—(a) "New Important Theory About the Nature of Self or Ego" or (b) "New Discoveries About the Size and Age of the Universe"?

    (a) ☐ S   (b) ☐ U

13. Assuming that you have significant ability to be assured of success, would you prefer to be (a) an admired major artist or musician or (b) an important and respected business executive or administrator?

    (a) ☐ a   (b) ☐ e

14. The main object of scientific research should be the discovery of truth rather than its practical applications:
    (a) yes or (b) no.

    (a) ☐ n   (b) ☐ e

15. In a doctor's office waiting room you see two books. Which would you choose to read— (a) *Hiking in the Sierras* or (b) *Techniques for Meditation?*

    (a) ☐ n   (b) ☐ m

16. Are you more interested in reading accounts of the lives and works of individuals such as (a) Ludwig van Beethoven, Friedrich Nietzsche, and Richard Wagner or (b) St. Francis of Assisi, St. Augustine, and the Buddha?

    (a) ☐ a   (b) ☐ m

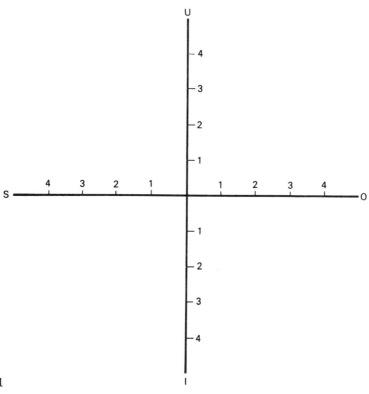

Figure 1

	S	O	I	U
1. a. Here	a._____			
b. There		b._____		
2. a. Flower			a._____	
b. Landscape				b._____
3. a. You		a._____		
b. I	b._____			
4. a. Area				a._____
b. Point			b._____	
5. a. Person			a._____	
b. World				b._____
6. a. Mars		a._____		
b. (your city)	b._____			

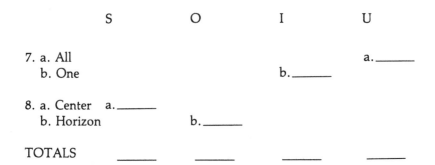

	S	O	I	U
7. a. All				a._____
b. One			b._____	
8. a. Center	a._____			
b. Horizon		b._____		
TOTALS	_____	_____	_____	_____

Figure 1 (*continued*)

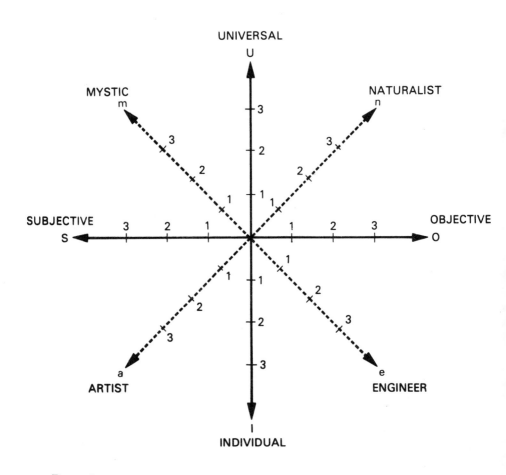

Figure 2

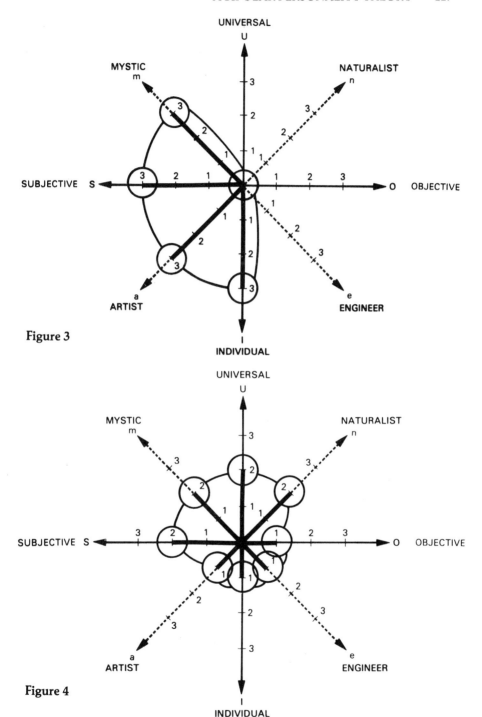

Figure 3

Figure 4

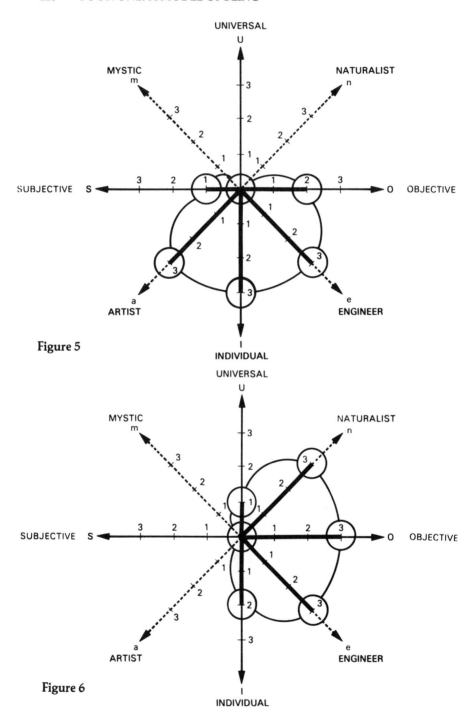

Figure 5

Figure 6

Philosophical Positions

It appears that the personality structures, world views, world designs, life-styles, cultural biases, and metaphysical orientations which are associated with positions along these axes and the resultant locations within the area of the profile or topology are quite clear. We get a lucid image of the type of human being present. What is not quite as readily available is a phenomenological description of these possible and different orientations carried out in such a way that they can be correlated with personality traits, theories of personality, and the like. However, the rather substantial explanatory power of this bipolar analysis of human potentialities is sufficiently convincing to risk the important venture of organizing a great deal of psychological and metaphysical material under its wings.

These orientations are not new to the history of philosophy. Major schools of thought have developed around each of them. Let us look at some examples.

Our analysis can cover metaphysics, epistemology, and axiology— reality, truth (or knowledge), and value. The subjective orientation on the horizontal subject-object axis corresponds to idealistic, spiritualistic, mentalistic, and subjectivist metaphysics. Reality is conceived as being mental, inward, and subjective. Consciousness is the ultimately real. In terms of epistemology (that is, considerations regarding knowledge and truth) this position demands that all knowledge is based on first-person experience. This is Kierkegaard's position that subjectivity is the starting point. It is also the view that to be objective is but one of the many decisions made by a subjectivity, so that absolute objectivity is impossible and even undesirable. Subjectivism in epistemology invites relativism.

A subjective metaphysics and a subjective epistemology can be oriented either toward the universal or the individual direction. In the former are metaphysical positions reminiscent of objective or absolute idealism (a subjective universalism); in the latter is traditional subjective idealism. We are reminded of Leibniz's monadism and even of solipsism. Objective idealism (which corresponds to the mystic personality structure) is a monistic idealism or a monistic subjectivism. Subjective idealism (which corresponds to the artist's personality structure) is a pluralistic subjectivism or a pluralistic idealism.

Metaphysics on the objective pole is exemplified by naturalistic or materialistic positions. They also include two varieties of realism—ultimate reality is material (Hobbes) or conceptual (Plato). This epistemological orientation is assigned preeminence by the scientific outlook. Knowledge is based on the examination of the hard realities of the external world. Absolutist positions (as opposed to relativism) have their origin in the objective orientation. Values and standards are external to the person. They reside in God, nature, or society—but not in the area of conscious sub-jectivity. The metaphysics corresponding to the naturalist personality structure is a monistic materialism, objectivism, or naturalism. Parmenides is the example par excellence of this position. On the other hand, the metaphysics which corresponds to the engineering personality structure is, quite appropriately, the pluralistic materialism, naturalism, and objecti-vism. The obvious examples are the atomists Democritus and Leucippus.

The metaphysical postures associated with the individual-universal axis are now quite obvious. The universalist metaphysics is monistic—the universe is one—whereas the individualistic metaphysics is pluralistic—the universe is made up of particular, atomic monads.

If we examine each metaphysical position individually, we will often recognize that a pure commitment to one pole of one axis is rare. At most, a metaphysical position is a direction or an emphasis. In fact, when we explore metaphysical positions such as those of Leibniz (pluralism) and Spinoza (monism) we notice how they also try to incorporate the non-emphasized elements in their viewpoints. (See Figure 7.)

Two developments that go beyond existentialism and phenomenology in contemporary European philosophy are hermeneutics and structuralism. Both are expressed in the bipolar topology. The two vertically intersecting polar axes are the basic structures that consciousness projects on the world. That is a structuralist conception, derived in this case not from the studies of empirical anthropology (as done by Lévi-Strauss) but by transcendental

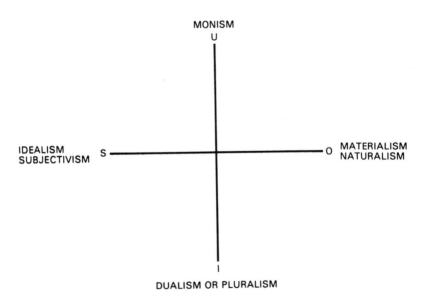

Figure 7   **Metaphysical Positions**

a priori researches (that is, direct inspection of our unique inner consciousness).

Hermeneutics is the search for principles of interpretation so that communication of realities rather than metaphors can be established. It is a way of going beyond rationalization and saying what we mean. The bipolar topology is a good example. We may talk of willpower, civil liberties, or atoms. Our real meaning, however, is that we have made the decision for individuality or particularity and are living it in both our inner and outer existence.

Personality Types

We can chart the personality types, structures, values, and orientations which can be mapped on a bipolar topology and for which we can get a profile based on a judicious use of psychometric devices. The following list incorporates a number of standard and important personality theories, political postures, and ethical viewpoints. The S-O and I-U axes, which lead to the primary types, provide us with interesting contrasts and parallels. The secondary types, the a-n, m-e axes, yield additional noteworthy descriptions of common types of human beings.

PRIMARY TYPES

SUBJECTIVE:

Stoic, ascetic
Idealistic
Inner-directed
Introspective
Reflective, detached
Highest value is love

OBJECTIVE:

Sensuous, physical
Materialistic
Other-directed
Outgoing
Involved, committed
Highest value is realism

INDIVIDUAL:

Active, ambitious
Concerned with personal success; believes that problems are solved through personal initiative and responsibility
Anxious, critical personality
Leads
Logical and analytic approaches to life
Highest values are power and strength

UNIVERSAL:

Passive, easygoing
Concerned with the well-being of society and the world; believes that problems are solved by communal and state actions
Relaxed, accepting personality
Conforms
Global and impressionistic approaches to life
Highest values are unity and harmony

SECONDARY TYPES

ARTIST:

Idealistic individualist. This is the life of feeling, sensitivity and, perhaps, narcissism (preoccupation with self). His or her highest values are depth, art, and empathy.

ENGINEER:

The prototype of our society. This person is practical; he or she harnesses nature and society for individual profit or social use. This is the engineer, technocrat, builder, and materialistic individualist. He or she is a manipulator and an activist. The highest values for this personality are wealth and/or efficiency.

NATURALIST:

Identifies with nature and/or the social order through devotion to pure science and art, as well as through the study of history and social systems. His or her highest values are truth, beauty, and compassion.

MYSTIC:

Identifies with cosmic consciousness. This person "goes with the flow" and allows events to happen. Has a predilection for meditation and Oriental philosophies. His or her highest values are peace and tranquility.

Following is a subsidiary chart of traits associated with the primary polarities. These traits are not as clear, as apt, or as exact in their discrimination as those of the above list. It is nevertheless important to mention them so that the meaning of these polarities can be further clarified.

SUBJECTIVE:	OBJECTIVE:
Active	Passive
Independent	Dependent
Nurturing	Needs caring
Feminine	Masculine
Stoic	Epicurean
Ultimate reality is spiritual	Ultimate reality is physical
Focus on persons	Focus on things
Poetic	Scientific
Concerned with the here-and-now	Concerned with the there-and-then

INDIVIDUAL:

Close minded
Emphasis on self-control
Atheistic
Focus on the individual and the particular
Alienated, alone, isolated
Negative, "no"-saying
Self-reliant
Believes in medication and in surgery for healing

Endorses humanistic and existential approaches to psychology

Private
Critical personality
Capitalist
Believes in the supremacy of the individual
Values whatever benefits persons, individuals

UNIVERSAL:

Open-minded
Emphasis on abandon
Theistic
Focus on the universal, worldly, and cosmic
Gregarious, familial
Positive, "yes"-saying
Trusting
Believes in holistic medicine and parapsychology (such as faith healing)

Endorses experimental approaches to psychology and behavior modification

Public, social
Accepting personality
Socialist
Believes in the supremacy of the community
Values whatever benefits society, history, and the world

A final comment on these personality traits is in order before we move on to other ways in which this map helps us organize the proliferation of ideas in the growth movement today.

First of all, human beings are combinations of all of these factors. In many, even most, there will be distinct tendencies in one direction or another. Second, there is neither likelihood nor need of consistency of direction. Some people are constant in their personality structure; others are or need to be variable. Third, there is no pathology directly indicated on this map. All possibilities are healthy opportunities for being. No value judgments are intended with any of these descriptions. Pathology and health are connected to the availability and uses of *freedom* with respect to these orientations.

Fourth, health and illness would be defined in terms of the amount of control and flexibility as opposed to the automatism and inflexibility that a person has over these various personality structures. Each person must analyze his personality structure himself; he must then evaluate it, that is, ask himself if that is the orientation he wishes to choose; and finally, he must be able and willing to make whatever changes in his orientation, world view, mode of perception, and life-style that he deems appropriate.

Fifth, a healthy person is not one who sees only one orientation as the true, the real, and the valuable. He may choose one and remain there but he cannot be inflexible and fixated. The freedom to change orientations, the wisdom to know there exist other and equally legitimate life-styles and world views, and an openness to these unexplored regions of one's possibilities are the hallmark of the healthy person. That is a philosophic definition of health.

The bipolar topology is a good example of how philosophy relates to psychological and health issues. The name *clinical philosophy* is thus an appropriately descriptive designation for this new and burgeoning discipline.

Types of Psychotherapy

The proliferation of growth techniques and healing methods—both orthodox and innovative—can be organized by this bipolar theory. Each approach has its place and represents a certain orientation of the field of consciousness within the map of bipolar being. Each results from and is associated with a unique structure of consciousness, a structure which, while sharing some traits (such as freedom) with all persons, is nevertheless different for each individual person. The outlines of this structure can be easily detected. And this structure influences the personality, values, attitudes, and being-in-the-world of each human being. Healing methods are thus neither contradictory nor mutually exclusive; they are instead complementary and supplementary.

There is no suggestion that a person who, let us say, has defined himself as relating best to the engineer (e) quadrant will do best with treatments emanating from the e orientation. It is likely that an e person would normally think that e-type healing procedures are the only ones to be taken seriously, the only ones that exist, or the only ones that are scientific or reliable. However, it may well be that precisely because of this fixation the person is ill or at least shows symptoms. Healing, then, would involve—under at least one criterion—approaches based on the opposite pole of the axis on which the person finds his profile situated; that would introduce both balance and flexibility into his life. It expands his field of consciousness and connects him with the power and the vastness of his freedom.

Below is a list of common psychotherapeutic approaches and their tentative place on the bipolar map. Since no authentic therapist is fully one-sided, in practice there exists a great deal of overlap.

> m-quadrant: Therapies of the center; meditation; asceticism; dis-identification therapies; holistic medicine; parapsychology; faith healing; Jungian analysis (focus on archetypes)

e-quadrant: Body therapies (bioenergetics, rolfing, dance therapy, massage, and so forth); use of medication and surgery; Freud's psychoanalytic *theory* (focus on the body as basic metaphor)

a-quadrant: Existential, gestalt, and reality therapies; focus on freedom, choice, personal responsibility, and confrontation; rational-emotive psychotherapy; Freud's psychoanalytic *practice* (focus on maturity and independence)

n-quadrant: Environmental manipulation; ethnotherapy; theories and psychologies of adjustment; radical psychiatry; experimental psychology; behavior modification

Along with psychotherapies, religious questions—especially the issue of immortality—can be placed on this map. Ashvaghosha writes, in *The Awakening of Faith,* "When the mind is disturbed, the multiplicity of things is produced, but when the mind is quieted, the multiplicity of things disappears."[1] This statement refers—in a religious context—to our potential for flexibility along the I-U axis. Translated into the jargon of phenomenology, the quotation reads "When consciousness constitutes, the individual (as a member of a pluralistic universe) is produced, but when consciousness deconstitutes (or performs the transcendental reduction), then plurality disappears and the sense of universality is achieved."

It follows, therefore, that the perception of the individual-pole of the I-U axis is of a finite and dying being, since the individual is constituted through the "invention" of death.[2] Correlatively, the perception of ourselves at the universal pole, while very personal and intimate, is perceived not as individual but as eternal and undying.

The last point to consider in this section on therapies is to make the effort to fit Jung's theories into the bipolar paradigm. The two diagrams of Figure 8 should be self-explanatory to anyone at all familiar with Jung's typology.

A Phenomenology of Freedom

The last theme of clinical philosophy that the bipolar topology can usefully organize for us is freedom. Consciousness—once understood, experienced, and integrated into life—yields two fundamental insights and rewards: it gives us a justified sense of being *centered,* which leads to *security,* and a legitimate feeling of *freedom,* which leads us to *action* and potency. Herein lies a fundamental contribution of existential phenomenology to the theory and practice of psychotherapy. It is this sense of freedom as a transcendental and ontological structure that we are now integrating into the map of being. (See Figure 9.)

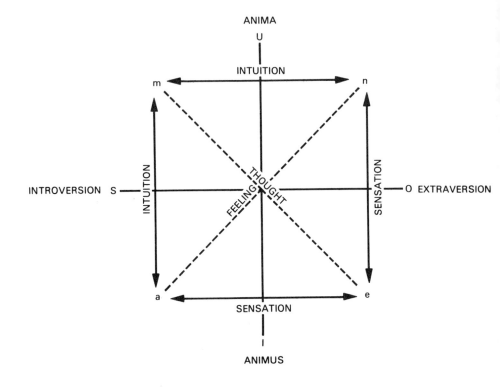

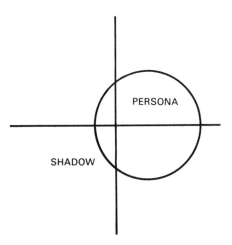

Figure 8

Let us begin with a brief phenomenology of freedom. (If we place freedom on the map it should be at the origin.) To discover our freedom is a powerful experience of illumination. To the extent that I am a *conscious center* I feel that I belong in the universe and that the universe belongs to me. The universe is my home and I am at home in it, regardless of whether or not my body is comfortable or, for that matter, even alive. To the extent that I am a *freedom* I feel hope, energy, and control. But as a freedom, I am also outside of the material and objective realm of things; in relation to the world my freedom is a supreme mystery and a sublime miracle. I do not understand it; I merely wonder about it. Transcendental freedom, properly understood, is thus worthy of reverence and even worship. The metaphor of a dry car battery, which becomes charged only when distilled water is added, is a helpful one. The discovery of my freedom is like charging a battery—tremendous potential energy, ready to go, becomes available to me.

There are many exercises (some of which are discussed in Book Two) which can assist us in experiencing the power of our freedom. One of the most useful is to literally force ourselves (in truth, "choose" to force ourselves) to reperceive, that is, to reconstitute, despair into hope. There are a number of ways in which persons can be urged to take responsibility for their obstacles. One can ask, for example, What are the obstacles you will put in the way of achieving your goals during any given time (a course, a therapy session, a marriage, a job, a vacation, lovemaking, and so forth)? Another way of urging a person to take responsibility for his obstacles is to assume that these have a hidden meaning. It is generally true that the obstacle helps you to experience your freedom. One should meditate or reflect on this thought. The experience of freedom may well be one of our greatest intrinsic values. And it may be equally true that the *only* way to experience and appreciate this holy sense of freedom is by placing obstacles and frustrations in its way, for it is in the struggle against these obstinate contraventions that the power and the glory of freedom rises into full view.

Another exercise that helps arouse the sense of freedom is, as in Freudian dream analysis, to interpret obstacles as the expression or fulfillment of an unconscious wish. If a patient is confronted with this interpretation by a person he perceives as an authority, then, through suggestion, he is forced to reconstitute his perception of the obstacle. We need not know whether or not in actual fact the obstacle was "set up" by the patient. The facts in this situation are not objective and causal but subjective and decisional. Let us avoid the trap of pure objectivism, of pretending that only the empirical realm is real.

Being is a subject-object encounter, an intentional subject-object continuum, a process, or an interface phenomenon. We need not know if an obstacle (such as an earthquake) is indeed the result of an unconscious wish. *It may nevertheless be perceived as fulfilling an unconscious wish;* once we learn to reconstitute our experience in this fashion, we are in contact with the enormous and beneficial psychological and physical healing power of our freedom. And that is a transcendental fact. The fact is that the patient *can* reinterpret the meaning of the obstacle from *given* to *chosen*. In so doing he forces himself to be in touch with his freedom rather than to remain out of contact with it. That crucially important change in perception is distinctly possible. It is the experience of transforming impotence into potency. The question is, will the patient do it?

Another approach to facilitate the experience of freedom is to interpret each obstacle as the expression of one part of you which you have denied. Such an assessment opens completely novel, possible, and unexpected self-concepts. The denied or negative aspect of our existence is either conscious—that is, we are clearly aware of it—or, if it is unconscious, it appears in our life as external, as projections. An insurmountable obstacle or a frustration leading to despair are good examples of projections. Jung put it well when he said that the unconscious treats you the way you treat it. If you deny it, it will reappear outside of you and haunt you. And that is how an obstacle must be perceived if we wish to make use of our freedom. Marriage counseling can serve as illustration.

In marriage counseling women often complain that their husbands are boorish, cruel, indifferent, weak, alcoholic, irascible, unfaithful, ineffectual, impotent. And men often complain that their wives are weak, aimless, hysterical, dumb, unaffectionate, frigid, destructive, unattractive, irresponsible.

These expletives are not accurate criticisms, for each person sees in a spouse that part of him or her which he has denied in himself. Therefore, a useful therapeutic interpretation follows these two lines of analysis: (a) the spouse *represents* the patient's unconscious wishes or repressed desires; and (b) the spouse *acts out* the patient's unconscious or lives that part of the patient's personality which he or she has denied.

The use of the denial-interpretation as a therapeutic tool is pragmatically true: it works in forcing the patient to assume responsibility for his own obstacles and for choosing to cope with them. And that construction of reality has as much right to exist as any other. It has the advantage, however, of manifesting the value of freedom in life. It is therefore to be preferred and has a superior claim on our loyalties.

The last exercise to facilitate the awareness of freedom can be called "the obstacle exercise." It summarizes much of the above material. The subject is presented, authoritatively, with three statements:

"There *are* answers to life's problems"
"We find *meaning* and *joy* in searching for these answers"
"Every obstacle turned over is a *stepping-stone*"

He is then asked to personalize these three insights by endeavoring to reperceive his primary problem or anxiety in this light. Again, this exercise in reconstitution does not depend for its efficacy on settling the matter of objective truth or falsity. It is one of choosing to cope or choosing not to cope with the problem or with the anxiety-producing situation. To consolidate and simplify this information for the general public, one may pass out "reminder cards" to students or an audience that look like this:

> I have a problem because
> I FORGOT THAT I EXIST and because
> I FORGOT THAT I AM A FREEDOM
>
> I chose this problem to remind me that
> I EXIST and to remind me that
> I AM A FREEDOM
>
> Now watch yourself make results happen

The reference here is to both the sense of *center* and the sense of *freedom*— the I-am experience and the experience of a potent core (the idea of the "creative erotic energy core" discussed in *Is There An Answer to Death?*)[3]— that emanate from an understanding of transcendental consciousness.

Four Types of Freedom

We are now ready to discuss how the idea and the sense of freedom can be placed on the bipolar personality chart. There are four ways—all different from each other—in which freedom expresses itself and can be experienced. Each of these manifestations corresponds to one of the four basic poles of the two axes.

Freedom on the I-pole of the I-U axis becomes or expresses itself as what is usually called *willpower*. It is the most common conception of freedom. There is nothing wrong with emphasizing and eulogizing willpower, self-discipline, and the power of determination and resoluteness. What would make such an emphasis unacceptable is to see it as the only, the exclusive meaning of freedom. Willpower works if we are flexible and recognize it to be one of four different manifestations of our freedom, but it does not work if we are inflexible and insist that it is the sole approach to solving human problems.

We can elicit the meaning and the experience of willpower through Sartre's philosophy. The Sartrean view is that a person is self-created or self-defined against a background of empty nothingness and is fashioned ex nihilo out of an absurd and valueless universe, a world bereft of absolutes, ground, or anchor points. That is a good image of how pure willpower functions at the basis of our being.

The alcoholic is often accused of lacking willpower. In fact, however, an alcoholic going to work Monday morning after a weekend drinking spree displays more willpower than most workers in his place of employment: They might be absent with a mere cold. Willpower, which he has but which has failed him, is therefore not the answer to alcoholism. Another mode of freedom must be tried.

The experience of willpower can be elicited by meditating and reflecting on the meaning of the following types of expressions, remembering them, and constantly using them:

> I have a choice
> I am responsible
> I choose to . . .
> I am doing it to myself
> I permit it to happen
> I tolerate this situation
> I put up with the problem
> I am in charge of my life

Furthermore, there is joy in confronting obstacles. Baruch Spinoza and Josiah Royce have noted that, and so have ascetics, stoics, and puritans. There is glory, satisfaction, security, and peace of mind in the knowledge that we do have willpower and that with it we have the strength to overcome obstacles.

The opposite expression of freedom occurs when we experience it on the U-pole of the I-U axis. There freedom is the sense of *spontaneity*. A common expression for or description of that sense of freedom is "going with the flow." "Trusting God fully" (or the body, or one's feelings or instincts, or society or the unconscious) yields a feeling of liberation. Spontaneity is the idea of freedom which is consonant with the belief that the mind-body heals itself. Therapists frequently discourage their patients from approaching healing through the willpower type of freedom and instead urge them to adopt a freedom-is-spontaneity attitude. As a result, the therapeutic focus frequently is on relaxation, rest cures, and externally imposed routines. Sleeping and hiking, meditation and travel lead to health because they utilize freedom in its mode of spontaneity. Sleeping and meditation are subjective-universal experiences, whereas hiking and travel are objective-universal experiences. The important point is that they are both experiences of the universality potential of human existence. Massage, nutrition, and relaxation are all approaches to healing which, because they direct the person toward the universal, utilize freedom in its manifestation as spontaneity.

The S-O axis yields two additional types of freedom—understanding and action. Much of the conflict between the theoretician and the activist lies in ignorance regarding the pervasiveness of this polarity. A thorough philo-sophic *understanding* of the reality and the nature of freedom—something that can be achieved through classwork, lectures, readings, and discussion —is extremely helpful in the therapeutic use of freedom. Many a patient would benefit from a class in the philosophy of freedom as preparation for or adjunct to intensive therapy, where the use of freedom is required.[4]

Freedom expressed on the S-pole of the S-O axis is the intellectual or conceptual *understanding* of the meaning and the reality of freedom. This approach includes a defense of freedom against determinism. It is also the *experience* of freedom, achieved perhaps through appropriate ac-tivities and exercises. Comprehending freedom in this conceptual and experiential fashion opens up the person to the vast transcendental di-mensions and the rich subjective possibilities of existence. Philosophies of psychological determinism and behaviorism (if they are general meta-physics rather than mere methodologies) tend to reject the reality of this important type of freedom. Both meditation and philosophic analysis remain good paths to the comprehension of freedom as a reliable fact.

We need early training in freedom—especially in conceptually entrench-ing it into the consciousness of our society. There must be sex education and death education in the early grades in school. That is needed for the creation of authentic individuals. But there must also be freedom education. And it must be cast not in a political, patriotic, or historical mold (which is freedom as action) but in a philosophical one of conceptual and experi-ential appreciation. One aspect, but only one, of freedom education is assertiveness training (that is, freedom as action). Training in relaxation would also be education in freedom, but in this case it is freedom in its mode of spontaneity.

The final expression or manifestation of freedom occurs on the O-pole of the S-O axis. Here freedom becomes action—the interface between mind and matter. This form of freedom can be expressed best as *risking action assertively*. The person who lives this kind of freedom welcomes challenges and feels comfortable in confrontations. Freedom as action "makes waves"; it is like having a child. The recent interest in consciousness raising, as-sertiveness training, political action groups, and national liberation move-ments are all expressions of this mode of freedom. The traditional self-reliant pioneer or self-made businessman, the executive and the military type, the "man of the world," all these personality structures identify freedom with essentially one mode of it—action. Often, of course, will-power is added, so that we see exhibited the engineering syndrome: action through willpower as the proper mode of being-in-the-world. For many freedom as action is the most important of all the manifestations of freedom.

We can diagram and thus summarize this analysis of freedom with Figure 9.

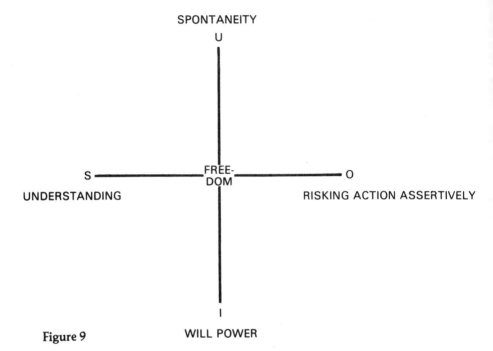

SPONTANEITY

U

S ——————————— FREE-——————————— O
                    DOM

UNDERSTANDING   RISKING ACTION ASSERTIVELY

I

Figure 9   WILL POWER

Interpretation

Now that we have an individual profile, the question of interpretation must be raised. This is not the place for a detailed exploration of the psycho-metric, diagnostic, and therapeutic possibilities of the bipolar map of consciousness and of being. A few comments, nevertheless, should be brought out to interpret the ensuing profile. The profile is likely to diagnose the overt personality structure of the person. It describes more or less what Jung has called the *persona*. It is also likely to identify those therapies which the person is inclined to choose for himself whenever he or she feels that therapeutic intervention is indicated. Finally, an individualized pro-file will suggest the meaning that freedom has for this individual. In sum, the closed area of the profile indicates the overt, manifest, or conscious personality of the subject taking a test based on these ideas.

However, through an inspection of the profile we can also take a look at the unconscious or *shadow area* of the person, represented by the region outside of the profile area. This would be the open area. We can in this way discover the personality-trait possibilities which the person has denied. The open areas are the deep unconscious. It is useful to reflect on them and investigate the degree to which this neglect and denial may be the source of symptoms and an avenue for therapeutic assistance.

Another use of the shadow or unconscious area of the profile is that it suggests therapeutic approaches which, while foreign to the person, may be precisely because of their hidden nature the ones most promising to elicit the unconscious material needed for added flexibility and control over the totality of a person's potential.

Finally, the shadow area of the profile suggests that the person in question experiment with his unused or denied forms of freedom. If a symptom exists, the individual is not flexible. He lacks the potential to shift—if that should be needed—from one quadrant to another. If there is no symptom, then we can infer that even if the person exists constantly in one quadrant he has the power to shift his emphasis. A man of action will benefit—if there are symptoms in his life and he is thus diagnosed as rigid—from understanding and reflecting on his freedom. A passive and relaxed person, for whom freedom is spontaneity, will benefit from the self-discipline of his freedom as willpower. The profile opens up the unconscious dimension—a useful tool for therapy. (See Figures 3-6.)

Health can now be defined. It rests on freedom. It is the ability to freely move one's profile along the topology. It means we are not fixated in any one orientation. It means we are flexible. This is not to eulogize indecisiveness. On the contrary, any posture adopted must be recognized to be freely and responsibly chosen (and rechosen). Nothing automatic is authentic. But the posture adopted must be responsibly, consciously, and deliberately assumed and it must be subject to change as needed.

The profile is also useful for matching partners or mates. If the chosen relationship is to be complementary, then opposite profiles are a good match. The husband's shadow area should be the wife's manifest profile content, and vice versa. However, if the choice of relationship is to be one of equality, then a good match consists of similar profiles.

Physics

One final observation about the explanatory power of the bipolar topology of being is in order.

It is not certain how one is to decide which perception of the world is prior, the universal or the individual. From the point of view of the post-analytic given, that is, the given as it emerges upon the deconstitution of our experience,[5] the universal is the primordial experientially given and the world of objects results from the archetypal decision for atomism, a decision made in the pre-Socratic days of the Western history of ideas. Many thinkers have felt, perhaps because of their respect for Oriental philosophy, that the universal is prior to the individual, but they are far from sure. If we view the given as a preanalytic datum, then the *Lebenswelt*—with objects already constituted in it—is the primordial experience. The archetypal decision is to do away with objects—which, we must assume, even animals perceive—by insisting on perceiving reality as continuous rather than discrete. If the preanalytic is our epistemological datum, then reality consists of individuals.

An interesting corollary applies to physics. Among the many conflicts in the theory of modern physics, some concern the particle-wave paradox of light. Another concerns the conflict between the world of visible objects—to which Newton's physics applies—and the world of invisible objects (macro- and micro-)—to which quantum mechanics and relativity apply. The visible world is the world of objects, of particulars; it is the world picture brought about by choosing the individual pole on the I-U axis. That is also the premise for the world of Newtonian physics—discrete atoms and points (objects, in short) are chosen as the ultimate ingredients of reality, a decision which began with Democritus and reached its apogee with Newton. Newtonian physics, roughly the physics of gross or visible objects, is thus the physics of the pole of individuality.

On the other side we find the world of subatomic physics and the cosmology of a four-dimensional space-time. That conforms to a field nature of being, to a sense of universality, process, and continuity where conceiving of individual, hard, material, and precisely delineated objects makes no sense. Micro- and macrophysics are thus clearly the products of shifting the focus of our vision on the universal pole of the I-U axis. To the layman the field theory of being is as invisible as is the subatomic particle or the curvature of space-time. The same is true of Eastern mysticism. All of these perceptions pertain to the universal pole of the axis.

Finally, the idea of a four-dimensional curved space—which derives from relativity theory—is no mystery if we understand that the region of the subject eventuates in the Eternal Now. And that stage of conscious subjectivity is achieved by making time itself into an object. It becomes then a matter of direct experience that time is the fourth dimension and that the universe is a four-dimensional space-time "surface" which is then "curved" by its mass. It is no mystery that the universe is a "stationary" space-time block and can be perceived "forwards" as well as "backwards." What is interesting is that research into the invisible in physical nature (modern physics) has forced us to recognize the primacy of first-person experience, which is the fundamental contention in the epistemology of phenomenology.

We can relate the nature of a complete Eastern mysticism to the I-U axis, as the quotation from Ashvaghosha shows. The S-O axis seems less relevant to a sympathetic understanding of Eastern thought, for it is the universal, which can be either subject or object, that is important in Eastern mysticism.

We can then relate the insights of modern physics to the S-O axis just as the basis of classical physics (mechanics) arose out of the I-U axis. In contemporary physics we have distinguished between the visible world (and *visible* here means *visible in principle*)—to which Newtonian analysis applies—and the invisible world (invisible in principle; in this context there can be no meaning attached to the word *visible*)—to which apply the macroscopic world of relativity theory and the microscopic, subatomic world of quantum mechanics. The visible world is the world of objects. But the world of transcendental subjectivity, the pure and objectless consciousness which is opened by reductive thinking, is considered by common sense (and even in the life-world) to be invisible. That is why most people do not understand it. In a religious context we say that consciousness—like God and the soul—is "out of this world" or *supernatural* (extra-natural, pre-natural, or paranatural would be equally appropriate). Similarly, the worlds of macro- and microphysics are invisible. Therefore, the study of contemporary physics yields insights which, while at first surprising and incomprehensible, are no mystery to the phenomenologist. When we study the invisible world, we study the transcendental region.

Beyond Phenomenology

Let us compose a variation on the previous themes. To think of experience as a dialectical subject-object polarity is only a first step in the development of a complete topology of the field of being. If the subject-object polarity is like a magnetic field, then we must allow for other intersecting fields of force, such as—to continue our metaphor—electricity and gravitation. The final phenomenological model of being incorporates a great deal of research and reflection beyond Husserl's phenomenology—in the humanities, in psychology and medicine, and in the sciences in general.

The first dimension of the field of being is given to us by the primary phenomenological contribution to philosophy, namely, the intentionality of consciousness. That first dimension is a subject-object, consciousness-world polarity. We symbolize it as follows:

$$S \longleftarrow \longrightarrow O$$

When the field "moves" or "acts" in a subject-to-object direction, we call that phenomenon intentionality, whereas if subjectivity withdraws itself from the object, we call that act the transcendental-phenomenological reduction.

The second dimension of the given structure of the field of being, diagrammed as perpendicular to the first, comes to us from the phenomenological notion of constitution, from the existential theory that to be an individual is to create the hard nodule of a self out of a universal void, and in general from the history of epistemology, which tells us that the world of perception is our subjective organization of the given. We can therefore perceive the world as one vast and universal whole or as a series of in-

dividuals and particulars. This second axis is then a universal-individual
axis. We diagram it as follows:

When in perception, consciousness acts to fashion an individual entity out
of a universal whole, then we call that constitution. Conversely, when the
individual objects or substances are disorganized and return to their primordial chaos—as they would be experienced in altered states of consciousness—we have the phenomenon of deconstitution.

The bipolar field so far described can organize for us most personality
theories. Also, we notice that Eastern culture is based on the decision
(Urentschluss, archetypal choice) to ascribe ultimate reality status to the
universal subjective region—and call it cosmic consciousness:

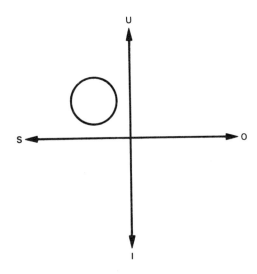

Western cultures have been based on the decision to call real that which is
objective and individual. This view becomes atomism:

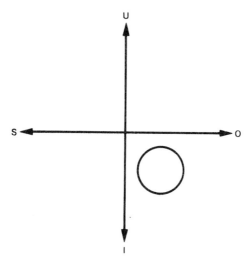

Both are legitimate organizations of being, as long as they remain flexible. Rigidity and reductionism are myopic. This much has been discussed already. Let us move on by experimenting with additional dimensions.

A third axis, perpendicular to the plane described by the first two, is given to us by the heavy existential emphasis on freedom. It is the polarity of freedom and facticity, and we diagram it thus:

When the conscious act attaches itself to a recalcitrant otherness—as when an individual identifies with a nation, or a mother with her child—then freedom moves towards facticity, an act we call cathexis. Passion, ego-involvement, and commitment are examples of freedom cathecting facticity. Disengagement is called decathexis. If the freedom in decathexis is conscious, then decathexis is the phenomenon of asceticism, whereas if the decathexis is not conscious, we call the ensuing phenomenon catatonic withdrawal. Our three-dimensional polarity of being is seen in this three-dimensional figure:

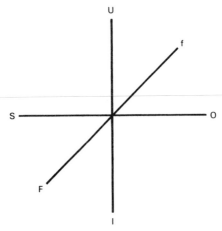

A fourth dimension introduces the notion of the unconscious, that dramatic idea invented by Nietzsche and utilized by Freud and Jung to revolutionize our thinking about the human condition. All aspects of the tri-polar field can occur in a conscious *and* in an unconscious context. We diagram it as follows:

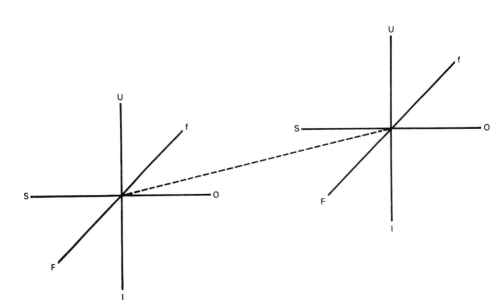

The conscious act which moves from conscious to unconscious is self-deception (Sartre called it bad faith) and its reversal is self-disclosure—which is the goal of therapy when it analyzes the resistance.

Our derivation of the categories of the phenomenological model of being leads us to a quadripolar or multiphasic description of the consciousness-being continuum.

Three added features must be emphasized: First, this polarity exists within and is totally suffused by a spatio-temporal and matter-energy continuum which is *experienced* in the inner and outer life-world. Second, the polarity exists in "packets," "pockets," or "clusters"—of all sizes—somewhat like Leibniz's monads. For example, the space-time within which exists a bacterium is of the same order, albeit smaller, as the space-time of a vast nebula. And third, we are a nonattached observer to this four dimensional continuum, an observer who is different from that which it observes and who therefore can be called descriptively the Eternal Here-and-Now. We can legitimately describe the Eternal Here-and-Now as either us or as going through us.

The hypothesis here presented is that this phenomenological model of being is a set of modern categories which describe the most general traits of the *Lebenswelt* as these disclose themselves to sensitive phenomenological analysis. This model as a four-dimensional polarity observed by an Eternal-Here-and-Now is thus the general pattern or structure into which the results of all our explorations (in any discipline whatever) will fall. These are philosophical facts about region A + B + C,[6] that is, ontological facts, accumulated through the systematic application of a phenomenological methodology. These categories are derived from a thorough analysis of immediate experience and then appear to be used by us literally as sophisticated anthropomorphic metaphors in the sciences. Success in basic scientific research may be proportional to the extent to which this model is used in theory construction and experiment design.

Notes

1. Ashvaghosha, *The Awakening of Faith*, translated by D.T. Suzuki (Chicago: Open Court, 1900), p. 78.

2. See Part III of Peter Koestenbaum, *Is There An Answer To Death?* (Englewood Cliffs, N.J.: Prentice-Hall, 1976).

3. Koestenbaum, *Is There An Answer To Death?* pp. 144ff.

4. In this connection it is advisable to read Peter Koestenbaum, *The Vitality of Death* (Westport, Conn.: Greenwood, 1971), chap. 5.

5. *Ibid.*, chap. 27.

6. See Book One, chap. 2.

Part IV • THREE
PHILOSOPHIC
FACTS

Chapter 10 • PHILOSOPHIC FACT ONE: MYSTICISM AND ALTERED STATES OF CONSCIOUSNESS

Now that we have developed what it is hoped is a comprehensive presentation of the phenomenological model of being, we must investigate some of the material with a more specific view toward practical applications. The essence of an existential personality theory can be presented in terms of three facts which we call philosophic facts. The expression *philosophic fact* has special meaning: Philosophy in the phenomenonlogical mold is the exceptionally sensitive description of all aspects, regions and zones of experience and perception. These descriptions clarify and bring into focus facts—data—about human experience. Whereas statistics can uncover "facts" in a horizontal sense, phenomenological descriptions disclose the vertical structure of the facts of human experience. Facts come in layers, layers which can be disclosed through the hermeneutic exploration—the bracketing and careful analysis—of the subtle nuances of human experience. Psychotherapy, poetry, wisdom—all acts and attitudes we call "deep" or "profound"—are means of reaching vertically into the treasure of experience.

Three basic facts are disclosed by these philosophic researches. These facts are not new, but we are now ready to concede their scientific character (or the mystical-transcendental aspects of science, if we prefer).

Philosophic Fact One, which has many formulations, runs thus: "A consciousness runs through me"; "A luminous, aware, clear, light runs through me"; or "A conscious stream runs through me." It would be technically more correct to say "A consciousness-world stream runs through me." Philosophic Fact One of the existential personality theory is the elaboration of the conscious universality of the individual-universal polarity of the phenomenological model of being.

Overview

Philosophic Fact One is the phenomenological description of the experience of pure consciousness. We refer to this activity as transcendental phenomenology, since the description is in the reflexive mode of thought rather than in the referential. It is not difficult to develop a reasonably accurate description of that consciousness, the phenomenon of universality, but the consequences of taking these descriptions seriously are staggering. Let us examine five descriptively discovered traits of consciousness.

The consciousness within me is first of all experienced as *universal*. Being an individual is not the irreducible given in experience. I am not born an individual. To be an individual is to have boundaries and limits and it is to experience one's alienation from the rest of being. But the boundaries which separate an ego from its environing non-ego world are neither precise nor obvious. They vary even for the most sophisticated, highly developed, and individualized ego and are therefore subject to choice and definition, constitution, and cathexis. Furthermore, the limits of the ego are not true limits, since they are transcended each time they are thought. In experiencing the limits of the ego we transcend the ego. A limit must be seen from both sides to be meaningful. But as soon as a limit is seen from the *other side of the ego* as it were, consciousness has transcended these limits. Finally, the experience of assuming full responsibility for being oneself, which is the experience of maturity, is also the experience of constituting an individual experience out of the larger givenness of a universal consciousness. These are therefore some of the reasons why we can legitimately talk about our consciousness as being universal.

Second, the consciousness within is experienced as *infinite*. This is a true infinite, in that it is the only infinite which can be experienced. But it is what we might call a negative rather than a positive infinite. The latter would be the experience of an actual infinity, which is a contradiction in terms, for anything directly and positively experienced will be finite. A negative infinity is simply the actual experience of the absence of limits. Consciousness is one of the aspects of experience which is given *only from the inside* as it were. The closer we get to whatever it is we mean by its limits, the more these recede into the distance. This peculiar experience of limitlessness is a fundamental fact of existence; it must be fully experienced, fully understood, and fully integrated into our ontology and our lived human existence.

Third, consciousness is coeval with *space* and *time*. Inner space and outer space can be distinguished only pragmatically, as William James has pointed out in his essay "Does Consciousness Exist?"[1]:

The whole philosophy of perception from Democritus's time downwards has been just one long wrangle over the paradox that what is evidently one reality should be in two places at once, both in outer space and in a person's mind. . . . If the "pure experience" of the room were a place of intersection of two processes, which connected it with different groups of associates respectively, it could be counted twice over, as belonging to either group, and spoken of loosely as existing in two places, although it would remain all the time a numerically single thing. . . . In one of these contexts it is your "field of consciousness"; in another it is "the room in which you sit."

The identity of time with consciousness is even more emphatically obvious, since we do not even attempt to distinguish inner and outer time. Needless to say, the time we speak of here is the primordial, lived, and originary experience of time and it is not any conceptual or scientific construct derived from these *Lebenswelt* experiences.

Fourth, consciousness is experienced as *indestructible*, since the experience or conception of the non-being of consciousness is totally meaningless within the context of an intentional theory of being. All being has connected with it, as an integral part of every object or event, a stream of consciousness leading to a transcendental subjectivity. Non-being itself is always an intentional object, that is, the object of an intentional and a self-transcending consciousness. If we should attempt to transfer the concept of non-being to the transcendental region we instantly discover that this project is impossible and self-contradictory. We then discern that such contention is meaningless. The difficulty of this point does not lie as much in understanding it—a few simple logical steps can accomplish that—but in applying and integrating this insight to therapy, medicine, and life in general. The severe consequences of this undaunted examination of presuppositionless experience must be faced not with the prejudice of tradition but with the courage of a new world view.

Finally, this consciousness disclosed as Philosophic Fact One, because of its universal and indestructible characteristics, can be experienced and recognized as the ground of being and thus is a basic answer to the eternal questions. Transcendental consciousness is one answer to the question, What and where is home?

Dreams are our daily reminders of both the reality and the importance of these ontological and metaphysical observations. If we understand the meaning of the concept *dreams* then we understand the distinction between the transcendental and the empirical realms. Dreams are both fascinating and evasive. But they allow for a trans-commonsense metaphysics. Dreams are our basic protection against the total domination of commonsense metaphysics.

Characteristics of Philosophic Fact One

We know of the existence of this inward stream of consciousness through direct inspection of introspective material. That is merely an application of the phenomenological method in general and of the theory of reductions in particular. Thus the evidence for the existence of an eternal stream of universal or cosmic consciousness that runs through us appears within the philosophical discipline of transcendental phenomenology.

We are a consciousness-ignorant and consciousness-denying culture. Eastern philosophy has helped us understand our own Western tradition in depth. The phenomenological contribution to philosophy and modern thought in general has been to call attention to the turn—the inward look, the reversal of the usual direction of consciousness, the reduction—away from objects and toward the source of observation and agency.

The stream has specific characteristics which are discovered through the careful application of the phenomenological reduction. First, it is eternal and unchanging. Beginning, ending, and changing are not relevant descriptions of the stream of consciousness. If we should superimpose the former concepts (that is, beginning, ending, change) onto the experience of the stream, a method of proof used in the early theorems of Euclid, we detect no congruence. This method of establishing the truth of philosophical positions derives from Husserl's method of imaginative variations. It is reminiscent of Mill's methods, except that variation occurs with mental or ideational rather than with physical experiments.

Specifically, to demonstrate the eternity of consciousness, we place ourselves into the kind of meditative mood which opens up for direct inspection the transcendental dimension, reduced experience, or pure consciousness—terms used here synonymously. We then try out certain concepts—possibly (but not necessarily) concepts derived from the empirical region, from the shadows on the screen in Plato's cave— which we attempt to place over that transcendental region to see if they correspond or fit. The phenomenological reduction has shown us (through a *reflexive* rather than a *referential* act of consciousness) that inward and transcendental consciousness is an infinite regress—as a fact which is directly observable. Similarily, consciousness as it reaches out to the world and becomes spatiality shows itself to direct inspection to be an infinite progress. Infinite progress and regress are complementary aspects of the field of consciousness.

The question of correspondence is answered intuitively. That is the only kind of evidence available when the subject of research is transcendental consciousness. Whereas the evidence is difficult to acquire, it is in principle no more difficult than other contemporary experiments. Instead of using complex and expensive equipment, we use our own being. It is more complex than the most convoluted technical machinery. The evidence for the existence and structure of consciousness is the same as it is for the existence and structure of the life-world: immediate experience. But since there are observable differences in how we perceive or intuit these two regions of being, we must use the terms *referential* to designate life-world perceptions and *reductive* or *reflexive* to designate transcendental (that is, pure consciousness) intuitions. If necessary, we can place the terms *referential* and *reflexive* in an epoche and describe in greater detail these two fundamental acts of consciousness, these two basically different—even opposite—intentions.

We first try the concept of temporal limits, of beginning and of ending, of a nothingness that precedes it and a nothingness that follows. We try out the concept of a prior and a posterior time which, while not nothing, is nevertheless something other than this stream of pure consciousness itself. None of these concepts fit. No meaningful correspondence can be detected. Such a transcendental experiment can be carried out by one observer many times and repeated by other observers as well. The result will be increased refinement in articulation. The criteria of public verifiability, of replicating experiments, can thus be met in this expansion of the scientific method (discussed at length in Chapters 25 and 26, *The Vitality of Death*). To realize the truth of these analyses is to say that the concept of *eternity* does fit. We have here the outlines of an adequate argument (through descriptions which are a form of radical empiricism or a *transcendental empiricism*) for the eternity of consciousness.

What has been said here about the meaninglessness of temporal limits applies also to spatial limits. It follows that the second characteristic of the stream is its spatial infinity. Just as this stream is the experience of time, so it also is the experience of space. Lived space, experienced space, and the experience of conceptual space (the experienced distance between subject and object, ego and world, consciousness and what we are conscious of, which we may call psychic and abstract space) is very real and very immediate. No concept of limits can be placed congruently over it. We again must conclude, with a kind of transcendental empiricism, an empiricism of experience as reduced, that the stream of consciousness which runs through every *me* is infinite.

A point discussed in Chapter 6 of Book One, in connection with the notion of cosmic consciousness, is the similarity of outer and inner space, as well as outer and inner time—*as these are perceived, lived, and experienced.* For one, it appears that the experience of external space per se as a perception is very closely similar to the experience of consciousness per se. In addition, the real physical distance between my body and some other physical object—a boulder on a mountain, for example—is the same kind of *emptiness* or *vacuity* as is the intuited psychic distance between what we may call the center or the source of consciousness (which is, of course, an infinite regress in the same way that external space is an infinite progress) and any eidetic, affective, or iconic object (idea, emotion, or fantasy respectively). The evidence is found in direct observation, in the intuitive viewing of the matrix within which the events of this world—outer as well as inner—occur. Consciousness as referential or outward-looking produces (or makes available) the sense or experience of external space. Correlatively, consciousness as reflexive or as self-conscious and inward-looking[2] produces (or makes available) the experience of inner space.

With the experience of lived time, the situation may be a bit different. There seems to be, prima facie, no significant difference between the experiences of the time-experience of the world, the so-called external time, and the time-experience of the psyche, the so-called inner time.

One consequence following from this type of description and analysis of the general traits of experience and of being is the significant similarity between whatever we call in consensual speech "consciousness" and what in that same ordinary language we refer to as "space-time." Any scientific uses of the terms *consciousness* and *space-time*, as these occur in psychology and physics respectively, are partially distorted derivatives of this essentially unitary lived experience of space-time. It is the derivatives which force us to discriminate between inner and outer.

Lived space-time is the experienced phenomenon of consciousness. Lived consciousness-space-time is continuous. Within it, in its primordial, pure, originary, and given form we cannot distinguish unequivocally between inner and outer consciousness-space-time. This distinction is thus constituted. And the processes of constitution include the invention of the scientifically useful derivatives of consciousness-space-time. In psychology, consciousness is transformed from the vacuity of an infinite regress into an object to be studied. And what distinguishes this object from others in the world is that it is supposed to be *internal*. With that demand for internality, lived consciousness becomes conceptual consciousness. A parallel situation exists when space-time is defined in terms of measurements. Manipulation of physical objects in the processes of measurement and observation helps bring about the phenomenon of conceptual space-time. It is this type of manipulation which is an integral part of the constitution of externality.

Philosophic Fact One is knowledge of these aspects of consciousness.

NECESSITY

A third characteristic of consciousness or of Philosophic Fact One is that the stream exhibits existential necessity.[3]

The necessary existence or being of consciousness is of the same order as the aseity of God, the theological view that God exists by virtue of His own necessity and is not produced or kept in being by any other thing. *Logical* necessity, as distinguished from existential necessity, is the cohesion of event and property, such as that of the concepts *triangle* and *three-sidedness*. The connection is either established to be true by definition or it is true by virtue of "the nature of things" (which includes Platonic Forms or Eternal Essences, where some of these necessary connections—such as *man* and *rationality*—are established for all time).[4]

However, the crucial type of necessity is existential necessity, the fact that certain phenomena or aspects of being are not only connected necessarily but also exist necessarily. We need not call existence a property and we can therefore refer to necessary existence merely as a discovery. But there should be no objection to saying that existence is indeed a property and that this property is necessarily connected with consciousness. This is a metaphoric and circuitous manner of speaking, acceptable, it appears, regardless of its logical impurities. Direct inspection and observation of consciousness (also of space-time) discloses the fact that its non-being is a meaningless, inconceivable, and unobservable phenomenon. Another equally empirically observed self-evident phenomenon is the fact that *I am that consciousness* or that this consciousness is a stream which is continuous with whatever it is that I call *me*. These are important discoveries, in that they provide—in clinical philosophy—the empirical evidence for the indestructibility of consciousness, metaphorically institutionalized in the myths of personal immortality and reincarnation.

Evidence for the indestructibility of consciousness is one of the achievements of a phenomenologically expanded scientific method.

Philosophers differ in their interpretation of which logical connections are a priori, that is, what it is that is known to be true without reference to experience and empirical verification. But that kind of necessity—the logic of connection rather than of existence—does not concern us here. We are concerned with existential necessity, a concept unfortunately rejected in much of the most respected forms of modern philosophy. Existential necessity comes to us from the rationalistic tradition in philosophy, which holds that reason connects mind and world, so that understanding the processes of reason also gives us access to the processes of nature. This notion of necessary existence must be revived in contemporary philosophy. The combination of the theory of reductions and the phenomenological description of the region of being thus opened—that is, the transcendental region—will reestablish the legitimacy of the concept of necessary existence, of the existential a priori, or of the idea that at least one event (namely, the pure stream of consciousness) exists by virtue of its own necessity.

When we are witness to that stream—when we perceive it through introspection, and when we examine phenomenologically the yield of the transcendental reduction—we recognize that it must exist. We discover, as an experiential fact, that the nonexistence of that stream is a nonvisualizable and nonconceptualizable idea. We cannot constitute the idea of a nonexisting stream of consciousness. To assert this and to say the stream exists necessarily are synonymous expressions. Furthermore, any apparent denial or rejection of the existence of the stream, any attempted contradiction to its presence, is seen—upon engaging in the introspective phenomenological analysis which is our premise—to have been made by that very conscious stream whose denial we think is possible.

In other words, whenever we deny the necessary existence of the stream, we immediately discover that far from denying the stream it is the stream itself that has done the denying, and thus the reality of the stream of consciousness has been reestablished. The firmness of our denial of the necessary existence of the stream is precisely the firmness with which its existence is demonstrated, since to deny it is really to affirm it. The greater the denial the stronger the affirmation. The apparent contradiction is explained by the transcendental-empirical polarity. In this fashion the stream has ensconced itself permanently into existence, for this process of denial-affirmation can be repeated as often as is needed, that is, indefinitely.

Chapter 6 discusses levels of consciousness, from animal consciousness to the Eternal Now. These levels are differentiated by degrees of reduction—stepping back, disidentification, or detachment. As a result of this hermeneutically available or layered character of consciousness, we find that there are many different and often apparently contradictory ways of describing consciousness. The ultimate description is the Eternal-Here-and-Now. From that stance, space-time (which is *both* a physical *and* a psychic or conscious reality) is an object to the observation and to the agency of the Eternal-Here-and-Eternal-Now (Eternal Now, for short) aspect of being.

Modern physics invites a similar view of being; it is a picture of space-time seen from *outside* of space-time. It is important to describe being not only from the perspective of space-time itself (that is, the world seen from within space-time) but also and foremost from the point of view of the Eternal Now, from a perspective which has its point of departure *outside* of space-time. That is the perspective of the mystic, of the meditator who now may be focusing on cosmic consciousness. In describing the world or being we cannot confuse perspectives or realms. The world from the perspective of the Eternal Now does *not* look like the world from its perspective of space-time. Yet the world or being are the same. What is different is the point of view.

We must therefore not talk of altered states of consciousness (ASC) but of *altered perspectives* only. Let us recall the parallel of the dream. To see the dream from the perspective of the dreamer is to take the position of the Eternal Now; and to see the dream from the space-time perspective is to consider the dream content to be the root metaphor for reality. When we confuse realms in dreaming, the meaninglessness of that confusion becomes apparent.

This analysis can be a point of departure for establishing hypotheses to account for and to stimulate paranormal phenomena. For example, we can hypothesize that a paranormal phenomenon occurs—or appears to occur—when we oscillate between perspectives. We can also hypothesize that what appears clear under an Eternal-Now perspective appears as paranormal in a space-time perspective. However, to translate these thoughts into experimental language confronts us with a unique problem. Let us return to the parallel with the dream. How can two dream figures (dream scientists) "experiment" about the reality of the dreamer? It would be much simpler to merely wake up.

IMPERSONAL FOUNDATION

Fourth, the stream of consciousness that runs through us is impersonal and nonindividual. There is considerable controversy on this point. Some persons in touch with meditation processes will insist that an experience of transcendental consciousness is a highly personal and individual phenomenon. It would appear that such a personal experience is nevertheless universal, in that it is unique. It is the experience of the universe as *me*.

If we call the stream of consciousness God—which would be justified by the history of religious thought, especially those strains with a mystical bias—then this God is not a person and does not have personal attributes. We cannot relate ourselves to Him on individual terms. These statements are made with a clear understanding of the unorthodoxy of this position in circles where religion is practiced and applied. Individuality, which is Philosophic Fact Two, is a different matter and will be discussed in the next chapter. It is precisely this attribute of impersonality that gives to God (or consciousness) its cosmic, soothing, loving, and protecting character.

We must remember that the sense of being an individual is constituted by denying our universality and by alienating ourselves from the vastness of being, which we thereby define as the non-ego. We accomplish both tasks through the invention of death. In other words, to be an individual means to reject God. The *individual* that we are is not to be found in the stream of consciousness which runs through us. Our individual ego is constituted by this stream and is observed or witnessed by it. The sense of universality runs through the ego, like blood through a capillary—as our metaphor indicates—but it is not the ego. It is for these reasons that we must say that the stream of consciousness is impersonal. But in its impersonalness lies its eternity, infinity, and the peace which goes with it. The hope for the immortality of an individual personality must be abandoned, because individuality and dying are synonyms. As long as we are dying we are individuals. But when we are dead, this is no longer true. However, and as a result, a different hope is kindled—hope for the eternity of the idea of personality and, what is a corrollary to it, hope for reincarnation as a meaningful and realistic symbol.

The last and crucial empirically discovered and reflectively understood characteristic of the stream of consciousness is its function or role as a ground or a foundation. This is not to deny the reality of other grounds. The reality and value of the spiritual foundation of human existence is what is stressed here. The stream is like the bottom of the universe, on which all else stands. The ground will be there when all else falls apart. It is our roots. The ground means peace and can give us strength and courage. The ground consists of answers, assurances, and meanings. It justifies our ethical convictions. The ground is the psychotherapeutic reason for this discussion of the conscious-universality or Philosophic Fact One. In short, the ground ends relativism and reintroduces absolutism. It is that on which the freedom for constitution and cathexis rests and is the realization that an absolute truth does exist. In theory, at least, before therapy can lead to change, before the character resistances and negative transferences can be broken through, a firm foundation, a secure base, is required. That base is Philosophic Fact One, a characteristic of being that each person can discover for him- or herself.

Dreams

Dreams—not the actual experience of a dream but the idea or concept of a dream or of dreaming as a human possibility—exist to remind us of the reality of Philosophic Fact One. Dogs dream; they have the experience, but they do not know that they are dreaming and they do not possess the notion or idea of a dream. Dogs, like all animals (called the animal consciousness in Chapter 6), are conscious but not self-conscious. They are aware of a world (*their* world), but they cannot perform a reduction, which would make them aware of the fact that they are aware. Their cathexis to the world is total. Dreams, therefore, are of paramount importance in both understanding and in managing the stream of consciousness in us as well as our permanent possibility for universality. Dreams are a daily, constant reminder of the reality of the stream of universal consciousness that runs through us.

There is a certain inconsistency about the concept of a dream: While we dream we do not know that we are dreaming.[5] If we adhere to strict phenomenology, we must say that a dream is not a dream while we are dreaming it, but is at that time simply part of our bona fide reality. That view is consonant with Medard Boss's theory of dreams as the continuation of our daily lives. In other words, a dream—while it is going on—exists as reality but not as dream.

On the other hand, while we are awake we are of course not dreaming, so that any dream is transformed into the *memory* of a dream. That is, when we talk of our dreams then the phenomenon in question, the object of our intentional consciousness, is not a dream but is the mere *memory* or the *recollection* of a dream. The object to consciousness is an iconic, fantasy object. A fringe area of that iconic object is the vector or external reference of that object. The iconic object (the dream) is not given as *dream*—that is, as real, so that the ego is fully cathected with it and the world which is the dream is not called in question—but is given as *recollected*, as pointing to its *past*, and as not part of the *real* world. A memory is a *here-and-now* fantasy, a here-and-now phenomenon, and that is not in turn a dream. In other words, the dream we talk about, which is the only dream there is, is not a dream at all, but the mere memory of a dream. The *real* dream is not given as dream but as reality. A dream, therefore, is never a given phenomenon.

In terms of epistemological analysis, a dream, like the external world, is an obvious and consensual object, but cannot be perceived as the phenomenon we believe it to be. A dream is as inaccessible as the external world. The latter is a theory and the former, a memory. Proof of this can be found in the fact that there is no way to confirm the accuracy of the memory of a dream, since even if another dream were to verify it (such as in a recurring dream) in the last analysis it is still a memory that verifies another memory.

For example, on Monday night one dreams of a bear (D_1). On Tuesday morning one has the memory of that bear-dream (M_1). On Tuesday night one again dreams of a bear (D_2), and on Wednesday morning one has the memory of that dream (M_2). One may use M_2 to verify M_1, and this cannot be construed to be a satisfactory confirmation of a dream. But it is crucial to note that no direct verificational contact can be established between the dream region (D_1 and D_2) and the memory region (M_1 and M_2). By definition, we cannot "photograph" a dream (D_1) and then compare that photograph with our memory of the dream. Freud was accurate when he held that a person cannot distinguish the *recollection* of having witnessed the primal scene from the *fantasy* of that scene.

It almost appears to follow that a dream, like Hume's idea of a miracle, is a logical impossibility. Hume argues, in his *Dialogues Concerning Natural Religion*, that a miracle as a violation of a law of nature is a logical contradiction. A law of nature is a generalization of observation. If the observational set is contradicted with an exception (which would then be the *miracle*) then the law or generalization was in error and a new, revised, and inclusive one must be developed. The crux of the dream problem is found in the concept of reflection.

A dream is a nonreflective activity; it is a condition of engagement, of cathexis. To dream is to be lost in the natural attitude. That is a necessary (if not sufficient) condition for a dream to exist. The sufficient condition is that dreams are not part of the consensual world we use as the basis for all our theories. Only memories of dreams are part of our consensual world. But to remember a dream is now to reflect on it. To say "I had a dream" is evidence that the phenomenological attitude (the reduction) has been activated. Dreams are destroyed by the phenomenological reduction in the same way as daylight destroys Dracula, since *to dream* means to be cathected to a phenomenon, which, once decathected, becomes a mere fantasy.

INTERPRETATION OF DREAMS

First, a dream is an *idea* and not an experience. Second, the idea of a dream is an abstraction of the basic bipolar structure of being itself[6] and is thus a permanent clue to the basic design of what we can call in clinical philosophy *ultimate reality*.

A dream therefore is a construct or a constitution whose primitive data are first memories of dreams and second, all experiences generally. Furthermore, the commonly accepted theory that dreams are possible and real is the only deeply entrenched everyday belief which can suggest to us the reality and importance of the transcendental stream of consciousness that runs through us. The belief that dreams exist is our only reminder of the truth of the transcendental-empirical distinction in existence. The stream is like the dreamer and the invention of the ego is like the creation or the having of a dream. Dreams change but the dreamer remains the same; egos and cathexes change, but the stream of consciousness remains unaffected. The dream-metaphor, known to all, carries within it the seeds of all aspects of the phenomenological model of being.

We are, in truth, the stream-ego polarity. *We are*, in truth, the transcendental ego-empirical ego duality. *We are*, in truth, the universal-individual polarity. That is first, primitive, primary, and axiomatic. Only then, as a secondary and derivative step in our constitution of the world, do we create a symbol for this important truth about ourselves. The invented symbol is the idea of a dream (or its memory) but not the direct experience of a dream. We superimpose that idea—the construct of a dream—on certain affective and mnemonic experiences, and thus the constituted objects of actual dreams are brought about.

Our idea that there are dreams, that they exist and are part of the real world, is the sole reminder in this world of our transcendental nature; it is the footprint in the world of the otherworldly (or prewordly) stream of consciousness that runs through us. We must preserve that reminder. As a result, we institutionalize it in common sense. The ultimate materialistic dictatorship would have to destroy the belief in the existence of dreams. That would forever enslave mankind, because it would rob us of access to the transcendental region and with it to our secure ground and our experience of transcendental freedom. It should therefore not come as a surprise that dreams have always been central to religion, philosophy, and mental health. Every time we think of dreams we remind ourselves of the universal and eternal stream of consciousness within us. And it should be no surprise that a person for whom dreams are not an integral part of life is an incomplete human existence and will develop corresponding symptoms.

Notes

1. William James, "Does 'Consciousness' Exist?" *Journal of Philosophy* 1 (September 1, 1904): 477-491. See William James, *Essays in Radical Empiricism* (New York: Longmans, Green, 1912). From Max H. Fisch, ed., *Classic American Philosophers* (New York: Appleton-Century-Crofts, 1951), p. 151.

2. The inward look is not just a different place, region, or object which is viewed, but consists of a *different manner* of viewing, a different positioning of consciousness itself. Whereas referential thought follows the metaphor of an expanding coil, reflexive thought is like the contraction of a coil. If the lines of the spiral are one-dimensional

only, and if the image of regress or of its collapse involves a slowing of the process, we can imagine a coil collapsing upon itself forever.

3. There are several notions in clinical philosophy which deserve the special attention of the philosophic community. One of these is the scientific character of phenomenology. It is the idea that phenomenology, as defined in clinical philosophy, is an expansion of the method of science or, conversely, that science is a specific instantiation or application of a more general or pervasive method of knowledge, namely phenomenology. Phenomenology as a method is presuppositionless (at least as much as such a goal is possible). Science makes certain constitutive assumptions; it presupposes a certain world-structure and metaphysics, and then proceeds effectively and pragmatically in making discoveries about that constituted world. Philosophers concerned with the philosophy of science need to pursue further these phenomenological researches. (The reader has been referred before to Chapters 9, 25, and 26 of Peter Koestenbaum, *The Vitality of Death*.)

A second notion in clinical philosophy which deserves very special attention is that of the necessary being of consciousness. This point has been developed in Chapters 18 and 19 of *The Vitality of Death* and in Chapter 18 of *Is There An Answer to Death?*

4. Today we would call some of these connections a priori (as *triangle* and *three-sidedness*), normative (as *man* and *rationality*), and empirical or a posteriori (as *heating water with fire* and *the production of steam*). The key word, however, is *necessary*. The connection between the stream of consciousness and its existence is of a necessary character. The nonexistence of the stream is a meaningless concept.

5. This statement is true by definition. A dream in which we know we are dreaming should be called a daydream, not a *real* dream.

6. Specifically, a dream is a metaphor for the bipolar—subject-object and individual-universal—possibilities of the consciousness-world field or of the experience-being complex.

Chapter 11 • CONSEQUENCES OF INTEGRATING PHILOSOPHIC FACT ONE

Philosophic Fact One is of immense psychotherapeutic importance, especially in a materialistic, object-oriented, individualistic, and alienated society such as ours. In the past it was religion that was charged with managing this fact. Today the interest in Jung, in Eastern thought and meditation, and in transpersonal psychology concerns itself with its vitality. Eastern religions are in the ascendancy in the United States to a great extent. As one study revealed, we will be a predominantly Buddhist society in fifteen years if present trends continue. This increase of interest in mystical philosophies further corroborates the view that our society sees the need to integrate Philosophic Fact One into its world view.

Philosophic Fact One is necessary to return consciousness to our culture. Without the clear and validated concept and experience of consciousness we can have no sense of inwardness or centeredness, no sense of eternity and peace, no sense of consciousness-expansion or intersubjectivity, no idea of freedom, and no concept of creativity. All of these crucial values for a meaningful human existence have their origin in the idea of consciousness as developed by the descriptions and discoveries of the method of transcendental phenomenology and are compressed in this philosophic fact. If we reject the idea of consciousness, that is, if we continue to pursue the biases of our culture—which are ignorance of consciousness and the denial of consciousness—none of the above values can be realized.

When Philosophic Fact One becomes integrated into the life of an individual or of society, certain changes can be expected:

First, coping becomes easy and natural, for a ground has been found. A visit to any of our large cities reveals endless numbers of Bowery bums and winos; it is also full of sick and sadistic faces. These pathetic people, often a danger to themselves and sometimes a threat to others, have written all over them the dominant contemporary diagnosis, "I cannot cope." The same is true of the despair that leads to marital tensions, unhappiness in school, dependence on drugs and alcohol, meaningless ambition, and often ulcer- and hypertension-producing competition for nothing of value.

Philosophic Fact One can form the basis for helping society cope in an age in which the traditional coping mechanisms have been eroded and have justifiably been shown to be inadequate because they are rooted in an erroneous ontology. The Bowery bum will not benefit from a lecture on Philosophic Fact One. However, he does express the reality that society lacks a meaningful understanding of that fact. Once that lack has been remedied, the general social atmosphere will change and the approaches of the healing arts will also be modified. In this latter sense, the alcoholic will benefit, and so will we all. In fact, in such a society he would never have reached the nadir where he now lingers and suffers.

Second, integrating this philosophic fact into society results in a euphoric sense of individual and political freedom and the glorious feeling of being in control over one's life and destiny. It is the insecurity of a lack of ground that produces a timid and placating personality and a totalitarian state. Once the ground is found and it is clearly understood that it is an indisputable ontological reality, the result is a confident command over one's life. Philosophic Fact One means that every person is a freedom. A person is a freedom in various senses: He is free to decathect and to see himself or herself in perspective or objectively. He need no longer be enslaved by, for example, his character defenses or the resistances of his body armor. His inwardness is liberated.

Furthermore, a person is free to deconstitute his or her self-concept. Then reconstitution can begin. And reconstitution starts with an organizing image. A human being to be philosophically healthy and authentic needs *space*—time and space that is his or hers alone. He needs the opportunity to be isolated physically and isolated emotionally—that is, isolation without guilt or pressures—to facilitate the experience of the conscious center. Overcommitment, over-crowding, and dictatorial rules are the enemies of the development of the inward strength and foundation of Philosophic Fact One. Furthermore, a person needs a model—an image, a hero, and so forth—who or which will organize for that person in a practical and speedy way the outlines of his newly constituted self. The excitement of seeing or finding one's hero rests on the sudden and hopeful insight that a new definition of self is possible—since the hero has been able to accomplish it. This excitement and hope are also the experience of reconstitution itself. And reconstitution means growth and future—the old self-image impeded expansion of self, creative self-transcendence; it made futurization and hope impossible. A new self-image, provided by one's hero, makes possible emergent and outward-moving self-transcendence.

As a third consequence of Philosophic Fact One, relaxation and peace of mind pervade the personality and the society that have found, experienced, and integrated this ground of being. Anxiety abates and emotional conflicts diminish, because the despair of groundlessness, homelessness, and abandonment has been overcome.

Fourth, energy is released. The ungrounded person is obsessed with the need to find answers, adjustments, solutions, life-styles, values, roles, and so forth. He feels panic; he is dependent; he is confused about authority because he believes the latter can give him answers and protection. He finds it increasingly more difficult to cope with his despair. His life is one of constant tension, convolution, rigidity, and exhaustion. The person who has discovered his ground—which has been there all the time—can relax fully and release the enormous amount of libido and *élan vital* which is the intentional, spatio-temporal, self-transcendent nature of the stream of consciousness that runs through us. His life is now simple and joyous, because it is easy and can be focused.

Fifth, now that placating is no longer necessary, unimpeded clarity of mind and thought and freedom of action are possible. In fact, it is likely that intelligence is a function of freedom and groundedness. We can argue that a person is by nature intelligent. His mind is clear to see logical connections and intuitive, global, truths. The panic of groundlessness clouds and petrifies the diaphanous purity of consciousness.

Furthermore, the structure of consciousness tells us that a person is by nature free. Intelligence and freedom go together, for freedom is lucidity about actions and directions. Freedom is ease of constitution and cathexis, and power for reconstitution and recathexis. The originality and creativity of genius can be fostered by wiping away the sticky cobwebs produced by a lack of ground. And that is done through the intense, permanent, and socially integrated experience of ground that is the stream of consciousness.

In other words, intelligence seems to be a function of freedom and pure consciousness; intelligence seems to be what happens when a person has achieved access to Philosophic Fact One. A phenomenology of intelligence informs us that intelligence means *vision* in the sense of inner space-time; it is the facility for bringing into focus eidetic objects, the capacity for connecting, dissociating, and reconnecting eidetic objects. It appears to be a hypothesis worth further investigation that the greater a person's facility with an access to his or her inner transcendental consciousness, the greater also will be his or her intellectual capacity. It should not be difficult to put this hypothesis to an empirical test. Meditation practices which emphasize the characteristics of Philosophic Fact One as developed in the phenomenological model of being should lead to improved intelligence. And intelligence must be defined to include more than the material covered in intelligence tests (but must not exclude that material).

If it is true that intelligence is a function of self-consciousness, then we can construct a series of hypotheses on how we can improve out intellectual performance at any given time: We must engage in meditation practices of disidentification, eventuating in disidentification from the empirical ego itself. For the inexperienced, this need demands a quiet, undisturbed place. The experienced are able to utilize each disturbance or obtrusion into the center of consciousness as a further object from which the center can disidentify itself.

We must experience the complete freedom—like that of a disembodied spirit floating above the world—which is an essential ingredient of the transcendental realm of consciousness. We must develop through practice the capacity to scan the eidetic objects (that is, the subject matters) which are of concern to us. This should increase the range of our imagination.

The only obstacle to realizing this enormous fluidity and flexibility of transcendental consciousness is that implementing it—applying it and demonstrating its existence—involves focusing, reconstitution, and re-cathexis. These are outward-moving forms of attachment which are inimical to the experience of the universality of the inwardness that is transcendental consciousness, or Philosophical Fact One. Discussing, writing, or calculating a problem's answer which increased intelligence should now have made possible requires worldly, empirical, and objective activity and commitment which are contradictory to the project of reduction, reflexivity, and subjective universality. It is in the resolution of this difficulty which lies at the heart of developing one's intelligence through meditation exercises.

The answer—which is part of this hypothesis—is that writing, calculating, and so forth, must be carried out with close to automatism. The skills in terms of which intelligence is to be expressed—playing a musical instrument, designing tools, solving problems in economics—must be so accomplished that they are carried out almost mechanically, in the service of the higher creative goal which this new intelligence has fashioned. Specific training programs can be set up on the basis of this pattern and results are subject to statistical testing in performance and creativity.

In sum, these changes are experienced as joy, as meaning, and as fulfillment. Philosophic Fact One leads us to the resolution of frustration and conflict and to a true *homecoming*.

Techniques for Teaching Philosophic Fact One

Following is a series of specific suggestions on how to enhance the presence of Philosophic Fact One in one's life.

LANGUAGE HABITS

One rule is to change one's language habits in such a way as to become constantly aware of the transcendental dimension, of the reflective or reflexive attitude, of the epoche, of reduced experience, which is the underlying universal stream of consciousness. One must not say "I hurt," which is said from the point of view of the natural attitude, but must change to the more accurate "I observe my hurt," which is a statement made from the point of view of the phenomenological attitude. One must not make these statements mechanically but allow their meaning to be clear so that it can gradually transform our world view away from the biases of common sense and toward conformity with the philosophical reality.

One should not say "I am depressed," but should'instead change that statement to the more accurate "I perceive that my empirical ego is depressed." This reformulation also implies the statement, "I am not the same as the depression or the depressed person that I perceive," just as the former restatement implies "I am not the hurt which I observe." We must not say "I am frustrated" but say instead "I perceive my frustration." The principle behind these reformulations is simple. Ordinary language reflects or mirrors incompletely the true ontological situation. The consensual assumption behind ordinary language is that only the object exists, the cathected empirical situation bereft of antecedent intentional streams of consciousness.

In *Managing Anxiety* reference is made to a comet theory of objects. The statements, "I am angry," or "I am an angry person," imply that there exists only a comet as a star, but not a comet which has also a tail. These statements assume that reality consists only of objects and not of our consciousness of these objects. We must therefore correct our language to fit our ontology and say "I am aware of the fact that I am angry" or "I observe that I am an angry person." By improving the representative quality of our language we assist ourselves psychologically, since we have integrated into life the permanent and ubiquitous undercurrent of the transcendental dimension.

This reformulation is of particular value when a person is under emotional or physical stress. An important element of the stressful situation is the denial of the transcendental dimension of all experience. Stress—in one of its aspects—is the experience of cathexis itself. Stress is the sense of being caught up in or identified with an inherently impossible or untenable situation. In fact, what makes a situation emotionally problematic is the existence of conflict. One is caught up in a situation which cannot be tolerated but from which there is no escape. A loves B but B does not love A. A cannot give up his love for B, but neither can A live with unrequited love.

The solution to most (perhaps even all) conflict is to first realize that all conflict is an expression of the fundamental dialectic or polarities of being—polarities which essentially are chosen to be real in order to create a sense of existence. But the second solution to conflict is to decathect or reduce it: to realize that all conflict—and especially this particular and painful conflict—is part of the empirical realm and is observed by the transcendental, but without participation. If we are in the habit of using transcendental language, that is, language which integrates Philosophic Fact One into itself, we will then constantly remind ourselves of the peace and security of the transcending reality behind our insoluble conflicts. Once distance has been accomplished, management of the conflict is possible.

Lack of distance is often expressed as depression. The patient is overwhelmed by an insoluble conflict with which he is totally identified. He steps back from the conflict, perceives his freedom, uses it to say *yes* to life, and he is now ready to adopt an aggressive, mature, and positive attitude toward the management of the conflict. This process, if successful, also spells the end of the depression.

One need not restrict one's linguistic reformulations to undesirable and negative experiences. In fact, this exercise works even better with positive and joyful experiences. We then become increasingly more convinced that the transcendental dimension is a reality rather than a mere rationalization or some inconsequential philosophical abstraction or speculation.

Action Habits

Another rule which helps integrate Philosophic Fact One into our daily lives is to change our action habits. We need to set aside specific periods of time—brief ones are sufficient—to practice withdrawing into the center. Every person develops his or her own style. Some rest; others go to sleep. Some withdraw from the world by going to a church, mosque, or synagogue. Others meditate. If one is accomplished in the art of detachment, as the *Bhagavad Gita* recommends, one can disengage oneself from the commitment to the work that one is doing (that is, from the natural attitude) at any time and for as long as one chooses. One may be operating a machine, computer, or calculator. If persons are experienced in the art of detachment, then they can change from the natural attitude, in which they enjoy what they are doing and are ego-involved with their work, to the phenomenological attitude, in which they *observe* the fact that someone with his or her name operates these devices. Assembly-line workers, as well as people with routinized and mechanical tasks, do this automatically—as a technique for psychological self-protection.

You may be an athlete or a musician. To practice and perform with detachment means that at this moment you become a member of the audience and you perceive yourself as a spectator. You see yourself run or play tennis; you hear yourself play the piano or the violin as if you had recorded yourself. There are divergent schools of thought as to what is the best method of practicing and teaching the performing arts. It is likely that the catechumen, the beginning artist, throws himself fully into his role, if he is an actor; into his instrument and score if he is a musician, and into his choreography and body movements if he is a dancer. The result may be great artistry, but the artist does run the danger of putting on an oversentimentalized, gushy, embarrassing, or exaggerated performance.

The mature artist, it would appear, is the person who can take a position of distance vis-à-vis his art and his performance. The actor needs a director or a videotape to see himself as others see him. He needs to be outside of himself, as the observer of himself, to perfect his role—much like a sculptor fashions his statue: he steps back and looks at it with each new chip of his chisel. The musician needs a coach or a tape that will make it possible for him to *observe* rather than *be* his playing. For example, it is easier to play the piano than to hear oneself play the piano as one plays the piano. And yet it is this latter posture which facilitates real self-criticism and true artistic excellence in performance. Such is the psychological power of the phenomenological reduction.

It is useful to study dance, acting, or musical performance not only for its own sake but also to achieve the skill of detachment. That skill will transfer its value to other aspects of life as well. In other words, to be a performer is a healthful activity. The philosophic basis for the value of detachment in the performing arts—both for the sake of the art and the condition of general health—is to be found in the phenomenological model of being: Through detachment we experience the intimate, pure, inward, and transcendental consciousness that we are. By practicing a detachment which runs concurrent with our attachments, and by doing it for even very brief periods every day, we teach ourselves conceptually and experientially the reality of the stream of consciousness that runs through us. And in doing this the human values of freedom, love, eternity, integrity, and creativity—all of which have their origin in Philosophic Fact One—are possible. Such must be the foundation, the logical beginning, of any psychotherapy based in clinical philosophy.

We must learn the art of distancing as a separate skill, just as we would learn to play the piano and how to swim. Once we have these skills, we can take time out to play a piece or swim a few laps. Similarly, training in meditation, contemplation, and reflection is an equally important aspect of the education of our children. But meditation must not be taught as a ritual or a cult. Nor must the schools be dogmatic or insensitive about it. Meditation can be used to illustrate experientially the general philosophic phenomenon of Philosophic Fact One.

In parallel fashion, confrontation techniques could be used to illustrate—by evoking or eliciting—the element of freedom within consciousness. In this way our young people can gain respect for the reality and importance of inner space exploration. The skills associated with the transcendental dimension will thus become as natural a part of their existence as is their ability to walk, bicycle, or drive. That knowledge will function like our faith in the independent existence of an external world or our conviction that inside the body of a friend exists a center of consciousness like our own, both of which are fundamental aspects of our world view. The consequences of such integration are an authentic existence.

An interesting example of taking time out daily for the transcendental is shown by the following anecdote: William T. Coleman was named, in January of 1975, to the post of Secretary of Transportation by President Ford, the second black to hold Cabinet rank.

A *magna cum laude* graduate from the Harvard Law School in 1946, Coleman was selected by Justice Felix Frankfurter to be the first black law clerk in the history of the Supreme Court. He and another young clerk, Elliot Richardson (who later, under Richard Nixon became Secretary of Health, Education and Welfare, Secretary of Defense, as well as Attorney General), used to *spend one uninterrupted hour each morning reading poetry together.*[1]

This practice is a good example of the daily reminder of the transcendental region, the universal stream of consciousness. Taking time out for anything is an act of reflection and distancing—phenomena which open up the realm of pure consciousness. Furthermore, the introspective activity of consciousness is an act of contact with our possibility for universality. The practice of Coleman and Richardson was thus a dual approach toward integrating the transcendental into daily life.

Another example of using Philosophic Fact One therapeutically, without theory or abstraction, is found in the work of Dr. Herbert Benson, a Boston physician, who has taught some of his patients to reduce their blood pressure by means of what he calls "relaxation response," a sort of transcendental-meditation technique.[2] Contact with the stream of consciousness, achieved through temporary withdrawal from the world, leads to the peace of mind that is reflected in a body with lowered blood pressure.

Finally, the crucial technique in learning how to integrate Philosophic Fact One into one's life is to repeat to oneself, as if it were a mantra, some formulation of the truth of the transcendental like the following:

I am not this thought; I am not this feeling; I am not this physical object; I am not this body of flesh and bones, nor am I this self-concept. I am not these feelings, these attitudes, and these responses associated with my personality. Nor am I the character defenses or body armor with which most of us so closely identify ourselves. I am instead and in truth pure and universal consciousness.

In saying *not this, not this* to the world, as is suggested in the *Brihadarañaka Upanishad's* famous *neti, neti,* we must understand that this process never stops. We will never exhaust all the objects to consciousness from which we can experience ourselves detached. Nor is this the only thing which we can say about ourselves, for in addition to Philosophic Fact One there are also two further and complementary facts to be considered.

In this way we can achieve direct experiential access to our pure, inward, transcendental, and universal consciousness. Detachment and withdrawal are of course always only approximations. Nevertheless, by repeating our formula, *neti, neti,* the ontological reality is drilled into our mechanism for constitution. As a result, our world view will be transformed away from objectivism, materialism, and alienation to take account of our possibility for universality.

The phenomenological model of being, or the bipolar personality theory, teaches us that healthy, normal, authentic being or experience is *dialectical:* It is always in a state of stress, opposition, contrast. Sometimes it is "on" and at other times it is "off." We know the light is off because before it was on. We know the light is on because earlier it was off. Philosophic Fact One corresponds, somewhat roughly, to a focus on the subjective-universal possibility (cosmic consciousness) of bipolar being.

We are now ready to examine the dialectical opposite of Philosophic Fact One, an event which roughly corresponds to the focus on the individual-objective possibilities of bipolar being.

Notes

1. *Time,* January 20, 1975, p. 19.
2. *Time,* January 13, 1975, p. 64.

Chapter 12 • *PHILOSOPHIC FACT TWO:*
INDIVIDUALISM AND THE
SCIENTIFIC OUTLOOK

The second basic philosophic fact in this more practical analysis of earlier selected themes is the converse of Philosophic Fact One. It is the constitution of an ego or an individual out of the universal matrix represented by Philosophic Fact One, that is, the individuality pole of the individual-universal polarity.

Although one cannot assign priority to either philosophic fact, from the point of view of a pedagogic exposition of the existential personality theory, didactic priorities are in order. In a clinical or therapeutic context it is useful to assume that the sense of individuality is in fact constituted out of more basic and primitive raw material, namely that which is designated by Philosophic Fact One. Furthermore, it provides the sense of security, the experience of self-worth, and the feeling of self-esteem, on which the important phenomenon of individuality and of personal identity can be constructed. Before a person, client, student, or patient can get a firm grip on his or her ego and can change the structure of his or her individuality, there must be a securely grounded base from which to operate. Before persons can take risks and before they can relate intimately with others, they must have roots, a home, headquarters, or a foundation. That base is provided by an appreciation of Philosophic Fact One.

Philosophic Fact Two

Once consciousness feels that it is (or has) a secure foundation, then the string of archetypal choices, the first decisions which define a human existence, can confidently be made; first and foremost is to *invent* the ego. (Some of this material has been touched on and thus anticipated in Chapter 3.) The religious symbol or metaphor for this primary act of constitution, this originary and fundamental act of organization and invention, appears as God creating Man. It must be interpreted to mean that God (who represents Philosophic Fact One) chooses to be Man (or a person, a human being), in short, the individual (who represents Philosophic Fact Two). This crucial and universal symbol is expressed in God's creation of Man in the *Old Testament* and in God's surrender of His Son to the Cross in the *New Testament.* If we want a reason or explanation for this archetypal decision to move from Philosophic Fact One to Philosophic Fact Two, we must argue, to continue with the Biblical symbolism, that God felt it was better to be human (and limited) than divine (and unlimited). In these Biblical stories God made the archetypal decision for finitude. This mechanism is the decision-set which is operative at this very moment to bring into being and maintain in that form the all-important sense of being an individual identity.

From the point of view of personal growth and progress in psychotherapy, there is real growth and progress—forward evolution—from the universality of Philosophic Fact One to the individuality of Philosophic Fact Two. And this growth is brought about by a decision—an archetypal decision to be sure—at least from the perspective of psychotherapy. The tool that implements this archetypal choice is our capacity for negation. We have (or consciousness has) the power to say no, the power of negation. Negation produces the phenomenon of alienation, of isolation, and separateness. The most powerful and unquestionably most dramatic form which negation takes is the anticipation of death. When I hold myself personally responsible for my own dying, when I appropriate or own up to my own dying, then I recognize my identity with the principle of death within me. It is at this time that I conceive and experience the meaning of being a self, an ego, an individual, and an identity.

Again, it is religion which has recognized the individuating character of death, well symbolized by Moses' death in the desert before seeing the Promised Land and Jesus' death on the Cross. Moses' death preceded the individuation of the Israelites as a people in Canaan; Jesus' death presaged the message of individual salvation (rather than the Oriental sense of cosmic oneness) central to the Christian doctrine.

The symbols of religion are projections of our innermost needs, our deepest choices, and of the roots of our philosophical substratum. Therefore, each of us, in our human and psychological development, must arduously and personally go through this philosophical process of self-creation—represented only symbolically in the myths of religion. The making of this archetypal decision for finitude is exactly the same as the choice of becoming and being an individual; it is the choice to be free, to be independent, and to cherish self-reliance; it is the affirmation of being inner-directed. In fact, many of the personal and psychological problems which are *not* connected with rootedness, security, and ground—that is, problems of adjustment, maturity, potency, and effectiveness as a human being—are related to this archetypal decision. Psychological problems exist at the level of this archetypal decision. In other words, problems in the area of personal potency exist because the archetypal decision for finitude has not yet been made. The experience of personal potency, strength, and effectiveness is, at its core, the archetypal decision for finitude. And when this decision is not being made and has not been made, it is because the person does not know how to make it. For one, he lacks the philosophical insight which makes that important archetypal decision possible and intelligible.

Philosophical elucidation of the ontological situation is a *sine qua non* for accomplishing the psychological desideratum of becoming an independent individual. It is because of this kind of a situation that an adequate—that is, accurate—philosophy of life is needed by both therapist and patient. Unless the archetypal decision for finitude is clearly integrated into a theory of psychotherapy, bringing about that decision can only be accomplished through an ineffective and unsystematic hit-or-miss, trial-and-error approach.

RESPONSIBILITY FOR INDIVIDUALITY

We must connect the idea of responsibility with the decision to become an individual. Ordinarily, we speak of being an individual first and of assuming personal responsibility for our life, character, and well-being second. In this context, however, we speak of a deeper and an earlier sense of responsibility. Consciousness, in its sense as a universality, before the experience of individuality has arisen, takes full responsibility for choosing to perceive of itself as individual. This is the ultimate reconciliation with our identity and, along with it, the final reconciliation with death. This position is tantamount to saying that the death we anticipate and the death which defines our lives is a self-chosen death, a freely chosen self-concept. In this sense we can say we are fully responsible for the individuals who we are. This attitude is the end of self-pity and the termination of buck-passing.

The authentic person takes full conceptual and emotional responsibility for making the archetypal decision of being an individual. He takes conceptual responsibility in that he understands it; he takes emotional responsibility to the extent that he both lives it and acts it out behaviorally. If this archetypal decision for finitude is fully understood, disclosed, known, and implemented, then life is joy. Joy can therefore be a symptom of authenticity. The presence of joy is proof that the archetypal decision for finitude has been fully made, and that it has been made without any secret qualifications or unconscious reservations. On the other hand, if this archetypal decision is ignored, or if it is not understood, or just plain not made, then the ensuing symptoms are suffering, depression, ennui, and meaninglessness.

Not to make this personal decision for finitude is to choose not to live a human life. The person who resists this is in truth living a conflict. While he thinks of himself as an individual—and not a mystic totally, permanently, and indifferently submerged in the cosmic consciousness or the Eternal Now—he does not willingly, fully, and without qualification participate in the life of being an individual. This person wants the advantages of a human and individual life without any of the attending toughness and self-discipline. And that indecisiveness is a condition of retardation and regression, as well as of depression. We can therefore conclude that the person who suffers—and who may concurrently wallow in self-pity and blame others for his misfortunes—is not making or has not made the archetypal decision for finitude.

The choice to be an individual is a constant condition and a permanent need. It is not something done once and then forgotten. Life as human and as individual *is* (in principle) the constant, conscious, and deliberate rejection of universality and the unwavering acceptance of finitude. Therefore, it is also the unfailingly continuous choice of dying. The polar stress between these two philosophic facts is always present (a tension and a dialectic which then becomes Philosophic Fact Three).

The archetypal decision for finitude is the choice to be an adult. And to be adult is to repress, deny, or overcome the childish. The childish does not disappear; it is merely put out of action. And the denial of that which is childish is the bedrock on which adulthood stands. As one upholds upwards the weight of adulthood one exerts precisely the same pressure downward on dependency, weakness, excuses, and childishness. This is not to deny the beauty of being childlike and the acceptance of weakness. Only the strong know when it is proper to be childlike; only the mature know when and under what circumstances it is right to surrender to one's weakness and dependency.

The archetypal choice for individuality, which is the same as the decision to be a mature adult, signifies that we know what it means to take full responsibility for our life. That this decision is actually being made manifests itself in the freedom and control that a person has over his or her space and time.

This resulting freedom and control over one's existence first appears as an attitude, a way of perceiving the world, as a self-concept, and as a philosophy of life. Gradually this subjectively philosophic aspect of individuality projects itself on the concrete world of things, objects and people. The *subjective* self-image of an individual gradually translates itself into *objective* reality. The translation, transformation, or projection is almost automatic. If the decision to be an individual has been made on the level of pure consciousness so that a self-image of individual identity has been produced, then the projection of that image on our world is close to automatic. This is the power of our self-concept and this is also the meaning of willpower. The proof that we have made the archetypal decision for finitude is then found in our ability to risk new forms of behavior and new methods of adaptation. We can have full confidence in the fact that the world responds favorably and supportively to intelligent risk-taking, since the world appears to be made specifically for the mature individual.

METAPHORS

We are engaged in phenomenological descriptions and it is important to bring out the full meaning of being an individual. That is done not through proof and inference but by describing how it actually feels to be an individual. Even more important is to uncover the layers of consciousness, constitution, and decision-making that lie beneath the conscious surface of our everyday awareness. We need more than a glimpse; we need a total revelation of the subsurface structures of consciousness which support our pervasive sense of individuality. It is in this spirit that we use metaphors to clarify further our role—the role of human freedom—in bringing about this sense of individuality.

We can represent the act of choosing individuality through two metaphors. First, let us assume a heated and supersaturated solution of water and epsom salts is cooled quickly and suddenly. As a result, crystallization occurs. Each crystal that appears is individual and was created directly out of the total fluid environment. Although it was at one time fluid and indistinguishable, once created it is completely different from its environment. Its existence actually negates its environment. The individual crystal cannot return to meld with its environment (unless of course the temperature is raised again). In a manner of speaking, the individual crystals create themselves by saying *no* to the environment, by alienating themselves from their matrix. They become individuals by being different, unique. The image of a beaker filled with a homogenous liquid suddenly producing hard nodules is how we must conceive the archetypal decision which leads from Philosophic Fact One to Philosophic Fact Two. If we now carry this metaphor further, of particular interest is the question of which molecules are *chosen* by the total mixture to congeal into crystals and which molecules are *chosen* to remain as part of the liquid matrix. That raises the issues of how consciousness (which is universal and well called Philosophic Fact One) chooses zones of individuality which then become the *I's* and *you's* of the world.

Let us use a second metaphor. Children in Germany used to celebrate the New Year by dropping molten lead which had been heated over the stove on a spoon into a bucket of cold water. The lead would harden instantaneously and produce an infinite variety of rather fascinating and interesting shapes. Like snowflakes, no two were alike. We can now think of these unique pieces of lead in the water, formed by the merger of two liquids which show their total alienation from each other, as individuals formed through the archetypal decision of saying *no* to the water which surrounds them. This is a good image of the decision to be a solid individual within a sea of consciousness. And the separation of the individual out of the totality is an act of negation which leads to estrangement and alienation.

These are only approximate metaphors, of course, and we must neither take them too seriously nor be carried away by them. But they should help engrave in our minds a workable image of the archetypal decision for finitude.

The Power of Saying No

The constitutive tool in the construction of the self or ego is the power of saying *no*. And to say *no* to an environment is *ipso facto* to say *yes* to the individual who is thereby being isolated. Therefore, the key technique for achieving not only the sense but also the reality of individuality is to learn to say *no* intelligently and judiciously. The technique must be based on an understanding of the true nature of the risks involved, because it is in recognizing that these risks are irrevocable that the threatening isolation of being an individual is first appreciated. We find a notable illustration of this power in the contrariness of the protagonist in Dostoevsky's *Notes From Underground*.

I am a sick man . . . I am a spiteful man. I am an unattractive man. I believe my liver is diseased. However, I know nothing at all about my disease, and do not know for certain what ails me. I don't consult a doctor for it, and never have, though I have a respect for medicine and doctors. Besides, I am extremely superstitious, sufficiently so to respect medicine, anyway (I am well-educated enough not to be superstitious, but I am superstitious). No, I refuse to consult a doctor from spite. That you probably will not understand. Well, I understand it, though. Of course, I can't explain who it is precisely that I am mortifying in this case by my spite: I am perfectly well aware that I cannot "pay out" the doctors by not consulting them; I know better than anyone that by all this I am only injuring myself and no one else. But still, if I don't consult a doctor it is from spite. My liver is bad, well—let it get worse!

I have been going on like that for a long time—twenty years. Now I am forty.[1]

As the protagonist rejects everything for the sake of rejection itself he gains a sense of being an individual. But his is an approach of last resort. The writer in Dostoevsky's *Notes From Underground* talks about spite. He is spiteful, and he rejects even the very idea that his reader might understand or sympathize with his spite. The short piece is layer after layer of no-saying and rejection, ending with the final "no," "I wish to declare once and for all that if I write as though I were addressing readers, that is simply because it is easier for me to write in that form. It is a form, an empty form —I shall never have readers. . . ."[2]

There is an obvious albeit surface connection between what is known today as assertiveness training or consciousness raising and the power of saying no. The difference lies in the special emphasis on the dangerous, threatening, and anxiety-producing aspects of individuation accorded to it by the existential analysis. To recognize accurately the negativity of the structure of negation—that is, negation really does mean negation—is simply being realistic.

Camus' idea of the rebel against life is a further and famous example of how no-saying leads to the sense of individuality.

The story of Adam and Eve's Original Sin is another interesting and important illustration of how no-saying is the archetypal decision for the creation of a person. In Paradise—a place where human beings and nature are a total harmonious unit and where personal responsibility is a frivolous concept—Adam and Eve must be understood to represent the person as Philosophic Fact One. Human beings are visualized as still universal and divine. What precisely was it that expelled them from Paradise? What severed their coalescence with the Divine? It was their first free act, saying no to God.

Adam and Eve were created in the image of God: they were created as centers of consciousness and as freedoms—both prime characteristics of God. God was obliging in making no-saying easy. He cooperated in making it possible for Adam and Eve to demonstrate the reality and aliveness of their free conscious centeredness by challenging them to create their own limits. He said, "All is yours, but do not eat from the tree of knowledge." *Knowledge* in this instance must be understood to mean the fundamental act of self-constitution, that is, the archetypal decision for finitude. It was essential for Adam and Eve to confront the one forbidden act in Paradise, so that they would have the opportunity to say no to God. It was that single act of negation—with "fatal" consequences—which made Adam and Eve into human beings. If God is omniscient and all is planned, then we can argue that it was necessary for God to give Adam and Eve a chance to say no. In setting up His rule for the tree of knowledge, He gave them the opportunity to be human. That, in fact, is Adam and Eve's only opportunity, since it challenges and then evokes their freedom, which they then use for the archetypal decision of self-creation, namely, saying no.

The expulsion from the Garden of Eden can then be interpreted as the archetypal choice that each person has to relive in his or her maturation to move from universality to individuality. The expulsion from the universal is not a punishment added to the act of disobedience; it is rather the natural individuating and anxiety-producing consequence of saying no. To disobey in the universality of Paradise is in effect to say no to this universality. The fruit, in Milton's words, had a "mortal taste." The effect produced by saying no is to acquire mortality and finitude, in short, individuality. And the symbol for the individual is to be *outside* of or different from the universal bosom-of-God that is represented by the Garden of Eden. Expulsion from Paradise is the denial of our sense of universality. The phenomenon of individuality is indeed a free act, as was Man's disobedience in eating the forbidden fruit. The fact that Man has committed a "sin" means that individuation introduces anxiety into existence.

The individuating power of saying no to our possibility for universality is also illustrated in the religious representation of these ideas by Peter's denial of Jesus and by Kierkegaard's proud Lutheran minister father's stentorian curse of God upon the death of his wife. The potency for individuation pregnant in the act of saying no is further illustrated in how great religious leaders defined themselves by saying no to the temptations to be God rather than Man. The Buddha was tempted under the Bo tree. He said no and thereby established his identity as the Enlightened One. Jesus was tempted in the desert and in saying no defined himself as the Savior. In general, religious symbols are strong metaphors for philosophic realities. The above are typical examples.

On the psychological level we find people who need self-pity and suffering to feel loved or worthy. They act as if their mothers would only love them if they suffered. On the nonmetaphoric level these persons say no to even (or especially) what they love—leading in extreme cases to battered wives or children—as a desperate and last attempt to be their own identity and experience their own individuality by saying no to that which matters most to them in life. In actual fact they are not saying no to what matters most but to their second highest value. Their top priority is to establish an existing individual identity. And that they achieve by saying no to their second most precious values—their wives, children, meanings, or valuable possessions. But this confused project is a total failure.

ACTIVISM

There are even more extreme examples of how risking no-saying creates the sense of being an effective individual. The more dangerous the no-saying, the more authentic or at least the more successful it seems to be. As the danger increases, the adamantine implacability of the alienation thus produced also increases. And only when the alienation has become total can we say that the pure and true individual has been created. Let us consider three examples which are altogether different: Vietnam war resisters, headhunters, and the infamous "Zebra" murders in San Francisco during 1974.

The Vietnam war resisters often overstepped the line beyond which there was no return. Refusing induction was one common example; desertion was another. Once the act of refusing induction or desertion was committed, or the alienation brought about by this implemented decision became final, reconciliation was really never again possible. That type of peremptory and irreversible act illustrates the fact that no-saying is a risk which alienates totally and thereby creates a complete insulated but concrete individual. The war resisters became individuals through their act of defiance and they created a definition of their country and its values through their act. They created themselves as individuals at the moment in which they reached and passed the point of no return. Self-creation is always an authentic and commendable act. It is the foundation of human existence. But there are also instances in which no-saying, while having an understandable goal, is distorted and highly immoral.

Headhunting as an initiation rite forces a young man to make permanent enemies with the tribe on which he preys. To exhibit the courage which provokes permanent mortal enemies is indeed to have risked the archetypal decision for finitude, to have said no in the most dangerous way possible and created therewith the kind of definitive alienation which insures that the initiate becomes an individual. Such is a philosophical explanation of the meaning of some initiation rites: the person says no in such a way as to make forgiveness and redemption forever impossible. This act of permanent, final alienation produces the sense of individuality. The person is henceforth totally responsible for continuing the decision to be himself and not someone else. We can see how honor and individuality are connected. The return to innocence (the state prior to the completion of the initiation rite) is no longer possible. Should it become impossible to maintain the chosen identity, the chosen self-definition, then the only alternative is death. That is the meaning—that is, the philosophical explanation—of the attitude expressed in the phrase "death before dishonor."

On a less intense level, the same *philoso-dynamics* exist in the motivation behind tattoos. A tattoo is a commitment; it is an act from which there is no turning back. It is a self-definition, achieved by saying no to (injuring or defacing) a certain part of the body. Since there is no turning back, the rest of that person's life must be spent rechoosing that initial self-definition.

The notorious Zebra murders were arbitrary killings of white men by a Black Muslim splinter group. In that organization, points were given for dead whites and acceptance in the organization was contingent on killing them. These men evidently lacked in a most unusual way any sense of individuality and identity. Only by this ultimate risk which created a situation of permanent and total alienation—being forever hunted by the police and estranged from society—could they establish a sense of individuality and of self-worth. This identity was made possible through membership in a tightly cohesive group. Murder is final; it cannot be taken back. Therefore, an archetypal decision for finitude, for alienation from society, which has been achieved in this demonic fashion is irrevocable and irreversible. It is the irremissible character of the act which gives it the potential for individuation.

Here again we can learn to understand the pyschodynamics of certain asocial or criminal acts. They are distortions of what is essentially a normal and an understandable philosophical act—the constitution of the individual through the act of saying no. And if a person has never said no and thus has no sense of individuality, then the pressure of the frustration builds up and when that person finally does say no it becomes a stupid, violent, and criminal act. Rather than call this analysis the psychodynamics of the situation, we ought to use an expression more appropriate in the context of clinical philosophy—*philoso-dynamics*.

Certainly no one recommends or endorses such excessive behavior. However, these extreme examples do show that in the matter of becoming an individual, that is, moving from Philosophic Fact One to Philosophic Fact Two, we are dealing with an extremely basic and dangerous process. These philosophic considerations may explain many an otherwise bizarre or meaningless act of violence.

Further Illustrations

FREUD

Freud was aware that the individual (or ego, for him) is constituted out of the plenitude of universal being when he wrote, in *Civilization and Its Discontents* (p. 13):

Originally the ego includes everything, later it detaches from itself the external world. The ego-feeling we are aware of now is thus only a shrunken vestige of a far more extensive feeling—a feeling which embraced the universe and expressed an inseparable connection of the ego with the external world.[3]

It is of course a pleasure to cite such distinguished support. However, clinical philosophy does differ with Freud in several respects. Its view may be more extreme than Freud's, but it is also a position which is more consistent than his and which is philosophically and epistemologically purer. Clinical philosophy has taken the method of phenomenological descriptions and the theory of reductions seriously, and has had the courage to allow these ideas to follow their own direction. And it has done that without any interference whatever which might be based on the fear of contradicting even the most widely accepted consensual opinions and the deepest prejudices of the most respected academic establishments.

To be specific, the differences between Freud's position and that of clinical philosophy are these: The constitution of the ego out of the universality to which he refers is surely conceived by Freud to be automatic and inevitable, since he must have felt that it is brought about by causes external to the to-be-constituted ego. Furthermore, the constituted ego-world separation was in all probability thought by him to reflect a true perception of the real world, whereas the pregenital amorphous universality out of which it grows is but an immature delusion of childhood. Should the latter world view persist at maturity, it would surely be construed to be a psychopathological and regressive phenomenon.

Clinical philosophy does not evaluate these two perspectives. It does not give either the seal of absolute ontological approval. In fact, it considers both to be authentic possibilities, but we must also be fully aware of the serious consequences of choosing either. Clinical philosophy bases its opinion on the reality of the freedom of the transcendental region, on the principles of constitution and cathexis, and consequently, on the relativity of empirical reality. As a result, clinical philosophy cannot believe that the process of ego constitution is fully automatic. It is, in truth, a passive constitution, in Husserl's terminology. But to the extent that it is constitution at all it does contain the element of freedom. Therefore it *can* be changed. And *I* can change it. Transcendental consciousness can transform passive constitution into active constitution. That is the meaning of taking control over one's life. That is the meaning of being an individual and having made the decision for finitude. In short, it becomes possible for each person to say, *I am responsible for my constitutions!*

CRISIS INTERVENTION AND PRIMAL SCREAM

There is an excellent psychologist who trains police departments across the nation in family crisis intervention techniques. Since an unusually high percentage of all police calls concern family quarrels, training law enforcement personnel in effectively managing such situations is of great value. One of the basic techniques he teaches is in effect a direct application of Philosophic Fact Two. Rather than give advice or settle the dispute, the officer is instructed to hold the disputing parties directly responsible for solving their quarrel, without offering any judgment. After each party is given an opportunity to air his or her complaint, the officer asks "What are you going to do about it?" "How are you going to handle your problem?" The idea is to challenge the person to assume responsibility for the constitution of his own existence. The officer points out—by simply making the assumption and inserting it as a suppressed premise in his question— that the person involved is indeed an individual and is in fact fully responsible for the conduct of his life and the structure of his existence. The police officer makes the assumption that this philosophical point is not debatable or negotiable. There is no need for theoretical discussion, but the officer must operate on the assumption that it is true. Since he is much in demand, it is logical to assume that this simple and coarse application of Philosophic Fact Two seems to work in practice.

A former student, a therapist, wrote the following in a term paper about her patients in primal scream therapy:

> The therapeutic process that they experience is a regressive subjective one that usually proceeds from the present day and recedes to the historical residue that has been repressed. Almost without exception these patients eventually experience stark, utter terror in connection with the black, empty, cold, bottomless pit, a feeling that is at least universal with my patient population and also is expressed in your book *Managing Anxiety*. Resistance to feeling this is intense; it is often described as death; however, there are no adequate words. This feeling does represent the turning-around point for the patient. It is as though he must experience death in life somehow before he can live and fully accept his own death. The phenomenological existential theories are graphic for my work in this regard.

Here she argues that the abyss experienced in primal scream therapy finally leads to psychotherapeutic resolution because that is the moment at which Philosophic Fact One turns into Philosophic Fact Two, when our possibility as universalities transforms itself into the sense of individuality. And this transformation is an act of free will; it is the phenomenon of self-determination and self-definition. She describes in this passage the experience of making an archetypal decision for finitude. And she seems to feel that it is precisely this decision which is the therapeutic cure. Screaming alone will not bring about this archetypal decision. Screaming, however, can facilitate it because it opens the abyss and shows how the individual is different from the gaping nothingness. The individual says no to non-being and thus establishes and upholds an identity. All therapy is an adjunct to a philosophy of life. This type of philosophic understanding deepens the meaning and efficacy of any therapy, including primal work.

We discussed above that becoming an individual is one of the two great psychotherapeutic problems. Primal scream therapy seems to be one of the many adjuncts to the development of a philosophy of life which can help a nonindividuated consciousness to become a *bona fide* individual identity.

The Act of Embodiment

One of the most useful examples of the archetypal decision for finitude is the phenomenon of embodiment. To experience oneself as an individual is also to experience oneself as *embodied*. In a society in which we wear clothes, we also feel disconnected from our bodies. In a culture dependent on automobiles, we are tempted to identify our consciousness with the box of steel which encases our bodies. A separate decision is needed to re-establish the sense of intimacy and identity with the body.[4]

The contention here is not that there are minds floating in the world and soulless bodies wandering aimlessly, and the two unite. It is that there are many different ways in which the dialectical, bipolar field which is being can be interpreted and perceived. The argument is that the atomization of being into individual realities is not an observed fact but an archetypal decision—made by Democritus, Leucippus, and later Lucretius, in Greek and Roman antiquity. To experience or perceive existence as *mine* and as focused on and centered in *a body*, which we then constitute into something we call *my-body*, is an act of constitution by being, and from within and out of being. These are facts—transcendental facts, to be precise—which emerge upon a sensitive phenomenological (that is, unbiased) description of experience. But the fundamental turn which brings out these realizations is the reduction of experience.

A PHENOMENOLOGY OF THE BODY

My-body (technically, the body-qua-mine) is a most unusual phenomenon. It is a unique event in this world. It is qualitatively different from all other phenomena. There are *other bodies*, but these are different from my experience of *my-body*. The experience of my-body is unique because my-body is literally the incarnation of the two philosophical ideas of polarity and intentionality. My-body is, in the religious metaphor, the incarnation of ultimate reality.

In the world we find separate and isolated subjects, egos, individuals, minds, souls, selves (subjective things), and we find objects: bodies, trees, clouds, birds, houses. But in *my-body* we find these two metaphysical regions combined in one interface. In *my-body*, and only in *my-body*, are the subjective and objective regions combined. In *my-body*, subject and object meld, merge, are one. There exists nothing else in the entire universe which prima facie has this extraordinary characteristic of being both subject and object at the same time. This insight has been a contribution of the French philospher Merleau-Ponty.

In existential phenomenology we use the expression *the body-subject* and *the body-object*. My-body, or any part of it, can function as a subject, as an organ of sensation, in the general subject-object intentional field that is being.

The reverse is also true: any part of my-body can be the object in a subject-object field. For example, how can one find out that the bottom surface of a swimming pool is rough rather than smooth? If one is a good swimmer, then one can use any part of the body as the organ of sense which will detect how that surface feels. One can close the eyes and go under water. One can use the head, the nose, perhaps a big toe. In this sense one is using the body as the subject in the total experience. The object is the pool floor.

But that very same body can also be the object of your perception. Let us say a person breaks out in hives. He can call his doctor and say, "Doctor, I have hives all over my body." The doctor asks, "Where?" "I can see some of them," the patient replies. In this case, part of the body, the eyes, becomes the subject, whereas the hives that are observed become objects. If he has hives on his arm and he looks at his arm, then the arm is now in the role or position of an object while his eyes are the subject. His body is now subject and object simultaneously. If hives are on his back, then he can feel them with his fingers. He then tells the doctor, "I have three hives on my back. I can feel them with my fingers." He is now using his hands as subject while his back has become the object.

The doctor now asks, "Does it hurt if you press your stomach?" Again he uses his fingers as the subject and his stomach as the object.

Or, assume someone has a pimple on his nose. He feels it to describe it. The nose then becomes the object and the finger the subject. If the person now views this action in a mirror, then his eyes become the subject, his nose the object, and his feeling finger, both subject and object at the same time.

Someone has a callus on his finger. He uses his nose as a sense organ. He now examines the callus on his finger and he uses his nose to feel it. The nose, which in the previous example was the object, now becomes the subject, and the finger, which before had been the body-subject is now the body-object. The same organs of the body-qua-mine have been both subject and object.

We can interchangeably use the body as both subject and object, which is not true of anything else in the universe. That is why the body—the phenomenon of being incarnated, embodied, made flesh—is a philosophically extraordinary event. The body is the central symbol of all existence. It is the one region in which the subject and object poles of the field of consciousness coexist.

Thus, the body is the interface; it is the locus where a purely conscious phenomenon, an idea, or an act of consciousness, is translated into incarnate action. My-body exists in the precise middle between subjective consciousness and objective flesh. My-body exists in the middle of and between two worlds: the world of consciousness and the world of the flesh, of matter. In another sense, my-body exists between cosmic consciousness and the cosmos.

Embodiment also means that the body expresses consciousness. Consciousness manifests itself in our muscles, posture, and in the general shape of our body; it shows itself in those aspects of our body over which we have voluntary control and which are built up over the years. Does our conscious structure cause our bodily configurations, or is it the reverse? Does our body's form affect our mind? Do thoughts influence our body's looks, or does the muscular tension in our body influence modes of thought? It appears that we move both ways: we can change our bodies by the way we think, and we can change our thinking by the way we change our bodies.

Some therapeutic techniques utilize the notion that mind and body are intentionally connected, that they are a continuous field. It follows that we can influence either one by manipulating the other and—as would be the case with an electrically charged field—it does not matter which we manipulate first, the mind or the body.

Biofeedback is an interesting development in this connection. The experience of biofeedback—where one is made intensely aware of how states of consciousness affect bodily processes, how our freedom and our conscious center can affect, cause, or bring about surprising changes in the body—accentuates the awareness of embodiment. By doubling, let us say, the instances in which consciousness produces changes in the body—such as blood pressure, temperature, rate of heartbeats—the experience of embodiment, the perception of the fact that the body is the active and living interface between consciousness and the world, can be clarified enormously and made exceptionally obvious. It is likely that persons, especially children, who grow up in a biofeedback-saturated environment will find the accuracy of the field-theory of the person a perfectly normal description of existence. And they will also therefore live its benefits.

My-body is thus the experience of intentionality and self-transcendence. We can express experientially the consciousness-world connection in the body-qua-mine through what Alan Watts called the Zen *power yell* and the Zen *morning laugh.* They are *decisions for embodiment,* decisions to be the body—which is the transcendental consciousness deliberately entering and being the empirical world.

The Zen power yell and morning laugh can illustrate how we affect the spirit by manipulating the body. The morning laugh consists of simply standing (alone, so you won't look foolish) with your open palms against your hips, laughing uproariously. You laugh unselfconsciously until your laughter is carried by its own momentum. Initially, as you start laughing, your laughter is purely physical and mechanical. Gradually, your body's convulsions connect with the spirit. As your body makes contact with consciousness, your laughter becomes funny. The moment it is truly "funny" the laughter arises from *within* you. When your laughter starts to be funny, then it becomes intentional; it develops into a continuous subject-object field.

Let us be specific. Think of your body and then think of your consciousness; perhaps you feel that the latter is "behind" your body. You now start laughing by shaking your body. Gradually, this bodily shaking will connect with the consciousness "behind" it, shaking that consciousness also. Your body has activated your consciousness, at which time the laughter becomes a continuous subject-object, ego-body, field phenomenon. The vector is reversed, so that your quasi-hysterical "convulsions" have their origin in your consciousness and flow outward and forward into the body. The experience of embodiment is now flowing through your being.

That is a good way to start the day; it integrates your consciousness with your body by establishing the continuity of consciousness with the world. The exercise-experience helps achieve what we call in phenomenology *self-transcending* or *emerging*, which is the fundamental spatio-temporal process of our human existence. You start the day having become yourself.

The exact sequence is as follows: First, one makes the decision to do the Zen morning laugh exercise. The decision itself is a purely conscious, that is, transcendental act. However, this same decision results in an intentional, self-transcending act or event, which is the convulsing body laughing hysterically. The second step is that the conscious center detaches itself from the laughing body and now *observes* it. But specifically what is it that is observed? Observed is not merely a laughing body but a *consciousness forcing a body to laugh*. The observer in this second stage is, therefore, a reduction of (a stepping back from) the first stage. What is observed is the constitution and the cathexis of the act or phenomenon of stage one. Such possibility for regression—in fact, the reality of an eventually *infinite* regress—is the essence of transcendental consciousness.

The third stage in this sequence is a new cathexis, in which the reduced, transcendental consciousness of stage two *identifies* itself with the phenomenon which is stage one. Of course, *explaining* the inner dynamics of the Zen morning laugh, as we are doing here, is again a reduction of stage three. We now *observe* how the morning laugh is constituted in three separate steps. This analysis is, therefore, a fourth stage. In this way we achieve control over the experience and the existence of intentionality. We become the subject-object, consciousness-world interface. This analysis uncovers the philosophical details of the phenomenon of embodiment.

Let us now look at one version of the Zen power yell: Sit, kneeling, on the floor, resting on the back of your feet. Place your arms on your hips, and get into breathing exercises. Take a deep breath, then breathe out, and count "one."

Most meditation exercises include specific prescriptions for breathing, since that is an obvious way to experience bringing together the inside (subjectivity) and the outside (objectivity). Inhaling brings the outside in. It establishes contact from world to you. In exhaling, your inside merges with the external world. Exhaling is the experienced connection of the inside world with outside existence. It follows that concentration on breathing is in itself already an adequate exercise in experiencing the intentionality of being. Breathing fully expresses the continuity, process, and field aspect of experience and of being. Awareness of breathing is therefore good preparation for the Zen power yell.

You are sitting, resting your arms to the side, focusing on breathing, and counting "one." Concentrate on the cycle of your breathing five times. Now get ready to leap. Raise your arms, make fists with your hands, cross your arms over your chest—left fist on right shoulder, right fist on left shoulder. You are in a preparatory stance. You again breathe in deeply, then hold your breath. Count, going up to eight. Then lunge forward with maximum explosive force and roar with a leonine power that rattles your bones. You are now prepared for experiencing in your personal body the actual integration of subject with object. You have experienced the intentional field of being through breathing, laughing, roaring, and choosing to thrust yourself forward. You are expressing through your body this subject-object emerging forward and futurizing movement or process which we call, in existential phenomenology, self-transcendence. By *thinking* of yourself as a lion, you are using—not only breath, body and voice—but an image, a metaphor, a symbol, even a myth, to experience your nature (and the reality of being) as self-transcendence. This experience is therefore not only one of embodiment, but also of *enworldment*, since one experiences not only a connection with the body but with the environing world.

We saw earlier that primal scream therapy is another way of living our incarnation, of forcing us to live the intentional subject-object relationship. There are certain regions of our field of consciousness in which the body and mind, subject and object, are *not* intentionally connected, where they are disassociated and lead their own independent lives. That is not a *human* existence, but an emergency, saintly, artistic, or even a schizoid one. A human life, an individuated and individualized life, is one that exists on the interface between consciousness and the world, between subject and object, incorporating and participating in both regions.

Directed, controlled and profound screaming will help to connect areas of subjectivity with areas of objectivity that had been heretofore severed. The scream makes a subject-object connection; it creates a field in regions of the person where such subject-object connection did not exist before.

Screaming or yelling, while extremely useful, is not automatically therapeutic. What matters is not *that* but *how* one screams. Two features of authenticity stand out. First, the goal is subject-object connection. And that *connection* must be sought, fantasized, and experienced. Second, the person must understand and experience the meaning of the two isolated dialectical poles which are to be connected. A consciousness fantasy or meditation exercise must precede the scream. The person must experience his consciousness as cosmic, as detached from body and world, and as proceeding from a region of infinity which is past, below, or behind. Correspondingly, the person must conceptualize and experience, therefore fantasize, that the world toward which the scream is going to reach is equally infinite, in the future, forward, and up. The scream itself, then, is the experience or the act of being in touch or of getting in touch; it is the act of intentionality and of self-transcendence; it is the phenomenon of growth. The scream is the subject-object interface, the experience of embodiment and incarnation.[5]

Let us mention briefly a few other growth-facilitating techniques that apply the hypothesis that the body-qua-mine is the incarnation of the intentionality of consciousness, the lived interface of the subject-object field of being. Bioenergetics and many of its related body therapies incorporate the existential hypothesis that the body reflects our past conscious history, that it is a map, relic, or fossil of all our past decisions. By appropriate manipulations of the body, one achieves access to past conscious history. The client can then perform changes in his consciousness, not by direct behavior modification, but by reaching, through the body, the core decisions of his being.

Let us return to the metaphor of an electric field, as in a capacitor, in which an equal number of positive and negative charges assemble on each plate. The space between the plates is the field or flow of consciousness. The positively charged plate represents the body and the negatively charged plate, the inner consciousness. Bioenergetics and body therapies assume that a change of the charge on the positive plate (the body) effects a corresponding change on the negative plate (pure consciousness). The reverse effect can also occur: a change in insight, will, or decision leads to a corresponding change in body, behavior, or life-style. This latter process is the common one in orthodox counseling.

Attitude psychology has discovered that often an emotion, attitude, or psychological state—such as anxiety, joy, unhappiness, fear, depression, hope—one is about to enter is announced by a characteristic bodily posture or muscular tension. This posture precedes the emotion, thereby announcing it. This discovery leads to the hypothesis that one can manipulate the body's emotions, its psychology, as it were, by manipulating the muscles. Such a view is the theoretical foundation of Ida Rolf's structural integration, sometimes referred to as *rolfing*, as well as the work of Nina Bull. There have been some dramatic changes in personality, and even in urine content and metabolic rates, in people who have been exposed to rolfing for as little as ten times. If we want an explanation for these phenomena, we can find it in the analysis of the existential concept of the body-qua-mine, of my-body as the incarnation of the fundamental structure of being itself, in the view that the consciousness-world and mind-body continuum is the basic and irreducible unit of explanation of all being.

The opposite therapeutic technique, in which a change in ideas leads to change in the body and its behavior, is older. Traditional psychoanalytic approaches are a good example. Psychoanalysis is talk which affects the emotions. Also, Eric Berne's transactional analysis is a simple conceptual framework which helps us reconstruct our perceptions. Rethinking of experience can change feeling and behavior. Transactional analysis illustrates likewise that a change of ideas becomes a change of the physical.

The same is true of Albert Ellis's *rational psychology* or *rational emotive psychotherapy*. According to Ellis, there is a sentence behind every physical expression. There is an idea, sometimes suppressed, behind every physical act. To achieve growth and develop our human potential, we must find that idea. This approach is similar to transactional analysis, where one searches for the script or the game of one's life. For example, let us say you are depressed, or have an anxiety attack, or are frustrated, or unsuccessful, or bitter, or angry, or lethargic. What is the idea or sentence behind each of these emotional states? What are you saying to yourself with each of these emotions? When you bring that concept or idea, that "constituting" act of consciousness, out into open consciousness and make it an object to your consciousness, you know what causes your problem. You have the power to change the image. With a change in concept, there will be a change in physical appearance, emotions, nervous condition, the cardiovascular system, the endocrine system, and so forth. The ultimate hope, not often realized, is that a change in self-concept, self-image, a change in model, will lead to a transformation (deconstitution and reconstitution) of deep-seated character structures.

We have seen that a phenomenology of the body is ipso facto an analysis of the intentionality of the consciousness-being continuum. Embodiment— the archetypal decision to be an individual—is also the principal project of being, to which the religious myth of incarnation testifies. Personalism, the view that *person* is our most successful root-metaphor for being, may not be far off the mark.

Notes

1. Feodor Dostoevsky, "Notes from Underground," translated by Constance Garnett, in W. Kaufman, *Existentialism from Dostoevsky to Sartre* (New York: Meridian, 1956), pp. 53-54.

2. *Ibid.*, p. 82.

3. (London: The Hogarth Press, Ltd., 1949).

4. The chapters on embodiment in Peter Koestenbaum, *Existential Sexuality* (Englewood Cliffs, N.J.: Prentice-Hall, 1976) cover this topic in some detail.

5. See Book Three, chap. 2.

Chapter 13 • TECHNIQUES FOR THE CONSTITUTION OF THE INDIVIDUAL

Techniques to Bring About Philosophic Fact Two

There are specific procedures one can follow to aid in the constitution of individuality. Most of these involve *action*.

A first technique is to constantly confront oneself, or those we might be counseling, with the question, "What am I or (are you) going to do about it?" This phrase automatically places the responsibility for successfully choosing to be an individual on one's own shoulders or on that of the patient, client, or student. In terms of pure logic, this challenge is an instance of the fallacy of the complex question, since it assumes without stating and certainly without proof that we *can* do something about our problems. Slipping in a suppressed premise of this kind—if the intent is ethical and we have the cooperation of the client—can be highly effective psychologically. In terms of the system of clinical philosophy the suppressed premise is of course a correct assumption. The question tolerates no discussion, doubt, or qualification. The sense of personal responsibility has been injected into the mind, which now restructures its experience accordingly. And this is healthy.

A second technique, a related confrontation, also leads to the sense of individuality. It is the admonition, "You are doing it to yourself" or "I am doing it to myself." These statements imply not only logically but also experientially that we are *choosing not to be* individuals. The client's preauthentic state is not neutral, but is a condition of *choosing against* individuality; it is a state for which he must hold himself fully responsible. It is often the case that once the client realizes he is making that inauthentic choice himself, he finds it relatively easy to make a different choice, namely, the one for finitude, limits, and alienation, the one that makes him into an individual.

Strictly speaking, if it is true that "I do it to myself" then it is also true that

"I *want* to do it to myself." This latter statement, even more forcefully than the previous one, makes clear to us that we are responsible for *not* choosing individuality and that we can therefore just as readily *choose* the archetypal decision for finitude which is Philosophic Fact Two. Once the condition of philosophical pathology is seen in this light, the transformation from inauthenticity to authenticity is not excessively difficult. The difficulty usually lies in helping the client fully reach this level of insight for there are character resistances against fully accepting the meaning of freedom and personal responsibility. These defenses are not merely problems that an individual faces and the result of each person's unique history and genesis, but are ensconced deep in our culture which—by denying consciousness and therefore being ignorant of its structure—does not teach its children the meaning of inwardness, choice, freedom, and responsibility.

A third strategy revolves around the insight that *to be is always to say either yes or no to individuality*, yes or no to the human way of life. *To be* means to constitute or deconstitute, cathect or decathect. There can be no being, no ego-world stream, without these concurrent conscious acts. But to be human, as usually understood, means to constitute and cathect the individual possibility of the bipolar field of consciousness. As one exists through life, the voice that one is always chooses to say either yes or no to life, which means being an individual. Not being an individual is as much a free, deliberate, and reversible choice as is that of being an individual. Not making the archetypal decision for finitude is not necessarily pathological but it does run counter to the consensual and civilized sense of rational, educated, effective, and productive humanness. Furthermore, this kind of archetypal choosing goes on all the time; it is continuous and relentless. The experiences of being conscious and of choosing, while qualitatively different, always coexist. Knowing that makes accepting life and coping with it natural, normal, and easy.

Within the limits of Philosophic Fact One, we know we are in the act of choosing to say *yes* to being an individual whenever we are joyous, feel fulfilled, have meaning, and are in control of our destiny. Conversely, we know we are choosing to say *no* to being an individual whenever we feel depressed, impotent, frustrated, and worthless while at the same time choosing the life of a human being in the consensual world. Knowing that we are condemned to be choosers is likely to make us more effective choosers. Of course, if an archetypal decision for mysticism or cosmic consciousness has been made, then the experience of joy and glory, as opposed to the cloudiness of depression, follows the converse pattern. But our focus in this chapter is on eulogizing the individual and on developing techniques to help us make the archetypal decision for finitude.

A fourth technique for constituting individuality is a rather powerful exercise that is often used to help persons cope with death. The certainty of death is the underlying motivator or constituting mechanism for the decision toward individuality—a point which was established earlier, in the theoretical section. More precisely, we teach individuality, we bring about the archetypal decision for finitude, we urge the cosmic consciousness of the child to learn to reperceive itself as an individual by indoctrinating him or her with the constructs of both birth and death. We teach the child "you were born; at one time you were not; and then you came, as it were, out of nothing." The child does not and cannot experience or confirm this lesson. We also teach a child "you will die; your consciousness will end." And that is another construct, because no person can experience either the beginning or the end of consciousness, which is how the birth-of-oneself and the death-of-oneself, respectively, are here defined.

We must reperceive children's questions—or curiosity or anxiety—about birth and death. These are not biological questions, although they do produce biological answers by our educators. The question underlying a child's curiosity about the birth process—its inherently interesting and fascinating character notwithstanding—is that birth means the beginning of a consciousness which is experienced as infinite and as eternal. It makes no sense to the child to be told that at one time he—as consciousness—did not exist.

The same applies to death. The child, whose primordial self-experience is that of an infinite cosmic being—both consciousness and nature—can make no sense of the concept of the non-being, at some future time, of that consciousness. He learns to reconstitute his mystical world by forcing the beliefs in both the beginning and the end of his consciousness into his perception of the world. These two concepts (birth and death) function like indoctrination. They force him to think of himself as finite, as limited. And the only way this decision to think of himself as a finite being can be made is by his creating the idea of an ego, the notion that he is a *self-object*. And the most accessible candidate to be that object is his body.

Educators must remember that, whereas the biological processes of birth and death as well as their social concomitants are important aspects of a child's education, the underlying philosophic issues are even more important. The child is learning to imagine—or reconstruct—his or her self-concept as a limited, alienated, isolated, alive, substantial, and anxious entity. These constitutional philosophic phenomena must be brought out in helping a child cope with his feelings about birth and death.

In the retired or older adult the connection between a decision for authentic individuality and the threat of upcoming death can be made simple and concrete by confronting the client with the message, "The next five years (or any other time span that seems appropriate) of your life either will be your best or will not be your best. There is no third alternative. Futhermore, you are today better equipped than ever before, in terms of maturity, experience, knowledge, and accomplishments, to choose success in living. At the end of those five years you will discover what your decision has been!"

Such a theme can be used in conducting a funeral service. John, a bereaved and elderly widower, was assisted in coping with what was for him an almost unmanageable situation: the death of his wife. Here are excerpts:

. . . When faced with the change of death, how does an authentic I—any I—react? By affirming "I choose to cope with death." Coping is always possible, because to cope is a decision. And that is good news. "In one year I shall find out if I did or did not choose to cope. Only I can choose not to cope with death. And only I can choose to cope with death. How do I choose?"

. . . John is a hero, and like the mythical hero with a thousand faces, he travels through clearly discernible stages. He is now ending one stage on life's way so that tomorrow he can move on to the next. What stage does he come from? From the period of life in which he searched, in his words, "for the universal lady." John the cadet has been the knight in quest of the Holy Grail. . . . That is where John, the hero, comes from. To what stage is he now stepping? What is next in his heroic journey? What noble rebirth awaits him?

Allow me to admonish all of those present: WATCH HIM CLOSELY OVER THE NEXT FIVE YEARS AND YOU WILL SHARE HIS JOY IN FINDING OUT.

This device has frequently made it possible for patients, clients, or students —in a myriad of contexts—to cross the abyss of inauthenticity and finally succeed in choosing themselves as individuals.

Fifth, we must practice saying no. Each *no* is a risk. We must not be foolhardy in our risking. To know the proper dosages of risk-taking is not a science but an art and requires experience. Risking, to be therapeutic, must be done in small doses, but not so small as to be ineffective.

R E A L I T Y - N O

The important phenomenon of saying no must be discussed in two phases —as reality and as fantasy. In saying no to the world, the inner-directed person says yes to his or her own inner destiny and individuality. In real life, the reader or the client should make a contract with himself or herself to actualize specific and prearranged *nos* by planning and scheduling their expression. It is helpful to make a list—short and manageable—of *nos* that one must say. That list should be specific enough to include location, person, and time. And saying these is not enough. The contract people make with themselves includes the provision that they mean what they say. In preparing this list they must use good judgment; the items or projected acts must be intelligent, sensitive, humane, kind, understanding, and realistic. Crude and excessive *nos* are like temper tantrums; they are immature and ineffective. They are demands for attention—in short, no more than requests for permission to be free and independent from authority figures. Or they may become requests to be restricted and dominated. Crude, immature, and excessively "loud" *nos* are manifestations of dependency, not independence.

A strong no is one that works, one that brings result. It is a no confirmed by the actual facts of the real world, not by empty words from those authorities to whom one may wish to appeal with a tantrum. A strong no is like a powerful and heavy airliner; with little noise and less fuss these behemoths make unstoppable turns and altitude changes. A strong no is silent and unwavering, as firm as the force of gravity from the sun, which keeps the earth in its orbit. It is like a glacier; its movement is as irresistible as it is imperceptible. A strong no is known by its effectiveness. It does not hurt but is kind, because it is right and known as such.

Let us look at an offensive, unreasonable, and integrity-violating directive or order bellowed by a parent, boss, manager, or spouse: "Do this, and do it now!" A weak response is likely to be of the order of an "expletive deleted." The person may have an explosive reaction but in the end will follow the instructions anyway. A strong response, on the other hand, exaggerated, perhaps, may run as follows, "Your request is legitimate, important, and understandable. You of course realize that it must be postponed until its time has come. I appreciate you!" And then of course one must mean this kind of answer and proceed to do what one thinks is right and rational.

It is useful to take a closer look at an example of the no-saying self-contract mentioned here. Jim is a graduate student in psychology at a French University. He writes,

I am inspired by my surroundings. There is history and excellence in every structure. I walk the ground on which lived and created some of France's most notable intellectual giants. I visit the buildings in which some of the world's great ideas were first thought.

But I also fear deeply my dependency. I think that dependency is a personality structure that harms me but I feel tied to it. I have tried to understand my character problem by imagining that to be independent is to be a man. And I have difficulties being a man because I still compete with my father for the attentions of my mother. In this conflict I cannot win. My mother conspires with my father—she fears him. And my father—and in this fantasy I'm still but a small boy—is far too strong for me to even think of taking over his prerogatives.

Impressions enter my mind and I tend to react to them. I almost panic at the thought that my identity and my life are run by these external data and my response to them. My inner voices are in constant danger of being silenced.

I must first learn to say no to my father. Even though he is now old, these insidious Oedipal conflicts still operate within me.

But I must also address myself to what is immediate and presently external.

I must learn to say no to these loud external forces. I am sick and tired of being an other-directed type of person. This school has been made great by the inner-directedness and the fierce independence of its illustrious sons and daughters.

I must also say no to the weather. If it is hot and humid I tend to react with laziness and a soporific stupor. I do not work but instead go to an air-conditioned movie or restaurant. If it is sunny and dry, I respond to that and go to the beach. In each case, my inner voices are squelched and my work remains undone. In my life I am not an agent who acts on the decisions he has made with his inner voices but a *reagent* who responds only to external stimuli and allows himself to be buffeted by the waves and the wind. I must resolutely say no to the weather.

On the other hand, I must also say no to my tendency for intemperate overwork. In another sense, I never stop working and thus exhaust myself utterly. Exhausted, I am tired and uninspired. My work is then not joy but drudgery. I must know what my good hours are and say no to sleeping late, no to my girlfriend's entreaties to see her in the morning, and no to the endless busy work that surrounds me in my study.

I make a list: *no* to weather; overwork; busy work; early morning distractions, and excessively long hours of work.

The growth movement has been attacked as the new narcissism. Although such criticism has its healthful ingredient, it does not apply to clinical philosophy. The old uses of reason, objectivity, and commitment to ideals, traditions, and to society were a form of essentialism. Essentialism is the position that a person must conform to certain standards of being, meaning, and behavior which do not have their origin in the intentional stream of consciousness-body-world in which we participate and which we are. Essentialism demands that the inner core, process, or flow make the decision to be subservient to these externally imposed definitions, goals, and meanings. Existentialism—at least as the existential personality theory —on the other hand, assumes that there is an inner nature to persons and to being, a nature described in the phenomenological model of being, and a nature referred to in this book as a higher-level natural law theory. Aspects of that deeper nature are eternity, freedom, self-transcendence, encounter, dialectic polarity, and so forth.

An authentic existence is one which is self-disclosed in this existential-metaphysical sense and which is lived out in accordance with its desiderata. A person whose philosophic self-disclosure has been facilitated is not a new narcissist but a deeply authentic person. A person whose center is self-understood has the strength to make commitments—and total ones—to the enormous realm of the Other. The existentially self-disclosed person is one who experiences the outward-bound inner flow (Philosophic Fact One), the process emanating from an infinitely distant source and growing toward an infinitely far-off destiny. He has an *elan vital* which has a clearly describable character—the strength, the solidity, the rivets to withstand confrontations, and to grow through opposition. These commitments are based on firm and secure foundations. The essentialist on the other hand has a hollow core and sooner or later the shell will collapse.

A dramatic example of the failure of essentialism is seen in the mid-life crisis of some successful professionals. These are unhappy people who have everything: health, status, education, possessions, freedom to travel, and beautiful families. Their unhappiness—often bordering on depression—

leads them nevertheless to leave their spouses, without apparent cause. And not uncommonly they turn to drugs or alcohol. In many cases the problem is that the reason for their success is that they have adopted an essentialist view of the world. From childhood on they learned to deny their inner core —to silence their inner voices—to accomplish their elaborate, difficult, and competitive educational goals: medicine, law, or dentistry, and research and scholarship. Intense self-discipline is what was required.

They have enough integrity left, however, to feel the hurt of the silenced inner voices. A dramatic act—leaving the family; even a suicide attempt—is a statement (which they themselves often fail to understand) by their whole being that the inner, existential voices *will* be heard before it is too late.

Once this crisis point is understood and met, once the individual recognizes the nature of the stream of consciousness-being that he is, his behavioral, physiological, and psychological symptomatology usually disappears. The crisis is not a middle-age sexual problem. The inner existential, unique, and individual core has been denied for most of his or her lifetime. The symptom, the act of leaving or the act of the affair, is the rebellion of that inner core. The core is asserting its right to *be* and to be *free*. The escapade must be seen as an expression of a legitimate demand for authenticity. Once that demand is satisfied, the spouses are often reunited.

Following is a sample sequence of events to illustrate this point:

A woman leaves her husband and her four children for another man. The existential therapist supports her act. He says, "You are expressing or being your freedom. That is long overdue. As a woman you have been trained not to say *yes* to your inwardness. You have finally chosen to do so."

The husband calls the therapist and accuses him of encouraging his wife to leave him. That is not true.

What the therapist *is* doing is respecting the woman's long-suppressed freedom. He is reasonably certain that once her freedom is fully confirmed she will make a rational decision, a decision for integrity. The chances are excellent that, given the opportunity to experience the choices as *free* and as *hers*, she will return to her husband.

Thus, to accuse the growth movement of narcissism is mostly narrow and unthinking. There is great danger that in making this accusation these important existential insights about inwardness may be missed.

FANTASY-NO

The second major way of saying no is a matter of fantasy, also known as the *guided daydream*. Here we can say it with as much power and violence as is necessary to be completely cleansed of foreign objects, to be totally disidentified from non-ego phenomena. Only when we are totally free of what is not ours or ourselves (or better said, that from which we have decided to alienate ourselves so as to create a sense of a precisely circumscribed identity, as a white mountain on the moon is sharply cut off from the black sky beyond) have we chosen ourselves as individuals. Fantasies are composed not only of mental imagery but also include the kind of powerful, vocal, bodily, and total no-saying that is practiced in some of the recent psychotherapeutic innovations associated with humanistic pyschology such as primal scream therapy and bioenergetics—where the verbalization while kicking a mattress on which the patient lies is commonly a variant of "no! no!"

It is useful to isolate five different and cardinal types of fantasy no-saying. All these nos are directed at the sources in the world that define the self we are to be. Each of these sources against which the no is directed is a major well-spring of energy that tries to define us. These nos are all directed at the essentialist forces of socialization which define the self, which assign roles and natures to it. Socialization is not bad in itself. Life is a constant conflict between inner freedom and the outer forces of definition. The consensually well-adjusted person is the one who has learned to balance the opposing forces. Character reconstitution—which is the same as reconstructive psychotherapy—requires access to this vast and rich realm of freedom. Full access to it is terrifying and even psychotic. It is brought about by this series of fantasy nos. And it is necessary for decathexis of a worn-out self-image and the reconstitution and recathexis of a fresh and more authentic self-image, that is, one in keeping with the basics of the phenomenological model of being.

The person who opts for the possibility of individuality is *self*-created, *self*-defined. And it is against the idea that self-definition has its origin outside our center that the authentic no is directed. All a person needs is a first name, his or her given or self-chosen name—one which frees him or her from family and tradition. The surname is superfluous. And the uncompromising individual must reject all efforts from the world outside his inward center to define who he is. In other words, we must, in fantasy, say no firmly and irrevocably—as a minimum—to *God*, our *parents*, our *children*, our *society*, and to the *child in us*.

No to Parents

Although not essential, fantasy violence, even to the degree of fantasy homicide and, beyond that, the complete elimination of any physical traces, must not be ruled out. To eliminate a parent in fantasy is to free oneself of the superego and make room for genuine self-creation. Saying no to the parent in fantasy may not be enough, in that it is unimaginative and therefore ineffective. The fantasy may also have to involve punishment, harm, pain, death, and burial. Even death did not remove Hamlet's father. He returned as a ghost. In these fantasy exercises, the ghost must also be destroyed so as never to return. Thus, even fantasy "exorcism" may be a psychological necessity. These are, of course, uniquely personal matters, and can be accomplished variously by burying the parent (who serves here as example only), covering the grave with a huge boulder that no one and nothing can remove, cremating the parent, or even plowing him in the ground.

Sometimes in actual practice none of these fantasies works to extinguish the parent as a psychological reality to allow room for authentic self-creation: the parent continually reemerges in fantasy. Another example might therefore be used: the patient can in fantasy *eat* the parent—in any way that fantasy permits. The person then imagines the digestive system assimilating the parent and that may well silence the fantasy parent forever. Primitive and aboriginal practices, including cannibalism—which to us may seem excessively crude and even bizarre—seem to originate and gain psychological justification from the fact that these practices are a working through of these philosophical necessities in the creation of an authentic individual.

The extremity of these exercises does not prove the perverse and evil nature of man. Not at all. They are primitive dramatizations of the power of the external world over our self-definition and the resoluteness with which we must fight these alien incursions if we cherish the decision for individuality and inner-directedness. The demonic is thus, at least in part, the defense of the individual's integrity. Some people become "locked" in these fantasies. As fantasy, their anger is detached, in an epoche. If the anger is cathected, if identification does take place, the control which can reestablish the distance—reintroduce the phenomenological attitude or the reduction—is never lost. Should it be, then the patient goes through a psychotic episode (one definition of psychosis in clinical philosophy is loss of the capacity for reflection, reduction, or distancing). To be psychotic is to be fixated automatically in the natural attitude.

The obvious is scarcely worth mentioning. Nevertheless it is crucial to understand that the fantasy violence is most certainly not directed at real people. The parents killed in fantasy are not even replicas of the parents of today (these may even be already dead). At best, they are representations of parents who existed decades ago and, as introjections into the personality, are operative today. The ontological status of the parent who is killed is indeed a fantasy in itself. And a real fantasy can be confronted only with one similar in kind.

In these fantasies we are saying no, not to real people, sometimes not even to the memories of real people, but to general types, to sources of domination, to the nonindividualistic archetypes, to the archetypal enemies of individuality. We are saying no to certain Platonic Ideas, to a class of essences.

Violent fantasy work, even when accompanied with violent but safe physical expressions, represents no danger that it will translate itself into reality—at least not in the case of normal persons.

Violence is sometimes pure and unadulterated evil. It is then a decision for evil. But violence can also be the last protest or life-affirmation of a squelched center. In that sense, violence may be desperate, unethical, and inefficient, but it does have its element of authenticity. Finally, violence can be a way of getting in touch or being in touch with another person. Violence as an explosion which responds to frustrated or blocked self-transcendence and intentionality can be inefficient and also unethical. But sometimes it may be the only way to get past one's armor and get through to another person.

There is a greater danger that *repressed* anger—that is, fantasies *not had but needed*—will become uncontrollable impulses which act themselves out automatically. Furthermore, these violent fantasies tend to improve rather than deteriorate the actual relationships with the persons concerned, as well as with others. Before these violent fantasies of rejection and destruction, for example, the relationship with a father may have been bad. However, after this kind of fantasy work, and in direct proportion to its violence and unacceptability on ordinary standards, the actual living relationship with a father can become greatly improved. The inner psychological obstacles to a genuine physical and social encounter have been eliminated and meaningful person-to-person contact can be established.

An authentic relationship with a parent can be blocked by the child's deficiency in becoming an individual. But the grown child relates himself or herself to the actual person that is the parent no longer as if he or she were still a child, but as if the parent were another adult, a friend, an equal. This transformation, necessary as it may be, is often a difficult adjustment for both parent and child (or, more accurately, for both ex-parent and ex-child). Now that a person has become an individual he or she is ready to establish mature encounters—with relative independence of the maturity of the other person.

Not all angry fantasies are self-affirming. A *no* to the parent may not be an expression of alienation, that is, it may not be a manifestation of the archetypal decision for finitude, but may instead be a form of dependency. The destructive no-saying may in fact be an "I hate you" which quickly leads to "Because you don't love me." That in turn can easily become "I am dependent on your love for self-validation."

We are dealing here with important but dangerous material and must therefore tread with caution.

No to God

Let us consider another no. Nietzsche helped us say no to God in his famous passage from *The Gay Science* in which he declared that God is dead. We can argue that the modern age has destroyed God through war, through the scientific outlook, and through overpopulation, a point discussed at the beginning of this book. And we can argue further that alienation of modern man is the result of the death of God, that is, the death of inwardness, the denial of the conscious center—with its sense of freedom and responsibility—and ignorance of the mystery of subjectivity. The death of God means, among other things, the denial of the transcendental dimension. To this extent, the death of God is bad. But the death of God can also mean the end of the essentialist, objectified God. That would signal the end of an incomplete and inadequate metaphysics. To this extent God's death is good. The implication is that if God could be reinstated alienation would be overcome. However, there is no need to present such a gloomy outlook.

One other interpretation of Nietzsche's message is not bad, but good, even from the point of view of a person with a religious perspective. The death of God can be seen as a critical phase in the development of consciousness. Through the death of God, consciousness says no to God Himself to affirm its own independence and integrity. God—as concept, myth, or reality—represents the most powerful source of standards, essences, values, and definitions that the world has ever known. That type of God is already established in primitive societies, where God embodies or systematizes and sanctions the local mores, traditions, and roles. Such a God was introduced into Western philosophy with Plato's theory of ideas. Constant references to the threat of hell and purgatory further underscored the defining—as well as the suffocating and strangling—power of God.

Introduced by Nietzsche, the modern age, through its commendable democratic movements toward creating the individual, has found it necessary to say no to God, in fantasy at least, by destroying and even killing Him. Nietzsche writes, "What was holiest and most powerful of all that the world has yet owned has bled to death under knives. "And later he writes, "Must not we ourselves become gods simply to seem worthy of it? . . . There has never been a greater deed; and whoever will be born after us—for the sake of this deed he will be part of a higher history than all history hitherto."[1] No to God—the Father, and sometimes even the Mother—is a no to the most potent infringement of isolation, independence, and self-affirmation, in short, individuality. No to God is the most dangerous of all nos. It is the ultimate risk, and with it, it becomes the most successful mechanism for the constitution of the sense of individuality. That is how the individual is created through the power of *no*.

When Nietzsche said that God is dead we can argue that he meant that the modern age has created the individual—who by nature is anxious, isolated, and alienated—at the price of saying no to the world's greatest source: God. Modern individualism is thus bought at the price of deicide! As with parents, this act has profound philosophic meaning as a fantasy. It is not blasphemous; it does not affect the reality of God—whatever your philosophic position may be. As free individuals, we can now—if we choose—return to God on our terms, as equals, without threat or compulsion. That would then be an authentic Man-God relationship. That is genuine religion; it is mature theology.

No to Children and Society

We now turn to another fundamental area of no-saying. Saying no to our children is a rather obvious exercise. Many parents are alienated from their children and what is indicated under these circumstances is intensified yes-saying to these children. Discussion of more no-saying would here be dangerously out of place. But there are other situations in which the otherwise legitimate demands for love and responsibility nevertheless truncate the parents' independence and individuality. Under these circumstances, saying no to the real child is realistic and teaches the child about the equal reality of the parent.

Furthermore, some parents use their attachment to their children as excuse or explanation for failing as individuals. These parents are dependent on their children. The extent of the failure may not be apparent until the children are grown and have left the home. They may then discover that their sense of failure is still with them even when the excuse of the children is gone. In this case of dependency, saying no to children in fantasy is of crucial importance for the creation of individuality in the parent. And it is only through the example of an independent parent that a child learns to understand the meaning of individuality. The fantasy child can symbolize an archetype of dependency. Then, saying no to one's fantasy child can be the optimum act of independence and self-definition.

Saying no to society and tradition is again a common experience in the evolution of the individual and because it is well known and generally understood it requires only brief mention. Its importance must be recognized; its salubrious consequences for establishing the decision for individuality must be supported. The principles of adaptation which worked half a century ago are no longer relevant. The world at large no longer supports the world view which was meaningful in the ghetto or in the native state. Contemporary social reality requires all of us to be self-defined. That can be accomplished only through the rigorous rejection of whatever atomistic remnants remain of one's ethnic tradition, social, background, and political heritage. Of course, once we have established ourselves as free individuals, we can take any posture we choose with respect to these rejected social elements. This situation parallels the rejection of God.

A person's ethnicity is as important in understanding the parameters in which he perceives and conceptualizes his world as are his earliest Oedipal connections. Ethnicity means race, nationality, religion, tradition, and so forth. These powerful ties must be cut and denied, at least in fantasy, to achieve a true sense of individuality. If a Catholic wishes to experience his individuality, if he wants the sense of being a truly self-made person, he needs to deny the Church. He may or may not return in his own time as a free and inner-directed and self-chosen act of commitment and self-definition. A black man, to be individual and self-made, must first deny his tradition of the Negro Soul and the Black Experience. He may rededicate himself to it as a new and free act, a self-determined and autonomous creation out of nothing. Then he is a freely chosen and individual black, not a born and determined black.

No to the Child Within

Let us conclude this section on techniques which use no-saying to achieve the independence that characterizes the constitution of the sense of individuality with a reference to Antoine de St. Exupèry's famous and charming book, *The Little Prince*. Many stories which are ostensibly for children actually carry within them sophisticated existential teachings. This lovely fable is an excellent example of the last of the regions which require no-saying, namely, the child within us. *The Little Prince*—and this may well be a debatable and controversial interpretation—is the story of a man growing up. He reaches adulthood only when the child within him is dead. And since his death is for a good cause—namely, the birth of the man, the adult—St. Exupery makes the child die cheerfully.

The basic message of the book is that adulthood—which means inner-directedness and independence, that is, individuality—is bought at the price of the destruction of childhood dependency, trust, and self-pity. This view may seem unfeeling, uncompromising, and even harsh, but it is only by means of this peremptory approach to maturity that a genuine understanding of the unilateral, single-pole choice of what it means to be a self-sufficient and potent individual can be fully experienced and implemented.

The protagonist is an adult pilot—adult in body only, but still a child at heart. His childishness is exhibited by the fact that he always carries a drawing from his boyhood: a hatlike pencil sketch which everyone sees as a hat but which for him was a boa constrictor that had swallowed an elephant. He did add, as a child, a dot on the rim of the hat to serve as an eye—but to his great disappointment people nevertheless insisted on perceiving this "improved" drawing as a hat. He thus carried with him into adult life this symbol of being misunderstood, of being a lonely, rejected, neglected child. He remained a dependent person, even in adulthood, all the while hoping to cover up his childishness with the presumptively mature and manly profession of pilot.

Not being an adult, he had to fail at the business of being an adult. And adulthood is symbolized in the story by successfully piloting an airplane. As a result, the flight to independence ended instead with an emergency landing in the Sahara desert. Having thus failed in his attempt to be an independent adult, the source of this failure now appears to him in the desert: a little boy—a prince—materializes before him. The little prince is the child within him, the beautiful child, the lovable child, the profound value of childishness, but nevertheless, the explanation and the source of his failure as an adult and thus the cause of his emergency landing. The pilot has lengthy coversations with the boy, all the while working to repair his airplane. In other words, the adult speaks to the child within and, of course, the reverse is also true. Only when the child finally dies in the desert—he dies a voluntary, self-chosen death, by asking a snake to bite him—is the airplane repaired and the pilot able to fly again, this time successfully. The child's death means that the total person—the adult-child polarity—chooses at this time in his life the option of the adult over the child. The magnetic field chooses to emphasize, identify itself with, or make a commitment to its positive pole. The ultimately mature life-style may be a synthesis of the two—the child *and* the adult, the dependent *and* the independent, the negative *and* the positive poles—but such synthesis is not the developmental stage represented by Philosophic Fact Two. That is the province of Philosophic Fact Three.

It may be sad, and it is no less true because of it, that independence (or adulthood—effective, potent, and autonomous functioning) requires the destruction of the child within us. Childhood must be overcome for us to become an adult. The independent adult stands up and by that act holds down the childhood from which he came. The adult stands on the child within as a painter stands high on a scaffold. If the support gives way, the adult dies. This act of inner-child overcoming is not a one-time accomplishment. On the contrary, it is an act of constitution and decathexis, of archetypal self-definition, which must be reinvoked fully each time the decision for being an individual is made. A person may drift into dependency when the world is good to him. But as soon as adversity frustrates him, the urgent need for strong and independent action becomes apparent. How does he draw his forces together? By denying the child in him and through this no-saying creating his own individuality.

None of these statements contradicts the other element of maturity, which is that childishness has its proper place in a whole life, but not at this time and not in the present context of constituting a sense of Philosophic Fact Two.

Property

A final technique for developing the sense of individuality is based on the idea of the right to property, as that concept was initially understood by John Locke. Thomas Jefferson wisely changed Locke's *property* to *happiness* in the *Declaration of Independence.* To achieve individuality one must demand and risk control, that is, property rights, over a specific spatio-temporal region, over a specific meaning, a constituted object— in the widest possible sense of the word *object.* That region concretizes what would otherwise be a purely abstract notion of individuality. There are innumerable levels at which this "real estate" can exist. It can be a room, a hobby, a garden. But it is more effective as education, a skill, a business, or a profession. Excellence, competence, and perfection are words that describe the extent to which control is exercised. To search for excellence in a narrow field is to make that field one's property. In that way the individual becomes visible in the world and concrete to himself. The highest level of property over a spatio-temporal region is character and integrity, since the world exercises minimal control over them.[2] A man's reputation or his worth are constituted meanings, created objective regions in the world over which he exerts almost total control. A man's integrity is his property, and in that lies his sense of individuality.

In *Is There An Answer To Death?* the sense of individuality is called the *creative erotic energy core.* That core is our potency, and it can appear to us in dreams and fantasies as the demonic. It can emerge as snakes, monsters, fire, earthquakes, and so forth. We often disattach ourselves from the demonic. But once we make it our own we have permitted the creative genius to take over our existence and with this integration our sense of individuality is complete. The experience in question is the convergence of the individual created out of the transcendental ego—which is pure consciousness—and the individual created out of the empirical realm of nature—which is pure material substance. When these two join, a true sense of concrete individuality is established. (See Appendix B.)

This discussion of the archetypal decision in favor of our possibility as individuals assumed that the decision for individuality is the *right* one; that individuality is an absolute, an unqualified value in clinical philosophy. In a practical sense, this is of course the case. Counseling should help develop a person's individuality and potency. Most tasks in life, including loving, demand as prerequisite the sense of individuality. It is difficult to be an effective person without a commitment to the archetypal decision for individuality.

However, from the point of view of the highest metaphysical perspective, that exclusivity is of course not true. It follows from our basic metaphors (the magnet and the bloodstream) and from the discussion of the phenomenological model of being that a third stage in the evolution of the personality exists. This stage is the dialectical, polar, and stressful relationship between Philosophic Facts One and Two. We now turn to Philosophic Fact Three, and with it conclude the expanded exposition of the phenomenological model of being and the existential personality theory.

Notes

1. Walter Kaufmann, *Existentialism from Dostoevsky to Sartre* (New York: Meridian, 1956), p. 105.
2. This point is developed in detail in Book Two, chap. 10.

Chapter 14 • *PHILOSOPHIC FACT THREE: POLARITY*

Experiencing Polarization

Now that we have developed in detail the two contradictory options made possible for us by the polar character of being, we must return to the original metaphor of the dialectic. We proceed in Hegelian fashion, in that we return to the beginning but only after we have developed the component antitheses. The resulting synthesis thus has a meaning which could not be suspected at the very beginning.

Philosophic Fact Three is the synthesis of the opposing Philosophic Facts One and Two. The concept of synthesis was anticipated in Chapter 9, which is the discussion of the bipolar personality theory.

Real life, authentic existence, and self-actualizing experience is not likely to make a unilateral and permanent decision either for universality or individuality. (A similar type of reasoning applies to decisions between a subjective and an objective emphasis.) The themes heretofore developed, when used for living and for therapy, must be applied with artistry. We cannot overlook the complexity and variations of actual experience.

Philosophic Fact One and Philosophic Fact Two are in conflict, and that is an aspect of their essential nature. Life *is* that conflict (as well as the subject-object conflict) and not its resolution. Contradiction, polarity, and dialectic are permanent and desirable structures of experience and existence. The ambiguity they represent and the stresses they embody are in actual fact the experience of feeling alive, of existing and of being. Let us be more specific. If we ask for a phenomenological description of the experience of being *alive*—a condition which can be equated with the experience of the passage of time, with the flow about which Bergson wrote, with joy, with excitement and excitation, with energy, and even with anxiety—then the unequivocal answer must be *the experience of polarization*. And it is the polar unification or synthesis of Philosophic Facts One and Two that is here called Philosophic Fact Three.

The therapeutic value of this position becomes apparent. In most cases, Philosophic Fact Three shows that what is given as a problem is not in reality a problem at all. What torments the patient and what appears to him or her as an inextricable problem is often no more than the urge to choose a single polarity. But it is this urge itself to choose a nondialectical, nonflowing, nonfieldlike self-concept or mode of being-in-the-world which is contrary to the nature of existence. The solution to this agony often is increased philosophical understanding, and with it, a recognition of the value, even the necessity, of the polar contradictions.

We must remember that existentialism rejects the idea that a human being has an essence. In clinical philosophy, however, although we agree with this existential analysis, we do distinguish between a nature (or an essence) and a higher-level nature or essence. The dialectical character of being and of the person is not an essence in the Platonic or Aristotelian sense, but it is the essence of essences, a higher-level nature or essence. It is in this fashion that the phenomenological model of being hopes to reconcile the existential insight that a person is essence-free with the added view that human beings do have some kind of absolute and describable nature. The experience of the dialectic is also the experience of feeling alive. The phenomenological description of aliveness yields the descriptive trait of the dialectic, of polarization, stress, and oscillation.

Possibly our best example is to be found in human relationships, especially marriage. Many romantic love affairs start with the choice of one polarity. Either the woman is totally devoted to the interests and projects of the man, or vice versa. As a rule, such a relationship changes over the years, possibly into what family counselors call the "Bitch-Nice Guy" type of marriage—which happens to be common in middle-class America. If and when such a marriage breaks up, the romantic relationship which started it is frequently reestablished with a new partner. The devotion of the present philosophic analysis to Philosophic Fact Three should show that the authentic and mature resolution of these marital troubles is for both partners to recognize that an adult relationship *is* polar. Two persons are two poles. The meaning they find in their togetherness lies in the ambiguity and the stress—hence the experience of reality and of life—that is produced by the merger of two independent centers of consciousness into one "magnetic" totality.

Life occurs essentially on the interface of this polarity between Philosophic Facts One and Two. That point is also the intersection of subject and object, of consciousness and world. It appears that this interface is also the locus of the experience of power, energy, control and, in the last analysis, technology. It is possible that here psychology and physics meet. The concepts of physics which are of central use to technology—such as energy force, work, light, and so forth—are derived from the life-world. The lived experiences from which these engineering abstractions originate are the phenomena which occur at the interface of the polar dialectic that is the being of man. It is likely that the assiduous analysis of the process of derivation from the subject-object and individual-universal interface in the life-world to the corresponding conceptual abstractions in physics and engineering can bring about new theories of energy with as-yet-unsuspected implications for technology.

The mutually exclusive polarities *together* comprise the feeling of wholeness that defines the authentic person. These polarities are as real as they are irreconcilable. By choice and tradition, not by nature, the individual-universal polarity has been connected with gender, so that the man is the individual and the woman is the universal. Or that man is the subject and woman the object. This point must be understood to discuss intelligently the issues involved in the prevailing contemporary practice of redefining sexual roles. It is useful to give up the words *masculine* and *feminine* and replace them with subjective-individual and objective-universal or, if we prefer, with potent, independent, and assertive, and nurturing, trusting, and dependent respectively. Sex organs have nothing to do with these personality traits based on polarities. Choices and socialization are the sources of this identification.

All human beings are persons first and foremost; they are freedoms and choosers. They can choose which aspects of the bipolar field of possibilities that they are shall be realized at any one time. If gender is now to be made relevant to these decisions, then we are confronted with the kind of archetypal decision which defines the basic structure of a society, the basic configuration of a relationship, and the basic character of a person. Through this double-level approach to sexual roles we can understand both the equality of men and women as well as the importance of their self-chosen differences. The solution to sexual-role problems is not to autocratically prescribe androgyny for everyone, but to recognize the enormous freedom given all of us in this respect. The only givens are the parameters of human freedom and responsibility on the one hand and the sanctity of each subjective conscious inwardness on the other. These principles must never be violated. Many of the most perplexing problems faced today by men and women can be resolved by the proper application of this philosophic insight and clarification.

Love, compassion, kindness, intimacy, and intersubjectivity are also in themselves dialectical phenomena. These highly evolved states of human consciousness conform to the structure of ambiguity and stress that any self-disclosed person finds at the heart of his existence. To understand the polarity of Philosophic Fact Three is therefore to help oneself along the path toward intimacy or personal encounter. Love is a dialectical phenomenon: it means *one*, in that two conscious centers experience the fact that they are part of a single field of consciousness. But love also means *two* in the sense that each person experiences and confirms the unique individual identity (the creative-erotic energy core) of each partner. Whereas unity means empathy, duality means confrontation.

Principal Polarities

It may be helpful to list some of the principal polarities that comprise Philosophic Fact Three and with which human beings are confronted. In each case we must remember that the polarities of Philosophic Facts One and Two exist in conflict with one another and that a resolution of this contradiction is found (if at all) only in the higher synthesis of a holistic world view and clearly not in the unilateral choice of only one of the two poles. It is a useful counseling practice to expect Philosophic Fact Three to emerge alone, without help, in the patient. The role of the therapist is to underscore the polarities in the life of the patient. It should not be the responsibility of the therapist to resolve or synthesize the polarities for the patient. The patient will learn, unaided, to live with the uncompromising reality of both poles in his life.

PARENT-CHILD

One significant polarity, and one for which therapists will find much use, is the parent-child or adult-child dialectic. The parent represents the rational life-style, whereas the child is the symbol for the irrational and impulsive mode of being-in-the-world. The parent represents the adult and mature mode of behavior and the child the innocent mode. The parent represents distance and objectivity whereas the child stands for attachment and subjectivity. The parent seeks freedom; the child needs unconditional commitment.

When problems occur in life or in therapy so that a client lives in despair because the conflict is irresolvable, then the following formula may be of help. Clarification of these issues can be obtained by emphasizing individual polarities. These are the options. The client should be helped to see and experience clearly what the alternative polarities are. Resolution of the issues, on the other hand, can be facilitated by emphasizing the health, naturalness, and inevitability of the dialectical field. The power of the phenomenological model of being must then be established unquestionably. A new form of perception of old realities can follow; the experience of adaptation emerges; a new freedom of action is instituted.

MASCULINITY-FEMININITY

Another important polarity that is significantly relevant to therapeutic questions is the masculine-feminine contradiction. We have touched on this matter on pages 203-205.[1] A few additional and summary comments here should suffice. Each of us has a masculine potential—strong, individual, aggressive, independent, leading, hard—and a feminine component—trusting, accepting, loving, compassionate, caring, mothering, passive, nurturing. That we identify these polar possibilities of personality structure with gender is purely a matter of historical reality and social convention. By no longer using the words *masculine* and *feminine* we make clear that each person has the opportunity to develop his or her potential for leading as well as for accepting. And no intimation whatever is made that these divergent personality characteristics are connected to sexual organs and biological destiny. We might thus use expressions like *the aggressive gender* and *the passive gender*, without there being any need to specify and fix the sex of these chosen personality characteristics.

SUBJECTIVITY-OBJECTIVITY

Another daily, culturally and therapeutically relevant paradox is that between subjectivity and objectivity. We ask whether we should utilize the intuitive mind in our quest for values and choice of life-styles. That would be the subjective approach. Or we want to know to what extent we should be analytical and discursive in our problem solving. The academic establishment still rewards the analytic over the intuitive mind. Intelligence tests and college entrance examinations still principally measure analytic, not intuitive thinking. Another form this polarity takes is the conflict between the interests of our feelings, our inward needs, and the reality demands of an external world. This is a conflict between understanding and forgiveness and contracts and justice. Again, we can assess personality in terms of which pole an individual favors. But the authentic person is one who in the last analysis embraces both poles in the fashion of an electro-magnetic field.

ADDITIONAL POLARITIES

Death and immortality is another important pair in the polarity of human existence discussed as Philosophic Fact Three. Death belongs to the individual—with all the advantages, meanings, joys, and possibilities for fulfillment associated with that archetypal decision—whereas immortality comes after the surrender of individuality through asceticism and the cult of indifference.[2]

Philosophic Fact Three is also defined through the contrasts of the active and the passive personality, the inner-directed and the other-directed self-definition. The active life-style organizes, directs, and controls. The passive life-style accepts, nurtures, and adapts. Again, when confronted in life with these issues, the answer is not to choose between them—except to clarify the specific nature of the field of stress—but to understand that in the conflict itself between the active and the passive personality the experience of being fully alive emerges.

Another important and frequent occurrence of the active-passive polarity found in a therapeutic context is the conflict between the directive and nondirective approach. Unqualified positive regard has advantages that have been amply demonstrated in theory and substantiated by practice. For one, the client-centered approach of active listening is easy to teach and easy to use. And it is effective. It is a method by which the client is given the opportunity to express his feelings and, in having them, experience a catharsis, and in observing them, develop rational solutions. The nondirective approach has the further advantage of placing the client in an environment in which his center is accepted for what it is. This psychological environment has the effect of providing the client with a sense of ground. The method may be artificial, in that the ground produced by the therapist is illusory. That does not matter, because the illusion of a ground reminds the client of the reality of the ground that has been his all along but which he had refused to recognize.

The negative aspect of the nondirective approach is that it may well be the rationalization of grave timidity in the therapist. The client-centered approach is a timid, nonrisking approach. It entails no commitment on the part of the therapist—no opinion, no strength, no philosophy of life, no leadership.

A clearly directive approach also has its value. Directive psychotherapy, confrontation, and the like can be based on the orthodoxy of the phenomenological model of being. The therapist may decide to expect the patient to conform not to a lower-level orthodoxy, such as narrow religious or psychological views as to what is normal and what is not, but to a higher-level orthodoxy (or natural-law theory or essentialism) such as developed by the phenomenological model of being. This orthodoxy does *not* tell the individual he must fulfill his sexual needs—that is a desideratum based on a biological model. But it *does* tell the individual he must understand and exercise his freedom for the sake of authenticity. This latter orthodoxy or directive psychotherapy is based on a higher-level ontology than are the conventional psychologies of adaptation. Whereas traditional psychology requires adaptation to biological, social, and psychological realities—such as sex, family, and happiness—clinical philosophy gives itself the right to demand adaptation to ontological realities, such as freedom, self-transcendence, ambiguity, and death. It is because of these latter considerations that we are entitled to call clinical philosophy a *higher-level* orthodoxy, natural-law theory, or essentialism.

The practicing therapist must be sensitive to the needs of his client and adapt the directive and nondirective options of his own technique to the circumstances of the person for whom he is responsible. The psychotherapeutic significance of Philosophic Fact Three is that it forces on the client a fundamental reconstitution of his or her life-world, from a perspective which demands impossible choices between equally valued alternatives, to one which is free and at peace with eternal conflict, and is thus energetic. This reconstitution, this accommodation to the dialectic and acceptance of the rectitude of polarization, makes possible the continuation of life. Conflicts which demand unilateral commitments bring life to a standstill. The reality of Philosophic Fact Three reintroduces forward movement into life.

Independence-dependence (or trust) is another underlying ambiguity and stress which expresses the consciousness-world field that we are. Both of these poles represent authentic values. Any person choosing one pole exclusively over a lifetime becomes thereby an artificial, dishonest, and truncated human being. The independent person is independent at the price of sorrowing over having relinquished the sweet support of dependency. The dependent (or trusting) person is dependent at the price of feeling guilt over denying the dignified posture of self-reliance. Philosophic Fact Three teaches us that it is not a question of whether we are independent or dependent, but which side of us is up and showing and which one is down and temporarily hidden.

Throughout the history of ideas, the conflict synthesized in Philosophic Fact Three emerges also as the struggle between Man and God. Man and God, even though mythologized as real and independent entities, must be understood as projections or metaphors of the fundamental condition of being as disclosed through phenomenology. Man is the finite possibility of being; God is the option for infinity. The same reality can be seen (or interpreted) from either the perspectives of time or eternity. If we choose to see being from the point of view of time, we record or register those perceptions which are found in our consensual world view—the split between the inner self and the outer world, the supremacy of the atom and the individual, the finitude of man, and so forth. However, if the point of view of eternity is chosen, then that same world is perceived as ego-less, as atemporal, as unified. If it should come to pass that the actual data or the material content of these two perspectives are different, it is due to selective perception. We do not register all possible data, only those which fit into our prechosen world view.

For example, humanism and transcendentalism are metaphysical positions that are as incompatible as they are true. The authentic person is one who can integrate both in one philosophy of life by recognizing that the friction between them is the substance of life itself, the experience of time, the phenomenon of intentionality made perceptible. That is the beauty of the study of the history of philosophy. Students often worry over which of many conflicting viewpoints to adopt for themselves: idealism, naturalism, pragmatism, Platonism, or what have you. The history of ideas teaches us that there is merit in each view and that the history of thought is like a rolling and growing snowball.

A related manifestation of the underlying dialectic of being is the conflict between the individual and the state, or, to a lesser extent, the corporation. This paradox leads to the liberal-conservative confrontation. On the one hand, the individual must be revered and protected. It is therefore true that the function of the state is to protect the freedom and the integrity of the individual. That is the role of the Bill of Rights, the first amendment to the Constitution. To be a liberal is thus an authentic political posture. But there is another side, which is equally true. The individual exists in a state. The state provides the security and embodies the structure that makes the individual life possible. Furthermore, the state has solidified the values, laws, and institutions that make up the culture which creates the individual. And even a corporation provides the individual with a job and perhaps also with the opportunity for meaning. Without the shell of the state or the corporation which encases him, the individual may well be nothing.

The Constitution which the Bill of Rights amended was to give cohesion to the life-world of the Pilgrims' descendants, so that the individual could flourish. These are the conservative views, and they are equally true to the facts. They merely represent another pole in Philosophic Fact Three. The liberal-conservative and individual-state controversies are not resolved by opting for one pole over the other—even though specific legislative decisions may involve one such actual choice—but by recognizing that the vitality of society lies in precisely the creative interaction, the stress and the fascination of the polar or dialectical process itself. In other words, the solution to the liberal-conservative and individual-state controversies is not to take sides but to recognize the legitimacy of both positions and to realize that the mature *truth* lies in the fact that the experience of life, the experience of social reality, and the experience of *Existenz* (Jasper's term) consist of the polar conflict itself. That is the authentic return to the phenomenological model of being.

Another version already mentioned of the polarity of Philosophic Fact Three is the conflict between time and eternity. Time is human; eternity, divine. Time is the decision for finitude which gives us the sense of life; eternity is the atemporal, pretemporal, or posttemporal experience of ourselves as the Eternal Now, the mystical consciousness. Even in sex the polar distinction between time and eternity is of significance. Foreplay is the experience of time; it has a future, a goal, a destiny. The orgasm is the experience of eternity; it goes nowhere, it merely is. It is always at its goal. Again here there is conflict leading often to emotional problems between the partners. The world seen from the aspect of foreplay is in no way the same as the world of the orgasm. The healthy resolution of these conflicts is the mature acceptance of polarity as the nature of things.

The distinction between the transcendental and the empirical egos—often restated in dreams as a ship on the ocean, a room in a house, an airplane in the sky, or a rock in the desert—is a root symbol of the polarities of Philosophic Facts One and Two. A ship in the ocean is a unified image synthesizing, as Philosophic Fact Three, the individual-universal as well as the subject-object polarities. If the dreamer is in the ship, that becomes the region of the subject; the threat of the ocean—or its support—becomes the object in the experience. And this observation returns us to the phenomenological model of being.

This discussion concludes the extended illustration and application of the phenomenological model of being to specific and therapeutically useful themes, which have been presented as the three basic philosophical facts.

Notes

1. These points are covered at some length in Peter Koestenbaum, *Existential Sexuality* (Englewood Cliffs, N.J.: Prentice-Hall, 1974).

2. This point is the main topic of Peter Koestenbaum, *Is There An Answer To Death?* (Englewood Cliffs, N.J.: Prentice-Hall, 1976).

BOOK TWO **Revelations of Anxiety**

Part I • DEFINITION OF ANXIETY

Chapter 1 • INTRODUCTION

Leah

One afternoon, as I was ready to begin a seminar, Leah, a student I had never seen before, approached me. In her twenties, she was desperate and affectionate, manic and thoughtful. She quickly told me she was dying of cancer, was divorced, and had three children. She recently had a double mastectomy, and now she was facing the prospect of a hysterectomy, since she apparently had uterine cancer. "Since you had written about death," she said, "perhaps you could be of some help to me."

This brief episode demonstrates the urgent need to bring to bear immediately and forcefully, but also responsibly, abstract philosophy onto living issues which are crying stridently for solution.

We have had, since then, many talks. Some of my earliest responses to her follow and can well serve as introduction to the spirit and the content of Book Two. These responses were discoveries and revelations we made mutually. She was bright, sensitive, and insightful.

"Your agony," I said, "which we should call anxiety, is a source of wisdom. It reveals certain truths about you, about human beings in general, and about larger cosmic issues as well."

"Because of your condition, you feel like a stranger in this world. You think of yourself as a pariah. Other women your age can be happy and 'normal.' You have been condemned to be the exception who will die young and in suffering. You feel that life has cheated you. And you feel angry But you also feel inferior since you secretly believe that the world, which is stronger than all of us, must have rightfully judged you. In some deep and dark unconscious recess you are convinced—like the child whose parent is dead—that you deserve your fate. Your fate embarrasses you. You feel self-conscious, guilty, and worthless. You feel that your unfortunate condition is proof that in you, unlike others, there is a dark ravine in which flows a polluted river of depravity.

"And yet the contrary is the case. You see the truth about life. You know about dying. You are the realist. The world that you secretly envy represses death; it postpones coping with dying. You alone, with your so-called 'unusual problem,' your 'abnormality,' are in actuality part of the real world. You do not participate in the death-denying fantasy world of the majority. If any envy is in order, the world, which is blind, should envy you, who can see."

Both of us realized that to learn how to take philosophy seriously is indeed a human emergency. Perhaps the most fundamental point of all to share with her was that she should consider the following:

"There is something universal in us all. There is a consciousness that runs through us which is indestructible and eternal. Immortality and reincarnation are myths, that is true, but we ourselves place them where they are so that they will remind us of this unquestionable underlying philosophical reality. Our consciousness does not result from brain activity, but brain activity is what consciousness thinks about. Your brain cells do not reproduce or renew themselves, like other body cells. Therefore, deterioration or damage to them becomes a severe threat to the functioning of the brain. But consciousness is not dependent on the functioning of the brain but is rather the spatio-temporal matrix of being in which the brain, like other objects, phenomena, and essences have their existence. Perhaps the most worthwhile activity of life is to seek to demonstrate the truth of this insight and to allow that truth to suffuse our finite existence."

Insight in therapy is important and necessary, but not sufficient. Insight alone is not enough. Philosophic healing also requires contact and intimacy, in short, compassion. Ludwig Lefebre told of it when he wrote about intersubjectivity and how it can be established:

A patient who was acutely suicidal for more than three years trusted me sufficently to tell me that she was saving sleeping pills. I promised not to tell either her husband or her physician but asked her to give me the pills whenever she felt that she might carry out her plan to take them. She promised but stipulated that I return the pills to her when she felt that the accute desire to kill herself had passed. I promised. This situation occurred two or three times. A long time afterwards, when she had recovered and was about to stop therapy, she told me that the trust experienced in my returning the pills had been the turning point. By honoring her request I had at the same time confirmed her reality and given her a chance to trust me. In my terminology I had conferred relevance on her suffering and in so doing had made it possible for her to admit me into her world.[1]

We have here the elements (philosophic understanding and human encounter) which make healing possible.

Overview

The key to Book Two is that anxiety reveals the truth about the person and thus contributes centrally to the healing process. Healing is not an automatic occurrence produced by medicine but a synchronicity and resonance between the patient and the most basic structure of being. The total picture of the person presented here in terms of anxiety and the proper functioning of the transcendental dimension makes up what here is called the existential personality theory. The table in Appendix D summarizes the seven revelations of anxiety, their diagnoses, treatment, and even their political implications.

. What traditionally are known as neuroses may correspond roughly to ignorance about these revelations of anxiety, that is, neuroses may result from an inadequate understanding of the possibilities of human existence as these are compressed in the existential personality theory. That condition is inauthenticity. Schizophrenia may similarly be a diagnostic category which corresponds roughly to the malfunction of crippling of consciousness itself. We must call this condition the nonintentional consciousness. Schizophrenia is thus allied to a malfunction of the basic structure of the field of consciousness itself.

Note

1. In an unpublished paper delivered at the Annual Meeting of the Association for Phenomenological Psychiatry, Los Angeles, California, May 1974.

Chapter 2 • DESCRIPTION OF ANXIETY

Definition

Anxiety is a common word in the English language; it is a family of experiences drawn from the life-world; everyone who reads these pages can use the word *anxiety* correctly. In addition, a person with therapeutic experience—both theoretical and practical—will have developed some theories about anxiety. As a result he will have used that word as a principle of organization for his own life and that of his client. If, in addition, the therapist has a philosophical background of the kind discussed in Book One, he can use anxiety as a principle of organization that has moved from the provincialism of the person to the catholicity of being itself.

On the horizon of our analysis is the phenomenological method. We must endeavor to describe anxiety without the ordinary assumptions that any science, especially psychology, expects us to make. We have earlier singled out some of these assumptions: consciousness, if it has any meaning at all, is in no way different from the world; the world of nature has ontological priority over the world of consciousness; all events are causally determined; a fact is something that can be measured with precision; the axiom of existence is the individual, who is severed absolutely from his environment. Common sense also assumes that when we touch a rock in the forest it does not touch us back with a cooling caress. We assume that the rock is not us and that we are not it. These are but sample assumptions.

Having dispensed with assumptions, we then carry out the presuppositionless description by not *being* anxiety but *perceiving* anxiety from a distance—which invokes the epoche. The reduction aspect of the epoche is of particular interest. Through that methodological device we become aware of any transcendental aspects that are inherent in the phenomenon of anxiety. We then ask ourselves how the family of experiences that ordinary language classifies as anxiety can be explained by the ontology of the intentional theory of consciousness and integrated into the metaphysics of the consciousness-world field.

We do this by using the method of free imaginative variation of examples established in Husserl's phenomenology, a concept which we must adapt to

our own purposes by connecting it with the method of science. The definition of anxiety that follows from identifying presuppositions, describing
anxiety, measuring the results against our model of being, and using
imaginative variations is a description of anxiety that is of the order of a
phenomenological-scientific hypothesis. The elements of the hypothesis are
plucked from the data of experience (phenomena), from available concepts
that float in our consciousness like the debris from previous ages (essences),
and the presumably absolute metaphysics of the phenomenological model
of being (ontology), which represents a higher-level philosophical consensual world. (The latter, of course, is subject to as much modification as
any other metaphysical position.)

The reader is requested to develop a feeling, a closeness, an openness
toward these attempted phenomenological descriptions of anxiety and then
ask himself to what extent they are or could be his own. Research in phenomenology consists in varying these hypotheses and checking them against
our experience—which itself expands and contracts as we go through life—
until we reach maximum congruence.

It is premature to define the important and well-known distinction
between existential and neurotic anxiety. This distinction will be examined
in detail in the section on diagnosis (Chapter 4). But it must be pointed out
at the beginning that this discussion is primarily about existential anxiety.
Neurotic anxiety is not a separate type but rather a dysfunctional derivative
of the basic anxiety, which is existential. Existential anxiety is healthy and is
the natural condition of the person when in a state of self-disclosure.
Existential anxiety is the condition in which the individual understands
conceptually and realizes experientially the intimate ontological structure
of being. Neurotic anxiety is diseased and is the denial of existential anxiety.
Existential anxiety leads to creativity, whereas neurotic anxiety leads to
symptom-formation. Thus neurotic anxiety becomes a function of existential anxiety: $A_n = f(A_e)$: The function is denial. The basis is existential
anxiety. This distinction is important because it reverses the conventional
trend to view all anxiety as pathological. We are then surprised that cures
do not work!

A philosophical discussion of anxiety, regardless of its theoretical interest
and importance, appears to have therapeutic side effects. Perhaps these are
like desensitization. Even a perfunctory lecture on the philosophy of anxiety
can alleviate the anxiety of some persons in the audience. To be accurate we
should say that a lecture on anxiety can change the unpleasant experience of
neurotic anxiety into the elevating condition of existential anxiety. Furthermore *desensitization* is not at all a precise phenomenological description of
experience but an all-encompassing and somewhat blurred behavioristic
word which refers to the very complex philosophical dynamics of what
happens when consciousness is fully revealed to itself. These dynamics
describe in minute detail what actually happens in the experience of anxiety.

Another reason why a philosophic discussion may be therapeutic is that it provides a positive and life-affirming rather than negative and depressing description. Philosophy introduces the thought of anxiety's normalcy, thus forcing a fundamental reconstitution of the common-sense world.

The best way to define anxiety is in a series of sequential steps.

Description

Existential anxiety is a sui generis experience. Like the concept being, but not for reason of its generality, anxiety does not lend itself to classification. To describe it is therefore difficult and mostly metaphoric. As a result of its uniqueness it occupies a pivotal position in existential philosophy: It is the phenomenon fundamental to achieving an understanding of personality and of human existence. It is the one phenomenon which does not give us conceptual analysis alone, as would be true of a logical truth, nor does it give us experience alone, as would be the case with a feeling or an emotion. Anxiety is unique in that it is a concept-feeling complex, a concept-feeling interface. And our first discovery in the careful phenomenological analysis of anxiety—that is, in our presuppositionless description of it from the distance of an epoche—is that anxiety is ineffable. It cannot be readily classified or described; it cannot be named with literalness. It is indeed unique. And we will shortly see why.

Contrary to conventional psychological theories, anxiety is not an illness, not a disease, and not a dysfunction—neither mental nor physical. Therefore, it is not something about which we should be embarrassed, or something which makes us feel inferior or inadequate. We should not worry about it or want to get rid of it. On the contrary, anxiety must be recognized as healthy, normal, and natural. It gives us strength because it is creative; it can give us joy because it is alive. It need not lead to symptoms but can be the raw material for an authentic existence.

We must examine anxiety in terms of a field-theory rather than a medical theory of the person—as these concepts have been defined in Book One. If we do, the result is that anxiety is conceptualized in terms of a growth- and knowledge-model rather than in terms of a disease-model.

Furthermore, anxiety cannot properly be called a feeling or an emotion, although these may be its accompanying characteristics. Again, the contrast between conventional pyschological and phenomenological-existential descriptions of anxiety must be recognized as radical. One can still a feeling with behavioristic desensitization techniques, ventilation in psycho-therapy, or ataraxic medication in psychiatry. But to treat anxiety in these terms is like fighting a shark by smashing the glass in the aquarium. Anxiety cannot be silenced and attempts to do so should not be made (except as a temporary expedient or as an emergency compromise when philosophical integration is not possible). To treat anxiety with a head-on collision, that is, with a pharmacological confrontation, is like expecting to understand physics by burning the textbook, or hoping to cool a heat wave by dislodging the earth from its sun and sending it spinning endlessly into dark and empty space.

The results of this philosophically proposed shift in our perception of anxiety (from being an illness to not being an illness) are that we can cope confidently and in a relaxed manner with anxiety, rather than feel obligated —as we would on the basis of the disease model—to escape or deny it. To run in anguish from anxiety is futile, since anxiety will not go away anymore than our breath will go away. To be "cured" of anxiety makes as much sense as to be "cured" of heartbeats or of metabolism. Once we have accepted anxiety as right and proper we can begin to build creatively on the experience. That new peace and relaxation removes blocks and releases the natural flow of energy that accompanies the perennial stream of the field of consciousness that we are. We therefore feel no longer obliged to assault anxiety destructively with Thorazine or divorce, with straitjackets or alcohol, or even with Librium and psychotherapy. To confront anxiety with the conviction it is the enemy drains us of our natural creative energies because we must uphold an artificial structure, a self-concept contrary to the philosophically discovered facts of human existence.

The preferred metaphor for anxiety that seems to come closest to symbolizing what is essentially its indescribable nature is that it is *cognitive.* Anxiety is a revealing, an illumination, a seeing. In fact, anxiety is the act of philosophical perception itself. To be anxious, in the pure sense of existential anxiety, is to stand on the mountaintop that reveals being to us. (The conceptual equivalent for anxiety is the phenomenological attitude or the transcendental reduction.) Anxiety is our window to the truth about being. The textbook which supposedly teaches the student to think philosophically and to *do* philosophy should not invite him into the realm of logical analyses but give him instead one simple instruction: "Permit yourself to be anxious!"

We can be a bit more precise in our description of anxiety as cognitive if we go back to our epistemological fundamentals. That anxiety is a *revealing* is substantiated by the etymologies of certain crucial words. The Sanskrit equivalent for philosophy is *darśana*, which is best translated as a seeing, a revelation, and an illumination of reality. The earliest records written down by these seers (called *rishis*, the visionary wise men among the Aryans of ancient India) are the *Vedas*, a word which, like the Latin *video*, refers to the openness and illumination to being that these scriptures reflect. Heidegger's analysis of the Greek *aletheia* is well known. He says that for Plato (in his Allegory of the Cave of Book VII in the *Republic*) truth meant unhiddenness, openness, that is, revelation—as the etymology of that Greek word suggests. Phenomenology endorses this direct openness to being as the meaning of truth. In all of these epistemological positions the intuitive and global mode of answering philosophic questions predominates. The analytic and detailed approach usually associated with science and technology and made possible by mathematics and computers does not lend itself to the examination of the phenomenon of anxiety as a first-person experience. The phenomenological method, especially through the reduction, is the effort to touch being directly, to achieve unmediated access to being.

This view of truth is to be contrasted with the more conventional definitions of truth developed in the history of philosophy, such as correspondence, coherence, and pragmatism. There truth is defined through criteria which are external to the experience of being itself. Furthermore, these theories of truth do not give final authority to the structure of immediate first-person experience, as that is revealed through presuppositionless description, because these alternative definitions of truth do not yield certainty but only guesses or empirical-inductive testing (correspondence and coherence) or probability approximations (pragmatism). The existential personality theory adds the insight that when this direct seeing of being is actually carried out, the total experience is best described by also using the word *anxiety*.

Anxiety is therefore the act of reflection itself. Anxiety is the act of looking *at* the empirical realm—the body, the emotions, society, and the world—without being the empirical realm or being *in* that realm. Anxiety reveals all the hidden nuances of the act of reflection itself, because anxiety is the reflexive experience of our ambiguities and struggles in that epoche, in addition to the referential revelations about the structure of being which it makes available.[1] Anxiety is thus the experience of bracketing—when what we bracket is of ontological significance: death rather than, let us say, grasshoppers. Also anxiety is the act of looking *at* the transcendental realm—pure consciousness. It is therefore also the experience of reduction. In the field-of-consciousness model of being, anxiety is the act of reflection which looks *both ways* (noematically to the empirical realm and noetically to the transcendental realm). To define it in empirical terms alone may be a necessity of convention but is philosophically inadequate.

Anxiety is also the experience of deconstitution and death, that is, of the world's disorganization into its primary data and of the withdrawal of consciousness from its worldly attachments and identifications. It is correct to call that unconventional and anti-consensual experience painful, but it is equally obvious that such an experience is a prerequisite for meaningful change and growth. The latter, in phenomenology, is called reconstitution and recathexis and invokes the full use of our transcendental freedom.

Thus, anxiety reveals directly and phenomenologically the truth about being, for biases and presuppositions—which are the interpretive constitutions and cathexes imposed on uncontaminated primordial data—are eliminated or at least put out of action. Anxiety, because it is the experience of deconstitution and decathexis, gives us the world free of belief-systems, world views, world designs, and other and lesser constructs. Anxiety can reveal being to us before the constitution and cathexis of the ego, soul, or self, and can thus show that perhaps even the ego is merely an accent on eternity, a derivate construct rather than an irreducible atomic core. The converse also follows, namely, that these constructs—from world designs to the reality of the ego—have a psychological function: They are defenses against anxiety; they bind anxiety. They help us manage anxiety, escape anxiety, and pretend that we can avoid it. Anxiety is the illumination that invades us when these defenses are no longer in operation.

NORMA

Norma, a college student, illustrates that anxiety means both deconstitution and its transcendental revelations, and that we have a tendency to defend ourselves against this anxiety by invoking—through magic or other ceremonies—tried and habitual constitutions. She is deeply interested in the transcendental aspects of a phenomenological philosophy and she has frequent nightmares about such things as maelstroms, tornadoes, typhoons, hurricanes, earthquakes, and other assorted disasters. We can call these "Wizard-of-Oz traumas." She routinely wakes up and feels the need to drink a glass of warm milk. Her nightmares mean deconstitution and decathexis, and with it the transcendental revelations that she secretly wishes. This dream, like most others, is wish-fulfillment. While anxious about deconstitution, she at the same time desires it. Drinking warm milk, on the other hand, is a regressive phenomenon. After the traumatic experience of deconstitution-decathexis she automatically repeats her earliest childhood experience of world-constitution and cathexis. It was then that her constitution of the consensual world began, and she hopes it will be repeated each time after a dream through the magic of her milk-drinking ceremony.

A more authentic response for Norma would be to accept the health and normalcy of her anxiety of deconstitution-decathexis and to take charge and responsibility herself for courageously reconstructing her world according to the so-called natural outlines of human existence (developed in the phenomenological model of being) and her own decisions and choices, that is, those values and life-styles which present themselves to her as *right*. Above all, however, she begins to fulfill in her dreams what she seeks while awake and in college: transcendental illumination. To carry out that program in real life is to assume personal responsibility for tolerating anxiety and its revelations.

Anxiety is thus an experience or a phenomenon belonging to the transcendental possibilities of human existence. It discloses, as does any reduction, the pure, objectless consciousness that, depending on our terminology, we are or that courses through us. Anxiety is the experience of the transcendental-phenomenological reduction explicated by the metaphor of a young child totally cathected to his mother who is suddenly cut off from her (through her death, illness, or abandonment). The child, understanding nothing but experiencing everything, is left with a pure look, an objectless consciousness, an intentional stream that says "Mommy! Mommy!" but faces only a wordless blank. That is the paradigm for the experience of pure consciousness, the metaphor we use as adults to remind us of and to clarify the transcendental nature that we also are. That vacuum is both the experience of transcendental consciousness *and* of anxiety. They are one experience.

If we think of the death of the biosphere as the paradigm for anxiety, then the image of the earth-deprived consciousness is a further metaphor for transcendental consciousness. As said before, the philosophical image of transcendental consciousness is not produced by mother-child separation early in life. The contrary is true; the loneliness of pure consciousness is a truth about being. We have developed the images of separation and abandonment in order to dramatize metaphorically these philosophical realities and to incarnate the abstract philosophic truth in the life of flesh, bones, and in our origins as children. Anxiety thus opens up the full realm of the transcendental dimension, the realm of eternal consciousness, and absolute freedom. That is the realm where the source for all meaningful and deep answers in psychotherapy and in philosophies of life are to be found.

Kierkegaard defined anxiety in this way: "So when the danger is so great that death has become one's hope, despair is the disconsolateness of not being able to die."[2] It seems that the psychological metaphors of rejection, abandonment, and separation used to describe anxiety are most effective in eliciting both experientially and conceptually their underlying philosophic meaning.

We cannot of course deny the obvious, in that from a common-sense point of view many people literally suffer from anxiety. Nor do we mean that this despair is covert joy. However, two causes account for this condition of distress. First, the anxiety neurosis or psychotic episode which brings a patient to a hospital may be neurotic anxiety. His defense against anxiety may no longer be effective in repressing the insights that his unconscious demands to disclose to him. The rhinoceros, which was a baby when we got it and lived docilely in its wooden cage, has now grown to a full-sized, ill-tempered monster which can no longer be contained by the fragile cage. It is now breaking loose.

The second cause for the upsurge of unmanageable anxiety is that the patient has no, little, or limited toleration for the truth. He thus fights to be blind. That is his anxiety neurosis. He also discovers—a point to which Thomas Szasz and R.D. Laing have been sensitive—that his friends and society around him are terrified by his visions of the ontological truth. Like the fate of visionaries of an earlier age, the social consensus is that the patient is possessed by the Devil and must be purified of his contamination by the *auto-da-fé* of burning. The "normal" condition is to have much of the philosophic truth about us permanently repressed. The more this truth can be tolerated, the more authentic is the individual. Many individuals can tolerate little and would rather die than see. Part of the problem is social bias against the phenomenological model of being. Ignorance of philosophy leads people to recoil in terror when philosophic truth becomes revealed.

To continue our description of existential anxiety we must take an excursus into the contagiousness of anxiety and how that affects the practice of the healing arts.

Notes

1. See Chapters 2 and 3, Book One, for definitions.

2. S. A. Kierkegaard, *The Sickness Unto Death,* translated by W. Lowrie (Garden City, N.Y.: Doubleday, 1955), p. 151.

Chapter 3 • PROVOCATION OF ANXIETY

Anxiety Is Contagious

Anxiety is highly contagious. It is contagious in that all insight is "catching" and all knowledge is "communicable"—regardless of whether it is existential or neurotic. Existential anxiety is contagious because insight is communicable—even without declarative, abstract, and discursive language. Neurotic anxiety—because it cripples existential anxiety and distorts the vision of existential anxiety—is also contagious and for the same reason. Its authentic residue is transmitted in human interactions. In other words, a person with neurotic anxiety communicates nonverbally and from his unconscious to the unconscious of others the bitter struggle of repression and crippling against the existential anxiety raging within him. Just as the heart of an atomic explosion starts fires all around it and in distant places, so does the neurotic anxiety of one human being remind those around him of their own unresolved struggles. If a highly anxious person enters a room or participates in a discussion, the anxiety levels of the others are raised to a high pitch even though that person may not manifest any obvious signs of anxiety. That is often the reaction a layman gets from meeting a schizophrenic. He is upset by the meeting but does not understand why. As a result, he is likely to put it out of his mind. But what he has just experienced is the contagiousness of anxiety.

Medical and Therapeutic Provocation of Anxiety

The single most difficult problem in the therapeutic management of anxiety is the fact that anxiety in the patient arouses anxiety in physicians, therapists, or other healers. Because of the importance of this condition, it must be discussed in some detail. Specifically, the issues are two: First, the patient's anxiety arouses anxiety in the health practitioner. Second, the healer's independent anxiety provokes anxiety in the patient. Both conditions interfere with healing. The medical and therapeutic problem of anxiety does not gravitate exclusively around the question of how to treat the anxious patient. It also concerns itself with how to treat the anxious therapist who is treating an anxious patient. Moreover, and all too often, the therapist provokes anxiety in his patient. We then frequently have a situation in which the anxiety originates in the healer and then through its contagiousness reappears in the patient, where it is then treated (or mistreated) as part of the latter's symptomatology.

What goes on when a healer's anxiety (physician, nurse, psychologist) is transferred to the patient? This is a strictly neurotic and inauthentic situation. It does not occur when the healer experiences his own authentic, that is, existential anxiety, but when it has been distorted into neurotic or pathological anxiety, and when the healer uses his patient to work out his own anxiety.

What kind of person is this anxiety-provoking healer? The initial anxiety in the healer may be based on his own personal situation or lack of philosophical self-disclosure, his lack of phenomenological self-consciousness. The healer who exudes provoking waves of anxiety because he has not resolved his neurotic anxiety into its existential or ontological underpinnings, who has not worked through his own inauthenticity, should not be in a healing position. Being a competent surgeon, for example, is not in itself enough to make the physician an authentic healer. Even though the surgeon performs his healing function while his patient is supine and unconscious, it is the personal contact both before and after surgery that provides the frame of mind which—as many experts on holistic and psychosomatic medicine now maintain—will help insure a speedy recovery, not to mention the purely moral issues involved.

A second common reason for the existence of inauthentic anxiety in the healer is based on a dual fear: He feels incompetent; he feels he cannot handle the specific problem with which he is confronted, a situation typical mostly in young physicians and inexperienced therapists. And the healer may also feel that he cannot meet the excessive expectations of his patient or client. The dying patient expects to be saved; the surgical patient wants a painless operation; the alcoholic thinks his therapist will cure him of his habit; the client with a bad marriage assumes that his counselor will transform years of bitterness into a future of uninterrupted bliss. These expectations are often categorical demands. The healer who internalizes these unwarranted expectations either has no inner-directed sense for his own self-image and thus depends entirely for what he thinks he is on how others perceive him, or he has the need to think of himself as a kind of god. He is therefore flattered when his patients recognize him as such, but he is also dismayed when he discovers what a trap that narcissistic and egomaniacal need turns out to be. This type of healer is too immature to be fully effective.

A third form of anxiety in the healer, an anxiety which is contagious through provocation, results in the subtle expression of sadistic impulses. All healers can be tempted to abuse their power. Women sometimes complain of this, rightly or wrongly, in their treatment by male gynecologists. The healer's unconscious has residual and unanalyzed primitive sexual and aggressive impulses. The patient's unconscious responds to the healer's unconscious sexual aggression. When the sadistic impulses are not blatant, then they become at most an invasion of privacy.

Certain inherent and unavoidable aspects of medicine and therapy are of a provoking character and thus produce anxiety in the patient or client. Medicine and therapy are unavoidably invasions of the privacy and violations of the integrity of the patient. He (or she) loses control over the territory—his body, his feelings, and his world view—that is legitimately his and his alone. This problem can be greatly ameliorated by encouraging the patient to *participate* in his own therapeutic procedures. (More on this in Book Three.)

Anxiety provoked in this fashion can be legitimate or illegitimate. It is legitimate, and producing it is thus an authentic act, when the assaults on the body are both necessary and unavoidable *and* when the practitioner uses every known device to avoid provoking anxiety in the patient. *Not* using all safeguards *is* a provocation. (A smallpox innoculation for a trip abroad is one example.) The anxiety provocation is illegitimate if it is unnecessary. We are not here talking about obviously gratuitous medical procedures—these are illegal. We are talking about the much subtler abuse of a patient's privacy and disregard of his or her sensitivities when more thought and increased competence could avoid unethical situations. Problems of this kind often occur with particularly sensitive operations, such as hysterectomies, mastectomies, and even vasectomies.

This discussion does not intend to suggest that all complaints against physicians are valid. On the contrary, often the complaint of induced or provoked anxiety may be no more than an inverted wish or a covert desire by the patient to be just so violated. We could risk going even beyond that: Let us assume that a patient feels violated and has in fact been violated (on some objective criterion we need not go into). It is still useful to *blame* the patient by accusing him or her of expressing a secret wish. The result of this interpretation may well be that the patient is shocked into taking full responsibility for what happens to him—even in a hospital. If he does not like it, he will then do something about it.

Following are a few suggestions on the management of the provocation of anxiety in a medical and psychotherapeutic setting.

MANAGEMENT

Health practitioners must be healthy themselves. Specifically, those who hope to facilitate the development of authenticity in others must also be authentic. It is strongly advisable that training for therapy include significant therapy for the trainee himself. And this convicion holds as much for those trained in psychoanalysis as it does for the practitioners of humanistic psychology, of clinical philosophy, or of personalized education in philosophy. The rule which mandates the health of the healer does not imply that a practitioner must not be neurotic. In fact, a healer with problems is often more sympathetic and helpful than one with none. It does mean that an authentic healer must *possess the permanent possibility for establishing and maintaining distance,* an epoche, from his own problems and those of his patient. If the healer has problems he must be able to recognize them, put them at a distance and out of action. In short, the authentic therapist may be neurotic but must place his neurosis in an epoche. And he can never fail in this task and still be effective as a therapist.

In addition, an authentic therapist permanently makes the binding decision—a commitment that has its origin within the region of consciousness exposed by the transcendental-phenomenological reduction—to be devoted solely to the interest of his patient, to care only for his patient's welfare, and never to use him for his own neurotic purposes. The transcendental region exposes several characteristics of consciousness that must be invoked by the authentic therapist, regardless of his own psychological health: his freedom, his rationality, his objectivity, and his capacity for maintaining distance, that is, for not getting involved with the patient in the sense of the natural attitude. He must be capable of maintaining, at all times, the phenomenological attitude. Simply, this means the therapist must be ethical (make a free commitment for the welfare of his patient) and rational (maintain the epoche). The authentic therapist makes the decision, which is to be permanent, that all dealings with his patient have their origin in the transcendental realm of reason and not in the empirical realm of feelings, in the transcendental realm of freedom and control and not in the empirical realm of deterministic subservience to impulses. This rule is part of the general principle that all therapeutic relationships are to be transcendental or transpersonal.

Another rule for the management of anxiety in the healer is honesty about his feelings and his shortcomings. The honesty in question is not only with himself (which means he can perform an epoche on *all* aspects of his being-in-the-world) but with his patient (which is an act of courage and thus a free commitment to the patient's reality and integrity). The therapist will have established a commendable relationship with his patient, one with great healing potential, if he can share with the patient his own anxieties about their relationship, his own inadequacies in his treatment of the patient. An honest articulation of this issue of anxiety in the therapist can be the hallmark of an existential therapeutic encounter.

True, the patient will find it more difficult to project his unconscious on that kind of an honest therapist. But he will early in the treatment be exposed to the dual notions of personal responsibility and human finitude. That exposure will make up for whatever difficulty there may be in establishing the projection typical of the transference. Also, healing by authoritative suggestion—which many patients demand tacitly, is ruled out by the type of existential honesty here recommended.

Furthermore, problems with the provocation of anxiety can be managed if the therapist is a truly caring, concerned, understanding, and compassionate person. This rule—if we can call it such—follows from the three earlier considerations, since they are all meant to direct the healer toward his own authenticity.

One rule remains. A patient should not be kept in ignorance of his treatment. All treatment, from major surgery to minor marriage counseling, should involve both *education* and *participation*. The client should be told what he wants to know (and his curiosity should be encouraged) about the theory with which he is being treated and the research supporting it. Also, he should be encouraged to participate in his medical and therapeutic procedures—examine himself, give himself injections, take his own blood pressure, and meditate through fantasies on surgical details should these be part of his healing program. Enlisting the patient in his treatment through education and participation applies to all aspects of the healing process: *examination*, *diagnosis*, *prognosis*, and *treatment*. We are touching here on an undeveloped branch of the healing arts. We can be confident that building in this area can do much to improve health care. Book Three deals with this issue.

Chapter 4 • *DIAGNOSIS AND VALUE OF ANXIETY*

The definition of anxiety in Part One consists of three independent discussions: description, diagnosis, and value. Having now completed the description of existential anxiety, we now move on to its diagnosis and value.

Existential Versus Neurotic Anxiety

Existential anxiety, also called ontological or authentic anxiety, is the unique phenomenon of human experience that reveals our transcendental truth. As such, it is a healthy, normal, and desirable phenomenon, something to be cultivated and cherished, to be chosen voluntarily, and a condition that leads to strength, peace, and creativity. Existential anxiety is also called ontological because it reveals the structure of being (ontology). It reveals the reality of consciousness, our nature as a field, the abyss and the search for ground residing in our depth, the vastness and the anguish of our freedom, and all of those characteristics of our essence needed to achieve true health.

Yet it turns out that human beings, because of their tendency to conceptualize their experience in terms of objects alone rather than in terms of a subject-object field (a distinction called the ghost-in-a-machine theory of man as opposed to the field-of-consciousness theory of man), fear their own nature. They deny the truth about themselves, and they deny their source of insight. They try to kill the anxiety that is in reality the messenger of the gods. When anxiety is denied our nature is denied. And that denial leads to the condition of inauthenticity called, variously, mental illness, neurosis, maladjustment, maladaptation, melancholia, and so forth. But above all, the denial of existential anxiety leads to a lack of meaning in life, to an existence without a task, to a condition of despair—because we *must* live yet *cannot* live. Furthermore, the denial of existential anxiety produces symptoms. We can now understand why this denial is properly called neurotic, inauthentic, or pathological anxiety.

Neurotic anxiety, beyond being denial through ignorance, is also the fear of anxiety. It is second-order anxiety, that is, anxiety about anxiety. When we are anxious, we experience the truth. But when we are anxious about being anxious, we are sick and needlessly limit our potential for enjoying life—and we do not experience the truth.

The mechanisms by which we deny existential anxiety are endless and include but are not limited to those traditionally isolated in clinical psychology: repression, projection, and displacement, as well as rationalization, reaction-formation, dissociation, compulsion, obsession, compensation, sublimation, and on and on. What is denied by all of these strategies, directly or symbolically, is existential anxiety, ontology, transcendental consciousness, the truth about being. This denial is experienced as an unhappy life, or worse.

The specific causes for the denial of existential anxiety are various and we can list but a few. Philosophic ignorance or general metaphysical misinformation is the generic cause for the denial of existential anxiety; specifically, materialistic and objectivist metaphysics are prime cultural culprits. Fear and the avoidance of pain, as if these were intrinsic evils rather than conditions to be evaluated in perspective, are also causes for denial. These causes point out that the person who denies his existential anxiety is still immature and seriously underdeveloped in view of the vast potential for self-understanding of which a human being is capable.

As a result, the price we pay for the denial of existential anxiety is severe. The dominant consequence is a stricture on life. Rather than fulfilling his potential, he who denies his existential anxiety seriously limits the realization of his range of possibilities. The conventional name for imposing these strictures on life is the psychoneuroses. These must be defined as acts which *deliberately* limit life for the sake of protecting it from anxiety. "Sacrifice living but at least be protected from seeing anxiety" is the operative rule. The word *deliberately* is here used with emphasis. A person can be held responsible for limiting himself. His reason may be good and logical, given his environment, but the reasons for not limiting himself are even better. Holding the individual responsible enables him to discover his free will, which is a transcendental phenomenon, and puts him in touch with the only device known that can help him—the power of his freedom.

Another consequence of this denial is the formation of symptoms, the most obvious being somatic.[1] But there are other conditions properly called symptoms that result from this denial. Sexual dysfunctions are a good illustration, as are *intimacy* dysfunctions (the difficulties many people have in allowing for intimacy in relationships). Margaret is always tired. She laughs compulsively to protect herself from facing sad feelings and insights. Her fear is like a phobia. She wants unlimited love: she wants to both love and be loved. Yet she stops herself and as a result expends all her energies in repressing her insatiable need for intimacy. She cannot take a mature leadership role in establishing love relationships. She cannot help men handle her love. She cannot assert herself by demanding that her love be expressed. That intimacy dysfunction results from denying her existential anxiety, because that anxiety could make her into an authentic self-affirming individual and give her the strength to demand the love she wants.

There are also behavior dysfunctions, which include difficulties with nonintimate human relationships and, finally, spiritual dysfunctions, which refer to the impoverishment of the life of consciousness, to the loss of meanings occasioned by an almost animalistic lack of spiritual values.

In denying our anxiety we also pay the price of self-betrayal. At the core of many a person is the dismal fear or recognition that he has betrayed himself by not fulfilling his possibilities. That is the underlying sense of worthlessness and self-contempt that is the root of many an inauthentic existence. And no amount of rationalization can convince such a person that there are excuses or exonerating circumstances for his self-betrayal. Conscience is merciless and indomitable. A life of neurotic anxiety is thus an existence of self-deception. Freedom is used not to grow and be strong, not for joy and love, but only to disguise itself. When man uses his freedom to hide his freedom from himself, he is expending all his precious life-force, libido, and the temporal stream of consciousness that runs through him on the single goal of self-deception. The quintessential price that emerges from denying existential anxiety and thereby producing neurotic anxiety is a living death and a life of intolerable self-immolation.

Toleration for Anxiety

The health of a person can be measured by the extent of his toleration for anxiety. His authenticity is a function of how much and how well he integrates the negative aspects of life into his existence. Toleration for anxiety measures one's capacity to cope.

The authentic person is not unanxious, but he has enormous capacity for being comfortable with anxiety. He has well-toned psychic muscles. The experience of tolerating anxiety is difficult to describe. It is similar to that of the skydiver who, upon reaching certain speed, ceases to accelerate downward. Still not opening his parachute, he feels as if he were sleeping on a cloud. He leaps into the abyss and discovers that the abyss supports him. Anxiety is tolerated when the individual abandons himself to it and gains strength and stature, reality and authority. It is like dreams of falling. At first we try to arrest the fall; and that feels like a cramp. Then we relax and abandon ourselves to the fall. At that moment we achieve ego-strength through the toleration for anxiety.

How does one acquire toleration for anxiety? Can it be cultivated? In the final analysis, toleration is the result of an archetypal choice. Toleration for anxiety, and thus a self-actualizing life-style and an authentic existence, is a condition that can be brought about fully through our own efforts.

Earl is a man with four children. He lost two sons—to him an absolutely irrecoverable tragedy. His wife *chose* (in existential terms) not to cope and had a total breakdown, becoming as dependent on his most meticulous care as a tropical plant would be in Alaska. Not only did he have to cope with his own feelings about this disaster, but he had to protect and provide a home for his remaining children. Suicide was not an option for him primarily because his remaining children had an ethical claim on his continued and sane existence. His situation was terrible; there can be no question about that. But whether he would open himself up to the enormity of anxiety and allow it to engulf him, to permit it to swallow him like a whale, or whether he would deny it, close his eyes, run away, blame others or suffer a pyschotic episode—these were his free decisions. The decision is difficult only because the alternatives are alike and because our man would give anything not to be confronted with these two disagreeable options. Other than that, however, he is completely free and his freedom is easy to carry out. For him, tolerating anxiety is no more and no less than a simple decision.

This decision is another manifestation of the archetypal decision to be an ego. The statement "I cannot make the archetypal decision to tolerate anxiety" is an incomplete analysis. Only the object of the total intentional stream is recorded. The subjective or transcendental stream leading to it requires the following complete statement: "I, as a transcendental freedom, choose not to make the archetypal decision to tolerate anxiety." We have difficulty with the second statement only because we somehow feel it is inherently wrong or false. However, at the archetypal level, right and wrong have not yet been established (that is, constituted); therefore, to choose toleration is really no better than not to choose it.

The Value of Anxiety

We have up to now covered principally the negative aspects of anxiety. But it is only neurotic anxiety that is really negative. Existential anxiety, even though mistakenly feared, is a very positive experience. It is important to end this definition of existential anxiety by emphasizing anxiety's positive values.

What, exactly, does a person feel in a fully blossoming state of existential anxiety? First and foremost, anxiety is the concrete experience of living. To be anxious is to feel alive. Consider these questions: How does it actually feel to be alive? What is and how can we describe this sense of existing, this fact of being? The answer is anxiety. Anxiety is the conflict of polarities, the opposition between the natural and the phenomenological attitudes. It is the oscillating stress which makes us aware of the fact that we exist, the tension between contradictions and thus the vibrancy of life itself. *To be* and *to be anxious* are therefore synonyms. The excitement of being a body, of being sensuous, of being finite are the richly concrete experiences described by the phenomenon of existential anxiety. Anxiety is an openness to being; it is a receptivity to reality; it is being properly fitted to absorb existence.

Anxiety forms part of a continuum which we can call excitement, excitation, or the throb of life. One extreme of that unitary continuum we call anxiety and the other, joy. The similarities are more important than the differences:

However, we sometimes cut off anxiety from the continuum and think it to be bad and different:

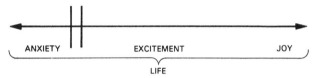

When we do that, we *deny* the truth about anxiety. Anxiety as part of the continuum is existential anxiety. In an inauthentic life that anxiety is denied. And cutting it off is what we call neurotic anxiety. Merely understanding this point can put your anxiety in perspective. Experiencing and then applying or integrating it is even more meaningful.

An individual spins his past like a cobweb. He sees what his empty consciousness has created by looking at his past. But he no longer *is* that past— he only *was* it. He is now and always a present-creating-its-past. Thus, the experiences of ambition and accomplishment are the values inherent in the reality that is anxiety, since they are the process of creating the past. Consequently, anxiety informs us of the meaning of life because anxiety is that meaning. To be anxious is the meaning. Anxiety discloses our substantiality to us. It tells us how to go about creating our past. And to create ourselves in the future into a concrete past is what we mean by the content of the meaning of life.

Second, anxiety is the motivation to meaning. A life without anxiety is static like a rock. Anxiety introduces disequilibrium; it creates an imbalance which develops a goal of resoluteness. The *search* for meaning is brought about through the phenomenon of anxiety.

A third value of anxiety is that it arouses us to the significance of love and compassion; it alerts us to the incontrovertible need for care and concern. Anxiety proves to us the value of tenderness. The emptiness of anxiety, its sense of isolation, separation, and abandonment, urgently points to the axiomatic need for closeness, oneness, and intimacy. What is there to share if it is not one's anxiety?

Fourth, anxiety is also the experience of time, and with it, of futurity and hope. Anxiety discloses our structure as intentional beings; it therefore purifies for us the experience of time that we are. And being time, we are also that toward which time moves, which is the future. And in disclosing to us our futurization, anxiety is the experience of hope.

Finally, anxiety is the experience of creativity. All creative acts—artistic, loving, scholarly, scientific, political, social, and so forth—are born of anxiety and made possible through anxiety. All great creative people have translated the experience of anxiety into the act and product of creation. Time and creativity together fashion growth. Anxiety is thus essential to growth. In fact, the experience of anxiety *is* the experience of growth.

Those are the experiences of a person who is fully open to existential anxiety.

NOTE

1. The logical connection between the denial of existential anxiety through the power of our transcendental freedom and physiological symptoms can be explained only in terms of a field-theory of the person. The Cartesian mind-body dualism, which is an essential albeit often suppressed element in the medical model of the person, cannot explain how psychosomatic symptoms are possible, much less how they are to be treated. It is likely that to the extent that psychiatry has been successful in treating bodily illnesses psychologically it has tacitly adopted the phenomenological model of being—without really understanding its philosophic base and justification.

Part II • REVELATIONS OF ANXIETY AS EXISTENTIAL ANXIETY

Chapter 5 • BIRTH

In the previous definition of anxiety, the basic contention was that anxiety reveals the structure of being. We now embark on a detailed exposition of precisely how and what anxiety reveals, what happens when these revelations are suppressed, as well as a detailed presentation of strategies for coping with these revelations about the structure of being. The presentation of these revelations has been formalized into seven types of existential anxieties, each revealing a unique characteristic of being or of being human: *birth, evil, nihilism-ground* (that is, the question of grounding), *freedom, death, individuality,* and *guilt.*[1] The table in Appendix D summarizes the results of these phenomenological researches.

To make the reading of the revelations of anxiety personally meaningful it is helpful to do an exercise. Focus on one particular and troublesome anxiety in your life at present. Spell it out as specifically as you can. As you read each revelation of anxiety, ask yourself to what extent that revelation is the specific secret meaning which is trying to reveal itself in your feeling of anxiety.

Birth

The first type of existential anxiety is the anxiety of birth or the anxiety of being born. This anxiety reveals the fact that to exist authentically is to permit oneself—and even beyond that, encourage oneself—to be born or reborn. The presence of anxiety does not mean that we are sick but that something within us is trying to be born. The experience of anxiety is (or can be) the realization that an old self is dying and a new self is trying to appear. To grow is to experience anxiety. There can be no growth without it.

Conversely, the presence of anxiety may well be the experience of growth itself. To interfere, hinder, or impede this growth is the equivalent of shoving the baby back into the womb, when what is needed is to tolerate the pain so as to facilitate the wonderful event. The wise man is glad for his anxiety and recognizes it as his friend. He encourages the anxiety and with it facilitates the birth of his own meaning, task, fulfillment, and integrity. The fool fears his anxiety and squelches it with repression or drugs; he suffers the loss of meaning as a result. It may not be an exaggeration to say that salvation was offered him and he was too ignorant to take advantage of the opportunity.

If we do not feel anxious it may be appropriate to encourage it for the sake of rebirth. For therapy to be effective and truly reconstructive or re-constitutive it must seek out the maximum amount of tolerable anxiety. Changes which occur in intensive therapy do so by undermining the deepest suppressed assumptions—a condition of grave anxiety. Such anxiety must be encouraged for rebirth to take place. We can mobilize the anxiety of birth, and thus facilitate growth, by giving the client, first of all, a "shock-ing" diagnosis. However, the therapist must be an artist. The *shock* must be loving and it must be perceived as such. It must also be based on an accurate assessment of the client's project or his being-in-the-world. The shock must be strong enough to undermine the old and nonworking world design of the client—in other words, powerful enough to establish instant deconstitution and decathexis—but not so violent as to arouse more anxiety than the client is prepared to cope with and thus lead to a psychotic episode. It is here where one needs artistry and a genuinely supportive environment in addition to appropriate knowledge in the behavioral sciences and in philo-sophy. It is this shocking and anxiety-producing diagnosis, this quick grasp of the new possibilities of one's existence, that—in a philosophically oriented therapy—makes the arousal of the anxiety of birth worthwhile.

One client discovers how grossly he has neglected his freedom, how he has neglected taking charge of his life. His whole existence reflects his free-dom's desuetude. Through the anxiety of birth he can see in one flash how his life can be reorganized in its very foundations. Another client discovers that throughout his life he has allowed external circumstances, publicly broadcast values, and accidental relationships to determine what is to be of meaning in his existence. He suddenly is helped to realize the philosophic fact that he does have an inner foundation, an internal resource, and that this ground is of far more vast proportions than whatever his social en-vironment could possibly offer. He also realizes that the world in general and history—if not his petty immediate social world—will support and re-spond to his inner voices and values. A third client discovers how he has never learned to affirm himself effectively, to assert himself irrevocably. His old self-concept is life-denying. The anxiety of birth is the experience of a new possibility: life affirmation. It is also the actual experience of this tran-sition. He is helped to discover the philosophic fact that he can choose, literally, to be reborn to be someone else: unmistakable and consistent self-affirmation is as close to him as his prebirth decision of self-denial.

In the lives of all these clients there may be a childhood origin or explana-tion for the old self-concept. It probably was logical, rational, and reasonable for the child to respond to his early situation as he in fact did: he relinquished his freedom, he developed an other-directed identity, and he became self-effacing. In short, he tried his best to adapt to his childhood world by approximating as close as possible the state of nonexistence. A five-year-old child overhears his mother: "Junior has grown in the last year. Thank God! We feared he'd never be of decent size!" One can imagine how the mother blames her son for being short. She expects him to solve her own feelings of inferiority. The five-year-old is expected to take on his mother's burdens. He must take responsibility for being too short to satisfy his mother—at five years of age! The child will internalize that perception of him, accept it as his own, and go through life thinking of himself as deservedly crippled. A father, complaining about the cost of an item while shopping for his little daughter, tells the salesperson—in "jest," of course—"She isn't worth even two dollars!" It is logical for these children to learn to experience themselves as ungrounded or as not existing. In mobilizing the anxiety of birth, the client transforms himself or herself from nonexistence to existence.

All these persons, when grown, will need to learn that their self-image is philosophically without foundation and perform an act of massive reconstitution (specifically, first deconstitute and decathect and then reconstitute and recathect). To do that is to experience the anxiety of birth. To the extent that this process occurs, the client experiences existential anxiety; but to the degree that the client fears he cannot handle this existential anxiety and therefore chooses to deny, fight, or repress it, he is experiencing neurotic anxiety. Existential anxiety leads to health; neurotic anxiety produces symptoms.

In an authentic existence we are, as in the myth of reincarnation, reborn again and again. Birth therefore also means rebirth. It also means the forward movement of life, the experience of time, growth, and with it the embrace of hope. Birth comes after death just as a beginning comes after an ending. The process of birth involves the risk of novelty and the risk of death. Rebirth is like the second discovery of fire in Teilhard de Chardin's beautiful words, "Someday, after mastering the winds, the waves, the tides and gravity, we shall harness for God the energies of love, and then, for the second time in the history of the world, man will discover fire."

But birth can only be accomplished through anxiety. That is true of both biological *and* philosophical birth. Rollo May points that out in his book *Existence*, when he calls attention to the interesting etymology of the word *anxiety*. The German *Angst* (Danish, *ængstel*), and the English *anguish*, derive from the Latin *angustus*, which means narrow and difficult. And that word comes in turn from the Latin *angere*, which means to press together. The word anxiety thus seems to give us a direct etymological confirmation of the fact that in the primordial or originary dawn of mankind's consciousness, biological birth and philosophical anxiety were recognized as connected. For our purposes we must remember that birth, as the experience of growth, transition, change, transformation, and creativity—including what Rogers means by his apt phrase "becoming what one is"—is an anxiety-producing experience. Without birth there is no authentic existence; without anxiety, or at least the toleration for anxiety, there can be no authentic existence.

In the phenomenon of birth, the pain (or anxiety) is in the ending that precedes every beginning, the ending of the familiar that also makes room for a beginning. Snow White and Rose Red are good examples of one's need to die (an anxiety situation) before one can live. Snow White dies by the poisoned apple (anxiety) before she is kissed by her prince and brought back to life and fulfillment (birth); Rose Red sleeps for a hundred years (death, anxiety) before she is rescued by her prince (birth) for a life of meaning.

All fundamental changes in life (as well as in therapy) follow this pattern. The increasing presence of anxiety is not a sign of regression or failure but a sign of openness and hope. It is a sign that an old world is dying to allow a new one to be born. A simple but subtle example can serve as illustration.

Lilly played the oboe. Her life was devoted to the instrument. She practiced nine hours each day. After some time of intensive counseling, she began to develop anxiety and some unexpected changes appeared in her life. She observed that these changes were happening in her behavior, but she did not feel that she was making them happen through deliberate choice. The changes were these: increased anxiety, switching oboe teachers, rescheduling practice habits (by edict of the new teacher) from nine to two hours daily, and accepting students herself. None of these changes was planned. They gradually and unexpectedly emerged in her life. Changing teachers, for example, started with a dislike she developed for her first teacher, and a decline in her respect for him as a teacher. She stopped the lessons having no other conscious plans and accidentally met the person who was then to become her next teacher.

The psychological meaning of these changes was profound. Her practicing before had been a panic reaction to her lack of self-confidence as a musician. Her incessant toil anesthetized her against feelings of failure. Her new teacher severely reduced her practice schedule, which made musical sense due to the strain on the lips and the limitations of a quality attention span. Less practice time meant faith rather than panic as her mode of being-in-the-world. She filled the empty time (which had initially produced anxiety and panic) not with self-deceiving busy-work (which could include even musicology courses at a university or repetitious practicing) but with teaching.

Teaching and learning are interchangeable activities. Alan Watts once said, "I don't know much about death. I think I'll write a book about it!" An old Hassidic saying is "The teacher learns five times as much as the student."

Sometimes a therapist benefits emotionally more from a therapeutic intervention than does the patient. For Lilly teaching meant reflecting (epoche) on playing in addition to just playing. It was at that time that she started taping her playing so as to be able to criticize herself. She had not noticed the connection between taping and teaching. Both are experiences of reflection, reduction, distancing, and disidentification.

Teaching also meant contact with others and self-exposure. Those were expressions of faith in the object-pole of her existence. To *be* does not only mean to be in control and to constitute. To be can also mean to let be and deconstitute. That was for her the fundamental experience of birth. *Her big change was the discovery of faith in nature,* including her nature. She had made a quantum jump of growth. She had broken the barrier which had stopped her from becoming a significant musician. All of that growth occurred above a persistent organ tone of anxiety. The task of her self-therapy was *not to interfere* with this growth process. Only toleration for the anxiety of birth and the knowledge that existential anxiety is healthy can make possible her transformation from a mechanical practice-machine to a genuine musician.

The following symbol represents the death-leads-to-birth, ending-means-beginning or anxiety-reveals-birth syndrome:

This symbol aptly reflects that to be born—to be renewed—makes sense only if there is some kind of death or ending connected with it. The total situation is good, normal, and healthy, but is also anxiety-producing because of the negative, downward, and regressive turn the lines take. In fact, the loop—which is the essence of birth—is experienced as anxiety. Anything that tends to allay anxiety also flattens the loop. And that, as would be true of any wheel, stops its progress. The initial curve moves down, representing a negative, depressive, and unsatisfactory life-style or self-concept. The final curve points forward and upward—the traditional symbols for self-transcending expansiveness in space and futurization in time. The loop, which is the anxiety zone, is the needed change of direction. The diagram can be a helpful phenomenological description of the anxiety of being born into a new life-style, a new world design, or a new personality.

We can state this situation formally as follows. If the existential anxiety of birth is denied through any of the many defense mechanisms, then we reach a state of pathology or neurotic anxiety which is characterized primarily as being uncreative. Life is then experienced as dry and pointless and joy is relegated to the escape from meaning in busy-work, job, hobbies, fights, resentments, and the neglect of body, mind, and relationships. However, if we accept the existential anxiety of birth as revealing an important structure of human existence, if we welcome it as a messenger of salvation and hope, then our life will have taken a fundamental turn from jejune death to joyous birth.

The obvious therapeutic strategy for coping with the anxiety of birth is risk. The existential anxiety of birth is the anatomy of the experience of risking. To learn to risk, to use risk judiciously, and to press risking just beyond the comfort point are birth-giving acts. The "treatment" of the "pathology" which results from risk-denial (the neurotic anxiety of birth) is to be prepared to take risks. If systematic risking becomes a way of life, then life becomes a perpetual birth. Both the prominence and the tragedies of the Kennedy family resulted from systematic risking as a life-style. Each person has to decide for himself whether or not that family risked excessively.

Each of the seven revelations of anxiety has political implications as well as psychological ones. The anxiety of birth describes well the agony of our age. We are a dying age, but *ipso facto* also a birth-giving age. The convulsions of the present age are, it is true, the last gasps of a dying age, a dying image of the person, a dying value-system, and of a dying world view. But they are also the labor pains of birth. This anguished hope assigns to us a three-fold task: We must understand the age that tries to be born; we must not interfere with that birth by pushing the fetus back into the womb; and we must facilitate the birth, help it to be what it is striving to be. In summary, we must understand and facilitate the transition of our age from one of technology to one of inner-space exploration. We must, together, invent the new symbols and meanings for the age that wishes to be born. We must allow ourselves to be the prophets through which our culture invents these symbols—such as the birth-sign above. This is not a time to lose faith in the future of mankind; nor is it a time to lose our nerve. The knowledge that we are in a historical anxiety-of-birth cycle can give us as a society hope and meaning for the future.

Note

1. What is the difference between a person and being? At the level of presuppositionless philosophy, the existence of this distinction cannot be assumed. In other words, does anxiety reveal the structure of human existence or the structure of being in general? The answer is both. Whether the individual or the universality is the unit of explanation depends on the processes of constitution which occur along the I-U axis. The revelations of anxiety occur at a more primitive level.

Chapter 6 • COPING WITH THE ANXIETY OF BIRTH

General Characteristics of Coping With Anxiety

We must concern ourselves now with therapy or coping strategies. For the existential anxiety of birth these gravitate about the general phenomena of learning how to risk. Contending with the anxiety of birth means coping with the existential anxiety of affirmatively welcoming birth *and* coping with the neurotic anxiety of denying birth. Coping with anxiety philosophically involves both an avoidance-reaction and an approach-reaction. The general rule with neurotic anxiety is to recognize it as ignorance and suppression. We counter it with philosophical understanding and deliberate provocation. *Understanding* means we know anxiety is healthy and *provoking* means we neutralize the suppression with a deliberate attack. The general rule with existential anxiety is to hear its message and then live it.

Relationships

An absolutely basic principle of existential therapy, clinical philosophy, or any personalized education in philosophy is that *all healing occurs in relationships.* Although absolutes are always dangerous, it is safe to say that pure self-help is rare and what heals is the encounter established between two or more persons. There are reasons for this. Authenticity often requires that we replace the suppressed premises by which we live. Self-help, more often than not, is based on the very premises that cause our inauthenticity. The client needs an encounter with another subjectivity —either as model or as challenger—to bore into those root premises. As model, the therapist confirms that the new premises work, and as challenger he demonstrates the need for the eradication of the old ones.

Successful therapy seems to depend more heavily on the quality of the client-therapist encounter than it does on theories of mental illness and the therapist's didacticism. The details of this healing encounter are highly specific. It has characteristics which can rigorously be defined. And the reason encounter works in healing can be explained in terms of the phenomenological model of being.

We could even argue that a counseling hour is successful in proportion to the amount of being-with, meeting, encounter, contact, sense of oneness, continuity between client and therapist, and intersubjectivity that have been established. Perhaps we can even detect, measure, and time the moments of authentic encounter, so that we have as it were an efficiency-index for the therapeutic hour. It is the time spent in this transcendental healing atmosphere—rather than in the specifics of a theory of the person that may have been transmitted or in the impersonal application of technique derived from the behavioral sciences and used mechanically—which is the actual healing process or coping strategy for anxiety.

Anxiety reveals the cosmically significant consciousness which I am and which connects me intersubjectively with others. To be *healed* means also to acquire the confidence that this anxiety can be tolerated. These phenomena occur in an expanded consciousness, the most available form of which is the intersubjective consciousness. That is why all healing occurs in relationships. That is the therapeutic meaning of encounter or being-with. In other words, when we discuss the insight that all healing of anxiety occurs in relationships, we must recognize that interpretation, teaching, and understanding do not heal as well as does the actual relationship of client and patient, the actual experience of being-with.

To say encounter and intersubjectivity heal regardless of interpretation— so that it is the client-patient relationship and neither the teaching of a world view nor the intellectual underpinnings that establishes the framework of treatment which produces health—appears to contradict the emphases in these discussions on the didactic. Assumed throughout has been that understanding the phenomenological model of being and the existential personality theory is healing. The following distinction can bring back consistency.

The point was made in Book One that this theory and model of being must be understood in the spirit of natural-law philosophies. Contrary to the views which are popularly associated with Sartre, man does have a nature. However, there are two levels of natures or essences—transcendental and empirical. Traditional natural-law metaphysics—which may have either a theological or biological bias—tend to be narrow: "Contraception is unnatural" or "celibacy is unnatural" respectively. Since these natural-law theories legislate what is proper and authentic in the physiological, social, psychological, or worldly realm, we must call them empirical. Those are to be rejected. The existential personality theory has transcended them, as one must in this relativistic and pluralistic age. The phenomenological theory of natural law is strictly transcendental. The absolutes in human essence and health are found in descriptions of the transcendental realm. These absolutes, however, are highly general. They are overall guidelines, policies, and directions which leave the day-to-day regulations to each individual person.

One of these transcendental categories is the phenomenon of intersubjectivity. As was discussed in Book One, this is one further step back in the direction of understanding and experiencing the transcendental dimension. And it is in that region that reside both the *freedom* for reconstitution and recathexis needed for change in depth psychotherapy and the sense of *eternity* and indestructibility which provide the ground for self-confidence and the courage needed to act. Intersubjectivity, therefore, is in and of itself a healing (that is, grounding) experience. Consciousness expansion can be lateral or horizontal. Lateral expansion is a linear model in which reduction leads to ever deeper levels of inwardness, culminating in what Husserl has called the transcendental ego. (Book One has made additional distinctions within that concept.) Horizontal expansion is the spatial model in which the individual consciousness incorporates other individual consciousnesses. Since these are thought by common sense to be alike, the metaphor of a horizontal fusion seems appropriate.

A TRANSCENDENTAL RELATIONSHIP

The phenomenological theory of natural law says that to open up the transcendental dimension is natural and that any therapy which ignores it is superficial and defective because it is unnatural. The statement that it is the relationship and not the interpretation which heals must therefore be understood to mean the following: The kind of special relationship that heals is a desideratum of a transcendental natural-law theory. The relationship is transcendental and is illustrated by what is called *the therapeutic triangle*. The kind of contact that may be recommended by an empirical natural-law theory is therefore irrelevant to deep-level healing.

We see here the explanation of why encounter works, an explanation made possible within the context of the phenomenological model of being. A relationship as described here means deepened reduction and thus an *expanded consciousness*. The path from the animal consciousness back towards the Eternal Now has gone beyond the individual consciousness to the intersubjective type.

The following is a formal definition of a transcendental relationship and the therapeutic triangle. A transcendental relationship exists when the conscious center of the patient or client and the conscious center of the therapist or facilitator form one intimate and intersubjective field (and this statement is meant to be literally true and not just an apt metaphor). In addition, that transcendental relationship is part of a therapeutic triangle when the common object to this expanded common subject is a specific problem, situation, fear, or emotion (that is, an empirical phenomenon) of the patient or client. The relationship is called transcendental because it exists on the level of transcendental consciousness alone. The therapist's empirical ego is left out. The sole empirical phenomenon admitted into the realm of objects is the empirical ego of the patient. The unique features of this relationship are what make it therapeutic and they are especially the capacity for distancing (reduction and epoche) and the expansion of consciousness from an awareness of individuality to an awareness of intersubjectivity. But the relationship also includes the devotion of one transcendental ego to the integrity of another's empirical ego. This special contact can also be called *transpersonal*.

The encounter that heals is therefore not a neurotic, manipulative, or "using" kind of relationship. The empirical needs of the therapist are not being met by his relationship with his client. These may be his requirements to get approval, to be found attractive, to be loved and to have his sexuality confirmed, as well to be dominant, aggressive, powerful, controlling, and even omnipotent or sadistic. These needs are irrelevant to the therapeutic situation. If the therapist has them and can put them out of action in an epoche he can be a good therapist. But if he is cathected to them, so that he is not reflectively conscious of them, he cannot be accepted into the therapeutic community. Training and education are irrelevant to this aspect of the preparation of a therapist, which is a question of authenticity and not of learning. Personal therapeutic work is therefore mandatory.

The healing encounter is, on the contrary, transcendental, which is the matrix for a genuinely ethical and objectively rational relationship, one which is based solely on the authentic needs and interests of the client. What are these needs of the client? They are first an experiential understanding of his transcendental nature—which provides the guidelines for a "natural" existence and makes possible a life in conformity with his essence. Second, they are the discovery and subsequent free decisions about the satisfaction of his empirical needs, from his task in life, to a healthy body, to a good work and love life, to adequate economic means of support.

It should now be clear that encounter does not mean any being-with whatever, but only the special kind that can be called transcendental, a transcendental relationship, or a transcendental triangle. An empirical relationship can be maudlin and sentimental, and can border on the unethical. A transcendental relationship appears abstract and rational, but it is not unfeeling. It takes charge of the problems of living. An empirical relationship, because it presupposes cathexis and not decathexis, is the victim of the problems of living. The empirical relationship, which is the seat of projections and transference, produces novel—even surprising and often fascinating—information of our empirical or psychological ego. A therapeutic encounter can therefore be a shaking experience. However, the healing occurs when the unsuspected surge of new emotions is placed in an epoche and is jointly considered by client and therapist who are now poised in a therapeutic, transcendental, or transpersonal triangle.

The success of Carl Rogers's client-centered psychotherapy is due in great measure to the fact that he systematized the technique for establishing a transcendental encounter or being-with. It was an accidental, trial-and-error, and empirical discovery without any ready theoretical explanation. The theory of the expanded consciousness, leading to the sense of grounding that is in turn based on the indestructibility of transcendental consciousness, provides the theoretical base for his discovery. If encounter is established mechanically it will dutifully do its therapeutic work for a while. It gives the therapist time to think about future strategy, and gives him time to enhance his own authenticity. But sooner or later a deepened philosophic understanding of the meaning of being human is required to continue with the therapeutic process. If the therapy is short, neither client nor therapist will ever even notice the deficiency in their relationship. (Figures 1 and 2 illustrate two approaches to the transcendental relationship or the therapeutic triangle.)

In life we find four basic relationships: empirical, transcendental, therapeutic, and authentic. Each has its place. Inauthenticity occurs when the relationship is deceitful, dishonest, and therefore not appropriate for the occasion. (Figures 3-6 illustrate the basic human relationships.)

The small circle on the top of person P_1 and P_2 (Figure 3) represents the empirical or psychological ego—the body and the emotions of the individual. The larger bottom circle represents the transcendental ego, that is, the conscious center, the subjective inwardness of pure consciousness.

This is an empirical relationship. It is a business relationship. It is mechanical, legal, and governed by formal rules. The sense of inwardness is unimportant. Sensitivity, compassion, love, forgiveness, and so forth are irrelevant. The only issue is whether or not the rules have been followed. If such a formal, contractual business relationship takes the place of love, we call it prostitution.

Figure 4 is a transcendental relationship. That contact is basic for love. Two conscious centers form a tunnel between them and establish a larger, joint, and expanded conscious field. That is the chief ingredient of a love relationship. If it is expressed on the empirical and psychological level as well, then it becomes a loving sexual relationship.

Figure 5 is a therapeutic relationship. The empirical ego of the therapist is left out of the relationship. That is taken care of by the patient's fee. The patient is fully present—empirically and transcendentally. The patient is there as transcendental consciousness, as pure subjective inwardness. But

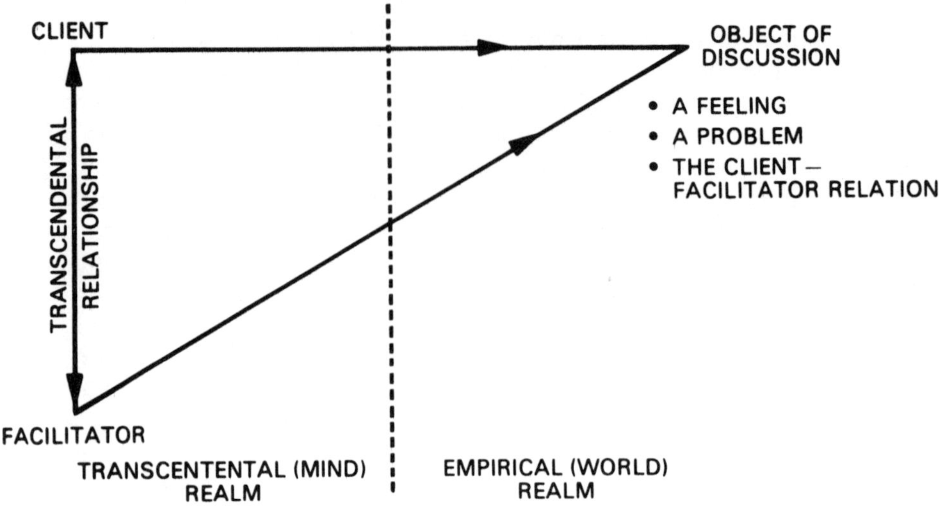

Figure 1

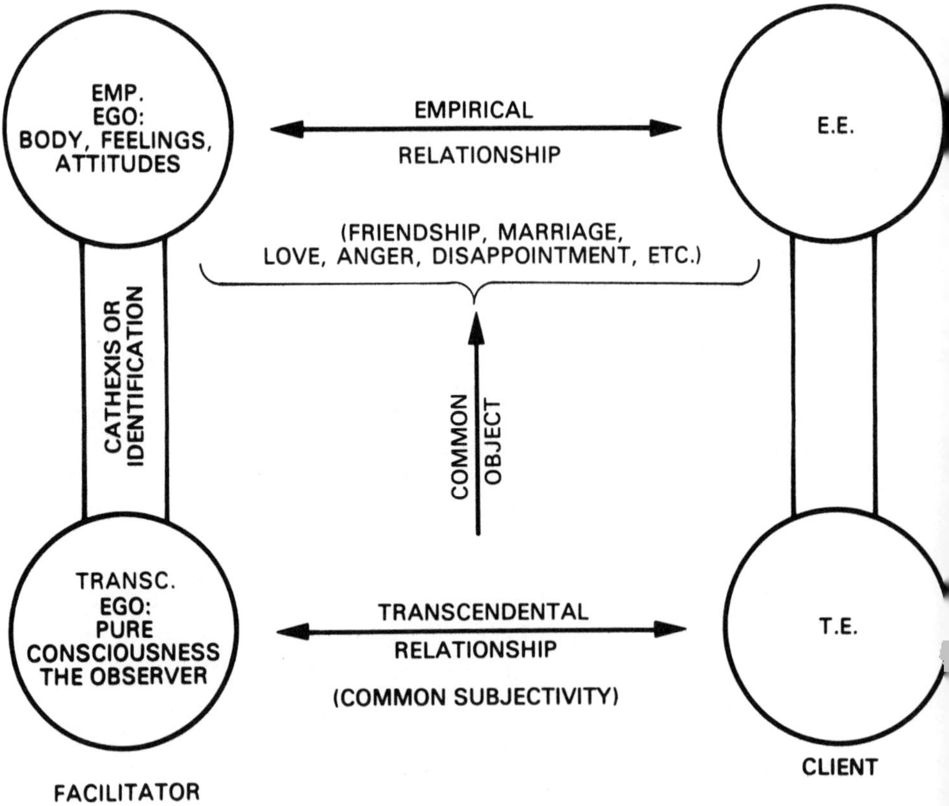

Figure 2

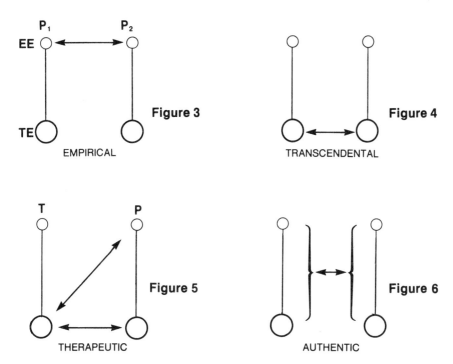

Figure 3

EMPIRICAL

Figure 4

TRANSCENDENTAL

Figure 5

THERAPEUTIC

Figure 6

AUTHENTIC

he is also present as a body, as a system of behavior, and as a plethora of feelings. The patient's empirical nature is the subject-matter discussed or treated in the therapeutic hour. The patient's transcendental nature connects with the therapist's transcendental nature. Jointly they establish the expanded conscious field from whose point of view the empirical ego of the patient is discussed, analyzed, shared, healed, and redefined.

Finally, Figure 6 is the authentic relationship of two lovers, fully integrated. It is a multi-relational contact in which every and all aspects of each person are fully utilized.

COMMITMENT

Another aspect of a relationship—in addition to the element of contact—that heals anxiety is the phenomenon of commitment. An existential therapist makes a commitment to his client to be with him as long as he is needed. Surely, he does not permit exploitation. Nor must his commitment have a neurotic source. It is based on the needs of the client, objectively and rationally assessed. It is also based on the human need and not on the fee, although the latter is a perfectly legitimate and even necessary ingredient of the therapeutic transaction. It insures equality, avoids exploitation, and shows respect to the economic realities of empirical existence. Commitment—to be an ingredient in the healing relationship—must thus have three characteristics: First it must be *inner-directed*. Its source must be within the therapist. The therapist decides he will make that commitment to his patient. He does not do it out of pity or for profit. He does it in response to objective need, on the basis of a rational ethical posture, as a result of his independent decision about his own life-style and professional development, and, finally, in voluntary responsibility to the presence of another human being in need.

Only the Kantian ethics explains this kind of motivation. Conventional psychology assumes motivation to be based on instinct, need, habit, pleasure, satisfaction, approval, conditioning, reward, or what have you. All these causes are of empirical origin—they are worldly events, events in the realm of objects. Phenomenology has added the transcendental dimension to psychotherapy. In this realm, the region of pure observing and spectatorial consciousness, motivation by reason is a meaningful concept. An act is chosen on rational grounds alone, and that choice is adopted without pushes or pulls but spontaneously and autonomously, that is, freely. The categories of reason and freedom, which are the motives for a truly moral act, have their origin and meaning in the transcendental realm. That is the Kantian ethics and that is the definition of an authentic therapeutic commitment from the point of view of an existential personality theory. As a result, the client owes nothing to the therapist. When "cured," the therapist fades away and becomes but a flicker of a memory. The effective therapist has neutralized the patient's need for him to practically zero.

Second, a therapeutic commitment must be *"forever,"* in the sense that it will cover a prearranged period in the client's life, and during that time—with all the usual ups and downs—the therapist will not abandon his patient. And that guarantee includes, at least theoretically, provisions *by the therapist* against illness, change of area of residence, death, and suicide. In other words, if the therapist abandons his client *for any reason whatever,* that act is to be interpreted as a therapeutic failure committed by the therapist. For the life of the need, the therapist's commitment is permanent.

Finally, the commitment is an *action* on the part of the therapist and not a reaction. The commitment does not depend on the cooperation of the patient or his friendliness, not even on his regular attendance or payments. On these terms, a client is still a client even if he has not been in the office for a year. The client knows the therapist is there, committed to him in the sense that the door is always open and the client is always welcome, understood, and accepted.

These are then the elements of commitment, which, in addition to inter-subjectivity make up the complex phenomenon of encounter. And that is the crux of the healing process.

IMPLEMENTATION

To implement intersubjectivity two simple rules must be followed. If you are in the health professions or are a healer, you must offer to be-with, make encounter possible, invite intersubjectivity. You do this with understanding, compassion, patience, and perseverance, especially if you deal with disturbed or rigidly cathected persons. You can also challenge the client by stating categorically that the absence of intersubjectivity is a disease. In catatonic and related states, in paranoid conditions and in highly impersonal and distant relationships, such an absolute challenge is helpful. If on the other hand you are in the client, student, or patient position, then take the initiative and ask that someone of your choice *be with you*. You are entitled to intersubjectivity; you have a claim on life that it give you the right to intersubjectivity when needed. If you understand that in demanding intersubjectivity you are neither attacking, squelching, nor suffocating anyone, but simply affirming a transcendental fact, then you will also discover that the world can be surprisingly responsive and supportive. The world will in fact thank you for demanding intersubjectivity. If one person is not responsive, do not obtrude yourself on him. Another will recognize your right to intersubjectivity.

A physician described the effects on him of his meetings with his therapist as "soothing." He said he was a better physician to his patients after the sessions. The reason he gave was simply that the being-with which defined patient-therapist relationship gave him a sense of peace, that is, security and self-confidence, and this feeling carried over to the office and was transmitted to his patients. The physician was referring to the benefits derived from the simple fact that once a week he existed in a transcendental relationship.

Several women clients were making significant changes in their lives. One was going through a divorce, another was moving away from her parents, and a third was changing careers. All three primarily needed support. But it is not enough to say only that much. They needed a home, a headquarters, a base of operations, a ground, a source. And that was found in the experience of transcendental intersubjectivity, the intimacy of pure consciousness, that an authentic counseling relationship can and should provide. Only with that transcendental intersubjective field as foundation is it then possible to make use of the philosophic insights embodied in these existential and phenomenological views. They were able to come in and talk. They felt understood; they felt connected; they felt safe. All are transcendental characteristics: expanded consciousness and no empirical (that is, physical or emotional) demands. The expanded consciousness spelled security; it was a taste of ground. The absence of empirical demands spelled an ethical relationship, which means that someone they respect made a commitment to them. It was this relationship which gave them the strength and the base from which to reconstruct their lives.

A psychiatrist commits suicide. Some months before he mentioned that the demands of his patients had become unendurable. He perceived being-with as burdensome. And yet his problem seems to have been that intimacy, intersubjectivity, or being-with as transcendental experiences were not part of his professional, intellectual, or personal equipment. To him all relationships were empirical, something that followed from his exclusive reliance on the medical model. His alternatives were aloofness—which limited his therapeutic potential—or empirical involvements—which were correctly perceived as unendurable and crushing burdens. He needed, we might say, his own being-with, that is, being-with himself. In other words, he needed to say no to his patients. These had wormed themselves deep into his psyche and he was incapable of the transcendental relation through distancing which could have saved him.

ENDINGS

Since relationship is essential to coping with anxiety and thus to successful clinical philosophy, a word must be said about endings. Intensive work means intensive relationships. Endings are notoriously difficult. The situation parallels the adulthood of children and the problems surrounding their leaving home. Endings are as various as clients. Three common ones are friendship, disappearance, and rational decision.

The time comes when the intensity of the therapeutic triangle or the power of projections can be transmuted into the empirical relationship of equals, friends, or of colleagues. At first, the expectations of independence are frightening. So is the increase in responsibility. The fee is eliminated, and rational, considerate, and ethical demands are made mutually. The relationship of friendship is indefinite. Each person is aware of the limits in the life of the other. The client, for example, understands that the counselor has his own personal commitments, his own family, and profession. The client also understands that the counselor's time is tight. Actual contact may be limited to an occasional post card, call, or even visit. But no fee is paid; and it is that which signalizes the end of the therapeutic relationship and the beginning of a rational, mature, and sober friendship. Conversely, the counselor makes modest demands on his new friend, demands which in no way are to be neurotic, and which the ex-client can easily meet and willingly does. This ending is totally within the context of authentic human relationships. Once ended it is difficult to reestablish a deep therapeutic relationship, because when you are someone's friend it is unlikely that the one-way relationship which is characteristic of therapy—that is, a transitive rather than symmetric one—can be reestablished. The end of therapy is therefore real and final.

In a second type of ending, the therapist disappears; his reality is neutralized. Whereas during the intense period of the relationship the client may become fiercely dependent and the counselor is an image of enormous mass in the consciousness of the client, at the termination of the relationship the counselor shrinks drastically in size. Eventually the therapist disappears as a relevant presence to the patient. The therapist is no longer needed. The patient finds himself alone, and happily so. The relationship with the therapist was always purely transcendental. No empirical contact existed or exists. And at the termination of the therapy, the two are like separating stars in an expanding universe. As their distance increases so does their speed of recession, until they are no longer visible to one another.

The third ending is a rational decision. Patient and therapist openly discuss the issue. They confront the need for ending and its difficulties. The opportunity for reopening the relationship is always present.

Significant Others Are Watching

Another and most effective coping device for anxiety is to recognize that one's response to anxiety serves as a living example for other persons on what to do with anxiety, how to manage it, and how to cope with it. And those watching to whom we should pay attention are the so-called "significant others." Your children are watching if you are a parent. Your patient is watching if you are a therapist. Your wife is watching if you are a husband and vice versa. Your constituency is watching if you are a political leader, and so are your colleagues. A manager is watched by his subordinates, and the general is watched by his army. The teacher is watched by the student, and leaders in literature and the arts such as Solzhenitzyn and Toscanini were watched by mankind.

All these individuals in the "audience" may be tempted away from their integrity and need you to set an example. In the United States, it is the president who has the maximum opportunity to serve as example, an opportunity often neglected. To realize that one's authenticity, that is, one's coping with anxiety, is being watched by and serves as an example for significant others is a potent stimulus toward taking charge of one's anxiety-management.

The guilt of a divorced man for his children can serve as illustration. When Jim divorced his wife the court gave her custody of their three children, aged eight to three. His marriage counselor felt Jim had little choice in the matter. After the divorce, Jim's former wife manipulated his children against him by such strategies as talking against him, asking the children to call him frequently and make him feel guilty ("Daddy, we didn't have meat for supper tonight because you don't send Mommy enough money!" which, incidentally, was not true), bringing men to the house whose presence she knew would trouble the children, and by interfering with his visitation rights. Jim got no court relief, although he tried. In fact, and as one would expect, his former wife's hostility increased with each court action, exacerbating an already bad situation. Of course often this situation is reversed, and it is the former husband who makes life miserable for his divorced wife. Since Jim had exhausted all legal actions and since one could not recommend anything illegal, he pursued the following program, which illustrates this second principle for coping with anxiety.

The essence of the device used by Jim is that his actions as well as his emotional health are focused not on what they will do for him but on serving as example to his children, even given only sparse contact with them at present. He coped with anxiety by translating it into meaning, by realizing that it is the core ingredient of meaning. He restructured his life from the narcissistic pursuits of pleasure and self-fulfillment to the other-focused (not self-focused) goals of charity, love, commitment, obligation, and even duty. Jim demonstrated to his children that maintaining a relationship with them was a lifetime project, which if it does not succeed today will perhaps succeed tomorrow, or next month, or next year, or possibly in the next decade. They may hate him today but they might also perceive him and his relationship to them a few years hence in a better light. He exhibited loyalty to them in his life (given the irreversible fact of the divorce). Even if they never respond to him, someday they may realize that their father made a life-long commitment to them under difficult circumstances.

In short, Jim coped with his anxiety of having left his children by defining himself as a loyal person, as a father whose essence is the eternal, unqualified, and inner-directed (which means that the decision stands, with or without response from the children) commitment to his children. In so doing he knew he was choosing this self-definition not for his benefit but to serve as a model for his children. He acted not out of a need for self-satisfaction but because his children needed him. He expressed through his life the kind of commitment that was described above as an inescapable ingredient in the therapeutic encounter. They would always know the quality of person that their father was. They would also always experience the intersubjective field of intimacy, because the irreversible inner-directed commitment to them had been made, which then refers to the intersubjective ingredient of the transcendental encounter which defines existential therapy.

The opposite of this commitment was illustrated by a newspaper article in which a young comedienne responded to a question about the whereabouts of her father with "I don't know what he's doing; but I'm sure that whatever it is, it's illegal," to which her father responded with a $4 million law suit. For a father to sue his daughter is the grotesque antithesis of commitment. An authentic father would not make what amounts to an anticommitment to his daughter.

A second step in the technique used by Jim was to share—whenever possible and at a level of depth and openness that seemed appropriate— his negative feelings of guilt, failure, frustration, and anger with them. But he also shared his positive attempts to cope, his feelings of love for them, and his decision to be determined to succeed with them; he did that by demonstrating to them that he was the model of a good father. He taught them, in words and by example, that he loved them, that he cherished them, that he trusted them, that they were important to him, and that he respected them.

A third aspect of Jim's coping device was that he chose strength, courage, success, and life-affirmation, rather than surrender to despair through alcohol, crime, drugs, neurosis, neglect, psychosis, revenge, bitterness, or even suicide. He demonstrated to his children that strength is a choice —open to all. He chose to affirm life not as much for himself as for the sake of his children. They needed his self-affirmation. Jim's meaning in life became to teach his children how to develop into authentic individuals by serving as their example. It is difficult under normal circumstances to serve one's children as a model of authenticity. In Jim's case, with guilt and inaccessibility added, the difficulty was increased a hundred fold. His task was that much clearer; his authenticity that much more precious; his example that much more inspired. It was up to him if he would betray them or not. To betray himself was bad enough. He could, however, live with that. But to betray his children was more than he could face. Consequently, he had no choice but to choose to cope with his anxiety.

A middle-aged woman in a workshop was near suicide until she saw that a teenager who meant much to her was watching her closely. For her own sake she did not care and she would have gladly destroyed herself. But for his sake she did care and she had to be strong. She owed him the decision to say *yes* to her life. For him she would do it . . . , and not just for that night in the group, but for the rest of her life.

If Jim can show his children that he can cope honestly and maturely— and thus successfully—with one of his life's most difficult problems, then he is giving them man's noblest gift and leaving them the richest inheritance there is. And that is an authentic solution to the problem of coping with anxiety. The anxiety is not overcome; but it is internalized, integrated creatively into life. It is tolerated and is translated into strength and health.

Anger

Anger is one of the most important and effective coping devices against anxiety, for anger is protest, and protest is proof that the indomitable spirit of man has not been squelched. Indifference is the absence of a core, the experience of being an empty shell. Indifference is an empirical ego which is hollow; it is only an envelope. Anger, however, is the experience of the archetypal decision to be an ego, a self, a core, an identity. Anger is the last vestige of self-affirmation. A person may have been squelched since childhood. The child may never have been fully confirmed. His parental message in life may always have been "You're not quite good enough. In fact, you can never try hard enough to satisfy me." If that child grows into an indifferent adult, he will have been defeated. But if he grows instead into an angry adult, he will maintain the posture of protest. His anger is his self-affirmation.

But anger is negative. His next step is to translate that anger into something constructive and creative. That translation is not sublimation but is the continued growth of the anger. Anger is not a pure emotion. It is the brutal, direct, and unadorned life-affirmation in the face of ultimate danger. The anger is not transmuted into a socially acceptable emotion or life-style. Instead, the self-affirmation that is the anger is developed further and is expanded into the world. Perhaps the angry client is now ready to proceed to a life of excellence, accomplishment, and competence. He will then gain deserved respect, recognition, and even power. He will not need to apologize or hide, because his expanded self-affirmation is a contribution to society.

Jill, a middle-aged woman with three grown children, complains she has an unhappy marriage. Her relationship with her husband is one angry episode after another. Yet years of therapy, she says, have brought about no changes other than to intensify the anger. Whereas in fantasy she wants to leave her husband, she is surprised that in actual fact she does nothing to break up the marriage. On a deep level she prefers the status quo. In her marriage there is anger everywhere: from her to her husband and from him to her. Anger need not be directional; it is rather the pervasive horizon against which a person's life is experienced.

Jill, it seems, is not really unhappy at all. She *believes* she *should* be unhappy because that is what the social model demands. She could have a "happy" marriage by totally squelching her anger. Then society would approve. The truth lies elsewhere. Jill needs self-affirmation and not social approval. Her anger—which is safely embedded in her marriage—is her self-affirmation. Jill is happier being angry than having a "good" marriage. In fact, she does have a good marriage because it is an arrangement in which her anger can exist. A better marriage would be for her not one in which there is peace but one which begins with her *expanded* anger. That is, she must expand her anger to become a creative life. Only then will her marriage change.

Chapter 7 • EVIL

Anxiety when it performs its existential function reveals the reality of evil. This is the second revelation of anxiety. It reveals separately the evil in the world and the demonic in us. It makes known the eternal paradox between good and evil. The focus on evil is not orthodox in therapy. Evil is not a psychological perception as much as an irrefragable reality. Evil is a metaphysical problem; it is an issue of theology. The problem of theodicy is still one of the most deeply moving issues in philosophy. To any sensitive person, to any decent individual, who appreciates the values of civilization, the existence of evil—which is the destruction of civilized values—is absolutely intolerable. Adjustment to evil is the denigration of the soul. Yet evil is real and remains real; the polarity of good and evil—witnessed with a clarity unequaled in this century, at least in sheer numbers—is one of the most unbearable burdens of human existence. And at least three kinds of evil exist: man-made destruction, natural destruction, and the demonic in the soul. The next time anxiety strikes ask yourself, What does it reveal? The phenomenologically revealed answer may well be that what you see is the conflict between the crass reality and the unquestionable impermissibility of evil, in any of its infinite forms.

It is common practice in therapy—resulting perhaps from Freud's discovery of aggression as fundamental and Jung's discovery of the pervasive presence of what he called the shadow—to encourage clients to accept their dark side, to accept negative emotions as natural. The patient is urged to express his gut-feelings; he is told that he has problems expressing his anger; he is allowed to kick, scream, or hit. But this attitude is quite different from recognizing that evil is both without redemption and ineradicable, and the two must not be confused. Anger is not of itself evil. Perhaps the frustration against which it cries out is a genuine evil.

The severe conflict between the unavoidable reality of evil and the fact that it is unforgivable is in fact a revival of the Manichaean heresy and the Zoroastrian dualist theology. Anxiety reveals the absoluteness of evil: a terrifying thought, but nevertheless one fully warranted by our commitment to realism and truthfulness. Anxiety shows evil in its full horror, but it also reveals a resulting noble task—if we allow the anxiety to completely unfold itself. For if we restrict the anxiety it becomes neurotic and it chastises us by withholding its revelations. It reveals only when it is in full bloom. And we call that the existential anxiety of evil. (In Chapter 3 of Book One the issue of the permanence of evil was discussed in the epistemological context on dualism.) And what that reveals to us is that we human beings are the only answer to evil that exists in the universe. Our freedom is capable of withstanding evil—of saying no to it. Our freedom is our only opportunity to choose to be noble, to stand up to evil, to counteract evil. The existential anxiety of evil reveals the preciousness of our freedom, and its enormous cosmic responsibility to uphold the values of civilization; it uncovers the much-neglected meaning of duty and obligation. These latter categories of ethics and morality—in the rigid deontological Kantian sense—must be reintroduced into a comprehensive existential theory of therapy.

And what is evil? In one word, inconsiderateness. Evil is the denial—from insensitivity to murder—of the sancticy of the inward, conscious, and free center of any human being.

The Structure of Evil

In essense, evil reveals itself in terms of five of its elements. First, *evil is completely unacceptable.* Once it is understood and its horror perceived with total phenomenological clarity, there can be no compromise and no adjustment. Just because evil is impregnable does not excuse us, regardless of how much we may be tempted. If either compromise or adjustment does occur, then our integrity has been violated and our authenticity tarnished. We cannot rationalize ourselves out of this predicament, even though we may not be able to do anything about it. To adopt Alexander Pope's position that "evil is good, not understood," is a distortion of the basic facts phenomenology reveals. There are events which inexcusably and unforgivably destroy those values which have an unqualified and absolute claim to be. These destructions can be either headline-grabbing catastrophes or minuscule degradations in interpersonal relations. We will look at some illustrations later.

Second, *evil is completely real.* Evil is well described by all those metaphysical dualisms which accord evil a place of equality next to God. God, in this important myth, is the power of absolute goodness and infinite love, but is also powerless to eliminate evil. The proper descriptive word is respect. We must recognize that evil is worthy of respect—not because it embodies a value, but because it has the same kind of necessary being as does God. This type of respect is not a form of reverence, only of contempt. But the respect acknowledges with permanently open eyes that evil is always there before us, demanding our attention. Evil deserves the respect, acknowledgment, and recognition given to a mad kidnapper or a grenade-packing terrorist on a crowded airplane. If we as much as blink our eyes, we have lost the sense of realism that our phenomenological integrity requires, for in that fraction of a second we deluded ourselves that there are moments without evil.

We may, for example, enjoy a beautiful concert. But we also know that people are being tortured in totalitarian jails at that very moment. The fact that we can do nothing about this horror, especially at that particular moment, and the knowledge that it is also impossible for us to worry over everything at all times, do not by a scintilla change the reality and atro-ciousness of the evil of torture. We must analyze this conflict-at-the-concert situation as follows: one of the evils in this world, in addition to torture, is that we can make fully integrated (in the polar sense) and therefore authen-tic decisions to limit ourselves in and ignore (sometimes or always) the struggle against evil. This is a difficult position to accept ethically, yet the bitter realities of existence make it inevitable. This kind of compromise is nevertheless an adjustment to and an acceptance of evil, and is thus grossly insensitive to those who suffer.

This point suggests the third element of evil, which is that *to be human is to struggle against evil*. In our religious metaphor, God leads the struggle against evil. We struggle against evil but do not conquer it. We can be successful in searching for meaning without ever making the claim that we have found meaning. Similarly, we can be successful in struggling against evil without ever being able to claim that we have overcome or conquered it. Because of our polar nature, we exist on the interface between good and evil. Our freedom chooses which side to take and how far to go. This type of choice is archetypal. The choice between good and evil is the choice between reason and unreason—and for that fundamental choice there is no good reason. Choosing between good and evil is choosing between the affirmations of life, consciousness, and freedom and their denials. To the extent that we opt for decency, we must look upon human existence as the permanent struggle against evil.

The fourth element in the phenomenon of evil is the discovery that *the struggle against evil gives meaning to life*. That was Viktor Frankl's great insight while in a Nazi concentration camp. Whatever activity we find meaningful is meaningful to the precise extent that it is a struggle without quarter against evil.

The fifth and last element of the phenomenology of evil is that *our pos-ture towards evil is freely chosen and we are fully responsible for it*. There is nothing automatic about the struggle against evil. It does not get done un-less we do it. It takes some persons a lifetime to learn this lesson. Further-more, our attitude towards evil is a free and autonomous decision, a point which is central to the stoic, Kantian, and existentialist ethics. It is indeed unfortunate that in our ordinary language *sick* (which deserves compassion) is a stronger ethical pejorative than *evil* (which needs punishment or destruction). On this analysis, therefore, Hitler was not a sick man but an evil one.

Examples

It seems hardly necessary to illustrate the reality of evil with specific cases. All one needs is to read newspapers or history books, or simply look around, to become aware of its onus. Furthermore, evil, in retrospect, loses, like all experience, some of its immediacy and depth. The revelations of the anxiety of evil that gives us the greatest access to the structure of being are easily lost as the experience of a particular evil recedes into the past. Around the time of the fall of Saigon in 1975 and at the beginning of the "orphan baby lift," the rear door of a transport plane opened, some children were sucked out, and the plane crashed. Many survived; all were injured. There can be no extenuating circumstances for a situation of this kind. Blaming individuals is senseless. If we find a culprit we are momentarily relieved of apprehending the reality and absoluteness of evil. We think we found the cause. And if we now eliminate it, we have extirpated evil from the world.

Alas, this demand for evil's unconditional surrender is never to be met. It was in fact being itself that permitted such a tragedy. It is the nature of things that such evil is possible. And nature, because it possesses that possibility, is therefore itself tarnished and partially evil. There can be no redemption, no recovery for that occurrence, no adjustment to that tragedy—without a loss of integrity, and a betrayal of the values of authentic human existence. Our anxiety regarding this situation—as it occurs, as it is fresh and immediate, and as one is a witness—reveals the immutable reality of evil as a given and self-evident phenomenon.

At that time a photograph was circulated in the newspapers showing a Vietnamese woman—a refugee escaping south on a dusty road—carrying a baby on one arm and, breast exposed, nursing him, while with the other leading her husband who hobbled behind her on a crutch, since he had lost a leg. This picture demonstrated to a world which all-too-soon forgets that evil is as intolerable as it is real. Any attempt to rationalize evil away is a tendency toward monistic metaphysics, whether we believe it leads to good or whether we feel that our struggle against it ameliorates evil. Only when we recognize evil as a final barrier, which is the gut-level experience of metaphysical dualism, do we experience the truth of our finitude. Only then do we live without illusion.

Another widely circulated photograph that brought back the years of agony of the Vietnam experience was one in which American servicemen were seen kicking and punching their Vietnamese friends, to whom they had promised protection, to keep them off their fleeing airplane. It had been risky for a Vietnamese to work for the Americans. If the South collapsed, he might well be shot. The reason given for forcing the South Vietnamese refugees off the airplane was that a stampede would result if even one non-American were admitted, and then no one would be saved. One serviceman was quoted as saying, "I have never felt as sick in my life. I will never again work for my goverment. I cannot live with the memory of this betrayal."

Scenes like these are reminders of the realities of evil. What we must avoid is permitting scenes like these—and millions of others—to be forgotten, to recede into the past and lull us into the illusory dream that the problem has gone away or, what is even worse, that it has been solved. Generalized, they teach us that world morality is bankrupt, that the existing concept of the person on which social and governmental actions are based is bankrupt, and that our manner of solving problems—that is, the willingness to use violence—is also bankrupt.

Further proof (as if it were needed) of the absolute and irremissible character of evil is that we do live in a world which has the answer to just about all our global problems. We know about morality; we understand psychology; we have the results of extensive research in anthropology, sociology, and history; our technological competence is boundless. Nevertheless, none of this progress has in the slightest affected the recurring presence of naked evil. Such a paradox would be metaphysically beyond comprehension were it not for the undeniable reality of evil. One needs only to read the newspaper headlines to become ashamed and embarrassed for our spaceship earth. Is it any wonder that sanity demands blindness to evil?

The three examples given satisfy the five elements or criteria of evil. It is intuitively clear that tragedies such as the crash of the baby-lift airplane, the nursing refugee with her crippled husband, and the American servicemen kicking their Vietnamese friends are totally and completely unacceptable. That this is true is self-evident to anyone who permits the full anxiety of this situation to reveal itself. All that is needed to discover the unconscionableness and unacceptability of evil is to permit these events to penetrate every pore of our being. That is what we mean by confronting the existential anxiety and opening ourselves up to its revelations.

Furthermore, these examples prove the unexceptionable reality of evil. We cannot argue it away as part of a Divine Plan without distorting the phenomenologically uncovered facts of experience. The only available response for self-respecting persons is to struggle in whatever way possible against these evil events. And it is precisely that struggle which gives life meaning and worth, that gives birth to the phenomenon of *morality* in human existence. Morality is a non-natural event; it is a transcendental phenomenon. It is an archetypal decision made ex nihilo by transcendental freedom. And it is the reality of evil which makes possible and gives meaning to this transcendental choice for morality. Finally, our decision to devote ourselves to the eradication of evil, hopeless as the task might seem, is taken freely, without promise of reward or fear of punishment, but as an expression of the archetypal decisions for rationality and for life-affirmation.

Israeli journalist Elie Wiesel writes about his childhood in a German concentration camp, where he watched the oven in which his little sister and his mother were going to be thrown.

"Never shall I forget that night, the first night in camp, which has turned my life into one long night, seven times cursed and seven times sealed. Never shall I forget that smoke. Never shall I forget the little faces of the children, whose bodies I saw turned into wreaths of smoke beneath a silent blue sky. Never shall I forget those flames which consumed my Faith forever: Never shall I forget that nocturnal silence which deprived me, for all eternity, of the desire to live. Never shall I forget those moments which murdered my God and my soul and turned my dreams to dust. Never shall I forget these things, even if I am condemned to live as long as God Himself. Never."[1]

Francois Mauriac writes of that statement,

"Have we ever thought about the consequence of a horror that, though less apparent, less striking than the other outrages, is yet the worst of all to those of us who have faith: the death of God in the soul of a child who suddenly discovers absolute evil?"[2]

Notes

1. E. Wiesel, *Night* (McGibbon and Kee, 1960; Avon Books, 1969), p. 9.
2. Ibid., pp. 8-9.

Chapter 8 • COPING WITH THE ANXIETY OF EVIL

Morality

Probably the most effective response to the existential anxiety of evil is the knowledge that it generates the whole syndrome of morality, ethics, integrity, goal, destiny, purpose, and task. In other words, the reality of evil brings about one fundamental recognition: it gives meaning to morality. And the capacity for and expression of morality is one of the defining characteristics of being human. When a person is moral he does not act automatically. He makes the archetypal and ex-nihilo decision to be moral. He does not consider thoughts of reward or punishment. Nor does he consider psychological, sociological, or behavioristic matters, in the sense that the behavioral sciences are irrelevant to our understanding of morality.

Morality is not the result of causes or motives whose origin is in the world of nature and described by science. Quite to the contrary, in the act of choosing himself as moral, a human being has stepped outside of the natural order. The non-natural character of the person—his structure as a being which does not exist exclusively in the world—is made most clear by the possibility of morality. In short, morality is not an empirical phenomenon. Morality is not part of the world of objects. Instead, it is strictly a transcendental phenomenon associated with the operations of the center, of pure consciousness, and of freedom. Within the pure conscious center, freedom creates ex nihilo the response of moral resoluteness and outrages against the evils in the world. These can be evil objects or situations, but they also can be evil decisions of other human freedoms.

These seven terms—morality, ethics, integrity, goal, destiny, purpose, and task—circumscribe a central, perhaps even *the* central, significance of personhood. The sense of being a person is the constitution that consciousness brings about in response to the existence of evil. Let us cover each briefly.

The stiffening self-assertive posture toward life, self, and values implied by such terms as morality, ethics, and integrity is the individuation of the person. Individuation occurs in synchronous yet dialectical response to the confrontation with an alienated, opposing, and threatening Other. And that Other is what we call evil. The muscles tighten to brace against the onslaught. An armor forms around the center to insure the preservation of its integrity. Evil is the opposing negativity which produces such alienation; evil is the terrifying confrontation which brings about the courage which preserves individuality. The isolated and exposed condition of individuality is the exact opposite of the uterine and protected condition of the fetus. The latter is a universalizing melding and surrender to the environment. The former is an individualizing hardening against it.

Whereas morality, ethics, and integrity are the natural responses to evil, we must ask if—in addition to their negative value of protection—they are positive values to be cherished for their own sakes. Would we want them even if they were not needed as protections against evil? An answer can be achieved only through strict adherence to phenomenological methodology. We must enter this posture through fantasy, through memory, and through action. How does it feel to be a person of integrity? What is it like to be honest under difficult circumstances? What is the experience of doing what is "right" rather than what is "expedient"? We also enter the experiences of morality, ethics, and integrity by recalling and reliving instances from our past in which we stood up for an unpopular cause, or lost something of value because our conscience bid us make a difficult decision. Perhaps we went on strike because of a principle—and lost our jobs. Perhaps we did not go on strike—and lost our friends. How did we feel? Was the action merely a necessity, or did it embody a positive value as well?

Finally, we enter this experience through action. We risk morality, ethics, and integrity. We follow Kant's famous position that ony when we act *counter* to our inclination do we know we have acted on principle rather than feeling. How do we actually feel having risked a moral stand, when the easy way out would have been to lie, to cheat, to ignore, or to appease? The child next door is battered. Do we call the authorities and risk neighborhood enmity? Or do we ignore the problem and allow the child's suffering to continue? If we do what is right and stand up for morality, does that indeed feel like the positive value of choosing the solidity of one's integrity and the weight of one's individuality?

Exploration in depth of these experiences constitutes a phenomenological description of the meaning of morality, ethics and integrity. And through this kind of investigation we can discover whether being moral and ethical, and preserving our integrity "feels" good or "appears" good to us in, by, and of itself. And if the answer is yes, these same phenomenological investigations will tell us why, by yielding a detailed analysis of these experiences. We reach an answer by establishing the hypothesis that the decision for morality is a stand against evil and that the consequence of this decision is a sense of individual identity, solidity, and strength. The hypothesis further asserts that this feeling is experienced as an intrinsic value. The evidence lies in individual introspection *and* in intersubjective comparison. In this manner, by appealing to the scientific character of phenomenology, we can confirm or disconfirm the hypothesis. If confirmed, the answers are (a) that these experiences are intrinsically valuable and (b) that the reason for their value is the sense of personhood to which they lead, which is in turn experienced to be inherently valuable. We must return to the metaphor that God saw it was better to be human and finite than divine and infinite. That is the message of the Creation, the Covenant, and the Birth of Christ. Let us now describe in greater detail the value of integrity which results from confronting the anxiety of evil.

A positive value is experienced. The concrete sense of selfhood is a value in itself, as well as being a response to evil. It feels good to be an individual. It feels healthy, joyous, and potent. One feels the vibrancy of agency in the blood, the excitement of action, the glory of having all of being condensed onto one point, the intensity of being a concrete here-and-now. These are difficult descriptions, but they do tell us that being an individual who is moral, ethical, and who has integrity is clearly experienced and is accurately described phenomenologically as an intrinsic value. Direct intuition confirms that to us. That is the philosophical basis for the therapeutic device of encouraging the client to "do something good to himself," "to explore his own feelings," "to look after his own interests," "to not allow himself to be used," "to assert himself," "to express his gut feelings," "to recognize that he has needs, too, and that he is entitled to respect and consideration," and so forth.

The second set of terms—goal, destiny, purpose, and task—refers to the futurization of the individual whose self-creation is expressed by the three discussed above. The anxiety of evil produces the character and the sense of integrity and worth. But it also produces meaning and the motivation to create a future for ourselves and for the world. The individual is like the projectile in an atom smasher: a small individual who develops enormous momentum by moving forward, into the future, as it were. Evil provides the task which generates the energy to propel a person forward into his future. An exercise will illustrate how the anxiety of evil leads us to discover our destiny.

Ask yourself "What evil troubles me most?" "What bothers me most about life in general? About my life particular?" Do not allow public opinion to influence what specific wants you consider evil. A person can find his meaning, his future, by focusing on his own anxiety of evil, by discovering the greatest evil in his life. Here is a range of evils that might concern you: *ignorance*, which includes lack of understanding or the inability to understand; *ugliness*, in nature, in the social structure, in politics, in human relations, in interpersonal transactions, in your own feelings and emotions, in your fantasies, your self-image, and in your life in general; *weakness*, ineffectiveness, lack of potency, lack of respect, failure; *alienation*, lack of contact, injustice, a feeling of separateness from society; *poverty*, which can mean world poverty, national poverty, personal poverty, or merely the inability to manage your finances, your job, and your business affairs; *chaos*, which may be a sense of separation from the oceanic, that is, from God.

If you can produce a profile diagnosis of yourself in terms of these six types of evils—by asking which of these evils troubles you most (or by ranking them)—then you may find your goal, destiny, purpose, and task in the future-oriented struggle against them. You may already have achieved this aspect of coping with the anxiety of evil. However, you can now bring it into consciousness, use your freedom, and assess and revise what you have done. Here are some illustrations.

If *ignorance* is your evil, then the life of a scientist or a scholar, the "theoretical man," becomes your way of responding to your particular evil with your particular task.[1] And of course we need much greater specificity. Your evil is not likely just ignorance in general, but a very specific type, such as ignorance about cancer, brought about perhaps by having been a witness to the tragic death of a loved one. More knowledge would have saved that person. You now demand to develop that knowledge. Such an experience, occurring early in life, can determine the course of one's life. Here, then, is your task. Since these tasks may start early and are therefore now deeply entrenched, we can reverse the process of discovery. You can examine your present interests and then assume that they are in fact your current response to a deep-seated and even unconscious confrontation with your individual and unique supreme evil. And in this way you can discover—through inference—the particular evil buried deep in your empirical ego.

For example, if you discover that your interest lies in psychology, then perhaps ignorance about human consciousness or human behavior is the kind of evil that lies buried in you. The focus of all the evil forces in the world is, for you, ignorance about what it means to be a person. It is against this evil that you must struggle. You must therefore intensify your study and research in psychology, now that you understand the personal ontological origins of your interest. If your interest is astronomy, then perhaps the ignorance you struggle against is of a cosmological sort. You are surrounded by infinite space, you see it every day, and you are permanently frustrated in your need to reach into it. You cannot grasp the universe, physically or intellectually. The world is a stranger to you. That may be your evil. You repeat the struggles of ancient Chinese, Indians, Egyptians, Israelites, and Greeks and study the stars and feel good when you understand even a modicum of their mysterious doings. Or maybe your interests are technological, and you are fascinated by engineering, possibly electronics. Your evil is of a practical sort. You recognize that problems can be solved through technology, and it is safe to say that the kind of technology that interests you most does so because it struggles against the particular kind of evil that disturbs you most.

Interest is a function of rebellion against evil. We have a philosophic hypothesis in answer to the question of how interests originate: A person's interests, values, goals, or meanings are reactions to his perception of what is evil. An interest is a way of saying *I am* in the face of destructive opposition, confronting otherness, and threatening evil. The anxiety of evil comes first; the discovery of meaning is a reaction, not an action. That is a therapeutically valuable generalization to keep in mind.

If your evil is *ugliness*, then art, which is the pursuit of the "aesthetic man," is your life-style. If *weakness* should be your evil, then your goal, destiny, purpose, and task are the acquisition and uses of power. You then become the "political man." The counterphobic life-style of the "tough guy" is a denigrated example of this reaction. If you discover that your most grievous evil is *alienation*, then your task is to establish and cultivate social relations, either in your private life, or to encourage this for society as a whole. You then become the "social man." If your evil is *poverty*, then economic achievement—either as a personal goal or a social remedy— becomes the task that will give meaning to your life. You then become the "economic man."

Finally, if your evil is what has here been called, for lack of a better word, *chaos*—meaning thereby mostly the search for immortality and for an ordered universe—then the life-style which responds to it is that of the "religious man." These evils and our responses can occur in various combinations and intensities, and the resulting constellations of values can change during our lifetime.

A goal gives meaning to one's life not because it is achieved or even because it can be achieved. On the contrary, a goal already gives meaning if our eyes merely face in that direction and even more if our life begins to move toward it. Our goal is to face our specific evil. In this struggle we achieve substance, which includes morality, ethics, and integrity, and we achieve meaning, which includes goals, destiny, purpose, and tasks.

This outline on coping with the anxiety of evil can be systematized into a therapy program, in which coping with evil is accomplished by establishing a goal. A detailed diagnosis and therapy program can be worked out for each individual. In the face of evil we can make a decision for hope by spelling out a *contract* with ourselves. The contract specifies how, in detail, we are to struggle against the particular evil we have singled out as our enemy. The contract also needs a realistic timetable. In that way we can cope with the anxiety of evil. With sensitivity and imagination, a complete therapeutic program can be built around this particular approach.

"I Have No Goal"

Many a client will argue that he has no goal. If he could only find a goal, his life would have meaning. He knows all about evil and he knows everything about tasks and destiny, but still no meaning appears. He searches through school catalogs; he takes courses in careers and employment opportunities; he takes vocational interest tests. He has still to find *his* goal. How can this person cope with the anxiety of evil?

Some make a virtue of having no goal. That can be legitimate and authentic. The pursuit of *goallessness* assumed by the here-and-now subculture and the quest for satori in Zen and Nirvana in Buddhism—the search for timelessness and for desirelessness—are also bona fide goals, with specific tasks designed to achieve goallessness. They are not exceptions to the rule, because a goal in life means much more than merely a middle-class value. The presence of a goal, even if that goal be the elimination of all goals, injects passion, life, enthusiasm, vitality, energy, direction, and joy into human existence. Jeremy discovered his meaning in satori. He worked doggedly in the shipyards to save enough money for a trip to Japan. Purposefully he joined a monastery, where he assiduously followed the prescribed regimen. He approached his goal of goallessness with business-like efficiency. He knew what he wanted. His behavior was goal-directed. And his goal was in the future.

However, the real lack of goals and meanings in a person's life is the experience of ennui, depression, unhappiness, irritability, and general dissatisfaction with life. That condition is proof that he has not yet made the decision to assume responsibility for being himself or, more specifically, responsibility for confronting evil with meaning. The fundamental archetypal decision which differentiates the person from his environment and creates him as an individual identity has not yet been made. This person is running away from dealing with this issue, and that is the source of his goallessness. The decision to be an individual has been postponed successfully, for to have a goal is to continually choose to say yes to oneself.

The therapeutic question therefore is not, "Let's review goals and see what 'turns you on,' " but "Let us explore your resistance against being yourself." The decision to be oneself is the underground fire which surfaces as boiling water in the geyser of a visible goal. The analysis of the resistance then becomes the indicated healing task. The gaze of life for the individual without a goal is looking outward for direction rather than inward. He reacts but does not act. He is other-directed rather than inner-directed and probably has a history of not being validated for being himself but only for his performance—or perhaps not even that. His center is ungrounded and underdeveloped. The truly goalless person experiences the absence of his inner and solid core. He does not understand the meaning of becoming an individual and therefore lacks potency and efficacy. He has to understand why remaining underdeveloped made sense in his childhood environment. He can then work toward neutralizing that nefarious script and replacing it with one of his free and rational choosing.

Epitaph

The analysis of this resistance can be facilitated in at least two ways: through the *epitaph exercise* and by *attention to inner voices*. Imagine your epitaph. What do you want written on your tombstone? What do you want to say about yourself after all the meanings you have been are finalized, after the openness of what you were is forever closed? That is a useful exercise to help a client focus on his own personal and real evil and to help him deal with it.[2] As he struggles to create his epitaph, he will be forced to discover what troubles him most in his life and how the struggle against that evil can give meaning to him. Some of that material will be empirical—such as (and these are merely examples) saying to his parents or children "I love you" or returning to the religious faith of his youth. But much of it is likely to be transcendental, that is, he is not using his freedom fully or he is suffocating in busywork and detail and thereby out of touch with the larger philosophical perspectives on his life. His epitaph is a marker that points out the authentic way for him.

Lack of meaning is caused by the absence of a sense of individuality. And this results from the ignorance and desuetude of freedom. To be an individual one must make the free decision to be one and to assume full personal responsibility for one's life. Finally, the foundation for freedom is to be centered, an insight dependent on a clear understanding of our transcendental dimension. Consequently, if a person cannot find meaning, no matter how hard he tries, the difficulty lies in the absence of an inner core, a core whose existence he can bring about by an act of free will and choice. But this archetypal choice has a special structure. The core is threatened by non-being. The universe itself—and certainly each center within it—is experienced or perceived as contingent. It makes more sense not to be than to be.

Heidegger asked "Why are there beings rather than nothing?" Tillich talked about the threat of non-being. Aquinas told us that the contingency of the world demonstrates the necessary existence of God. To be is the sole value. Augustine told us that the evil man is good to the extent that he exists, although his acts may be evil. The threat of non-being is evil— but that is also the threat of death and the threat of nihilism. Although the latter two are additional revelations of anxiety, all three are experientially connected. The center, our individuated *Existenz*, our sense of core identity, is, as Tillich put it, the experience of the power to resist non-being. That is indeed the ultimate miracle, properly called the miracle of being.

Only through the evil of non-being, including death and nihilism, does the value of emerging as a center come into full relief. To be is the ultimate meaning, the ultimate affirmation—and it is made as a reaction to the experienced presence of pure evil. The miracle of being is the answer to evil.

Once the supports of this *pyramid of authenticity* are established (see Figure 1) we discover that love is possible only if there is meaning first. We use love to share and reinforce our meanings, not to create them. Furthermore, love will strengthen and validate all the other human values needed for establishing meaning. These insights must be both conceptual and experiential, and ultimately they must be integrated into one's full life so that this pyramid is not only thought and felt but also lived, made public, and visible.

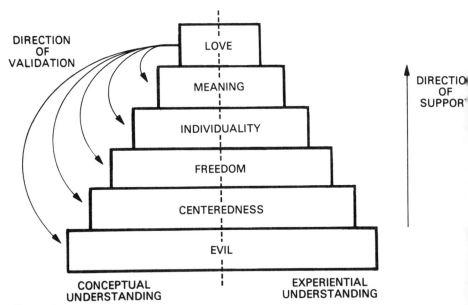

Figure 1

Inner Voices

Also of special importance for the analysis of the resistance against a goal is to learn to listen to our inner voices. Most inner voices come from the empirical ego. They are like psychological X-rays: they inform us of what is going on inside of the rich source that is our empirical or psychological ego—the body, our emotions, and our unconscious. Our inner voices appear when we permit and especially when we encourage the body to speak its mind. But our feelings, emotions, and attitudes are not be to be confused with our pure transcendental consciousness proper. Our pure consciousness is always available to us (except when we are in the animal consciousness).[3] Each of us has an emotional nature—an aspect of the empirical ego here called the psyche (discussed in Book Three)—which is stimulated and sometimes generated by our past decisions and influences, both parental and cultural. The psyche can make itself heard—through behavioral symptoms, somatic illness, and body presence. We can train ourselves to *listen* to our empirical ego and its being-in-the-world. What we then hear are our inner voices.

If we still the noises of all external inputs—including internalized external inputs (ancient scripts)—we may begin to hear these inner voices. To accomplish that requires rest and relaxation, a change of human, social, and physical environments and time, peace, and patience. These inner voices will come out of our unconscious—collective or individual— out of our past, out of our heritage, out of our childhood experiences, and out of our bodies. We are not forced to obey these voices. Only a psychology that does not have a theory of the transcendental ego is bound by these empirical commands. However, these voices do reveal to us delicate and hidden details about our empirical structure. They are a microscope placed on the pysche. They unravel the knots produced in our empirical ego by unconscious and unresolved conflicts. If we listen to them, we gain a clear view of who as empirical egos we are and who we have been; we get a comprehensive and lucid picture of the empirical ego that we have entered.

We have made the decision, as individuals, to live in the consensual world. These voices are part of the same empirical reality which gives rise to the consensual world. Consequently, they have considerable, although not final, authority. We are now ready to allow these voices to speak to us. We then *decide*—and this is a transcendental and not an empirical act— whether we are to do their bidding or proceed differently on our path to ascribe meanings to existence. These voices tell us what we must do to live in peace with our empirical ego, in its particular being-in-the-world. There is merit in accepting our biological, historical, and social destiny (the components of the empirical ego), just as there is value in turning over that destiny and creating our own. That is one of our archetypal decisions. If *we* made that decision and do not allow it to be made for us, then we have achieved the sense of self-affirmation and ego-strength which expresses itself in life as goal-directed behavior. We are then coping with the anxiety of evil. If the decision is not made by us, that is, by the transcendental aspect of us, then we are not coping authentically.

We can summarize these two chapters on evil as a revelation of anxiety and our strategies to cope with it as follows: Existential anxiety reveals to us the reality of evil. To deny that revelation leads to the pathology of purposelessness or meaninglessness in life. However, to accept this revelation of anxiety, that is, to courageously confront it and permit oneself clearly to see the evil it reveals, leads to the richness of meaning and the fulfillment of purpose in life. The essential treatment strategy for this anxiety consists of making a contract to first discover the evil that is uniquely ours and then constructing one's life around the fight against and the conquest of that evil. On the political level, this insight can lead to the awakening of the moral rededication of America, something sorely needed and eminently appropriate for the nation's Bicentennial and after.

The Statue of Liberty in New York harbor is a good example of the idea that the meaning of America is to adopt a moral stance toward the future of mankind. The origin of the statue—a gift from France—and the museum at its foot—depict touchingly the contributions of all ethnic groups and nationalities to the amalgam that is the United States of America. It is time once more for America to be a moral leader by being a moral example. Our nation can become unified by the moral decision to struggle for the preservation of the sanctity of human rights.

Notes

1. It should be obvious that this allusion is to Spranger's *Lebenstypen*, used in Gordon Allport, Philip Vernon, and Gardner Lindsey, *Scale of Values* (Boston: Houghton Mifflin, 1960).

2. This exercise is discussed at some length and with illustrations in Peter Koestenbaum, *Is There An Answer To Death?* (Englewood Cliffs, N.J.: Prentice-Hall, 1976).

3. See Book One, chap. 6.

Chapter 9 • THE NIHILISM-GROUND ISSUE

Nihilism and freedom are two very special revelations of anxiety. Together they can help us develop a theory of mental illness within the context of a phenomenological model of being and an existential personality theory. That theory of illness must stand on its own, for it cannot necessarily be correlated with the conventional nosology of psychopathology. On the surface, it may nevertheless be worthwhile to explore the relation, if any, that exists between inauthenticity and schizophrenia on the one hand and neurosis on the other. There are two qualitatively different categories of field-of-consciousness dysfunctions: the ignorant consciousness and the crippled consciousness. It is possible that a tenuous correlation between neurosis and schizophrenia respectively can be found. The discussion of the crippled consciousness in particular is carried out in Book Three. It is discussed only after all seven of the revelations of anxiety have been explored. However, nihilism and freedom are the primary relevant aspects of being necessary for an understanding of the crippled consciousness.

Nihilism Defined

If we ask, all subtleties aside, "What is anxiety?" the answer must be given principally in terms of the idea of nihilism. The revelation of anxiety which is here called nihilism, or the nihilism-ground issue, is likely to be the single most important of all these revelations, important in that it is the least adulterated and most primitive representation of the structure of being itself. And it is not only here, but throughout the entire history of existential thought that nihilism or nothingness has been assigned its position of prominence. With Nietzsche's announcement of the death of God, the chill wind of nihilism began to be felt. Humanism and existentialism—from Desiderius Erasmus and Giovanni Pico della Mirandola all the way to Soren Kierkegaard and Jean-Paul Sartre—have tried to give significance to man in the face of the abyss of emptiness that is a godless world or at least a world uncertain about the reality of God or His equivalent.

It is not necessary to decide whether or not God exists to avail oneself of the concept *God*. God is a word in the English language that goes back into deeper ancestral and unconscious material than do any words, such as force, power, principle, or what have you, in terms of which God might be defined. *God* is the word in the history of mankind which better perhaps than most evokes the need for ground. And that need is as real for the theist as it is for the atheist.

In trying to provide a phenomenological description of anxiety—especially the anxiety of nihilism—several points must be kept in mind. The descriptions are transcendental. At least they are intended to be such. Descriptions of anxiety are reflexive, not referential, and they deal with transcendental and not empirical material. We are therefore here engaged in transcendental phenomenological researches. The region to which anxiety points is the region of inner space, the region of the center, the region of pure consciousness. We therefore encounter all the difficulties inherent in performing and then describing the transcendental-phenomenological reduction. Also and even more important are the difficulties inherent in any description of fringe phenomena. There is no easy way and no obvious metaphor in terms of which the threat of groundlessness or the threat of non-being can be evoked and recorded. Nor is there any readily accessible formulation which can make clear to a mind brainwashed by the medical model of the person (or by the ghost-in-a-machine theory of man) the profoundly effective coping devices developed throughout the history of ideas. The transformation of nothingness into being, of anxiety into security, is the image of God creating a world out of nothing. That is the universal foundation of the human condition. But to make that point clear is in itself a desperately difficult and anxiety-producing enterprise.

NOTHINGNESS

Anxiety in its purest form is the experience of attempting to confront nothingness as one's intentional object. It is encountering ultimate panic, as is the case when one sees an apparition so esoteric and exotic that it undermines any residual sense our world might still make. The *spiritual possession* that terrifies does so because it evokes the possibility of total nothingness. Imagine waking from a profound sleep in the middle of the night, in a strange place, in pitch darkness. The night and darkness are experiences of nothingness, because they are the absence of all objects. Since you just awoke, you are further disoriented because you are frustrated in your attempt to organize this nothingness in terms of your memories (how you got here and where you are), your present experience (you stand on solid ground and can feel perhaps a wall and a door), and your future anticipation (the sun will soon rise, it will be daylight and normalcy returns). In other words, with practically no signposts or guidance, you try to establish at least a minimal constitution. But the constitution of some reality amidst the darkness is only tenuous. The world thus constituted is very brittle, but it is the best you can do at the moment. It is your best effort to defend yourself against the anxiety of nihilism through structure and organization.

Suddenly you have a fright. Something appears or occurs which has two basic traits: it is very obtrusive and it in no way fits into your just-now constituted scheme. A loud noise would be obtrusive as would the unexpected softening or moving of the floor. A rat that might leap on you, a scorpion that might sting you, or a spider that threatens to bite you—all are obtrusive events. You cannot ignore these apparitions—even though they may be physically small. The noise, for example, is totally unexpected —it does not fit your fragile construct. Furthermore, you anticipated sturdy ground, so that if the floor caves in your expectations are catastrophically violated. And of course you expected no threatening animal or insect. But when you brush by what looks like one, even your most tenuously constituted world will be destroyed.

These are the elements of the experience of panic. They add up to one simple truth: no semblance of world can be sustained. The darkness, which is at least consistent, is also the phenomenon of anxiety. But the sudden destruction of the gossamer world design constituted in the face of this emergency produces terror and panic.

Through this phenomenological description we can spell out in detail the structure of anxiety as a function of the experience of nothingness. The anxiety of nihilism appears in all three areas of philosophic expression: understanding, experience, and integration. As understanding, nihilism is the concept, idea, fantasy, or icon of nothingness. As experience, nihilism is panic, anxiety, and terror. As integration, nihilism can be manifested as a life of disintegration, as an intensely defensive life, or as a life in the process of rechoosing and redefining itself. Since anxiety can eventually be translated into either joy or security—as it is in mysticism—the total commitment to a deeply spiritual life is one more expression of the integration of the anxiety of nihilism.

Nihilism Described

Nothingness is a phenomenological term. In the context of strict logic, *nothing* may simply be a vacant place in symbolic notation. But the word *nothingness* is an English term that everyone can use, and use correctly.

And it is one of the best words available to record, describe, and evoke the feeling one gets when he realizes that all his supports have been withdrawn —in fact, that they never existed. It is when the illusion of an organized and reliable world becomes the reality of chaos and the absence of foundation. The supports in question are these perennial philosophic and theological themes: The fact that I exist rather than not; the fact that the world exists rather than not. There must be a support for that ego and that world, and yet the history of modern and contemporary philosophy seems to have shown conclusively that this foundation is an illusion. The idea of a necessary being, of an *existens a se,* that is, a being that exists by virtue of its own necessity, that is self-created *(causa sui)* has been abandoned by contemporary thought. The result has been inner turmoil and social disintegration.

A paradigmatic symbol of this lack of foundation is found in our attitudes toward the heartbeat. The heartbeat is a primary sign of life. As long as it beats its regular rhythm, the person exists. But neither the person nor an observer can control the continuity of these life-supporting heartbeats. It seems to be a matter of sheer and incomprehensible luck that they continue. This is the discovery that the world and I do exist but that there is no reason and no perceptible foundation for it and there is no guarantee that being will endure. Such is the perception of the contingency of the world, of the miracle of being, of the wonder that things are rather than not.

Other apparent supports or defenses against the phenomenon of nihilism are our values and our self-concepts or self-definitions. What is an authentic life-style? What is our meaning and our destiny? What is the proper social order? These questions, crucial as they are, need answers, and answers which are true. There is no room for error among the things that matter most. And anxiety is the discovery that these answers do not exist. In fact, they never did exist and never will. If we do have answers, we only think we do. They are illusions, but necessary ones, for they protect us against the anxiety of nihilism.

Finally, the absence of supports that is the anxiety of nihilism touches deeply on the question of immortality. Is life limited to its brief span of a maximum of one hundred years, assuming further advances in medicine? Or is life, as pure consciousness, forever, eternal? Needless to say, the structure of the anxiety of nihilism and our perception of it are profoundly affected by how we answer these questions, for deathlessness means support. But most contemporary philosophic and scientific thought has insisted that even this foundation is a cruel illusion.

We therefore perceive in this century and with clarity the absence of these needed supports and we know that this is the experience of nothingness. Its affective-conceptual and lived correlate is the experience of total anxiety.

Anxiety is what happens when we recognize that there exists nothing at all that is permanent, secure, dependable, reliable, and forever. Living even one additional minute—in fact, the existence of the universe itself for one additional minute—depends on the continued successful connections of our brain cells—over which we have no control. It depends on world peace—for all we know, a nuclear-tipped intercontinental ballistic missile may be right now on its way to our city. Our children, wives, husbands, and parents are exposed to constant and innumerable dangers. The children ride bicycles and drive cars, the cities teem with crime, jobs are difficult to find and even then may be insecure, and on and on and on. Kant—referring to Aquinas's argument for the existence of God "from possibility and necessity"—called this perception of a universal characteristic of the world the contingency of the world, a fact we have disucssed earlier. The world need not be, nor does anything within it exist necessarily. If we attach or identify ourselves to or with anything in that world, we immediately notice that there is no guarantee that the values thereby created will be preserved. This constant uncertainty, this ceaseless doubting about the permanence and reliability of all that we cherish, is experienced as emptiness, as a vacuum, and that is the same as the experience of the existential anxiety of nihilism. Existential anxiety is thus the discovery, in Bertrand Russell's eloquent words, "That all is passing in this mad, monstrous world, that all is struggling to snatch, at any cost, a few brief moments of life before Death's inexorable decree."[1]

ESTRANGEMENT

Anxiety discloses nihilism, the groundlessness of existence. It shows to us our alienation and estrangement—the schizoid depersonalization and lack of commitment to ourselves and to others typical of modern man —toward what Binswanger (after Heidegger) called our three worlds: *Eigenwelt, Mitwelt,* and *Umwelt* (the world of my ego, the world of intimacy and social relations, and the world of nature). For example, we in the twentieth century no longer feel that we belong in nature. We are estranged from the *Umwelt*. We artificially restructure our lives with indifference to the seasons, the weather, and the hours of the day. We work at night— the time nature intended for sleep. We adhere to a rigorous clock-schedule, disregarding the body's rhythms. We need the convenience of so-called civilization to feel comfortable. Our bodies show the flab of desuetude and the stoop of physical inactivity.

We are estranged from the *Mitwelt*. We are pro-forma members only of a society, a history, and a tradition. We live as independent modern couples or families; each member goes his own way, narcissistically preoccupied with his or her own destiny. The security afforded by generations of family unity is on the wane. Love, devotion, care, dedication, and commitment to another person are today, if they exist at all, often only temporary at best.

Finally, self-estrangement, alienation from the *Eigenwelt*, may well be the most insidious of all, since it seems to be the source of the other types of alienation. In this aspect of the anxiety of nihilism one feels fragmented. What we usually call *me* is a composite of transcendental and empirical dimensions. To be fragmented or estranged from the *Eigenwelt* means that these parts do not fit together. For example, the ego does not recognize its transcendental nature—it is thus split off from understanding its freedom for self-definition and life-styling. More commonly we talk of being out of touch with one's feelings. That is the reverse type of fragmentation, in that what is repressed is not the transcendental dimension but our empirical richness. And even within the empirical ego proper there can be fragmentation, as when we cannot meld love and sex, care and anger, and so forth.

ADDITIONAL CHARACTERISTICS

The existential anxiety of nihilism discloses to us that we are abandoned, that we are homeless. But it also reveals the world as ambiguous and truth as relative in that there can be a near infinity of world views, world designs, and belief-systems, each of which conforms to the facts and is internally consistent. One such metaphysics uses the waking state as its point of reference, and it gives us the consensual world. Another metaphysics uses the mystical experience as reference point, and we get other-worldly, religious world pictures. One metaphysics insists on the cohesiveness of society, the importance of tradition, whereas another insists on the overarching value of the individual and his choices. Relativism—which can be both responsible and respectable—leads nevertheless to chaos. It creates chaos in the mind and produces chaos in society. Dogmatism in metaphysics brings about rigid personalities and monolithic states, all of which are defenses against the transcendentally revealed truth of relativism. Camus's famous question about suicide in *The Myth of Sisyphus* is still with us . . . unanswered.

Some of the most dramatic statements about the anxiety of nihilism are in Kierkegaard's elaborate analysis of the story of Abraham and Isaac in *Fear and Trembling*, where he examines the problems of repentance and faith:

And God tempted Abraham and said unto him, Take Isaac, thine only son, whom thou lovest, and get thee into the Land of Moriah, and offer him there for a burnt offering upon the mountain which I will show thee.[2]

Abraham must decide, among many other things, if God exists or not. On that decision hinges his son's life and his own self-respect. If God exists and he kills his son, dreadful as that act may be, it would nevertheless be authentic within the general outlines of his world design. The directive was, after all, the will of the Creator. But if God does not exist, Abraham would be nothing short of a hallucinating paranoid schizophrenic of the worst sort. On the other hand, if God did exist and Abraham disobeyed, his sin would be unconscionable. Abraham's dilemma is not about obedience to God but about the prior issue of the existence of God. But religious metaphysics makes no allowance for justifiable doubt. God does not seem to have compassion for the fact that Abraham could legitimately question His existence. Abraham must decide, and he must decide now about the existence of God, and the consequences of his decision are as severe as any could be. The loneliness and the abandonment that Abraham feels at this moment are shared by us all; it is our condition as well, because each of us must, with no support or evidence of any kind, make a decision about the nature of the universe, make a choice of metaphysics—in short, decide what is real and what is true. This isolation is the philosophic truth about man. It is the nihilistic abyss of nothingness opened up before us by existential anxiety.

Nietzche's famous God-is-dead passage from *The Gay Science* is another version of the anxiety of nihilism. The death of God chills and darkens the world; the abyss of nothingness has now become visible. The earth is unchained from the sun; the symbol of ground is receding. There is no up or down left; the consensual world is deconstituting, leaving us face to face with a structureless emptiness. He says we have killed God—a reference to our responsibility for the existence of the condition of nihilism. We are responsible in the sense that we do nothing about it. We are responsible in the sense of self-deception or of neurotic anxiety. It is the essence of this period in world history that we do not face the anxiety of nihilism. We choose to repress it—and in that neurotic act we have killed our ground which has been called God. The problem of nihilism is without doubt *the* issue of our age.

NIHILISTIC DREAMS

Philosophical insights are commonly reflected and revealed in dreams. Nightmares or dreams of falling without end are the direct and unmediated experience of the anxiety of nihilism. Falling is the experience of being ungrounded, of the abyss, the absence of an answer, the presence of the darkest and the emptiest nothingness. Other nihilistic dreams are about storms and earthquakes; in them, the world is violently deconstituted. In fact, the violence with which the foundations are shaken is the experience of the resistance against deconstitution. In other words, the resistance of the buildings to collapse is the experience of the resistance against deconstitution. The buildings represent the constituted and cathected world; their fall is the transcendental act of deconstitution which bares the nothingness of pure consciousness. Conversely, deconstitution without resistance appears in dreams as dissolving, melting, or sinking. Surrendering to that profound anxiety and to the total nothingness can become an oceanic and even glowingly erotic feeling.

Losing teeth in dreams often means losing one's grip on whatever supports, grounds, or holds up. Whatever it is that is "out there" and is real enough so that we can "put our teeth into it" is no longer working. For the phenomenon of grounding need not be restricted by the metaphor of the earth. Grounding can also mean leaning or inclination, or holding on or hanging on. Another typical dream is one in which we find ourselves on a steep mountainside. The soil is loose and slides down with us—slowly but relentlessly. Now and then we grasp a shrub, but its roots do not hold and we pull it down with us. There are many dreams which depict the anxiety of nihilism.

What if we have a dream of the anxiety of nihilism? Should we quickly run to a psychiatrist? Not at all. The above analysis can be simplified (or oversimplified) as follows: A person who does not have nihilistic nightmares is ignorant of the philosophic realities of human existence. He is the one who needs psychiatric help. On the other hand, the person who does have nihilistic nightmares is healthy because he has insight into the structure of reality. He is in the state of being that follows rather than precedes a successful series of psychiatric consultations. He may now wish to proceed further and use these insights to achieve more growth. This sequence reverses the socially accepted understanding of mental health. The conventional view—the medical model of the person or the ghost-in-a-machine theory of man—holds that ignorance is healthy and normal and leads to a fulfilled life. And that philosophic insight is a sickness and must be treated medically—hopefully with the result that the state of ignorance will be restored!

Despite these ancillary considerations, we must never forget that nothingness is a descriptive metaphor for consciousness itself. Sartre recognized this when he titled his *magnum opus* *Being and Nothingness*, where nothingness functions like an adjective describing consciousness or the *pour soi*. In the end, the identity of consciousness with nothingness is the explanation for the pervasiveness of anxiety. But since consciousness is also the basic world category in Oriental philosophy, the converse of anxiety is security (and bliss).

Notes

1. Bertrand Russell, "A Free Man's Worship," in *Mysticism and Logic* (New York: Norton, 1929), p. 47.
2. Genesis 22:1-2

Chapter 10 • COPING WITH THE
ANXIETY OF NIHILISM

Four Responses

The enormity of the aloneness and isolation adumbrated by the anxiety of nihilism leaves us only a paltry list of responses. Rebellion or *protest* is a youthful and Promethean defiance toward this hollow fate. Both art and ambition can be successful albeit ephemeral anodynes, for every work of art has limits. A painting has a frame; a play or symphony begins and ends. Defiance against nothingness, however noble, also has its limits.

Our response to nihilism can be *commitment* to a goal that is larger than ourselves. To participate in something that will live beyond us and to be involved in matters transcending our own limited individuality are also solutions to the problem of the anxiety of nihilism, solutions that mankind has investigated, proffered, and used. These two responses to nihilism— rebellion and commitment—do not depend entirely or necessarily on a religious or idealistic metaphysics. They must be classified as essentially nonreligious responses.

Some answers, however, do presuppose a theological view of the world. One is *resignation*. We can resign ourselves to the lack of foundation and to the envelope of non-being. We then say to God "Thy will be done" and accept with full resignation the incomprehensibility of our fate. History has proven that we can do this. In this posture, we do not understand and we do not wish to understand why there is nothing behind appearances. But in the end we accept it as right and true even though it is incomprehensible in its unfairness. Perhaps we have faith that the apparent emptiness is really full and that the anxiety has an unfathomable but real purpose. We do not feel that and we do not understand it; but we are persuaded that in some absolute sense these answers exist. Perhaps in another life, or at some other time, or when the moment of grace touches us, nihilism— or at least what appears to be nihilism—will indeed make sense. That is why St. Augustine said we must first believe so that we may then understand (*credo ut intelligam*). Such is one possible legitimate and respectable answer that most Western religions have given to the anxiety of nihilism. It is called faith.

The final response to nihilism that mankind has historically investigated and used is that of *mysticism*. In this resolution, the anxiety reveals nihilism itself to be an illusion. It is the dream quality of this world which proves that the consensual world is without foundation. The mystical solution is very important because it transforms the experience of nihilism into its opposite, namely, the sense of ground. It is therefore with ample justification that the insights of Eastern philosophies are slowly being incorporated into Western psychotherapy—a prediction Schopenhauer had made more than one hundred years ago. The philosophical foundations for humanistic psychology must enable us to do precisely that: They must create for us an ontology which translates these Eastern insights into *bona fide* Western possibilities.

Coping Strategies

When we apply these philosophic ideas to psychopathology and psychotherapy, we will find that this analysis of anxiety may be of considerable use. Conditions of high anxiety, such as anxiety neurosis, and the vast amount of free-floating or unbound anxiety found in psychoses and schizophrenias can be illuminated by relating them to the anxiety of nihilism. We can argue that a life organized around the defense against anxiety—which may be true of all of us, except that anxiety neurotics, psychotics, and schizophrenics may do it expensively and inefficiently—is one that says "I must repress at all costs the truth of nihilism; I must spare no effort and no expense to run away from the truth of nihilism." These conditions are correctly diagnosed as neurotic because they do not confront openly the revelation of that anxiety. Repressing nihilism leads to the panic of an anxiety neurosis—because suppression in the end will fail. Confronting nihilism leads to truth and to whatever authentic answers and solutions there are.

THE NOTHINGNESS-GROUND TRANSFORMATION

The West says we are a field of consciousness and the discovery of this field is the experience of nihilism, of nothingness, and of foundationlessness. The East likewise says that we are a field of consciousness, but that its discovery is the experience of peace, bliss, and joy. We must always remember the intimate connection between two apparently incompatible views: despair or joy. We must compare resignation to anxiety in a consensual world with mystical resolution to anxiety in an otherworldly metaphysics; either reality is anxiety or reality is peace and bliss. There are several possible philosophic resolutions to this cultural and historical conflict. One is to view anxiety and peace as two poles on a continuum of the experience of consciousness. Another, undoubtedly related to the first, is the idea of transforming nothingness to ground and anxiety to peace.

The first coping device for the anxiety of nihilism is to translate that nothingness into concrete being. How is that to be done? When we think of coping with nihilism we can fantasize climbing K-2, a Himalayan mountain more severe even than Mount Everest. We picture the icy winds of nothingness cutting sharply into our faces as we scale the snowy cliffs. This fantasy—with its purely intuitive illogic—then shifts to the beginning of Nietzsche's *Zarathustra*. We now see another mountaintop—a steep and beautiful Alpine hill with a commanding view rather than the forbidding Himalayan peak—with Nietzsche's eagle and serpent, symbols for the highest and the lowest in the human spectrum. There, Zarathustra has been absorbing the overflow of the sun's radiance for ten years, and now, being filled to overflowing himself, he descends to share with mankind his new "inward morning."[1]

All these images have one meaning: we open ourselves to the anxiety of nihilism. We no longer fight the terror of nothingness, the dark night of the soul. On the contrary, we abandon ourselves to it. In so doing, the nothingness itself becomes our nature; the nothingness hardens; the nothingness even feels comfortable. We exclaim, *I experience the ground!* The secret of this transformation is not to fight, suppress, or repress the anxiety but to *allow it to happen*. We witness a miracle in this transfiguration. Most anxiety, including psychosis and schizophrenia, may be a growth stage that we must work through. By facing the anxiety we move to the other side, where we find our answer. Under these circumstances pills or escapes, Meprobamate or alcohol, sex or divorce, all these devices try to halt the progress of anxiety-consciousness. Escape from anxiety is also escape from truth and wisdom. But the consciousness of the anxiety of nihilism must move forward. Only the courage to know that anxiety is existence and life can get us past the obstacle and to our destination of complete self-disclosure and self-realization. In fairy tales the anxiety, which is the obstacle, must always be confronted, attacked, and overcome —be it sleep or death, be it dragons, enemies, fires, forests, rivers, caves, or any number of assorted monsters. We must do that in real life as well.

Solutions

There are essentially two ways to cope with the anxiety of nihilism. One is to use naked willpower to establish an identity. That is the way of Sartre and Camus, perhaps partially also of Heidegger. We have developed an image for it in the fantasy of the mountain climber. The willpower approach to the management of the anxiety of nihilism is also found in the image of God as the ex-nihilo creator of the world. This is the powerful and noble image of a human being forever capable of choosing to say no to any fate and thereby eternally asserting the dignity of an undaunted and indomitable human spirit. The other way is to discover, through the phenomenological exploration of the anxiety of nihilism itself, a universal foundation and then willingly be it or surrender to it. In this case anxiety shows us how non-being becomes being or how nothingness is transmuted into ground. This is the image of God as a necessary being or as the foundation. We surrender to the fall; we trust the chilling emptiness.

The first of these solutions is humanistic or atheistic. It is Camus's rebel against life and it is expressed in the myth of Prometheus. The second is the answer of faith and religion; it is theistic. It is the dimension of trust and of belief. The first is proud and the second, meek. The first is defiant, the second, submissive. The first shouts danger and the second whispers protection.

In either case we must allow anxiety to happen. When anxiety occurs ultimately, and when nothingness is thereby revealed in its full nakedness, then that hollow emptiness gradually congeals into a solid and permanent ground. We take a closer look and we see the world of Heraclitus transformed into the world of Parmenides. We then make the momentous discovery that the answer is not to find that after all somewhere within nothingness there floats a God or a support (in infinite space it could always be at an infinite distance from us) but that the nothingness itself is in fact the ultimate reality of our very own consciousness. We discover that our consciousness *is* nothingness. We discover that the word nothingness is used only as contrast to the empirical realm of objects. It is not to be feared. The emptiness terrifies us only as long as we insist that we are not this emptiness, that we do not want to be it, and that it is radically different from us. Our fear of nothingness is then seen to be but our resistance to it, merely a reflection of ignorance about the transcendental dimension. The anxiety of nihilism teaches us that we ourselves are this nothingness and that we are not opposed to it at all. It is our pure inward consciousness. And thus we experience the mysterious and wondrous release of ultimate reconciliation.

Transcendental Revelation

The significance of the above introspective descriptions is that the anxiety of nihilism actually reveals to us the transcendental dimension in its fullness. Nothingness and consciousness are experienced to be coeval.

These are phenomenological descriptions of the anxiety which is manifest in the vision of nothingness. It is a nothingness which stares at us when we look for our roots, our foundations, our home, and our security. At that time we make another momentous discovery: We recognize the important equivalence in the meanings to which the following seven words refer (none is a technical term but each is plucked from our experience and our life-world): consciousness, space, time, energy, illumination, language, and nothingness. All amplify phenomenologically the most general use of the verb "to see." They mean and refer to the transcendental dimension as it is uncovered through reductive or reflexive thinking and focus on the outward meaning, self-transcending, and intentional direction of the field of consciousness. This septagonal structure revealed by the anxiety of nihilism is our entry into the eternity and concreteness of our transcendental nature. Seeing is—or these seven aspects of being are—like a peaceful rainbow over a torrential waterfall. And that is the experience of ground revealed to us by the existential anxiety of nihilism and not available to those who neurotically deny that anxiety. Once we have established that nothingness is consciousness we have touched, paradoxically as it may seem, the indestructible aspect of that nothingness.

In fact, we can add to the above seven words the terms God, being, and nature. They all possess a level of equivalence, if we accept these words as primitive to the life-world and thus as nontechnical, and if we are sensitive to the fringe meanings and the poetic connotations to which they allude. Each one of the ten can be used to describe or define the others. The anxiety of nihilism makes these equivalences experiential, because when we search for words which will describe for us or evoke in others the direct intuition of nothingness, we find ourselves using terms such as consciousness, space-time, God, being, and so forth predominantly. We will then have discovered, experientially, the reality of immortality associated with the archetypal choice for universality discussed in Book One.[2]

The Sea

The fact that the anxiety of nihilism has the power to transmute terror into security, abandonment into home, and nothingness into ground is importantly illustrated by the universal symbol of the sea. We can work out within ourselves the problem of nihilism indirectly through the symbol of the sea. Poetry, fantasy, dreams, and other uses of the imagination can help us transform the terror of the sea into a phenomenon of great aesthetic value. The sea is both a threat and a home. We come from it ancestrally through biological evolution. Our largest cities are built on its shores. Our dreams and vacations float over its waves. The feel of water enveloping our bodies renews us so that we feel reborn. We think of young Christopher Columbus, sitting on a pier, looking distantly into the horizon and dreaming of future lands beyond. These are the positive, secure, and home-coming aspects of the image of the sea. To this extent the sea is our ground.

But it is also the symbol of nihilism. We may dread the vast amount of water below us when we fly over the oceans. The ocean proverbially is the abode of monsters, some of which in fact exist, like killer sharks, clutching octopuses, and enormous whales. The ocean is dark and it is deep. It is cold; powerful currents crisscross it. The sea is the world's largest symbol of suffocation. So the ocean terrifies us as well as soothes us. And as Rudolf Otto has pointed out, when bliss and terror combine we get fascination.

In dreams the ocean can be both death and salvation. It depends on whether we conceive of ourselves as individuals—in which case the sea scares us—or as universalities—in which case we are the vast and the eternal sea and its image is soothing and peaceful.

Thus, the transformation of anxiety to ground is one of the fundamental coping devices for the anxiety of nihilism.

TRUTH

Another coping device, derived from the above, is to realize that the anxiety of nihilism reveals a profound truth to us. A therapist who chooses to operate in this philosophic context can convey to his client, in whatever way is effective and appropriate, that this anxiety demonstrates not that he is sick but that a starving and thirsting philosopher-artist exists within him. Throughout history, devotion to the realization of the pervasive truth of nihilism and dedication to the understanding that the empty consciousness (the consciousness of dreamless sleep) is that very nothingness has been one of the supreme and noble functions of the philosopher and the artist. To be pregnant with such vast understanding, to be in touch with history—in other words, to be in contact not only with the world of space but with the world of time or historicity—are experiences and insights to be proud of, not pathologies to be treated with Mellaril or phenothiazine.

Therefore, the anxiety of nihilism is not exactly a severe illness but rather a clarity about the ultimate truth of being itself. And the question of truth may well be more important than the precise nature of the affect which accompanies the insight. Furthermore, we can cope with the insight. In fact, it is desirable to cope with the insight. What is not desirable is to deny it. The former is existential anxiety; it leads to meaning. The latter is neurotic anxiety; it leads to symptoms. Any client can take heart in this insight, although it requires creative imagination on the part of the therapist to find ways of facilitating it. The great philosophers, saints, writers, and artists, the great seers and the courageous reformers have all shared this insight. They understood deeply the real meaning of the anxiety of nihilism. They also knew that a human being is real and noble to the extent that he or she copes with that anxiety.

Illnesses—mental, physical, and social—arise only with the denial of this ontological truth. Medication, although not always contraindicated, often helps to strengthen the very forces of denial it wishes to conquer. Paradoxical as it may seem, the uncanny sensitivities often found in schizophrenics may be due to the fact not that they are sick but that they are truly in touch with these perennial and profound philosophic insights. The trouble is, we reject these insights during "business hours," that is, in the consensual world; neither we nor the schizophrenic have acquired the wisdom to both appreciate and manage the anxiety of nihilism. An excellent example of the conflict between the neurotic and the existential anxiety of nihilism is seen in the following letter. Medication means the denial of the anxiety of nihilism. For this patient, the denial approach was worse than irrelevant. It was destructive and dehumanizing. This patient needed a secure atmosphere in which to confront her existential anxiety. In so doing, she experienced growth.

You did me a huge favor in suggesting [the existential therapist] Dr. _____ as a psychiatrist. My previous therapist did much damage and in fact probably caused me to remain sick longer than I would have otherwise. My previous therapist kept me on Mellaril which is a very strong mind-altering drug which causes lack of memory, function, and so forth. (The therapist stated that these effects were symptoms of my disease and not the effect of the drug, but I strongly feel otherwise.) My previous therapist also told me I would have to take Mellaril the rest of my life, that I would always be an "invalid" and that I must accept myself as an invalid who could never work at the capacity of other people. Dr. _____ immediately disagreed. He told me that I was not as deeply sick as she had stated, but that I had a "poor script" which I followed. Dr. _____ has helped me outline the direction I want my life to go in, the changes necessary to bring about that direction and a general idea of my problem areas. He is also a very human, personable individual whom I can relate to very well.

In pursuing the theme that bearing the burden of the anxiety of nihilism is one of mankind's noblest tasks, it would not be an exaggeration to ask the (sophisticated) client, "Why do you want to bury the Plato, the St. Augustine, the Galileo, the Mozart, the Michelangelo, or the Shakespeare within you?" If the patient does not cope well with the anxiety of nihilism, it may be due more to his or her escape from it than it is from the anxiety itself. Once faced and understood the anxiety of nihilism need not be feared.

HISTORY

In another and related coping device, the client can be informed that this anxiety is in truth what it feels like to have the current of history running through him or her. History—seen *sub specie aeternitatis*—can be interpreted to be the world's movement toward ever increasing philosophic understanding. The thrust of history is the demand that consciousness fully reveal itself as human self-consciousness. History is the movement toward ever greater clarity about the structure of the field of consciousness that we are and of our transcendental possibilities. It is thus the development of consciousness—from the darkness of total nonexistence to the sunburst of its fullest potential. And the client must be made aware that this current is running through him or her and that it is going through the business of evolution right there in his or her empirical existence. This current of historical electricity is experienced as the anxiety of nihilism. The patient should not squelch it with a pill but wear it proudly and develop it confidently. Suffering and pain are then perceived in a new perspective. Pain has been deconstituted from its meaning as illness and reconstituted into its meaning as task.

Of course when dealing with a client in these terms limits must be placed on this strategy. It could lead to unrealistic world views and there is always the danger that these ideas, injudiciously used, feed the delusions of some patients. But the essence stands: the anxiety of nihilism is but the experience of being in touch with the current of history, with the evolutionary development of consciousness out of lifeless matter. Only through a comprehension of the transcendental aspect of being is such a world view possible and contact with that aspect of existence established. Supremely anxious persons—anxiety neurotics, psychotics, or schizophrenics—may have their eyes permanently forced open against their will to the transcendental truth about human existence. Allowing for such an unorthodox interpretation of psychopathology is one of the basic contributions that existential psychotherapy can make to conventional views. (This point is developed further in Book Three.)

TASK

A third coping strategy is to transmit to the client the realization that the anxiety of nihilism assigns to him or her a noble task and even a prophetic destiny. As it did through a prophetess in ancient Greece, being speaks through the client's anxiety of nothingness. But like a prophet among the Israelites, the client is entrusted with the active role of implementing the message. Stated differently, we must *respond* to the knowledge that anxiety reveals. We do that by finding our task. And our task is simply to manage that anxiety, or, which is the same, to manage the human condition. The anxiety of nihilism gives us the challenge of defining human nature; it gives us the purpose of learning how to cope with being human.

We are not performing this noble task only for ourselves. We are doing it for all mankind; we are choosing for history. Confronting the anxiety of nihilism is the specific task that history has assigned to our age. Everyone is watching to see how each of us copes with that anxiety. Since history runs through us, every person can be a hero and a leader. Confronted with these realities, the client may well measure up to the challenge. And the client will find joy and meaning, a sense of being alive, in taking up that challenge.

A good example of how the discovery of a historical task helps us cope with nihilistic anxiety is the problem of a woman who must redefine her role as woman and as feminine in our changing and liberalizing society. Being now roleless, or feeling her role undermined, or undermining it herself by feeling dissatisfied with the roles assigned to her by society, many women today are justifiably concerned. Women, as a class, perhaps even more than men, are exposed to the anxiety of nihilism by the mere fact of being women. First, many women feel justly that they have been oppressed. The inability to fully say yes to herself may make her feel in certain contexts like a zero. And what invariably accompanies the experience of a zero center is either almost catatonic withdrawal and ennui or an apparently inexplicable and frighteningly irrational rage. Second, once a woman liberates herself, she is again faced with the anxiety of nihilism, in that she must create out of nothing her new set of values, self-concepts, roles, and world views. Since now she is divested of her roles, she is also structureless. She therefore faces the abyss of nothingness. Her roles, which were her surrogates for ground, support, and security, have finally demonstrated their fraudulence. There is no other ground that can readily replace what she has lost. It appears once more that women are entrusted with the emotional business of our society.

This problem, faced by many thoughtful women, must not be construed to be a personal issue. As a personal issue it may look maladjusted, neurotic, or pathological. But in truth it is a world issue, an issue perhaps unique to this period of history. She experiences in her being-in-the-world the high level of development that freedom has achieved in this period of history. Freedom is a transcendental phenomenon; it is another trait of pure consciousness (discussed in the next chapter). At this very moment, she is living the awareness of freedom as it is evolving itself through her. Her coping with that anxiety is really history coping with that anxiety. The woman who faces her task of role redefinition is more advanced and mature than the one who still hides from it.

The erosion of roles is both a natural development of social and historical progress and the unfolding of the intrinsic truth of a person's ontological freedom for self-definition. For a woman to cope with that situation means to understand it, to grasp her freedom, and to use it to either rechoose her ancient roles or create a set of new ones. The precondition is to embrace the anxiety of nihilism, because by transforming nothingness into ground and anxiety into security, she has the ego-strength and the foundation to carry out her redefinition. And she is most positively not doing it for herself alone. She is accomplishing this task for all women, eventually, for all men as well. At this level, a philosophically oriented psychotherapy becomes a political issue. Counseling becomes prophetic.

If these analyses are integrated into counseling, the client can achieve a justified sense of health, importance, and worth. He or she is now a person of true substance, and does not need to affect solidity through any kind of bravado such as fancy clothes, big cars, expensive homes, or obtrusive mannerisms.

Adrienne Rich perceived these insights beautifully when she wrote that we are "living through a time that needs to be lived through us."

The moral and political dimensions can thus be introduced into the therapeutic framework on the same grounds and with the same certitude as any scientific discovery. The phenomenological model of being, by assigning equal reality status to both the empirical and the transcendental regions, can justify in terms of a general theory the scientific character of ethical and political obligations. We see once more, as we did in analyzing coping devices for the anxiety of evil, that clinical philosophy is not only therapy but also morality. There is thus essentially no difference between coping well with life in general and coping well with conditions of psychopathology.

We now turn to more narrowly practical ways of coping with the anxiety of nihilism. Our eventual hope is that through them we may also find our ground.

GROUNDING

The search for the sense of ground must be deliberate. When Jefferson, addressing the French *philosophes,* wrote in the *Declaration of Independence* that all men have a right to life, liberty, and happiness, he had changed what was the prior Lockean emphasis on *property* into the utilitarian principle of *happiness.* We can learn how to find our ground by examining the symbolic value of an "unalienable" right to property in the Lockean and Jeffersonian interpretations. To have property means symbolically to be rooted or grounded, since the most primitive sense of property is land or ground. The expression, "the land of our fathers" still pulls at our heartstrings. Displaced persons, be they Jews or Palestinians, East Germans or Mainland Chinese, Africans or Europeans, suffer more deeply and create more political disturbances than most other types of individuals. They do so because they are uprooted, because being landless is to be ungrounded. It is not true that nations want and argue over land because in primitive times grazing, hunting, and agriculture meant sustenance. People want land—especially land over which they have political sovereignty—because land is the symbol of being grounded or having a foundation. Philosophical anthropology precedes scientific anthropology.

The struggle among Christians, Moslems, and Jews over Jerusalem is a controversy over one universal and popular symbol for ultimate ground. Jerusalem is the source and homeland of all three religions. The worldwide interest in the fate of Jerusalem seems to be in part a projection of the world community's need for a sense of home, for feeling grounded. Jerusalem is a most likely object to lend itself to such projections.

To have a right to property means, in general terms, to exert absolute control over some region of space-time. That this region be earth and that it support agriculture or cattle are essentially romantic atavisms anachronistic for our age. It need not be land, or even a nation. All persons must choose their own private symbols for property, for property is a person's ultimate home. They cannot afford to ape advertisers' enticements that real estate or motor homes, mountain property or outboard motor boats are true homes. Overpopulation—even though it limits actual land—does not therefore stand in the way.

Education

There are some genuine pieces of *property* where we can find our home and can capture the sense of being grounded. Education is a good example. It is both an intrinsic value and, obviously, a commonly used coping device for grounding us against the anxiety of nihilism. Aristotle said that the best provision for old age is education. Education is pursued not for the sake of a better job; nor is it meant to please one's parents or impress one's peers. Real education is not a ladder to status; on the contrary, education is one of the few things that a person undertakes exclusively for himself or herself. To become an educated person is to follow one's very own curriculum; its rewards are the satisfactions one achieves within oneself. Our education is the region of space-time over which we have precisely as much control and jurisdiction as we choose. A scientific researcher who has command over his material is respected and respects himself as would be true of a chief or a king in older days who might have earned his exalted position of control through his military exploits. Education without standards is a gift-wrapped box that is empty. It is standards for excellence that give education the substantiality which qualify it to be property and therefore serve as ground. Education which fails to insist on excellence defrauds the student. To become educated is only one symbol for ground, only one strategy for managing the anxiety of nihilism. But it is indeed one of the most important answers that civilization has given to the anxiety of the nihilism-ground issue.

Let us review. Out of the emptiness, the nothingness revealed to us by this anxiety we develop the decision-making capacity to conquer completely one space-time region of being. There are two distinctly different ways to create meaning and ground out of nothingness. One is through exerting sheer ex-nihilo willpower and naked determination. The other is to transform this emptiness into our very being; through a catharsis we discover our ultimate strength hidden within what appeared as our ultimate weakness. How completely we own this property is therefore the result of our own decisions and determination. To find our ground is then neither a matter of automatic nature nor of grace, but the result of our own actions. In therapy this means that the client (and the therapist for that matter) is responsible for finding his own ground and security. Like all freedoms, this insight is both painful and supportive, anxiety-producing and hope-giving. But it should provide a real answer in this age of anxiety and death-of-God morality.

The Pursuit of Excellence

This analysis of grounding shows the central role occupied by the pursuit of excellence. It demonstrates the ontological status of integrity. Character is not a cultural or a psychological trait but a metaphysical reality. Any denigration of excellence undermines the search for our ground. In a musical performance we want excellence of the artist and perfection in the composer. To witness proof that excellence and perfection are approachable or even attainable realities is a deep aesthetic experience. Why? Because it fills us with the joy and enthusiasm of a person who is once more reminded of the ontological truth that human beings can through their own efforts either create or find a ground. That is why we stream to concerts given by the world's greatest musicians, queue for hours before museums, or travel thousands of miles to appreciate an original painting or sculpture. To be informed—through the example of accomplished artists and other creative persons—that perfection can indeed be approximated and therefore meaningfully pursued is to experience a therapeutic cure for the malaise of the human condition in its form of the anxiety of nihilism.

Whereas we seek excellence in education, we demand competence in the professions. Great surgeons or great jurists are important not only because of their influence or the good they do. They are important above all because they serve as models: They are inspiring examples of the answer to the anxiety of nihilism. They have created their ground by being identified with and extended over as many nooks and crannies of their property—that is, the space-time region of being that they have designated as the symbol for ground—as is at all possible. And that proprietary region is their specific professional specialty and contribution. Thus, accomplished professionals are what they are not due to any need, or instinct for recognition, or compensation for feelings of inferiority, or because of an overdeveloped superego, but because their competence is the secret to the experience of foundation and ground. That is their working answer to the anxiety of nihilism. The specific means they use to achieve this experience may in themselves be but surrogates, symbols, or metaphors. But the experience thus attained is indeed a genuine perception of the authentic ground of being and the real answer to nihilistic anxiety.

The same considerations that apply to education, the arts, and the professions are relevant to business, to labor, and to skills. Freud, in praising work, recognized this coping strategy, although he was not equipped to conceptualize it philosophically and was thus limited by a narrowly physiological and mechanistic version of the medical model of the person. But work is not busy-work. The kind of work which binds anxiety because it elicits the experience of ground must have character, integrity, and be creative. Busy-work, on the other hand, produces neurotic anxiety because it is work used to escape rather than to confront the search for foundations.

The Empirical Ego

Another area in which we can locate our symbol for ground is in the vast land that is our particular empirical ego. The empirical ego consists, minimally, of the body, feelings, needs, attitudes, behavior, and the unconscious. We can find our ground, we can feel rooted and at home, if we adopt an unalienable-right-to-property attitude toward any one of these elements of the empirical ego. The Third Force in psychology has done precisely that, and it has been done in response to the dissolution and erosion in our age of more traditional grounds, such as the family, children, the state, religion, myth, and tradition, as well as the arts and crafts handed down from generation to generation. These older grounding techniques were appropriate to static social organizations, but they no longer are relevant to a highly mobile society where global and instantaneous communication has become an axiom of life. Humanistic psychology has therefore stepped in and discovered that the empirical ego can indeed serve effectively as a replacement for ancient grounds. To be rooted in the empirical ego is to be a humanist; it is to choose to make our individual and finite life on earth into the meaning of our existence. And that was the original message of existentialism, especially in such existential precursors as Kierkegaard and Nietzsche. And that is one proper and historically proven way to experience our ontological ground.

The Body

To consolidate the above position, let us examine separately several of the six enunciated elements of the empirical ego. We can be assisted in finding our ground in our body through several body therapy techniques which have been popular at various times—bioenergetics, rolfing, massage, polarity therapy, the Feldenkrais method, and so forth. The popularity of these particular growth-facilitating approaches will change in time. And the level of competence and sophistication with which they have been applied also varies greatly. Sometimes these are well integrated into a total philosophy of life, in which case they can be very effective; at other times they are used in isolation and are therefore only peripherally meaningful experiences. Nevertheless, one fact remains: The emphasis in therapy to work with the body, to help the patient to find a home in the body—as an adjunct both to life in general and to a professionally supervised overall therapy program—will remain as a permanent contribution to the healer's toolbox. There is very little question that body therapies are a powerful instrument for grounding. But the technique itself is not enough; its place in a larger philosophic context must also be understood. In this therapeutic approach the body has become the lived symbol for the ground of being. Only when body-work is placed consciously in such a total context of a philosophy of life, and only when it is understood in terms of a philosophic view of the person, does it reach its fullest value.

Feelings

Acquiring respect for our own personal feelings, needs, attitudes, and behaviors—learning to discriminate between our genuine ("gut") feelings and those artificially imposed upon us by the demands of our parental and social environment—has been a traditionally important element in therapeutic techniques. Its philosophic significance rests on the general principle that we can experience our ground in the affective region of the empirical ego. We have empirical (as well as intuitive) evidence that it works. The orthodox therapeutic techniques of acceptance and noninterference and of maintaining an optimum level of anxiety—possibly most clearly embodied in Carl Rogers's client-centered approach—stir up dormant and unsuspected emotions. Healing can occur often without interpretation, in which case the richer feelings themselves bring about the experience of ground. It is the life of our feelings that provides the exuberant sense of foundation. If we *are in touch with our feelings*, we also have a concrete sense of being a ground. We experience in the intensity and the richness of our feelings the fact that we are indeed the power to resist the threat of non-being.

The Unconscious

The unconscious is a particularly important part of the empirical ego. It undergirds all its other aspects. It snakes continuously through life like an underground river. The techniques for tapping the unconscious are well-known. New ones are discovered all the time, and this is not the place for a compendium of them. Nevertheless, a few reminders may be useful. Fantasy work in general (psychosynthesis and the guided daydream are good examples) facilitates access to the unconscious. Primal scream therapy, dream analysis, hypnosis, drugs—all these devices help give access to the unconscious. Also effective are the older techniques of free-association and anxiety-producing interpretations. The unconscious can also serve as ground—and a very potent one indeed.

The unconscious is part of the empirical ego, buried in the same way our liver and our pancreas lie beneath the skin and are hidden from consciousness. The unconscious is a mystery only to those who confuse consciousness with the objects of consciousness. Consciousness can have as its objects physical events (rocks, bodies) and psychological events (feelings). All objects can be hidden from sight. What cannot be hidden is subjective consciousness, the observer of all objects. The philosophical question (called the problem of the existence of the external world or that of the ontological status of universals) is "Where are our feelings, memories, and so forth, when we do not perceive them?" The implication is that feelings are made up of consciousness and consciousness exists only to the extent that we are conscious. But once we realize that feelings are objects and not consciousness, the mystery either vanishes completely or becomes one with the mystery of the whereabouts of unperceived physical objects. (This point is discussed in Book Three.)

The unconscious, therefore, is a vast mass of out-of-view body experiences, feelings, attitudes, hopes, and fears, which are of the same ontological order as their physical equivalents—that is, out-of-view objects. The only difference is that unconscious material, precisely because it has been repressed, is judged by the psychic censor to be a threat to the integrity of the ego, something which is not the case with unconscious or unperceived physical objects. Furthermore, the concept of the unconscious becomes meaningful in a theory of *layered* reality—a reality that is not only surface but also contains depth.

The *individual unconscious* consists of memories from our childhood. They are hidden memory-objects, and it is we who are hiding them daily. The *collective unconscious* consists of memories of the human race, which the race hides daily from itself. The explanation for the existence of a collective unconscious can come from three directions. It may be transmitted in some chromosomal fashion. It may be transmitted through a social language that is not verbal. Or it may be evidence for the continuity of consciousness from person to person and generation to generation, so that each individual is in reality less isolated and less separated than he believes himself to be.

Philosophy must thus subscribe to the investigation of the unconscious. That is an extension of the exploration of conscious feelings. Appropriating these unconscious feelings is a way of achieving the sense of ground. It is a way of acquiring property, command over a slice of space-time within the plenitude of being. Consequently, what philosophy adds to psychoanalysis and other approaches to the unconscious is the dimension of understanding. Explorations in the unconscious are therapeutically important because they are strategies to countermand the anxiety of nihilism by the *creation* or the *discovery* (both approaches are possible; each case must be evaluated individually) of a ground. The unconscious is the *ne plus ultra* in the continuing therapeutic effort to find the experience of grounding in an age of alienation.

When dreams or parapraxes are interpreted as wish fulfillments then we own up to them. This act of integration, crucial for successful psychotherapy, is the experience of being grounded in the unconscious. The unconscious treats you the way you treat it, said Jung. If we reject it, we feel incomplete and hollow. If we make it our own, including the demonic and the shadow, we feel whole and secure and therefore grounded. This is a fundamental principle of all depth psychotherapy.

Beyond the Self

The individual unconscious (as opposed to the collective unconscious) facilitates grounding when our approach is in line with or a reflection of the individual consciousness.[3] It establishes contact between our consciousness and the totality of our empirical ego. There is, however, another way.

If we now search for coping strategies based on the expanded intimate and social consciousness, and we look for their reflections in the world, we move into the areas of love and tradition. We can find our ground in our relation to another person, such as a husband, wife, child, parent, lover, friend, patient or student. Strictly speaking, we are then moving beyond the *pure* empirical ego into the gray area beyond that we call *world*. But a relationship is as much "ontological real estate" as are our feelings and bodies. What is important to keep in mind is that a relationship can serve to make us feel grounded not only in and of itself, or in an axiomatic and irreducible fashion, but above all because we can use that relationship as our personal symbol for the ground that counteracts the anxiety of nihilism. If we find our home in a relationship, then it is this empirical encounter which is our own lived symbol for the reality of the intersubjective or intimate consciousness. And the phenomenon of transcendental intersubjectivity, because it is an expansion of pure consciousness, is clearly an experience in the direction of an absolute ground. In the last analysis this is the experience of the universal ground of being as the field of consciousness.

If in our search for ground we now move even beyond the intersubjective consciousness and into the regions of society and tradition, then we contact the worldly equivalent of the social consciousness, which is what is evoked by the collective unconscious. In phenomenology we assume that each conscious or noetic, that is, transcendental, act has a noematic, empirical, or worldly correlate, which is the strands of meaning constituted by transcendental consciousness.

Specifically, these individual, intersubjective, and social coping strategies work in the following way: The client explores with his counselor the possibility that there may be significant threads in the fabric of his heritage. He may wish to recommit his life to them. Examples can be found in the family. Family ties are often broken. Grounding might be achieved—these are of course strictly individual matters—by reestablishing relationships with lost or ignored relatives, including in-laws, cousins, and relatives in distant lands. Another source of social grounding might be found in matters relating to tradition. The client may choose to reestablish an identity with his religious background—perhaps once abandoned—or his ethnic tradition. He may find it of value to accentuate his ethnicity rather than to minimize it. He may take pride in it and wish to transmit it to his children. *My people* will then become a phrase of profound emotional meaning. Each time it stirs him he in actuality touches his sacred ground. Whereas patriotism may be out of vogue in many quarters, it can still serve as one more method of grounding. So can devotion to a cause and an ideal. And the same function can be served—perhaps less conclusively—by associations of some standing such as Masons, Boy Scouts, Alcoholics Anonymous and new organizations such as the Delancey Street Foundation.

Although prima facie there is no connection between tradition and the collective unconscious, contact between them can nevertheless be established. Whereas using the body and the empirical ego, in its narrow conception, as ground-surrogate is a reflection in the world of what in the transcendental region is the individual consciousness, using historical and societal events for this purpose is a reflection in the world of what in the transcendental region is the social consciousness. And that consciousness extends both in length and amplitude far beyond either the individual or the intersubjective consciousness. The social consciousness therefore encompasses the region of the collectivity, whether conscious or unconscious. That is the collective unconscious. He who finds his roots in society and tradition is finding them in the empirical correlate of the collective unconscious.

We must argue here as we did above that the collective unconscious refers to that part of the world psyche which is hidden from our conscious view in exactly the way the collective material unconscious—such as the uninhabited jungles of the Amazon, the earth's molten core and the planets of a foreign star—is hidden from our physical eye. The existence of collective archetypes is no greater mystery or logical contradiction than were Platonic Forms or are those material objects which, while theoretically accessible to all, are in practice beyond the collective reach.

For our discussion of the last of these coping strategies we revisit the two kinds of universality—the conscious and the bodily—covered in Book One. The transpersonal, the religious, and the mystical client on the one hand and the nature worshiper on the other will find their experience of the ground in transcendental consciousness and universal nature respectively. Their urgent medicine is to recover contact and identification with their pure and transcendental conscious center through meditation and asceticism or to restore their oneness with nature by exposing themselves to the experiences of renewal made available by nature, art, or backpacking.

SUMMARY

We can now summarize the nihilism-ground issue as follows: The name of the revelation of anxiety, or existential anxiety proper, is the anxiety of nihilism or the anxiety of the nihilism-ground question. When the reality of that anxiety is denied and thereby becomes neurotic, it leads to the symptom of insecurity. If we need one word which describes the pathology of the neurotic anxiety of nihilism, that word is *insecurity*.[4] If we are to choose a second word that gives us the essence of this neurotic anxiety, it is *weak* or *weakness*. The answer to insecurity and weakness lies in accepting and integrating existential anxiety. The result can be a sense of homecoming, strength, and grounded security. The treatment suggested to translate anxiety into security has the following framework: Either use naked willpower to establish an identity (which is the ex-nihilo procedure adopted by humanistic and atheistic existentialists)—an example of which is the experience of embodiment—or discover that a universal and real foundation—such as pure consciousness—does in fact exist (which is a religious approach). If you choose the latter, then surrender to this universal consciousness; identify with it; be it.

If we politicize these psychological themes, we get a desideratum something like this: Demand that a world government permanently preserve an aesthetic biosphere as the absolute home of mankind. The emphasis is that spaceship earth is the only objectively real home that we have. In fact, on the earth it is only the wafer-thin layer called the biosphere that is our legitimate and only possible home. And only a world government can deal effectively to preserve a home that is hopelessly interdependent. The biosphere must be aesthetic because it is through that quality that we can identify with our true material home. Only through the beauty of the world can we sense our oneness with material nature.

Notes

1. Thoreau's felicitous phrase.

2. The anxiety-ground transformation is developed in detail in Peter Koestenbaum, *Is There An Answer To Death?*, where it appears as the death-immortality sequence.

3. See Book One, Chap. 6.

4. We all remember Alan Watts' *The Wisdom of Insecurity* (New York: Random House, 1968).

Chapter 11 • FREEDOM

The Nature and Importance of Free Will

Anxiety reveals me as a freedom. The revelation of freedom, because of the enormity of the topic, deserves a massive analysis which can only be presented here in outline form.

Existential anxiety reveals that I am free, or, as we should say, that *I am a freedom*. Neurotic anxiety represses the knowledge that I am free. In a normally functioning field of consciousness, the denial of freedom is in turn a free act. In fact, all types of neurotic anxiety reduce themselves to an act of freedom. The denial of anxiety is the free act of repressing that anxiety. It is thus an act of self-deception. Strictly speaking, inauthenticity and neuroticism are therefore not the destruction of freedom but the use of freedom to repress the use of freedom *and* the use of freedom to repress the knowledge of this repression. Although the neurotic anxiety of freedom results in our putting freedom out of action for all practical purposes, freedom itself is not destroyed. And as long as freedom is not destroyed there is hope that authenticity can be recovered. This complex condition of self-deception is the inner structure of the neurotic anxiety of freedom. That is what happens when we deny our freedom.

All revelations of anxiety can lead to transcendental, empirical, or *noetic-noematic* material or insights. To be specific, being, as an *ego-cogito-cogitatum* continuum, consists of three regions: subject, object, and the connection between them (see Chapter 2 of Book One). Anxiety, because it is an ontological disclosure of the totality of being human, can therefore reveal aspects of all three regions, although the principal emphasis here has been its disclosure of the transcendental dimension. Similarly, in the case of freedom, the most important feature of its revelation is of course its transcendental aspect. In short, existential anxiety reveals to us that freedom is a transcendental phenomenon—a world-constituting phenomenon, a *creatio-ex-nihilo* phenomenon. Inasmuch as existential anxiety is the revelation of freedom, it reaches directly into the very source of being. But it also touches a source of profound agony: The fact that I am a freedom means I have no answers for those questions that absolutely need answers. And these questions are, What is true? and What is real?

Freedom is to the world as God is to the world. Both are external to nature. Freedom is *supernatural* or *extranatural* just as God is conceived to be. The arguments for the existence of God are often misunderstood because God is incorrectly conceived as an object in the world. When that object can neither be found nor demonstrated to exist we are told to conclude that God does not exist. But what does exist is the searcher for God, the questioner, the consciousness that seeks. And that observing consciousness is immediately misjudged to be another object, whereas detailed descriptive and reductive analyses show that this consciousness is not of the order of objects but of an infinite regress not unlike space and time.

It is quite appropriate therefore to call that consciousness God. God must be understood to be the observer of the world, which is the same as the consciousness that we ourselves are. We are like God, not to the extent that we are members of this world, but insofar as we are the consciousness *of* or the perceivers *of* this world. The same is true of freedom. Freedom is not an object nor is it a process or even a relationship in the world. On the contrary, freedom is the constituting and cathecting aspect of transcendental consciousness. Freedom may leave footprints in the world, as does God. But in itself it is other-worldly. Freedom is the act of organizing into meanings the world's visible raw material. Since freedom is intimately connected with the experience and act of individuation, freedom becomes the identification of cosmic consciousness with certain specific regions of the transcendental realm, regions which we then call me, mine, or myself.

The *discovery* of the region of freedom in existence (or—in terms of another philosophy of history—the *evolution* of the consciousness and self-consciousness of freedom) coincides with the discovery (or evolution) of morality in the development of the human species. The discovery (or evolution) of the region of transcendental freedom makes it possible for us to ascribe as much reality to the moral dimension of human existence as we do to the physical. This is a central message for today's world of the phenomenological model of being. The spiritual is exactly as real as the physical. Our society is still not based on this insight, due to the influence of a scientific outlook which is excessively objectivistic. Moral laws are not matters of convention any more than are physical laws. Both are discoveries made by carefully observing the field of consciousness or the consciousness-world continuum which we are or which courses through us.

Statements about freedom are therefore either true or false, depending on whether or not they correspond to transcendental reality. Moral laws then become descriptions of the structure of consciousness—that is, their existence encourages our respect for and the generous use of transcendental freedom—just as physical laws are descriptions of the empirical realm. To be moral is as important as to be healthy. It has the same relation to the consciousness of human beings as does being sturdy and well designed (that is, earthquake-proof) does to a skyscraper. Unfortunately, our society, which is objectivistic, materialistic and mechanistic, that is, it operates on the principles of a ghost-in-a-machine theory of personality, is not organized around these principles. The revelation of transcendental freedom is withheld from the foundations of our culture.

There comes a specific moment in the life of any authentic person when, like a divine afflatus in a conversion, the ideal of free will becomes of paramount importance. As a result, one's whole perception of life changes. Suddenly we see that there truly exists the phenomenon of human freedom, that indeed there is an unquenchable element of free will in our consciousness. Once one becomes conscious of the fact that one is a freedom, that there exists within us a zone which is absolutely free—as free as empty space and as free as God—then all else in one's life and one's world sparkles with new possibilities, new hopes, and new joys. The discovery of transcendental freedom is an experience of conversion; it has the power of transformation of the first infatuation of love. For days after this initial discovery one goes through ordinary daily activities exhilarated by the knowledge that one is free, that one is a freedom which no one can destroy, that this is a treasure which no one can take away from us. We now understand that freedom is one's essence and that it expresses itself wherever we are and in whatever we do. That insight, which is as old as the discovery of consciousness itself, is one of the all-time powerful ideas of mankind. It is a pity that this idea is being threatened by the materialistic and thing-oriented world views of today's prevailing winds of doctrine.

Appendix C summarizes the implication of these ideas for education and crime. We can reach consensus in the exploration of inwardness by using methods similar to those which help what Peirce called "the fixation of belief" in the sciences. But a science of subjectivity can be accomplished only after we understand and perform the transcendental-phenomenological *reduction*, that is, when we understand the meaning of reversing the usual direction of the stream of consciousness. A science of subjectivity discovers the structure of freedom and its pervasiveness. It explains once and for all the meaning of personal responsibility. It clarifies the meaning of the phrase "I take full personal responsibility for being myself." The exploration of transcendental consciousness, a type of research which leads to cumulative and publicly accepted data, can place morality on a genuinely scientific basis—a basis which, far from denigrating our humanity, ennobles it.

Self-Definition

Whenever anxiety reveals to us that we are free, that we are freedoms, it demonstrates that we make our decisions ex nihilo, out of nothing. One of the most important functions of the creative spontaneity called freedom is to choose an identity, an essence, a world view, a life-style, a self-concept, or a self-definition. Freedom chooses, out of nothing, a set of values, a belief-system, a metaphysics, or a world design. These are all objective correlates of the freely chosen self-definition. While indeed conscious, that immense freedom is not always *self*-conscious. World constitutions and cathexes as well as self-constitutions and self-cathexes are always free. Much of that freedom, however, is also freely, rationally, and voluntarily repressed, so that in daily life we also have a set of passive constitutions and passive cathexes. These can, however, be activated or reactivated. Self-deception is necessary to successfully carry out the life of the limited consciousness, which is what we normally mean by human existence. Self-deception is therefore part of the archetypal decision for finitude, which lies at the roots of our characteristically finite human existence.

In other words, to live a normal life—rather than either a saintly or schizophrenic life, or the life of a fiery creative genius (these are not the same)—we need to deactivate much of our freedom. We therefore establish in our being-in-the-world a set of passive constitutions and cathexes. However, and at least in theory, these can always be made active. But the price in terms of anxiety of transmuting passivity into activity is very high indeed.

A good example of the experience of transcendental freedom is the fear of heights. It is my freedom, operating out of the abyss of nothingness, which chooses not to jump. Imagine yourself on a gigantic, high, single-span bridge, like San Francisco's Golden Gate, but with the railings removed. The chances of falling into the treacherous and cold currents of San Francisco Bay are no greater than falling off a sidewalk. Yet the anxiety is enormous. Why? Because the decision not to jump is never automatic; nor is it rational. In fact, it is strictly the prerational decision to affirm life rather than to deny life. The fear of heights is thus the experience of the fact that we choose world views and value systems in a prerational realm. Reason itself, as a method of solving problems and as a way of organizing consciousness, is a choice. That is, a life which adheres to rational considerations (as Kant has effectively demonstrated in his discussion of the categorical imperative in his *Metaphysic of Morals*) is chosen not on rational grounds in turn—nor on emotional grounds for that matter —but, strictly speaking, on no grounds at all. Kant calls this choice, in effect, autonomous and spontaneous.

To describe this transcendental freedom, this possibility for transcendental choices, is as difficult as it is important. The experience of the phenomenon of pure freedom can be evoked peripherally, since it is always present in us as long as we are conscious, through Kant's expression: freedom is "spontaneous autonomy." The full depth of one's transcendental freedom is thus apprehended and appreciated as one looks down three hundred or so feet to the bay from atop Golden Gate Bridge. The waves below are diminutive and the drop far greater than one would think when viewing the bridge from the city. A queasy feeling and tingles inside the bones are the physical equivalents of the vision of transcendental freedom which is suddenly forced upon us with full luminosity. The height and the absence of barriers are klieg lights which suddenly illuminate what was the total darkness of the transcendental realm. All at once transcendental freedom is there, naked before us. And we discover that we are it, that we are that freedom. As we look down into the water we realize that not lunging over the side and plunging down into the abyss are no more than our decision not to jump and another's decision not to push us. We are also forced to realize that these decisions have no cause, no antecedents, no reason, no guarantee, and no right or wrong. Since most of us repress our transcendental freedom—and the conscious decision to deny our freedom is an authentic act—we usually avoid situations which expose us to our inner subjective nature.

All that which is the basis of our civilized and human existence must be created instantaneously and continuously. For a moment, as we stand on the bridge, all that which up to this point in time made sense and was logical is now questioned to its very foundations. The civilized and the consensual world must be re-created, reconstructed, and reaccepted. That is the phenomenological essence of the feeling of dizziness. This mental complexity is the phenomenological description of what eventually will be our ex-nihilo decision not to jump. Anxiety states and some schizophrenic reactions often are the uncontrollable experience of this total and excessive freedom. The obsessively fixed openness to transcendental freedom reveals the cosmic enormity of human responsibility. Anxiety neurotics and schizophrenics are then not sick but *too* healthy. They have lost the comfort of passive constitutions and must avail themselves of inefficacious and expensive emergency measures to cope with the unmitigated access which they have to the abyss of their freedom.

There is an added point. To be free means that we are our actions. We are not only our free thoughts, but also the consequences of these thoughts when translated into action. We are our waves of influence. It is therefore a fact of being that the expressions *I choose* and *I am responsible* are synonymous. This point is developed in the next section.

When we apply this philosophic analysis of transcendental freedom to some current social issues, certain insights suggest themselves. While it is of course true that one of the prime functions of society is to preserve freedom, it is also true that the rigidity of society provides the important passive constitutions and cathexes necessary to retain the small amount of freedom we can manage effectively. We need restrictions on our absolute freedom so that what freedom remains can be profitably used. Too much freedom is schizophrenia or total anarchic chaos, whereas insufficient freedom is the death of consciousness itself. Optimum freedom, like optimum life, exists only in the context of an archetypal decision for finitude. Laws, if they are just, can represent these necessary and freely chosen limits to freedom. In the context of managing our freedom, forgiveness and compassion are less important than the dependability of the legal structure of society. Laws must be consistent and predictable in both their application and their enforcement. A social system respects the freedom aspect of human existence through humane considerations— through compassion, flexibility, and forgiveness—but it responds to responsibility, that is, the need for the limits that make freedom available to us in a practical sense (which is the other side of the coin of freedom) through a system of dependably rigid accountability. The present disintegration of our society is due in part to the fact that this philosophic point is being ignored. We do not seem to fully understand—in structuring our society and in raising our children—that freedom, to exist, needs limits. And even if we do understand, we lack the skill to reconcile the ensuing paradox, since we have not yet fully integrated into life its polarity and the need for dialectic.

Thus, existential anxiety reveals to us the fact that we are a freedom. When we deny that freedom and develop the pathology of neurotic anxiety we experience our lives as restricted. On the other hand, if we confront our existential anxiety of freedom, we feel a justified surge of self-determination. The treatment of the pathology involves emphasis in all states of consciousness on the underlying refrain *I choose*. If we know that to be and to choose are simultaneous occurrences, then therapy is taking place. Finally, the political repercussions of the idea of freedom can be succinctly stated by realizing that we must never compromise with independence, for a society is human the precise extent that it is free.

A Phenomenology of Freedom: Action and Interface

In developing a phenomenology of freedom, that is, a discussion of the nature of transcendental freedom and its importance in the affairs of life, there are two particularly useful models or diagrams. They seem to answer many questions that arise in an exposition of the idea of freedom. One of these deals with the concepts of action and interface and the other concerns itself with the freedom-facticity distinction.

Let our first model of freedom be an oval which represents the totality of the field of consciousness. The left side stands for the transcendental region of consciousness, that is, the part of us which is free, reflective, detached, peaceful, and silent. The right side, separated from the transcendental with a vertical wavy line, is the empirical realm, the worldly, bodily, emotional, mechanical, social, and unfree world, which runs its course independently of us and over which we have no control.

What has been here called the medical model of the person places our human reality in this empirical realm exclusively. But when human beings reach their extremity—as they do in death, love, meaning, and responsibility—then that medical model fails us. The medical model of the person is useful for coping with those aspects of human existence which are exclusively empirical, such as viruses, nutrition, and the removal of gallstones. But human extremities reach into the transcendental realm, and that model does not equip us to cope with decisions, with self-definitions, with intimacy, with finitude, and with our possibilities for eternity. Many people who are defined as mentally disturbed suffer instead from an unworkable philosophy of life. They wish to help themselves. Society's message is *manipulate, do not take personal responsibility*. When manipulation does not work, the patient tries harder: he looks for new and more intense forms of manipulation. The harder he tries the more painfully he fails. Only when he changes his world view to one where freedom, consciousness, and subjectivity are understood does he have a realistic chance for successfully coping with life.

The medical model of the person does not explain the transcendental aspects of the human condition, and it is for this reason that it cannot lead to solutions involving any transcendental aspect whatever. However, the philosophical truth is that we as total human beings exist in the middle of that oval; we live out our lives *on* the wavy line. It is our destiny to reach into *both* the empirical *and* the transcendental regions at one and the same time. A human being is the only phenomenon in the world which exists in *both* realms. We exist on that line and we must find a *modus vivendi* on the border zone between these two regions of being. We are neither pure disembodied souls or spirits—who live on the left, the transcendental, the purely conscious side only and who are thus totally free— nor are we animals or plants that are completely mechanical and instinctual and live only as bodies—who exist on the right, the empirical, or objective side. We, as persons, are condemned to exist on the interface between these two regions. Since we live in the wavy zone of being, the one word that will help us understand the connection between the two worlds is *action*. It describes the wavy line that is the interface connecting the two regions, the integument or membrane which links the two polar regions of being. The identification of personhood with action has been a central theme of twentieth century existentialist philosophers and it is what accounts for both the political and therapeutic activism associated with this philosophic position. (See Figure 1.)

HUMAN EXISTENCE

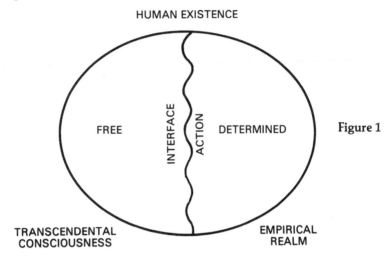

Figure 1

TRANSCENDENTAL
CONSCIOUSNESS

EMPIRICAL
REALM

The word *world* traditionally describes the empirical zone; *God* frequently means the transcendental zone. And the word *human* designates the narrow membrane which describes the interface zone, the region which exists in both worlds. Thus, to be human means to exist precisely on that interface and definitely not exclusively in either of the other regions alone. As a practical matter, the idea of free will makes sense only to the degree that it is understood that we exist on this interface, for the interface is the region of *action*.

A free action is the translation of an occurrence in the realm of consciousness into one that occurs in the realm of the body or world. Action is thus the essence of our *human* life, our existence as individuals. A decision is not a full-bodied decision until its conscious content is transformed into physical reality. It is at this moment that a thought becomes a decision and a commitment. It is at this moment at which consequences emerge.

For example, you are making decisions right now—as you read this page —regarding what to think and what not to think, where to look and where not to look. You will then make decisions on how to spend the rest of your day or evening, the rest of the week, the rest of the season, the rest of the year, and the rest of your life. At present, these decisions are thoughts only. But when these thoughts become translated into a commitment, when they begin, as it were, to make waves in the world, then they acquire a reality of their own, beyond our control. That is the mystery of *action*—the interface between mind and matter, consciousness and world, subject and object, ego and body that is the essence of our life and existence. If we are intellectually aware of and emotionally in touch with that interface, then our life can be changed, for it is at this interface that thought and feeling become integrated into visible living. Life is then experienced as new because it is now philosophically realistic.

The metaphor of the interface is very useful. It explains why existentialism emphasizes action. In action free will becomes real. Action is lived freedom. A free deliberate action is the translation of a conscious state—which by itself has no consequences—into worldly waves or phenomena, which are now part of the world and can never be retracted. They can be changed or redirected, but the waves themselves can never be taken back. Consequences have now attached themselves to the conscious state. Freedom is now real. Pure transcendental freedom is like the thought of having a baby. The child is part of the empirical world; it is the waves of consequences that emanate from you like ripples from a pebble in a pool. The act of impregnation itself is the interface, the action, where consciousness and freedom become matter and determinism. Once a woman is pregnant, which is the result of a free action, her life becomes the consequences of that action. The interface action begins with a fantasy of pregnancy or intercourse. It is first only an idea or thought, an anticipation, but nothing more concrete. However once this pure conscious state is translated into action, waves of material consequences form, and these can never be reversed or retracted in the sense of never-having-been.

The act of conception is one of fertilization. The moment of ejaculation is the interface between the idea—the thought, the desire, the wish, the intent—and its now inevitable translation into worldly consequences which will run their course regardless of our protestations. The interface has translated the diaphanous purity of the consciousness of our freedom into the opaque thickness of the animal world, the empirical world of nature, the world of determinism. All the anxieties, possibilities, and joys of pregnancy—for both parents—are experiences characteristic of this interface. The act of getting pregnant compresses within itself the universal aspects of all free acts. Free action is the phenomenon of creation. Any act of creation is therefore a magnificent metaphor for freedom.

Actions are like our children: we are fully responsible for them because they have their origin in our consciousness, but once they pass the interface they lead a life of their own. We have no final control over the life we have freely created. The act of conception is a potent metaphor for the meaning of free will as interface, action, and consequences. And the common and therapeutically useful name for this complex experience is *personal responsibility.*

The toughest part of any job is to start it. Why? The beginning moment is the act of creation, of conception. The beginning is the interface and it is here where the resistance to action is revealed. An Indian saying holds, "If an elephant blocks your way, cut him up into little pieces and eat one at a time." It is good advice to divide your project into smaller pieces. It makes the moment of creation less momentous, less cosmic. Nevertheless, that first step is the creative moment itself. At the precise moment at which you begin, the creative moment is upon you—with its anxiety, joy, and frustration. If you plan to write a novel, then the moment you actually start researching and taking notes is when you reach the interface. That is when your decision is translated into worldly consequences. To fully comprehend that beginning of creation is crucial, because our entire life is a sequence of such conceptions. It can be the creation of the world, the conception of a child, the writing of a paper, or the cooking of a meal. Life stretches itself out into one continuous interface moment of creation. We waste much time running away from that insight. We seem not to want to live it. We often fear creation as a burden. We think that creativity is only for the occasional genius, when in truth we all are condemned to live the creativity of freedom.

We can also make a decision by not acting. Since we are condemned to be human, choice is unavoidable. If we pretend that we can avoid choices—if we choose by not choosing—we are in fact opting to let someone else make the choice which is rightfully ours. When we choose by not choosing we become aware of the interface of inauthenticity and self-deception: we are freely allowing someone else to choose for us.

LAUREL

Let us consider the predicament of nineteen-year-old Laurel, who is pregnant because she was seduced, even though she had resolved that this would never happen to her. She now says, "I couldn't help myself. It wasn't my decision; it just happened." She analyzes her problem in terms of an interface that is past. She feels that the problem arose because of her ignorance about her freedom. She had been living in a state of self-deception. Her freedom was not fully disclosed to her. But in the last analysis, even that self-deception was a choice. She resisted full and deliberate awareness of the region of her freedom. Her decision to get pregnant was the experience of an interface. Ignorance of this type of analysis caused her lack of control over her life and produced this unwanted predicament.

But this situation also has a present interface. She must consider the choices open to her right now: It is a now-fact that she is pregnant; that is of course no longer open to choice. However, she can now choose to learn from that experience. For example, she can choose *never again* to say she is not free and therefore choose to never again allow others to make decisions for her. Now that she is pregnant she can choose to learn from the consequences of having previously rejected her freedom. She can now decide whether she will continue to reject her freedom or whether this is to be the last time she will have denied her freedom.

The result of this new-found resoluteness is expressed when she says, "Now that I am pregnant, I shall choose personally all my future decisions. I choose to realize that I am responsible and free, and that I will never again choose to hide this fact from me."

At this point she also chooses to recognize that various options are open to her: marriage, abortion, the life of a single parent, adoption. She now chooses to recognize her freedom with respect to those options. She now knows that even in denial she is choosing; in that case the free decision would be *not* to take charge of her life. Not to take charge of one's life is a choice. Rejecting responsibility is a choice. At that moment she experiences her authenticity because she will have understood her freedom. When she realizes that a refusal to decide is really a choice, she has already broken the vicious circle of defensively rejecting freedom. She is thereby forced to be in touch with her freedom and to accept it. Laurel faces options; this brings us to our second diagram of freedom.

Freedom and Facticity

The second model which explicates the existential concept of free will as revealed by existential anxiety also uses the oval shape. (See Figure 2.) The oval, which stands for being, is divided into three zones. The middle zone is the region of freedom. In unhappy, unfulfilled, or inauthentic people, that region is narrow. For people in touch with the optimum (not maximum) breadth of their freedom, that region is wider. In fact, a person is authentic precisely to the extent that he has access to his free will, and up to a point in proportion to the width of this zone. Too much freedom means mania and delusion. On the other hand, a person with an extremely narrow band of freedom (Figure 3) is almost dead. The role of the therapist is to touch that freedom, to nurture it, to cultivate it, to reinforce it, and to expand it. However, an excessively wide band of freedom (Figure 4) means that the person totally lacks a sense of limits and of reality and feels that nothing is impossible. These two diagrams represent the extremes of a manic-depressive psychosis. The authentic person finds an optimum middle ground.

The two regions on the right and left in the oval are the regions of facticity. Whereas both represent facticity, they are nevertheless different; one consists of alternatives, the other is the need to choose. Both are untouched by freedom. They are determined, set, and fixed.

The right realm of facticity is the region of the alternatives or options open to us in life. Often, we are not fully aware of how vast our options are; we see only a narrow range of alternatives. However, if we view

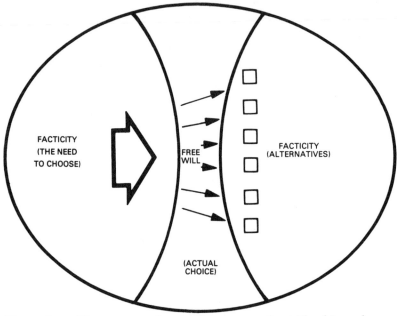

Figure 2   The more authentic the person, the wider his or her zone of freedom. The band of freedom may be reduced to a thin thread, but it will never disappear altogether as long as the individual is conscious.

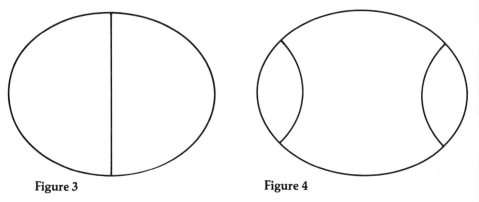

Figure 3   **Figure 4**

the world not as rigid but as full of options, new hope is often possible. Executives and government leaders frequently depend on imaginative and well-informed assistants whose full-time responsibility is to develop options and catalogue alternatives. There are also therapists who operate in this way. They help their clients discover the full spectrum of options.

When you, for example, list your options for an overdue decision, you will realize that a previously rigid world is transformed into a flexible congeries of alternatives. There is more freedom (choice) in this world than you may have thought. But since these options are not your invention, they are not part of your zone of freedom. Instead, they are part of the independent real world, the hard world of facticity.

The left side of the oval is the motivation for action. We are compelled to choose; we are forced to be free. We are not free to not be free; we cannot choose not to choose. Nor can we choose to choose, since we are forced to choose. We are condemned to be free. The best we can do is to choose self-deception. We often forget that we are born free, even though that may be against our will. We sometimes delude ourselves into thinking that we can ignore or even destroy our freedom. However, those who know they are condemned to be free find ways to use that freedom constructively.

Often, when we know there is something we *must* do—like pay taxes or obey a court order—we find a way to do it, although at first we may have been convinced that it could never be done. Once we understand that we have been irrevocably condemned to be free, we have no choice but to be free and to cope with our freedom constructively. In fact, we find it a principal source of joy and meaning. The same is true with anxiety in general. Once we realize it is natural, we can cope with it gracefully. Behind us the need to choose hems us in; in front of us our alternatives restrict (or free) us. Now, seeing that, we can take charge of our existence and start truly living.

For example, Jonathan discovers that he has arthritis. He had secretly believed that he would remain forever unscathed, that he would never develop a degenerative disease. Yet that hope proved false. But now he must adjust himself to a new physical and psychological condition. He will make his peace with it; others have done it. And he will do that freely. Claudia discovers cataracts in both her eyes. She will lose her eyesight and then she may submit to a cataract operation. She does not want that operation; it terrifies her. Nevertheless, she does make up her mind to have it. She then discovers she can adjust herself to this new reality. Some options that she now invokes and even lives had previously not been even part of her vocabulary. What was incorrectly seen yesterday as impossible is today recognized as a legitimate option.

Loren needs false teeth. "Well, I never thought I was going to need false teeth," he exclaims. In fact, however, he does have all of his teeth pulled and has dentures installed in their place. Carol thought she would never become pregnant. Yet now she finds out that she is. She will have a child. Once confronted with inevitability, she makes her peace with it. Whereas before her own pregnancy she thought that going through with labor and parturition were not options for her, once she finds she is pregnant she recognizes that these are legitimate and possible options. If any of us is confronted with what at first appears to be dismal news, we will nevertheless eventually accept it and freely make peace with it. A human being is capable of enormous amounts of desensitization. New alternatives become visible at all times. Once discovered, these alternatives of accommodation *can* be freely chosen. This insight used to be called adjustment.

Once we realize that we are ineluctably free, that we are stuck with creative, godlike freedom, we will *make* it work. Because once we recognize a possible solution as a bona fide option we can *choose* to make it work. This is the power of freedom. We then realize that the same world which has condemned us to be free also provides us with the helpful options and alternatives. Basic among these alternatives is the fundamental option to be realistic or unrealistic about freedom. And those who are realistic about their freedom are liberated human beings.

If we experience our life within this conceptual framework, we will be elated at the amount of freedom, space, time, and control that it releases. The residual sense of being trapped will vanish. Since we can adapt to almost any real and irrevocable condition, we can certainly adapt to the fact that we are free. And now that we understand our freedom we can live it.

The experience of free will can be evoked with additional clarity if we observe its occurrence in religion and if we understand how religion contains metaphors which help us to codify and manage our freedom.

Free Will and Religion

There are many ways in which the experience of freedom appears in the context of religion. Religion is rich in lived metaphors through which we can understand and manage philosophically revealed ontological realities. In existential theology, the idea of God stands for, among other themes, the notion of a free transcendental consciousness. God is a historical and mythological, that is, symbolic repository of insights about our transcendental freedom. God means creativity. God means consciousness. God means free will. When we are in possession of the idea of God, then we understand—theoretically, mythologically, or symbolically—the idea of a *pure consciousness* which is also a *freedom*. And religion can sometimes teach us how to manage this idea in our daily existence. On this view, whenever a person is in any way affected by the idea of God the Creator he is in truth working through, by means of a lived metaphor, the problem of his transcendental freedom. If for him God is the Creator and if he identifies with God through prayer and religious ceremony, then he is in effect striving to manage the reality of his own freedom. If we fail to conceive of God as a living Creator—as may be the case when in deism God becomes depersonalized into a distant and mechanical force —then we are not using this religious metaphor to manage the issue of freedom in our existence. Religion then becomes a convenient escape from freedom. It effectively denies freedom, for it deludes us into believing that since we are at least intellectually concerned with the Creator we are in fact dealing with the problem of freedom after all. This process is an excellently efficient form of self-deception.

There is in addition an entirely different aspect to religion which illuminates the phenomenon of freedom. A religious commitment—even the most fundamentalist and orthodox one—is itself a free choice. In fact, it is not just a choice of belief-systems but a choice of world view. The decision about the existence of God is an archetypal one. If, for example, you convert to Christianity through the efforts of a charismatic evangelist, then you make a *decision* for Christ. Your act is not a matter of argument, proof, or of being convinced; it is an expression of the fact that you are at all times responsible for freely choosing or freely rejecting God.

Pascal wrote about the religious wager. He implied, with William James and others, that there is no rational way to establish or disestablish conclusively the existence of God. In the end, therefore, a belief in God is a wager, a choice which each individual is condemned to make. As in all cases, we are fully responsible for the choice we make. All persons, religious or not, are forced into the fundamental choice of accepting or rejecting God. They may be coaxed, urged, or threatened into it, but they nevertheless fully know that the final decision is theirs.

Even the most fundamentalist forms of Christianity recognize that it is a person's *free will* which makes (or does not make) the decision for Christ. Even though Calvin and his followers may threaten mankind with horrendous eschatological suffering if we do not make a decision for Christ, we are still *free*—even in terms of their approach—*not to make that decision*. The fundamentalist approach to religion is especially aware of the fact that the ultimate source of religious faith and commitment is a decision, a choice. Thus, the truth of even the most orthodox fundamentalism rests on the pillars of the individual freedom of the believer. There remains little doubt that religious determinism is as much an illusion as is its scientific counterpart.

A final point can now be made in the exposition of the experience of free will. It is to uncover the element of the demonic in freedom, which is a direct derivative of the source of freedom, namely, anxiety.

The Anxiety of Pure Consciousness

What is the relation between the demonic or the shadow in the collective unconscious, or the threatening residual material of early childhood in the individual unconscious, and the transcendental ego? For one, the transcendental ego is not the collective unconscious. The threatening elements which are compressed in the one amorphous concept of the collective unconscious can be refined phenomenologically into several components. First, threatening material or the demonic is empirical and part of the empirical ego. These are the frightening objects and situations common to all. Included here are also threatening or forbidden desires and impulses. The impulse of the *id* coupled with the prohibition of the *superego* is one empirical or objective complex.

Second, the demonic can appear also in the transcendental region. And it appears in the form of nihilism and freedom. The demonic as nihilism is the fearsome experience of the transcendental ego in its purity, which is the sense of total abandonment. The demonic as freedom is the realization that choices of self-definition are indeed free, spontaneous, and groundless. A murderous impulse, for example, is threatening or demonic not only because it is forbidden (which is an empirical phenomenon), but also because it can through retaliation lead to the non-being of one's own transcendental center (nihilism). Above all, it is threatening because it can be spontaneously implemented (freedom).

Let us consider some details:

Transcendental freedom is related to the demonic. It comes out in dreams, because a part of us exists with which we are not in touch. It may be violent. It seems foreign to us. Transcendental freedom is a mixture of negative, hostile, aggressive, and violent feelings resulting from everyday frustrations and from unconscious unresolved Oedipal material. It also results from our transcendental nature, which is that part of our freedom in terms of which *everything* is possible. An individual may be a perfectly nice, decent, and civilized person but that individual is also free to be a scoundrel, a rascal, or a criminal. There is nothing in our transcendental nature that stops us from turning our freedom in an immoral direction; only our free decision preserves morality and civilization. There are of course social controls, and people become conditioned—sometimes—to be nice, civilized, polite, gentle, and kind. But within everyone there always exists the dangerous freedom to deny that which is good and to choose that which is evil. If we now combine the violent primitive impulses within (which are the empirical phenomena of the demonic and the shadow in the unconscious) with the transcendental phenomenon of being free to choose criminality, we open up a double-barreled dimension of human consciousness that is indeed frightening. This scenario is then the structure of the existential anxiety of freedom as it relates to Jung's ideas of the shadow and the demonic.

This view is supported by the very existence of the transcendental ego itself. We have discussed before the fact that I am not only my body, personality, ideas, thoughts, emotions, hopes, and feelings, but I am also that part *which is conscious of these things.* That part of being which is conscious of me, but is not me, is the transcendental ego. Thus I am two egos: I am the empirical ego, the psychological ego—my body, my feelings, my emotions—but I am also the transcendental ego, which is the pure consciousness *of* these objects. Most of us are not fully aware—that is, self-conscious—of this transcendental ego. We realize that we are a person, with a name and certain feelings and hopes, but we do not think of ourselves as also the consciousness which is "behind," "looking at" the empirical or psychological ego. If we suddenly discover that inside of us there lurks another consciousness—that we are and always have been pregnant with another consciousness—and that this inner and other consciousness is more truly us than the surface phenomena, then we are overcome by the uncanny and the eerie.

Imagine that you discover that there is someone else living inside you, and that this other person is more real than you! And that Other, living inside you, gradually takes over your life, because it is the only reality that has ever been. That is a frightening experience. The fight you put up against the inner Other taking over is in actual fact your resistance to accepting the universal consciousness that you are. And that resistance is one of the roots for the choice for determinism. It is the source of energy with which our culture denies free will. Since freedom is one of the paramount characteristics of that consciousness, the transcendental freedom of self-definition is thus experienced as the total vacuum of nihilism.

Education for Freedom

Benson and Engeman[1] have written an interesting book about crime and corruption in America. One source of immorality, they contend, is a lack of ethical teaching in American schools and churches. A philosophy of freedom has an important contribution to offer. At first glance this philosophy appears to espouse relativism and thus it undermines rather than strengthens ethical convictions. It is true that existential philosophy has called attention to the fact that life-styles and value-systems are chosen and that it is difficult to support a philosophy of absolutes. As long as human beings are free, they are free to define anything as good and they are equally free to choose evil (or any definition of that term).

On the other hand, the existential emphasis on freedom of choice and on personal responsibility can have the opposite effect. It holds every individual personally responsible to make and to support ethical choices. Furthermore, existentialism does not teach a code of ethics in a doctrinaire fashion. It teaches that freedom of choice is a *fact* of human existence, and that we choose to either measure up or not. This teaching is very much in the spirit of science and not of moralizing, preaching, or pontificating.

In addition to teaching the reality of free will and the resulting personal responsibility for making ethical choices, the existential-phenomenological position can give two additional directives. Certain values—such as justice —are perceived almost universally as having a claim on us, even though the details of implementation may vary. Furthermore, the outlines of a field theory of the person give us a criteria of sickness and health, which then in turn become moral imperatives. Thus, the facts are that we have two sets of absolute values—eidetic objects (Platonic ideas of values) and the transcendental-empirical field (the self-transcending intentionality of consciousness). We are personally and freely responsible for implementing these values and conditions of health and authenticity. The truth remains, however, that we retain our freedom to reject these values.

It therefore seems that exploring the phenomenological model of being, with its focus on exploring the transcendental nature of freedom, can well serve as the modern, professional, and respectable way to teach values and ethics in our schools. No established religion or ethical posture will have its rights violated. A universal foundation for a pluralistic society will then have been found.

We would not destroy the cosmos, space, and time, even if we could. On the same strength of philosophic argumentation we would never destroy a consciousness (with either outright death or with mere inconsiderateness or insensitivity) if we understand its nature. Teaching the nature of human consciousness in schools—its centrality and sanctity— is another way of teaching ethics. Consciousness and subjectivity are to be revered; direct inspection of their sacred nature makes that clear. (See Appendix C.)

EXISTENTIAL ETHICS

Some more sharply focused comments about the complex question of ethics in existentialism are in order. Because of the centrality of freedom in the existential personality theory, this philosophy is often seen as cynical relativism. In truth, existentialism has its ingredients of absolutism. Specifically, the absolute values are those characteristics which reflect the phenom-enological model of being. Among them we find the sanctity of conscious-ness, the respect for freedom, the admiration for unique individual identi-ties, the importance of contact (with *Eigen-*, *Mit-* and *Umwelt*), and the need for both reflection and commitment. These are absolute values. Nevertheless, nature does not guarantee that these values are realized or implemented. It takes a separate, and crucial, step—an *act* of freedom, of free will, of commitment, of risk—to either affirm (which is good) or deny (which is evil) these views.

Any holocaust experience demonstrates the fragility of the values of civilization. It demonstrates that nature does not automatically support the values of a civilized society. It shows that any person can choose evil (that is, choose to perpetrate a holocaust) and that any person can decide to follow a leader like a sheep. But it also follows—and this is really the important point—that a person can choose civilization. Civilization is supported on pillars, and these pillars are the ex-nihilo decisions of free-doms which create a personality structure and a society where the values of civilization are embodied, preserved, and made non-negotiable. Each of us has the glorious opportunity and the fearsome responsibility to know that whether we are civilized or not *is up to us!* (See Appendix C.)

Now that we have covered an exposition of the nature of freedom and its importance, we must address ourselves to the more theoretical but no less significant issue of the justification of freedom. A philosophic foundation for psychology must be able to argue convincingly for the reality of free will.

Note

1. George C. S. Benson and Thomas S. Engeman, *Amoral America* (Stanford: Hoover Institution Press, 1975).

Chapter 12 • IN DEFENSE OF FREEDOM

Freedom As Experience

It is still fashionable, even after close to a century of existential thought, to be convinced that freedom is not a philosophically disclosed fact or, even worse, that it may be even a contradictory idea. Because of the importance of freedom in the existential personality theory and on account of the resistance against its legitimacy, a review of ways of arguing in favor of the reality and the existence of free will is needed, for that is the pivot of a humanizing philosophy.

The fundamental existential position is that freedom is real; it is not an illusion. Free will is a pervasive and legitimate experience. But free will is also a transcendental phenomenon, so that any denial of consciousness or of the transcendental region is also a denial of the possibility of freedom. Philosophy has an ethical and a psychotherapeutic responsibility to society to establish with finality the reality of free will. The exigencies of human dignity and personal meaning can no longer tolerate the denial of the human region of subjectivity, with its central and unequivocal core of freedom.

We know that the existential personality theory tries to describe, in presuppositionless detail, the human condition. It does not argue, nor does it seek to prove; it merely describes—with sensitivity. In phenomenology one focuses on facts and not on interpretations, theories or speculations. And that fact-orientation means that one is being scientific. Therefore, any attempt to strictly *demonstrate* or *prove* that free will exists—as would also be the case with proving the existence of God—is an error. The enemies of freedom will maneuver us to consent to the false notion that free will is the conclusion of a lengthy argument chain, resting on unexceptionable axioms; or that it is the result of some intricate, computer-assisted experiment, frosted with impeccable statistics. We can of course legitimately be expected to use logic and scientific experimentation to demonstrate the reality of free will. However, these approaches also have the dangerous tendency to place freedom among the world's objects, whereas in truth, freedom is a structure of inwardness, an element of subjectivity. Freedom is a transcendental phenomenon, accessible only to reductive or reflexive thought and not to referential thought or consciousness. But free will *is* an experience. It is an irreducible experience, and therefore it has the epistemological authority of all primary and uninterpreted experience.

Whereas the validity of logic and scientific experimentation is not to be denied, the defense of freedom avails itself of more primitive methods. We must appeal directly to the basis of all knowledge—immediate experience. And we must be equally open to the transcendental as well as the empirical dimension. We must be willing, in searching for the facts of immediate experience, to look both referentially into the world and reflexively into our inwardness. When we gaze into our inwardness we see with clarity—and with both hope and anxiety as well—our transcendental freedom; we perceive it also as irreducible and as logically and epistemologically primitive, primordial, or originary. Let us now be specific.

There exists in the transcendental realm of all experience an element which mankind has learned to call freedom or free will. It matters little if these terms are thought of as good or bad, as appropriate or inappropriate, as licit or illicit. What does matter is that the expression free will, however described, has the capacity to evoke the unique experience we are discussing. It has the power to suggest that zone of being which reveals a central feature of our transcendental consciousness. This freedom can be hidden or open, clear or obscure. And it is the philosopher's responsibility to make the experience of freedom available, accessible, and clear. Furthermore, it is the philosopher's task to expand that experience so that it can be made central to everything that we are, do, think, and feel. In following this philosophical prescription, all of us can fulfill maximally our human potential.

To ask whether or not free will actually exists is a meaningless question. In fact, its reality can perhaps be most clearly established by turning the tables in the defense of freedom and instead describing the mind which denies free will. The attack on free will holds, in the most simple and conventional terms, that since every event is known to have an antecedent cause (or necessary and sufficient conditions) which fully explains, rationalizes, or determines it, there can be no meaningful freedom, spontaneity, choice, or self-determination (all of which are elements of freedom).

The Case Against Determinism

A determinist makes the assumption that every effect or event has an all-determining cause or an antecedent that fully explains or accounts for that effect or event. There is no way to prove the truth of this generalization or sufficient evidence to render it absolutely certain. We can achieve only approximations or probabilities, but that is not in the spirit of the determinist argument. A determinist does not search for some event without a cause and then accept or reject his hypothesis in view of the available evidence. He holds, rather arbitrarily, that all events have causes. This position is not an empirical generalization, but an absolute or a priori statement; consequently, no empirical evidence can be found, on principle, to substantiate it. Determinism, therefore, is an assumption with which we approach experience. It is an interpretation of experience not derived from observations of experience.

We must therefore conclude that an accurate phenomenological description of the constitution of the meaning which is determinism is as follows: A determinist freely chooses to make his assumptions, since there is no way to arrive at them except to choose them. But as soon as we discover and understand that an assumption is indeed chosen— that it can come into being in no other fashion than through some kind of archetypal decision—then we have ipso facto recognized the primacy of choice and the certainty of free will. Thus in existential phenomenology we do not seek to prove anything but only to describe the primary and raw data of uninterpreted experience.

If we now describe a determinist phenomenologically, we see that it is impossible to portray his inner conscious structure without inserting the root fact that *he* arbitrarily, freely, and without rational or experiential grounds *chooses to view the world in terms of the assumption that every event has a cause which fully determines it.* There can be no other explanation for his belief in determinism.

Does the capacity to make statistical predictions invalidate the reality of free will? In totalitarian countries, propaganda works. Newspapers can decide what people will think and talk about and what they will consider important simply by a judicious and Machiavellian choice of headlines. Any country, up to a point, can be manipulated and controlled through advertising, behavior modification techniques, and propaganda. It is therefore true that we can predict the behavior of population groups. However, the ability to predict group behavior via statistics does not disconfirm a belief in free will; on the contrary, it confirms it.

The expression *statistical generalization* means precisely that there are numerous exceptions to the rule. If there were no exceptions we would not have a statistical generalization but an absolute and univocal certainty. All that is necessary to confirm the existence of free will is to admit to a single exception for any causal generalization. Specifically, in a totalitarian nation it is always possible for a person to say, "I will not be brainwashed. I will not go along with the majority. I will not accept the messages of advertising or propaganda. I will rebel; I will say *no* to that to which all other people say *yes.*" Furthermore, every individual human being possesses the potential for independent, maverick thinking and a few people usually will carry it out. Consequently, in a probability and statistical context there is room for free will. As long as we speak in those terms, which we tend to do today in the sciences, we do not at all deny the existence of free will. We talk about tendencies and not compulsions, thereby leaving ample room for free will to maneuver. All that freedom needs is the knowledge that I, the individual and not the average, could have acted otherwise than in fact I did.

Everyone who reads the following passage from Sartre is touched by the reality of human freedom. His phenomenological analysis clearly shows that the exception to the statistical generalization of totalitarian propaganda and repression is incontrovertible evidence for the reality of freedom.

The Resistance

We were never more free than under the German Occupation. We had lost all our rights, above all the right to speak; we were insulted daily and had to remain silent, we were deported, because we were workers, because we were Jews, because we were political prisoners. All around us on the walls, in the newspapers, on the screen, we met that foul and insipid image that our oppressors wanted us to accept as ourselves. Because of all this we were free. Since the Nazi poison was seeping into our thinking, each accurate thought was a victory; since an all-powerful police was trying to force silence upon us, each word became precious as a declaration of principle; since we were hunted, each gesture had the weight of a commitment. The often frightful circumstances of our struggle enabled us finally to live, undisguised and unconcealed, that anxious, unbearable situation which is called the human predicament. Exile, captivity, death, which in happier times are skillfully hidden, were our perpetual concern, and we learned that they are not avoidable accidents nor an external menace; in them we had to recognize our lot, our destiny, the deep source of our reality as men. At each moment we were living to the full the meaning of that banal little phrase: "All men are mortal." The choice that each of us made of himself was authentic, because it was made in the presence of death, since it could always be expressed in the form, "Rather death than—."

I am not speaking here of that elite who were actual Resistants, but of all those Frenchmen who by day and by night, for four years, said "No." The cruelty of our enemy drove us to the limits of our condition, forcing us to ask those questions which can be avoided in peace. All those who were aware—and what Frenchman was not, at one time or another—of some information about the Resistance, asked himself anxiously, "If they torture me, can I hold out?" Thus the question of freedom was posed, and we were brought to the edge of the deepest knowledge a man can have of himself. For the secret of a man is not his Oedipus complex or his inferiority complex, it is the limit of his freedom, his ability to resist torture and death.

For those involved in underground activity, the circumstances of their struggle were a new experience: they were not fighting in the open as soldiers; hunted alone, arrested alone, they resisted torture in the most complete abandonment; alone and naked before torturers who were clean-shaven, well-fed, well-dressed, who regarded this wretched flesh with contempt—torturers whose smug consciences and enormous social power gave every appearance of their being right. Nevertheless, at the depth of this solitude, others were present, all the comrades of the Resistance they were defending; a single word was enough to trigger ten, a hundred arrests. This total responsibility in total solitude, is it not the revelation of our freedom? . . . [1]

Situations III, 11-13.

Let us now amplify these observations.

A Phenomenology of Determinism

What is the frame of mind, the world view, the perception of reality of a person who says that free will does not exist? Or a person who insists on a deterministic and mechanistic world view, that perceives the world as rigid? First of all, the determinist does not *prove* that every event has a cause; he *assumes* it. He says, "I shall consider meaningful only those events, sentences, and occurrences for which I can find an antecedent and determining set of situations or causes." He says, simply, "I assume that every event has a cause, and I assume further that the cause fully determines the nature and the existence of that event. If I can*not* find a cause for a specific event, I conclude that it has not yet been discovered but that at some future time will be."

Let us illustrate these assumptions of the deterministic rejection of the reality of free will. We have not yet found a universal cause for cancer despite the fact that we have looked for it more extensively than in any other comparable type of scientific research. If science teaches us that we learn from past experience, which is inductive logic, then this tends to confirm that cancer does not have a cause. The critical question is, "When is there enough evidence accumulated to establish the 'causelessness' of cancer?" The answer given by the determinist is, of course, "never," which proves that no evidence will ever be permitted to suffice in establishing causelessness. He then violates his own commitment to the inductive method of science, where past experience guides us toward future theories.

It is clear that the determinist does not *argue* for his position but assumes it before any argument takes place. The existentialist rejoins by appealing to the facts of experience rather than to blind prejudice. (We are not arguing here the merits of cancer research but analyzing the concept of causation. We must of course continue our search for cancer cures. But we must also make room for free will in the scientific outlook.) No matter how conclusive may be the experimental evidence that cancer has no cause—even one hundred years of concerted and futile research—the determinist will always demand that we continue the search until something is found which satisfied our criteria of *cause*. If we still fail, he will insist that we cannot find the cause, not that it does not exist. And this situation will never change.

The scientific outlook, which includes the medical model of the person, thinks of persons as objects (ghost-in-a-machine theory of the person). A researcher who functions within this model is therefore subject to the same a priori demands for causal explanations as he would expect to apply to any physical object. But when we begin to integrate into medicine the field theory of being then we can overcome this archetypal decision for determinism. We then become capable and willing to realize that, since persons are not objects but also transcendental subjects, a legitimate place for free will can be found in behavioral science research. Medicine, psychology, and psychiatry will change drastically when free will becomes fully integrated into these fields as a meaningful and logical truth, one which is completely consistent with the most rigorous application of the scientific method.

This analysis shows that the consensual world makes a *decision* to perceive the world as having causes and that it *chooses* to be blind to contrary evidence and experience. No real empirical evidence is brought to bear on the validity of the deterministic position.

That we have not found the cause for cancer can never mean to the scientist that cancer does not have a cause. On the contrary, he redoubles his efforts and spends more energy and money than before to search for it. Thus if there should ever be an event for which we do not know the cause, we never say that it does not have one, but rather that the cause is hidden. And common sense is absolutely rigid on this point. We are a culture of determinists, and the determinist assumes—in fact, *insists*—that everything is determined. The phenomenological disclosure is that he does not *discover* this fact. Indeed, the requirement that every event have a determining cause then becomes the very test for meaning itself. Unless his experience can be interpreted as cause-and-effect sequences, he chooses not to understand it. Our selective perception does not notice an event if it does not appear in a cause-and-effect context. Determinism is therefore a decision about how to perceive and interpret experience; it is not a scientific discovery or description about the nature of our human experience. That is how the deterministic frame of mind operates.

Thus, determinism is *freely* chosen and the belief in free will is *freely* denied. A determinist *freely* chooses and accepts the assumptions that he makes. He is personally *responsible* for these assumptions. He is not *forced* to accept them. Nothing in his nature coerces him into making them. However, our culture and the scientific outlook, common sense and the consensual world, do encourage him to make these assumptions. But there is another deeper reason why this is so. Religion has called it the Fall of Man. Others call it materialism or plain ignorance of the philosophical realities of human existence. We might here call it the objectivist fallacy—the rejection of subjectivity, of consciousness, of the reality of the silent and solitary center. Objectivism is the malaise of our age, and the convulsions of the resultant symptoms are almost beyond coping.

In sum, a careful phenomenological analysis, one that is sensitive to the intentionality of all experience and fully recognizes the reality of the transcendental dimension present in all experience, discovers a zone of freedom every time determinism is asserted, every time the world is perceived or conceived as causal. Determinism is a conscious act, a constituted meaning, and as such it emanates from a center; one of the defining characteristics of that highly specific center is its freedom.

In particular, the decision *for* determinism is the decision *against* freedom. It is a free choice to deny freedom. That decision is made deep in the unconscious, deep in the personality, deep in the body, and deep in the roots of society. The decision for *determinism* is thus an archetypal one, that is, one of the very first decisions (logically *and* chronologically) made and continuously being made whose effect is to organize the most basic structures of our world. Furthermore, determinism is repressed self-deception; it is philosophical suicide: Our last free act—after which no further free acts are possible—is to deny that we are free. This process is the mechanism of dehumanization and the dynamics of depersonalization. Because of the pervasiveness of this denial of freedom we live in an age of alienation, an age that cannot manage its anxiety.

A determinist *freely chooses to reject any consciousness of freedom* because of the pain, agony, and suffering—in short, anxiety—which accompanies that discovery. Freedom is a volcanic discovery; there is superficial merit in aligning oneself with the forces that deny and resist it. But ultimate authenticity can never be achieved without being in possession of the fullness of our freedom. This is the whole issue of the neurotic versus the existential anxiety of freedom.

A Mental Experiment

If you are tempted into determinism, you might perform the following exercise. Put yourself in the frame of mind which says, "I cannot accept free will; there is no free will. Even though I may not immediately recognize the causes for my actions, thoughts, and feelings, as I explore myself further and increase my learning I do begin to discover these causes. Eventually I will uncover the antecedent situations that forced me to accept certain ideas, and to speak as I do and be the kind of person that I am. As John Doe, I have been *determined* by the causes in my background to talk and to write about *free will.*"

Now that you have fantasized yourself into this deterministic position, try to describe it. A careful phenomenological description of your own frame of mind should make it clear that you are *choosing* to be a determinist. All experience is intentional; and so is the experience of determinism. Even the deterministic world design is perceived by an ego and is constituted by an ego. And all acts of constitution contain an element of freedom, since they can be chosen, rechosen, preserved, and undone.

Furthermore, in choosing determinism, you are also choosing the consequences of determinism. These are, among others, that the universe is explainable, not mysterious; that the universe is rigid, not loose; that the universe is predictable, not unpredictable and that the universe is clear, not ambiguous. In choosing determinism you deny the shadow region (Jung's term) within you which is represented by the objective ambiguity of the world and by its subjective correlate, the absolute freedom for self-definition. The choice for a deterministic world view is furthermore the decision to avoid responsibility. Your world has now been constituted as rigid, and as purely black and white. The gray areas, which are ambiguous and which retain their flexibility to willingly accept our projections, have been blotted out.

A deterministic world view therefore gives the illusion that it protects you from anxiety. Specifically, the free choice of determinism shields you from the anxiety that is inherent in the dual indeterminism of human existence itself. In sum, the decision for determinism says, "I will not *look* at my freedom. I will not *accept* a world view which tells me that I am free. I will use my freedom to *deny* my freedom. I will use my freedom for *self-deception*." That is the voice of the neurotic anxiety of freedom.

Note

1. Editions Gallimard, *Situations III*, 1949. Reprinted in Robert D. Cumming, *The Philosophy of Jean-Paul Sartre* (New York: Random House, 1965), pp. 232-233.

Chapter 13 • COPING WITH THE ANXIETY OF FREEDOM

Risk

The basic strategy of coping with the anxiety of freedom—that is, over-coming the paralysis brought about by the denial of freedom, by avoiding the confrontation with and integration of freedom—is the same as it is for coping with the anxiety of individuality: Risking action. We must learn to risk in small doses. By so doing we will gradually increase our toleration for the anxiety of freedom and we will also be able to take advantage of the existence of freedom. However, we must not identify toleration with desensitization—although they are related phenomena. Desensitization is a purely mechanical conception; toleration implies a comprehensive phenomenological description and a complete ontology. Above all, toleration implies a decision. Through risk we become aware that the anxiety of freedom can be tolerated, that freedom is our nature, and that it *feels good* to integrate the anxiety of freedom into our total personality. Intelligent risking gives us a sense of space and solidity. Furthermore, the world has a tendency to validate and confirm our risks. But we have to learn how to make our demands of nature and the world and be judicious in applying this principle. Risking effectively is an art that matures through experience.

Language

A second coping device is to program our speech to enhance our aware-ness of freedom. We must use frequently and with full awareness of their meaning expressions such as "I choose . . ." and "I am responsible for . . . ." So that when we would otherwise be tempted to say "I am depressed" we must now say "I choose not to cope with my experience of depression" and "I am responsible for choosing not to cope with my experience of depres-sion." We must be careful, however, that our expanded statements are correct. Thus, the statement "I choose to be depressed" is not accurate. The element of choice does not pertain to the appearance of the feeling of depression but to our response to and attitude toward that feeling. The response either does or does not reflect the prior decision to cope with those feelings and with the situations that give rise to them. Our consciousness can be stretched, our inner space expanded, and the interface of freedom widened with the systematic and deliberate use and reuse of the phrases "I choose to . . ." and "I am responsible for . . . ." And all we do in them is speak the truth. We insert an awareness of the transcendental dimension into our everyday language, while before we had limited our focus exclusively to the empirical region.

In using these expressions freely and repeatedly we are indicating to ourselves and reminding ourselves of the intentional character of all experience. We thereby remain aware of the transcendental dimension of all experience. We recognize that every object—the feeling of depression in this case—is connected to an inwardness and that this inwardness is an intrinsic part of the total situation, object, or experience. When one says "I am depressed" then one is a camera that shoots a wilted flower. But with the use of this statement the camera is ignored and all one recognizes as real is the wilted flower. It is as if the subject and verb of the sentence did not exist—only the predicate. We ignore in our metaphysical conception the "I am" of the sentence and see only the "depression" aspect. Whereas in truth all experience follows the *ego-cogito-cogitatum* model of analysis, in the case of the wilted flower we accept as real only the *cogitatum*. That viewpoint is contrary to the empirically given facts of immediate and first-person experience and it must therefore be considered scientifically disconfirmed.

However, we can take advantage of the constitutive and reconstitutive powers of our language. Our mode of speech must recognize that the *depressed* has an *I am* attached to it and that the *wilted flower* has a *camera* before it. This greater precision of language will lead to a more accurate perception and conception of the world and will therefore be reflected as an improvement in our whole life-style. When we add to "I am" the phrase "I choose" and get "I am choosing to be depressed" (or better "I am choosing not to deal with my depression") we clearly remind ourselves that subjectivity is free. If we recognize that the camera is part of the wilted-flower complex, then we realize that it is the clicking of the shutter—which here symbolizes a free act—which produces the picture. In expanding our language in this way, our mind increases in accuracy. If it is true that language constitutes experience, then we can expect that our life will develop a tendency to increasingly conform to the phenomenological model of being. Thus, by focusing also on the subjective dimension whenever we are in the presence of an emotional object we maintain a clear awareness of our freedom. And that is precisely what we must do to cope with the anxiety of freedom.

Finally, by adding the subjective element to all statements about the feeling (or affective) objects which have invaded us or are present to us we remind ourselves of our capacity for reflection or reduction. The statement "I am depressed" occurs in the natural attitude. No awareness of any self-consciousness is inserted into it. However, if we say "I choose not to cope with these feelings of depression" then self-consciousness (that is, the conscious constitutive and cathecting attitude we take toward the feeling-objects) becomes part of that sentence, and the sentence now occurs in the phenomenological, reduced, or transcendental attitude. And we have discussed in Book One the power of the act of reflection. It is wasteful to permit our language to hide the epoche from us.

Thus, by choosing our words with care—and visualizing what we are saying—we can greatly assist the process of philosophic self-disclosure. Simple linguistic changes can help assure us that we are living more fully in harmony with the intentional and polar structure of human existence.

A third coping technique with the anxiety of freedom is an expansion of the first—taking risks. When a person reaches a crisis point in life or in therapy, when an individual experiences himself "open to his feelings," when new patterns and new personality structures suddenly appear reasonable and thus become available, then it is time to seriously consider risking these new life-styles, value-systems, beliefs, and relationships. Persons in therapy who suddenly solve a problem that has remained insoluble for half a lifetime, who see the possibility of giving up alcohol, drugs, or cigarettes, who leave a marriage, or enter a marriage, are ready to risk a major change in life and to cope with the larger consequences of that change. If they persist and if they know that a person can choose never to give up but to always push ahead they will find that the world confirms their choices. The world belongs to those who risk and who persist.

A further way of implementing these coping devices is to make an inventory of our freedom.

Inventory of Freedom

To maximize the use of our transcendental freedom, it helps to make ourselves aware of all our alternatives. We must locate not just a few, not just the peripheral ones, not only the ones that trouble us, or those that we find palatable. We need all of them, even those we have repressed. This is often difficult to choose because there may be alternatives not yet discovered. We owe it to ourselves to complete the list, for once this is done, choosing can become natural and easy. But we must choose to accept the list as complete or we will be deflected by ceaseless and unwarranted opportunities for procrastination. If we did not choose X before, it may have been because we had hoped for a way out; now that it has become clear there is no such way, we will have no difficulty in opting for X.

What if several options are equally valuable and real? When this occurs we are in touch with the purity of our freedom and not with an objective fact about the alternatives. We are also experiencing the objective correlate of our freedom, which is the ambiguity of the world. At that moment we make an arbitrary choice—because that is the nature of all choice. We must recognize that all choosing has a transcendental core which demands an archetypal choice. When the alternatives are equal and when both subjective freedom and objective ambiguity stand naked before us, then choice is seen to be both a transcendental and an archetypal phenomenon. Thus choice is a phenomenon which is capable of an ex-nihilo act and through it one chooses to define the organization of being—as God was said to have done when He created the world. We must recall that the paradigmatic image of God creating the world contains two central elements: centeredness and freedom. In fact, it is only when the alternatives are of equal value that we experience in its full depth the reality of our transcendental freedom. We recognize that choosing among alternatives is the sacred process by which we define our future, choose our life-style, and decide on the structure of our empirical nature.

Perhaps the choice is one of career, or one relating to marriage or children. When several options appear to be truly equivalent in value and meaning, then we are in touch with the ambiguity of existence, which—as was stated above—is the objective correlate of the absoluteness of our freedom. We then understand the existential point that we alone are responsible for hewing out a path for ourselves in the world's jungle of ambiguity. No one looks over our shoulder with the authority to say we are right or wrong. We must make the choice and we are stuck with the consequences, because we *are* the consequences. We thus constitute our empirical ego, which is then the accumulated consequences or crystallizations of our previous free choices. At the moment of choice we just go ahead and do it. And then we realize that we can indeed choose without actually knowing whether or not the decision is *right*. Choices are risks into which we must plunge. In taking those risks, the nihilism of anxiety becomes the concreteness of individuality.

A word of psychotherapeutic caution is in order. In practice there can be danger in encouraging too much freedom. While freedom is a truth about the human being, so is its correlate of anxiety. Some people come to counseling with an already weakened and loosened sense of structure. While it is correct to say that they have an accurate perception of the underlying philosophical reality of their being, they also have legitimate fears of intensified anxiety and, consequently, the possibility of a psychotic break, with the total disorganization of their experience. In practice, therefore, it is important to help this type of person minimize freedom and maximize structure. That can be done through appeal to absolutes, authority, and suggestion, as well as by appropriate environmental manipulation to establish consistency, predictability, and security.

Exercises

Here are some general suggestions on how to create a specific inventory of freedom: First, become acquainted with decisions you have already made. On a sheet of paper, divide your life into past, present, and future. Then review what your key decisions have been and still are. Begin with the past. How have you used your freedom in the past? Have you been able to experience your life in terms of the concept of freedom? Or is the idea new? What are some of the important decisions which you have made in your life? Which are still with you? Can you recapture some of them? Can you put yourself in touch with the process of making them? How did you finally take action? Do you feel proud or guilty? Do you, in retrospect, believe that these decisions were right? If not, what would have been a better choice? What would have been the consequences had you done otherwise?

In this exploratory philosophical surgery you lay open the history of your freedom. You will get into both painful and joyous material. Some people exclaim, "I was an idiot in making that decision. How could I ever have permitted it!" In becoming acquainted with past decisions you will discover important strengths and weaknesses within you. Being in touch with why you allowed inauthentic decisions in the past may lead to authentic decisions today. Through this exercise you can also be in touch with the resistances which *stopped* you from making authentic decisions. That resistance to authenticity, that escape from freedom, may still be working within you today. Now think of the present. Focus on decisions that you *are* now in the process of making as well as on those that you are now *not* making.

To facilitate getting in touch with the decision-making process, it is useful to prepare a list of five overdue decisions: Write down five decisions that are overdue. Then rank these in the order of difficulty or importance to you. After they are ranked, add the one you were afraid to put down. Some subjects wait for this last instruction to commit to writing their highest priority decision. This exercise was once done in a group by an apparently happily married couple. To everyone's surprise, the husband's highest-priority item was whether or not to leave his wife. That entry, understandably, had dramatic consequences, leading eventually to actual divorce.

Once you have written down the overdue decisions and ranked them, try to be in touch—through observation and experience—with your *re-

sistance against making them. There are direct and indirect resistances. You can *feel* direct resistances in your body and in your emotions. Indirect resistances can be *observed* in your defensive behavior and in the way you set up failures for your needs, but you do not feel them viscerally. You can feel in your body that you stop yourself from making decisions by asking in what organ you feel the resistance against making a specific and needed choice. In this way you can develop a map of your freedom. It is a useful device in developing a program of coping with the anxiety of freedom.

Connett

Let us conclude this analysis of freedom and of ways of coping with the existential anxiety of freedom by examining the following incredible story. It is one that cannot be explained in terms of a nonexistential theory of personality. In fact, if we presume the assumptions of the medical model or of the ghost-in-a-machine theory of the person, the events— including the process of rehabilitation—would be impossible to conceptualize.

Time Has Healed Archie Connett

Time is a patient physician. It cures ugly memories and yellows newspaper files. It can do all things—even lift the shadows and cloud the visions that haunt a murderer's mind.

Time has healed Archie V. Connett.

Even those with good memories and a penchant for such things wouldn't recognize today's Archie Connett—lecturer, author, and behavioral science researcher.

Their memories are frozen to that monstrous tableau in a Cupertino home two days before Christmas 1952 when a young school teacher went berserk and bashed and battered the life from his three small children, then tried to kill himself and his estranged wife.

That also was Archie Connett.

But the two views of the same man can't be blended without explaining what happened before and since that mad happening.

Archie Connett started out with a firm grip on the world's tail. A star athlete in high school, he breezed through the University of Colorado with a sociology major and a Phi Beta Kappa key.

After graduating in 1941, he served as a Navy officer in World War II and made a success of that, too.

After a stint teaching at the University of Texas and a fling at fiction writing, newly-wed Connett earned a master's degree at Stanford and a job teaching English and social studies at San Jose's James Lick High School.

Had Connett kept his life on schedule, he would today be a respected, graying 50-year-old senior teacher at James Lick with a healthy retirement fund, a comfortable home, a middle-aged wife, and three grown children. Except for one nightmare, 1951's dream would be 1971's reality.

Let's see, Michael would be 24, Teresa, 22, and Carl, 20.

But Michael died at 4, Teresa at 2 and Carl didn't survive four months, because their father arrived home one day and was confronted by his wife: she wanted a divorce. Wyona wished to marry a young professor he had brought home a few times, Archie believes.

Stunned, Archie didn't know what to do. All he knew was that he didn't want his family broken up, so he went to Mexico to escape the process server. However, he found the separation intolerable, so he returned and was served with the inevitable papers.

Archie guides us along his path to infanticide:

"I got a job in another school (in San Lorenzo) and I worked in a cannery. I was working about 12 hours a day. I couldn't seem to relax or settle down. I couldn't sleep.

"My wife had been in San Francisco for four days and I was in a heavy depression. She came back on the day I was going to do some Christmas shopping.

"I was feeding the children when she walked in and the little girl fell off her chair. I began stroking and consoling her. My wife tried to take her but I wouldn't give her up. Then my wife struck me in the face. Not a slap. She hit me with her fist.

"I felt strange. I just kind of patted the baby for a little while, then all of a sudden, I went berserk. Something snapped, I guess.

"I attacked my wife and almost killed her. I thought she was dead. Then I turned on my children and killed them. All three of them. (Accounts at the time say this was done by slamming them against the walls and floor.)

"Then I tried to kill myself. I cut both wrists to the bone with a razor blade and then severed my esophagus completely."

A surgeon at Santa Clara County Hospital did for Archie what he couldn't do for his kids: he saved his life.

A month-long sensational trial ended with Connett's conviction on three counts of second-degree murder. He was sentenced to 10-years-to-life.

While in San Quentin and four other prisons, Archie had to decide whether living held any preference over dying. Suicide seemed an attractive alternative to living with himself.

"I came to where I saw that no matter what had happened or what I had done, I still had the potential to go on living and loving and creating and it was up to me to do it," he explained.

Archie tried to put his past behind him. He never again communicated with his wife who eventually got her divorce. He wrote her a letter once, he said, but he destroyed it before he could yield to the temptation of mailing it.

"My biggest problem was to forgive myself for what I had done. This was absolutely necessary. Eventually—I was able to forgive myself."

On July 1, 1968, after 15 years of forced penance, Archie Connett reentered society.

In the two and one-half years since, Archie has gained a measure of revenge on fate. He's turned it all around.

He is president of Ex-Offender Resources, Inc., a group which tries to help ex-cons repay society; he has been honored by Gov. Reagan for serving on a task force for the State Council on Criminal Justice; he teaches "The Prison Community" at San Diego State College; he also serves as a correctional counselor in honor prison camps.

This fall, Connett will collaborate with such luminaries as Norman Carlson, federal director of prisons, and Dr. Karl Menninger on a symposium entitled "The Purposes of Corrections."

As an authority in penology, Archie has cracked the big time.

Last April, Archie remarried. He's trying to build a solid life out of the wreckage and it looks like he'll finally make it.

Archie Connett has deserved the right to dream again; but for the remainder of his life, every dream will have a nightmare in its background.[1]

ANALYSIS

First, Connett went berserk. One can understand, if not forgive, the pressures, taunts, and frustrations that led to his sudden and total rejection of all that is human. An act of free will was involved. At a particular moment in time he made the archetypal decision to choose irrationality over rationality. The change from civilized to uncivilized behavior, from reason to unreason involves an archetypal choice. All being changes with this choice. Civilized reality is kept in existence by the opposite choice of that made by Connett. We are always choosing between rationality and irrationality. But we become aware of it only in extreme situations—such as those that confronted Connett. It is on the autonomous and ex-nihilo decision between rationality and irrationality that rests the existence of all that is prized as human. Only free choices protect us from barbarism. The responsibility assigned to us by our free will is thus enormous.

The specific free aspect of Connett's emotional and criminal explosion was the archetypal decision to *give in* to the emotional forces that invaded his ego. His first decision was to abandon himself to these powerful forces. Cornered by anger and a lust for violence, he chose to surrender and become their slave. His second choice was to deny the reality of his distancing consciousness. He chose the animal consciousness (total identification with instinct) as the definition of man. He chose *against* the reflective or reduced consciousness as the definition of man. We know that consciousness always has a core of freedom. Therefore, as long as he was conscious, he made these choices. Understanding this point of total personal responsibility—in addition to self-forgiveness—is essential to rehabilitative therapy.

These two decisions—irrationality and animal consciousness (or lack of impulse control)—are not minor or isolated decisions but are in reality choices of self-concepts, choices about the definition and meaning of the person, and choices of fundamental metaphysical commitments. The fact that the decision to surrender to psychopathy was difficult and slow in coming and that it was made in response to enormous adversity does not change by a scintilla the truth that Connett was indeed responsible for his act: He chose it; he decided for complete abandonment to his emotions and impulses. Some other options to his freedom were self-control and stoic discipline, physical escape from the situation, soliciting help from a friend, suicide, or psychiatric consultation.

Connett's decision to go berserk was not the choice for merely one isolated act but for an altogether different and new world. He transformed himself from a human being into an animal, from a civilized creature into a barbarian. He chose to transform the world from a place where barbarism is completely unacceptable to a world where barbarism is indeed a viable option. To be humane is to retain the capacity for rational control; it is to keep open the possibility of reflection and epoche. But to choose to abandon that rational control is as much an option open to free will as is to continue such control. There is nothing automatic about being either civilized or uncivilized under difficult circumstances. Anxiety in human extremity discloses to us that the rationality in the model of the universe and in human interactions is constantly upheld but only and exclusively by an archetypal decision. That crucial decision is one which is groundless, free, autonomous, and spontaneous, that is, a genuine case of *creatio ex nihilo*. Nor are we condemned to reject automatically the consensual definition of man when under stress. Definitions of personality are chosen freely and maintained freely. (See page 504, IV.)

There is a kind of proof that the crime was a free act, and it is Connett's rehabilitation. Rehabilitation is possible only when two conditions exist: The initial act was committed freely, thus confirming the existence of free will in the individual. Then, the individual undertakes the arduous tasks of self-forgiveness and redefinition. These are possible because of the previously confirmed reality of his free will. Connett's subsequent recognition of that freedom and his willingness to assume responsibility for his self-definition eventually made possible what we must assume to be his full rehabilitation. His total rehabilitation could never have been possible had he not been aware of his freedom to reconstruct his life.

His most serious problem was self-forgiveness. To live a normal human life he must be able to identify himself with his past. However, Connett's past is subhuman. He must do what most individuals find impossible—integrate a most unusual and heinous crime into his present existence. There is but one way this integration can be accomplished, and it is through the realization that the consciousness of man, which is his essence, is in itself neither good nor bad, neither human nor subhuman, but only free. And this preaxiological freedom is the power to decide whether civilization and reason shall or shall not be part of the meaning of human existence. To forgive himself means to accept his true transcendental nature—which is to be free. He can then say that the Connett who killed his children and the Connett who is now a sane and useful professional is one and the same man—without any need to allude to theories of split personality, and without denigrating the transcendental freedom within him. He is one and the same man—criminal and rehabilitated—because he is one and the same freedom throughout his existence. His self-definitions change; his empirical nature can be modified; but his transcendental essence perdures. Changes in self-definition means changes in attachments. But the transcendental consciousness that does the attaching remains the same.

Furthermore, once Connett accepted himself as a transcendental freedom and not as an exclusively empirical ego, a human being with a certain set psychological makeup—hysterical, psychopathic, or what have you—he was in touch with the power which can transform his life. This is the reconstitutive and recathective capacity of freedom. He now chose to affirm his human possibilities from within the profundity of the freedom, the freedom that is the real *he*. He redefined himself as civilized, concerned, rational, and educated. It is no more natural for Connett, or anyone else, to be rational and civilized than it is to be barbaric. The ultimate support of civilized behavior is the responsible and individual choice to define and affirm one's humanity.

THE FUTURE

Can Connett be trusted in the future? How should an associate, unaware of his sordid past, react to its sudden disclosure? Could the associate, who has learned to like and trust Connett, maintain his feelings for him and his confidence in him after such a revelation? The answer—and it is a crucial one to the matter of reaccepting ex-convicts into society—depends entirely on the theory of the person against which the experience is measured and on the world view in terms of which the experience is understood. Connett's associate faces nagging fears: Can Connett be trusted? Will it happen again? Is he capable of managing stress as successfully and reliably as any man? The answers to these crucial questions depend more on how we define man than on any statistical correlations, theories about the unconscious, or the glandular physiology of rage. In other words, the reliability and character of Archie Connett are what his free will makes them. Correlatively, the truth about Archie Connett's psychological makeup is what our free will freely chooses to be our definition of man. Connett has to live with his past the way a person lives with schizophrenia or diabetes—he makes a decision to cope. We cannot predict that he will continue to make the decision to cope, for decisions are made and do not unfold themselves automatically or predictably.

Let us be more specific. Connett's associate may *choose* to view all men as conditioned and caused, determined and fixed biological and material organisms. In that case he has chosen to constitute or invent Archie Connett, and with him the race of all men, as a mechanical device predictable on the basis of statistical correlations and causal connections.

He will therefore perceive him as permanently tainted and in constant peril of repeating his crime, since his past predicts his future. On the other hand, Connett's associate may choose to recognize and reflect the freedom that exists within both of them and is the source of their unique *I am* experience and their true humanity. In that case, he will recognize that complete forgiveness and consequently a totally new start at self-definition are possible. In fact, these possibilities stem from the ontological, that is, ultimate and absolute nature of man's consciousness. The question is mostly how clearly Connett is aware of these philosophic structures. The associate will recognize that Archie Connett is no different from any other man. If there are distinctions, it is that Archie Connett achieved access to his freedom—with all the terror, power, opportunity, and salvation made possible thereby—and others may not yet have accomplished that.

"My biggest problem was to forgive myself for what I had done." Connett said. "This was absolutely necessary." In the end, what does self-forgiveness mean? Does it mean to ignore, forget, or be callously indifferent? Not at all. Archie Connett discovered that he is a freedom capable of holiness as well as bestiality. He discovered that whatever life-style and self-concept he chooses is arbitrarily the result of his foundationless and free choice. He must forgive himself for being human—which means he must accept his humanity. That means, not to accept his feelings, his childhood, his abilities, and his body, but to accept his freedom. He is the godlike freedom of creating a world out of nothing, with no blueprint and no cause. Civilization, for all of us, rests on the blind yet holy decision to define ourselves out of the vacuity of nothingness, as rational, just, and caring. Archie Connett appears to have done that.

One might be forgiven for introducing as frightening a story as Connett's in order to dramatize the power of freedom. Freedom is indeed like nuclear energy—a deep truth from the universe, a terrifying danger, and the possible salvation of mankind's energy crisis in the millenia to come. It again points up the enormous responsiblity which falls on the shoulders of human beings, for they live in both worlds—the world of freedom and the world of facticity. We are being's interface, with all its anxiety, power, and glory.

Note

1. *San Jose Mercury-News*, April 18, 1971, p. 22.

Chapter 14 • DEATH AND INDIVIDUALITY

Of the seven revelations of anxiety, four have been discussed in detail: birth, evil, nihilism, and freedom. The next two are death and individuality. Since the revelation of death has been developed in detail in *Is There An Answer To Death?*,[1] included here are three aspects of this revelation not covered in that book. The revelation of individuality is discussed at length in Book One (Chapters 12 and 13) and requires no additional comments. The next chapter is devoted to the final revelation, guilt.

Death

Existential anxiety reveals that death is real. And the reality of death makes possible the sense of being alive and the joy in living. Imagine that death is unknown. You are raised like Gotama Sakyamuni—Gotama, the wise man of India's Sakya tribe. He was destined to be the Buddha, but his father, the king, wanted him to inherit his throne. He wanted him to become a king and military leader, not a holy man. He therefore hid suffering from his son and studiously kept from him all forms of human pain and frailty. Consequently, Gotama grew up knowing nothing of death. Imagine that you are like him. You have never heard of any death— not even in history. You have never seen anyone or anything die, not even a flea. Therefore, the concept of death does not exist for you.

Now ask yourself if you know that you are alive. You may agree that if we lack even the slightest adumbration of death, we cannot conceive of the fact that we are alive. It is as if we must first invent death so as to achieve the experience of being alive. In Book One, mind and matter are defined as reciprocal functions. A similar consideration applies to the present analysis. Life is a function of death: $L = f(d)$. And the function is life's finitude. Life is perceived as life only to the extent that it is finite. Our hope for its infinity is but intensified awareness of its finitude. Finitude gives life its value—that is why we strive to overcome finitude with self-transcendence or eternal life.

Death can thus be a positive aspect of life. And when we as philosophers talk of death, we do not mean exclusively the dying patients in the cancer wards of hospitals. Not at all. We refer to the universal fact of mortality. The healthiest persons with the longest life stretching out ahead of them are mortal. A person does not only die in the time period shortly before his actual death. All living is a form of dying. To die is a verb, an action, performed during every living moment. Mortality is a (maybe the) central ingredient in the meaning of life. One's mortality is created at the moment of conception—even before birth. And when we say that death is a revelation of existential anxiety we mean this pervasive element of dying or mortality which is the everpresent essence of human existence. We are mortal at all times in our life—whether we think of it or not and whether we are anxious about it or not.

Preparation for actual death must occur early in life. People who are close to death are usually in no condition to ready themselves for it. Preparation for death is not morbid, for it is also preparation for life. When a young child begins to show anxiety about dying it is time to realize that the child is becoming an individual and that he is developing an awareness of life. The child, when anxious about death (which occurs earlier than curiosity about sex), is showing healthy signs of normal development. Education for death is therefore a task for the schools. Similarly, persons who deal with death-related situations—from the police to hospital personnel—need training in a philosophic approach to death management.

The basic themes of a philosophic understanding of death lead in two different directions. For one, death is crucial for producing a sense of individuality. The knowledge of our mortality individuates us. It gives us, in being finite, the experience of being a unique person. On the other hand, the everpresent anticipation of death also forces us to explore the possibility of immortality and thus can also lead us to an understanding of the eternity and universality of our consciousness. The issue of the individual versus the universal interpretation of the consciousness-world field, which was a central theme in Book One, is brought into the focus of integrated and lived experience by the knowledge that we are always dying. Each of these two "solutions" commits us to a different life-style. One path stresses worldly achievements; it means success and potency, individualism and creativity. The other path is meditative and peaceful; it stresses eternity and peace. Each person must choose for himself and he must do so with his transcendental freedom: He cannot know which path is the right one.

The existential view on death has rarely been expressed more movingly than in this remarkable quotation from Wolfgang Mozart to his father, upon hearing of the latter's illness (1787):

. . . I have accustomed myself always to expect the worst in all circumstances. Since death, when we come to consider it, is the true end of life, I have made the acquaintance, for some years now, of this best and truest friend of man, so that his image no longer frightens me, but suggests, on the contrary, peace and consolation. And I thank God for giving me the opportunity . . . of coming to recognize Him as the key to true happiness. I never go to bed without thinking, that young as I am, I may perhaps never see another day; and yet no one who really knows me can say that I am morose or sad with my fellows! I thank my Creator every day of my life for this blessing, and I wish with all my heart that I might share it with my fellow men.[2]

Coping with the Anxiety of Death

Elisabeth Kübler-Ross has shown that a patient when coping with death goes through five distinct stages: denial; rage; bargaining; depression; and finally acceptance.There are implicit in this analysis two philosophically debatable assumptions. One implication of this sequence is that it occurs only toward the end of life. Another is that when death is finally accepted the anguish is gone and a happy death, or at least a mature death, is possible. However, the philosophical approach changes this view in two ways. First, as discussed above, preparation for death is really preparation for life. It is sad, therefore, to find oneself ready for life only minutes before death. The denial-to-acceptance sequence must therefore be brought to a successful conclusion as early in life as possible so as to insure the longest possible life of fulfillment. Second, philosophic coping with death does not consist of these five stages but *begins* only after the last stage has been reached. Only when a person clearly accepts death is that individual ready to understand the choices between individuality and immortality. Then that person may embrace either of these respective life-styles. Let us now take a closer look at some specific philosophic ways of coping with death.

VENTILATION AND BEING-WITH

Philosophic devices for coping with the anxiety of death apply equally to life and to death. In other words, we can use them to help dying patients with their pain and their anguish; we can assist their grieving relatives and friends. However, we can also apply these suggestions to the young, the healthy, and the exuberant who are just beginning to savor the magnificent possibilities of life. These first two philosophic phases may be called *ventilation* and *being-with* respectively. Ventilation of feelings and being-with are of course two central methods of beginning any philosophic-therapeutic process. Ventilation of feelings is simply the phenomenological project of uncovering the multiplicity of details inherent in any pain or problem. Ventilation helps us to explore the many dimensions of the anticipation of death. And before we can manage this pain or this problem, before we can translate the anxiety of death into the creativity of living, we must understand the vastness of its emotional detail and ramifications.

Being-with as a philosophic coping device for death expresses our deference to the fact that most healing occurs in a relationship. Having someone present, knowing someone cares, simply *being-with*, facilitates experiencing and dealing with the plethora of emotions and thoughts that emerge when we confront death. The sick child is comforted if someone just sits in the room by the bed. No words are exchanged and the child dozes off. The child is comforted by the mere presence, the being-with, of a human being. The companion must care, for if he or she does not then there is only physical and not conscious being-with.

Being-with is the experience of intersubjectivity or intimacy. It is a replication by the sickbed of the important therapeutic triangle. The person who holds the hand of the dying patient need not be a relative. The empirical or social relation to the patient is philosophically irrelevant. What heals is the establishment of a common conscious space between them. Body language, touching, silence, as well as words, of course, can bring about this common tunnel of consciousness, where each knows the other is present.

What should they discuss? As visitors (friends, relatives, lovers, physicians, therapists, ministers, nurses, or volunteers) we must settle several issues. First, we must avoid taking unwarranted burdens upon ourselves. It is not our role to "cure" the patient. Nor is it our function to answer the problem of death for the patient. We are dying just as the patient is dying. It is only a matter of time, and in cosmic time these moments are relatively so close together that they are for all practical purposes simultaneous. These realities remove a major obstacle to true contact. What shall we talk about? We can encourage the patient's verbalization. But we may also talk about ourselves, our lives, and our needs. That is one legitimate way of establishing contact and confirming the reality of our presence. Above all, we must be sensitive to the need to establish this contact. We must *reality-test* it. We will discover soon enough what words and gestures, what topics of conversation, and what periods of silence facilitate the phenomenon of intersubjectivity, and what obstructs it.

The explanation for the fact that being-with is therapeutic was discussed in Chapter 6 of Book Two in the context of healing as occurring mostly in and through relationships. Being-with expands consciousness, because it is a "larger" presence of consciousness than is the individual consciousness. The more expanded our consciousness is, the more security and eternity will we experience. And this expansion can occur in and through other persons or it can move directly into a sense of cosmic consciousness—as would be the case with a mystic who is also a hermit.

DECISION

Coping with death is possible because it is based on a *decision*. And that is the third philosophic coping device. The decision to cope with death—in health or in sickness, in youth or in old age, in safety or in danger—is made from within the transcendental depth of our freedom, the insight revealed to us by the existential anxiety of freedom. We either make the decision to cope with death or we do not. The decision itself appears in a purely ex-nihilo manner. The language of the deepest center of our soul speaks one of only two sentences—there are no others from which it can choose. It either says, I choose to cope with death or, I choose not to cope with death. The first is the choice of maturity, individuality, inner-directedness, courage, and a willingness for confrontation; the second is the choice of immaturity, escape, other-directedness, evasion, cowardice, and placation. The first is calm, the second, hysterical; the first is transcendental, the second, empirical. The first is natural, in that it is made in the daylight of our freedom, and the second, unnatural, since it is made in the night of our unfreedom.

An issue related to the one of the enormity of our freedom is that successful coping with death, which seems to be prima facie inconceivable, is nevertheless possible, for a human being can adjust to anything. Any condition of life can be accepted, *if such a choice is made*. In psychology this phenomenon is called desensitization. We can desensitize ourselves to almost anything—if we so choose. The interminable chain of brainwashing "successes"—from Stalin's purges in the Russia of the 1930s to Patty Hearst in the United States in the middle 1970s—is ample proof of the correctness of this generalization. Resistance against desensitization is a chosen defense. Those of our prisoners of war in Korea and Vietnam who successfully resisted brainwashing did so because they understood that their human nature guaranteed them that choice.

This is far from suggesting that such blanket desensitization is desirable. Quite to the contrary, brainwashing through sleeplessness and fear-induction is a most inhuman and immoral, albeit no less effective, form of desensitization. It is the rape of the mind. The prisoner, as Solzhenitsyn has told us in the *Gulag Archipelago*, finally chooses to accept whatever belief-system and path of action his interrogator demands. We must bring up these painful themes only to call attention to one fact: when survival is at stake we discover that all of us can make decisions to accept and endorse *anything* as true and good. Such endorsement is always a choice, and many courageous human beings have made the contrary choice to deny and reject these encroachments on their dignity.

In the Third Reich many Germans accepted horrors as values simply because they chose to acquiesce, while others chose to denounce them. The Nazi holocaust of World War II could never have happened if this philosophical principle—the possibility of choosing total adaptation—were not operative. Many ask, how could Nazi Germany and World War II have ever happened? This episode of history is indeed impossible in the context of a theory of the person which says decency is innate. It is, however, possible within a personality theory which understands that freedom, not decency (or indecency, for that matter), is innate, and that decency and civilized behavior are fully dependent on archetypal choices made by individual freedoms.

On the positive side of this dismal picture we have the fact that coping with death, which is based on accepting the reality of death but not necessarily resignation to death, is really a simple possibility for any human being. We must merely perform the primordial and archetypal decision to cope. Each person has within him a hollow, an empty space. If he looks closely he discovers that this emptiness is a window to another cosmos, to another world. That world is one and not many, infinite and not finite. He then discovers that the empty spaces within other persons lead to exactly the same universal region that he has discovered through his own opening channel to infinity and to eternity. When we are in touch with that space, and see how it begins within our body, then we are also in touch with our archetypal and transcendental freedom. It is that freedom which can choose, with equal facility, one of two entirely different trails: coping with death or not coping with death. The full experience and integration of this knowledge makes a firm decision between these two paths not only possible but easy.

UNFINISHED BUSINESS

Coping with death means, and this is our fourth device, to *complete* the *unfinished business* of one's life. But that decision, except over the narrow compass of financial affairs and related matters, is also not limited to the end of life. Even at the beginning of life it is important to complete the unfinished business of living because what is unfinished is finding the meaning that one is to assign to his life, the meaning that will help overcome the everpresent threat of death and extinction.

Unfinished affairs of life tend to fall into two categories: *relationships* and *tasks*. Many people, in theory at least, want to love and be loved but will in practice obstruct and interfere with intimacy—either physical or spiritual, or both. Many marriages and many parent-child relationships are a constant conflict between the need for intimacy on the one hand and the fact of alienation on the other. Death makes clear that if we do want intimacy the time to decide for it is now. It makes clear that intimacy is a supreme value. Confrontation with death thus gives us the motivation and the strength to pursue intimacy immediately and effectively. Old resentments can then be overcome and early training about the virtues of tough-minded isolation and empty pride can then be rejected. In the lives of most of us many I-love-yous remain unsaid. Death helps us say them. If one knows one will die tomorrow, one can summon the fortitude to say the unspoken I-love-yous today. If one knows one is mortal, one can acquire the rationality to express these emotions in the immediate future.

Also, in the lives of many, some I-hate-yous or I-am-angry-at-yous have remained unsaid. To be angry is to have a relationship. Finding ways to creatively express anger will establish closer relationships. Anger is often a healthy albeit explosive form of self-affirmation.

A third kind of unfinished business in human relationships, and one scarcely worth mentioning, is the unsaid I-am-indifferent-to you. Too often in life we are angry at persons who do not deserve the intensity of our ire but who instead have earned the contempt of our total indifference. Often we have relations with people with whom we should have none. Either our own unresolved projections interfere with our authenticity, or our equally inauthentic decision to permit a fascistic intrusion into the sanctity of our center have transmuted proper indifference into improper anger. Only when we are assaulted by what in most instances constitutes a criminal act is it true that a person literally does not permit us to be indifferent. In sum, the confrontation with anxiety's revelation of death makes possible both clarity in and the execution of these unfinished relations.

In addition, death points out to us our unfinished tasks. Our tasks are the meanings we will have achieved (or which we are in the process of achieving) to protect us from the threat of having lived in vain, of having been a mistake, of having wasted all there is to us, namely, our life. Our tasks are our meanings, our goals, the dictates of our inner voices; they are what fulfills us or what we experience as our duty and obligation; in short, our tasks are our dearest responsibilities. To have a task in life need not mean a success-oriented middle-class value-system. The demand that life have goals and meanings can move from the narrowly focused point of selling one million dollars worth of life insurance in the coming year to the broad and amorphous search for a totally detached, ascetic, and undemanding here-and-now existence. Achieving saintly desirelessness can be as much a goal and a task as selling large quantities of soap or cereal. What precisely our task looks like when seen before us concretely must be a matter of individual discovery and decision.

EXAMPLE

A fifth philosophic coping device that helps us profit from the anxiety of death is our opportunity to serve as *example* to those we love. This approach is a general anxiety-coping strategy, as discussed in Chapter 6. The dying patient and the living mortal can show love to the significant others in their lives by teaching them through example how one dies. For once you teach a person how to die, you also teach him how to live. Is there any greater legacy you can leave your children? Is there any more effective way to demonstrate your love and your capacity for love? Socrates did that in the *Phaedo*; all of us can do it now. In a New York medical symposium on death one presenter was a beautiful and brilliant young woman (who was attending the symposium with her husband and young child), the other an older priest from the Greek Orthodox Church. The woman spoke eloquently and reported on an impressive body of research she had done on how to assist the hospitalized dying in coping with their plight. The priest did not speak with either eloquence or scholarship. It was therefore inevitable that one man in the audience would ask, "Which of these two persons would I like next to my bed as I lay dying?"

What counts in the management of death is the example, not the words. What is therapeutic is the *presence* of the person, not the ideas. The listener said that "the beautiful and brilliant woman would merely remind me of what I shall be missing as I leave this world. While I may have reached the sought-after stage of accepting death, I might be aroused by her presence to rekindle my despair and my rage all over again." He continued, "The priest, on the other hand, exhibits an entirely different presence. Whereas he had little to say in a purely intellectual sense, and his power of theological analysis and his research methods were severely limited, it was obvious to me that he had dedicated his life to the ministration of those who suffer. His life represents the unflinching commitment to cope with death and to share that coping with others. His presence tells me that his life is a devotion to the management of death. I know that in helping others he helps himself. And I know that in living for the management of his own death he lives for the management of the death of others. It was his total presence—not charisma—that served as example. I—even though I am an atheist—want him at my bedside when I die." The priest had coped with death by being an example to significant others. He demonstrated the seriousness of his commitment in many ways, including the sacrifices that his priestly vows demand: poverty, obedience, and chastity. He therefore served as example on how to cope with death by having clearly made the religious and the sharing (or being-with) aspects of coping with death the central projects of his life.

The woman in the symposium was no less authentic. Her task in coping with death was to do death-research and live well in the pleasures of the here-and-now that the success of her research made possible. For a different person and under different circumstances, her example would be excellent—but not to someone dying in a hospital. The presence of all that is life is insouciant to death.

IMMORTALITY

Another way of coping with death is by exploring open-mindedly *the possibility of immortality or reincarnation.* This then is our sixth philosophic coping device. It should be possible to reach the insight that personal immortality and individual reincarnation are myths—important myths, myths to live by—which call attention to the indestructibility and eternity of the consciousness that runs through us all. This is a point that has been developed in Book One. These myths—which include religion, mythology, literature, and the arts—make possible the integration of this philosophic insight into our lives here and now. This integration, because it seems to be a genuine answer to death, gives us both the peace of mind to allay our anxieties and the strength to make creative changes for genuine growth in our lives. This particular way of coping with death is of the greatest importance. On the one hand, this solution has hardly been neglected in the history of Western thought. On the other, a reaction against medieval dogmatism about this matter set in during the Age of Reason and reached its apogee during our present age of science. It is hoped that considerations regarding the deathlessness and indestructibility of pure and transcendental consciousness are gradually becoming acceptable to the scientific community—not as extraneous and irrelevant additions but as the intrinsic results of scientific research expanded by the phenomenological method. Immortality defined not as a ghost leaving the body but as the moment of eternity and the universally available experience of the indestructibility of consciousness, should become part of routine medical teaching and practice. This hope rests on exploration of inner space and respect for meditation.

Two additional coping devices for death should be mentioned. They have been used elsewhere, but they are also appropriate in the management of the existential anxiety of death. One of these is to raise the challenge with clients that the next few years of their lives can be their best—they have the experience and the maturity to make that come true. The end of that period will tell how they chose. In this way one can make it crystal clear that finding joy and meaning in life is not an automatic occurrence but a matter for personal decision.

The other coping device—in keeping with what was said earlier—is to use meditation, not only to lower blood pressure and relax the system, but to give the client quick evidential access to the eternity of his transcendental region. Periodic reminders of this simple philosophic insight—and occasional reminders or brief moments to refresh the memory is all that should be required—will reestablish the strength and courage which have their origin in the transcendental sphere and which are needed to help create one's meaning in life.

PARTICIPATION

A final coping device for death is *participation*.[3] This topic is a major one and can only be touched on here. It concerns the use of philosophy for strictly medical healing. It deals with psychosomatic medicine. It is the question of what happens if medicine begins to take the phenomenological model of being seriously. What happens to research? What happens to healing practices? What precisely is the mechanism in operation when the mind influences the body? New ideas for imaginative and novel hypotheses can emerge from this wedding of philosophy and medicine.

To participate in one's death (whether at the end of life or at the beginning) is to establish a connection—an intentional continuity—between the conscious center that knows about death and the phenomenon of death that is the object for that center. And the object that is the phenomenon of death is really the empirical ego. Therefore to participate in one's death means to participate in one's empirical ego; in short, it means to be embodied. Since mental illness is defined in the context of clinical philosophy as in part a split between the subject and the object, the dissociation from death may often be the reverse of coping with death. Whereas it is true that we can cope with death through ascetic withdrawal from our identification with worldly matters, to cope through participation is to cope as an embodiment. It is to choose one's death, to will one's finitude.

In this sense, to cope—or to be authentic—means to establish and reinforce a subject-object continuity. The subject, which is consciousness, intentionally appropriates the object, which is the anticipation, reality, fear, or invention of death. This act then becomes the phenomenon of participation. In other words, coping with death can mean to participate in death. Control over death then becomes a reality (not in the sense of changing biological facts but definitely in the sense of changing psychological facts). The management of death becomes possible and successful under these circumstances. However, not to cope with death in this way means that the participatory continuity could be broken. In that case we experience complete alienation. Consciousness can exert no effective control over the management of death when the phenomenon of participation (or intentionality, as discussed in Chapter 2 of Book One) has become inoperative.

Participation, which derives from the intentionality of consciousness, speaks directly to the issue of bridging the subject-object split in experience. If necessary, participation can be a deliberate choice and become part of a planned program. Participation is the answer on how to use consciousness to bring about changes in the material world—without appealing to the occult. Let us examine some details.

Participation means protest, anger, rebellion, and fight against a fate which condemns us to death. This attitude means that we vigorously and deliberately participate in the act of living. We affirm life and we affirm the self. They are decisions to be resolute. Self- and life-affirmation are both archetypal decisions. Archetypal decisions are easy to make, but because of the primitive depth from which they spring and their cataclysmic world-reconstruction consequences, we choose to resist them. Consciousness' powers of self-deception constitute them into passivity and deposit them in the unconscious. When we do make an archetypal decision we experience abundantly our existential anxiety; but when we resist or deny the free decision for authentic change then the anxiety thereby experienced is neurotic.

The structure of the decision for participation is to choose to establish continuous contact from the inward and purely conscious subject to the outward and material world. The decision for participation is also the decision to implement, make real, or integrate into life the nature of intentionality. Since we are not dealing here with metaphor but rather are describing literally the structure of human existence (through our use of the phenomenological method), we discover that this decision to bridge the subject-object gap is simple, direct, explicit, and unadulterated. It is not hidden behind a morass of symbol, technique, and slow and gradual growth. We may have to break old habits. But each time we do so we have "solved" the problem of changing personality and life-style. We may have to solve the problem not once or twice, but again and again. Choices, after all, are continuous and not isolated events.

In a practical sense, this analysis leads to two important hypotheses. First, a person who participates in life by choosing to throw himself or herself into self-transcending meanings will be healthier, physically and mentally, than a person who is self-reflecting, or whose life-style is reflexive. The latter may become narcissistic and perhaps, as a result, even hypochondriacal. The participating personality will pay less self-conscious attention to health than the self-conscious one. He or she will give less attention to the perfect diet, exercise, rest, recreation, medication, and medical checkups than will the self-conscious, world-isolating and withdrawing person. The hypothesis is that the participators will live longer and healthier lives than the mere observers. This view is not to contradict the values of asceticism—or medical checkups, for that matter.

All too often, however, the world makes self-transcendence extremely difficult. Political circumstances under which freedom is severely restricted, including imprisonment, make it logical for a person to withdraw into an inner shell—for the sake of sanity and self-preservation. Even under these conditions self-transcendence can occur elsewhere, as in the case of exiled dissident writers. Nevertheless, asceticism as a life-style—from difficulty with communication, difficulty in being understood, and difficulty in loving, all the way to autism and catatonic withdrawal—can be a logical response to children's emotional or even physical isolation in their home life. In this case, isolation has become a habit: It makes sense. The hermit's existence can be experienced as resulting from a decision for asceticism. But it can also be reversed. A new decision can be made. The decision for asceticism is archetypal; it may be logical but it has no antecedents. Consequently, a series of new decisions can be made—to recognize the inauthenticity of one's environment and then to change it. These get one ready for a new archetypal decision: to *participate* in life, in relations, with objects, and to throw oneself fully into the world.

Debbie, a middle-aged woman, exhibited in her life a clear subject-object split (which is the decision *against* participation). In a seminar, she wrote a fantasy visualizing the flow of her life. She saw in the distant future the solution to her present problems. But she could not visualize the immediate future, the time directly before her, where the *connection* between now and then would have to be established. In other words, she had not made the archetypal decision for direct contact. She said repeatedly that she was always misunderstood. Both seminar coleaders responded by emphasizing alternately the need for independence in life as well as the contrasting need for intimacy. She reacted almost thoughtlessly by saying, "You don't understand what I am trying to say," confirming thereby once more the earlier diagnosis. She indeed is making and living the decision not to be understood, that is, the archetypal decision for alienation. She then read what she had written in her fantasy, expecting, she said, that it would make no sense to anyone. And yet, when she finished, her face blushed with a healthy glow, and with uncharacteristic feeling she said, "My God! It felt good to read; much, much better than I expected!" In a small way, by reading to the group, she had overcome alienation and made a living decision for participation. This fact was then pointed out to her, and there is no reason why she cannot make further and continuous decisions for participation—decisions which are direct and deliberate. Her environing world will gradually adjust itself so that her decisions for self-transcendence will increasingly be confirmed.

PHYSIOLOGICAL CURES

We can go beyond the purely psychological implications of participation and move on to our second hypothesis. Specific physiological cures—

and this is hypothesis only—might be facilitated by *participating* in the body's struggles toward health. This might be of particular relevance to cancer, where the body—by not developing appropriate immunities—does not seem to know that it is ill. Perhaps a participating consciousness can "inform" its body that it is ill and thereby assist in reversing this process. The body might then begin to fight.

There are essentially two ways to participate in one's body. One way is to look at and identify with either directly-seen, directly-felt-through-any-of-the-other senses, or imagined parts or organs of the body. We can see our hands, we can feel our lungs fill with air, and we can imagine the liver. This decision to be aware of one's body is one type of participation. It is self-conscious. We can call this mode of participation *viewing the body as object.*

A second kind of body-participation is *viewing the body as instrument or as subject.* In this case we use the body as vehicle for identifying with that which is *beyond* the body, namely, the world. We use the hand to clasp a friend. Our identification and self-transcendence is with the friend and not our hand. We use our lungs to appreciate the mountain air, and we use our fantasy about our liver to experience our relatedness to all other vertebrates in the animal kingdom.

Participation means that, in illness but also in health, individuals consciously and deliberately, freely and choosingly, identify themselves with all the aspects of the body. Transcendental consciousness makes the deliberate decision to cathect, that is, to throw-itself-out-into the world of objects that is the body. The transcendental ego "harpoons" the body and then draws the two close together and experiences them as one. That is the first type of body participation. In the second, the body itself serves as "harpoon" for the world beyond. A dramatic expression of this decision is to use the body for political purposes, as is the case in nonviolent resistance, even to the ultimate extreme of self-immolation.

Finally, participation as a philosophic adjunct to medical practice means family and social involvement in the cure. Death is an intimate and feeling family affair, not an asceptic and abstract hospital procedure. So is the cure, or at least the attack on it. Healing is a process in which all significant persons cooperate with full openness to the sick person's emotions. Perhaps the most obvious as well as dramatic examples are parent-to-child organ transplants and skin grafts. But lesser events can serve equally well for illustration.

Grete, a mother of a large family, comes to her physician with a broken arm. The illness or the problem is not exclusively the fracture. Even slight investigation discloses that Grete was having extended and severe emotional conflicts with one of her teen-age sons. For a week she had been close to complete nervous collapse. Finally, she lost her balance and fell in a bedroom of her house. The broken arm was merely the focal point for the total family crisis. No one was at fault. It was a problem of inter-action and interrelationships and not really one of right and wrong. It was a problem where everyone—including the husband and the other children—participated, at least, as witnesses and cosufferers, but probably much more. Curing the broken arm must likewise involve a resolution of the family crisis, the broken relationships. Articulation of all the feel-ings involved and openness in communication will also, on this hypothesis, improve the rate of cure. The broken arm was the symptom of a family conflict. Amelioration of the cause diminished the symptom. Healing the family conflict accelerates the healing of the cracked bone. In other words, participation by the family meant first and diagnostically that the family's *break* became the mother's broken bone and then, in terms of treatment, that the family's *healing* became the arm's healing.

No doubt, there are other models in terms of which this process can be explained. The explanation may be mechanistic, but we will find a field-theory link somewhere. If we argue that emotional stress weakens the body and that an improved emotional climate relaxes the body, we are implying, in the emotion-body link, a field-theory approach. If we are now freer than ever before in using this field-theory approach of par-ticipation, we have another philosophic tool in the medical management of illness and death—at least in the form of a testable hypothesis.

Aging

Let us conclude this brief description of coping philosophically with the anxiety of death with an analysis of anxiety in old age.

Old age is the end of the time of life. Time is a basic category of explana-tion in existentialism. Bergson, Husserl, Heidegger, and Minkowski have told us that *man is time*. We have discussed in Book One the suggestion that time (as well as space) is one of the synonyms for consciousness. The consciousness of old age—like all consciousness—can therefore understand itself when it examines its temporality. The most important dimension (Heidegger called it *ecstasy*) of time is the future. To have a sense of the distant future is to have meaning and hope. To have a sense of the mediate future—the future that mediates the present with the distant future—is to have connected present activities with future results.

The student who gets a good education now connects the immediate future that lies directly before him with the career he hopes for in the distant future. He therefore feels authentic. The concentration camp in-mate, the prisoner of war, and the felon with an indeterminate sentence have been robbed of their mediate future. They do not know when, if ever, they will be released. Because these prisoners often do have a sense of the distant future (release, freedom, and reunion with their families) they have hope and thus can be sane in the present. Without such hope they are dead, and suicide, disease, or homicide are merely natural expressions of a fait accompli. Letters are therefore important to prisoners, because they rekindle the truth of their hope. If the distant future is also destroyed, depression ensues, since hope has vanished. On the other hand, if the prisoners' sense of a distant future is heightened—they have faith in eventual although distant release—then hope has been rekindled and they can tolerate the present. However, their personality is likely to be permanently damaged because their present life, and the life lying before them in the immediate future, can in no meaningful way be connected with their distant future. The resulting fragmentation leads to painful and tragic inauthenticity. Prisoners confined for lengthy periods with indefinite sentences—and all three of the above examples qualify—have become habituated to experience the distant but not the mediate future and retain this pattern of organizing their experience of time upon release. As a result they find difficulty in holding on to mundane activities, like jobs, education, and family relations, which depend on comfortable access to the mediate future in our sense of time. What now is the sense of time in old age?

This time which is our being and which authentically runs from past to future runs backward in our society. Youth—with its energy, exuberance, physical beauty, and limitless possibilities—is epitomized in our culture as the goal of life. Goal or purpose and end are synonyms. End means both purpose and termination. Perhaps these ideas are connected. Youth means boundless futurity. But the underlying social conception of time, rather than extending itself indefinitely into the future, moves into the past. For youth is to all of us a matter of the past. And if it is not now, it will be soon. If not now, it will be that way in the future. For the middle-aged and for the old, youth is in the past. And for the young, all they have to look forward to is that in the future their youth will also be in the past. From the point of view of a philosophical anthropology of time and of the future, such cultural time-reversal will inevitably lead to universal depression and alienation, culminating in the totally unnecessary despair, ineffectuality, and senility of old age.

Old people—like the rest of us—have internalized and accepted as truth society's rejection of their condition. They do not feel entitled to get help; they do not feel their needs are justified. They "must stay out of the way of the younger generation." Old people often feel guilty, embarrassed, apologetic, defensive, and inadequate simply because they are old. That is because old age is seen, from infancy on, not as the future but as the past. The degeneration of the total person in old age is not really primarily a physical phenomenon. An aging and ailing body does not present much of a problem to persons for whom age means the future. They look forward to it; their families and society support it; the value that can be realized in old age, namely wisdom, is the highest in such a society. The aging persons see their age in the full context of their lives and the life of their society: fulfillment, understanding, and peace.

However, in our current conception of old age, life becomes a retrogression into the past. As one gets closer to this past, depression understandably sets in. Even the name for this period, *involutionary*, implies that time is like a parabolic curve. In youth it ascends but in old age it reverses its climb. It descends to whence it came. A more accurate perception of time informs us that life is an infinitely ascending line; evolution never stops. Only a body-model of the person identifies evolution with the suppleness and strength of the body. A field-of-consciousness theory of the person identifies experience, wisdom, knowledge, and understanding with authentic evolution, an evolution in which bodily growth is merely one phase or element.

The ability for consciousness to futurize itself is part of its internal structure. An archetypal decision can help us identify with that structure. An archetypal decision can say that one's life shall conform to the future-oriented structure of time. That is a decision affecting the greatest depths of the personality and of the culture. A deliberate and simple decision—like the decision to say yes to life rather than no—carried out with presence of mind, with courage, and over a lifetime, can bring a person out of the depression of time-reversal and into the energetic and creative hope of a permanent and growing future.

Futurization is not dependent on physiological circumstances. Oriental cultures, which identify meaning and fulfillment with wisdom rather than youth, look forward to old age as the culmination of a consistently future-oriented existence. If we could overnight change our cultural time-distortion, the corresponding transformations in self- and world-perception might well empty our old-age homes, cure or prevent many cases of senility, and in general revolutionize the retirement structure of our corporations, government, and institutions. Restoring time to its original meaning would create an entirely new professional group, persons in their third careers, purveyors of life's wisdom. One is tempted to venture the prediction that this straightening of time would improve relations within families and lower the anxiety level of the entire nation. But these are, of course, hypotheses only. The implementation of these ideas requires imagination and experimentation. But new hypotheses for gerontology suggest themselves by this field-theory approach to the person. Thus, participation and time modification are two suggestions of principle about the future of medical practice that follow from the phenomenological model of being and the existential personality theory.

Summation

We can summarize the approach to the existential anxiety of death as follows: The revelation of the anxiety in question is death. Its corresponding psychopathology—that is, neurotic anxiety which develops if we deny the existential anxiety of death—is timidity. The person who represses the reality of death becomes timid; he placates rather than confronts reality. However, accepting the existential anxiety achieves for us the courage to be. Therapy consists of developing the sense of individuality (by confronting clients with the reality that the next years of their lives can be their best) and the sense of immortality (through meditation exercises). The political desiderata emerging from a study of the anxiety of death are that we should insist that the threat of world apocalypse, which means the threatened death of the biosphere through nuclear war, hunger, and death by pollution (discussed at the beginning of Book One) give mankind a unified purpose: survival and cooperation, which are a joint search for meaning.

Individuality

Little or nothing can be added to the revelations of the anxiety of individuality beyond that discussed in Book One or in *Is There an Answer To Death?*. We can, however, summarize the anxiety of individuality in terms of the following schema. The name of the revelation of existential anxiety is individuality. Its corresponding psychopathology (or neurotic anxiety) is the need to conform and the feeling that one is worthless. However, accepting and integrating the existential anxiety of individuality helps one to experience his or her potency. The treatment of this condition consists essentially of learning to say no in both fantasy and reality. Finally, we can translate these insights into political reality by holding every government accountable to guarantee the integrity of each citizen. We need a totally humanistic world government, one which is dedicated to allowing for the self-fulfillment of every person on earth.

Notes

1. Peter Koestenbaum, *Is There An Answer to Death?* (Englewood Cliffs, N.J.: Prentice-Hall, 1976).
2. Howard D. McKinney and H. R. Anderson, *Music in History* (New York: American Book Company, 1940), p. 490. This quotation was called to my attention by Dr. Jim Luotto.
3. Discussed at length in Book Three.

Chapter 15 • GUILT

Existential Versus Neurotic Guilt

The last revelation of existential anxiety to be discussed is guilt. When the distinction between the existential and the neurotic was first developed, it was applied in particular to guilt. In brief, existential guilt is guilt about unfulfilled potential, about self-betrayal, and anger at one's weakness. Neurotic guilt has two layers: the denial of the existence of existential guilt altogether, and the internalization of external and essentially irrelevant rules and values. These are distinct and do not seem to be reducible to one another. However, they occur in sequence. If we deny our existential guilt we lose the weight and the solidity of the center. This is the condition of the first type of neurotic guilt. We then substitute for this vacuity—for this emptiness, this hollow that resides in one's chest in lieu of substance—a mere shell or crust consisting of whatever irrelevant values, roles, and identities we happen to find lying around in the axiological debris surrounding us. We thus acquire the second type of neurotic guilt, which leads to the formation of the superego.

Let us be more specific about the two different kinds of neurotic guilt. In the first place, neurotic guilt is the limitation placed upon life when one rejects the guilt about possibilities. A person who does not recognize that he is always betraying his most genuine intrinsic values is a person without depth, a superficial human being, who spends most of his time trying to forget the real values of his life. Second, neurotic guilt is more than the denial of existential guilt—a characteristic of all the revelations of anxiety. It is also the introjection of external rules and the formation of an overdeveloped superego. This second type of neurotic guilt leads to the defensive personality. It is exhibited by the person who does not feel entitled to his rights, does not feel he belongs in this world, and finds it necessary to apologize for actions, demands, and needs that most people find quite acceptable. He must therefore depend on others to tell him who he is and what he must do.

EXISTENTIAL GUILT

In what precise sense can we say that existential anxiety reveals us as guilty? One of the most profound pains in life, a pain impervious to medical and psychological treatment, is regret over unfulfilled possibilities, grief over unrealized potential. We say a suicide or a young death is a "waste" for precisely this reason. The missed destiny can be a talent undeveloped, a love-relationship not pursued, sensuality that is untapped and not expressed, or a mind that has not been stretched by education. Neglect, inexcusable and perpetrated on ourselves and by ourselves, is the nature of existential guilt.

Fulfilling one's potential—physical and mental, intuitive and analytic— has been for many ages in history the pinnacle of human ideals. Among the most notable have been the civilizations of ancient Greece and the European Renaissance. Furthermore, to enjoy life is to go beyond oneself (self-transcendence), to become what one is (self-realization). To enjoy life does not mean to fulfill a narrow duty or to fit one's life into the procrustean bed of some provincial value system. It does mean to give expression to our transcendental nature—to understand our freedom and to know about meanings—and to pay attention to our inner voices. And a person who has denied his or her authentic potential, who has conspired in its imprisonment, feels a resultant deep twinge of guilt. The reason that he *is* guilty is because he has denied his nature. A person who follows all the rules of parents and society may suffer deeply from existential guilt precisely because the rules, which he freely chooses to continue to adopt, prevent him from hearing his inner voices and hinder him in living out what he secretly knows to be his authentic destiny.

Existential guilt therefore is the pain of the experience of self-betrayal. To be betrayed by another person—as by the mother in the Oedipal situation who locks the bedroom door and goes to bed with father—is one thing. But it is quite another matter to betray oneself, for this is so painful that few have the strength to admit it. Guilt means *I* have done the betraying; existential guilt means *I* have used my very own nature, which is my freedom, to betray my nature, which is to deny my freedom. It is as important as it is difficult to be able to distinguish in one's own soul between neurotic and existential guilt. Is the guilt I feel about a specific omission a response to early training? Or does there exist a deeper human commitment to the realization of that value? To complicate the problem even further, we must ask ourselves if perhaps one's authentic depth has willingly accepted and made a loving commitment to one's early training.

Religious attitudes can serve as examples. Early religious training is externally imposed. To accept it on these grounds alone in later life is neurotic. To violate these ukases—as when a person marries outside of the Church—leads to guilt. This guilt is neurotic. But it is quite possible even likely, that in the years of maturity a person makes the independent choice to identify himself or herself fully with the religious training of his or her childhood. An adult rechooses his childhood; he is no longer victimized by it. If he now violates this renewed commitment, his guilt is no longer neurotic but existential.

Rollo May writes that early in his psychoanalytic career his women patients would feel guilty going to bed with their boyfriends. A generation later, his women patients feel guilty for not going to bed with their boyfriends. Both guilts are neurotic. They exemplify the second type of neurotic guilt—the introjection of external authority. Social expectations have changed; the tacit rules for the new roles have changed. In each case, the woman is ruled by an external directive and arbitrary standards unrelated to the voices of her own inwardness. Existential guilt refers to the knowledge that she is betraying what her own inner voices tell her is the proper behavior and the right life-style for her. What does *she* want? What is right for *her*? These are the questions which must be answered. The doubt about them and the refusal to heed them are existential guilt.

Only extensive introspection, meditation on one's inner needs, can help a person resolve these important issues. How does one learn to hear these inner voices? How can one assess their truth?

INNER VOICES

Our inner voices come from a variety of regions. Some come from our universal nature and some from our adventitious empirical circumstances. We have essentially two levels of inner voices. The first and most basic level is ontological or transcendental. It is our philosophic nature; it speaks to us from out of the depth of the inner space-time which is our transcendental consciousness. For example, our inner voices can tell us that our possibilities for eternity and universality have been neglected. These are authentic possibilities and guilt at this transcendental self-betrayal is as intense as it is real. Or these voices inform us that our freedom and our potential for individuation have been denied. And it is always we who have done it. In this case we have rejected our potential of assuming responsibility for choosing our own identity. We then are guilty and feel guilty—not because of some introjected external authority but because we recognize the structure of our ontology. Our potential for individuation has been denied.

These three examples—eternity-universality, freedom, and individuation—reflect the type of existential guilt that is transcendental or ontological. Our inner voices tell us that we have betrayed our basic, that is, transcendental human nature. But there also is another, more specialized, type of existential guilt.

We have an individual, temporal, or local destiny in addition to our transcendental one. This is the second level of inner voices. These come from the outer spatio-temporal reality with which our ontological and transcendental natures have identified themselves. To give up these inner voices is to contradict the archetypal decision to be one's empirical self. Each of us has a childhood, a tradition, and a social identity. Each of us has an individual unconscious and a collective unconscious. Each of us has an empirical ego and an empirical nature and destiny. That also is a source of inner voices. Many persons have rejected their childhood religion but found it necessary in later life to either recapture it or find a mature substitute. The ontological or transcendental identity is inevitable and is the deepest. But the personal, ethnic, religious, or social identity, while not absolute, nevertheless runs very deep. It is set in early childhood. Similarly, the sexual identity is set (or chosen) early. These inner voices thus may require of us that we fulfill our sexual and ethnic destinies as well as our ontological-transcendental one. These ethnic, religious, and sexual identity choices are also archetypal. They can be reversed, but frequently one discovers that one *wants* to make them, and even that one *wants* to intensify them. Some individuals of course do discover, upon hearing these inner voices, that they desperately *want* to change them. The ensuing choice is then again obvious.

These alternatives among which we must choose belong to the empirical ego and the voices that tell us about these options for meaning come from the empirical realm. Missed opportunities in the realm of these options leads to empirical regret, empirical loss, or empirical guilt. However, we may in addition experience guilt for not using our transcendental freedom in making these choices. When our conscience tells us that we are neglecting the use of our freedom, that we are neither considering these options nor making commitments to them (both reflection and commitment are free acts), then the inner voices are heard originating in the transcendental ego. The desire for a specific heterosexual, homosexual, or lesbian erotic act or expression, for example, is a voice from the empirical ego. But the choice to refuse to listen to that empirical voice or the decision to confront that empirical voice, if it is indeed heard, is a voice emanating from the transcendental ego. The question, "What is my sexual interest?" is answered by voices originating in the empirical ego. But the questions, "Am I expressing my sexual interest?," "Am I dealing with these feelings?," "Am I in charge of my life or is my life in charge of me?" are answered by voices originating in the transcendental ego.

Changes in sexual or ethnic identification are possible and real even though they may be rare. They are rare because they are archetypal decisions and remaking them involves the earth-shaking reorganization of the entire life-world of the individual. Specifically, Bill has homosexual interests. After significant therapeutic exploration of the feelings involved he discovers that he wishes to change his life-style to a heterosexual one. This voice comes from the empirical ego. If he now chooses to change his sexuality, he listens to the empirical voices. If he chooses not to change his sexuality, then he does not listen. Whatever ensuing guilt there may be here is empirical guilt. However, if Bill adopts a fatalistic position, if he decides to let fate take over, or if he permits other people to direct or to manipulate him, then he is neglecting the very essence of his true decision-making power. Not to use his freedom (for either acceptance or rejection of the empirical voices) is transcendental guilt.

In terms of this schema, to freely choose homosexuality leads to empirical but not transcendental guilt. The guilt is empirical, because the empirical voice has spoken "heterosexuality." The guilt is not transcendental, because the decision was made freely. Conversely, to permit heterosexuality to happen automatically leads to transcendental guilt but not to empirical guilt. Bill has done what the empirical voice demanded: adopt a heterosexual life-style. But he has not done so freely and with personal responsibility. He therefore experiences transcendental guilt.

Let us reflect on a further example. There exists a whole class of persons who suffer deeply but refuse to rally the power of their freedom to effect a change in their lives. They are genuinely tragic figures. The decision for joy and happiness never seems to be made. They have learned to love their tragedy, and to depend on it for their self-concept and their meaning. To them, tragedy is beautiful and it is even supported by society. Symptoms develop when it becomes clear that lack of self-assertiveness deprives them of some of the pleasures, loves, and successes of life. Their sad world seems truly to reflect their self-concept as tragic figures. Some of the individuals who fit this description often turn out to belong to persecuted minorities. Their living decision to say no to joy and yes to tragedy results from an inner voice which comes not from their childhood but is of much more ancient vintage—their ethnic origins. This ethnic inner voice may overstep its bounds by souring a marriage or creating a psychopathological depression. It then becomes obvious that redefinition must be cast into an ethnic and not a psychological mold. The therapeutic conceptualization must be in terms of a collective ethnicity and not an individual set of childhood experiences. Ethnotherapy is thus indicated.

The Black must know that historically the tormented slave, with his melancholy spirituals, transformed himself into the aggressive militant. He must recapitulate in his own lifetime the history of his race. The Jew must know that the tragic pariah in the Diaspora transformed himself into a powerful Israeli soldier. And the Jew, as an individual, must do likewise with his self-concept and life-style. In other words, both minorities must apply these collective ethnic solutions, from a decision for negation to a decision for affirmation, to their own and more narrow individual personal situations. When every tool in the psychologist's bag of tricks fails, this anthropological or social redefinition of the person will work. The ethnic voices come from the empirical ego. The conscience which obligates us to use our freedom to endorse and activate these ethnic voices or reject and neutralize them comes from the region of transcendental subjectivity.

A convenient way to illuminate this important region of inner voices is to meditate on what Progoff calls *stepping-stones*: a few key events in a person's life. These will give us a sense of the flow that is our life today. We can then meditate on how it feels today, right now, to experience the flow that is our life. Then we proceed to write it all down, in the style of free association. This process reveals, among other things, unfulfilled potential. It reveals values that are experienced as real but are not being realized.

In doing such an exercise one avails himself first of the power of reflection, epoche, or reduction. One steps outside one's life and observes that life. One moves from the natural attitude, the commitment to and cathexis of the empirical realm, to the phenomenological attitude. One withdraws from the empirical ego to the transcendental ego.

Second, the hidden regions of the empirical ego—both in its collective and in its individual aspects—reveal themselves: hidden feelings, hidden aspirations and expectations, and hidden desires and needs. We then make a decision to integrate these insights into our daily lives and to realize these values in our empirical existence. Our inner voices have come from two sources. The transcendental voices tell us we must reflect, we must choose to see clearly what reflection reveals, and we must implement these insights. Reference is here made to reduction and the realm of pure consciousness it reveals, to freedom, and to cathexis or identification. All these are transcendental phenomena. All have been elicited by meditation. These are our inner voices speaking from the transcendental realm. "I am neglecting my freedom." That is an inner voice from the transcendental realm. "I rarely reflect; I am always involved with my life." That is another inner voice from the transcendental realm.

Empirical voices tell us the demands of the empirical ego. "As a child I wanted to be a great football player." That is an inner voice from the empirical realm. "My divorce was the most important stepping-stone in my adult life." That is an inner voice speaking from the empirical realm.

Thus neurotic guilt is the uncritical and automatic introjection of externally originating values, self-concepts, and life-styles into the structure of our existence. Also, neurotic guilt is the denial of existential guilt. Both types of neurotic guilt lead to symptoms. Existential guilt arises when we violate the commands of our inner voices. These can be empirical, in which case they are either collective (ethnic) or individual (psychological), or they can be transcendental.

SYMPTOMS OF EXISTENTIAL GUILT

Existential guilt, as the betrayal of one's possibilities, leads to self-hate and contempt for one's weakness. It leads also to loss of self-respect. Whereas persons who in their own eyes are unsuccessful experience this guilt early in life, so-called successful persons may postpone experiencing it until well into middle-age. That guilt is sometimes referred to symptomatically as the menopause, especially the male menopause. It is useful to discuss the symptoms of existential guilt in middle-aged men, since for them the excuse of physical menopausal symptoms does not exist. Success often means that external values and demands have been realized. The person then discovers that success is not the satisfying and durable value or state of being that he had expected. But after forty or fifty years in pursuit of these values, the price of saying "I was wrong" and "I am sorry" is indeed prohibitive. Existential guilt is then interpreted by our ghost-in-a-machine-theory-of-man society (or by the medical model of the person) not as an ontological structure but conveniently as a sexual dysfunction or loss of libido. Furthermore, existential guilt frequently becomes conceptualized exclusively as missed sexual opportunities. And while sexual opportunities may indeed have been missed, they are only one small aspect to the guilt about an unfulfilled existence.

In this way society and science deflect us from the contradictory and dialectical realities of living a life without illusion by seducing us into the belief that the polarities of existence are a curable malady. Existential philosophy is a philosophy without illusion about our reality. The first stage of absolute realism is to know that some of our dearest wishes and deepest needs are blocked by steel walls. The second stage is the knowledge that the wish and the need are equally absolute and uncompromising. That is the meaning of contradiction as the essence of human existence.

The pain of self-betrayal becomes translated into a variety of responses. Some seek "more of the same" and seek adventuresome affairs. Far from recognizing that their values are wrong, they think they did not pursue their earlier values with sufficient intensity. But they soon discover that the materialistic and objectivistic approach to life's problem of meaning, worth, and destiny does not work any better by increasing the dosage than it did in the first half of life. Self-contempt, on the other hand, can also be completely internalized, in which case the person becomes depressed. Or it can be expressed as anger, in which case the person projects his self-contempt on others. He wears signs on his face which read "It's your fault!" "If it hadn't been for your defects I would be a happy and fulfilled person!" Finally, self-hatred can be repressed, so that it leads to symptoms such as high blood pressure or alcoholism.

Many persons discover deep inside them two fundamentally contradictory self-concepts. One is an often untapped reservoir of strength. Another is a tremendous anger, hate, embarrassment, and disappointment at their own unconscionable weakness. That sense of worthlessness, to the extent that it is based on the factual comparison of reality with potentiality and to the degree that it is perceived in a context of inwardness and freedom, is existential guilt.

A woman in her early thirties—an unmarried professional—has a recurring and lurid dream of unsuccessfully trying to kill an ugly gopher. She finally decides to shoot it. The gopher is at that moment transformed into an attractive and charming young girl, who is not hurt by the bullet but swallows it instead. This dream has many possible meanings. One of these, however, is that being a charming young girl and an attractive young woman are and have been some of her unfulfilled possibilities. The ugly gopher is her existential guilt, and the repeated and bloody attempts to kill the animal represent her anger at her own self-betrayal. And her self-betrayal, like the gopher, will not go away or die.

It is important that we not develop guilt about existential guilt. The answer to existential guilt is not to "do something" but rather "live with it acceptingly." We can therefore be more specific in our examination on how to deal with it.

Coping with the Anxiety of Guilt

The general principles of coping discussed in connection with other forms of anxiety apply of course equally well to existential guilt. To see the application of this analysis to the problem of guilt, it is helpful to catalogue some of the prevalent types of existential guilt that one finds in personalized education in philosophy. Each of the following groups of persons experiences the pain of self-betrayal and the guilt of unrealized potential, even though in each case the circumstances of life are different.

THE CONTEMPORARY BOHEMIANS

One group consists of young people—from their early twenties to middle thirties—who are healthy in every aspect but at the same time severely alienated from their society. They are the heirs of the flower children, the hippies, and the beat generation. They live in the best regions of the country —beautiful mountains and stunning seashores. They are professionals or semi-professionals, often teachers or engineers (but most want to be poets, writers, painters, or therapists—and they would make good ones), but their primary concerns are artistic creativity, personal growth, intimacy, and love of nature.

These contemporary bohemians are superior people by every measurement. Their sexual lives are free, unorthodox, and unstable. But they also feel that they fail at family life, future planning, and financial security, and they are anguished about the lack of a stable structure in their lives. They cannot integrate their life-style with the established society, although they do feel a deep need for such integration. Their constant problem is the conflict between peace of mind and integrity. Their alienation is based not on illness but on health. They are the healthy ones. They are free, ethical, and committed to authentic human values. Their surrounding society is mostly sick and inauthentic. They feel forced, as healthy persons, to adjust themselves to a set of unacceptable institutions. Like all prisoners, they are powerless against the establishment.

These young people demand that their occupations be creative—a legitimate request but one that is difficult to realize. Their marriages as a rule do not work out, because they seek and require new life-styles. Because they have internalized the quasi-totalitarian demands of their society they feel guilty. Specifically, they are torn between the two kinds of guilt. They feel neurotic guilt because part of them still accepts conventional social rules. They feel existential guilt precisely because they accept the inauthenticities of society and therefore find that they betray their own personal and true meanings.

There does not seem to be anything like a solution to the problems of these people. They reflect a defect in our culture, or perhaps even a defect in being itself. They mirror the fact that we speak of one value-system— depth and liberation, respect for human beings, and reverence for the exploration of inwardness—but practice another: materialism and axiological rigidity. They do what we teach and are then punished for being good pupils. They cannot be integrated into the society which they need without at the same time violating the integrity of their inner voices. They cannot respond to their legitimate and valuable inner needs without suffering the fate of pariahs.

Two recommendations seem appropriate. First, never contradict or compromise your inner integrity. However, do not be boorish or immature, because you want more than protest: you want success. Second, never use your alienation from society as an excuse to fail in your own tasks and meanings or to transmute your joy and zest for life into bitterness, cynicism, and depression. In other words, you must realize that you *are* the consequences of your actions, that you *are* fully responsible for the success or failure of your life, and that basically the world does not care if you fail or succeed. But one person does care: you yourself. There can therefore be no excuse for failure in your life.

These young persons must recognize that they need beauty, creativity, meditation, art, religion, philosophy, and poetry as much as they need air, water, and bread. And they must pursue these needs with the alacrity of one who fights for his survival. These people are artist-philosophers, bohemians, perhaps. And they are condemned by their integrity to be such. Their life will be a continuum of struggle, frustration, opposition, and rejection. But they must persevere, for there is no other path that conforms to the truth about life as they and many others see it.

Some, but only very few, will be recognized by the surrounding culture and validated as great artists. Some, like Nietzsche, will even become prophets for a future age. But the fate of most will be one of suffering. Their guilt will be minimal, but their pain intense. They will feel real and satisfied but maladjusted. They will derive some comfort from the frail hope that there is a chance for recognition. Some have been catapulted into the forefront of our culture—and therein lies the feeble hope of others that they might likewise overcome their alienation from the establishment.

They can gain inspiration from other persons in other ages who have followed the same unswervingly independent path of creativity and integrity. We will never know of those resting in unmarked graves, but we do know of such as Boethius and Erasmus, Wycliffe and Aquinas. We know of Schubert and of Bartok, of Spinoza and of Kierkegaard, all of whom were great and wise but also socially maladjusted nonconformists.

MENOPAUSAL PROFESSIONALS

A second group of persons who experience the existential anxiety of guilt is successful middle-aged professionals and executives who are beginning to show symptoms of meaninglessness. Perhaps they are the parents of those discussed above. This group is discussed earlier in the exposition of existential guilt and as exhibiting the (mostly male) menopause. Their symptoms are depression, ennui, and marital boredom. The cause of their symptoms is the discovery that their careers, precisely because of their success, distracted and deflected them from hearing and listening to their inner voices. While their original professional commitment may have been in response to an inner voice, they may discover that by middle age the message of these voices is entirely different.

Their existential guilt, once exposed, can be colossal. Their existence suddenly becomes one massive symptom: their authentic meaning has been repressed, the fruitful insights of existential anxiety have been denied, and now their life is one big neurosis or neurotic anxiety. Now that their "success" is almost total, the fraudulence and bankruptcy of the values to which their lives have been devoted and which their society had proferred them as absolute and reliable becomes apparent. The values have been fulfilled. They have no place to go. And the meaning is not there.

The enemies to growth, in these cases, are the resistance against admitting a gargantuan mistake as well as the adulation society accords to successful people. Physicians are a good example of both problems. The time, expense, and difficulty of their preparation and the subsequent establishment of their practice rules out any chance that they can readily accept a fundamental error in judgment that might have occurred initially in their career or a change in values and attitudes that might have occurred in later years.

There is no suggestion here, by any stretch of the imagination, that medicine is an inauthentic career. In many instances, however—as is also true for the rest of us—this profession was chosen at a time when those concerned were certainly not at the height of their philosophic powers. Wisdom comes late in life and is the result of long experience in living. And no younster in college or even before can be expected to be in full command of these philosophic insights. But there is a further phenomenon operating here. All professional commitments lead to ennui unless there is continuous and significant growth and creativity. A successful politician, for example, may have high status in society. Others may envy him, praise him, and need him. He believes them (why shouldn't he?), but it may be that the din of their adulation deafens his inner voices. Even the best ear-specialist tires of looking into patient's ears. He needs new growth and new challenges. In a profession held in as high esteem as is the medical profession, the rewards of status, prestige, respect, and income seduce one away from his existential guilt.

It is, thus, extremely difficult for a person who became a physician at his parent's urgings to admit that perhaps and in view of what his inner voices are telling him he was wrong, or that what is wrong is his present neglect of other areas of development. Again, existential guilt is not allayed by "trying harder." Our success with anything in life must not cloud the constant presence of unfulfilled possibilities and therefore the permanent undercurrent of existential anxiety. People who perceive themselves as failures have no problem with this. But those who regard themselves as successes can use that illusion to deny neurotically the reality of their existential anxiety.

Thus, the problem of those facing a second career in which their unfinished business in life will be completed can be impeded by their very success at coping with the problems of the first half of life.

POTENCY IN WOMEN

Another group of clients who question their meaning and exhibit existential guilt about unfulfilled possibilities in the context of personalized education in philosophy are women concerned with women's liberation. A great deal of value has been accomplished with the ideals of liberated women and liberated relationships. Nevertheless, liberation should not be imposed but must be freely chosen. For example, a woman who makes an informed and deliberate choice to be conventional or traditional is indeed a liberated woman. On the other hand, a woman who reads current magazines and thoughtlessly chooses to be "liberated" so that she conforms with the latest fad is far from liberated. Liberation is a matter of the heart more than of visible behavior and audible verbalization. Some individuals mouth the jargon of liberation not because they truly believe it but because they hope that by voicing these views often enough they will become actualized in their own lives both as ideals and as realities.

Some women are in conflict about their potency. Many seemingly timid and placating women will eventually say, with a gleeful grin from ear to ear, "I would *love* to have power!" The issue involved in this situation is understandable. The overreaction may be unfortunate. Some implications are tragic. Our culture used to teach, and occasionally still teaches, that potency is male. As a result, some women feel ambiguous about their own potency and power while, at the same time, they envy men their power. They want to embrace them, be overwhelmed by them, and take their power into them. But they hate men at the same time. And they cannot in this subservient and slavish way appropriate a man's power any more than they can grow a male sex organ. Their envy and supplications are thus condemned to failure. But there is a deeper and more authentic source for their anger. It is unfair that potency should be unevenly distributed. And it is proper to rage against that injustice. Women had in the past been taught to surrender to this condition, but that can lead only to resentment.

The solution to this problem of guilt with respect to potency is to realize the obvious, namely, that potency already exists in women to the same extent that it does in men. The distribution of potency is indeed even and nature has not created an unjust situation. It is the social institutions that have brainwashed us into distorting these basic realities of human existence. The problem is artificially created by society, and there is no need at this point to speculate about its causes. Potency is the act of being. Potency is self-transcendence, freedom, and intentionality. Potency is the archetypal decision for individuality. It is the commitment to one's sexuality. Potency is to choose embodiment.

Potency is thus equally available to all. A person is not potent because he is male or impotent because she is female. On the contrary, a person is potent first, because that person is a consciousness-body-world field, and *then* that person avails himself or herself of this potency to choose and define the meaning of masculinity and femininity. Many problems between men and women as well as conflicts within the ego itself can be traced to this philosophic confusion. The ontological primacy of our here-and-now consciousness and the freedom to choose a sexual role are philosophic fundamentals about human existence which, if understood, can reintroduce harmony into the sexual lives of many people.

Psychoanalysis has named some of these dynamics *penis envy* and has tied them to its biology-is-destiny premise. Such a materialization of consciousness is a distortion of the primacy of consciousness and follows from the medical model of the person or the ghost-in-a-machine theory of man. To identify potency with penis may be alliterative and it has its uses. It is dramatic, anxiety-producing, and effective in certain circumstances. But it is a metaphor only and it tempts us away from the philosophical reality of the field of consciousness that we are. It therefore deprives a woman of her freedom and a man of his flexibility.

Potency comes first: it is the energy that is consciousness; it is the energy that is the flow of time; it is the security of the Eternal Now; it makes possible the archetypal decision to be an individual. Then we develop its symbols. Jung preferred to deal in terms of myths. Freud was more primitive and preferred to use the human body, especially its most basic functions, as the mnemonic or metaphoric devices which summarize and concretize the philosophical dynamics of our human experience. It is false and therefore unfair to seek to deprive women of their potency and burden men with it by our conviction that a person is a body and not a consciousness.

One solution to the problem of women's uncertainty about potency has been for them to take full personal charge of their sexual gratification. The emphasis on female masturbation and on the clitoral rather than the vaginal orgasm—associated with the movement for women's liberation—are expressions of this desideratum. A woman's sexual arousal and sexual satisfaction can be literally in her own hands. She can and must assume personal responsibility for it. Autoeroticism is simply a symbol of liberation. It is the bodily counterpart of philosophic freedom and self-reliance. Lesbianism is, similarly, an expression of the fact that a woman can take personal charge of her sexual needs. Many so-called lesbians are really bisexual. In embracing another woman, a woman often for the first time embraces her own femininity. Furthermore, in heterosexual relationships, a woman must then feel free to be fully aggressive and demanding, unashamedly asking for what she wants. In this way she confirms the rebirth of her potency and responds authentically to her existential guilt.

Summation

We can consolidate the discussion of existential guilt in terms of the following highlights. The name of this revelation of existential anxiety is guilt. When we deny this guilt, thereby producing neurotic guilt, we experience depression. But when we work through this existential guilt by confronting it we develop a sense of wholeness. The "treatment" of this condition consists of developing or pursuing excellence in life. The ideals of human perfectibility and of achievement are authentic antidotes to the existential anxiety of guilt. And if we now extrapolate the insights about existential guilt onto the political scene, we discover that this guilt leads us to measure all institutions—such as the state, the family, education, the law, commerce, and medicine— by the degree to which they facilitate the development of human potential.

BOOK THREE Pathology

Chapter 1 • *THE COMPLEAT THERAPIST*

The Liberal Versus the Conservative Therapist

Who, in the context of clinical philosophy, is an ideal therapist? Such a question can have no definitive answer, and even to attempt an answer is a risk, perhaps a foolish one. However, this important question does need to be asked and deserves at least the outline of a hypothetical reply.

Three factors are to be considered: (1) the open or liberal therapist, (2) the closed or conservative (or orthodox) therapist, and (3) the lifelong therapist, philosophic friend, or therapeutic supporter.

Ideally speaking, philosophic therapy deals with the deepest zones and structures of not only human existence but of being in general. Consequently, all therapeutic rules and opinions, all guidelines and procedures, and all psychological theories of personality must trace their origin and find their justification within the very structures of being itself that they endeavor to disclose. In this purist sense, laws and social conventions, as well as accepted techniques, are irrelevant and even can endanger the success of the therapy proper. To be brutally frank, the issues that can arise in extreme cases include these: the patient chooses suicide, or homicide, or the patient chooses heterosexual or homosexual relations with the therapist.

Whereas the average therapist understandably and rationally does not wish to expose his life to the personal, social, professional, and legal risks and pressures implicit in such dramatic and unorthodox archetypal choices, a purist self-uncovering therapy can tolerate no such conventional limits. For a person to fully disclose to himself his psychological (unique) as well as his philosophical (generic) foundations, total openness and permissiveness are mandatory. And we cannot prescribe in advance what form this openness ideally should take. On the other hand, if the goal of therapy is adaptation, adjustment, coping, and reality-testing—which are commendable and legitimate albeit limited goals—then total openness is contraindicated and restrictiveness is required.

Nevertheless, openness is needed not only for the inherent value of full self-disclosure and for total ontological knowledge, but also for the more immediate therapeutic goal of change—for reconstitution, recathexis, and character reconstruction. The closed life-style is needed to succeed in the world of practical affairs.

Openness means deconstitution and decathexis; openness, in the last analysis, is the unmaking of whateever the archetypal decisions have been in this particular life. Moreover, openness is fraught with frightful anxiety. But it can also be the source of the deepest revelations of the mystery of the person and of the miracle of being. Openness may lead to total despair, but it also can lead to total truth. Openness is the *sine qua non* for a real change in one's self-definition. It is good but difficult; it is also dangerous. And to encourage this fully unmasking openness—for its own sake as well as for the sake of psychotherapeutic reconstruction—is the role of the liberal therapist.

The conservative therapist resonates to the practical. To live a normal life in the consensual world—and this for most individuals is indeed a genuine value—there must be controls. The empirical ego is created by instituting controls. The character or the personality is constituted through specifiable archetypal decisions for limitations. The usual names for these self-chosen, self-adopted, and internalized rigid constitutional structures are the processes of *socialization*, the development of the *super-ego, habit, conscience*, and the like.

The *normal* person is, therefore, one who, in his perception and behavior, exhibits a substantial set of passive constitutions and passive cathexes; the normal person must therefore live in a significant state of self-deception. However, these passive constitutions are chosen as passive, in that they are chosen to be placed into a state of passivity and then they are chosen to remain as such. We are entitled to call these habitual patterns of self-deception constitutions and cathexes nevertheless; and we retain consistency with our philosophy of freedom, because we can choose at any time to reestablish contact with them, and make them active. We can change our sexual preference, for example, if we (1) choose to decathect ourselves from our present archetypal decision for a specific sexual role—this act of reduction puts us in touch with our freedom—and (2) if we choose to recathect our silent and solitary transcendental centers with a different sexual role. However, to the extent that we have a mass of passive constitutions—and this represents the vast majority of us—we are closed. Therapy which respects these passive constitutions is closed, orthodox, and conservative. Such is the *normal* and in most cases realistic mode of being-in-the-world.

Openness, on the other hand, means that all (or most) of these passive and self-deceiving constitutions and cathexes, these rigid skeletal bones, become active rather than passive, conscious rather than unconscious, visible and perceptible rather than remain invisible and imperceptible. Conscious freedom means active freedom, self-controlled and autonomous freedom; it means accessible freedom. Unconscious freedom, which the open therapy seeks to overcome, means passive freedom, uncontrolled freedom, inaccessible freedom.

Let us sharpen this distinction through an example. A man sees a car burning in an airport parking lot. Fire engines arrive and extinguish it. He thinks no more of it. Later that evening he is told that there were four persons trapped in the burning car and that all of them perished. Upon hearing this, the man collapses into uncontrollable sobs. What is the explanation?

This situation can be analyzed on two levels. The first we might classify as an orthodox psychotherapeutic conceptualization: We can hypothesize, for instance, that the fire triggered both memories and guilt feelings in him. The fire perhaps reminded him of childhood traumas. Or, possibly, he needed to do much grief work in his life, and the jolt of the news shocked him into mourning over lost years and abandoned opportunities. These explanations, and many like them, may well be accurate, as far as they go. But in clinical philosophy such accounts are viewed as being only symbols of the deeper philosophic reality for which they exist as metaphors. The philosophic truth, the ontological reality which supports this breakdown, is the sudden vision into the abyss of existence; it is the truth about being and man. The sobbing body is the embodiment of the experience of deconstitution. The man is literally falling apart. In addition, the fact that he has no control over his convulsions divulges to him that he is a transcendental ego, a cosmic consciousness which observes the realm of the empirical and the physiological. The phenomenon of realizing there is no control is really the experience of being a disengaged spectator who, in an out-of-body experience, observes his body sob and convulse uncontrollably.

He grieves because he recognizes the profound, tragic, and totally unacceptable reality that the things that matter most are contingent; they are fragile and ephemeral. These four burned people were someone's children or someone's parents; someone's brother, sister, or lover. As conscious centers they were infinitely precious beings. Anyone who carefully observes a human inwardness perceives its preciousness, discovers, as a directly observable fact (called in Chapter 3 of Book One a transcendental fact) the holy nature of that center. To see it squelched, suffering, or even dead is directly perceived to be absolutely and unqualifiedly unacceptable. Yet it does happen. These transcendental facts are of the order of a higher level natural law theory or a higher level Platonism.

Burning is the most horrible of deaths. The experience of being burned is the same feeling of utterly unacceptable condemnation just mentioned: the victim cannot die, nor can he tolerate the excruciating pain. This feeling of being stuck, trapped, and condemned is also the feeling of being an individual and unique *Existenz* which is brought into being through the archetypal decision for finitude. Burning is then not just a trigger for the inviolable "stuckness" of being an individual; it also contains the elements of guilt and responsibility—as if the holocaust represented a hidden, secret, and unconscious wish, a demonic, satanic desire—of any archetypal decision. There is something deeply frightening about being an individual, and it is this: I am not born individual but I am self-created as individual. The cosmic universal totality from whence I came is secure because it is eternal. But the creation of the sense of being an individual—which is replete with a mass of passive constitutions (that is, archetypal decisions)—is a self-chosen risk; it is the denial of the environment; it is born in a bed of anxiety.

All these passive constitutions and ontological realities have suddenly obtruded themselves on this man. He can no longer repress his transcendental freedom. He sees his enormous freedom for identity- and individuality-creation. He experiences the groundlessness of existence, in that there is no guidance from within the cosmic universality for the constitution and the cathexes of his individual *Existenz*.

Let us review. The given facts are that our man (a) sees fire, (b) is told of death, and (c) breaks down. The breakdown includes the experiences of anxiety and guilt. The anxiety is the experience of nihilism: values, such as life itself, are not guaranteed; answers do not exist; human beings do not have a home. There is no foundation to the things that matter most. Being rests on nothingness. This is the first response to pure consciousness. But the anxiety is also the experience of freedom: values are eidetic or axiological objects which consciousness cathects; such identification is a free and ultimately ungrounded choice. There is no compulsion that I will choose certain values over others; and, by the same token, there is no guarantee that those people who share the world with me, and with my family, and who will marry my children and provide the environment for my grandchildren will choose the same values that I do. This calamitous insight is the first response to the discovery of the real meaning and the true depth of one's transcendental freedom. That discovery is therefore first an experience of unbridled panic, but it is also one that can be transformed into the power and the glory that is our freedom and the subsequent control achieved over one's destiny.

But what about the guilt? The guilt exists. In some unfathomable way, the man feels guilty because of these deaths. The term *survivor guilt* has been coined to describe this phenomenon. It is common among the survivors of holocausts. But what *is* the connection? To say he feels guilt because he survived whereas others died may be true; but that statement is not a clear and complete analysis of the content of this guilt. We can still ask meaningfully, why should a survivor feel guilty? Or more specifically, what is the exact nature of the guilt felt? These are demands for phenomenological descriptions of both an empirical and of a transcendental nature. One hypothetical answer is that guilt signifies choice, that the experience of guilt—like the experience of freedom—is either proof that a choice has been made or is the actual process of choosing itself. And the archaic choice which this fire reveals is the decision to be an individual. Individuation is right and good; it is important, natural, and normal. But it also involves infinite risk, great danger, and concomitantly the unconscionable destruction of true and authentic values.

In Chapter 13 (Book One) we discussed the constitution of the individual. It involves difficult *nos:* to God, tradition, society, parents, mate, children, and to the child in us. To be an individual is to choose to say no to many valuable possibilities: the surgeon is not a musician; the poet is not a politician; the practical person is not idealistic, and so forth. These *nos* are freely and responsibly chosen. They are necessary *nos.* But since they are chosen ex nihilo the guilt produced by the values denied is there and it can be enormous. The present phenomenological hypothesis is that this profound ontological guilt suddenly surfaced when our man heard of the deaths by fire. Of course, no claim is made that fire will always elicit these insights. The subterranean truth is always there, but what brings it forth is a highly individualistic and unpredictable matter.

The truly professional therapist needs to know all this. Whether or not the patient needs to or does know depends on the goals of this particular therapy. This example should also help explain the importance in a normal life of the state of repression. But this case also underscores the fact that what from the consensual perspective is conceptualized as a breakdown and as severance from reality is from the philosophic point of view recognized to be no less than a revelation of the ultimate nature of being itself.

Many difficult problems arising in therapy have no easy answer. For example, how much anger or how much sexuality can or should be expressed in the therapeutic hour? Is the therapist a friend of the patient or not? Is the relationship a professional and business one, or is it also a personal one?

These questions can be clarified and decisions made about them through the conceptual categories of clinical philosophy. *Empathy* means a transcendental (conscious-center-to-conscious-center) connection or relationship. *Confrontation* means that the therapist uses his empirical ego to challenge into existence and action the empirical ego of the patient or client. Hostile and loving acts must be understood in this latter sense: two empirical egos meet. Through this process, the empirical ego—or the creative erotic energy core—is experienced and validated, in short, created and nurtured. Specifically, the creative erotic energy core, the individual and unique identity which is called an *Existenz*, is neither the transcendental nor the empirical ego. It is instead the cathexis by the transcendental ego of the empirical ego. This is the ultimate experience of existing.

However, confrontation is not only experienced in the sense of identification and cathexis but is always observed as well; it is reduced, discussed, examined, analyzed or explained. In real life, that is, in an empirical relationship, performing a reduction or an epoche on an angry or a loving transaction is not necessary. But what makes a transaction therapeutic—and has healing effects—is that all empirical encounters, and in particular one which arouses into being the empirical ego, are eventually seen from a transcendental perspective. In that way the encounter is assimilated into the therapeutic process itself.

Before outlining further the characteristics of a totally open philosophic therapy, we should look at what may be for many a workable compromise. No supervisor or teacher should ever recommend open therapy to his or her trainee. For practical purposes, conservatism must be the rule. It is therefore useful to look at therapy as an underpinning, support, or adjunct to life.

People often complain that the time therapy takes to heal is excessive. There is some truth to it; but the statement is also misleading. Therapy is all too often conceptualized on the medical model. On its terms, the person in need of therapy is sick. Sickness means the presence of a morbid condition, maybe a bacillus or a virus. What is expected of therapy is an instantaneous, or at least quick, antidote or antibiotic. However, if we use the philosophic field model, we recognize that the need for philosophic or therapeutic support to life is permanent. We always will benefit from expert and caring discussions of the failures and successes in our lives. We may wish to restrict clinical philosophy to particularly difficult or emergency situations only. But ideally, the need for it is never exhausted.

To do without philosophic analysis in life is like doing without love or vacations; it is like dispensing with all recreation and forcing ourselves to live in cramped, ugly, and unhealthy neighborhoods. To feel that therapy is too slow is not unlike the complaint that a symphony is too slow. To accelerate therapy may be like playing music faster, or growing up—from child to adult—faster. Furthermore, addiction to clinical philosophy is like addiction to good poetry. It is healthy rather than malignant. It is one part of a harmonious and fulfilled life. In other words, therapeutic support is, ideally, a lifelong process—like regular medical checkups, or continuing education, or love, meaning, or art.

Let us now approach the issue of ideal therapy in the setting of clinical philosophy with greater specificity. (See also Appendix H.)

The characteristics of an open philosophic therapeutic encounter include these features:

1. *Permissiveness.* Permissiveness is total revelation of all feelings, hopes, fantasies, and fears. Permissiveness also means unlimited acting out. Finally, permissiveness means that the therapist is willing to risk total involvement in the needs and acts of the patient. The therapist must use his or her full empirical ego (body, emotions, power, commitment, risk) in the service of the authentic needs and genuine growth of the patient (genuine is defined as being in conformity with the phenomenological model of being, the higher-level natural law). This is not to say the therapist will permit manipulation

or neurotic use by the patient, nor will the therapist use the patient in any way for any of his or her own purposes.

The therapist's empirical ego is the instrument and the technique which he makes fully available to the patient. The therapeutic hour belongs to the patient. This means that the total attention of the transcendental ego of the therapist—and of course the patient also—is devoted to a reflexive posture (understanding, analysis, and detached action) on the problems or concerns of the patient. The therapist chooses—at all times maintaining in his own mind distance and detachment, that is, uninvolvement—total focus and total concern on the problems of the patient. That is accomplished by surrendering the empirical ego (of the therapist) and putting it to use for the needs of the patient. In this *ideal* or *pure* open therapy, such surrender does not exclude wrestling, fighting, lovemaking, rocking, nursing, defecating, screaming, sobbing, and many other activities which would ordinarily be termed as highly unorthodox.

The therapist has a tool—his or her empirical ego, which includes both body and feelings—which he or she uses exclusively to meet the therapeutically valid needs of the patient. Never does the therapist participate emotionally in these needs. His transcendental ego is at all times conscious of the ontological-psychological structure of the patient—the phenomenological model of being in clinical philosophy gives the therapist a competent grasp of exactly what is happening in the life of the patient. Training in traditional psychology gives the therapist a perspective on the patient's personality structure and on how environmental factors, especially early childhood experiences, have led logically to his or her present behavior patterns. But training in clinical philosophy gives the therapist a deepened grasp as well. Clinical philosophy makes clear what underlying universal and generic structures of being have been activated and expressed in this unique way in this patient's individual life. The therapist does of course act, but does not participate in these acts. There is no cathexis, no natural attitude, only reduction and the phenomenological attitude. The therapist acts but does not benefit (in the sense of either primary or secondary gain) from these acts.

The powerful empirical-ego-to-empirical-ego interaction elicits important psychological material for examination. The patient discovers that he or she has a far greater, more interesting and complex empirical ego than could have been imagined prior to this kind of denuding therapy. However, the goal of therapy in clinical philosophy goes far beyond uncovering. The therapist's eventual purpose is to enable the patient to adopt the same kind of detached epoche, the same kind of reflective and disengaged attitude toward his or her empirical ego and being-in-the-world as he, the therapist, has been able to adopt toward the life of the patient. Patient and therapist thus establish a transcendental relationship, in which their empirical-ego-to-empirical-ego interaction is now itself the object of observation and analysis. In this way the patient achieves access to his or her conscious center, with the characteristics of freedom, creativity, integrity, intimacy, and eternity that reside therein. The first experience upon discovering pure consciousness is anxiety. Eventually the anxiety is tolerated, which leads to a sense of security.

The patient is now fully self-disclosed. The patient knows who he or she is (that is, understands the empirical ego). This is a psychologically oriented task. The patient also knows his or her transcendental nature (consciousness and freedom). And this is a philosophically oriented task. True reconstruction is now within reach.

Whereas everything is permitted, there are the following qualifications:

2. *Honesty.* Whatever it is that is experienced, felt, explored, or acted out must arise naturally from the therapeutic encounter. There can be no automatic application of therapeutic techniques. The acts must be open and honest. There can be no hidden agenda or neurotic duplicity. There can be no manipulation. The therapist must be fully self-disclosed and so disclose himself to the patient. In this way directness, openness, and honesty can be assured. There can be in the therapist no undisclosed search for sexual, sadistic, masochistic, egotistical, or power gratification.

3. *Unmasking.* The complete unmasking of the constitutional and cathective lines of the empirical ego is permitted, even encouraged, sometimes even challenged or aroused through confrontation. This means the total revelation of the most intimate and archaic structures of this particular empirical ego. The structures revealed are not only psychological but also and preeminently philosophical and ontological.

4. *Transcendental relationship.* Unmasking occurs within the absolute parameters of a transcendental relationship. In other words, both patient and therapist know (that is, discuss, reduce, place in an epoche) exactly what it is they are doing. While they may act out anything they choose, the acting out itself is observed, seen—first by therapist and then by patient—from the distance of detachment and disidentification. Their true connection is the "spiritual" conscious-center-to-conscious-center contact. They understand and fully trust each other. They may be sexually attracted to each other or repelled—or indifferent; they may be angry or resentful; they may be fearful of each other or anxious about some dreadful and shadowy intimation; they may fear one or the other is insane. To have a transcendental relationship means to be able to join in one field of consciousness and share, discuss, analyze, and observe any and all of these fundamental feelings and threatening concerns. To the extent that anything at all is taboo for discussion—and this may even be the issue of the fee—the therapy does not operate completely in the coordinates of the transcendental triangle. It is the taboo that is the resistance; the taboo is the one empirical region that has been resistant to decathexis and reduction. And in

that resistance lies the residual problem (of either patient or therapist or both).

If these empirical feelings (cathected affective objects) have first been acted out, then their power is just that much more noticeable. Whereas acting out (cathecting the affective objects) may be in itself moderately therapeutic, the real therapeutic work occurs when acting out brings into awareness feelings and behavior patterns and makes decathexis possible. Decathecting feelings which have been acted out is of course considerably more dramatic—and thus more of a learning experience—than reflecting on feelings that are still unexpressed. The imperative that therapy occur within the coordinates of the transcendental triangle is thus one fundamental but authentic limitation of an open therapeutic relationship.

It is this *capacity for reducing experience*—as well as *the actual experience of consciousness-to-consciousness contact*, forming one transcendental ego which observes the affective objects of the patient's empirical ego— which is precisely what makes the relationship therapeutic. Should that capacity and the resulting experience ever be lost, the relationship descends to the level of an empirical (ordinary, consensual, loving, or business) relationship or, even worse, to a psychotic episode. We must define a psychotic episode as a cathexis to a feeling, to an idea, to a mode of behavior, or to a self-concept which *cannot* or is *chosen not* to be decathected or reduced.

5. *Respect*. The conscious stream which courses through us can be *observed* to be *holy*. This is a basic theme in clinical philosophy. The sanctity of the conscious center is seen to be a fact, philosophically discovered and, through the scientific character of phenomenology, verified scientifically and publicly confirmed. The fact that consciousness is seen to be holy is one result of phenomenological researches. This is a very important type of science. Respect—mutual respect—is thus a second critical limit to open therapy in clinical philosophy.

6. *Defenses*. The patient's (and also the therapist's) defenses exist for a purpose. The defenses and the resistances do not exist exclusively so that they may be broken down. They have a logical function. The first obligation of both patient and therapist is to learn to accept, even love and cherish, these defenses. The patient must know that his defenses are accepted, understood, considered, and respected and that he or she can therefore feel comfortable in the therapeutic encounter. A balance must be struck between two ways of giving the patient confidence: to respect his or her defenses and be willing to break them down (or, better said, overcome them) if that is what the patient's inwardness really wants.

7. *Therapist commitment*. The therapist makes a commitment to care for the patient. A commitment is a decision and not a feeling. A therapist can *decide* he is going to care for a patient even though he may not *feel* that he

wants to help the patient. A decision can be consistent; most feelings are variable. The therapist is thus interested in the well-being of the patient—by choice rather than by feeling or inclination. Such interest is not indoctrination. The therapist is available to help the patient do whatever work he or she really wants to do, that is to say, "wants to do" as seen from the perspective of full self-disclosure—which the experienced therapist sometimes can anticipate.

8. *Patient commitment.* Finally, the patient understands and makes a commitment to learn, to grow, to resolve, and to change. This is not to say that all therapy in clinical philosophy is reconstructive. The *change* referred to here can also be one of moving from rejection to acceptance, from manipulation to adaptation, and from maladjustment to adjustment. This commitment to change could also be called *motivation.* The therapist cannot provide the patient with the motivation, the desire, the resoluteness, and the decision to work therapeutically. But the therapist can point out the *philosophical fact* that the lack of motivation is not an object, not an empirical phenomenon, but is the motivation to be unmotivated or the *choice not to be motivated,* and is thus a transcendental phenomenon. In other words, lethargy and ennui are acts and choices. This is a fact, but not a scientific fact, or even a poetic fact. These choices are transcendental facts.

9. *Therapeutic hour.* The hour is a limit. Since full permissiveness is the character of open therapy, that permissiveness is strictly circumscribed by time. Patient and therapist do not live together and do not see each other socially. By limiting their relationship to a specific hour, to a circumscribed time period, they are free of any empirical or cathective encumbrances and can therefore operate in an atmosphere not only of unqualified acceptance but above all of unmitigated and unimpeded *intensity.*

10. *Pragmatic limits.* The above are ideal parameters. In actual practice, pragmatic parameters also exist. Whereas they limit the theoretical efficacy of therapy, these parameters are nevertheless to be recommended. The empirical ego of the therapist has limits. Also the average therapist chooses to function in only a limited range of his or her possibilities. A therapist is limited by the practical exigencies of his or her own private life, by the extent of the commitment made to the practice of psychotherapy or clinical philosophy, and of course by the laws of the state and the rules and expectations of the profession.

Chapter 2 • THE EMPIRICAL EGO

Objects: Conscious and Unconscious

We need a phenomenological clarification of the empirical ego, since it is the usual subject matter of psychology. If we wish to explore in full detail the relation between philosophy and psychology, we must also spell out specifically what the relation is between the transcendental ego and the empirical ego. It is not enough to distinguish between the two. The nuances of their interconnection must also be analyzed, for it is in those details that the precise relevance of transcendental phenomenology to psychotherapy can be worked out.

The empirical ego, like the world itself, is an aspect of the objective zone (the noematic, empirical region) of the consciousness-world field. The empirical ego shares with the rest of the world its status as the object of the intentional field. Only in phenomenology, however, do we view the body not as principally a subject but as also a bona fide object. We must study in particular our manner of appropriation of the various elements of the empirical ego, because it is in the phenomena of cathexes that the object which is the empirical ego differs from other objects in the world. Through this type of analysis we gain clarity to help us understand such controversial topics (and these topics are in dire need of clarification) as the unconscious, psychosomatic medicine, and paranormal phenomena (the latter two topics are discussed in later chapters). We accomplish this task of clarifying constitutions and cathexes by describing in detail the phenomenological structure of the objects which present themselves to consciousness (consciousness as the transcendental ego) and with which consciousness then identifies itself (empirical ego and world). This act brings about the transcendental ego's archetypal decision for finitude. In the process of understanding the relation of the transcendental ego to the world, that is, through our understanding of the transcendental ego's being-in-the-world—which involves both constitution and cathexes—we also learn to conceptualize the important notion of the unconscious in a therapeutically useful fashion.

The first object of perception and identification, that is, the first object toward which the intentional field of consciousness is directed, is the world. We see the world before we know of a self. The world is the most distant object, the largest object, and its most general. However, the world is, strictly speaking, not an object but more like the background or horizon for all objects.

One key issue in the constitution of the empirical ego out of the totality that is the world is the unconscious, since that is the most important source of therapeutically relevant material. Thus we must find an even more specific place for the unconscious in all types of intentions than we have done before. All constituted and cathected objects contain two elements or regions. One of these we can call conscious, visible, or literal, whereas the other must be referred to as unconscious, invisible, and not literal. Both presences can be clearly and distinctly described phenomenologically. The dominant characteristics of the former include what Hume called *vivacity*; the outstanding characteristic of the latter is its peculiar yet definitely experienceable *presence as hiddenness*—like a memory we know we have but cannot remember; yet we have no difficulty in recognizing the memory as accurate once it does "come to mind."

Part of the world is presented to the transcendental ego (or to the transcendental region, since in preconstituted experience we cannot properly talk of an ego; the ego is not yet constituted) at any one moment as visible, experienced, and explored. That part of the world is conscious, as it were, and we must name it the *conscious world.* Another part of the world presents itself to us (or to the realm of consciousness) as prima facie inaccessible, as unexplored, as inferred, or as implied. That hidden part of the world—and we must be certain to keep in mind that *it presents itself to us as hidden* (we cannot speak otherwise within the confines of the radical empiricism of phenomenology)—is the *unconscious world.* Between the specifically conscious and the specifically unconscious world there exists a gray area of memory and future accessibility. It is the area which is potentially and readily accessible, although it is definitely not given at the present moment.

We can illustrate the conscious world, preconscious world, and unconscious world (the given or manifest, the partially hidden, and the permanently or totally hidden) respectively as a tree that we see now, a specific shrub on the south side of Mount Kilimanjaro, which we could see if we climbed there, and the molten lava at the very center of the earth, which is inaccessible to present-day technology although it is certainly not something whose existence we doubt. The unconscious world is an empirical matter; it is an *empirical unconscious.* But, as we shall see later, there are also unconscious decisions involved in the construction and appropriation of the empirical ego. Since freedom belongs to the transcendental and not the empirical region, we must also establish the category of a *transcendental unconscious,* an unconscious which consists principally of the repression of freedom, but also of the repression of other characteristics of consciousness, such as eternity.

These distinctions, which draw a parallel for all objects between the conscious and the unconscious, take the mystery out of the notion of the unconscious and place at least one aspect of it in the realm of objects, where much of it belongs. The conscious world is what we see and the unconscious world is what we believe to exist. This *belief* is of course absolutely central to our world-constitution. Without it we would be solipsists or phenomenalists. And this principle applies throughout our entire discussion of all intentional objects.

A similar distinction between the conscious and the unconscious part of objects (making of course added allowances for the intervening gray areas) exists in our perception of each individual physical object. Think of a cube. At most three sides are visible at any one time. We call what we see the *conscious cube.* Three more sides as well as the interior exist only by inference. These sides are easily reached and must therefore be relegated to a preconscious, or postconscious gray area. However, the interior of the cube, especially if it is made of steel, is not readily accessible at all, and certainly not in full detail—since the interior of any mass is usually not as exposed to vision as is a surface. In this context we call the interior of the cube the *unconscious cube.*

We can thus assign meaning to the conscious, the preconscious, and the unconscious in connection with the world as a whole, the background or horizon of all experience, *and* to physical objects within it. Let us now carry this analogy from the analysis of the question of the existence of an external world to an exploration of the empirical ego.

It is at this point that we distinguish between the ego and the non-ego. The distinction between man and world, person and cosmos is not given but constituted. When philosophy, especially as metaphysics, is defined as the study of man's place in the universe, it is clear that the precise distinction and separation is inexact. Decisions are made to establish what is man and what is world before the question of their interconnection has any meaning. The primordial or originary given is a person-world continuum or complex. Separating man from world is neither automatic nor unambiguous. If there are any ultimate principles of classification these would be pragmatic or axiological. And even here we are speaking of what at bottom is an ex-nihilo decision.

In excising the empirical ego from what now and by this act becomes the enormous mass of the non-ego, world and physical objects become decathected. We no longer call them ours or part of us. Through an archetypal decision we alienate ourselves from them. But that is not an ultimate and irreducible fact of experience but is subject to the powers of decision-making. Those objects in the world which we call the empirical ego (the mind, the body, and the psyche) are in every way as objective to transcendental consciousness as are the world and physical objects. In fact, the psychic distance between any physical object and the transcendental ego is the same as that between any and all parts of the empirical ego and the transcendental ego. The difference in distances is intended, that is, constituted. Physical objects are intended as objects. However, there is of course an enormous difference between physical objects, which are intended as *not-me* and objects that are eidetic (ideas, concepts), affective (feelings, emotions), iconic (fantasies, dreams), which—while existing at the same psychic distance from the center as do physical objects—are intended as *me*, nevertheless.

In other words, aspects of the empirical ego are cathected, which means they are incorporated into the zone of the ego or the here-zone of experience. Also, these aspects of the empirical ego can be used as subject-surrogates. The body-subject is an expression that makes sense quite readily. The same cannot be said of a cube or a tree. We cannot talk about the cube-subject or the tree-subject without seriously distorting the facts of experience. We *can*, however, talk of a hearing-aid subject or glasses-subject, even of a microscope-subject and telescope-subject. Pilots who do instrument flying, knowing that hundreds of lives depend on them, will perceive their gadgets as subject-surrogates. When Pablo Casals said "My cello is my best friend" and "My cello is my weapon" he demonstrated that even a physical object can be a subject-surrogate. But even here there is a gray area.

We can say therefore that the psychic distance is constant but that the intentional space—or the space intended, the distance that is either inferred from or projected onto the object—varies greatly. And this variation is subject to choice, a choice which is, in the last analysis, free.

In other words, these presentations to consciousness in the world which are encompassed by the term empirical ego are objects chosen to reside in a here-zone rather than a there-zone; they are cathected rather than decathected; we identify with them rather than alienate ourselves from them. We appropriate rather than disengage ourselves from them. These are potentially free acts, therefore cathexis results from our freedom.

The Specific Structure of the Object Called the Empirical Ego

The empirical ego is a complex constituted object which essentially consists of three aspects—a *body*, a *mind*, and a *psyche*. The psyche is, in turn, an amalgam of *emotions*, *fantasies* (icons), and *self-concepts*. (See Figure 1.) Each of the above intended and constituted objects has its conscious as well as unconscious elements (and also its preconscious, gray area). Let us analyze each subelement.

The *conscious body* is the visible or perceptible body. Specifically, it is the body-qua-mine (Merleau-Ponty's term). Its perceptible aspect is mostly its surface, and of that only the front, and certainly not the back of the head. The inside of the body-qua-mine is given to us in actual experience only as a conglomerate of inferences, theories, memories of physiology texts, and analogies from the human anatomy laboratory. The inside—fortunately—is not given to most of us directly. This is true of our own

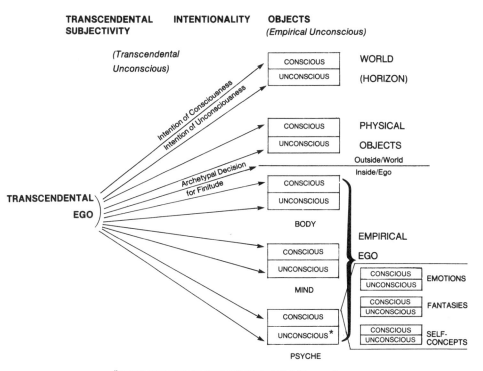

Figure 1

bodies, but it of course does not apply to the bodies of others. A surgeon, a coroner, or an advanced medical student in human anatomy has direct (that is, conscious) access to the insides of the bodies of others, but the same is certainly not true about the inner aspects of his own body. That remains forever a matter of inference, analogy, theory, belief, and speculation. The inside of the body-qua-mine is thus the *unconscious* body. But we do believe nevertheless that the inside of the body, that is, the unconscious body, has an independent existence and a reality of its own, just as we believe this to be the case with the cube and the world in general. Here the concept of the unconscious is less of a mystery than when we deal with the field of our emotions, and yet the parallel is legitimate. Evidence for the unconscious body is found in surgery and dissection. Similarly, evidence for unconscious emotions is found in therapy through fantasy, body work, dreams, drugs, and confrontation.

The *mind* is the intellect or the conceptual apparatus. The transcendental ego has before it ideas, concepts, inferences, theories, hypotheses, logical connections, in short, eidetic objects. The archetypal decision has been made, at least if we are not Platonists or realists with respect to universals, that eidetic objects are part of a *me* and not part of the external world. They are constituted to belong to the empirical ego and not to the alienated non-ego world. Within the mind itself the *conscious mind* is composed of actively thought ideas, which are then intended or constituted as *mine*, as well as of memories of ideas (the gray area). In addition, the mind contains ideas *yet to be thought*. The latter then make up the *unconscious mind*.

For example, relativity theory was unconscious to Newton. Newtonian physics was unconscious to Ptolemy. The calculus was unconscious to Pythagoras. The categorical imperative was unconscious to Homer. The ideas still to be thought—which include deeply buried memories—have the same reality as does any unconscious material. The truth of these ideas exists now but it has not yet been discovered. The technology of the mind has not yet been devised which can get us to them. And by technology we mean the thinker of genius, like Einstein, Newton, and Kant. In other words, when Einstein thought his ideas known to us as relativity theory, he was confronted with one or several eidetic objects. One aspect—and it is a fringe datum—of this particular eidetic object is its *external* reference. A careful description of the eidetic object called relativity theory uncovers the fringe fact that, even though only now discovered, this theory has been true since the beginning of time. It divulges itself as an *eternal verity*. It is an aspect of this truth which is "seen" (with the inner eye) as well as perhaps inferred from ratiocination. We now know that it has existed in an unconscious, unknown way forever.

The *psyche* is a part of the empirical ego which consists of emotions (affective objects), fantasies (iconic objects), and self-concepts (narcissistic objects). The emotions in the psyche have a perceptible and an imperceptible part. It was here, in this distinction, that the term unconscious originated. It is peculiar that no systematic connection had so far been made between two kinds of apparently disparate situations which phenomenology discloses nevertheless to be similar: an unconscious feeling and an unperceived object. *Conscious emotions* are here-and-now feelings, experienced emotions; they are the surface affect easily perceptible to the transcendental consciousness. *Unconscious emotions,* on the other hand, are the feelings that can be aroused, and which, once they appear, are a surprise. They exist, but they exist as hidden; they can be recovered, especially if they are in the preconscious, gray area. It is much more difficult to reach them if they are truly unconscious.

Unconscious feelings or emotions represent the individual unconscious, a concept we associate mostly with Freud. The evidence for unconscious feelings is the same as for unconscious physical phenomena. We know about unconscious anger (turned inward, for example, as in depression; or resisted and neutralized, as in alcoholism) because it is needed to explain conscious phenomena. It gives them meaning and sense. But we also know of it because of the transformation which occurs in therapy. Similarly, we know of the molten core in the earth's center by extrapolation from evidence found in petroleum geology and in astronomy. But the day will come when our diggings will reach that center. Philosophical solutions to the problem of the unconscious have been attempted through the use of such ideas as potentiality and dispositional properties. However, unless these words can point a phenomenon in or a characteristic of experience they are but empty verbiage; they are names naming ignorance. Only when intimate feelings *and* fringe phenomena—such as *hiddenness* and *external reference*—are both recognized as bona fide objects and data do we have the epistemology to account for the reality and meaningfulness of the unconscious. Phenomenology as a philosophy has brought us to this position. The reader is reminded that this analysis is justified by the scientific character of phenomenology, especially the distinction between scientific data and poetic data.

The *fantasy psyche* consists of *conscious fantasies*—those daydreams which we have at the present time, fantasies that can be easily stimulated, and, finally, also of *unconscious fantasies*. These latter are the archetypes, which we may never see directly but which are required as principles of explanation; their existence has the same reality as the world beyond the horizon, the other side of the moon, and the inside of the earth. While indeed they are inferences, they are at the same time part of our consensually constituted world, having their own special kind of givenness as hidden. To the extent that the meaning of our fantasies is that they point to archetypes, the unconscious fantasy is part of the collective unconscious. There is thus no theoretical obstacle to Jung's theory of the collective unconscious.

Finally, the important area of *self-concepts*, the basic scripts that run our lives, must be assigned a separate compartment in the psyche. What the ego thinks of itself is the self-image issue. It is here that character and personality are formed. Basic response patterns and coping strategies are compressed in what we call the self-concept. The basic psychological categories defining personality traits are closely related to the idea of a self-concept. Most of these are, of course, unconscious to the average person who nevertheless clearly exhibits them in his life: passive-aggressive, schizoid, paranoid, obsessive-compulsive, hysterical, manic-depressive, sociopathic, and so forth.

The *conscious self-concept* is what is obvious. It is the literal answer we get when we ask, Who are you? Or Who am I? Or, How does it feel to be you or me? It is the mask, the persona we laboriously fashion to show to the world. It is probably true universally that each person perceives himself differently from the way others do. Either he thinks of himself as exalted, that is, not in terms of his present actuality but of his future possibilities, or as depraved and worthless. It is likely that others disagree with both self-estimates. Yet it is precisely these self-estimates that are the conscious self-concept. The *unconscious self-concept* is either the secret script by which we live and which only intensive depth psychotherapy can bring to light, or the script that is only potentially ours, the healthy script of a future rebirth. To the extent that the scripts have therapeutic value, they are real. An *as-if* philosophy is inadequate to account for them fully, since description of immediate experience discloses them to be operative psychic realities—regardless of their origin. These scripts are mostly in the gray area, since they are accessible to varying degrees of self-analysis and self-observation.

An unconscious self-concept is a script on a tape which organizes our life for us. For example, a man has a script which reads, "(a) being a boy, or a man, I must be strong, especially vis-à-vis women; (b) in truth I am weak; and (c) women—maybe mother—will accuse me of being weak and will make fun of my weakness." This self-concept script is a tape which is constantly played in the unconscious of this particular man. His life is set up on this principle and fulfills the demands of the tape. His profession is that of an aggressive and confronting military leader, which compensates for the "truth," as described on the tape, of his inner weakness. His profession is external and visible evidence for the unconscious machinations of his self-concept. In his practical life he overcompensates for a truth which he understands and which in this way he hopes to hide from himself.

His first marriage was a castrating one and ended in divorce. Here, too, he set up his environment to conform to the demands of his unconscious self-concept. He is fiercely jealous, potential violence lurks just under his thin skin, and he is interested in very young women. His excessive jealousy is his anger at women for their anticipated attack and rejection, his retaliation for the anticipated fear that they will discover his weakness and then laugh at it. By dating younger women he sets himself up to be rejected either by them or by the knowledge that when he is old they will be interested in men younger than he. All of these circumstances set up situations for him in which he will be ridiculed by a woman for his weakness. This unconscious self-concept constitutes, passively and automatically, his whole life. His conscious self-concept is that of a powerful, charming, aggressive, loving, and successful man. Most of his friends buy that image. But a sensitive observer finds in the less successful aspects of his life signs of the underlying, unconscious self-concept.

Therapy is indicated to raise that unconscious self-concept to consciousness, which is accomplished first by placing the constitutional lines of his life in a epoche and then, in this way, giving him access to his passive constitutions and cathexes. This unconscious self-concept tape can now become conscious, and obvious. His task is to erase it and then reprogram it with the truth that he is strong or that it is all right to be weak, and that all women are not castrating. If they should be, he is powerful enough to stand up to them.

This common situation, which is a phenomenology of jealousy and its philosophical dynamics, is a good illustration of the functioning of an unconscious self-concept.

The Constitution of the Embodied Individual

We are here discussing the manner in which the sense of individuality comes about. This point has been covered in Chapters 12 and 13 of Book One and in Chapter 16 of *Is There An Answer To Death*? But because of the overarching importance of this point for clinical philosophy, there can be no end to the refinements to which this process should be subjected. The sense of being an individual is constituted through a series of conscious acts. Some of these are the archetypal decisions listed in Appendix B and discussed in Chapter 3 of Book One. Others are the unexamined assumptions which *organize* for us the kind of world—and persons within it—which we see when we open our eyes. Some of these are listed in Chapter 8 of *The Vitality of Death*. A complete study of these would be a detailed phenomenology of the constitutional lines and the intentional streams through which we produce the sense of individuals who are in or who have a world.

It is, strictly speaking, incorrect to say that these archetypal decisions were made at a certain point in time. To be absolutely accurate, and to remain true to the first rule of the phenomenological method—the primacy of first-person experience—we must hold the following to be the accurate description of the structure of immediate experience: The past is not ex-perienced. The past is constituted out of present experiences. We do ex-perience memories. We do experience the *anterior* reference (anterior in time) of these memory-experiences. It is their anterior reference or vector—which is a fringe fact, as that concept is discussed in Chapter 2 of Book One, and in *The Vitality of Death* Chapters 9, 25, and 26—which entitles us to call them memories. The fringe datum (given) of anterior reference becomes the empirically given or discovered defining charac-teristic of the phenomenon that we call memory. These memories are then intended or constituted into what we call *our own past* as well as into a *past* that others have whom we know.

Thus, the strict phenomenological analysis of our present experience is that (a) at this moment (since first-person experience is not only a *here*-experience but is always also a *now*-experience) we are *constituting* a past (out of the raw material which is the fringe datum referred to earlier) and we are *cathecting* that particular constitution. The cathexis of that consti-tution then becomes one aspect of the constitution of our empirical ego. These constitutive and cathective acts do not in turn refer to an actual past, a past at which time these archetypal decisions, constitutions, and cathexes were actually performed. Quite the contrary is true. These com-plex layers of constitutions and cathexes, that is, archetypal decisions *are being performed here and now!* These acts are quite properly called archetypal. Furthermore, (b) these constitutions and cathexes are experi-enced at the time as being passive. In some sense it is true that these de-cisions are not experienced. But this vacuum does not prove that these passive constitutions are not decisions. The real decisions are buried. They form part of the passive constitutions and cathexes which are the "archaeology" of the self, the sedimentation which provides the founda-tion substance for the self.

We must instead postulate, with Sartre, that (c) consciousness exists in layers—is hermeneutic (Chapter 6 of *The Vitality of Death*). This state-ment does not violate the principles of radical empiricism entrenched in phenomenology. In fact, it is in keeping with the pervasiveness of polarity and dialectic in the phenomenological model of being. Consciousness itself is dialectical; it is living; it is excited; it vibrates; it oscillates; it is a condition of taut stress and a phenomenon of interacting in a field. It therefore makes sense to talk of unconscious decisions. The reasons for that are, first (as we shall see later) that the censor must know that certain material is dangerous before it knows that it should be repressed and, second, we do have the experience of saying—especially in the context of psychotherapy—"I knew it all along but I wouldn't admit it to myself." That sentence expresses the experience of the multilevel character of con-sciousness (which in itself is one pole of the consciousness-world polarity).

We are making now (d) the decision to constitute a past for ourselves as part of the constitution of the empirical ego. We are also choosing at this time to repress these archetypal constitutions. Also (e) we are repressing the fact that we are repressing, a series which can go on to infinity. Finally (f) all these layers of choices, freedom, decisions, constitutions, cathexes, and intentions are *recoverable*. Their accessibility is the key to depth psychotherapy, to character reconstruction, to the reversion of sexual roles, and to changes in life-style. Ontological self-disclosure as well as reconstructive psychotherapy are based on the assumption, buttressed by clinical experience, that this large mass of dormant decisions is recoverable and accessible. In fact, to achieve such access is one of the primary preliminary goals of therapy. However, access is coupled with anxiety and, as we have discussed already, the *normal* person is always a partially repressed person; the normal person binds anxiety.

Another consideration in the constitution of the empirical ego which takes place *continuously at this moment* is the act of bringing about the all-important sense of being an individual *existence*, for to constitute the empirical ego is not the same as to constitute the experience of personal existence. The empirical ego is an object like any other. But the sense of individual existence is *owning* that object or empirical ego. To explicate the full meaning of this theme of the nature of an individual existence has been one of the principal contributions of existential thought to this century. There are many words which elicit this theme: embodiment, individuality, creative-erotic energy core, *Existenz*, subject-object or consciousness-world interface, identity, uniqueness, and the like. The idea that God creates the world or becomes man or in some way intercedes in the affairs of human beings is the existentialist answer to the essentialism of Plato and Aristotle. We require a more detailed phenomenological description of this act of individuation—so that we know in therapy what we are doing and what our goal is and precisely what our progress has been. The terms used here are meant to elicit philosophic concepts; but essentially they are metaphors: Nevertheless, they are events *chosen now* and disclosed as such through intensive phenomenological analyses.

Cosmic consciousness (that is, the transcendental region *in toto*) constitutes itself into a conscious *atom*. A common word for this atom of consciousness is the self, ego, mind, or soul. But these are imprecise terms as currently used. Cosmic space-time—the realm of the external world—also constitutes itself into an *atom*. This entity is usually referred to as the body: it, like the self, is also one atomic or molecular ingredient plucked —through constitution—out of the plethora of external being. We now have, symbolically speaking, a conscious and a material event, a subjective and an objective phenomenon. The union of the two, the cathexis of this object—the body—by this subject, the act of embodiment in which consciousness becomes world, is the best phenomenological description of what processes are involved in the constitution and cathexis of an individual we can provide. These events occur, not sequentially, but simultaneously. While they do not occur instantaneously, they do occur all *at once*, at least from the point of view of the Eternal Now perspective. The therapist must know this to make adequate diagnoses, to locate the precise area of the problem for the patient, and to have an idea of the direction in which the therapy is or should be going.

Artists and all creative people need this kind of background information to understand the creative process. Let us say a musician plays the trumpet. His or her technique is good. But the tone lacks "soul." To get soul, the artist must first understand the act of creation as an act of embodiment. Then he or she must develop a fantasy to experience the fundamentals of this act of creation: to step back into his inwardness, detach himself from the world, experience cosmic consciousness. Once this vastness of inner space-time is experienced in a reasonably traditional meditation exercise, the equal vastness of outer space-time must be experienced in fantasy. Now the artist is ready for the experience of embodiment: cosmic consciousness (that is, the entire transcendental realm) forces itself through the mind-body-trumpet continuum and out into the vastness of the world beyond. This is the experience of incarnation, of self-transcendence, of the transcendental-empirical interface, of individuation. To the extent that the musician can actually live this experience, he or she is facilitating the process of creation; he or she is giving birth, like God creating the world, to the incarnation of being through the Holy Host that is, in this case, the trumpet.

Let us now continue with a full discussion and disclosure of the elements in the constitution of the empirical ego and cover briefly some of the peripheral theoretical issues orbiting about the concept of the unconscious.

The Problem of the Unconscious ·

CONTRADICTION

Now that we have seen the common division among *all* objects to consciousness between the conscious and the unconscious, we can make an effort to resolve in phenomenological terms the so-called problem of the unconscious.

There are essentially two issues of considerable theoretical significance that cause difficulties in accepting the concept of the unconscious as useful without qualifications. First, it can be argued that the expressions *unconscious emotion* or *unconscious idea* are self-contradictory. It is thought in the prevailing objectivist, nonprocess, nonhermeneutic, nondialectical, and nonintentional metaphysics that emotion (or an idea, a fantasy, or a self-concept) consists of consciousness. The *substance* of an emotion or an idea is thought to be some objects called consciousness. That is, the raw material out of which emotions and ideas are fashioned is believed to be consciousness. This view is part of a general confusion hopefully clarified through phenomenology. A nonphenomenological theory of consciousness places consciousness in the realm of objects or objectivities for the simple reason that nonphenomenological ontologies do not include reference to a transcendental realm. But consciousness, in transcendental phenomenology and clinical philosophy, is never observed but is instead the act of observation itself. The unconscious in traditional psychology is an empirical unconscious, which is just as dubious an entity as would be an empirical consciousness. In the primary analysis of the constitution of the empirical ego we used the expressions conscious and unconscious to designate the fact that certain objects or parts of objects were perceived (conscious objects) and that others were either not perceived (unconscious objects) or, which is more accurate, were perceived as not there.

However, a genuine theory of the unconscious must recognize that in addition to an empirical conscious-unconscious structure we have a transcendental consciousness, a centered region of freedom, infinity, and eternity.

It therefore follows that the above objection to the meaning and thus the existence of the unconscious holds true most easily in a nonintentional theory of consciousness. On that view, consciousness is but one of the many objects in the world; it is thereby thought to be a certain type of raw material—like water or sand—out of which certain objects can then be manufactured. Under these conditions, an unconscious idea would then be as impossible as glass without silicone, a woodless tree, or an invisible dike. However, in the intentional theory of consciousness, where real consciousness is transcendental and ubiquitous and consciousness is a stream attached to every object, emotions and ideas are objects to that consciousness in the same sense that more obvious physical things are objects to the acts of perception. If this analysis—this shift from the constituted to the given, to the originary, or the primordial—appears peculiar it is because language and thought habits have so distorted our perception of the immediate structure of experience that we barely recognize an unadulterated datum when we see one. We need the *distortions* of modern art to recover for us the experience of the uninterpreted.

The empirical unconscious—to which we turn first—is one part of the total and intentionally given object called *emotion* or *idea*. The empirical unconscious part of that object is given-as-hidden. That may appear to be a problem, but it is not one which is unique to the various elements of the psychic unconscious. This type of unconscious, the empirical unconscious, is instead one instance of the generic epistemological problem of the existence of an external world. That problem is a malaise affecting not only those phenomena which we have constituted as internal (emotions, feelings, concepts, and ideas), but equally those which we constitute as external, such as stars, rocks, trees, and houses.

The problem of the existence of an external world is due mostly to the verbal confusion brought about by not analyzing in clear detail the subtleties found in the manner in which the world is given to us. Consequently, there should be nothing mysterious or uniquely inexplicable about the concept of even an empirical unconscious emotion or idea. And to the extent that a phenomenological epistemology has solved the problem of the existence of an external world it has also solved the problem of the empirical unconscious. The outlines of the solution include the fact that the world is what is immediately given to first-person experience. But what is given is not a simplistically conceived congeries of objects but a series of meanings intentionally constituted. There is both flexibility and truth in these constitutions. Among them we find indices which point beyond—in both space and time—the initial datum. The beyond is given to us as hidden and as potentially accessible. This is the general condition of the experience and therefore of the world, and the notion of the empirical unconscious fits comfortably into this general framework.

Therefore, a first solution to the problem of the unconscious is that *given-as-hidden* is a genuine phenomenological fact, describable in terms of the notion of fringe data. The fringe datum given-as-hidden is attached not only to emotions but to *all* objects, especially all of the many different kinds of objects which make up the empirical ego. Second, the given-as-hidden is realized under a variety of circumstances, usually called discovery, recollection, insight, conversion, transformation, and so forth.

Finally, consciousness as transcendental (we are now not focusing on objects but on the subjective realm) is itself a polar phenomenon, operating —like air and ocean currents—on various levels, each going in a different direction. The phenomenon of self-deception is crucial to making comprehensible the multilevel, hermeneutic character of transcendental consciousness. This important point was developed earlier. It will also be analyzed in more detail in the next section.

THE CENSOR

The second general problem with the unconscious is that of the *censor*. Unconscious material is repressed because it is threatening. An important distinction is in order: threatening and therefore repressed *material*, since it consists of objectivities, is the empirical unconscious. But the *act* of repression, because it is a constitution, is the transcendental unconscious.

The empirical unconscious is a poetic or fringe fact, but the transcendental unconscious is a transcendental fact. (See Chapter 2, Book One.) The painful material must be held down in the cellar of the unconscious so as to protect the constitutional stability of the ego. The empirical unconscious is precisely what it is because of the transcendental and unconscious defense mechanisms of the ego. The name of the agency which passes on the safety of material and chooses whether it is to be released to the public or stamped classified, sensitive, and secret is, after Freud, the *censor* of the ego. The censor is the transcendental unconscious. What it censors becomes the empirical unconscious.

The problem which presumably arises is that the censor must know, that is, be conscious of the forbidden material to determine its degree of danger to the ego. Someone must read a document to classify it as secret. But it is impossible for the person who legitimately classifies a document to then withhold that same document from himself and forget the contents. The theory of the unconscious is therefore confronted with this obvious logical impossibility: How can an idea or a feeling, or any material for that matter, be unconscious if the ego's censor is capable of discriminating between what is safe and what is not? Either everything is repressed (in which case we get the problem of the ontological status of unconscious states of consciousness, which is discussed above) or nothing is repressed (which means that everything is at all times conscious, which is simply contrary to the facts of experience). What cannot be understood is differential, discriminating, or selective repression. But the problem is with the censor-metaphor and not with the experience of the phenomenon of unconscious material and unconscious processes.

A young mother, very much dependent on her husband, has a quarrel with him the day before he is to go off to fight in Vietnam. He had spent the evening in a bar saying good-bye to his buddies rather than with her and the baby. He storms out, drives, crashes, and kills himself. At the funeral, the woman, upon seeing the body of her husband, cries, "Oh, that is not he. Thank God he is still alive!" For a month she converses with an imaginary person.

Her husband's death is too threatening to be integrated into her life. Her censor therefore denies his death. The act of denial is the transcendental unconscious. But the content of this denial is the empirical unconscious. It is not easy to describe this empirical unconscious. Given is the fantasy of her husband. That is an iconic object. Anyone can have this kind of a fantasy. The nonreality of that iconic object is empirically given but repressed—that is, not acknowledged as such—by her transcendental processes.

This particular problem with the censor, developed by Sartre (in the existential psychoanlysis section of *Being and Nothingness*), can be resolved through the multilevel theory of consciousness already discussed, as well as through the notions of the phenomenological concepts of reflexive against referential consciousness that are central to the application of the epoche. The real issue that has been brought forward by this puzzle about the unconscious is the question, How is self-deception possible? How is it possible to know and not know at the same time? How can we know what we do not know? How can we not know what we know? This paradox is central to life, essential to psychotherapy and the most telling definition of the transcendental unconscious. It is also unintelligible in a philosophy which says that a person is a thing or an object (even Descartes looked upon consciousness and the ego as objects to a consciousness which he left totally unanalyzed). The transcendental unconscious is meaningless in a world view that ignores the intentionality and the bipolarity of consciousness.

We must therefore seek a solution by invoking the transcendental-ego-empirical-ego distinction and by relying on the intentional field connection between the two. We must fully integrate into our being-in-the-world as philosophers the insights that the self is not simple but consists of an empirical and a transcendental layer, a subjective and an objective layer, and that the self is a field and not a thing. One layer knows while the other does not.

Specifically, the transcendental layer constitutes and cathects the empirical layer. We live, as individuals, on the empirical layer, but as observers of ourselves we live also on the transcendental layer. All we need to penetrate the mysteries of the unconscious is to open the transcendental region for examination—and we do that by activating our capacity for reflexive thought—and then observe the strands of the constitution of our empirical ego. Self-deception is known to be possible since it is given to us as an actual and central fact of immediate experience. This fact forces us to accept a bilevel, or even a multilevel, multipolar theory of consciousness. Conversely, however, this bilevel or multipolar theory of consciousness is derived from an analysis of the structure of immediate experience, the analyis of perception, and the examination of how we acquire knowledge; evidence for it is also found in the possibility of fantasy and meditation, because of the transcendental elements in these activities. We then discover that this bilevel or multipolar theory of consciousness explains the possibility of our repression of threatening material while we know all along that it *is* threatening.

In the last analysis we must grant that to the fully self-disclosed person these layers exist obviously and concurrently. It takes a trained ear to identify and follow all the voices in the polyphony of a Bach fugue. We can with training develop clarity in the perception of these layers. The same applies to the polyphony of consciousness. The uninitiated hears only the top melody, or at best a confused amalgam of chaotic sounds. But the experienced person hears all of them, distinctly and sequentially. The animal consciousness experiences only the empirical region. The Eternal Now consciousness experiences all levels of consciousness concurrently.

If we think referentially, we do not observe what would be given to the reflexive consciousness. In the case of repressed material, the referential consciousness sees nothing, because it only looks at the empirical realm. But in turning upon itself and becoming reflexive, it will soon enough discover that behind the scenes, in its noetic rather than its noematic capacity, it is the transcendental consciousness thus revealed which performs the act of censoring the threatening material from empirical consciousness. What we need to solve the problem of the unconscious is familiarity with this more complex but also closer-to-the-actual-facts-of-immediate-experience version of the self attempted here. And even though the evidence of the unconscious forces us to postulate a polar self, the evidence for polarity comes also from other sources. It comes from a simple analysis of any conscious act whatever. Evidence is found in the discovery —through immediate experience—of intentionality. The edifice is therefore upheld by buttresses on both sides.

The unconscious is only a mystery to the medical model of the person. It is paradoxical that in practice experience with the unconscious occurs predominantly under the auspices of the medical model. It is ironic that this model in its application avails itself constantly of the one item of conclusive evidence for the failure of that very same model: the centrality of the unconscious. The unconscious is a crucial concept in any therapy. But it resists explanation and conceptualization in any purely empirical or objectivist ontology. The existence of the phenomenon of the unconscious forces us to reject our cultural and scientific object-worship and replace it with a truly intentional, bipolar, and field theory of the consciousness-body-world continuum that is being.

Chapter 3 • *PHILOSOPHICAL*
CLASSIFICATIONS OF
MENTAL CONDITIONS:
THE NATURAL AND
THE AUTHENTIC
CONSCIOUSNESS

The Value of Philosophy to Psychopathology

One of the most important insights to be derived from the phenomenological model of being, a revelation also made possible by the analysis of
existential anxiety, is the structure of mental illness. We thereby develop
a philosophical theory of mental illness or an existential or philosophic
psychopathology. Whereas this philosophic-phenomenological analysis
gives us a legitimate and workable theory of mental illness and an instrument which can help us distinguish sanity from insanity, there may nevertheless be only a limited correlation between this classification of inauthenticity and the categories of conventional or orthodox psychopathology.
We must therefore use our words with caution and leave the final decision
of correlation to subsequent empirical studies. But what is important is that
we can use the phenomenological model of being and the existential personality theory to describe with accuracy and utility those things that can
go right and go wrong in the manner in which consciousness relates itself
to the world. Beyond that, many conditions which, when diagnosed in
traditional terms require a procrustean bed, become easily understood in
the terms of clinical philosophy.

Let us now develop a phenomenology of mental illness by examining in
detail the various philosophic categories of classification introduced in the
previous chapters.

What is the value of a philosophic classification of diseases? For one, it
contributes to demonstrating the success of a phenomenological model

of being in unifying psychological and psychiatric material. Philosophy and psychology make a good marriage. In no way is either partner denied the full measure of his or her individuality and creative development. Neither becomes subservient to the other. Together they produce a new offspring. Second, this classification illustrates that a philosophical anthropology or an existential personality theory can—in both theoretical and practical ways—deal with bona fide therapeutic material. Specifically, the phenomenological model of being gives us descriptions and concepts which can serve as basis for diagnosis. Therapists can understand the nature of a problem by recognizing precisely where the patient's difficulty lies. The philosophic conception lends depth to the diagnosis. Finally, a philosophic psychopathology helps in suggesting treatment strategies.

Specifically, in some instances a therapist may wish to explain to a patient the philosophical dimensions of a particular problem or condition. An extreme example is when a therapist explains to the patient that he (or she) exists only as a transcendental ego, that is, as an amorphous, infinite, and pure consciousness, but that the condensation of that transcendental consciousness into an identity-core has not yet been accomplished. The reason, for example, that patient P is impotent—there are no circumstances under which he can have an erection—is that as an individual, as an embodiment, as a creative-erotic energy core—he simply does not exist. The patient's help can be enlisted to find ways of experiencing his ground. As a transcendental consciousness he exists, but as a cathected empirical ego, as an embodied transcendental ego, he does not yet exist. This condition is pervasive and severe and can neither be diagnosed nor treated readily in nonexistential contexts. Treatment includes all of the material concerning the constitution of the individual and the empirical ego—from saying no, to finding a ground, to making the archetypal decision for finitude out of an abyss of freedom and nothingness.

We can be directive in the use of clinical philosophy in the sense in which authoritative commands and rational discussion, as well as sample experiences and body work with philosophic explanation, can sometimes bring about strength that might otherwise be missing. Such quasi-didactic work is particularly effective in borderline cases. The problem with severe cases is that the resistance is so strong that their condition prevents them from understanding—even through metaphor—the basic philosophic issues in their lives. A person who is not in touch cannot understand the meaning of being in touch.

Furthermore, a paramount consideration is that these ideas are useful in the area of prevention. Healthy persons can develop programs to maintain and even enhance their mental health by understanding the simple rules that define the authentic consciousness as well as the theoretical background of these principles. A deliberate act of the will is often sufficient.

Finally, the basic questions which medicine, psychiatry, and psycho-therapy will ask—for research, diagnosis, and treatment—are dramatically different if they are based on the field theory of clinical philosophy and on field-, dialectical-, and process-concepts of interpersonal relationships rather than on object-concepts of the person and on molecular- and thing-concepts. And, as would be immediately obvious, the field of psychosomatic medicine is deeply affected by these ideas, especially through the notion of *participation*, which is the attempt to use philosophy directly for healing. That will be discussed later.

The basic unit of world conceptualization in the medical model of the person is the atom—the individual object. Questions in research and diagnosis and proposals for treatment are based on this archetypal decision. We can construct a medicine and a psychotherapy on alternative archetypal decisions. This task is as important as it is difficult. One alternative archetypal decision is for cosmic consciousness (the opposite emphasis to the decision for atomism in the bipolar map of being). This decision leads to an Eastern type of medicine. And responsible research in that area, from a Western point of view, is just beginning. However, the most promising unit in terms of which a new medicine can be built (or an old one rebuilt) is a different element. The ultimate unit of analysis, explanation, and reality —a kind of modern phenomenological version of Russell's logical atomism —that conforms to the higher-level structure of being (that is, its intentionality, embodiment, and *Existenz)* is the subject-object continuum, the *mind-body*, the consciousness-electron. The interaction between the two is a given. What is not given is the isolated existence of consciousness and/or the isolated existence of material objects. The consistent development of this idea promises to be a breakthrough in psychosomatic medicine.

A new profession of clinical philosophy is thus possible. We need people trained in the use of philosophy in the various areas where its relevance is most obvious. Medicine and psychotherapy are obvious examples. Equally important are philosophical applications to education and political theory, to criminology and rehabilitation, to management and personnel problems, and related fields. The profession of *applied philosophy*, of which personalized education in philosophy and clinical philosophy are spinoffs, requires training in the customary relevant practical disciplines. It requires *in addition*, however, intensive theoretical and practical training in the phenomenological model of being and the existential personality theory.

Outline

The basis for our discussion, description, and classification of the serious type of mental diseases is the phenomenological model of being. Since we define human existence as a field, the field must be intact and functional for health to exist. As long as it is essentially unscathed, the person exhibits what is usually and legitimately called *normalcy*. *Unscathed* means that the criteria of authenticity are met. An existence is authentic if the life conforms to the structure of the consciousness-body-world field; *structure* refers to what earlier was called the higher-level natural laws. Thus a life which expresses the transcendental characteristics (among others) of freedom (creativity), eternity (security), self-transcendence (intentionality or being in touch), and reduction (capacity for reflection and disidentification) is in fact a higher-level essentialism, or what is more appropriately called an *existentialism*. A life which manifests these values is then an authentic life, a life in conformity with the structure of the transcendental-consciousness-world field. However, a special kind of extremely serious inauthenticity develops when that field becomes in any way distorted or crippled and one or several of these transcendental field structures are no long exhibited. We call this latter condition the crippled field, or preferably, the *crippled consciousness*.

There are many different kinds of crippling, and each can lead to a separate disease category. For example, the object-zone of the field of consciousness (or of the subject-object polarity) can be cut off from its subjective aspect so that the person in question is forced into a constant condition of total openness to his or her transcendental nature. We can call this type of crippled consciousness the *cut* or the *truncated consciousness*. Avenues of escape from and defenses against these coerced visions of the transcendental dimension are blocked, inoperative, useless, or ineffective. These defenses are usually learned as part of the child's process of socialization or adaptation to the consensual world.

The traditional defense against this vision of the universal, the infinite, the abyss, and the eternal is the constitution of the ego. The ego as a strong, solid, and secure identity is the usual fortress which protects us against the storms which announce the vision of pure consciousness' nihilism and freedom. To the crippled consciousness that retreat into safety is impossible and the ego—necessary for a *normal* life in the consensual world—becomes fragmented, shattered, dissolved, illusory, fraudulent, or nonexistent. The individual afflicted with this condition finds it impossible to conduct his life, and the incessant openness to the transcendental region leads to persistent and ungovernable anxiety. Anxiety, it must be remembered, is the first response to the transcendental; *cure* lies in discovering that it can be tolerated and even translated—after the expenditure of much risk and courage—into the bliss of security. But this profound sequence is carried out only by the most enlightened souls. (The case of Don in *Is There An Answer to Death?* is an example of this transformation.)

Another kind of crippling is one where the continuity between subject and object is blocked. Both exist, but the intentional self-transcendence connecting them is blocked. Whereas nothing can replace the missing pole in the truncated consciousness, a good push can break through the barrier separating the two poles. In the blocked consciousness, no energy, libido, time, or sensation can flow from one region to the other. A person suffering from either condition is withdrawn from the world. He has schizoid, dissociative, antisocial, and catatonic characteristics in both his perception and his behavior. Furthermore, he has difficulty looking into the future; he has problems reaching out to others and understanding their feelings; his body and its needs, including his feelings, are equally foreign to him and thus feel numb. Consequently, the ability to spatialize his experience and to conceptualize himself as a being-in-the-world are seriously impaired.

The reasons for these personality traits are easy to trace: The phenomenon of connection cannot be experienced by either the truncated or the blocked consciousness. It appears that not much can be done in the way of treatment to help the truncated consciousness to experience or develop its intentionality and thus be in touch with forms of being not its own, because to its perception there exists nothing outside of its subjective center. However, the blocked consciousness is *curable* if the breakthrough can be motivated, risked, and carried out in a safe environment. *Dissociation* from all aspects of the *Eigen-*, *Mit-*, and *Umwelt* and uncontrollable *anxiety* are thus the two pervasive symptom syndromes of extreme cases of both the truncated and the blocked consciousness. (An illustration of this type of crippling is found in the next chapter.)

We should reserve the name *natural consciousness* to stand for ordinary health. There are other forms of crippling but we shall discuss these in the next chapters as well. Since these forms are severe types of alienation, it is possible that in some respects they resemble the hard-to-treat schizophrenic reactions.

However, there is an entirely different and much less serious type of inauthenticity called the ignorant field, or preferably, the *ignorant consciousness*. Here our model for inauthenticity derives from the existential personality theory, which is summarized by the revelations of anxiety as well as much of the material in the Master Table developed in *Managing Anxiety* and found in Appendix E. In this condition consciousness is intact but self-deception is uncontrolled and ignorance is pervasive. The ignorant consciousness is not educated to the characteristics of the field, its potential and its nuances. It is ignorant of what is *natural* in and to that field of consciousness. The ignorant consciousness lives out its life in painful blindness to the possibilities and needs of its own higher-level essence. The remedy for the ignorant consciousness is mostly education.

These two conditions then—the crippled consciousness and the ignorant consciousness—are totally distinct in their phenomenological manifestation, in their etiology, and consequently in their treatment. It is again conceivable that there is some significant overlap between the ignorant consciousness and the psychoneuroses, but only empirical research can confirm or disconfirm this hypothesis.

The Natural Consciousness

The most common condition which occurs and should be described is when the field of consciousness is uninjured; it is whole. We call this the *natural consciousness* in deference to the discussion on natural law at the end of Book One. Persons living this type of life approximate the ontological structure of that field. They manifest its characteristics in their life-styles. The full development of this field (also called the intentional consciousness) has of course been the topic of Books One and Two.

Specifically, the life-style of the natural consciousness can *reflect*. Flexible use and adaptation of closeness-distance capacities is understood and implemented. The principles of reflection, adaptability, and contradiction—all derivative of the fundamental act of reflection—are in force. These are of particular importance because in the unnatural or crippled consciousness these principles are not working. The natural consciousness *understands*. It has transcendental understanding and is in touch with transcendental ontology. This person has a grasp of the philosophical specifics, illustrated by the other items on the Master Table, such as freedom, self-reliance, love, and commitment. Furthermore, the natural consciousness is *free*. It has a life-integrated grasp of the transcendental character of freedom, including the notion of archetypal decisions. This person understands Sartre's analysis of Genet (in *Saint Genet, Actor and Martyr*) in which he argues that a human being can only be understood in terms of his freedom. He also understands the dialectical, stressful, oscillating, or polar nature of the field of consciousness that he or she is.

We can summarize all these characteristics of the natural consciousness in the expression *intentionality*. Succinctly stated, health means that the intentional connectedness of the various poles of human existence—primarily the subject-object contacts but also the individual-universal flexibility—is intact. And intentional connectedness is the dialectical phenomenon in which the integrity of the poles remains unassailed in the act of touch. It is now crucial to realize that this is *both* a spatial *and* a temporal phenomenon. Spatial connectedness—and here *space* means essentially psychic space or lived space—means that the person is in touch with reality at all of the three levels: *Eigenwelt, Mitwelt,* and *Umwelt.* Temporal connectedness means that the person has a sense of the unity and continuity of his or her own life. The person feels that the present is connected with—and is an unfolding of—the past, and that the future is the direct consequence of how in the present he uses the material from his past. This person learns from experience and has a sense of his own history.

A healthy person's conscious focus provides him with an expansive spatial and temporal panorama.

The natural consciousness exists on three levels—*authentic* and limitless, *limited*, or outright *inauthentic*. If it is authentic it is superior and fulfilled, centered and in control, joyous and meaningful. If inauthentic it is ignorant—unhappy, depressed, meaningless, unfulfilled, guilty, and inadequate. If it is merely limited it is average.

THE LIMITED CONSCIOUSNESS

The limited natural consciousness represents the so-called average person. He or she has made a reasonably satisfactory adjustment to life. These people have their problems and their questions; they manage their crises fairly well. They are never fully satisfied; their lives never (or only very rarely) have any real meaning. They die, not fully understanding what they missed and not being able to ask the kinds of questions which would bring into focus their vague dissatisfaction. Their only insights into the great issues of life come through isolated religious and aesthetic contacts and perhaps arise ephemerally at critical moments, such as birth, death, marriage, illness, economic catastrophe, and confrontation with the law. The limited consciousness is *un*developed, not *under*developed.

THE AUTHENTIC CONSCIOUSNESS

The natural consciousness can also be authentic and self-actualizing or at least be moving successfully in that direction. We call that the *authentic consciousness*, and it refers to the whole range of modes of being-in-the-world and experiences that Maslow called peak-experiences, that pertain to B-motivation, and are embodied in the lives of the self-actualizing individuals. These persons exhibit all the desiderata of the natural consciousness mentioned above. They have maximum freedom; they know they are on the path to fulfillment. They are strong. These are superior, supernormal, superhealthy. They are self-realized and feel fulfilled.

Maslow described them in terms of these fourteen points:

1. Efficient perception of reality; comfortable relations with it
2. Acceptance of self, others, nature
3. Spontaneity
4. Problem centering
5. Detachment
6. Independence of culture and environment
7. Freshness of appreciation
8. Limitless horizons
9. Social feeling

10. Deep but selective social relationships
11. Democratic character structure
12. Ethical certainty
13. Unhostile sense of humor
14. Creativeness.

Their freedom empowers them to reconstitute and recathect their lives and their world. They are individuals in that they can experience their concreteness. They are surrounded with ample psychological or lived space and time. They have freedom of movement and a large territory in which they function. If we are asked to single out one trait of authentic persons which more than any other accounts for their success it would be that they are in full conscious self-possession of their transcendental freedom. The Master Table, especially Section C, expands the coverage of the desiderata for the authentic consciousness.

THE IGNORANT CONSCIOUSNESS

Another type of natural consciousness is the outright inauthentic or the ignorant consciousness. Persons suffering from this condition—and this means the majority of the neurotic population—are not sick in the sense that their consciousness is injured. Their consciousness is whole and intact, but their ignorance of its natural structure is close to total and their self-deception is untrammeled. Self-deception is part of normalcy. In the ignorant consciousness, however, self-deception is not a concept. Consequently, individuals have no opportunity to cope with problems arising out of self-deception: both positive and negative. Sometimes self-deception is to be encouraged, as when a new life-style is finally chosen and it is time for action; but at other times, self-deception must be overcome. Self-deception is resistance to reflecting on one's being-in-the-world, and this resistance is the most common obstacle to growth and change.

The ignorant consciousness is strictly an underdeveloped consciousness. It could be neurotic but also mentally retarded; then again it may simply be grossly immature, restricted, narrow, or incapable of fulfilling itself. Persons with an ignorant consciousness have their field of consciousness severely narrowed. They are blissfully innocent of some of the most basic features of the existential personality theory. They do not know (because they deceive themselves) about the need for meaning in life. They waste their lives; they know that they do, but have no solution which realistically assuages the pain. They do not know what is means to be an individual. They cannot act on their own judgment. They have no truly personal and independent opinions. At best they can only parrot what they read, hear on the radio, or watch on television. They live the life of sheep.

Furthermore, the ignorant consciousness knows nothing of the meaning of responsibility. Such individuals do not act responsibly because this all-important phenomenon makes little or no sense to them. In severe cases, the ignorant consciousness cannot support a family or even himself or herself alone. These individuals cannot hold a job. They cannot discipline themselves enough to handle schoolwork. They neglect their children; they drive irresponsibly. Their most ardent promises are but empty gestures.

The ignorant consciousness is generally unaware of the meaning of encounter and the subtleties of intimacy. The intersubjective dimension is something that it just cannot understand; as a result, such individuals are selfish, self-centered, and uninteresting. Finally, they do not know that negative experiences can be creative; they are unfamiliar with the revealing powers of anxiety. They thus seek pleasure and anaesthesia as the goals of life.

Another important trait of the ignorant consciousness is difficulty with self-transcendence. But it is a problem brought about by sheer ignorance—by never having learned either by being told or through example about the self-transcending nature of human existence—and not by any inherent and irremediable defect in that person's unique individual consciousness. The future is therefore blocked; time and movement are restricted. Expression is hindered. Explosive anger is one response. This is primitive and direct, and is a natural albeit simplistic way of demolishing the obstacles to self-transcendence. More common, however, is the reaction of withdrawal from the obstacle, expressed as depression.

We can *treat* both the limited and the ignorant consciousness through psychotherapy. The difference between the two strategies lies in the amount, depth, and intensity of the counseling work. Also, we can treat these two types of consciousness with education. This includes classroom work, concept-formation, reading, lectures, group discussions, and the like. This type of *treatment* is called *didacticism*. We must, however, at all times illustrate this education with appropriate experiences and sensitivity training.

Much education can be carried out in a didactic, directive, instructional fashion. Whereas the ideal is the facilitating and midwifery approach, the authoritarian approach—if used with sensitivity and discretion and if applied within an impeccable ethical setting—also has its uses. Some therapists are very successful in combining didacticism and simplicity by utilizing the hypnotic-suggestive powers entailed by the position of authority accorded to them by some of their patients. These therapists have learned to state both dogmatically and simply a few but highly relevant philosophic insights. Examples are legion: "You may feel that your life is so hopelessly screwed up that you feel you'd be better off dead. However, *it is a fact that you do have a choice.*" Or, "You are not bound by the role of housewife that you have adopted. You are a center who is different from that role. You can risk standing up to your husband and your children and change your role." Or again, "Your job is indeed impossible; it hopelessly overwhelms you. I know of people who in the same circumstances have learned how to fight back! And what's more, they have succeeded!"

Encounter group work should be part of any academic training in philosophy and psychology when these disciplines deal with theories of the person. This type of *treatment* is called *experiencing*. Most themes in the phenomenological model of being and the existential personality theory can be illustrated experientially with exercises and applied therapeutically with analyses of specific situations in the lives of the students.

Also, a model is important. The client must see what in talk and in experience can only be theoretical. When he or she sees the authentic man or woman in action, then and only then does the ideal become part of the client's world. Finally, the space in which this treatment can take place is in the relationship with someone who cares and is competent.

Let us now move from the various types of natural consciousness and examine in some detail the uses of the concept of a crippled consciousness for a philosophic psychopathology.

Chapter 4 • THE CRIPPLED CONSCIOUSNESS

Principles of Classification

The description of the crippled consciousness is not based on clinical observations in hospitals, where one starts with raw data but avoids any preliminary or a priori principles of organization. This exploration of the crippled consciousness is a transcendental analysis, in that it is a description of the many ways in which the field of consciousness can be distorted. This task is not a priori in the rigid philosophic sense of that word (that is, being a matter of definition only) but it is a priori in the transcendental *and* experiential sense. In other words, we engage in transcendental phenomenology or, what is the same, develop a description of transcendental facts, facts open to the reduced or reflexive consciousness rather than the referential consciousness of the natural attitude. We are not engaged in descriptive phenomenology, that is, in the exploration of scientific or poetic facts. We are analyzing one unique phenomenon, the only consciousness there is (or the only consciousness to which we have access and of which we are therefore aware). We must call this activity a transcendental and experiential a priori, not a conceptual or definitional one. In Kant's language, our task is synthetic rather than analytic.

Conventional research in psychopathology, leading to the classification of diseases, is an a posteriori activity. We start with clinical data and then search for principles of organization. The phenomenological model of being presents itself as a high priority candidate to be that principle of organization. The various modes of the crippled consciousness are deductively derived from this model. The remaining question is the practical or applied one of how useful these philosophical categories are for explaining, diagnosing, and managing bona fide forms of mental illness. The following outline must therefore be taken in this spirit of hypothesis and as a preliminary guideline for the use of philosophy in psychopathology and psychiatry.

One implication of this philosophic analysis is that most persons diagnosed as schizophrenic or as chronic—even as incurable—are probably much less sick than is usually thought. In other words, the difference between the schizophrenic and the better-adapted individual is not as pronounced as many people believe. However, this philosophic classification also leads to the conclusion that a few people are disturbed in a far more profound manner than the nonphilosophical categories of explanation imply. Whereas there is a continuum with unclear boundaries from sick to well, there exist also conditions of extreme alienation and disturbance which are not explainable in terms of a natural condition of human existence. In short, the following philosophical analysis suggests that many schizophrenics are far less sick than usually presumed, but a few are much more disturbed than is ordinarily believed.

All statements made in this chapter represent extreme conditions. In real life these are never present either alone or in pure form. But a philosophically experienced therapist can see these various types of crippled and ignorant consciousness interweaving with each other as themes in a contrapuntal composition. Furthermore, in developing a phenomenology of the crippled consciousness we need not make any commitment to its etiology. It is perfectly reasonable to assume either that a person is "born" that way, or that his or her consciousness is distorted as a result of chemical influences on the brain. But above all it is possible that such profound dysfunction is a response or adaptation to an impossible environment, especially in the early years.

Of greater interest perhaps than the natural consciousness or the ignorant consciousness discussed in the previous chapter is the unnatural, nonintentional, injured, or crippled consciousness. This is a much more serious condition and it differs from even the ignorant consciousness not in degree but in kind. The ignorant consciousness is still whole. One can still communicate with it and recognize it. However, the crippled consciousness is of a fundamentally different sort altogether. It does not operate on the same assumption as others do; one cannot communicate with it. It seems to exist in a world apart. Sometimes the crippled consciousness does appear to act as if it were natural consciousness; it feigns naturalness and for a while gets away with it. But it does not understand its naturalness. Naturalness is not born on the inside and then spontaneously bursts and radiates to the world outside. Naturalness for the crippled consciousness is vacuous mimicry; it sometimes pretends to be natural because social punishment awaits those who do not conform to the standards of naturalness. But sooner or later the radical strangeness of the crippled consciousness becomes apparent. That sudden realization is not an emotional or an intellectual discovery. The crippled consciousness is revealed by what must be vaguely known as the *presence* of the person.

To discover that the person with whom one is conversing or to whom one is related is (or has) a crippled consciousness is therefore more accurately called a transcendental revelation. The reason for this nomenclature is that the crippled consciousness is the distortion or even destruction of all or part of consciousness itself, and is thus truly a transcendental phenomenon. Physical, behavioral or, in general, empirical symptoms and correlations are erratic, unreliable, and unpredictable—at least at the present level of investigation. When we deal with a crippled consciousness, the common field does appear to exist, at least for a while. We think that we experience a *common space* between our two subjectivities and that we are indeed in direct touch with another *conscious center*. These two characteristics of the relationship define the loving as well as the therapeutic encounter. They make it a transcendental relationship, which is a defining characteristic of philosophic therapy. But in the crippled consciousness we are gradually forced to realize that even though there may be another body in the room with us, we are really quite alone. The intersubjective connection is just not there. The intersubjective field has shown itself to be an illusion. It is the concept of the crippled consciousness which makes it possible for us to understand this experience. Without this concept we may be deceived and manipulated indefinitely by the severely disturbed individual.

AN OVERALL VIEW

We begin the detailed exposition of the crippled consciousness with an overall view which is more specific than the outline in the previous chapter. Some of the general characteristics of the crippled consciousness are these: *freedom* and control over constitutions, cathexes, actions, perceptions, and thought processes are diminished or lost. The crippled consciousness has, above all, lost its ability to constitute and cathect the consensual, common-sense world. The all important ability to *reflect* on one's experience, rather than just to be it—to step back, distance, disengage, and disidentify oneself —is also severely crippled or lost. The correlative capacity for *contact*, for being in touch (intentionality, self-transcendence, and futurization) is marginal at best.

Flexibility in choosing life-styles and adaptability in choosing responses to life's unpredictably variegated demands and opportunities, a concept discussed in particular in connection with the bipolar personality theory (Book One), is replaced by a rigidity nothing short of *rigor mortis*. As a result of this paralysis, the whole range of distance-closeness activities— behavior and experiences having to do with flexibility, adaptability, adjustment, polarity, dialectic, ambiguity, and contradiction—present unique difficulties to the crippled consciousness. This latter phenomenon shows itself particularly in the problem that some patients have with closeness. They demand closeness, but they panic when they get it because they feel that either they will be gobbled up or they recognize that they want to gobble up the other perscn.

Finally, the crippled consciousness does not understand the inevitable and unique dialectic or *polar*—the living and interweaving—property of being.

In the crippled consciousness the individual is not responsible for his acts and cannot be so held. Furthermore, he may not even be conscious of his acts. The crippled consciousness' contact with all aspects of the empirical world is minimal. It is said, for example, that Haile Selassie, absolute Emperor of Ethiopia for forty-five years, never knew he was deposed by an army coup d'etat and imprisoned during the eightieth year of his life. He thought he was emperor to the end.

In defining more specifically the crippled consciousness it is useful to distinguish five types: (1) The field is cut, or blocked, while the person nevertheless remains aware of the reality of the two now unconnected poles of existence. We can call this the *split consciousness*. (2) The field of consciousness is collapsed. The field character of consciousness, its intentionality, dialectic, and polar nature have literally disappeared, and only simple objects remain. This is the *collapsed consciousness*. For it, space, time, and energy—since they are the raw materials for the experience of a field, for the very existence of intentionality itself—are not disrupted (as they are in the split consciousness) but are mostly absent, inconceivable, or inexperienceable. We can be even more specific and define two kinds of collapse. After all, if a box is crushed and thus collapses, either the top hits the bottom or the bottom is pushed against the top. There can be a collapse by the *object* of consciousness *onto* the subjective region of the field: the world crashes onto the subjectivity and becomes coeval with it. That is the *consciousness of subjective collapse*, which is a total withdrawal from the world. The second kind of possible collapse is the reverse, in which the subjective region of the polarity that is the field of consciousness is completely absorbed in and by the object pole. We can call this crippled condition the *consciousness of objective collapse*, and in it all sense of subjectivity, pure consciousness, and centeredness is lost.

(3) The third type of crippled consciousness occurs when constitution and cathexis are fully automatic and utterly inflexible, and seem to be forever out of the control of the person so afflicted. We call that the automatic or the *rigid consciousness*. This is the person who not only believes he is a mechanical man but also acts the part. It is the person who cannot tolerate ambiguity and who is locked into ineradicable compulsions, as well as plagued with constant obsessions turning into delusions and hallucinations. (4) Another type of consciousness dysfunction is the *ungrounded conscious-*

ness, which is the experience of being hopelessly separated from the entire real *field* of consciousness. The person lives "next door" to the full and rich field of consciousness that is being. It is a life that comes complete with subject, object, and intentional connection, but in it all three of its elements are *ersatz* only; they are substitutes for the ground of being and are in no real way connected with it at any point. This person may be *ethereal,* excessively cerebral, floating, and disembodied. It is the truly homeless and alienated individual.

(5) Finally, we must refer to the permanently deconstituted and de-cathected consciousness, a consciousness which is condemned to a state of irreversible and ceaseless reflexivity and transcendental disclosure. We call that the open consciousness or the *deconstituted consciousness.* It is a consciousness condemned permanently to the full and clear vision of the ultimate ontological reality of being without the respite of self-deception and without the defense of a belief system. It is a punishment worthy in its refinement of the very best that Dante's *Inferno* has to offer. It is a consciousness which experiences the extreme anxiety of being exposed to the elements of nihilism and freedom of the transcendental dimension. And it is a consciousness which has not yet experienced the mystical serenity that suffuses those minds that have learned to tolerate and assimilate this initial state of anxiety. Given this danger, it is indeed strange that many people should be interested in full philosophic disclosure.

We are now ready to examine each of these categories in greater detail.

The Cut or Split Consciousness

When the field is cut or blocked we find the split consciousness. This person clearly perceives and even identifies with both poles of his dialectic or field-nature, for the split consciousness is not the same as the collapsed consciousness. However, he does not experience himself as a continuous intentional field. In this condition of inauthenticity, he feels that his transcendental ego is dissociated from all those objects in the world which he thinks ought to be dear or near to him. They include all three of Binswanger's worlds—*Eigenwelt, Mitwelt,* and *Umwelt.* With respect to the *Eigenwelt* (the world of the intimate inner empirical ego), the authentic consciousness experiences itself as a continuous field, beginning with the silent, solitary, and pure conscious center and ending with the inner feelings, the inherited traditions, and the secret, unfulfilled desires of its identity. In short, the authentic *Eigenwelt* experience is that of the intentional and dialectical transcendental-ego-empirical-ego continuum. In it the subject of the dialectic is the inmost inward conscious center of the person and the object is the empirical ego—the feelings, hopes, and fears that derive from the particular historical situation of the incarnated individual. There is a subjective dimension to the object that I am, and there is an objective dimension to the subject that I am. That is the philosophical and phenomenological equivalent—in terms of the epistemological fundamentals developed in Book One—of the experience of subject-object continuity. So much for the authentic *Eigenwelt* experience, which is precisely that experience which is absent in the split consciousness.

Thus, the split consciousness, while in touch with both ends of the polarity (its subjective consciousness and its psychological and physical needs) does not know how to connect the two. Moreover, this consciousness does not have the capacity to experience a connection of this type. The individual knows he has feelings and he knows he has a center. But he is not able to connect them in one experience. He experiences the duality and the bipolarity of the magnetic field that he is. He fails, however, in experiencing the oneness, the monism, the unity of the two, a oneness that is as much part of the field as is its twoness.

But dissociation is not limited to the *Eigenwelt*. In the authentic *Mitwelt* experience, the subject is the ego (either transcendental or empirical) and the object is another person (either as transcendental ego, as empirical ego, or as both). In the *Mitwelt* (the world of human beings), the split consciousness is fully aware of the existence of an I-Thou field. The split consciousness knows that in reality two persons exist: you and I. But this person cannot experience the connection. The I is the transcendental ego and the Thou is another person. We therefore need, in this discussion of the relation between the transcendental ego and the *Mitwelt*, to investigate the various ways persons can be related and assess which are natural and which are crippled forms of interpersonal contact. This matter becomes a significant analysis within the context of the consciousness which is split off from its *Mitwelt*. In this split, the possibility for establishing a polar intersubjective field has become crippled or atrophied. When two people are related, their relationship can exist on various levels. Since each person has a diadic self, there exist by the law of permutation four possible relationships: transcendental-ego-transcendental-ego, empirical-ego-empirical-ego, transcendental-ego-empirical-ego, and empirical-ego-transcendental-ego. But the complete and ideal relation lies elsewhere—in a field the two poles of which are fields in turn.

If I am authentic, then my own personal transcendental-ego-empirical-ego relationship is of the order of an intentional, polar, or dialectical field. Furthermore, if the person I relate myself to is also authentic, that individual is a functioning transcendental-ego-empirical-ego field. I then relate myself authentically to others by presenting myself to them as a field. An authentic encounter between two authentic persons (in the lived world and not in the therapeutic hour) is therefore a field-field relation or, to use an unforgivably repetitive circumlocution, a field-field field, or a field-to-field field. (See Figure 1.)

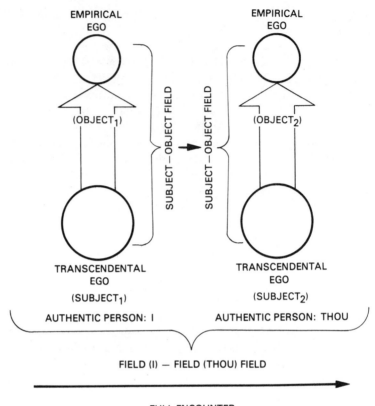

Figure 1

This figure illustrates the structure of a full and total authentic relationship. It is not contact limited to either a transcendental or an empirical relationship (see Figures 1A and 1B), but is a relationship in which the total field of one person resonates to the total field of another. The inauthentic person is aware of both poles of this authentic field and believes (rather than *feels* or *experiences*) that an intentional continuity in both the *Eigenwelt* and the *Mitwelt* is right and desirable. In actual fact, however, the split consciousness fails to experience or feel this all-important element of continuity from one authentic person to another. In the *Mitwelt* split, the subject may experience two authentic persons, but he cannot experience the connection between them. In the *Eigenwelt* split, the cut occurs between transcendental ego and empirical ego within one and the same person. The additional *Mitwelt* split may or may not be present. That is a separate issue. (See Figure 1C.)

The therapeutic relationship is unique in that it is either a transcendental-ego-to-transcendental-ego field or a transcendental-ego-to-transcendental-

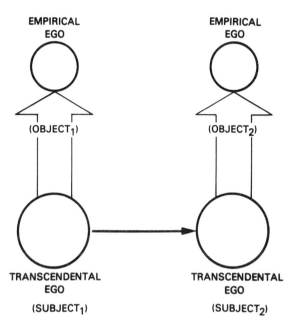

Figure 1A   Transcendental Relationship

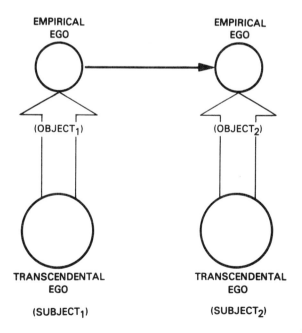

Figure 1B   Empirical Relationship

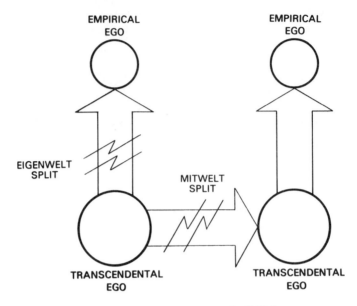

THE SPLIT CONSCIOUSNESS

Figure 1C

ego-empirical-ego field. The first is strictly the therapeutic triangle, and the second is not (Figures 2 and 3). Both relationships are authentic. However, in the split consciousness any one of these many possible levels of continuity can be broken so that we can have either a schizophrenic patient, a schizophrenic therapist, or a schizoid (that is, broken or nonexistent) relation between the two.

An exclusively empirical-ego-to-empirical-ego relationship is something entirely different; it is a formal business or legal relationship. The warm and comforting values of love and compassion, the devotion of commitment and care, these are not part of the formal relationship. Only formal adherence to contractual, that is, legal rules governs the transaction. That relationship is illustrated in Figure 4. It is governed by logic and not by feelings, by justice rather than by forgiveness. The transcendental ego is not part of this perhaps most common of all interpersonal exchanges. Again, in this purely empirical relationship, the split consciousness perceives the two empirical object-poles but they are not experienced as *connected* (Figure 4A).

Finally, a similar problem in the area of connectedness exists with the *Umwelt*, the world of nature. The authentic person is capable of feeling continuous with nature; the split consciousness, while aware of both nature and of the self, is nevertheless detached from and indifferent to the nature

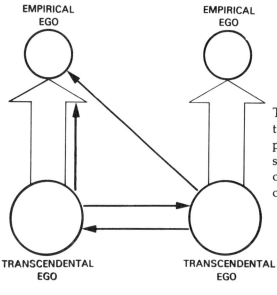

Therapeutic encounter: The therapeutic triangle. Therapist and client from one subject. Their common object is the empirical ego of the client.

Figure 2

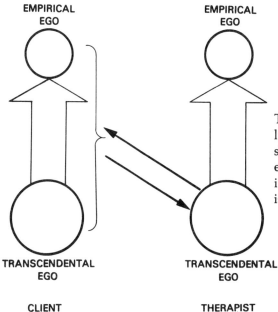

Therapeutic encounter: A linear therapeutic relationship. The transcendental ego of the therapist relates itself to the total field that is the client.

Figure 3

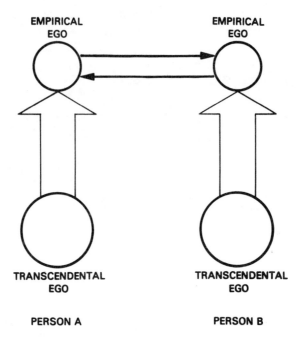

Figure 4   Contractual Transaction

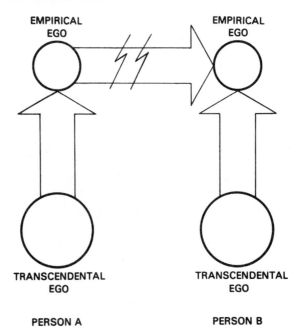

Figure 4A

in which he lives. The consciousness which is split off from the *Umwelt* is not only a condition resembling many traditionally described psychopathological syndromes but is a diagnosis for our age. Increased pollution, crime, and irresponsible denuding of the ecology have visibly lowered the quality of life in less than one generation. It therefore becomes necessary for us to live like blind men, like people separated from the lovely nature that gave birth to us millions of years ago. We must be satisfied to live in our houses, our offices, our stores, and our cars. Communion with nature, that paean of joy so superbly sung by Henry David Thoreau, is a luxury rather than a right. Alas, it is the exception rather than the rule. The split consciousness with respect to the *Umwelt* is a society devalued through the misuse of technology.

The above reflections invite the conclusion that the general symptoms of the split consciousness are these: the person is out of touch with reality, for the intentional structure, the binding continuity of the field of consciousness, is interrupted. One of the most painfully obvious manifestations of this interruption is that the person so afflicted has grave difficulties in establishing an intersubjective field. That individual has severe problems in bringing about and preserving intimacy, either transcendental or personal (that is, empirical). This person feels continually isolated from other human beings. Nor can he enter therapy successfully. Any attempts at love will usually end as disastrous failures. He cannot understand the respect, deference, care, and consideration that is to be accorded another subjective center, because, whereas he can conceptualize the other center, he cannot actually *feel* it. Binswanger refers to such a condition as the absence of love, and Minkowski calls it not being in touch. It is the tragedy of the split consciousness.

In sum, the split consciousness is a malfunction of the act of polarization itself. When we say that all authentic experience is polar we do not mean that a specific event (either object or subject) always occupies the same position in the ubiquitous polar field. On the contrary, the very idea of a pole is in itself a relational term. The varying and relative positions and the differing relationships determine whether any particular event is either in the place of an object or in the position of a subject. The event itself may well be neutral.

The astute and experienced therapist detects quickly what range of experience is to be considered the subject or its surrogate and what the object. For example, in Figure 1 there are various fields: transcendental ego_1 is one kind of subject, transcendental ego_2 is another kind of subject, and the transcendental-ego-empirical-ego complex or total field that is person 1 in turn acts as a subject (or subject surrogate) in the larger field established by the I-Thou, person-to-person encounter. Similarly, in Figure 4, it is the empirical ego in that situation which is the subject or subject surrogate. It is important to keep in mind that, just as in empty space the concepts of up and down, right and left, and here and there are clear but relative, so in the polar field of human experience the subjective and objective regions can be isolated clearly and are distinctly separate even though they represent positions that vary from one experience to the next and are thus relative.

Is there a disease-category that, even approximately, corresponds to the condition of consciousness that we have here called the split consciousness? The answer appears to be yes. Problems of alienation and schizophrenia, simple type, seem roughly to correspond to the split consciousness. Two characteristics of schizophrenics can be explained in terms of the split consciousness. Some schizophrenics fear closeness; others are dominated by irresolvable contradictions. The fear of closeness should be interpreted as the inability to achieve any kind of real and meaningful conscious continuity: the consciousness is split; therefore the experience of an intersubjective consciousness is unattainable and subject-object intentional connections are also beyond the rale of experience. Closeness means being in touch. And it is the latter which is not a possibility for the split consciousness. The more this consciousness tries closeness the more obvious and the more painful becomes the recognition that its goal is unattainable.

Contradictions are the essence of life. (See Chapter 14, Book One.) But the authentic perception of contradiction is one of synthesis, integration, and *coincidentia oppositorum*. The field of consciousness is a unity within a polarity. The split consciousness experiences the subject-object polarities of existence (pleasure-pain, love-hate, feeding-starving, giving-taking, men-women, and others) but does not experience the intentional connection between them, since this field is cut. Closeness-distance ambiguity is the essence of the dialectic. To feel comfortable with ambiguity means to have adapted oneself to the polar and field character of consciousness. The split consciousness cannot make such adaptation—due to its very structure—and therefore finds no way to cope with the closeness-distance ambiguity of life.

RICHARD

Richard is a middle-aged lawyer with chronic medical problems in the area of his neck: stiff neck muscles and a tight throat. Massage, coupled with the fantasy of encouraging a flow of energy between head and torso were significantly helpful treatments. His dominant behavior symptom at this stage of his life was impotence. Richard's past included the traumatic murder of his mother by his uncle: she was shot to death in his presence when he was four. In the light of this background, let us look at a rationale for the symptoms. The head is a common and logical symbol for consciousness or subjectivity. It can therefore be a surrogate for the transcendental. Furthermore, the head signifies the abstract, the intellectual, the cerebral, the mental, the ethereal—that which is detached and disengaged, that is, ungrounded. The torso represents the empirical ego or the world of objects in general; it stands for feelings and for the fire of passion. The torso then is the symbol for the bodily, the worldly, that which is the object to consciousness. In other words, we believe that the head contains the organs for consciousness, whereas the torso contains the organs for reproduction, defecation, alimentation, and respiration.

The neck then becomes a ready symbol for the interface between the subject and the object in what is normally a continuous field of consciousness to object. If there is no feeling of open space between these two regions, that is, if the flow of experience, consciousness, or energy does not pass the narrow canal of the neck, then subject and object are cut off from each other, and the split consciousness emerges. And what is cut off is not just *this* object from *this* subject (Richard's body from his head) but any object from any subject in the world of this particular person. The object can be another person; it can be a feeling, an unconscious idea, and so forth. The split consciousness blocks any and all subject-object connection. It is no surprise that this condition becomes embodied through a stiff neck and tight throat. It stands to reason that one way in which the split consciousness can express itself bodily is through chronic tension around the neck and throat. The split is the block.

What prevents the free flow? Certainly not the actual muscle tightness about the neck. That is only a somatic expression of the psychological or even philosophical reality. The impediment to free flow is the split in the field of consciousness itself. The consciousness-body or consciousness-world field is the primary fact of existence. It has absolute ontological priority. We use the body only as its surrogate. If we were to ascribe different meanings to our organs, then the symbolic use to which we would put the body will also change. We do not acquire a field philosophy of being because of the structure of our body; on the contrary, we interpret our body to suit our philosophic base. If we can experience our body as corresponding to the field, then by manipulating our body there is a good chance that we can modify or rectify the structure of the field.

We have a right to ask for the cause of the split. One reason is that it is chosen and kept in place voluntarily and through self-deception. An archetypal decision, one with an interesting structure, makes this so. Richard's empirical ego (symbolized by his torso) is a combination of the holy and the demonic, light and shadow, passion for love and passion for hate. In other words, polarities exist not only between subject and object (consciousness and empirical ego) but also between good objects and evil objects. Richard carried in his torso (unconsciously) the heavy burden of guilt and terror connected with the homicide of his mother. The positive part of him—civilized, rational, dutiful, and socially acceptable—was well-developed. He was a responsible family man with five children. His income and his habits were stable. He had difficulties, however, in *connecting* his consciousness with his torso. One of his symptoms was problems with his neck. He thought he had no trouble establishing an intentional field from head to torso in the area of his positive feelings, such as his interest in women. But he repressed his negative feelings, such as his guilt over his mother's death.

The torso, as a holy-demonic empirical ego, is one. But for Richard holy was light and thus visible, whereas the demonic was darkness and to him invisible. We cannot establish contact selectively with only part of the torso. Richard tried to reserve the field phenomenon to a connection with the holy in his torso, to the exclusion of the demonic. The result was that any and all contact between subject and object, head and torso were out of the question. His head cannot cathect his torso selectively without completely distorting human existence. It was not until he learned to accept the negative, to identify himself freely with his murderous hate, guilt, and emotions of worthlessness—to embrace all the ugliness within him—that he could establish contact between his consciousness and his total empirical ego. We cannot cathect a partial empirical ego. Once the empirical ego is constituted we cannot accept part of it and reject the other, any more than we can own only one side of a coin or a dollar bill. They come together. Richard's problem was that his transcendental ego (the head) decided to cathect only the positive in the empirical ego that life gave to him. He chose to decathect the negative aspect of his empirical ego. This bivalent subject-object attitude is one example of what can lead to the kind of crippling that we have here called the split consciousness, or the consciousness of the blocked field. The following diagram illustrates this analysis.

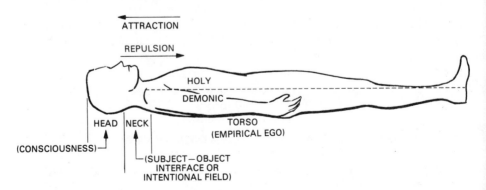

Chapter 5 • THE COLLAPSED CONSCIOUSNESS

There is a significant difference between the disease category (or condition of inauthenticity) which in clinical philosophy is called the split consciousness and the collapsed consciousness. In the former, the person is aware of the reality of both poles in any experience whatever. He knows of the dialectical interplay of life's contradictions, and he can perceive the bipolar stresses—like taut bows—between the object- and subject-poles in all of his experience. He cannot, however, live this dialectical and intentional connectedness; he cannot act on it; he cannot be it. In the latter case, however, the collapsed consciousness, reality is experienced as if it were made up of only one pole. The element of polarity itself is missing, and that would indicate a major crippling indeed. This malaise is the experience of one of the dialectical poles collapsing upon the other and becoming like it. We can generalize from this condition and aver that whenever a person feels that the dialectical polarity of existence is resolved, he has in fact moved away from experiencing himself (correctly) as a process and has succumbed to our cultural temptation to experience himself (incorrectly) as a thing or object. Such a person is like a magnet which imagines that it is a positive (or negative) pole only—and then lives that belief. This is a dangerously unrealistic, that is, one-sided view of life and of the person.

As a rough approximation, we can advance the hypothesis that the split consciousness represents an ambulatory or borderline schizophrenic, a person who is generally out of touch with reality but can still function in the world and may even be aware of his dissociated state. On the other hand, the collapsed consciousness in all probability represents a person with a schizophrenic reaction requiring hospitalization.

If the collapse is in the direction of the transcendental ego—the subjective and inward pole of the dialectic of the consciousness-world field—then the person can be expected to display symptoms of total withdrawal. The world is collapsed onto the inward ego. The world thus becomes and is the inward ego. The world's existence is then reduced fully to the subjective inwardness of the person. The world is indeed experienced, but it no longer appears as "out there," as intentionally distanced from the transcendental ego; it has been absorbed solipsistically by the transcendental ego. This person is not as much cut off from reality as he is lacking any sense of what reality is. The sense of space and time is also then essentially eliminated. Spatial and temporal projections, essential to any being-in-the-world, become impossible to this type of consciousness. This person lives in his own world, detached from the consensual, distant, and real world of the Other. To the consciousness of subjective collapse the world is a purely subjective phenomenon. The person so afflicted is a practicing solipsist. The conventional disease category that seems to come closest to the consciousness of subjective collapse is the manic-depressive psychosis, depressive type.

The collapse of consciousness can also occur in the opposite direction. In that case the reality of subjectivity is completely ignored. Subjectivity has projected itself completely onto the realm of objects, the empirical realm of matter. This type of condition, in its most general form, is also a diagnosis of our culture. In it the person becomes a thing, a human being becomes a body, and the conscious, spiritual, and value-dimensions are not accorded the equal ontological status which is warranted by an accurate phenomenological description and analysis of their givenness. It is important to reemphasize the fact that the materialistic and objectivist aspects of our culture are not forms of the split consciousness but of the consciousness of objective collapse. Materialism and objectivism tell us—not that mind is cut off from body—but that consciousness does not exist, an even more severe position. That is the objectively collapsed consciousness, with total denial of dialectic, polarity, and intentionality, and complete ignorance of any transcendental dimension whatever. Reality has become a comet without a tail.

Any person, physician or layman, who thinks that a bacillus or virus is exclusively responsible for even as much as a sore throat and who ignores such equally relevant factors as anxiety and life-style adheres to this type of cultural inauthenticity. We must train ourselves to think in systemic forms and not individual entities. The total mind-body, subject-object, consciousness-empirical-ego, and awareness-world system is what is dysfunctional in all so-called purely mental or bodily diseases.

All aspects of our culture which have to do with human engineering represent this particular type of inauthentic or crippled consciousness. Let us look at the following representative problems: How to motivate employees; how to improve efficiency in an organization; how to bring about teamwork; how to interest employees in the goals of the company; how to motivate a customer to buy; how to manipulate a prospect so that a sale can be closed. In each of these tasks, the premise is that persons and the organizations of which they are a part operate on the principles of objects. It is a world view in which human beings are expected to conform to the essence of objects. The culture thus exemplifies the consciousness of objective collapse.

Ramifications

There are other aspects to this form of inauthenticity. Consciousness can identify itself with the world in its totality, rather than with specific objects within it, which means that for it only the world exists and only the world is real. A consciousness which reaches out to the world, which perceives and thinks it but cannot be part of the world itself, simply does not exist on this view. That is our cultural malaise, and it is also the source of much of what we call mental illness and general unhappiness. We gain a picture of a lifeless world, the world before the dawn of the creation of life.

Consciousness can also identify with only one very specific object within the world. In that case the person thinks he is someone else, like Napoleon or Teddy Roosevelt, or he may believe himself to be a tree, a mountain, or even the sun. Looking at the sun the authentic or natural consciousness says, "I see the sun," meaning that *I* and *sun* are different and are intentionally connected by a field of perceptual as well as conceptual space. In contrast, the consciousness of subjective collapse says, "The sun is *in me*" or "The sun *is* me" and then acts on that belief. He withdraws from the world and does not recognize its reality. And he may try to act the way he thinks the sun would act. The consciousness of objective collapse, on the other hand, says, "I am *in the sun*" or "I have *become* the sun" and then behaves as if he in fact were that object among all other objects in the world.

We can further clarify the collapsed consciousness by isolating the amount of control which an individual exercises over this collapse. If the collapse is controlled, flexible, and reversible, we might call it identification or cathexis, but if control over collapse is absent, if it is automatic and essentially permanent, we call it fusion.

The difference between fusion (which is pathological) and role- or model-identification (which is authentic) lies also in the dimensions of distance and freedom. Gordon thinks he is Napoleon; whereas Murray models his life after Napoleon. The difference between the two can be described as follows: First, no psychic distance exists between Gordon and Napoleon. The field of consciousness has collapsed—onto the object which is Napoleon. (And *object* can have many meanings here: it can be a conceptual object or an iconic object.) Second, and as a result of this collapse, Gordon has lost his freedom and his control over the cathecting powers of consciousness. The subject that acts, the subject which is the repository of freedom, has literally vanished. The fusion is therefore automatic. And herein lies his illness. Murray, on the other hand, has retained his sense of psychic distance. He likes Napoleon; he wishes he were him, and he consciously imitates him. Napoleon is his model and his idol. It is fun for him to pretend and fantasize that he is Napoleon. But the truth remains clear to him: he is *not* Napoleon. In consequence of that distance, Murray retains his freedom and control over the cathexis or identification. He can give it up or intensify it at will. He can analyze and judge it. And this is a manifestation of the intentional consciousness, when the field is intact. Murray is thus a healthy person, but Gordon is not.

In addition to identifying with the world as a whole, or with one object within the world, the consciousness of objective collapse can also identify itself with what we for lack of a better term might call the *essence of objectivity*. That is, this consciousness collapses onto the *concept* of objectivity. We might even refer to it as an eidetic or noematic collapse, since the conscious stream or field collapses onto the idea or concept of objectivity. This consciousness acts like objects without thinking of itself as being any one object in particular. Its self-concept is that it is an object or a thing by nature, even though it has no clear idea of what specific and particular object it really is. This view represents the theological as well as the scientific search for a soul-substance, a consciousness-substance, or a mind-substance.

An alarming amount of current research in consciousness is not a true transcendental investigation but an empirical analysis. Consciousness is examined as if it were one more object in the world, albeit an unusual one, a mercurial, protean, evasive, cloudy, and amorphous one. What happens in this case—a situation that is also more of a cultural malaise than individual pathology—is that the person behaves and thinks in an objectlike, mechanical manner. Spontaneity, which is a trait of transcendental freedom, is thus lost, since this consciousness has managed to destroy its transcendental dimension. All forms of human engineering, and techniques such as motivation, goal-setting, rewards and punishments, token economies, and similar controls and forms of behavior modification —while useful and even necessary under some circumstances—result from the premises of what is here called the consciousness of objective collapse, where objectivity is eidetic or noematic, that is, it is the idea or the essence of objectivity itself.

This dysfunction becomes loss of impulse control and results in a lack of rational governance over one's actions. Another aspect of this pathology is the loss of control over the direction of one's life. Whereas one may feel detached from individual objects, and thus see them in perspective, one may not be detached from the object "my life." There exists in this condition a loss of control over the concept of "my life" and then over the experienced phenomenon "my life," since the capacities for distancing or disidentification are needed for control, for rational analysis, and for perspective. The consciousness of objective collapse, however, cannot see his or her life in any kind of perspective, because this consciousness is fused with its life. It cannot assess its value. It may not even know that it is a life. Some otherwise highly authentic persons find themselves in the position where the total course of their lives is running out of control, like a car that has lost its brakes or its steering wheel. Control over impulses is achieved by the agencies of distance and free will. But that freedom is lost with the loss of the distance of the transcendental dimension. Rational and reflective direction over life is achieved by *distance*. But this consciousness *has* no distance and is thus incapable of reflecting on its actions.

Nor can the consciousness of objective collapse see itself as others do. It cannot see itself reflected in others. It does not respond to the signals of others which could tell it how others perceive it. This consciousness cannot have, as it were, out-of-body or transcendent experiences: it cannot fantasize itself outside of its body and behavior and *observe* rather than act out its being-in-the-world. This lack of perspective, distance, and capacity for reflection and this absence of objectivity—as we already saw—makes rational behavior impossible. As a result, this person lacks both direction and consistency in life. And he is thus incapable of mature and adult behavior. He exists in a constant state of regressive behavior and ideation. He remains a child forever, and may even give the appearance of being retarded.

We have therefore three subsidiary types of inauthenticity in the consciousness of objective collapse: the world-consciousness (the world is the object), the thing-consciousness (the physical object), and the objectivity-consciousness (the eidetic object).

Because this particular possibility of the crippled consciousness—the fusion of consciousness with an object—is representative of what is usually thought to be "healthy" in our culture, it is especially important to discover which traditional disease categories correspond to it. There appear to be many. Essentially, the dominant disease category would be a manic-depressive psychosis, manic type. Whereas one feature of the depressed person is to withdraw, the manic individual is excessively involved with the world. He is not "objective" (that is, detached, observing, and reflective) in his response. He is neither rational nor controlled. In addition, the hysterical personality and the epileptoid personality disorder seem to occur in persons who are completely absorbed in the events and objects around them to the almost total exclusion of their own silent and solitary center. These individuals, having lost the security, courage, and decisiveness (of their core)—in short, the inner-directedness that follows from a life that is centered—react rather than act. Their resulting excessive sensitivity is in fact a heightened awareness of their surroundings and their environment, that is, of the external world. The sensitivity is excessive in that it occurs to the detriment of the inward dimension. And the explanation for that sensitivity lies in the exaggerated or exclusive identification or fusion with the objective part of the intentional field of consciousness. In other words, the explanation for these personality disturbances can be found in the collapse.

The depressed person, on the other hand, responds hardly at all to external stimuli. The depressed individual acts as if there were no external world, that is, the only reality for this consciousness is the transcendental region. In contrast, the hysterical personality acts as if the external world were all-important and as if the inner reality lacks all independence and integrity altogether. These are the experienced effects of a field of consciousness that has collapsed.

Furthermore, the mechanical behavior associated with what we called above the objectivity-consciousness suggests a similarity with the obsessive-compulsive personality. Compulsions and obsessions are rigid, mechanical, and objectlike acts, quite unbecoming to a free, flexible, and detachable consciousness, a consciousness whose essence is freedom, self-determination, choice, and spontaneity. This type of individual acts exclusively by rules, because it is the rules that help him experience himself as a thing. Freedom to him is unknown. As a consequence, so are change and growth.

Finally, we have to ask ourselves what role hallucinations play in this analysis of mental illness. Hallucinations are iconic objects reconstituted into physical objects. The conscious act that does this is paying more attention to objectivity, is assigning it a greater value, than is done consensually. To some degree, then, hallucinations are encouraged in the consciousness of objective collapse. In other words, it is customary to constitute or interpret iconic objects or data as part of the ego. The meaning that is ascribed to these data is that they are *inside* me. Physical objects, on the other hand, are data which are interpreted as part of the external world, as being *outside* of me. The question of whether in truth (in terms of a thorough phenomenological description of what differentiates these data from one another) iconic and physical objects have a different givenness or mode of presentation, whether these data can be *distinguished* from each other, whether we can discriminate between them on the basis of their pure givenness alone need not be resolved at this time. What this analysis does show is that the consciousness of objective collapse assigns a greater degree of objectivity to iconic data (regardless of whether this is justified by their pure phenomenological givenness) than is common.

And the explanation is obvious. This consciousness—because it fuses itself with objects—has a proclivity for such exaggeration. That is precisely its illness. We see this propensity at work not only in the interpretation of hallucinations as real but also in its emphasis on metaphysical constructs and wild speculation.

The consciousness of objective collapse is likely to be a delusional one as well, since it will confuse any eidetic object or speculative system with reality. The system is real not because of independent evidence (which can be sought and understood only by a detached consciousness) but simply because it has been thought.

The Rigid Consciousness

In this dysfunction the constitutions of either the world design or individual objects in the world, as well as of self-concepts, are automatic, fixed and inflexible. The freedom for constitution and the adaptability of cathexis are lost. With it, the capacities for deconstitution and reconstitution are also atrophied. Rigidity can of course be a matter of degree, since much of our authentic experience of the world is already rigidly—and passively —constituted: Houses and trees, people and cars, all these realities are no longer consciously and deliberately organized out of primitive and primordial data. They appear to us automatically as these specific objects and substances. For example, ordinary telephones require that we dial each number in its entirety, no matter how many times we do it. However, we can design special telephones in which frequently dialed numbers are programmed into the telephone memory and can be activated with the push of only one button. The number is then dialed automatically. That is how passive constitutions are formed.

It is therefore important to distinguish between passive constitution and the rigid consciousness, because one is natural and the other is crippled. For the natural consciousness not all experience is constituted passively. The already-constituted world serves as a background and base of operations for a focused and limited area of freedom. By having thus narrowed the range of our freedom, we can exert a laserlike effectiveness in that slim band where we do exert control over our world. We can then use the passively constituted regions as the tools with which we express and exercise our region of freedom. If we should face what in truth is a totally deconstituted world, a world where there exist no passive constitutions, we would be like a carpenter who has to grow the wood and build the tools with which he can build the machinery to till the soil to grow the wood. And he must accomplish all this before he can build the house which is his initial goal. In fact it is that house in which he must live while he builds his tools and tills the soil and builds the house . . . .

The natural consciousness needs specific passive constitutions to avoid such impossibly mercurial and disintegrating situations. In the natural consciousness there remains considerable freedom for constitution and cathexis in spite of (in fact, because of) the existence of numerous lines of passive constitution. And the limited nature of this freedom in the natural consciousness is its strength and not a weakness. It means the individual is well organized, devotes his energies to those areas of his life where he can be creative and productive, and does not waste his time on excessive details and needless busy-work. For the rigid consciousness none of these conditions holds. The world is stiff like a rheumatic leg. The world design is not selectively rigid, but is totally fixed, like a still photo in a film.

The second difference between the natural and the rigid consciousness is to be found in the area of flexibility. Even though the natural consciousness is loaded with a large mass of passively constituted material, this passivity is not rigid. The carpenter can change his tools and the authentic individual can change his already-constituted and already-cathected world and self-concept to meet whatever new requirements he has decided upon. The rigid consciousness sees the world as always the same. It responds to all demands and challenges with the same inflexible pattern. It attempts to solve all problems in a uniform manner. Deconstitution, which would open up the flexibility of freedom, is impossible. Reconstitution is equally out of the question, since there is no deconstituted material available for reconstitution. This person, because he is totally certain he is right, is likely to turn to political extremism of either the right or the left.

The etiology of this condition varies. It seems rather evident that such rigidity would be a defense against anxiety. To the extent that this is true, the rigid consciousness is the result of a decision for repression. The material repressed is the ontological truth about his being or his human nature. This kind of rigidity should then be classified under the ignorant consciousness, since the essentials of the stream of consciousness are present although misused. On the other hand, the rigidity may be independent of anxiety. It may be the logical adaptation to childhood circumstances; it may even have been taught, either by example or by the child's social environment. And it is important to stress this point. The rigid consciousness need not uniformly be a defense against anxiety. It can be the given condition of consciousness, either through atrophy, because of childhood circumstances, or as a bona fide "birth defect." In other words, to the extent that the rigid consciousness is a defense against anxiety it can be treated and should be classified as a psychoneurosis. However, to the extent that it is a crippled or an atrophied condition, it may well be essentially untreatable. We may then compare it to a schizophrenic reaction.

There are three particular symptoms which can be associated with the rigid consciousness: illusions, hallucinations, and delusions. (Symptoms overlap, since we have similar responses to different conditions, as is illustrated by fevers and headaches.) An illusion is an automatic constitution of a world design. It is a belief system or a metaphysics that is projected automatically on all experience. It becomes the permanent background of the person's experience. What distinguishes this pathological projection from an authentic constitution are the criteria of the dual supports of flexibility and testing. The pathological projection is neither flexible nor tested. As a result the individual so afflicted constantly runs into the bankruptcy of his world design.

A hallucination on the other hand is the automatic constitution and cathexis of an object within the world. We all have fantasies, dreams, ideas, thoughts, and visions. A fine musician hears sounds in his head. A competent painter fantasizes colors and shapes. And a playwright or novelist hears voices and sees people act in his mind. None of these phenomena are either hallucinations or in any way pathological. On the contrary, they are healthy, inspired, and important. The rigid consciousness is different from the creative artist in that the former adds the constituted element of *reality* to these iconic and affective objects. These data— fantasies of sounds and colors—are constituted by the rigid consciousness as *objects in the world* rather than as *objects in the empirical ego*. Furthermore, and contrary to the natural consciousness, these "objects" are inflexibly assigned independent reality status. And it is this characteristic of inflexibility and lack of control that produces the symptomatology of the rigid consciousness.

Finally, delusions are automatic constitutions of self-concepts. If a person has megalomaniac ideas, delusions of grandeur, then his self-concept is rigidly fixed and impervious to contrary evidence and unresponsive to any and all reality testing.

Illusions, hallucinations, and delusions are three areas of automatic constitution which correspond to the three classes of objects to consciousness represented on the ontograph (see Figure 1, p. 446): the world, objects within the world, and the empirical ego.

The disease categories which seem to correspond most closely to the rigid consciousness are schizophrenia, but in particular the paranoid states.

The Field Is Not Grounded

This type of dysfunction is well illustrated by one aspect of Ludwig Binswanger's classic "The Case of Ellen West."[1] In contemporary terms, Ellen West would probably be diagnosed as schizophrenic. One way of interpreting her condition is that she was unable to make contact with many, perhaps all, aspects of reality: persons, constancy in meanings, her body, and the like. *Reality* is here defined as the authentic and existing realm of being, which consists of the consciousness-world flow. Leaving aside the question of whether "in actual truth" she was detached from all possible groundedness in the stream of being, we must nevertheless claim that her perception of herself, seen from inside her and described in phenomenological terms, was that of a person who did not have a home in this consciousness-world stream. Her one good, healthy, and authentic day was apparently the day she decided on suicide. And death grounds— a fact that emerges clearly in the analysis of the creation of the sense of individuality. Whereas she had attempted suicide before, this time she succeeded. She meant it this time. It was thus not her first attempt, but it was the first time she made the decision to succeed. In other words, her decision was really about suicide, about really being dead, rather than about such psychological issues as revenge, attention, or pity.

During her lifetime Ellen West had felt uprooted and disconnected from anything that one can call reality, ground, foundation, security, answers, or roots. She lived, as it were, next door to the stream of being. It was only the individuating act of death which removed her from her identification with an ethereal and foundationless, floating self-concept and brought her down to the solid ground of the actual experience of being itself. It was therefore no surprise that facing death grounded her, since the decision to die—or to perceive or to constitute oneself as a dying being —is one of the key elements of the archetypal decision for finitude. It was therefore the phenomenon of death which gave her the sense of being rooted and of being a concrete individual. When she made death real, she also cast an anchor into the realm of being, an anchor which may touch down in consciousness, in her body, in the love and commitment for another person, in an ideal, in nature, or in any other of the many regions of the stream of being that have served as ground, roots, and home.

Since suicide is indeed drastic medicine for authenticity, the "cure" is thus worthless; however, authentic individuality can be elicited and then enhanced through guided daydreams about death. And then we must become keenly conscious of the effects that these insights can have on the present. Figure 7 on page 447 illustrates this condition, which we can summarize in the following general philosophical terms: The ungrounded consciousness feels disconnected from its ground, which is the real intentional consciousness-world stream. This stream is ordinarily perceived as either being us or at least as going through us. Furthermore, the disconnectedness from the ground can be either general or specific. If it is general, the individual "floats" above the stream, and this is the condition that describes Ellen West. But if the disconnectedness is specific—a less serious condition—then the individual touches the ground of being in places but not everywhere. Let us consider some details.

It is possible to experience disconnectedness in either the subjective or the objective regions alone, as well as on their interface, which is the body-qua-mine. To the degree that Ellen West experienced herself as ethereal, she was disconnected primarily from the objective, material, or natural pole of existence, since we would ordinarily think of the transcendental, conscious, or subjective pole to be symbolized by the ethereal. With most of the persons in our objectivistic, materialistic, mechanistic, organismic, or technological culture, however, the pervasive sense of disconnectedness is from that region of the stream of being which is the realm of consciousness or of the spirit. It is the ethereal realm and its possibilities which we deny in our culture.

To be grounded in the realm of transcendental consciousness is to experience the security of the Eternal Now, the indestructibility and the peace of pure consciousness. These are the roots of the mystic. To be grounded in the realm of the world is to feel at one with nature and at home in the material world. These are the roots of the nature lover. Roots can also be established on the interface, the body-qua-mine. And this may be the most popular way to achieve a sense of groundedness, at least in view of the current popularity of body therapies. Finally, one's ground can be found somewhere between the body-qua-mine and the world, which places it in society, tradition, ethnicity, nation, and the like. The ungrounded consciousness cannot make contact at any point with the stream of being. And a strict analysis of Ellen West shows that her ethereal nature did not mean she was grounded in the realm of pure consciousness but that even here she was uprooted. Ethereal does *not* mean *rooted in consciousness* but removed from all aspects of the consciousness-body-world field that is being.

We saw in her case that the technique for grounding, for reconnecting the satellite self to the real self, was through the decision for finitude. In fact, the decision for finitude is the specific constituting and cathecting act of rooting the satellite self onto the ground of being. And her decision for finitude was in her unqualified acceptance of death—which she accomplished through the decision for suicide.

Groundlessness is of course a central theme in the existential personality theory, illustrated by the extensive discussion of the nihilism-ground issue in Book Two. The symptoms of groundlessness follow from an analysis of the experience of *living next door to oneself*, and they are despair, meaninglessness, aimlessness, even suicidal tendencies. Also, depression, ennui, melancholia, and neurasthenia can be symptoms of not being in touch with one's ground. A person who is out of touch with the stream of being that flows through him is in a constant state of falling or suspension and is as such completely ineffective. He can be accurately described as a nobody, as not existing. It is no exaggeration to say that the ungrounded person *does not exist*.

Another obvious set of consequences following from the ungrounded state of consciousness is the lack of consistency. The stream is steady, the person removed from it is a will-o'-the-wisp. The stream has the will and the potency of a glacier, whereas the person removed from it is no more than a downy feather in a storm. As a result, the symptoms of fickleness, unreliability, and unpredictability can follow from the loss of direction and focus which are provided by contact with the ground of being or the stream that flows from consciousness through the body to the world.

The disease categories which we can associate with the ungrounded consciousness must include anxiety states. To be dislodged from one's ground is the experience of the anxiety of nihilism and of death. And being groundless is also to have no meaning; to be ungrounded is to have neither strength nor courage for self-determination. Frankl's discovery of the pervasiveness of noögenic neuroses is particularly applicable here (except that the ungrounded consciousness represents a more serious dysfunction than the term neurosis would imply). The person whose life has no meaning is so common an occurrence that the condition is often diagnosed as natural and normal. It may be normal in the sense that it is the average, but not in the sense of describing the structure and desiderata of the field of consciousness. The lack of meaning is thus unnatural, in that this condition does not conform to the structure of developed being.

Finally, the malaise known as involutional melancholia may not be due as much to the aging process itself as to the loss of grounding that occurs when the future is being cancelled and when the body no longer conforms to the standards of youthfulness which our culture extols as the *summum bonum*.

Note

1. In Rollo May et al., *Existence* (New York: Basic Books, 1958).

Chapter 6 • *THE DECONSTITUTED CONSCIOUSNESS*

Freedom and Nothingness in the Crippled Consciousness

The last category of inauthenticity to be discussed is the deconstituted consciousness, the state of being where the eyes of the person are forced to fall permanently on the primary reality of being, especially its transcendental characteristics. This condition is one in which the doors to inner space-time are flung open, with its chill winds blowing and deep darkness yawning into our faces. We are held with steel arms over the abyss—and our eyelids, with a paralytic cramp, are forced to remain open. This person sees the transcendental truth, is forced to see it and cannot ever escape from its terror. The heavy curtain which veils the transcendental is suddenly rent open. We may get just a brief terrifying look, or the curtain may never again close upon us. Furthermore, the deconstituted consciousness lacks the courage to plunge into it, to risk being it, to assimilate the realization that he himself is that yawning abyss from which he recoils.

The basic characteristic of this condition is the difficulty in creating a constituted state of affairs, and the equal difficulty with cathecting anything. This person lives in a continual state of deconstitution and decathexis. He has lost (or never had) the ability to avail himself of the security of passive constitutions, of invoking, like others, help from a mass of preset structures. Incredible as it may seem, the deconstituted consciousness has lost the capacity for self-deception. The mechanisms of defense against anxiety, which are the defense against the transcendental truth, do not work. While he is in the full presence of the transcendental truth about being, he is also in a continuous state of terrifying anxiety. This anxiety is brought about in particular by two of the seven revelations of anxiety: freedom and nothingness (nihilism). These two revelations (discussed in Book Two) were recognized as being central to the understanding of mental pathology.

Specifically, the deconstituted consciousness is fully and at all times—and automatically and quite unwillingly—exposed to both the total freedom and the total nothingness which undergirds being and out of which and by which the consensual world is fashioned for all of us.

In discussing basic ways of coping with anxiety (Book Two), we made a distinction between *choosing* a meaning, *inventing* an identity, or *deciding* on a ground and on *discovering* a meaning, *finding* an identity, or *experiencing* a ground that has always been there and is not placed there by us. This is the difference between atheistic and theistic existentialism. The deconstituted consciousness has taken neither step: it does not invent a ground or an identity for it; nor does it find one. With either solution, the initial anxiety produced by the vision of transcendental freedom and transcendental nothingness becomes transmuted into toleration and finally security. This step cannot be taken by this consciousness.

The medieval philosopher and theologian said God's production of the world was a *creatio ex nihilo* (a creation out of nothing). That famous phrase, that deep truth about world, God, and/or man, includes, unfortunately perhaps, both of the elements that make the ungrounded consciousness a pathology. We cannot deny or destroy this insight, regardless of its nefarious consequences, because it also happens to be a truth, and beyond that, a profound and important truth. The world, which means the constituted and cathected consensual world (not, of course, that which is the absolute and pure given in experience), is brought into being through *free acts*. But the world so created and organized has no antecedents, no blueprints, no model, no history. It appears, literally and in the last analysis, *out of nothing*. That is not to say, however, that the raw material for this structuring is created in the same fashion. It is the order and our identification with it, that is, our ascriptions to it as *real* and *as me* (or *not me*), which bring about what we call world. Thus, the expression *creatio ex nihilo* describes—as do many theological formulae— a fundamental truth about being.

The two most noteworthy revelations of anxiety are probably freedom and nothingness and this seriously mentally ill patient is condemned to see the world through these two aspects of metaphysical nakedness. This philosophic insight connects mental illness with truth rather than illusion, with insight rather than blindness, with realism rather than distortion, with philosophy rather than with psychology. If some mental illness is the vision of a truth, then working through it and beyond it, taking advantage of it and prizing it as an opportunity for transition, makes more sense than destroying it, eliminating it, meeting it head-on, tranquilizing it or excising it surgically.

One crucial difference between philosophy (or normalcy) and mental illness—both of which may nevertheless be disclosures of the transcendental reality of freedom and nothingness—lies in the flexibility of the transcendental vision. The authentic person can close, at will, the windows to his inner reality. The curtain can be made to fall again, and the succor of self-deception reappears—because the dialectical and bilevel possibilities of consciousness itself are reinstated in the normal person. The person afflicted with the deconstituted consciousness cannot attain this level of flexibility because his consciousness has lost the fluidity and polarity which characterizes a bilevel or multilevel consciousness. Instead, consciousness is more like a thing—it is obvious, simple, rigid, unambiguous; it is no wonder, no miracle, no mystery. It can therefore always be uniformly open to the transcendental truth.

Freedom and Nothingness in the Natural Consciousness

The natural consciousness also has in it vestiges of the dual abyss of freedom and nothingness experienced by the deconstituted consciousness. For example, the normal consciousness experiences the anxiety of freedom in fear of heights, such as looking down into the ocean from a very high bridge, or over the side of a highway which snakes along the steep cliffs overlooking a canyon, or glancing back while rock-climbing. This anxiety is the perception of the transcendental freedom that is suddenly aroused; it is the freedom to jump. Nothing but a free decision prevents us from leaping into the abyss. We may think that it is irrational to leap. What we forget is that rationality is the result of a leap into reason; it is not the cause of that leap. We leap first, and then we become rational. Before the leap we are neither rational nor irrational. Freedom precedes rationality. And it is this profound freedom, this prepredicative and transcendental freedom that is aroused by the experience of heights. Therefore, fear of heights is an ontologically revealing experience. It occurs in the natural consciousness and, in exaggerated and especially inflexible and automatic form, it becomes the deconstituted consciousness.

Other sources of the anxiety of freedom occur when we are given a dangerous and loaded weapon—or a potent poison. Children often fear they might choose to take the poison or do damage to themselves or others if they are given the opportunity. Their behavior is not yet comfortably conditioned. Their social controls are not yet calcified into the rigidity that gives them security. They have not yet developed a large mass of passive constitutions. The fact that they are uncertain of their actions and apprehensive about or threatened by the dangerous acts that they might perform shows that it is the experience of their pure transcendental freedom that terrifies them. As children they are still freer than is the average adult. The adult often feels proud that he does not use the weapon. He feels strong, resolute, and in control by not using what could easily become lethal. This feeling may account in part for the deplorable love of guns in the United States. "I have a gun; I can use it to protect or to kill. I have it in the house and I don't use it. That proves I am strong, constituted, and individuated. I have reason therefore to be proud." This is the language of the ego when it congratulates itself about having control over its freedom or uses its freedom judiciously.

The normal consciousness experiences the anxiety of nothingness in the anxiety of falling. To fall without hope of rescue is the experience of being ungrounded, of the nothingness which hits us when we understand that being could also not be. It appears in dreams of falling and in fear of airplanes. Flying over the ocean and seeing tiny waves and ships beneath can produce anxiety because it is *literally* the experience of not having a ground or a support; it is the danger of falling and the experience of nothingness in our bones. The airplane itself is not experienced as a real ground. If we were giants and our earth was to us only an enormous ball, we would also feel uneasy about the minimal amount of grounding that it provided for us. Since we are very small, we still live under the illusion, emotionally at least, that the earth is flat and that it functions as the ground of the universe. If we were to "live" the unvarnished astronomical truth, we would experience in the vast darkness of the cosmos, where our tiny earth is really lost, the brutal facts of the transcendental. This metaphor should be no surprise, since inner and outer space, described phenomenologically, are continuous with each other.

We can therefore conclude that the fear of heights in amusement parks and in skydiving is another element in the natural consciousness which reflects and is reminiscent of the deconstituted consciousness.

There is also much fascination in heights: Glacier Point in Yosemite National Park; the observation platform at the Empire State Building; the head of the Statue of Liberty; Mt. Everest; the Eiffel Tower, and of course, the allure of amusement parks. The element of fascination—which Rudolf Otto has isolated as one aspect of the universal religious experience —results from the cognitive character of anxiety. These height experiences, which combine terror and fascination, reveal the freedom and nothingness that are part of the stream of being. They reveal to us our human essence. In other words, we know unconsciously or tacitly that the fear of heights reveals to us, through metaphor and symbol, a profound and important truth about being: the existential anxiety of nihilism. It is that vestige of knowledge which appears to us in affective experience as fascination, that is, as mesmerizing interest.

We find in the natural consciousness traces of the experience of the anxiety of freedom and of nihilism. In the natural consciousness self-deception is still available to us. Not so for the deconstituted consciousness. Let us therefore investigate further what happens when the mind is forced without respite to face these two transcendental realities.

Phobias

The analysis of phobias, especially fear of heights, can benefit from a further examination of anxiety. Our hypothesis can start with the assumption that the individualized fears are focused symbols for the larger, deeper, and thus transcendental anxiety. Fear of heights is the most obvious. The advantage of such focused symbolization is dual. First of all, it narrows the anxiety from its terrifying cosmic or metaphysical compass to a relatively minuscule and thus manageable region of being. This condensation is of course merely one more aspect of the general process of individualization, particularization, embodiment, or incarnation. Second, a phobia expels the anxiety from its transcendental region and projects it onto a specific object or living situation—such as heights, closed spaces, and the like. By thus objectifying the anxiety, the individual hopes to transform his being-in-the-world from *being* the anxiety to *observing* or having the anxiety. The anxiety is no longer an intimate subjective or transcendental phenomenon; it is now one of many objects in the world.

These two devices lead us to the generalization that phobias are defenses against transcendental anxiety. Their psychodynamics involve fearing an individual object or situation rather than the total transcendental region, and experiencing—through the mechanism of projection—the transcendental situation as if it were an empirical one. The ego permits itself a massive illusion. In fear of heights, for example, the anxiety is an insight into the transcendental properties of consciousness, especially freedom and nihilism. But the ego defends itself against this anxiety by projecting it onto some external, objective reality. Now the ego believes that the anxiety is manageable *because the transcendental region can always detach itself*, in an act of reflection or reduction, from its empirical objectivities. Herein lies the illusion, because there is no way in which the transcendental ego can detach itself from itself.

We are thus led to the hypothesis that each phobia or each phobic episode points to its transcendental origin. To the sensitive observer, it demonstrates its source in the transcendental anxiety of freedom and nihilism in particular. The fundamental treatment outlines involve two philosophic consequences: learning how to manage existential (that is, transcendental) anxiety—which is the primary philosophic project of life itself—and understanding the mechanism of resistance against self-disclosure—which is best interpreted as an emotionally expensive, generally ineffective, misguided, *ignorant* (of the transcendental reality) and "unnatural" archetypal act of individualization.

The Pathology of the Deconstituted Consciousness

The type of mental illness associated with the deconstituted consciousness is in reality an increase in philosophical knowledge—that is, an increase in transcendental understanding and therefore a growing awareness of the structure of being—which is brought about precisely by the act of deconstitution itself. Whereas in philosophy or in the natural consciousness deconstitution is a free and deliberate act, in this form of pathology it occurs—at least in appearance—involuntarily and totally against what appears to be one's most redoubtable decisions.

As with all cases of self-deception which we wish to explain theoretically, we must assume the concurrent operation of the transcendental and the empirical egos. We avail ourselves of Kant's transcendental method, which asks what must we assume, or what else must be the case, for a phenomenon to be possible. If we use this method for our own purposes, we must ask what else is to be asserted if self-deception is to be possible. The answer then lies in the following schema: If the deconstituted consciousness can be healed, then a free act, an archetypal decision, is at its core. That decision is made by the transcendental ego; the empirical ego plays innocent and victimized. But it is the transcendental ego which has constituted the empirical ego as victimized and as in a state of self-deception. This stressful interaction fulfills a value. It protects from anxiety. It is kept in being because a solution—to cope with anxiety—seems unavailable. Philosophical clarification of the authentic nature of transcendental anxiety and its related archetypal decision for finitude offer a way to cope with any and all anxiety, including that of the deconstituted consciousness.

In Book One (Chapter 2) we discussed that traditionally in epistemology deconstitution leads to truth. Deconstitution is, in particular, an increase in self-knowledge. And it is that kind of knowledge which leads to control over life and destiny, and thus to happiness and fulfillment. The increase in knowledge is brought about by the constant presence of deconstitution. In a genuine and extreme case of the psychopathology of the deconstituted consciousness, deconstitution does not appear to be chosen; it seems to be automatic. But as a matter of practical fact it is not always clear whether the deconstituted consciousness is a case of repressed decision and thus curable or whether it is truly automatic and thus incurable. In the former case its cause could be early training; in the latter it would be chemical factors which, for reasons perhaps not yet understood, lead to a consciousness which is in a permanent state of deconstitution. Also, in the former case, it may have been that the early childhood environment made total deconstitution the logical free choice of adaptation—perhaps because all constitutions failed reality-testing—to a difficult environment.

Health means that we not only gawk at our freedom, which is possible also for some forms of the inauthentic consciousness and the crippled consciousness, but that we *use* it. And in using it we restrict it but also sharpen its focus; that is, when our freedom is total, which it accurately is, its power is also diffuse. However, when focused, all the energy of our freedom is concentrated on one high-intensity point. We must not discount the true condition of the deconstituted consciousness, which is that the individual is born, as it were, with a crippled consciousness. There are normal as well as abnormal types of the deconstituted consciousness, the criterion being whether the consciousness decides to be constituted or whether it is inevitable. This situation is somewhat parallel to the distinction between the manic-depressive personality—which is normal—and the manic-depressive psychosis, which is not.

As a result of this excessive clarity and illumination about the transcendental aspect of the human condition, especially freedom and nihilism, the deconstituted consciousness experiences uncontrollable anxiety. It also experiences confusion between right and wrong and can therefore lead to dangerous situations and acts; the deconstituted consciousness, in discarding all controls, has also abandoned its consciousness of right and wrong. The freedom thus uncovered is also the freedom which makes archetypal decisions. Some of these are also dissolved: the archetypal decision for morality being among them. An ethical system results from decisions which narrow the possibilities of the world design. But such decisions are not being made by the deconstituted consciousness. This person's values are therefore thoroughly confused. He does not know what hurts a person and what does not; he is unaware of what is kind and what is unkind. It is this state which we find in the psychopath and the sociopath, and in the antisocial personality, and which causes great danger to himself and others.

A few parenthetic words about existential ethics are appropriate at this point. On the view developed in this book, man's freedom is an inevitable philosophic *fact*. If he chooses to reflect that fact in his personal, interpersonal, social, and political life, he is conforming to his higher nature (that is, ontological and transcendental rather than purely social or even empirical nature). That choice is also a fact, but it is not an inevitable one. And since the choice is contingent, that is, not inevitable, the individual makes a value-choice in adopting it.

The schizophrenic who exhibits the condition of the deconstituted consciousness needs and often wants externally imposed limits and directions. This is further evidence that he is afraid of the freedom he has, for he welcomes restrictions. Even while he fights them, he appreciates the safety and security which are provided by this forced conformity to the commonsense and consensual world.

Why do psychotics and schizophrenics often make others anxious? In a group, one psychotic episode may trigger another. We have a genuine case of contagion. In less extreme cases, one psychotic episode raises the general level of anxiety, leads some to tears and sobs, and still others close to panic. There exist superficial explanations for this phenomenon, such as "it is the unknown," "someone might get hurt," "we lack experience," and the like. However, it appears that the genuine explanation lies elsewhere: Witnessing a psychotic episode reminds everyone of his or her own philosophic nature—in particular of the transcendental nothingness and transcendental freedom—and of its frighteningly infinite possibilities and the extraordinary attendant responsibility. Since the anxiety is cognitively contagious—it calls attention to a universal truth, open to all—it leads others to experience their hitherto dormant foundationless-ness, their freedom for world-constitution, self-definition, and value-choice. They recognize the relativity of such basic entities as self, world, and values.

In other words, when one person in a group makes clear to others that he is a deconstituted consciousness (not as theory but as experience), all members of the group are suddenly open to their own freedom in making archetypal choices. That sudden vision of the transcendental is a surge of electrifying anxiety. In perceiving the possibility of their own deconstitution —since their world is held together by a series of foundationless choices— they experience adumbrations and premonitions of the essential question-ableness and uncertainty of the consensual world. They experience a truth hidden from most of us through the protective veneer of our passive con-sensual constitutions. The crippled consciousness (probably schizophrenic) who is afflicted with the deconstituted consciousness is led by virtue of that condition to rediscover the inherent foundationlessness of man.

The symptoms of the deconstituted consciousness are intense anxiety, a life that is organized around the avoidance of anxiety, great danger to self and others, and controlled hallucinations. Except for the last, these symptoms should not be surprising. The latter refers to the fact that attempts at constitution are in their ultimate essence and in their philosophic and epistemological purity never better than consensually validated hallucin-ations, so that the patient will actually enjoy hallucinating. He can turn these hallucinations on and off at will. For a while this game gives him the illusion of not being deconstituted but having before him a consensually organized world. In the end, however, the world will disconfirm and disagree with his *ad hoc* constitutions. And it is because of these latter characteristics that we call them hallucinations.

Finally, the disease categories that might roughly correspond to the deconstituted consciousness are schizophrenia, paranoid type, as well as personality disorders, especially the antisocial personality and the paranoid personality. Phobias, anxiety hysteria, and somatic symptoms would also fall into this important and dominant category.

The Therapist's Power

One final point must be discussed in connection with this dysfunction, and that is the manner in which the therapist appears to the patient suffering from the deconstituted consciousness. Let us contrast an existential interpre-tation with more traditional ones.

A conventional therapist is one who follows the psychoanalytic or the nondirective pattern of serving mostly as a *tabula rasa* for the projections of the patient. The therapist says little; he allows the threatening unconscious feelings of the patient to gradually emerge and be accepted or at least tolerated. Under these circumstances, the therapist is often experienced by the patient as powerful and even omnipotent. Everything the therapist does acquires therapeutic significance: whether he grants approval or whether he refrains from doing so; whether he looks at the patient or does not; if he is late or on time—all these peripheral phenomena have meaning to the patient. What is the meaning of this "power"? Let us contrast conventional with existential accounts.

One explanation, of course, is that the patient invests the therapist with power as a result of his own projections. These projections may for example be the products of dependency wishes. But there is also another explanation, one related to the analysis of the crippled consciousness or schizophrenia in terms of the dual revelations of existential anxiety discussed above: freedom and nothingness (or nihilism). The therapist has become the repository of constitution and cathexis, the secret of the uses of freedom, for the patient. The therapist has become the locus for the freedom of constitution applied to the patient's world design, consensual world, and self-definition. The reason for this is that the patient sees himself mirrored in the therapist. In particular, however, it is his transcendental nature which is mirrored, since theirs is a transcendental relationship. It should therefore not surprise us that what the patient sees in the therapist is a reflection of his own freedom and his own nihilism. An alternative but related phenomenological description of this fact is to be found in the notion of the expanded, specifically the intersubjective, consciousness. The intensive therapeutic encounter enlarges the individual consciousness into an intersubjective one and thus reveals its structures through amplification or magnification. All these matters follow straight from the position in clinical philosophy that healing occurs in a transcendental relationship. And one of the prime features of this so-called therapeutic triangle is mirroring or the expanded consciousness.

Let us be specific. One meaning or function of the presence of the therapist in intensive depth psychotherapy is to assist in the deconstitution of the world of the patient. Deconstitution is safe only in the fatherly or motherly company of the therapist and in the secure embrace of the therapeutic hour. As a result, the therapist appears to hold the key to the entire constitutive process. He or she therefore is the repository of the freedom of the patient. Because the constitutive process has now been transferred from patient to therapist, it is the therapist in whom appears to reside the freedom to reconstitute ex nihilo the world of the patient; and this is a fact, not a projection. Also, the therapist holds the answer to the patient's abyss of nothingness. Confronted with such a situation, the patient responds in a religious way. He sees his transcendental freedom as external to him. He recognizes that it is embodied in the person facing him. He knows that the answer to nothingness is in the hands, as it were, of the other conscious center he faces in a transcendental relationship. That is a religious experience and the patient responds in kind: with anxiety, with helplessness, and with gratitude. A strong sexual transference could also be explained in these terms.

The patient exhibits what Rudolf Otto in *Das Heilige* (*The Idea of the Holy*) calls the feeling of infinite dependence. This is a central religious emotion, which can be replicated in the therapeutic context. The therapist now is in possession of the freedom which the patient needs in order to choose a reconstituted consensual world and to acquire a new self-concept. Furthermore, since the therapist is also invested with the knowledge of the structure of the field of consciousness, the patient needs his or her goodwill to establish a life-style that corresponds to the nature of the stream of being. Since during the period of maximum dependency the patient experiences all freedom to reside in the therapist, the aura embracing the total therapeutic experience is the phenomenon of grace. The patient realizes that the therapist owns his or her freedom. Therefore, there is no reason for the therapist either to give it back or use it for the benefit of the patient. The patient is grateful because he experiences the gift of freedom and reconstitution to be undeserved. That is what happens when another person becomes necessary for deconstitution, when consciousness becomes expanded beyond its manifestation as individual and spills over into intersubjectivity; one's very own freedom itself flows over to the consciousness of another.

The explanation of total dependency which makes the therapist appear as omnipotent to the patient is found in this shift or expansion of the center of freedom. The implication is that either the therapist must be unusually authentic—that is, strong and experienced—and supremely ethical, or the patient must do the work himself. In either case, to be effective, therapy must involve this transfer of freedom. But since the risks are great, such therapeutic successes are rarely permitted by patients and therapists alike. What goes under the name of personal relationship in many so-called existential therapies, rather than being a felicitous new approach to healing, is often merely an empirical relationship and, like any ordinary transference and countertransference, is in fact a resistance against this kind of transcendental contact and exposure.

Postscript

This chapter has emphasized exclusively the existential position that the disclosure of consciousness is coeval with the experience of anxiety. Anxiety is the natural condition of being. Anxiety is the experience of the revelation of transcendental characteristics of being. All persons share not only a common pool of transcendental consciousness but also a common pool of anxiety. Life is essentially a defense against anxiety, a binding of anxiety. The archetypal decisions and, in general, the constitutions of objects such as self-concepts, institutions, and ethical and political systems, are defenses against the primordial anxiety of transcendental being.

But this is not the only explanation. One response to this ocean of anxiety is the atheistic existential one: choose or invent an essence out of this abyss of freedom and nothingness, define the meaning of human nature in this fashion, hold on to it with your transcendental freedom and be a truly self-created person. The other way to deal with this primordial anxiety is a theistic one and it has been expertly developed by the mystical traditions of both East and West. This second view is that pure consciousness is the ultimate answer, the final security, the true nature of the universe. It is the position that the denial of this inward consciousness, the repression of the indwelling witness is the source of anxiety, and not the silent and solitary center itself.

We can combine these two important and apparently incompatible answers in the concept of *toleration*. The first glimpse of pure consciousness—because of its freedom, nihilism, and the deconstitution of the habitual consensual world—is revealed in the experience of anxiety; but this anxiety is existential, that is, it can be transmuted into life itself, into strength, and finally security. Anxiety can be the excitement of aliveness and the peace of final groundedness. But this subsequent insight and experience—a kind of enlightenment—emerges only after the avoidance response to anxiety is transformed into an approach response. That is the meaning of toleration for anxiety. And it is the other coping device for anxiety.

Summary

If we use three symbols to designate the intentional consciousness-world relation, we can diagram each of the constitutions and dysfunctions discussed in this philosophic psychopathology. (See Figure 1.) We use the circle (O) to represent the transcendental ego and the rectangle (□) to depict the realm of objectivity, the world, that is, the objects of consciousness. And we use the arrow (———→) to represent the dialectical—intentional —self-transcending relation between the two. The arrow, in the language of Husserl and phenomenology, represents the conscious intentional acts.

We can now draw diagrams to illustrate the fundamental acts of the authentic or normal consciousness. The fundamental diagram—which we can call an ontograph,[1] that is, a description of being in general—looks like that shown in Figure 1.

The most significant feature of this diagram is that it helps clarify the fundamental difference between the transcendental realm and the empirical realm in our constitution and cathexis of the emprical ego. Scientific psychology has as its subject matter the empirical ego. It ignores altogether the transcendental ego and its intentional acts. On the other hand, transcendental or phenomenological psychology, that is, a philosophically, phenomenologically, or existentially oriented psychology, has the transcendental realm, also called the realm of subjectivity, as its subject matter. Transcendental psychology recognizes that consciousness is *not* the empirical ego, but that the empirical ego is the object of the consciousness which transcendental phenomenology seeks to study. Once this distinction is understood and taken seriously, the significance and radicalness of the phenomenological and philosophical approaches to psychological problems can, as opposed to traditional and scientific ones, be more fully appreciated.

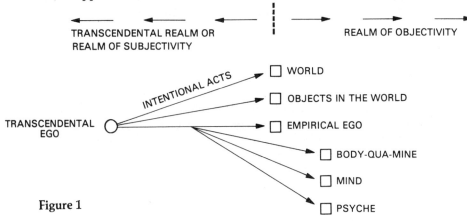

Figure 1

The authentic or natural consciousness is diagrammed like this:

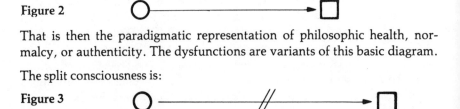

Figure 2

That is then the paradigmatic representation of philosophic health, normalcy, or authenticity. The dysfunctions are variants of this basic diagram.

The split consciousness is:

Figure 3

The collapsed consciousness is:

Figure 4

and

Figure 5

The figure consists of a horizontal arrow pointing right to a circle and a square.

It represents respectively the consciousness of subjective and objective collapse. The rigid consciousness can be represented by the following:

Figure 6

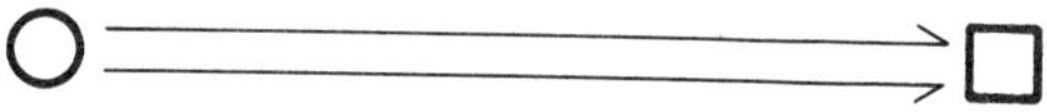

The figure consists of a circle connected by two nearly-parallel lines converging into an arrow pointing at a square.

The ungrounded consciousness is:

Figure 7

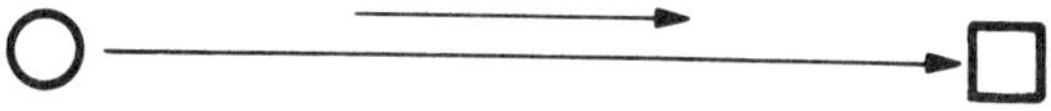

The figure consists of a circle connected by a horizontal line to a square, with a shorter arrow above the line.

Finally, the deconstituted consciousness becomes:

Figure 8

The figure consists of a circle and a square, separated, with no connecting line.

Note

1. The idea of the ontograph is discussed at some length in Peter Koestenbaum, *The Vitality of Death* (Westport, Conn.: Greenwood, 1971), Chap. 30.

Chapter 7 • *SCHIZOPHRENIA*

Selected Examples

To illustrate the explanatory power of this philosophic approach to mental illness we need to make some observations on selected theories of schizophrenia, as well as disease in general, from the point of view of the phenomenological model of being and an existential personality theory. Werner Mendel, in *Schizophrenia as a Life Style*, cites the words of schizophrenic patients:

I am like a zombie living behind a glass wall. I can see all that goes on in the world but I can't touch it. I can't reach it. I can't be in contact with it. I am outside. There is nothing there, absolutely nothing.[1]

This statement is a beautiful example of a phenomenological description of the split consciousness. The wall is the split. The wall is glass and the patient "can see all that goes on" because the person can experience both sides, both poles of the consciousness-world field, as is the case in the split consciousness. However, the person with a split consciousness feels himself or herself as existing on the subject rather than the object pole of the split stream. To this extent there is a trace of the consciousness of subjective collapse in him or her. The person cannot "touch," "reach," or be in "contact." Being in touch is an act of consciousness, perhaps *the fundamental* act of consciousness, of which this person is not capable. This is further confirmation of the split consciousness. In this case, the split occurs primarily between the transcendental ego and the *Umwelt*, the world in general.

The person writing the following passage is split from the *Mitwelt*, the world of people and intimacy. For him (or her) the intersubjective consciousness does not exist. The person is fixated in the individual consciousness. The conscious act, the intentional act which makes possible being in touch or being in contact with another subjectivity is not possible for this individual. This is a malfunction of consciousness itself. This passage is self-explanatory:

There's something wrong with me. I don't seem to feel about my family like others do. I know this mostly when I talk about my wife and children. I talk about them like my neighbors talk about their cars. I certainly like my family. But if they all went away it wouldn't bother me. They are really quite dispensable. I would just get somebody new, just like my neighbors get new cars.[2]

A similar case is illustrated by:

To me the world is peopled rather than populated. What I mean by peopled is that it is filled with people much like others' houses are furnished with furniture. It is all the same to me.[3]

Alienation or split from the *Eigenwelt*, that is, the world of the empirical ego, is seen in this passage:

Nothing is me, nothing is mine. I don't live in my body. I don't live anywhere. My body just is. It is just like the strings are pulled and it is moved automatically but I haven't anything in it.[4]

The deconstituted and the ungrounded consciousness are illustrated by:

There is a big hole in my chest. It is so empty it hurts. In fact it is going to explode with emptiness. It is an agony. It simply is that I have to stick something in it. I feel like I have to take a knife or a stick and poke it into my chest to try to fill the emptiness. The big emptiness in me is going to explode.[5]

The above patient experiences the deconstituted consciousness: His emptiness is the experience of nihilism, the agony of recognizing the nothingness which is coeval with the pure transcendental consciousness that we are. But it is also the experience of the ungrounded consciousness; the urge to "fill the emptiness" is the search for the experience of a ground.

The next example illustrates both the ignorant and the rigid consciousness:

It starts like a feeling of pressure on the back of my neck and head, and then the pressure spreads all over and I feel like I am a bomb that is about to go off. It's like if I looked at myself in the mirror I'd be all puffed up and colored bright red. That's when it is hardest to think clearly. Nobody seems to understand how close I am to blowing up. I feel so damn awful after I have done something or broken something or destroyed something. If only I could keep myself from going that far. There wasn't anybody who seemed to know that I am such a dangerous guy.[6]

The writer is frustrated because the intentional self-transcending stream cannot move outward and forward. To this extent he exemplifies the ignorant consciousness. Being-in-the-world, futurization, hope, temporality, all these aspects of the intentional stream are blocked and frustrated. Explosive feelings are the result. These can be hate, hitting, spitting, screaming—anything that is explosive in character. As a consequence of the intense frustration, the response has become both totally primitive—that is, originary and primordial. Also, the reaction can be pure explosiveness. In addition, the response is automated—it is fixated at this primitive level: "If only I could keep myself from going that far."

The following patient, in one simple sentence, describes his condition phenomenologically:

I don't have any feelings. I have nothing except the ache of emptiness.[7]

He (or she) expresses a split consciousness (first sentence), in this case split from the *Eigenwelt*. But the patient also illustrates the deconstituted consciousness (second sentence).

Following is a person whose consciousness is deconstituted and who cannot use his freedom to reconstitute his experience. He does manage to do so feebly, but his constitutions do not meet the standards of reality-testing:

Everything seems so mixed up, so disorganized. I can't seem to fit anything into place or put my fingers on anything. I can't seem to make my thoughts follow one another logically—I just sit in a confused muddle. It is a peculiar drifting feeling but not a pleasant drifting. And then in a way it is almost like a relief when I start to hallucinate. At least I don't just sit confused. I pay attention to what I am hallucinating. Even though it scares hell out of me, I can talk about it now like I knew it was hallucination. When it really happens I don't know, I am not at all sure. It is just like things were unreal in my confusion and then they suddenly become real when the experience happens that I am now later calling hallucination.[8]

A person with difficulties sustaining the constitution of the body-qua-mine writes:

It just feels like something is dragging my seeds down and like if I don't hold on to my belly my guts will fall out.[9]

Finally, this patient illustrates the rigid consciousness. In this case, he cannot use his freedom to reverse an unfortunate reconstitution:

I woke up this morning and I knew that it wasn't the world that was upside down or inside out. It was my eyes. They are completely turned in the socket. Everything was backward and inverted.[10]

Bleuler

Eugen Bleuler, in *Dementia Praecox or the Group of Schizophrenias*, defines schizophrenia in terms of four invariable symptoms: *associations, ambivalence, autism,* and *altered affect*.[11]

Schizophrenia is manifested by difficulty in thinking. The associations are loosened; thinking becomes tangential and reasoning is but a series of *non sequiturs*. And, according to Bleuler's observations, this defect in ideation is basic to the disease. What happens if we interpret the loosening of associations in existential terms, that is, in terms of the parameters of the phenomenological model of being and the existential personality theory? Thinking or reasoning is the process of constitution itself. In schizophrenia control over the constituting process is lost. Habitual patterns of constitution disintegrate. It is as if the program for the computer were suddenly missing. In the process of deconstitution, the transcendental freedom and nothingness, which are another crucial aspect of the schizophrenic consciousness, become uncovered. There are even physiological correlates to the loss of the power of constitution. When people age they often suffer from celulitis: the cells disintegrate—apparently from sheer age. The usual molecular organization falls apart. Similarly in schizophrenia, the usual and habitual streams of passive constitution disintegrate, making common sense and consensual life impossible and leading to bizarre and unorthodox conceptualizations.

This type of consciousness is related to the deconstituted consciousness. In a state rapidly approaching total deconstitution, it is not possible to sustain an organized existence of any kind. At best, residual snippets of organization appear, so that isolated segments of the patient's ratiocination still make sense, but the totality has become devoid of meaning. In other words, the constitutive powers and acts of consciousness, which are part of the essence of consciousness as intentionality, are absent in the person who has lost the capacity for thought. Thought is, after all, the capacity for organization. This capacity of consciousness is primitive and irreducible. It must be noted that constitution is not restricted to the creation of conceptual meanings. Quite to the contrary, constitution refers also to the organization and coordination of muscle activity—as in speech and in driving an automobile. Constitution means competence in living, grace and ease in moving about within the world.

Ambivalence, Bleuler's second defining characteristic of schizophrenia, means that in response to the world's ambiguity the schizophrenic patient becomes paralyzed. The philosophical analysis of this symptom is as follows: Ambiguity is real and natural. The subjective correlate of what appears as ambiguity in the objective world is transcendental freedom of the subjective world. If ambiguity paralyzes, the patient cannot use his freedom. The patient must choose ex nihilo a value, a world design, a belief-system, or any lesser meaning.

The capacity for ex-nihilo choosing is part of the authentic or natural consciousness. It results from contact and identification with the freedom that resides at the center of our inward and transcendental consciousness.

The inauthentic consciousness on the other hand expects to be influenced by external forces and determined by unambiguous direction signs in the world. When ambivalence becomes a problem we then witness with that the attrition of freedom. Rejection of ambivalence becomes the denial of freedom.

More specifically, if it is *denial* we mean, then the extinction of freedom is itself a free act and freedom—appearances to the contrary notwithstanding—has in reality not been extinguished. Denial of freedom belongs therefore to the ignorant consciousness. However, if freedom is altogether and truly nonexistent, then we have a genuine case of distortion or crippling of consciousness, for with the destruction of freedom consciousness itself is seriously injured. Another way to interpret ambivalence is to argue that it is part of the structure of the world which the patient does not integrate into his subjective being. Thus, ambivalence is in fact detachment or dissociation from the reality of ambiguity in the world. In that case, ambiguity illustrates the split consciousness.

Autism, which means withdrawal from the external world, is a condition of almost pure detachment. Autism is the consciousness of subjective collapse. It differs from asceticism and the mysticism of meditation in that autism, like all cripplings of consciousness, is automatic and fixed.

This is a distinction whose importance it is difficult to overestimate. Asceticism and autism are both withdrawals from the world, retreats into the realm of pure consciousness. Autism is automatic; it just happens. It appears—gradually or suddenly—or has always been that way, and the victim has no idea how it came about and exercises no noticeable control or power over the course of the illness. The victim's impotence may be quite genuine. This would then be a case of bona fide autism. But the impotence may be unconsciously chosen, in which case autism, perhaps because it engenders a secondary gain, is an act of self-deception. By touching the freedom of this person, the autism may be on its way to resolution.

Asceticism, on the other hand, is a freely, deliberately, and rationally (that is, metaphysically and theologically) chosen world view and life-style. It is far from automatic. On the contrary, the path to asceticism is arduous; it takes time, patience, perseverance, and self-discipline. Nor is asceticism a fixed state. It requires constant rededication; the practitioner is permanently in danger of slipping back into the consensual world. Asceticism can thus in no way be confused with autism.

Altered affect means that feelings are "flat and inappropriate."[12] This defining characteristic of schizophrenia lends itself to a variety of philosophical interpretations. For one, it means that consciousness is detached from the psyche of the empirical ego. There is a sense of artificiality about feelings which makes it appear that the subjective consciousness does participate in (cathect) its true feelings. Also, altered affect can mean that the region between the psyche and the external world to which it responds is split. The split or fissure, rather than occurring along the interface between the transcendental and the empirical, which is what one would expect, develops within the empirical realm itself, leading to a fragmentation between two objects in the world—the psyche and that part of the world of objects to which the psyche would normally relationally be connected.

OTHER VIEWS

Let us now examine another definition of schizophrenia. Mendel's view of the phenomenology of schizophrenia is developed around three notions: the failure of historicity; chaotic, expensive, and ineffective management or binding of anxiety; and painful interpersonal misadventures.[13]

Failure of historicity, which means difficulties with time, with the future, with the past, with the connectedness and the continuity of existence and experience, is reality failure or disruption of the field aspect of the field of consciousness. The intentional continuity from subject to object, expressed through the experience of time, and the phenomena of motion, futurization, and self-transcendence, is disrupted in the schizophrenic reaction. That disruption is what is here meant by the various forms of the crippled consciousness. In the inauthentic forms of consciousness described, the one characteristic they all share is that the field of consciousness ceases to function like a field, a process, a flow, or a dialectic. The metaphors of the magnet and the bloodstream—shown to be central to our understanding of human existence—do not apply to any form of the crippled consciousness. In other words, this aspect of schizophrenia may well be—on this philosophic hypothesis—the fundamental disruption, distortion, or crippling of the phenomenon of consciousness itself.

A second defining characteristic of this pathology is that the schizophrenic has great difficulty in developing defenses against his anxiety. Mendel writes that "Schizophrenic existence . . . stumbles and falls over pebbles . . . so small that the non-schizophrenic existence doesn't even see them. . . . Just getting through a day of life is an almost impossible task."[14]

The freedom and the abyss revealed to the schizophrenic by his anxiety are not bizarre pathological hallucinations but are revelations of underlying philosophic truths, existential realities, and transcendental structures. The schizophrenic is condemned to these visions of human truths. His protection against the blinding brilliance of the vision, his mechanisms of escape, his defense against these insights have all become inoperative. The reason for this excess of truth and for the elimination of the illusions which make life bearable is that his consciousness has lost its powers of constitution. Because the schizophrenic is the deconstituted consciousness, every act, regardless how small, has the character of world-creation. Even the most minuscule action evokes and invokes the full measure of transcendental freedom. As a result, the effort is understandably enormous and exhausting. By having his eyes permanently pried open—eyes which are forced into the transcendental reduction—the schizophrenic is condemned to experience the anxiety which the vision of pure consciousness entails, which the permanent reduction—that is, the loss of the object—implies. Moreover, in the process of simply living, the open-eyed schizophrenic must constitute anew the world in which even one step forward makes sense and is possible. His daily life thus clearly duplicates the process of world-constitution or constant creation. The burden is indeed excessive and beyond endurance.

Finally, interpersonal misadventure can be explained in terms of two philosophic factors. First, commitment—which means cathexis and tight subject-object connectedness—is impossible for the split consciousness. As a result, personal relations fail. Second, love is the establishement of an intersubjective field, which is equally impossible. The continuity of the field of consciousness is between subject and object or between consciousness and consciousness. To the crippled consciousness, intentionality as well as intersubjectivity are out of the question. One would therefore expect that a person whose consciousness malfunctions will not be able to cathect (that is, bind the ego with the world) or love (that is, establish a common and continuous field with another conscious center).

In this way we can suggest and briefly illustrate how the phenomenological model of being and the existential personality theory can serve as the ideology of the growth movement. They can bring together, in one system developed out of the history of epistemology, the various strands and forces of psychology today: experimental, psychoanalytic, humanistic, and transpersonal.

Notes

1. Arthur Burton, Juan J. Lopez-Ibor, and Werner M. Mendel, *Schizophrenia as a Life Style* (New York: Springer Publishing Co., 1974), p. 106. Also in Werner M. Mendel, *Supportive Care: Theory and Technique* (Santa Monica, Calif.: Mara Books, 1975), Chap. 18.

2. *Ibid.*, p. 107.
3. *Ibid.*, p. 107.
4. *Ibid.*, p. 109.
5. *Ibid.*, p. 109.
6. *Ibid.*, p. 108.
7. *Ibid.*, p. 110.
8. *Ibid.*, p. 110-111.
9. *Ibid.*, p. 110.
10. *Ibid.*, p. 112.
11. *Ibid.*, pp. 122 ff.
12. *Ibid.*, p. 122.
13. *Ibid.*, p. 123.
14. *Ibid.*, p. 126.

Chapter 8 • HEALING THROUGH PARTICIPATION: OVERVIEW

The Theoretical Foundations of Participation

The concept of participation stands for certain implications of the intentional theory of consciousness which have consequences for the theory and practice of healing. The study of participation, carried far enough and pursued systematically, can yield specific suggestions on how a phenomenological model of being contributes concretely to medical and psychological healing.

This analysis of participation, based on the intentional theory of consciousness, constitutes *adequate explanation* of the mind-body relationship. The ultimate unit of explanation and thus the guiding principle in research, both in formulating questions and in reporting results, is the mind-body couple, the subject-object continuum, the intentional field. All experience and all being consist of subject-object couples intentionally connected. What specifically serves as subject and what as object in any particular situation is variable and relative. The body can be the subject and a tree the object; the transcendental ego can be the subject and a feeling the object. One person's silent and solitary conscious center can be the subject and another, and witnessed, person's silent and solitary center can be the object. And even this latter subject-object polarization in experience can be reversed: "I love you" can be said by both the "I" and the "you" in this sentence, thus reversing the subject and object of one and the same actual field. Subject and object can also be of different sizes—from galactic to atomic. The consciousness that views the world is a massive subject-object connection. In fact, the entire universe is this cosmic subject-object field. When one nation perceives another, two large poles comprise this field. In all cases, the variable subject-object intentionally connected polarized field is the ultimate unit of reality, of fact, and of explanation.

This contention is the crux of the entire matter of analyzing philosophically various contemporary problems where breakthroughs seem to be imminent: One is the relation between the study of consciousness and the results of contemporary subatomic physics and astronomical cosmologies (well illustrated by Fritjof Capra's *The Tao of Physics*).

Another is in the area of parapsychology. It appears that we can view the world, correctly, either from the perspective of the Eternal Now or from that of time or the consensual world. Paranormal phenomena, it appears, seem to occur when a shift in world views is effected. The resignation and acceptance of dying may well be the time-to-eternity shift in world views.[1] Many people report paranormal experiences at that time (see Raymond Moody's book *Life After Life*).[2] Similarly, many people report paranormal experiences during moments of profound emotional attachment, or when these attachments are threatened, in short, at traumatic moments. At those times the reverse process seems to occur. It is the experience of embodiment, of incarnation; it is the experience of the archetypal decision for finitude, of becoming an individual. That is an eternity-to-time shift.[3] The phenomenological model of being seems to be able to provide the conceptual framework in terms of which research breakthroughs and explanatory breakthroughs may be possible. However, our concern in this chapter is with the problem of psychosomatic medicine, another area where the phenomenological model of being may offer possibilities for breakthroughs.

It is not enough to know that mind and body are connected and that some mental conditions are the results of bodily morbidity or that certain physiologic conditions are brought about by (or are the expressions of) conscious or unconscious mental postures. We must, in addition, have a clear phenomenological description of the mind-body, that is, of the body as a lived and experienced interacting mind-matter field. We may call the field that I am the *mind-body*. Our culture has little difficulty in mouthing this concept, but it faces insuperable difficulties in establishing adequate theoretical foundations, in developing its consequences for research and practice in medicine and psychotherapy, and in living this idea in daily life.

That description of the mind-body in no way corresponds to the body that is examined in a physician's office and even less to the formaldehyde-soaked cadaver in medical school. Nor is the body found in Gray's *Anatomy* even a simulacrum of the lived body. The lived body—as the subject-object, consciousness-world interface, as the direct experience of intentionality itself—is discovered strictly through a phenomenological analysis of how it feels to be a body and how it feels to live as a body in the world. The lived body is the membrane which connects the subjective and the objective, the transcendental and the empirical zones of being. The body-qua-mine is thus the universal essence of intentionality. Furthermore, we need a description of the mind, and we get that through sensitivity to the exploration of inwardness implied in the isolation of the transcendental dimension as a bona fide category of psychological investigation.

Finally, in order to adequately describe and conceptualize the phenomenon of psychosomaticism, we will eventually require a detailed phenomenological description of the field that is formed by the subject-object, mind-body, consciousness-*physis* continuity. One psychosomatically relevant possibility is for the center of consciousness (the mind, the freedom) to *participate* deliberately and voluntarily, through the use of willpower or surrender (or *mind-power*)—through an active or a passive cathexis—in the affairs of the body. Biofeedback training enhances the experience of the consciousness-body continuity and of the mutual interaction. Let us consider some examples and reflect on the questions they raise.

Sorrow over loss can be expressed as crying, weeping, or sobbing. Anxiety or panic can be expressed by the contraction of the blood vessels on the outer parts of the body. Is it possible and sufficient to explain this correlation in terms of the intentional model of being and use a kind of Spinozistic experiential double-aspect theory? Can we accept the reconstruction of the world in terms of the two polarities of the phenomenological model of being and consider that the ensuing explanation of the mind-body relationship is adequate? Or do we need additional hypotheses? Even if the intentional explanation would suffice, how are scientific explanations correlated with philosophic ones? Finally, if it is true that the intentional explanation is adequate, then why does it not always work? Furthermore, can we develop new and workable healing techniques through this philosophic hypothesis? If, for example, there is a field relationship between consciousness and the immune system, how is it—as may be the case in arthritis and cancer—that to exert mental control over these diseases is sometimes possible and most of the time impossible? These questions need further investigation.

Since the final test of any theory is whether or not it works, we must develop some experimental implications of these ideas by evolving testable hypotheses. All we can establish here by pure philosophy is the reasonableness and likeliness that these treatment hypotheses will work and heal. Philosophy gives us the creative imagination for new directions in research. It does not yet give us the full answers, which will always be interdisciplinary and cooperative ventures.

The difficulty of fully integrating participation into medical thinking can be illustrated by the following considerations. To what extent, let us say in weeping, is there direct mind-body contact? And to what extent are there—as the consensual world believes—"subterranean," implicit, inferred, and thus inaccessible events in operation? A series of diagrams can help us develop this rather significant distinction. Figure 1 illustrates the two levels at which a subject-object interaction can take place. A describes an *experienced* relationship whereas B represents an *inferred* relationship;

A is direct and B is an image garnered from a belief system. The particular belief system adopted is of course not wild speculation but justified by research, which is then called evidence. Experience and experiment disclose that both types of contact are efficacious and can therefore produce healing. In other words, the *right* thoughts and attitudes, which are events in the region of consciousness, can bring about healing and a healthy body. *Wrong* thoughts, on the other hand, deteriorate the body. What is needed are clues, from the philosophic analyses, made available in a comprehensive phenomenology of human experience, of what constitutes *right* and *wrong* thoughts followed by a test of the hypothesis at the sickbed.

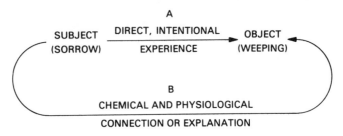

Figure 1

Sorrowful thoughts are expressed in weeping; joyous thoughts in laughter. These are examples of type A contacts. Another example of type A contact occurs when we learn to experience any disease, such as SLE (Systemic Lupus Erythematosis), no longer as caused by events external to the center of our consciousness but rather as an act—to cite only a crude example—of self-hate and self-destruction for which we take no personal and free responsibility. A different case is that of a woman who has been taught by our chauvinistic culture and by Freud's penis-envy theory not to affirm or not to be her potency (where affirmation means to give up being a wife and mother and to suffer loneliness). She may in actual fact indeed mouth the language of women's liberation, but she nevertheless counteracts her self-assertion with dramatic self-negation—through painful and disabling disease. It turns out that this negation is far more real and effective than her surface affirmation. Such situations occur frequently.

An uncompromising attitude of freedom and control seems to offer hope of recontacting directly the conscious center with my-body. In this instance we invoke the expression of freedom we call free will (cf. pp. 131 ff.). In other words, this person does not experience that she has direct control over her disease. One hope for bringing about this control is through the exercise of her willpower, which is the deliberate effort to directly force the inner consciousness upon the external body. Specific techniques can be devised to encourage this extrusion of consciousness onto the body. On the other hand, we can reverse this process and attempt to *control* consciousness through the body by exercising an equally uncompromising attitude of spontaneity—which would be the *willpower* of the body, the control of the body over consciousness. Body work and massage encourage the experience of direct body-to-mind contact. This experience of freedom is that of spontaneity rather than willpower; when the direct experience is mind-to-body it is appropriate to call that expression of freedom, willpower. These mind-body (and body-mind) or subject-object (and object-subject) contacts are direct, experienced, and of a field nature.

Examples of type B contacts—which are not experienced but inferred, which are mechanical, believed, and occur not on the experiential but are thought to occur on the molecular, atomic, or subatomic levels—include the introduction of pharmacological agents which alter the subject-object relationship or the total condition. Whereas there is evidence that both causal paths work in actual practice, there are instances in which one works but not the other. There are, for instance, cases in which medicine alone will effect a cure and in which no amount of psychological readiness, authenticity, or positive thinking seems to have any effect. These are cases of pure type B contact. Then again there are instances in which neither medicine nor surgery appear to have any effect and only consciousness or the spirit seem to have curative powers. These are clear-cut and pure cases of type A contact. Type B contacts are fully automatic. They occur irrespective of what the direct subject-object contact experience may be. Correlatively, type A contacts—and this is an important innovation—must occur irrespective of any changes on the molecular or inferred level. In other words, we must transcend the assumptions that the direct intentional contact is but a surface manifestation of underlying molecular activity. The direct, experienced, intentional contact is *sui generis* and it occurs quite independently of whatever inferred and molecular events may also take place at the same time.

It is of course reasonable to assume that most practical instances are a combination of these two types of interaction. In one current approach to the treatment of cancer, a combination of chemotherapy, radiation therapy, and a healthy mental attitude, a determination to live, the ability to take responsibility for one's life and to take charge of one's illness, as well as the capacity for joy and love are likely paths to whatever success is possible.

Figure 1 is an inaccurate phenomenological representation because it gives equal ontological weight to the given (A) and the interpreted (B). The principle of the primacy of subjectivity (Book One, Chapter 2) demands that A have ontological priority and that B be reconceptualized in terms of the requirement of the primacy of first-person experience. This epistemological fact implies also the primacy of direct (type-A) subject-object contact over the inferred (type-B) contact—which is the reverse of our prevailing medical attitudes. In other words, strict adherence to the phenomenological method demands the recognition that A-type experiences are the basis of all knowledge, and that B-type experiences are not experiences at all but theoretical constructs based on the primacy of direct, type-A contacts.

The phenomenological method leads to the nonconsensual but nevertheless inevitable conclusion that the direct experience of, for example, a headache has a higher claim to represent what is real than any inference that we draw from it; for we cannot be mistaken about the experienced presence of what we call a "headache"—a truism which does not hold for any interpretation we impose on that experience or inference we draw from it. As a first approximation, the headache is a unique and phenomenologically describable experience. An inference, after tests, would be that the pain is caused by a tumor. At the test stage, the tumor is only an inference. The headache is a type-A experience, whereas the tumor theory is a type-B experience. Then, exploratory surgery is performed. At that time, the tumor is actually seen, and it becomes a direct (type-A) experience—*but for another person*. For the person who has the tumor, it is still only an inference—and it will always remain an inference—although now it not only involves what we might call a pure inference, but involves in addition the report from another consciousness (the surgeon) with whom the patient is in direct touch.

We therefore get an improved and refined diagram describing the two ways in which the healing process (as well as the process of becoming ill) can be perceived:

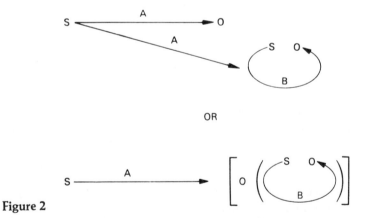

Figure 2

In this figure, the pharmacological connection between the state of consciousness (S) and the physical condition (O) is an object to consciousness, specifically an eidetic or conceptual object. In other words, the direct, experienced object of consciousness is the concept or the theory of the indirect subject-object connection. It is the theoretical model of this (type-B) connection which is what is given directly to consciousness. That is then the final model in terms of which psychosomatic or participatory phenomena are to be understood.

We need these preliminary epistemological and methodological considerations—all of which follow directly from the phenomenological method and the field structure of consciousness—to understand the theories of healing developed in the subsequent pages.

Illustration

The following considerations may confirm the primacy (and accuracy) of a direct and intentional subject-object connection over an indirect and inferred subject-object correspondence.

Most of us feel anxiety when we see the insides of a human or animal body—organs or skeleton—even under laboratory conditions. What is going on in that anxiety? What is it that we actually experience at that moment? This question embodies a typical phenomenological task: Get into that anxiety and explore the inward reality which exists at that moment. The following is a phenomenological hypothesis which others can use to test their own experience and to check if the present hypothesis conforms to the inward experiences of others. The present writing is a set of hypotheses about which phenomenological descriptions best conform to actual external and inward experience. The reader is the scientist, complete with a well-equipped laboratory (his or her own human existence), who then confirms or disconfirms through personal experience whether or not these phenomenological hypotheses do in fact conform to the givens in his or her experience.

The experience of seeing a body's entrails arouses the anxiety of nihilism. The anxiety of nihilism may well be the source of all anxiety, since it is the anxiety about groundlessness, about the absence of foundations, and the fact that we are all homeless.

When—perhaps in a college biology laboratory—we look at the entrails of an animal, we experience homelessness and foundationlessness. The message which the dissected animal communicates to us is that our being, foundation, and roots depend exclusively on the events and organizations that in life were going on inside that body. It is these very same events which are going on inside us now, covered from sight by the skin. Anything that serves as foundation, ground, and home to us is based on a skeleton, a heartbeat, a liver, fat, intestines, and the now collapsed lungs of the cadaver—all of which are simulcra of our own entrails.

What makes us think that our foundation in being depends on all these fragile and extraordinarily complex inside organs? That is the materialism of our age; it has told us that we are only physiological structures. It is this exclusively objectivist metaphysics, ghost-in-a-machine personality theory, along with ignorance and then denial of the vast transcendental region which is the source of our anxiety. We are forced to think that this grievous fragility, this frightening contingency, is all that it means to be us and our civilized values.

Let us go further. We envision, in addition, cells, DNA molecules, chromosomes, and so forth. Not only is our being totally grounded on organs like those inside the frog, cat, or cadaver, but our ground is also contingent on cells which we cannot see. And beyond that there are molecules inside the cells, and all kinds of incomprehensible, strange, and mysterious events—such as quanta, positrons, quarks and anti-particles—which occur within these molecules, and on which our being depends.

What is the message or the effect of these experiences on our security or anxiety? First, we are told that our being, our very ground, is controlled by events that are external to ourselves, external to consciousness, experientially completely removed from what we ordinarily call me. Even though the insides of our own bodies may be, in one sense, close, they are in experienced reality distant, in fact more distant even than Australia is to America. It is more likely that we will visit Australia in our lifetime than that we will see our own livers. And it is more likely that we will see a kangaroo in our living rooms than that we will ever see our pancreas. But we are not grounded on a kangaroo in Australia—which we could go and visit—but on our very own personal pancreas (among other things) with which we can never really be in touch. It follows that our whole being is rooted on many things and events that are not accessible to us.

A second consequence that follows when we allow ourselves to be dominated by the materialistic and objectivistic—consciousness-denying—world view is that we have no control whatsoever over our destiny. We have on this metaphysics no control over the very foundation of our being, because that foundation is independent of us. Heartbeats, biofeedback training to the contrary, are certainly beyond our control. We have no real power over whether or not our heart is going to beat. Our circulation, digestion, and temperature balance, and the fact that our skin does not break out in a rash, our eyes do not water, we do not stop salivating, our blood pressure remains delicately balanced, and the oxygen content of our blood is proper—all of these foundation events are completely out of the reach of our freedom and our consciousness. The materialistic model leads to the conviction that our very ground, like Nietzsche's God, "is dead." When we look at the inside of a body we become convinced that what makes us what we are is totally outside of our control. This feeling is intensified in modern research concerned with atomic and subatomic particles and molecules, which are not even visible by opening up the body or looking through a microscope. And yet we feel controlled by these mysterious chemical reactions and electrical forces inside our brain and throughout our nervous system, and once more we are overcome with the feeling that our essence and our substance are completely and totally beyond our reach and our power. Thus we feel alienated from ourselves. This lack of control leads us directly into the anxiety of nihilism, which derives from our materialistic metaphysics.

A third message that the *anxiety of physiology* discloses is the fragility of whatever grounding we do have, the contingency, the brittleness of our ground, its adventitious character. We are only a joke. We have no control over our ground. We are totally contingent, fragile, accidental, and adventitious; we depend on what we do not see and over which we can exert no direct efficacy.

The anxiety accompanying our seeing the insides of a body, or seeing blood reveals to us that we are alienated from our ground, that we are fallen and homeless beings, aliens to ourselves. We are coerced into this viewpoint by the objectivist and materialistic metaphysics of our culture. That is a deep-seated presupposition of enormous danger.

The view that I-am-a-thing is the moral bankruptcy of metaphysics. The exclusively materialistic, atomic, and objectivist view of the person is ruined. The I-am-the-inside-of-my-skin anxiety is the experience of the moral bankruptcy of the ghost-in-a-machine personality theory because it leads to anxiety about nothingness, anxiety about nihilism.

The good news is that the materialistic metaphysics is not presuppositionless at all but is itself one of the most dangerous of all presuppositions. The kind of metaphysics which denies the reality of the subjective or transcendental dimension is contrary to the facts of immediate human experience and to the facts on which all knowledge about existence must be based; it is contrary to the model of being, the consciousness-world-field model of being that emerges when we eliminate our presuppositions and experience our aliveness as it is . . . now.

Some Medical Implications

The full development of the philosophic idea of participation may hold out real hope for actually assisting physicians in the struggle against disease. Participation—in the context of disease and its treatment—means that the patient is fully informed of what is known about his condition. The expression *fully informed* is to be taken in a thoroughly academic, scholarly, and research sense. The patient, in the ideal case of participation, must be informed of the details of his illness to an extent usually beyond the time and even the competence of the average nurse and physician. He must be informed both generically (textbook and laboratory material) and individually (his own body and case). When so informed he must keep in mind that the subject matter is not *body* in the abstract but his own living body which his consciousness is at this moment cathecting. The hypothesis is that such a procedure, if carried out at all times, has curative consequences in most cases. We ask, assuming the hypothesis is confirmed, Why should it be? How does it work? What are the mechanics? The answer must be a fundamental epistemological one. The questions demand an explanation in terms of bodies in action, of forces in conflict.

The scientific establishment has transcended naive materialism and puerile mechanism. It has substituted the ideas of models and statistical correlations. These are no explanations at all, just summations of data. Common sense still lives with the mechanism and materialism of old. If we now take the field theory seriously, then we understand that mind and matter are different but also that they are in constant and direct contact. Mind-matter interaction becomes an axiom of immediate experience, a description of a presuppositionless reality, and not a mysterious theory. All mental events and all bodily events must then be explained in terms of the prior givenness of their intentional connection. The *direct* efficacy of the mind over matter, as well as the converse, is then one of the primordial facts of experience in terms of which all others are to be understood. We are now free to experiment imaginatively and artfully with the effects of direct touching of reality through the acts of consciousness.

Consider the following example: I look at my hand. I believe that the connection between the *I* and the *hand* is internal to the body—from head, through neck, torso, and arm to the hand. I overlook the directly given fact that eye-to-hand is an even more obvious connection. If the feelings in my hand are affected by my look and by my will, I attribute that to the internal and invisible workings of my nervous system. In truth, a field theory must claim that the causal nexus lies in the direct eye-to-hand act. Continual awareness of these realities tends to confirm this view. We can gradually accumulate knowledge of what can be done in this fashion and what cannot.

Participation also means the use of fantasy. It means that the patient goes through a guided (by self or physician) fantasy about how to fight his disease physically and chemically. He participates in this fight by identifying himself with the organs, the blood corpuscles, the cells, and the molecular structures that are active at this time. If there is truth to the physiological description of our own bodies, then there may be healthy efficacy in the deliberate connectedness established between consciousness and this organic aspect of our empirical ego.

What in reality does the patient do in this fantasy? He gives up a self-concept in which he is a passive victim of unknown forces with blind faith that techniques will, like magicians, correct the mechanical failure. He moves forward to a self-concept in which he attempts to achieve direct contact, an intentional subject-object field continuity, with those phenomena that affect him. He is not in touch with the phenomena directly but with what we hope is an accurate surrogate of them. However, if the descriptions from physiology and chemistry are correct, and if he focuses on that part of his body where these events are taking place, then he indeed and in fact is in direct contact with those parts of his body which are diseased.

A two-tier experiment suggests itself. First, we must carefully collect and evaluate evidence to see if there is in fact a correlation between fantasy work and healing. Second, assuming the answer to our first hypothesis is yes, we must investigate further to check specifically if the content of the fantasy is relevant. Is it true that a fantasy about the "correct" events inside the body is more effective than one based on an altogether false interpretation of these inner occurrences? Can we reverse this procedure and diagnose the physiopathology by the kind of fantasy work we empirically find effective?

If this approach is ineffective we may assume the specific fantasy or technique rather than the general principle is at fault. The general principle makes sense in the intentional theory of consciousness. The purely medical approach does not, in that it assumes a hiatus between the conscious center and the external reality of the body. The effect of philosophy on medicine should be to suggest new directions for investigation.

Notes

1. Compare the death fantasy at the end of Peter Koestenbaum, *Is There An Answer to Death?* (Englewood Cliffs, N.J.: Prentice-Hall, 1976).

2. Raymond Moody, *Life After Life* (Harrisburg, Pa.: Stackpole Books, 1976).

3. The myth of creation in *Is There An Answer To Death?* discusses this shift.

Chapter 9 • HEALING THROUGH
PARTICIPATION: DETAILS

Theory

Holistic medicine exists and is successful precisely because of and to the extent that it is one of the few modern approaches to medicine which has taken seriously the phenomenological model of being and the field-of-consciousness theory of the person. It has attempted to base its medical and psychological theories and practices on this model, a model which is gradually replacing the object-centered and subject-object caesura established by the mechanism and rationalism of the seventeenth century and which is replacing the Cartesian subject-object split with Husserl's concept of intentionality and the Heideggerian concept of being-in-the-world. The replacement is more than a change of models. It is progress toward accuracy and greater clarity and increased depth of analysis. While many hold to this view of subject-object connectedness, few understand it. To verbalize it is not to apply it. A patient may possess full conceptual clarity about his diagnosis, its etiology, and its theoretical analysis. Nevertheless, no change in life-style, perception, or symptoms occurs because the insights are not integrated into experience. The situation with psychosomatic medicine is parallel: We must train ourselves to redefine who we are in terms of the epistemological insight of participation, a process that should have started at birth. Since it did not, it must start at rebirth.

The principal contention of the phenomenological model of being used by holistic medicine is that the subject-object relation is *direct*, that subject and object are in direct contact with each other, and that each *participates* in the life, form, activity, and manifestation of the other. These ideas are inherent in the concept of the intentionality of consciousness, where subject and object, while different, are nevertheless in a constant condition of interaction. This connectedness—also referred to as a dialectical connection—is the accurate description of experience and thus of reality and is the epistemological foundation of all theories. This direct subject-object contact is the meaning of intentionality in Husserl, of being-in-the-world in Heidegger, of the *pour soi* in Sartre, and of the concept of participation in Marcel. All conflicting models and theories nevertheless have their origin and justification in this phenomenon of direct, participatory, and intentional contact. To account for certain phenomena in terms of this direct-contact model constitutes *adequate explanation*. For it is precisely this intentional continuity which is the irreducible, inexplicable, atomic, or axiomatic *fundamentum* component of experience. It follows that we must explain atoms and other particles and individuals through the manner in which they are conceptually developed or eidetically constituted out of the continuity of the intentional subject-object process rather than the reverse—which is to reduce continuity to particles (as when we say that a line—continuity—consists of an infinite number of points—particles) and which is our common scientific attitude.

In the human sphere this reversal of common prejudices leads to the important insight that the individual (alienated, alone, unique, and self-reliant) is not necessarily the ultimate, irreducible, and atomic ingredient in experience. We must also remember that it is the individual who dies and not the cosmic or natural universality with which he might identify. Many answers to human problems exist on the universal sphere (especially the security and peace of immortality). Most common problems however exist on the individual sphere (especially anxiety). In the last analysis, being is free to choose whether to make the individual or the universal the protocol of explanation. It appears that holistic medicine prefers to use the universal as its paradigm. A worthwhile hypothesis to explore would then be: "Conventional medicine works best for individuals. Holistic medicine works for universalities."

From the holistic point of view, the problem is therefore *not* how to explain immortality—or indestructibility—which is an existential a priori, an a priori given about being—but how to explain individuality, atomicity, and death—none of which are given and all of which are constituted or inferred. On this view it is thus *natural* to feel secure, immortal, and eternal. It is our alienation from the universal—which must be in the last analysis a possible free choice—which puzzles us and needs explanation. In physics, atoms exist as a matter of convenience—the atom is a mnemonic device which summarizes experimental data. In mathematics, points help us to calculate the dimensions of curves. In human relationships, it is the archetypal decision for finitude, that is, the choice of individual atomicity, which gives rise to that pervasive and peculiar perspective which we call human existence. And this decisions yields a *world view* of atomicity and not the *fact* of atomicity.

Whatever resistance there is to the view of the primacy of the universal is based on the staggering consequences of shifting from an individual to a universal world view. The consequences of choosing to perceive ourselves as individuals (more correctly phrased: the consequences of consciousness choosing to perceive itself as individual) are well known—they represent the world and the life that we accept without question as reality—until philosophers force us to examine the assumption of even the fiercest bias. Even in philosophic circles the attack on the premises of common sense—not that sensations are real but that *individuals are real*—leads not to counterargument but to laughter and ridicule.

The resistance to consciousness' choice of perceiving itself as universal rather than as individual is understandable, because it is due to the vastly—and even that word is an understatement—disruptive or reconstituting effect of that decision for reperception. The best illustration of the latter is the life of the extreme guru, from Sri Aurobindo to Baba Ram Das. In deciding between these two views, logic and philosophy end and prejudice, force, ridicule, and brainwashing take over. The ultimate philosophic truth is not the *Lebenswelt* or the mystical consciousness but (a) the ambiguity of the world, (b) the reality of the intentional field of consciousness, and (c) our freedom to constitute the given data of experience either way, that is, using alienated individuality as the organizing principle or the melding and flowing sense of universality as the principle in terms of which being is perceived. To look further than the continuous subject-object, individuality-universality topography for any underlying or irreducible true *indubitandum*, axiom, atom, or protocol is to deny the ontological and epistemological primacy of intentionality. The symbol for direct subject-object contact and participation—which is the phenomenologically established basis for all truth and knowledge—is the straight arrow:

Figure 1   S ————————————————→ O

The contravening and prevailing model of being which we have called the medical model of the person or the ghost-in-a-machine theory of the person is characterized by the belief or assumption that the direct subject-object contact is purely experiential and sensory and is therefore not to be taken seriously. The direct subject-object experienced connection is thought to be a mere appearance of the "true" underlying and mysterious connection. On this view, the correct analysis of any experienced subject-object relation is that it is *indirect, inferred, hypothesized,* and therefore *non-participatory.* This view can be traced throughout the entire compass of the history of philosophy. It expresses itself in the position, which is as old as the pre-Socratic philosopher Parmenides, that experience is not to be trusted as a guide to reality. Reason—which today means inference, system, or general theory—is our sole guarantee of truth. Plato espoused a similar view when he ascribed a higher region of reality to intelligible phenomena than to sensory phenomena. The empiricist tradition, beginning with Francis Bacon and culminating with William James and Edmund Husserl, has been successful in rectifying these historical confusions. The method of science, insofar as its intent is to identify truth with observation, is indeed empirical; but to the degree that it avails itself of heady amounts of inference, it contains massive doses of unanalyzed rationalism.

A significant way to diagram how these theories have entered our perceptions and conceptions of the world is this:

Figure 2

The real contact between the subject and object in our experience, such as the mind and the body, the mind and feelings, and the like, is thought to be somehow not visible nor experienceable directly. The connection is subterranean; it is *behind* (subject) and *beyond* (object) that which is visible, perceptible, or directly accessible. The prevailing metaphysics assumes that reality exists "behind" (that is, *before*) the subjective zone of the continuous intentional field of experience as well as "beyond" (that is, *after*) the objective zone of that field. Between the two poles, the connection is, shall we say, "subterranean."

It is useful to list the phenomenological descriptions which apply to each model or representation insofar as this analysis has implications for the healing process. The following table should be of help:

Phenomenological Model of Being	Medical Model of the Person
active	passive
personal responsibility for cure	physician takes care of patient
independent action of patient	medication, surgery, anaesthesia
patient participates in the etiology as well as in the treatment of the disease	patient is the helpless victim of germs, chemicals, and/or genetic influences
the physiological events are experienced as part of the center of the patient's being	bodily events are perceived as external to the existential center of the person

A final refinement in our model is required. Given the epistemological and ontological primacy of first-person experience, as embodied in Husserl's theory of the *Lebenswelt*, the medical model of the person does not have the same claim to truth, reality, and axiomaticity as does the phenomenological model of being. We can symbolize that insight by referring to page 460 and combining the two figure as follows:

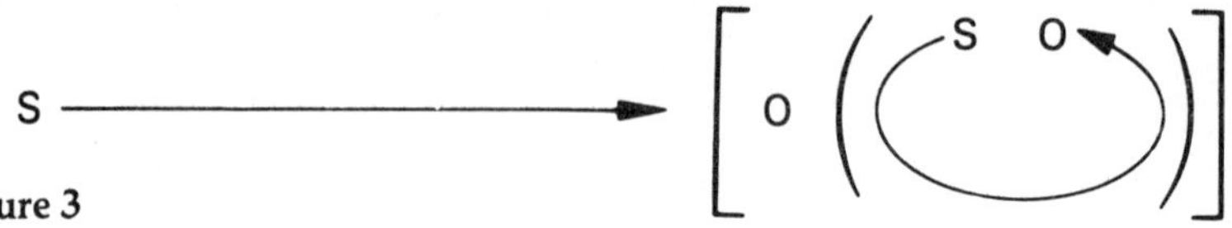

$$ S \longrightarrow \left[\; O \left(\overset{S \quad O}{\left(\bigcirc \right)} \right) \right] $$

Figure 3

The field of consciousness gives us the object directly, but the object is composite: It is an experienced front (O) to which is added a conceptual construct ($S \quad O$), which is the edifice of science. The immediate implication of the direct subject-object contact is in healing. It indicates that direct subject-object contact in bodily and emotional matters is natural, primary, and must be relentlessly explored to facilitate the control—if that is the right word—which the mind exerts over the body and its (or our) feelings.

It must be repeated that to explain certain medical phenomena in terms of this model (of direct subject-object contact) is *adequate* and it is not necessary to go beyond or elsewhere for additional or primary or more elementary explanations. The question, How can a phenomenon—specifically a psychosomatic phenomenon—be explained in terms of the medical model of the person or the ghost-in-a-machine theory of the person? becomes then, in selected cases, either peripheral, that is, additional, or even totally meaningless. We can therefore have greater confidence in the theoretical adequacy of the premises underlying holistic healing. If direct-contact healing does not seem to work then we are more likely to argue, as a result of these theoretical analyses, that our intentional technology is primitive or that we are not trying hard enough, rather than that the theory is false or inadequate.

A significant consequence of this analysis is that it should encourage rather than discourage research in unorthodox approaches to medicine. Traditional Western medicine and psychiatry—because of their reliance on the medical model of the person—find it difficult conceptually to support holistic medicine. And it is precisely because of this conflict that holistic medicine is called "unorthodox." What seems to save holistic medicine is that it, at least upon occasion, works. What phenomenology can do is to show that holistic medicine fits into the mainstream of Western thought. Finally, as a result of this shift in model, questions in medicine, experiments, research, treatment, and conception of diseases will change.

A few sketchy examples of the reorganization of our experience from a discontinuous (medical model of the person) to a continuous (phenomenological model of being) style of perception and constitution will be useful. It has been mentioned before that some of the basic concepts of physics—space, time, energy, motion, force, and illumination—derive from correlative experiences in the *Lebenswelt*. Thus, the epistemologically prior experiences or phenomena are *lived* space, *lived* time, *lived* energy, *lived* force, and *lived* illumination. We can call this *lived physics*. These lived phenomena have certain important characteristics in common: First, they are singular or unique (we cannot generalize); this gives them their *a priori* character. Second, they are both subjective and objective; they form a stream or a continuum from the so-called inner world to the outer. This property gives them their *synthetic* (in Kant's sense) character. Finally, these lived phenomena are descriptive of consciousness (*lived* consciousness, that is) which then leads us to conclude that the subject of physics is, at least in its originary or archetypal project, a transcendental study or a *transcendental science*.

Modern physics is discrete and atomistic. It is atomistic by accepting objectivism and it is discrete by accepting mathematics as its principal orientation. To this extent, *conceptual physics* borrows more than the above-mentioned categories of experience (space, time, and so forth). It also borrows the objective orientation. The combination of the two then leads to *conceptual physics*. The latter is useful for technology (that is, the manipulation of objects) but not for understanding. Conceptual physics must therefore return to the *Lebenswelt*, garner a renewed understanding and description of the phenomena of space, time, energy, force, motion, and illumination, and begin all over again the process of systematization. One recommendation is to divorce physics from its commitment to the discrete and the objective (expressed most clearly in atomism and a mathematics based on points) and marry it to the subjective and the continuous. This *physics of the soul* or the *physics of cosmic consciousness* becomes true metaphysics in the original sense of that word.

Let us explore a different issue—individuality—and see how it is affected by this type of participatory and phenomenological thinking. My-individuality is a belief system, an organizing principle. It leads to these important constructs: alienation, anxiety, objectness (the ego is constructed into an object, a point developed experimentally by Piaget in *The Construction of Reality in the Child*), responsibility, and finitude. The acts of consciousness which bring about, buttress, or at least accompany the constitution of myself as an individual are my-birth and my-death. These are inventions or heuristic concepts, because they are in principle unexperienceable. The net result of this analysis is the insight that my originary nature—at this very moment—is to be a universal consciousness-world stream and that this stream is constituting itself into an individual through the invention of the concepts of the birth and death of myself. Research in transcendental and constitutive phenomenology discloses that these passive acts of constitution are occurring at this very moment. What is more, we can achieve access to these acts—that is the purpose and the effect of the study of phenomenology and of the reductions—and reconstitute our experience. We can discover, right now, that we are making the archetypal decision for finitude and that it is this constitutive act which brings about the all-important sense of *my-individuality*.

There is, in all probability, a resemblance between the vertical experience of passive constitution of individuality now and the horizontal experience of ontogeny. We may assume that many archetypal decisions occur—that is, are solidified—during the first four years of life. We can thus hypothesize that the early development of the child corresponds to the constitution of the individual, perceptible now through an analysis of the passive transcendental constitutions which are present at this very moment in our experience of ourselves and which are revealed through a transcendental reduction.

What are the consequences of effecting a life-style which is consonant with the originary structure of being? First, when a child asks about birth his questions are not biological inquiries. He experiences the miracle and mystery of the being of consciousness and we teach him to conceptualize that question in terms of the premise that he is a biological organism and object exclusively (or at least primarily). In keeping with the principles of the existential personality theory, we must use the opportunity afforded us by the child's questions to give him or her this message: "You ask how you were born. This means you are becoming a real person, an individual. You are now truly beginning to grow up. That is wonderful and it is an occasion for celebration." The same response is indicated for the child's question about death. As he or she becomes anxious about death, the child also becomes conscious of being an individual, because *the thought of death is the thought of individuality*. The biological answers of hospitals and mortuaries, obstetrics and funerals, coitus and gerontology are not nearly as relevant to the child's question as are the philosophical answers about the constitution of the child's individuality.

A further point derives from curiosity, wonder, and anxiety. The wonder of the child (which can easily turn into apprehension or anxiety) should be interpreted in this fashion: "Becoming a person (an individual) is not something that just 'happens' to you; it is something you *make* happen and *want* or *choose* to make happen." Wonder, like anxiety, is the experience of constitution itself.

The child *chooses* to define and organize his or her experience as if he were *born* and as if he were to *die*. That is the joyous experience of the adventure of living the life of an individual. This is the message of modern religion—symbolically represented in traditional religion and mythology: God *wanted* Jesus to be born; God *wanted* Moses to be born into the palace of the Pharaoh. Jesus *wanted* death, hence he went into Jerusalem. The elements alluded to are all present here.

Now the child asks the truly overwhelming question: "What happens to me when I sleep? Where am I when I am asleep?" We are now in touch with the constitution of the self as an object. The phenomenologically given reality is that there is no gap at all from falling asleep to waking up. The moments before going to sleep are experienced as gradual deconstitutions of the archetypal decision for individuality into the deeper bliss of the universal, whereas the moments after awakening—usually very brief— are the experience of quick reconstitution of the world, a speedy rededication to the archetypal decision for finitude. These are the facts of experience disclosed by phenomenological analyses. I am not an object which perdures during sleep—rather, I experience the sequence constitution-deconstitution-reconstitution. And part of this latter reconstitution is the invention of the ego as an enduring object.

Furthermore, I am not different from others. The universe or cosmic consciousness that I am is, at least minimally, intersubjective. In constituting myself into an ego-object I also constitute others (that is, other minds) as ego-objects. These ego-objects presumably observe me while I am asleep and tell me about it—even show me photographs and electroencephalographs. In truth, however, what I experience is the consensual world: The intersubjective community "agrees," as it were, to uniform constitution of experience. I am you and you are I, and that dual or intersubjective field agrees or *consensually conspires* to constitute uniformly a world of objects. The conclusion is unavoidable: Life is a game that I choose to play seriously. There can be no reason for panic or despair—only joy, meaning, and forward movement—to those who understand this insight. The more responsibility we take for playing this game the better we will play it and the greater will be our joy in this process. We try to forget that life and individuality are games, because the more we succeed in forgetting, the more we enjoy the game—up to a point. If we forget totally then we enter a psychotic episode and despair overtakes us. We must train our children early to achieve facility in playing the game of life. We should begin by training ourselves.

Practice

The meaning of the idea of participation is clarified by exploring its application. What is the precise effect of these theoretical considerations on the practice of healing, including medicine? The answers are not very difficult. The problem lies in the establishment's resistance against implementing these ideas systematically and responsibly.

FREEDOM

In all forms of direct healing we must first recover access not only to our transcendental freedom itself—which means the experience of freedom—but also to our freedom for constitution and for cathexis. Specifically, we must learn to recover our transcendental center. This is done by first philosophically understanding the meaning of that center and then illustrating it through a variety of experiences. But the experiences are empty unless their meaning, context, and usefulness are first clarified by philosophic analysis. This process of freedom-recovery can be accomplished through many means already available and many more still to be explored and discovered. The philosophic outlines of this process involve a return, receding, or regression to the transcendental (an activity often referred to by common sense as going into the unconscious).

A philosophic approach to our transcendental freedom takes its departure from the two polarities of being. By *deconstituting* the archetypal decision for finitude we can recover the sense of universality. That is possible by operating within the framework of the individual-universal polarity. The other approach to pure consciousness is through the transcendental-phenomenological *reduction*, which gets us into the realm of ultimate inwardness and pure subjectivity. In a practical sense, philosophic understanding and intensive meditation help us achieve this access. The physiological and physical correlates of this return to the center of consciousness are incorporated in what is called the *alpha-state*. Achieving this state can be facilitated through any number of relaxation techniques, certain drugs, hypnosis, and biofeedback. The question is not whether this approach works or not, but what the most efficient techniques are to facilitate these philosophic insights.

It is important to point out that experience without understanding is inadequate. A general philosophic background is needed for the results of meditation to have meaning. Without philosophy, meditation cannot move forward and effect meaningful changes and healing. The importance of this cannot be overstressed.

Another point of major significance is that no healing occurs without access to this freedom. It is this freedom which enables us to understand our empirical nature and then to either embrace it, reject it, or change it.

SELF-TRANSCENDENCE

We must develop activities which encourage *direct* subject-object connection. We must learn to help consciousness "leap into" or "embrace" the body and its world beyond. We call this act self-transcendence. We define it as the experience of deliberately and directly connecting subject and object, consciousness and body. There are innumerable exercises that illustrate and encourage, by direct and deliberate action and through naive and innocent yet effective simplicity, the subject-object continuity, connection, and interpenetration. Screaming, jumping, laughing, dancing, and other activities which encourage bodily expressed spontaneity help bring about the sensation of joining in one experience the emprical and transcendental egos. Deliberately induced laughing is a particularly good example. It starts with shaking the body and feigning laughter. This is a purely bodily phenomenon. Gradually, consciousness or the mind-center recognizes how ridiculous this is and the laughter begins, as if it were contagious, to be initiated within. The body, which "contaminated" the mind with its laughter, is now in turn "contaminated" by the mind. We then have genuine laughter, which is the experience of consciousness taking over the body. Weeping and sobbing are parallel experiences and exercises, but less acceptable socially.

Body therapies are good examples of techniques which must be taken seriously by the medical profession not only because of their dramatic results but because they illustrate the power of a field theory of personality. These body therapies depend on a phenomenological model of being for their theoretical justification.

Perhaps the most interesting and widely applicable example of the technique of self-transcendence or of coercing directly the subject-object connection is found in humanistic athletics or philosophic or existential physical education. Physical education is not merely a series of exercises to develop muscle tone and skills. Jogging and exercising as chores are clear expressions of the belief that by forcing ourselves to do certain difficult actions we improve the inner and invisible condition of our bodies. To some extent that is of course correct. But if we approach athletics with a philosophy or see it in the context of a total world view, the results are far healthier and more pleasurable than if we operate mechanically. Swimming and skiing are two superlative examples. Fantasy work and philosophic understanding must be central features in all physical education programs. Many physical education teachers have made significant efforts in this direction.

We must see all physical education and athletics in the spirit of Herrigel's *Zen in the Art of Archery*[1] and George Leonard's *The Ultimate Athlete.*[2] We must learn to perceive physical education as a religious exercise, as the deliberate effort by our center of consciousness to throw itself blindly and with total force into every cell of the body and then move joyously forward into the world. Athletics and physical education can be understood as direct efforts to integrate subject and object, mind and body. They are deliberate attempts to establish an intentional field between subject and object. However, these physical activities do not work to our healing benefit automatically; their philosophic significance must be clearly understood.

Subject-object contact is the key to healing through participation. It can of course be established not only by the subject moving out to the object—which is the experience of self-transcendence, emergence, touching, jumping, running, screaming, and the like—but also by its converse, which is attraction, absorption, or ingestion. A total phenomenology of both methods of intentional subject-object contact is possible. By describing these we also describe methods of healing. It is important, however, to single out what may well be the two characteristics which discriminate between self-transcendence and absorption, and have to do with the sense of freedom. To self-transcend means to be an emptiness (Sartre's concept of consciousness) searching for an external (non-ego) fullness. It means to feel hungry and hollow, self-disciplined and in charge; it means to feel control; it is the sense of the ethereal. This is the experience of freedom, perhaps in its purity.

To absorb the world, on the other hand, is to be filled, to be acted upon, to appropriate, and to possess. If we view the objective as a "condensation" of the subjective—just as in relativity theory matter is a condensation of energy (after all, relativity theory is built out of the same conceptual blocks that comprise all phenomena and which have their roots in a common life-world)—then the experience or goal of consciousness or subjectivity absorbing the world is the sense of solidity. We want to be a thing; we want possessions, honors, and recognition. To be aware of these structures and their respective phenomenological descriptions and then to consciously further the pervasiveness with which they dominate our existence is the best medicine.

When we apply these insights directly to medicine proper we get such a book as *The Well Body Book*,[3] in which self-examination, mutual examination, and elementary self-diagnosis are recommended. This general procedure—which should become increasingly more refined and responsible —follows from the shift of world views here suggested.

Self-transcendence is a form of touching. In the general sense what is touched is the world. Touching is the direct and experienced subject-object contact prescribed by the intentional character of consciousness. Massage is one healing technique based in touching. Transference, in which the contact is perhaps spiritual or emotional rather than manual and thus physical, is another form of touching. The patient "touches" the person that is the therapist. Since we commonly find transference in therapy, we can reinterpret its meaning as a healing form of touching, as a lived form of the intentional field.

One type of touching to focus on is fantasy work.

CONTACT THROUGH FANTASY WORK

In massage touching we are in contact with a body; in fantasy we are in touch with iconic objects. We will discuss later the use of fantasy in the management of pain and addiction. There the emphasis in the contact-separation dialectic will be on the element of separation or distance. That technique is pain-management and addiction-management through distancing, detachment, disidentification, and dissociation. However, there is a type of fantasy work which underscores the *contact* and unification element of the subject-object dialectic which we are. Dramatic examples are attempts to heal physical conditions through fantasies. The following are interesting instances:

Consider the work of Carl Simonton, M.D. Depressed because so many of his cancer patients were dying in spite of X-radiation of the tumors, he utilized visual imagery in his treatment program. One case involved a B-52 navigator with a far-advanced malignancy of the throat. It had reached the size of a peach and was occluding the openings to the lungs and stomach. There was evidence of spread. Faced with certain death, the patient agreed to try the technique. He was taught to enter the alpha state by means of complete body relaxation. In this state, he visualized his white blood cells in the form of cowboys on horseback. The defenders were then seen attacking and destroying the cancer cells. The procedure was repeated three times daily for 15 minutes. Over a period of seven weeks the tumor receded in size and finally disappeared, leaving a normal throat mucosa. At the end of this time, he was taken back to the operating room, where biopsy specimens revealed only normal tissue.

In September of 1973, Dr. Simonton reported success in 128 cases using the combination of X-ray and visual imagery. The degree of success was proportional to the cooperative effort of the patient; Dr. Simonton's position as director of the prestigious American Cancer Society gives additional credence to his claims.[4]

My first patient . . . was a 61-year-old gentleman with very extensive throat cancer. He had lost a great deal of weight, could barely swallow his own saliva, and could eat no food. After explaining his disease and the way radiation worked, I had him relax three times a day, mentally picture his disease, his treatment, and the way his body was interacting with the treatment and the disease, so that he could better understand his disease and cooperate with what was going on. The results were truly amazing. . . . That patient is now a year and a half post-treatment, with no evidence of cancer in his throat. He also had arthritis, and he used the same mental process and eliminated that.[5]

In terms of the systemic approach to medicine or to human problems which results from taking seriously the phenomenological model of being, the direction of research and the effects achieved are no surprise. However, from the point of view of the medical model of the person, such occurrences must be evaluated as being bizarre. We ask, "How is it possible?"—a question which arises out of the instinctive need to find some indirect, obscure, and recondite model of mind-matter interaction. This interaction is conceptually impossible unless we make it the axiom, the very basis of the system itself. And that is of course what we do in phenomenology. Our evidence is simply the radically empirical and presuppositionless description of immediate experience. Certain aspects of these examples are worth identifying and isolating for the sake of accelerated future research.

For contact to work, the patient must possess the relevant and appropriate world view. It has been emphasized repeatedly that all activities and exercises, including efforts to accomplish the sense of self-transcendence, do not work well automatically; their philosophic significance, that is, their metaphysical or ontological context, must also be clearly understood. This point has something to do with faith and suggestibility. Faith means that the general world view within which the healing process occurs is accepted. The acceptance is not a surface intellectual one but is of the order in which the fish accepts the ocean and a mammal the air. The more willingly our social structure—especially the institutionalized healing arts—supports the phenomenological model of being the more faith will patients have in healing processes which follow its guidelines.

At the present time the patient has faith that if he is passive and willingly permits that prescribed and often tortuously painful procedures be carried out on him he will be healed. If the world view shifts—the medical model of the person is now three centuries behind the philosophic times—patients will have faith as well in a direct and unmediated approach rather than in the exclusively manipulative manner in which medicine and psychotherapy is often practiced. They will learn not only to appreciate but to understand that taking personal responsibility for healing and for staying healed is possible and it works; they will, above all, recognize that we frequently can approach the healing of a diseased condition directly. And they will understand in depth what is meant by *directly*.

We can then move on to specify the technologies which may bring about and intensify this direct intentional and self-transcending subject-object contact. It is hoped that by clarifying the theoretic foundations, medicine and psychotherapy can become increasingly more innovative, creative, and imaginative in developing new and holistic approaches to healing.

Criteria for Contact

What constitutes *contact* in cancer? One meaning is fantasy work. The fantasy object is the tumor and the fantasy manipulation is consciousness' effort, as in prayer, to feel itself close to the object of its anxiety. This is one inescapable aspect of contact. A second is the accuracy of the visualization. It is our hypothesis, which follows deductively from the phenomenological model of being, that the efficacy of fantasy work is directly proportional to the correctness of the physiological understanding. It appears that access to the center and to one's freedom depends heavily on understanding

—in addition to experiencing. In fact, the thought-feeling and theory-praxis controversies, for all their merits, may often be exaggerated. Clarity of thought is also an experience and a feeling. It is also true that adequacy of theory can lead imperceptibly to practical effects. The same holds with physiology.

The patient should be told in detail the surgical, chemical, and radiation procedures involved. He should also be given a maximum number of details in physiology, cytology, chemistry, and physics to achieve the best possible accuracy in his fantasies. And there is no limit to detail and accuracy. In this way we can give added reality to contact. If the patient fantasizes what actually occurs, he is indeed in closer contact with his tumor and his body's struggles than if his model were totally inaccurate. Even though the patient in the above example may have thought of cowboys and Indians, he knew what the reality of the situation actually was. Metaphor and symbol are not inaccuracies.

A third requirement for contact is the relationship with the surgeon. The person who guides the patient through fantasies must be the individual who has the closest possible access to the malignancy. In this case it is the surgeon. If a friend helps the patient with the fantasy, the actual physical contact with the malignancy is in no way as close as if the patient fantasizes directly with *the* surgeon (not *any* surgeon) who is in operative touch with the cancerous growth that is to be excised.

On the basis of these hypotheses and principles we can now develop research programs and construct experiments. This is not a proposal that philosophy replace medicine. It is a proposal that philosophic treatments be added, in selected cases, to accepted medical practice.

MEDITATION

Fantasy work connects us with the object, which is empirical; meditation connects us with the subject, which is transcendental. That is also a way of being in touch and was discussed at the beginning of this section.

Healing requires meditation. Meditation is the exploration of inner space. Inner and outer space are not as sharply different as most people think. Therefore the interpenetration of contemporary physics and research in transcendental pheonomenology is an obvious avenue for future research and analysis. We may then be ready to understand how meditation actually brings about physiological changes. Then we shall understand how consciousness contributes to producing illness as well as helps to heal it.

However, since these matters are still only at the most inchoate level of analysis and understanding, a preliminary discussion of this possibility is relegated to Appendix F.

Notes

1. Eugen Herrigel, *Zen in the Art of Archery* (New York: Pantheon, 1953).

2. George Leonard, *The Ultimate Athlete* (New York: Viking Press, 1975).

3. Mike Samuels and Hal Bennett, *The Well Body Book* (New York: Random House, 1973).

4. Irving Oyle, *The Healing Mind* (Millbrae, Calif.: Celestial Arts, 1975), p. 75-76.

5. *Ibid.*, p. 77, quoting Dr. Simonton.

Chapter 10 • PAIN AND NEED MANAGEMENT

We can further illustrate some of the dramatic consequences of shifting self-concepts and world views by discussing the philosophic management of pain and of pathological needs such as addictions. Let us concentrate on two examples: a migraine headache and the need to drink alcohol (or smoke cigarettes). Let us assume that both problems are postmedical, in that there are no discernible or manageable physiological underpinnings.

The patient must take direct and personal responsibility for handling the problem. In a ghost-in-a-machine theory of the person the problem will be solved for him. In a field-of-consciousness theory of the person he himself must solve the problem. That shift of attitude is in itself a shift from world alienation to world contact. The active, responsible, and touching or contacting person reaches out into the world; his being is truly in the world; he expresses self-transcendence in his behavior. To assume personal responsibility means to be centered, free, and in touch.

Some preliminary observations are in order. Phenomenological descriptions of pain and addiction disclose—at least as a first approximation—that these problem phenomena exist in or originate from *behind* the ego and *beyond* the body. This will tend to confirm further the accuracy of our paradigmatic diagram (see Figure 1). However, they have shown themselves to be unmanageable from the point of view of this model. The experience of the pain and the addiction must now be translated into the experience of direct contact. Let us see how this can be done.

Let us explore phenomenologically—that is describe the structure of immediate experience—what is involved in looking closely at one of our hands. We examine the experience of the stream of consciousness *from* our center (through the eyes) directly *to* the hand. The ultimate reality of this situation, according to the phenomenological method, is the direct subject-object connection exactly as given in immediate and first-person experience. Healing, to the extent that it is to follow the phenomenological model rather than the more traditional indirect and inferential procedures, must take its point of departure from this region of experience.

How do we conceptualize this particular example of a subject-object connection? The following is a rough approximation of how the medical model of the person—at best an inference and at most a Cartesian atavistic relic that is still entrenched in commonsense—visualizes, reconstructs, or constitutes what is thought to actually occur: The reality of my centered consciousness—that is, my *real* consciousness—is somehow *behind* that experience of awareness, behind what I perceive to be my consciousness. It exists in the form of glia, electric discharges, chemical reactions, and the like. We are convinced that it is these physical events which control and bring about our immediate experience of awareness and of centeredness. We are totally unaware of these physiochemical events and also feel ourselves entirely dependent on them; if they malfunction, our consciousness and with it our total being is disrupted and may even disappear. The arrow in Figure 1 which moves *in back of* the subject is thus placed there quite appropriately.

Now let us consider the hand which we are observing. Again here we have been trained, by the Cartesian encrustations in commonsense which have been transmitted to our sciences, that the reality of the hand is *beyond* it; reality is, as it were, on the *other side* of that hand. What we see is believed to be merely an appearance. The *true* hand consists of cells and blood, and complex molecules, and, in the last analysis, of electromagnetic waves. In other words, the hand is to be understood in the final analysis in subatomic terms. These in turn are completely inaccessible to direct experience. However, their reality is thought to be our very being, the very essence of our nature. We infer that whatever occurs at these micro-levels makes our hand what it is. These experientially inaccessible mocroevents make it healthy or morbid, pleasurable or painful. We have no direct control—just as we have no direct perception—over these microphenomena. Nevertheless we are wholly dependent on them for our very existence, for all our values, for all that is real and holy, meaningful and worthy. This phenomenological *beyond* is diagrammed by an arrow that reaches the object on the side away from the subject.

We now come to the connection. As experiential centers or as subject-object fields of consciousness, we are passive with respect to these obscure and scientifically inferred events. Their connection, as the diagram illustrates, is well beyond the reach of immediate experience. Let us consider once more the paradigmatic diagram:

Figure 1

The dotted line represents the only connection that we can experience. But the medical model of the person tells us that the real connection is elsewhere and thus, although crucial to our being, it is nevertheless altogether inaccessible to us. But it is precisely in that direct connection (represented by the dotted line) that reality transpires.

It may even be useful in this context to point out that many common diseases or discomforts come from *behind*, as in the case of chronic backaches, tensions in the neck, or headaches. Some come from what phenomenologically must be described as *below*, such as hemorrhoids and gastrointestinal distresses and colitis. Other conditions seem to have their origin—as described phenomenologically—*beyond* the objects in experience, as with paranoid reactions in which the world's otherness obtrudes itself on the person from a mysterious and inaccessible distance. The most apt illustration of the feeling of being totally dependent for one's being on the forces behind, below and beyond us is found in the condition of hypochondriasis.

Let us consider the issue of pain and addiction management through the use of a direct field approach as opposed to an indirect and inferred procedure.

The problem in cases of pain and need is the excessive fusion, cathexis, and identification of the transcendental ego with the emotional or psychic object (the pain and the need). The ego lives its life exclusively through the problem phenomenon, which is the pain or need. In other words, the problem is the object which, like the body, the patient uses as his means of or vehicle for his being-in-the-world. Because of this closeness, and since the closeness (or attachment, fixation, or cathexis) is the problem, the next task in the philosophic management of pain and need is to make the problem phenomenon into an object, to objectify it, rather than to continue to perceive it as an extension of the subject. The resistances against this act of disidentification are massive. An archetypal decision has been made to hold on to that phenomenon or psychic object at any cost. Even the health of the body is not too much to sacrifice for the sake of experiencing one's identity with the problem phenomenon. We can, but need not, go into its etiology to heal it. A trip to childhood clarifies a truth that can be also known without it: disidentification between subject and object (transcendental ego and pain or need in this case) is always possible—in the here and-now. We must remember that part of the problem is the fusion of the problem object with the transcendental ego. It follows that one of the primary tasks of philosophic healing is to defuse or decathect the identification.

There are many procedures which can facilitate this act of detachment. The first is to learn to describe the object, to make an image of it. The need to drink may start as a warm and supportive tingling in the neck and shoulders; it may then become a little man inside the chest, knocking in his little box, desperately demanding a drink. That may turn into the image of Mother as a vast cosmic figure screaming at the person. The client may be able to bring all of this material together into a single image or, what is more likely, end this fantasy movement with a final and representative image. This image must be described phenomenologically and understood fully. It would appear that the more extensive the description the greater our success in objectifying the problem phenomenon. A headache may be a graygreen rock or it may be a coarse and ragged marble slab. It may even be possible to draw a picture of it.

Through these exercises the problem phenomenon ceases to be *part of* the subject and becomes an experienced intentional *object to* consciousness. Through this fantasy procedure the pain or need is recognized as an effective object which is not the transcendental ego but which is given to the transcendental ego. It is distant, perceptible, knowable, and therefore manageable. The problem phenomenon is part of the empirical ego and by objectifying it we can establish a field between consciousness and that object. The sickness was in part the untoward closeness of the object to the ego. The dysfunction is a kind of consciousness of objective collapse. This analysis is simply an application of a basic philosophic and phenomenological truth. It must be clearly established that the primary truth is that we are in direct and actual touch with the headache and the need and that this direct contact is the actual and ultimate ontological situation. Any chemical inference about the fact that "in truth" the connection is a kind of dance of the electrons is inference and not datum, is secondary and not primary.

A second process which helps to objectify the problem is to *manipulate* the newly recognized object. After the object has been described and its reality and structure are thus recognized, we can start to do things with and to the object. These include giving it away, burying it, burning it, eating it, pulverizing it, and the like. This fantasy has the double effect of dislodging the affective or conceptual problem object from its fusion with the transcendental ego *and* eliminating it or transforming it completely. The problem (headache, addiction) is not really a physical condition at all. *The actual problem is the very act of fusion itself of the image with the center; it is the confusion of the pain or need with transcendental subjectivity proper.* The dysfunction is a case of excessive cathexis.

The act of separating the two and then destroying the offending object (in phenomenology we can say with justification that the pain or the addiction is a bona fide object) is the actual solution to the problem and will manifest itself in the ego's projection on its world. Success is directly proportional to the cooperation of the subject, that is, to the intensity with which and the depth at which this exercise is carried out. The exercise is difficult because it means taking charge of one's life. But that is precisely the key to all psychosomatic medicine. This exercise is also difficult because the resistances against it are powerful. They are related to the archetypal decision for finitude, which is not easily undone. It cannot be partially and selectively deconstituted. The difficulty of the exercise for the client is commensurate with the energy invested in the fusion or cathexis.

A question remains: What is the relation between the image of the headache and the so-called "real" headache? For one, we can experience the object (headache) as a concretization of consciousness. Rather than argue that this object is a symbol, the evidence suggests that it is indeed the reality. For example, I have a headache on both sides of my head. I do a phenomenological description of each side and draw two pictures, perhaps with crayons. These objects (let us say rocks) are then the real headaches; they are what the headache presentation looks like and feels like. These rocks are the given headache, the life-world foundation of the headache. All we need is accuracy in the phenomenological description. Visual imagery may not be enough. Now a consciousness-object equivalency principle (the life-world correlate of e = mc²) can be invoked. The act of consciousness is to force the two rocks into each other and, as long as we keep the hands that support the two rocks together, the headache may actually disappear. If it does not we have not established the proper epoche, reduction, decathexis, detachment, or disengagement from the headache in the first place, so that the object on which we operated was not the one we intended.

We can trace the nature or structure of the archetypal decision (passive constitution) of the headache by using the pervasive Freudian or psycho-analytic device to shock people into taking responsbility for their uncon-scious: We will interpret the headache authoritatively as an unconscious wish. It is an act of self-destruction, self-punishment, self-interference with meaning or success; it is protection against a greater danger. We will then operate not on the headache directly but on the deeper passive consti-tutions for which the headache is but the tip of the iceberg. We then experi-ence the conflict—alluded to earlier—between attachment and detachment. This conflict expresses the dialectical structure of consciousness itself from which, in this instance, we have not yet detached ourselves.

Another exercise in pain-management consists of reconstituting the meaning and value of the problem object. A headache, as pure phenomeno-logical presentation, is axiologically neutral: it is neither bad nor good, desirable nor undesirable; it is even neither painful nor pleasurable. These value ascriptions are in fact freely chosen interpretations. However, they are deep-seated, that is, originary and archetypal, and it takes an act of gargantuan free will to transform these constitutions and these assigned meanings. If the meaning we ascribe to the pain or the addiction is good, desirable, or pleasant, we have chosen to identify with it, to fuse with it. If, on the other hand, we choose to give it a bad, undesirable, or painful meaning we have chosen to reject it. The experience of pain is a conflict between the two; we choose to identify with the experience but reject it at the same time.

We can reconstitute the meaning of the problem phenomenon. We can interpret the pain as pleasure or as desirable, so that we welcome it and not reject it. The pain then becomes bearable. We can of course also interpret the pain as indifferent. The pure phenomenological givenness remains the same; our interpretation as ugly and undesirable vanishes. We no longer object to the pain any more than we would object to any other event in our lives to which we could be indifferent.

Diets benefit from this analysis: we can redefine (or reconstitute) the meanings of food and eating. If we define eating as filling the vacuum that is our pure conscious center with the world's objectivities, then we can perceive fasting as the meaningful and sanctified development of self-consciousness and eating as the meaningless and profane denigration of the center of consciousness that we are.

The situation becomes a bit more complex with addictions because of the withdrawal symptoms they produce. We must now interpret the presence of the withdrawal symptoms (as we would the hunger while dieting) as proof of our character and integrity. It is proof of our growth, our acquisition of meaning, and our destiny. Removing the withdrawal symptom—which can be done by taking a drink or indulging in another cigarette—would take with it proof of strength and pride in authenticity. This is not to say that we will now become addicted to the withdrawal symptoms (or the hunger, in diets) because once they disappear without the drug we know our character and integrity have triumphed: We have had the magnificent experience of seeing our freedom for reconstitution and recathexis victorious by finding confirmation in the world.

Again here we must recognize that whatever difficulties we have in redefining, reassigning meanings to, or reinterpreting the value of the problem phenomenon reflects our medical and psychological conflicts. Pain and addiction are, in philosophical terms, the excessive (even total) fusion of the transcendental ego with the specific psychic object in question. Discomfort, dissatisfaction, and even anxiety are the experiences of this fusion and express the need for subject-object separation. In those locations where the transcendental ego is fused with an object it is also vulnerable—as in castration anxiety. In fact, hypochondriasis in general or any specific phobia—like fear of cancer, acne, menopause, heart attack, senility, or impotence—can be attributed to excessive fusion between the transcendental ego and the specific bodily organs or functions involved. The vulnerability stems from the contingency of the object with which consciousness is fused and stands in sharp contrast to the indestructibility of the pure conscious center itself (a fact obscured by the fusion). The fusion may also be with objects or events external to the body—like a business, a jewel, a job, a degree, or one's reputation. The conquest over this sense of vulnerability lies in detachment, decathexis, epoche, or reduction, since in this way the center recovers the security of its indestructibility.

Any difficulties we may have in objectifying these fused objects and any problems which arise in our fantasy work represent the experience of resistance against healing that is the exact source of the illness. This phenomenologically given complex, that is, the experience of resistance against decathexis and deconstitution *is the disease itself*. It is not a symbol; it is not a manifestation, nor is it a surrogate. We are in direct touch here with the disease proper, and we can therefore deal with it directly as well. In terms of the medical model of the person or the ghost-in-a-machine theory of the person such an approach to healing makes little sense. But in the context of a phenomenological theory of the intentionality of consciousness, that is, in terms of the phenomenological model of being or the field-of-consciousness theory of the person, such an approach—in conjunction with traditional medicine—is perfectly legitimate and is an obvious suggestion. Such theoretical confirmation of holistic medicine can insure us that the direction may well be correct but that it is a deficiency in the theoretical model (at the present time mostly nonexistent) which prevents more imaginative and effective research, diagnosis, and treatment programs.

An important part of the healing process is the deep-down and thoroughly integrated acceptance of the philosophic world view in terms of which it is to be understood. This condition categorically does not exist in our culture. We must recall that the claim for acceptance of the phenomenological model of being is based on epistemological considerations and not on pragmatic, practical, or utilitarian implications. When we then find that this world view does have therapeutically beneficial implications, we find ourselves in a highly advantageous position. From the perspective of the phenomenological model of being, holistic medicine is an a priori science. It must work by virtue of the nature of being. If it does not work it is not the fault of erroneous theory but of incomplete or underdeveloped theory. Furthermore, the theory is more likely to work when patient, therapist, physician, hospital, and the culture in general operate on the premises of the phenomenological model of being rather than on the ghost-in-a-machine personality theory. Failures in holistic medicine are now due to inadequate theoretical work and insufficient theoretical support. We need a phenomenological model of being to suggest to us new directions for research.

A third technology for objectifying problem phenomena is to dialogue with them. We now ascribe life—or at least a voice—to the objectified problem phenomenon and in this way consolidate even further its objective, distant, and detached status. It now becomes not only an iconic or affective object, or perhaps a physical object, but it also becomes an other-mind object. Whereas up to this point the phenomenon has been a mere inanimate object, now, as we communicate with it and talk to it we establish a dialectical relation with it and a genuine field between it and us appears. We ascribe to it the reality of another living, free, and conscious center.

A dialogue with a pain or an addiction can be established by taking a piece of paper, dividing it vertically into two columns, and heading the first "pain" or "addiction" and the second "me." We then ask the pain such questions as, "What do you want from me?" "Why did you cause my illness?" "What are you trying to tell me?" "Are you mad at me?" "Are you helping me in any way?" "Are you protecting and supporting me?" "Do you think I am dependent on you?" "Is there someone else, standing behind you, for whom you are the spokesman?" It is then relatively easy to respond to the pain, addiction, and withdrawal symptom with either anger, acceptance, or insight, with reconstitution and recathexis. This exercise helps the client recognize the reality, independence, and otherness of the problem phenomenon. It produces subject-object detachment; it leads to an understanding of the phenomenological model of being; it helps establish the control of reconstitution with respect to the problem object. All these are healing experiences.

Talking to the pain or the addiction *forces* a field perspective on us. We can actually destroy or overcome the fused medical model of the person and establish in its place the disidentification of the phenomenological model. In the medical model of the person, which is a purely empiricist metaphysics, only the object exists. In the phenomenological model of being, we establish a subject-object field. We thus establish *direct* subject-object contact, since when the object is too close to the subject (which is the source of the problem, the anxiety, and the pain) we cannot really talk about a subject-object field, contact, or being in touch. You cannot observe the entomological nuances of the little insect that is stuck in your eye.

By performing these fundamental deconstitutive and reconstitutive acts on the problem phenomenon we assume responsiblity for the entire situation—its philosophic structuring as well as its manipulation into health. We respect the independent otherness of the pain and we recognize our interdependence on it, for to recognize accurately the Other is to understand another basic aspect of the structure of the field of consciousness-being.

There is little question that the effectiveness of these procedures depends on how imaginative and committed is our technology and procedure. As the phenomenological model of being becomes more and more the prevailing view, such new approaches to medicine and psychotherapy will be more acceptable to patient and physician alike and will, as a result, in all likelihood increase in effectiveness.

Peroration

We can exert *direct* control over the structure, focus, or organizational characteristics and meanings of our field of consciousness. That is one fundamental answer to mental and physical health, to meaning, and to the moral life. The bipolar view of existence maps out an area for us within which we can deliberately and freely move our consciousness to achieve basic differences of experience, of personality structure, and of life-styles. The analysis of anxiety presents us with another program on how to explore our field of consciousness, on what direction our consciousness is to take. The analyses of psychopathology, from neurosis to schizophrenia, and the analysis of participation as a form of healing again show us that we can approach the question of living well through direct maneuvers on structuring the stream of consciousness.

In other words, fundamental philosophic and psychological issues are the result of the functioning of the field of consciousness. The basic structure of that field must be understood. Each Book of this work develops one basic form of structuring consciousness: the bipolar personality theory (Book One), the analysis of anxiety (Book Two), and the meaning of psychopathology and of healing (Book Three). We now recognize that we have power and control over the structure of that field through direct action of our transcendental freedom. Therefore, we must develop consciousness-structuring exercises—like eye exercises—to strengthen our consciousness, to make it flexible. Let us say consciousness is an organ or a skill—it would then indeed be the basic organ or skill of existence—and this organ needs exercise, practice, and skill development. If we understand the material in this work we can devise ways of training and exercising our consciousness: We can move it around in the bipolar areas; we can enter the depth of inwardness in the exploration of anxiety; we can make the deliberate effort to connect subject and object in an intentional field (or sever this connection, for that matter). All we need is the imagination of teachers.

Specific suggestions are these:

Do all your living as an exercise in the organization of consciousness (transcendental constitution of consciousness).

Develop a *mantra*—or a *set of mantras*—which will remind you throughout all your activities—of the specific orientation you wish your consciousness to take.

You may, by way of example, focus on the fact that "reality is the individual" and make an effort to always see the individual aspect of any experience in isolation from its environment—be it a flower, a speck of dust, a thought, a person, or a business transaction. Or use as your mantra "reality is the object" or "reality is objective." You may then program your every experience and your total life-style to focus on or emphasize the object in experience. You *touch* what is before you; you *identify* with objects you see; you *feel* the solidity of the ground on which you walk; you make material things your meanings, values, and goals.

There are three levels at which exercises can be developed: *ideation* (visualization, altered states of consciousness); *activity* (touch, such as massage; art, including touch-arts like sculpture; and sports); and *life-styling* (integration into the total plan of one's existence). Ideation and activity must be performed as spiritual exercises, since their purpose is to restructure consciousness.

These exercises for transcendental reconstitution correspond to the three approaches to full philosophic comprehension: understanding, experiencing, and integration.

Appendices

Succinct summary statements of some of the cardinal points discussed in *The New Image of the Person* are covered in Appendices A-H.

Appendix A lists the essential points about death and immortality. Appendix B organizes the notion of the constitution of the individual. Appendix C outlines the uses of clinical philosophy in moral education. Appendix D summarizes the discussion about anxiety in Book Two. Appendix E is the Master Table, reproduced from *Managing Anxiety*, which is a comprehensive statement of the total existential-phenomenological position as it applies to therapy. Appendix F suggests some thoughts requiring further exploration on the relation between modern physics and the phenomenological model of being. Appendix G is a paper which extracts the essence of *The New Image of the Person* and which was read before the Philosophy Department at Harvard University on May 2, 1977. Finally, Appendix H summarizes the high points in the practice of clinical philosophy.

APPENDIX A • A Bill of Rights on Death: Twenty Philosophic Points

The following material was prepared for a meeting of the American Public Health Association on June 16, 1976, in San Francisco. It is an attempt to use philosophic insight for the management of death anxiety and to deal with the issue of the right to decide about one's own death.

1. The ultimate decision-making unit is the individual person. A consistent democracy demands that each person have unquestioned jurisdiction over his or her life.

2. Death education (DE) must become an aspect of education on a level with the "three Rs," with political education (civics), sex education, and self-esteem education (that is, consciousness-raising training). The law must provide for this expanded form of education by facilitating rather than obstructing DE.

3. As part of DE each person needs to create his or her own *individualized* and unique *death script* or death game plan (IDS).

4. Sample IDSs are:

   a. Traditional: Take no responsibility for your death. Let nature take its course and use any and all mechanical devices known to prolong life.

   b. Release physician and insist no artificial life-support methods be used.

   c. Commit suicide intelligently (perhaps as part of a pact) when senile or suffering needlessly. This decision assures death with dignity. The legal structure must be used only to protect the thoughtless, the immature, and the ignorant.

5. Through the IDS the person learns the meaning of death in his or her very own life. *To understand the meaning of death is also to understand the meaning of life.*

6. To work out one's IDS is a matter of the utmost importance, in line with confirmation, wedding, divorce, childbirth, wills, and funerals. One's IDS requires also the same amount of thought, reflection, devotion, and concern as do the other rites of passage.

7. *One's IDS must be worked out early in life*—continuously, thoughtfully, and carefully. Death education must therefore be explored at home, in school, in church or synagogue, even in the Boy Scout Handbook (right next to sex education), and in patients' contacts with the healing professions.

8. These important issues cannot be settled at the last moment. Each person must prepare early in life for his or her death, because *only then can there be fulfillment*

in life. A nation cannot protect itself against enemy attack after an invasion has begun. Preparedness for death starts at birth.

9. The result of early, personalized, extensive, and free discussion of and preparation for one's IDS—as part of one's education for death—leads to *maturity,* to *meaning,* and to *courage.*

10. The decision to accept, confront, and face death—and to have a plan for it—is equivalent to the decision to grow up and the resolute determination to become an individual. In the process of deciding one's IDS, one also takes full personal responsibility for one's life.

11. Legal constraints should be limited to guaranteeing the freedom of the individual and to providing opportunities for intelligent and informed IDS counseling. We should explore the possibility of even a responsible "Hemlock" society.

12. Nothing said here contradicts anyone's religious or ethical scruples. Each person is free to endorse his or her own religious or naturalistic views—but these cannot be imposed on others, especially not by law.

13. Our fear of death is vastly exaggerated. We fear death for lack of study, because of ignorance, and because of bad philosophy.

14. We are not by nature isolated individuals, nor are we born as isolated individuals. The consciousness of a child is a cosmic consciousness and a nature consciousness: The child experiences itself as one with a universal consciousness and as one with his or her environment (which we call nature or the biosphere).

15. However, the child *learns* to think of itself as an ego. The ego, as such disparate thinkers like Sigmund Freud and Alan Watts have held, is an invention. It may be our most important invention, but it is an invention nevertheless.

16. Our consciousness is *continuous* with cosmic consciousness; as William James has pointed out, inner space is continuous with outer space—just examine both spaces and see for yourself. The same is true of our bodies, which are *continuous* with the entire biosphere—and even beyond.

17. As permanent members and participants in the universe, *we are as indestructible as the universe itself.* The beliefs in personal immortality and individual reincarnation are important myths to live by: they are metaphors for the profound insight—which can be a direct experience—of the indestructibility of our innermost consciousness.

18. Our inner consciousness does not die; it is forever in the same sense that the atoms in our body have been and will be in the universe for an eternity. These truths are the source of our ultimate security, our strength, our confidence, and our peace of mind.

19. Life is our most important game. And the basic rule for playing the game of life is to choose to die. If you want to play with gusto then you will also want to choose your death with courage. Nietzsche wrote, "Many die too late, and some die too early. Yet strange sounds the precept: 'Die at the right time!' Die at the right time: so teaches Zarathustra." *That is the meaning of taking responsibility for being yourself.*

20. If these principles are taught early and explored over a lifetime, then death need never again be a problem . . . to individuals or to society, medically or legally.

APPENDIX B • Twenty Steps Toward Individuality

The following is a summary of the issue of constituting individuality, a theme which, as has been stated repeatedly, lies at the very foundation of the primary tasks of psychotherapy: the creation of an authentic individual. The essential meaning of these steps is to clarify at least one absolutely crucial issue in psychotherapy, and that is the meaning of the phrase "I take full responsibility for being myself." It is important to devise a simple and accessible formulation of the essential points in the construction of the sense of individual identity and in assessing its meanings and implications. The following list is an attempt to accomplish that goal.

1. Meditate on each item.

2. Applying the four characteristics of the phenomenological method reveals that (that is, there is evidence for the fact that):

3. I am or participate in a universal consciousness-world field.

4. It follows that I am continuous with all other consciousnesses, just as all objects are continuous with each other.

Continuous means (a) there is a uninterrupted field of molecules from object to object, that is, including air; (b) that the world (the empirical realm of objects or objectivity) appears to the observer to be on a screen (painters know this) and (c) that there is visible space connecting or relating objects to each other.

In one sense, one's consciousness is clearly *not* continuous with another's. However, we must (a) emphasize those aspects of human interactions (which include not only the meeting of actual persons but also such phenomena as "meeting the person that is or was Plato in reading his dialogues") in which continuity and unity are experientially present, (b) intensify and greatly expand and study those experiences which present themselves to us as consciousness-expanding phenomena, and we must (c) recognize that viewing the world from the perspective of what Husserl called "transcendental intersubjectivity" is a permanently possible point of view. It is possible, legitimate, and easy—at any time—to perceive the world from the perspective of conscious continuity. The world perceived is the same; only the perspective is different.

5. Discrete (atomic) objects—as both concepts and perceptions—are not given in immediate experience but are constructed (constituted) out of the continuum of subjective and objective being.

If we wish to understand individuality, we must postulate the primacy of the perspective of universality. If we wish to understand light, we begin by explaining darkness. However, if we wish to understand the sense of mystical universality, then we must postulate the primacy of the atomic perspective. Such a prescription follows from the basic tenets of the dialectic of the bipolar personality theory.

6. The objects I construct or intend include the belief in the independent and continuous existence of my empirical ego and the egos of others in a public or consensual world.

7. One of the most important of all acts of conscious constitution of objects is the constitution of the empirical ego. This is the creation of the sense of *my* individuality. The exploration of the structure and dynamics of this constitutive act may well be the single most important contribution of philosophy to medicine and psychotherapy.

8. The sense of individuality is constituted with or through the inventions of the concepts or constructs of my-birth and my-death (which are not the same as the birth-and-death-of-others) as ideas or myths by which we live.

9. Wonder (mystery) and anxiety are the awareness that in the last analysis I freely want and choose to perceive myself in the here-and-now as an individual.

10. That choice is the "archetypal decision for finitude." It is a *passive constitution* (unconscious)—we discover that it is operative at the present moment—that can become *active* (conscious)—we can make the decision deliberately; we can also unmake it. In any event, we are conscious of the fact that we take full responsibility for it.

11. The effects of performing this archetypal decision for finitude are (a) a powerful experience of alienation, (b) a feeling of objectness (of being an object, that is, the ego), and (c) an intense sense of personal responsibility.

12. The adjunct decisions to the archetypal decision for finitude that define the civilized and humane person are these: (a) a decision for personal identity (individuality); (b) the decision to experience myself as being a body, that is, the decision for embodiment (to explore the constitution of the body-qua-mine is a major and undone task of phenomenological philosophy); (c) a decision for the scientific outlook (atomism and inference); (d) a decision for life affirmation; (e) a decision for rationality, realism, and common sense; (f) a decision for morality and ethical behavior; (g) a decision for sexual and other role identifications; and (h) a decision for fundamental character structures and defenses, concepts crucial to successful reconstructive psychotherapy.

13. *Life as we know it is a game.* The archetypal decisions are *the rules*—all of which can be broken and all of which *are in effect not because they are ture or absolute but by virtue of continuous and free decisions.*

14. As is true of all games, the more we forget the game character of life the more we enjoy the playing.

15. However, *total* forgetfulness (that is, complete and irreversible cathexis) is the psychotic and animal-like complete and exclusive fixation on the empirical and objective region of bipolar being.

16. The object of the game—that is, how we define winning— is what we call the meaning of life. It consists of an authentic goal—which is philosophic self-disclosure—and of a game goal—which each person chooses for himself.

17. Intentionality means, in epistemology, (a) self-transcendence (participation) and absorption (ingestion), in short, a bidirectional ego-world contact; and (b) object-creation, meaning ascription.

18. We must practice intentionality. All of its aspects are essential to health. The archetypal decision for finitude is one form of object-creation.

19. To remake daily and continually the archetypal decision for finitude *and* the decision for intentional participation are the two legs on which stands all mental and physical fulfillment.

20. All our actions must express the two aspects of intentionality. Then we are mentally, physically, socially, educationally, and economically healthy.

A few additional items, not crucial to this list, should be mentioned:

21. The basic characteristics of the field are *space and time* (lived and not conceptual, both external *and* internal), which are the components of movement, life, libido, and process, as well as *energy* (which includes heat, electricity, force, and power), and *illumination* and *intentionality* (the capacity to organize meanings and objects out of the continuous reality that is the flow of being and the ability to be in touch with self, others, and the world).

22. Ignoring points 5 and 6, which is common, leads to most of the misunderstandings of the radicalness of the phenomenological model of being.

23. The study of the outer and the inner worlds coincides in the combined study of physics and consciousness.

24. We are both the inner and the outer manifestations of consciousness (that is, inner and outer objects).

25. Dreams as concepts (since they are by definition not experiences, not self-conscious) remind us of the game nature of life (those who do not dream cannot understand the subject-object, transcendental-ego-empirical-ego distinctions and go crazy).

26. These points must be taught to children and exhibited in the lives of adults.

27. Life, education, and therapy consist of exercises to constantly understand, experience, and apply these insights and rules.

APPENDIX C • Moral Education As an Answer to Crime

Part One. Crime

The following is an outline for analyzing crime and coping with it through moral education.

I. The Problem
  A. Statistics
  B. The Effects of Crime
    1. The deterioration of the quality of life.
    2. It is obvious and evident all day and night: we find it in fear, in sirens, and news accounts as well as in personal experiences.
    3. Examples:
      a. Air and water are *polluted* by individual and corporate irresponsibility. The world's most beautiful valleys ("How green was my valley!") are now ugly and their surrounding mountains mostly invisible.
      b. *Driving* is a constant confrontation with selfishness, aggression, inconsiderateness, contempt for life itself, and a blatant disregard for the common good.
      c. *Walking* has become nearly impossible for many. The love of and contact with nature (especially in our parks), with the stars at night, and with the history of our cities—rights even animals enjoy—are no longer ours.
      d. The sense of *homelessness* is widespread. There is anxiety in the home; there is fear of breakins, shootings, assaults, vandalism, and bombs. Most homes in our large cities now have iron gates and multiple locks.
        Please imagine the horrible fate of the elderly in the inner cities, where bands of young muggers roam like wolves waiting for them to cash their Social Security checks.
  C. Types of Crime
    These are not absolute distinctions, but they are interwoven. Each responds in its own way to philosophic education.
    1. Crimes of *passion*, due to loss of impulse control: 80% of murders (homicides) and aggravated assaults are of this type. The defense is temporary insanity.

2. Crime as an *occupation* or a way of life: muggings, theft, robbery, hold-ups, bank robbery, embezzlement; organized crime.

3. Crimes of *sadism*: child and wife battering; sexual abuse; crime for its own sake; random shootings; vandalism; "unnecessary" cruelty in the commission of other crimes.

These are sadly pervasive. They are the bizarre crimes, which make spectacular headlines, such as the Manson and Zebra murders.

4. *Terrorism* or crime as a political instrument: These crimes lead to statements such as "Today's terrorist is tomorrow's diplomat."

5. *Brainwashing* crimes: These are mind-rapes and should be legally included with physical rapes. The obvious examples are Patti Hearst and the so-called Moonies.

D. The Dangers of Complacency

There is great danger that we will continue on the path of increased adjustment to this deterioration of life—as if it were natural—and of complacency about crime.

Complacency and adjustment are *immoral*—like spitting in the face of God (that is, "I have contempt for the crowning glory of creation and evolution: a human being")—and *unnecessary*. There is real hope because there are workable answers.

II. The Causes

A. The philosophic causes of crime are in addition to the usual comments: poverty, racism, drugs, corruption in government. The philosophic causes are the underlying ones. They must and can be solved.

B. Contemporary problems expressed by crime are natural historical developments: the increase in *freedom* and the *death* of the world.

C. The development of FREEDOM is inevitable, in history and in evolution. Freedom is a value, but alienation is its side effect.

1. Freedom led to the *creation of the United States of America,* the writing of the Declaration of Independence, the Constitution, the Bill of Rights, and the Emancipation Declaration.

2. Freedom has led to (and continues to lead to) the *proliferation of world views* and self-concepts.

3. This is exemplified by the nationwide and worldwide political, social, sexual, religious, ethnic, and national liberation movements.

4. Freedom leads to *alienation*—people seem strangers to each other. It destroys the sense of common origin *and* destiny that characterizes a harmonious people: it destroys the sense of unifying myths about past and future. It eliminates a common ethnicity and tradition.

5. Freedom leads to the *discovery* (and subsequent dangerous experimentation with it) *that* to be free (which is a higher-level morality) means also *to be able to choose evil.* A modernized concept of evil must be reintroduced as a principle explaining human behavior.

D. Crime is a reaction to some depressing news: The world is dying or the forthcoming DEATH of the world.

1. C.G. Jung and A. Maslow—among many—have told us that health requires a sense of *eternity,* of the oceanic.

2. But the world is *dying*. The world is finally experiencing its imminent death in a series of convulsive spasms unprecedented in history: World wars, genocide, nuclear holocaust, population explosion, air and water pollution, the permanent dissipation of energy, and the irrevocable depletion of natural resources. Moreover, the communications explosion overloads the nervous system to the point of psychosis.

3. That there is and was *no life on Mars* dashes our hopes that life is prolific or common in the universe. Our fragile biosphere may contain the only life there is. Beyond that,

4. *The solar system* is not eternal. It *will end*, although not for a very very long time (6 to 10 billion years).

5. The *loss of a future* is the loss of hope, of strength, and of purpose in life. The death of the world leads to the hopelessness of despair, depression, anger, and alienation.

III. A Solution

Recognize that the anxiety of our age represents a transition, a birth, from ignorance and misuse of freedom and death to wisdom and integration of these two important historical and philosophic realities.

Specifically,

A. Teach philosophy—in the schools, through the media, through counselors, health professionals, lawyers, and administration of justice personnel. Why?

B. There are a number of important philosophic facts. To most of us they are not new. But there is real danger that an increasing population has never been informed of them.

C. These facts are rooted and compiled in a New Philosophic Image of the Person (clinical philosophy). They can be taught and applied.

D. We can therefore teach a higher-level morality, a morality which can be taught in the schools without violating individual rights or sensitivities.

E. A higher-level morality

1. Does not force but gives facts, does not threaten but informs, moves from external and imposed controls to internal and self-chosen controls. Example:

a. Lower, narrow, forced morality: "Do not bully Mike! If you do, the principal (or parent or big brother) will beat you up or God will punish you in hell!" This is morality through fear and terror.

b. Higher, factual morality: It states a fact and does not issue a command. "You are a freedom who makes the decision to respect a human being or who makes the decision not to respect a human being. You are personally accountable for all the consequences of your decision."

2. Furthermore, a lower-level morality *orders* specific, detailed, and narrow *rules*, such as:

"Children must be seen but not heard; therefore, don't talk so much."

"Children must sit still in school; therefore, don't move."

"Adultery is forbidden."

"Divorce is a mistake."

"Homosexuality is an illness."

"Boys must be strong: they don't cry."

But a higher-level morality *discovers* and reports the most general and pervasive philosophic *facts*, such as:

"Life is ambiguous."

"You are a freedom, a decision-maker, who is also fully responsible for the choices you make."

"Other persons, like you, are sacred, silent, and solitary centers, inwardnesses and subjectivities."

"Death defines life."

"Eternity and meaning are necessary for life."

3. In practice this means:

    a. Do *not* say, "Marriage is right and living together is wrong; therefore you are commanded not to live together without marriage."

    Do say, "It is a discovered general and universal fact that fulfilling human relationships are based on (i) reverence for inwardness, (ii) an understanding of the nature of intimacy, (iii) an appreciation of the value of honesty, (iv) free and responsible choices and commitments, and (v) the independence and maturity of the partners."

    These are facts (philosophic facts), not orders.

    b. Do *not* say, "Abortion is wrong, therefore you are ordered not to have one."

    Do say, "You are a freedom who will personally make the decision of whether a fetus is a bona fide human being or not. And you take full personal responsibility for the divergence of world views, metaphysics, and theologies implied by your act."

    These are philosophic facts, not commands.

4. Narrow ordered rules violate the First Amendment.

    General discovered facts are in harmony with the First Amendment.

5. The higher-level morality works statistically. People do not need orders, only information.

Part Two. Protocols for a Teacher's Manual in Moral Education

Each item is carefully phrased. Think about it, visualize it, and meditate upon it.

I. Philosophic *democracy* facts: The teaching of these facts will help insure the preservation (or reestablishment) of a democratic society.

  A. 1. Free will is a fact of human nature.

     2. Total personal responsibility is also a fact of human nature.

     3. The personality structures, life-styles, and sociopolitical institutions which manifest in themselves, which facilitate, and which protect the dual facts of freedom and responsibility are therefore natural—in that they are in keeping with the nature of the person—and healthy.

     On the other hand, the personality structures, life-styles, and sociopolitical institutions which interfere with, destroy, or deny the dual facts of freedom and responsibility are unnatural, sick, morbid, and pathological.

B. It is a fact that every person is a unique individual identity. The personality structures, life-styles, and sociopolitical institutions which respect, exhibit, and guarantee the integrity of each unique individual identity are therefore natural and healthy.

On the other hand, the personality structures, life-styles and sociopolitical institutions which disregard, deny, or obstruct the integrity of each unique individual identity are unnatural and sick.

C. It is a fact that each inward subjective conscious center is holy, worthy, and dignified. He who does not see this is blind to consciousness.

The personality structures, life-styles, and sociopolitical institutions which exhibit reverence for and assume protection of these inward, subjective, and conscious centers are natural and healthy.

The personality structures, life-styles, and sociopolitical institutions which manifest disrespect, ignorance, or destruction toward these inward, subjective, and conscious centers are unnatural and sick.

Recognition of this fact is evidenced in reverence for inwardness and for life, and in *responsible* and *considerate* behavior at all levels of human interaction.

He who does not revere consciousness and life, and who is irresponsible and inconsiderate, is one who is ignorant of the nature of human consciousness. The sanctity of consciousness is a directly observable fact, as is the color of one's hair.

D. It is a fact that truth (as openness, self-disclosure, and illumination) is the foundation of all that is human—as well as all which is nature and divinity.

Truth is the goal of education, of science, and of the arts—as well as of journalism and authentic politics.

II. Philosophic *morality* facts: The teaching of these facts will help reestablish a moral order in society.

A. It is a fact that you choose continuously between reason and unreason.

It is also a fact that you are personally responsible for all of the consequences of that choice, because you are your future, which is the fruit of your decisions and actions.

The consequences of the choice between reason and unreason are that you choose yourself either as a member of the human race or as not a member of the human race, as a participant in civilized society or as not a participant in —but as a pariah of—civilized society.

It is here our parents and teachers, as well as health and administration of justice professionals, have their most sacred obligations.

B. It is a fact that you choose continuously whether to affirm life or whether to deny life. This is the choice between success and depression, between joy and failure.

It is also a fact that you are personally and fully responsible for the consequences of the choice between life-affirmation and life-denial.

Example: The life of a criminal is a choice of life denial. If he is to be rehabilitated, he (and no one else) must make a decision for affirming life. No therapist can do that *for* him, only *with* him.

C. It is a fact that you choose honesty toward self and others or dishonesty toward self and others.

Which way have you chosen?

III. Philosophic *health* facts (a new definition of health):

A. You are physically, mentally, and socially healthy if you have taken personal charge to see that the following five psychological traits are fully integrated into your life.

B. You are physically, mentally, and socially unhealthy (sick) to the precise extent that any or all of these five psychological traits are *not* integrated into your life.

C. The way you choose is entirely up to you. This fact of choice gives you both pain and joy, both anxiety and hope.

D. The five psychological traits:

1. Freedom, responsibility, and self-reliance.
2. Integrity, worth, and a sense of identity.
3. Creativity, growth, and meaning.
4. Intimacy, commitment, and caring.
5. Eternity, a sense of the oceanic (immortality), and peace.

E. Teachers, health practitioners, counselors, and the like need philosophic background to understand the full measure of these ideas.

IV. Philosophic *sanity* facts (a new definition of sanity).

A. It is a fact that to be human is to be able *both* to participate, get involved, and identify with your emotions and your actions (for example, to make commitments and to experience spontaneous joy, but also to experience overwhelming anger) *and*—which is equally if not more important—to *reflect* on them, and detach, distance, and disidentify yourself from them.

B. The capacity for distancing is traditionally called rational reflection.

C. Human beings are born with the capacity for rational reflection; animals are not.

D. You *choose* to give up the distinctly human capacity for reflection; it does not disappear of its own accord. When you lose it you lose the right to call yourself human.

E. To choose to give up your capacity for reflection is to choose to become psychotic.

F. Know the warning signals: a history of irascibility, the sudden appearance of violent impulses, extraordinary stresses, even hallucinations and gradual disorganization of your world. It is your responsibility to own up to these signals and to take the necessary preventive health measures.

G. Remember that 80% of homicides are committed by persons who have temporarily given up their capacity for reflection. The legal term is temporary insanity. It is a legal defense; but it is neither a psychiatric defense nor a philosophic defense.

If you know this occurs, you could have seen it gradually develop and have taken steps to protect others and yourself.

H. Any and every loss of impulse control is your decision to choose not to take responsibility for preserving at all times your capacity for reflection; this includes the use of drugs and intoxicants.

V. Philosophic *reality* facts (a new definition of reality):

  A. It is a fact that you are a conscious, inward, and subjective center, and a body, but it is also a fact that you exist confronted at all times with a legitimate, hard, impenetrable, and inviolable external reality.

  B. This hard and unconquerable reality (which is exactly as real as you are, perhaps even more so) consists of:

   1. *Other* conscious, inward, and subjective centers.
   2. Their freedoms, values, and needs.
   3. The consequences, in the world, of all your actions.
   4. The demands of society, including laws (just or not).
   5. The laws of nature: birth, death, health, the need for shelter and for food.

  C. Society cannot be flexible nor can it compromise with essential human values.

  D. Your decision not to perceive at all times this external reality is your choice to exist with delusions and hallucinations.

  E. In sum, it is a fact that you choose continuously whether to acknowledge reality or whether to live in fantasy.

    Reality as opposed to fantasy has to do with the fact that you live with—and indeed are—the consequences of your choices and your actions.

    It is also a fact that you are personally and fully responsible for the consequences of choosing between reality and fantasy. What does it mean to choose reality?

    Society—and of course its individual members as well—has the obligation to recognize and implement the fact that you are the consequences of your actions. It must do this through a series of nonnegotiable demands it makes on its members, *for to be human is not negotiable.*

    An attitude of uncompromising outrage by society against crime expresses the nonnegotiable character of a higher-level morality.

    Therefore, an authentic society is one (a) which *demands* that people of all ages recognize that they are free and responsible for their actions and (b) which *facilitates* this development of the sense of responsibility through (i) compassion ("we love you and understand how difficult things can be, but we demand responsible behavior nevertheless") and (ii) hope, confidence, and respect ("it is perfectly possible for you to become a responsible person and you will be proud of your achievement").

VI. Philosophic facts about what is *right* (a new definition of right):

  A. The essence of what is right is *consistency* and *considerateness*.

  B. Consistency means self-imposed structures and controls. These—because they are predictable and reliable—make our consensual world possible. They define values, meanings, and goals.

  C. Considerateness results from and is evidence of the recognition that each person is a conscious center and that this consciousness is sacred, demands respect, and commands reverence.

VII. Philosophic facts about what is *wrong* (a new definition of wrong):

  A. Penology has three (not one) categories: rehabilitation, evil, and punishment.

  B. Rehabilitation as a goal is based on reason and compassion. It must be expanded. It is right and it gives hope. But it is not enough. There is also room in a higher-level morality for redefinitions of the concepts of evil and of punishment.

C. Evil:

1. Evil is a personal decision, a free choice, and not a law of nature. Causal and therefore permissive explanations from the behavioral sciences are not enough; they make evil appear inevitable. Some human beings who choose to define themselves as criminals are not sick, not deprived, but just plain evil. In other words, some persons—albeit too many—freely make choices for evil.

2. Evil is the decision to deny what is human. So that, among other things,
   a. Evil is disrespect for, disregard for, or destruction of any *consciousness* whatever, because consciousness is observed to be a sacred phenomenon.
   b. Evil is disrespect for, disregard for, or destruction of the *freedom* of any human being, for to be free is the essence of consciousness.
   c. Evil is disrespect for, disregard for, or destruction of the right to *love* and *security* for any human being whatever.

3. Some people do choose evil, and the only answer to their evil is another person's choice to stand up to it: Clearly label their choices as evil and be willing to punish. This attitude exists in addition to, not in place of, rehabilitation.

4. It is a fact that civilization rests exclusively and totally on the most fragile free (that is, uncaused) individual and collective human decisions for morality. Everyone has a personal responsibility to make him/herself and others aware, at all times, of this fragile freedom for morality.

5. A decision for evil is also a decision to leave the company of civilized persons. That is why in choosing evil one automatically loses his/her right to participate in human affairs.

D. Punishment:

1. Punishment is not revenge.

2. It is the Otherness—the concrete reality—of the other individuals in society.

3. Punishment is a statement made by the individual members of society: It is their way of making clear that certain precious human values are absolutely nonnegotiable, that they are as hard and as firmly embedded in reality as reinforced concrete or a granite mountain.

Part Three. Outline for Implementation

The premises are:

1. If these ideas are widespread and if these ideas are taught early, under accepting and pleasant circumstances, when, as it were, they are not needed, then they will come to the rescue of individuals and of society in moments of need.

2. People will think twice before acting out violent impulses.

3. People will exercise caution before destroying another person's inwardness.

4. Social demands and expectations for a higher-level morality will exert powerful and healthy pressures.

These ideas contradict nothing in our democratic culture. On the contrary, these philosophic facts are merely a modernized and teachable restatement of the very foundations of our country and of our civilization.

1. Parents, teachers, counselors, health practitioners, administration of justice personnel, the legal profession, and the like must understand the theory and the practice of a contemporary philosophy of the person.

This task is difficult but essential. It pays off.

2. All of these individuals and organizations must use their enormous energy, imagination, creativity, and resourcefulness to translate these philosophic facts into concepts and experiences understandable to their charges. Specifically,

3. These philosophic facts must be compressed into simple, formulalike phrases and statements so that their *conceptual* content is easily understood.

4. These philosophic facts must be made *experientially* available through exercises, stories, films, acting, and dramatizations.

5. We must develop extensive activities which will make it possible to *integrate* these insights into life, so that these philosophic facts will make an observable, noticeable difference in the lives of individuals and society.

6. Special responsibility rests on all news and entertainment media. It is a fact that they help to define society and the individuals within it—they helped to create the SLA, for example. Newswriters and newscasters, producers and writers must take personal responsibility for understanding these philosophic facts and be conscious of whether or not the material they produce and the emphases they give are indeed responsive to these philosophic facts.

APPENDIX D • Revelations of Anxiety

This diagram, using the important symbols of the triangle and the circle, can serve as a mnemonic device to recall the seven revelations of anxiety discussed in Book Two.

The following table summarizes the discussion of the revelations of anxiety as existential anxiety in Book Two.

PSYCHOLOGICAL AND POLITICAL DERIVATIVES OF AN EXISTENTIAL PERSONALITY THEORY

	Existential Anxiety	Pathology (Denial of Existential Anxiety)	Acceptance of Existential Anxiety Achieves	Treatment of Pathology	Political Equivalences and Desiderata
I.	BIRTH	Uncreative	Hope	Be willing to risk	Understand, facilitate, and trust the transition of our age from technology to inner space
II.	EVIL	Purposeless	Meaning	Make a contract to discover and fight your specific evil	Awaken the moral rededication of America for her third century
III.	NIHILISM	Insecure	Homecoming	Use naked willpower to establish an identity or discover a universal foundation and surrender to it	Demand that a world government preserve permanently an aesthetic biosphere as the absolute home of mankind
IV.	FREEDOM	Restricted	Self-determination	Always say "I choose . . ."	Do not compromise with independence and responsibility, since a society is human to the precise extent that it encourages freedom and demands responsibility
V.	DEATH	Timid	Courage	The next years can be your best; consider immortality and reincarnation	Insist that the threat of world apocalypse (nuclear war, hunger, death by pollution) gives mankind a unified purpose
VI.	INDIVIDUALITY	Need to conform	Potency	Say "no" in fantasy and reality	Hold every government accountable to guarantee the integrity (rights) of each citizen
VII.	GUILT	Depressed	Wholeness	Develop excellence	Measure all institutions (family, education, law, commerce, medicine) by the degree to which they develop human potential (individual, interpersonal, and social)

This can be a one-world philosophy since it is (a) based on the philosophic equivalent of scientific fact and (b) should not conflict with individual religions, politics, or value-systems. Implementation of these proposals must be through intensive educational campaigns—but only at the highest level of integrity.

APPENDIX E • *The Master Table*

The following master outline summarizes the insights about the nature of man and the character of his happiness developed by a hundred years of existential philosophy. The outline is carefully formulated to emphasize the practical application of existential philosophy.

A. The *Nature* of Human Existence (Metaphysics, Ontology)

1. The Field Theory of Man. "I am neither a body nor a soul but a continuous consciousness-body-world field." (Intentionality)

Explanation: I do not exist in isolation. I am one with other people and one with nature. Whatever affects other people and the environment also affects me, and whatever happens to me affects other people and the world around me.

2. The Two Selves. "I am a pure consciousness that has a psychological personality, a physical body, and many social roles." (Transcendental and empirical egos)

Explanation: I am more than just a body and even more than a personality. I am also a pure consciousness or a pure awareness that is different from the person that is known by the name that I carry and the likeness that I am. I am a center, the depths of which only I can plumb.

3. Five Modes of Consciousness. "Consciousness can be experienced as either individual, intimate, communal, cosmic, or as an Eternal Now." (Transcendental intersubjectivity)

Explanation: I understand that there is much confusion about the nature of the ego, because different cultures have different definitions of what it means to be a self. I am capable and willing to experience and identify with at least five separate and increasingly deeper and more universal ways in which the consciousness that I am or that runs through me can manifest itself in me.

The first, and most common, is the experience of consciousness as being an indi-

SOURCE: From Peter Koestenbaum, *Managing Anxiety: The Power of Knowing Who You Are.* Englewood Cliffs, N.J.: Prentice-Hall, 1974.

vidual. Individual consciousness is the silent and solitary center of all my experiences. Individual consciousness feels comfortable with itself but isolated from other people and from the world of nature.

I am also an intimate or intersubjective consciousness. I can experience complete oneness with another person. There exists a perceptible connecting conscious space between me and another person. I can perceive the center of another person directly; I can also sense how another experiences my center directly. These are the experiences of love and of communication.

Third, I have a communal awareness and I can achieve a sense of identity through social groups.

Fourth, I can experience the fact that I am part of a cosmic conscious stream and that I share and participate fully in the endless processes of nature. I am a wave in an ocean of consciousness; I am a well, as all others are wells (to use Ira Progoff's metaphor) which taps into a single underground stream, together with all the other wells. I am coterminous with empty space-time.

A fifth, final, and the deepest level in which consciousness manifests itself is what can be called the Eternal Now. In it, even space-time becomes an object to consciousness. The Eternal Now as the source of consciousness is experienced to be outside of space and time. A psychic distance has been inserted between the ego as the Eternal Now and its most primitive objects, empty space and time.

4. Responsibility. "I have created and am responsible for the organization of my world. I did not create the raw materials, but I am fully and alone responsible for the social reality that I have constructed around me and the life-style that I have organized for myself." (Constitution)

Explanation: If I am happy and successful, then it is essentially not fate and luck but my own efforts and decisions that have led to my well-being. If I fail and am unhappy, then I am prepared to assume full responsibility for my problems. I feel that my problems are basically my fault because I am in charge of my life—no one else is. It is good news to know that I help shape both the good and the bad in the world in which I live. I am prepared to fulfill my obligations.

B. The *Rule* for a Meaningful Human Existence (Methodology)

1. Self-disclosure. "I must be fully disclosed to myself both as a human being and as _____ (write your name in this space)." (Phenomenology)

Explanation: I am excited at the thought of both therapy and philosophy. I look forward to exploring the person that I am. I anticipate with pleasure examining my feelings and attitudes. I want to study my personality and my body. I am also determined to understand the philosophical nature of man. I recognize the importance of questions regarding human destiny and about the meaning of life. I also appreciate the significance of morality. I consider these questions fundamental to a free and healthy life.

C. The Sixteen *Principles* for Authentic Human Existence (Philosophical Anthropology)

1. *Pain. "I choose to value my pains." (Negation, Anxiety)*

Explanation: Suffering can be a learning experience. Pain is unavoidable. Death is a natural part of life. Anxiety and depression help me understand the meaning of life. I can successfully cope with the fact that evil is an integral part of life.

2. *Death. "I choose to value my limitations." (Negation, Finitude)*

Explanation: I can adapt myself to frustrations. I know that much of the time I cannot have what I want. I know that over a lifetime I will be forced to give up many of my most cherished dreams. I am successful in accepting that which cannot be helped. I can accept the fact that all life ends in death.

3. *Reflection. "I am able to both live my life and to reflect on my life." (Epoché, Reduction)*

Explanation: There are times when I am active and extraverted. I participate in life and I am involved. There are also times at which I am withdrawn and reflective —that is, introverted. If I so choose, I can meditate and be happy just being by myself and inside myself. I have control over these feelings and attitudes. They are usually appropriate to the circumstances of my life.

4. *Self-reliance. "I am an adult consciousness that exists alone: I choose to be independent and self-reliant." (Inwardness, Subjectivity)*

Explanation: I have outgrown childish forms of dependency. I can be comfortable being alone. I can go through life on my own two feet. I can take care of myself —and of others if necessary. I feel that this independence and self-reliance is an attitude that I voluntarily choose and not one that is imposed upon me from the outside. This theme is in contrast to the later themes of commitment (10) and love (12).

5. *Individuality. "It is right and normal for me to seem different from other human beings." (Uniqueness)*

Explanation: I am free to conform or not to conform as my value system dictates. I am not excessively bothered by the fact that I may be different from my peers. I am prepared to create my own direction and my own life, one that I know is right for me even though it may differ from the prevailing life-styles of those around me. I am not easily pressured by my associates and relatives. Neither am I easily pressured by my neighbors, by people that I meet, or by those who try to sell me something.

6. *Eternity. "There exists a consciousness within me which I am and which is eternal." (Transcendental ego)*

Explanation: This point is perhaps the most difficult one to understand. It means that I have genuine conception and perception of my most inner inwardness. I have a real sense of the center that I am within me amidst the storms, stresses, and changes of life. I understand what wise men of all ages mean when they refer to the pure consciousness within me that I am. I also recognize the universality of that center. The conscious center that I am is not susceptible to the flux of life and is therefore unchanging and timeless. It may not last forever, but it is outside of time.

7. Reverence. "Each individual human inward subjectivity is the divine consciousness in man." (Transcendental subjectivity)

Explanation: Reverence for subjectivity is the highest existential principle of morality. A person's character may be evil and his body diseased, but his pure inner conscious core is infinitely precious and eternally dignified. Man's inwardness is the source of his value; his inmost center is the foundation for his "unalienable rights of life, liberty, and the pursuit of happiness" with which each individual, according to the American Declaration of Independence, is born.

I am capable of respecting infinitely the inner ego of both myself and of others. I can "hate the sin rather than the sinner." I agree with Maritain when he says "the true connection among people is spiritual."

8. Freedom. "I always choose because I am always free." (Freedom)

Explanation: I have a realistic sense of the profound meaning of human freedom. I believe in the existence of free will. I believe that I am responsible for my actions and for my life. I believe that I set my own values and self-concepts and I am prepared to accept the full consequences. I am able to make decisions even while I realize that in most situations there are no definite truths and falsehoods, rights and wrongs.

9. Life. "My first and last choice is to say 'yes' to life." (Affirmation)

Explanation: If I say "yes" to life I recognize that I am fully responsible for whatever optimism or pessimism runs through my existence. If I am depressed *I* have said "no" to life. If I live with joy it is because *I* have said "yes" to life. If I say "yes" to life I freely choose to make living itself the highest value. In short, whether I love life or not, whether I am a positive or a negative personality is my own free personal choice for which I am fully responsible. I cannot blame others for my depression, anger, guilt, or lack of self-respect.

10. Commitment. "I am free to make commitments." (Commitment, Cathexis)

Explanation: Commitment and love represent a contrast to the theme of self-reliance (4). Commitment means that I feel connected with the world—I feel one with my body and one with the society and environment into which as a human being I am born. Commitment means that I can risk attachments to people, principles, goals, and life-styles. I can take it if I lose. Commitment means that I can live as a full-fledged participant in the affairs of society and of the natural environment. My life is experienced whole rather than fragmented.

11. Reality. "I clearly distinguish reality from fantasies, dreams, rationalizations, and wishful thinking. I am always in touch with what is real." (Ego-cogito-cogitatum)

Explanation: I have a well-developed sense of reality. Even though I understand that the distinction between dream and reality is philosophically ambiguous, I find no difficulty separating dream from reality in my daily and practical life. I know that there is a reality beyond my inwardness. I know that this reality is different from my subjective ego. I know that this reality may be other people or the objects of nature, but it can also be my body or my unconscious (as I see in cases of physical or mental illness). I know that this reality is independent of me: sometimes it joins me in my needs and wishes, sometimes it is indifferent and sometimes it opposes me. Nevertheless, at all times I feel that I am directly in touch with that external reality. I always sense that I am in contact with that part of the world which is other than me. Even while I am rationalizing, deceiving myself, or having fantasies, I know that what is real is that I am dreaming.

12. Love. *"As an adult I can choose to meet, confront, witness, understand, and be mirrored by another. I can also choose to love him or her and care for him or her." (Encounter)*

Explanation: I am capable of loving like an adult. I can love spiritually and I can love physically. I do not use love neurotically. In love I can accept the dignity and the needs of my partner in love. If I so choose, I am able to make love the central project in my life. I enjoy spiritual, emotional, and physical love and love is easy and natural for me.

13. Adaptability. *"I choose myself as one who is realistically flexible." (Flexibility)*

Explanation: I can be reflective and inward or active and outgoing, depending on my own choices and the circumstances in which I find myself. I can be self-reliant and independent if I want to and have to, but I also can be dependent and trusting if I choose that personality structure. I can be both a leader and a follower, as my decisions and the world's circumstances dictate.

14. Time. *"I experience time as living in a present which, while utilizing the past, connects directly and primarily into my future." (Futurity)*

Explanation: I experience my life as a continuous progression. My sense of time is not fragmented. My focus is on the future. I live in the present and I realize that both past and future are connected to me in the present. The burdens of the past exist for me in the present. The hopes and opportunities for the future exist for me in the present. I experience the time of my life as a river that flows always and smoothly in the direction of the future.

15. Growth. *"My life is an endless process of growing, emerging, and reaching out." (Self-transcendence)*

Explanation: For me, to live is to grow. I am not satisfied with achievements in life. My concern is rather with process and movement in my life. The meaning of my life is found in continual growth—in education, in human relationships, in occupational progress, in creativity, in building, and so forth. I feel that if my growing should end so would the meaning of my life. I know that either hate or disinterest are the results of a reaching out that has been frustrated.

16. Contradiction. "The inescapable ambiguities and contradictions of life are my powerful allies." (Polarity, Dialectic)

Explanation: When faced with contradictions in life I am not upset; instead, I am challenged. I realize that values and situations are usually ambiguous and unclear. There are many sides to most issues. I feel no compulsion to discover always the absolute right. I can act in spite of uncertainty. I can make decisions in spite of ambiguities. I can make commitments without being certain of the truth. I can tolerate disagreement, opposition, rejection, and denial. In fact, contradictions are to me a source of strength, because I find polarities within myself. I can integrate the polar opposites in me and achieve a mature sense of wholeness.

APPENDIX F • *Meditation, Physics, and Phenomenology*

Let us discuss the use of meditation in healing from the *highly speculative* and *mostly germinal* excursus of the relationship between the study of physics and the examination of consciousness.

Extremely interesting parallels exist between the phenomenological definition of intentionality and Einstein's theory about the relation between space-time and matter (as well as energy). Without matter there is no space-time. Kant thought that if we could remove all objects from space and time then pure and empty space and time would remain. Einstein, on the other hand, because he conceived of space-time as a function of matter, held that with the absence of matter space-time would equally vanish. This view disturbs the commonsense consciousness, but, after more than half a century, we have become accustomed to this "bizarre" kind of thinking.

Closely related is the view of the relationship between consciousness and its objects in the phenomenological model of being. That view, which is an analysis of the structure of immediate experience, holds that consciousness and its objects have precisely the same relationship as outlined in Einstein's view above. Consciousness does not exist without its objects and conversely there exists no object without being the object of some consciousness. This is a discernible fact that follows from the analysis of immediate experience—which is the foundation of all knowledge. We are even less comfortable with the dramatic impact of this phenomenological position than with the relativistic position. The phenomenological position is *radical* and *consistently empirical.*

One of the consequences of these insights is to make clear that consciousness is not the product of biological evolution but must be conceptualized as just as "ancient," shall we say, as matter itself. Thinkers like Chardin follow the Hegelian position that history is the development of consciousness' self-consciousness. The evidence for this view of the historical equality of consciousness and matter lies in the analysis of immediate experience, which must always take precedence over secondhand, deductive, mediated, or inferred constructs or references to distant or possible experiences. The result of integrating these ideas into our thinking, like Relativity Theory, is *radical* and *revolutionary.* The full impact of that reconstruction has not yet been felt.

Physics draws its metaphors from the field of consciousness. It is no surprise, therefore, to find residues of the structure of the field of consciousness in the theories of physics. In phenomenology—which means also in meditation and in fantasy work—a pure subject-object relation, such as any perception or any thought, is clarity and lucidity about the manner of appearance of an eidetic, conceptual, or iconic object. The clarity aspect, which is luminous or at least the effect of illumination, refers to the transcendental region, to the realm of pure consciousness. The object is the thing illuminated. The parallel between a radioactive object giving off energy waves—or reflecting them (sun and planets respectively)—is obvious. Furthermore, the older view in physics was, like the older view in philosophy, that mind and matter, consciousness and objects, space-time and things were separate. Resolution of conflicts consisted in dualistic or reductionistic metaphysics and cosmologies. A dialectical, interactive metaphysics, however, is new—or at least renewed.

Since it appears than we can identify energy with luminosity (energy is not a thing but more like an observation about a property of the transcendental sphere) we can explore the significance of another aspect of Relativity Theory, encapsulated in the notorious formula $e = mc^2$. Mass is a condensation of energy. Energy is the expansion of mass. If it is true that inner and outer space-time are phenomenologically related, and if it is also true that the metaphors or models of physics are fundamental anthropomorphisms (that is, the models of physics are derived from the lived experience of consciousness), then it may follow that the insights of modern physics are really descriptions of transcendental consciousness. It is therefore worth exploring whether or not the $e = mc^2$ relationship also describes the experience of subject-object connection.

For example, success in living entails, in each and every case, clear and uninterrupted clarity of perception and, above all, conception. We call that intensity or, more commonly, *alertness*. We also associate alertness with energy and the absence of alertness, which we call lethargy, laziness, drowsiness, and distraction with lack of energy or exhaustion. Furthermore, we equate *intelligence* with this kind of clarity and lucidity about objects, so that a dull person is one whose perception (or intellection) of conceptual objects is dulled. This type of description fits neatly into Plato's Theory of Forms. In the psychological and practical aspects of living, especially in the area of interpersonal transactions, this kind of *lucidity and energy equivalence* means rational and objective living. It means such traits as responsibility, reliability, control, commonsense, maturity, independence, and good judgment.

It would thus be a great service to mankind to find ways to further this kind of success, that is, lucidity, *creativity, intelligence*, and *energy*. Thus, the present *totally germinal and highly speculative* hypothesis, based on the suspected connection between the field of consciousness and research in physics, is this: an object (any object, including conceptual objects) is a source of creativity, intelligence, and energy—just as in physics mass is a source of energy. The translation of objectivity into subjectivity—in the lived rather than the conceptual area—appears to us as light, clarity, and control. We must learn to perceive objects—especially nonphysical objects—by sensing their direct connection with us, by experiencing the continuity they have with our (or the) center. That meditative or fantasy experience —which one can have under any and all circumstances of daily life—could make us aware of the illuminating and energy-producing effects of the objects of thought. That is, the ability to focus for long periods at a time on the solution of a single problem is a capacity called the power of concentration. At that moment subject and object are experienced as becoming interchangeable or at least mutually efficacious. This phenomenon is the atom bomb of the life of the mind; it is the atomic energy of consciousness. It may well be a practical way to greatly improve intelligence and performance.

Let us now examine some specific meditative exercises to illustrate and develop further the subject-object equivalence principle (derived heuristically from the $e = mc^2$ summation of the data of modern physics). Look at an object; think of $e = mc^2$. Now think of the fact that subject and object are one field, all aspects of which are immediately accessible to us. Then reflect on the fact that your experience of the object is an opposing condensation of consciousness and that your consciousness is an enormous expansion of objectivity. You now experience a great clarity (the "white light" of mysticism, perhaps?) and an enormous steadiness of mind. It almost appears as if you can absorb from the object increasingly larger doses of pure consciousness, which can steady you for any crisis.

We are trying to find a way for the object to increase the compass of our consciousness—to give us more energy, more intelligence, more creative genius, and greater powers of concentration. The history of meditative practices seems to provide us with ample evidence to substantiate this hypothesis.

What is far more difficult to accomplish is to use pure consciousness to bring about change in the object. If our metaphor holds, it would then be the case that we require enormous "quantities" of consciousness to bring about even minuscule changes in objects. In physics the problem is that of condensing energy to form matter, a feat already accomplished. Similarly, while it may be easy to experience the reverse, namely, that objects can give us energy and support (that is, that matter can become energy), we cannot demonstrate the reality of what in effect would have to be psychokinesis—even though the objects created are nonphysical. It is further worth reflection to examine the following: In the phenomenological model of being, nonphysical and physical objects are more like each other in manner of appearance than any object (regardless of how intimate) and pure consciousness itself. Does it follow, therefore, that since nonphysical objects can be instances of consciousness-transformed-into-objects (that is, the equivalent of energy transformed into matter), that consciousness can also transform itself into what we could legitimately call physical objects? Perhaps we should look for exceedingly small changes in the structure of objects.

These are speculations and notes for future research. But they are also risky thoughts. They are one further step in exploring the relation between physics and transcendental phenomenology. Let us now restate in more formal language the presumptive results of the above considerations. The life-world gives us a subject-object intentionally connected experience of being. The symbol that was used to represent this is:

S ⟶ O

Figure 1

The region on the left is consciousness (the transcendental dimension) and the region on the right is objectivity or matter (the empirical dimension). Consciousness is also experienced as space-time, as light, and as force and energy. But these experiences are lived space, lived time, lived light (the Heraclitean "fire," which symbolized both the light of the intellect and the warmth of the heart), lived force, and lived energy (not conceptual). Objectivity is also experienced as lived matter, lived otherness or opposition, lived solidity, and so forth. These are true and fundamental aspects of existence. The exploration of this dialectical structure of being is the task of a phenomenological model of being and is encased in the concept of the intentionality of consciousness. We must recall that the defining characteristics of intentionality are constitution and cathexis on the one hand and the continuity-separateness (dialectical) property of all field phenomena (such as an electromagnetic field) on the other. These are the data of the life-world. These represent truth and foundation; they are the epistemological source. All other knowledge is derived from these fundamentals.

The world as we perceive it is, however, constituted differently. We perceive not only the given but also the belief-system we impose on these data. Two historical **archetypal decisions were made millennia ago and are also made**—as is true of all decisions—continuously by all of us to this day. To grow up in our culture is to be indoctrinated—through tacit expectations and through the structuring powers of language—from the very beginning to always perceive the world in terms of the coordinates of the consensual system of beliefs. (This point was made in Book One, Chapter 9.) These fundamental rules of world organization are (a) the cultural or generic archetypal decision for atomism—which is a decision that affects mostly our perception and conception of the empirical realm, by denying the primacy of *continuity* through a point-oriented physics and mathematics—and (b) the cultural or generic archetypal decision for the supremacy of inference (or the denial of direct experience, and the corresponding preeminence of the indirect and invisible construct)—which is a decision that affects mostly our view of the transcendental dimension and above all the relation between the transcendental and empirical realms. It is this latter decision which gives us the heavily conceptual consensual world view, which distorts our given life-world into an inferred concept-world. The image which we used to describe this second world view is:

Figure 2

That view is produced by the two archetypal decisions mentioned above. It gives us technology and science. The ultimate function of the two generic, cultural, or historical archetypal decisions is to move us away from reflection, observation, and appreciation of being (which is truth and especially intuition, in the language of Bergson) and move us toward the control over being (which is praxis, utility, technology, and especially intellect, according to Bergson).

Both subject and object go through transformations as a result of these two archetypal decisions. Lived space becomes conceptual space and lived opposition (or solidity) becomes conceptual matter, and so forth.

The fundamental discovery of modern physics derived from the archetypal decision for atomism is the "discovery" of quanta of energy. Whereas for more than two thousand years we accepted the atomization of objectivity (the Greek atomists did talk about soul atoms) we have now concluded that subjectivity (in its derived form as conceptual energy) can also be atomized. More interestingly, two important discoveries in modern physics—the Heisenberg Uncertainty Principle and various aspects of relativity, such as the matter-energy equivalency and the interrelation between space, time, light, and measurement, that is, the existence of objects—seem to be the result of applying immediate, intentional (primordial, deconstituted) thought to what should have been mediate, nonintentional, inferred, and conceptual categories. Both of these discoveries in physics, going as far back as the Michelson-Morely experiments and the Lorentz transformation equations express fully the intentional relation between subject and object in experience. This insight seems to be significant but in need of much greater clarification and specificity. Also, its implications must be analyzed in detail. There emerge two suggestions which were alluded to earlier.

The key words are *intelligence* and *psychokinesis*. Relativity tells us that matter can be transformed into energy. If we now translate this view from physics, which is still more conceptual than lived, back to the life-world, we get the hypothesis that proper (to be defined) meditation on an object can translate that object into consciousness—which means clarity and creativity, but mostly intelligence. It appears that this is one explanation of what happens in many of the Hatha Yoga meditation exercises. It follows that a specific program of meditation to increase intelligence can be devised. Meditation on an object deconstitutes the object: it makes us aware not of what we think we see (our constituted meanings) but of what we actually see (the deconstituted given). The object perceived changes discernibly and dramatically as we see it from the point of view of the consciousness that we are and with the idea that it gradually transforms itself into consciousness or melds with the field of consciousness. In fact, we perceive that the reality proper of the object is called into question—experientially as well as conceptually. This experience is no mystery.

The other side of the issue is more complex. Energy has recently been converted into matter. If we now raise (or lower) this problem back to the level of the life-world we get reference to psychokinesis—the influence of consciousness on objects or the transformation of consciousness into objectivity. To experience that in meditation is difficult; to see it at work with so-called real objects is impossible for most (or all?).

APPENDIX G • *The New Image of the Person: The Theory and Practice of Clinical Philosophy*

The Topic

This paper outlines some theory and practice of clinical philosophy, defined as the confluence of a combined phenomenological model of being and existential personality theory with depth psychotherapy. Since many problems brought to physicians, psychiatrists, and psychologists are more philosophic than psychological or medical, a therapist trained in clinical philosophy will have an above-average diagnostic grasp of a patient's condition and can therefore create deepened and innovative treatment strategies.

The program of clinical philosophy is systematic and precise. We therefore begin with definitions of philosophy and phenomenology.

Philosophy and Phenomenology

Philosophy is the search for maximum precision and clarity in our descriptions of experiences and in our uses of languages. But it is also the discovery of distinctively philosophic facts. The organized accumulation of these philosophic facts yields a model of being that forms the basis for clinical philosophy.

Philosophic facts are discovered through the assiduous application of a phenomenological method. Its simplest formulation is "the *detached* and *presuppositionless description* of *first-person experiences*." Thus, phenomenology is first an attitude of distance and disengagement, known as epoche and reduction. For example, a patient in psychoanalysis reflects, in a single conscious unit with his analyst, on precisely those feelings to which he or she had been most deeply attached —including feelings for the therapist, known as the transference. To thus reflect on

SOURCE: This paper was read to the faculty of San Jose State University, April 19, 1977, and to the Philosophy Department at Harvard University, May 2, 1977.

Because this paper is highly compressed it may lend itself to several possible misinterpretations. The paper does not claim that emotional problems always respond to logical analysis or even that such an approach is necessarily therapeutically relevant. Also, the paper does not assert that every human being has total freedom in all respects. Far from it. All of us have only limited access to our freedom and some, due to the circumstances of their childhood and social and biological environments, have barely any contact at all with human freedom.

existence, rather than to simply exist—to be thus self-conscious rather than merely conscious—is a key phenomenological technique and therapeutic device. The resistance to reflection is the heart of the illness, and overcoming this resistance becomes the healing process. Why? Because this act of reflection on one's most intimate attachments reveals the region of inward and so-called transcendental consciousness and with it discloses the true meanings and strengths of every human being. We shall return to this important methodological step.

Phenomenology, second, describes rather than speculates; it reports but it does not infer. It must therefore be free to use poetic language and metaphysical symbols to elicit the elusive pure given on which rest all reality and truth.

Third, the goal of phenomenology is to make these descriptions as nearly assumption-free as is possible. In psychotherapy, patients' explorations of their feelings are therapeutic precisely to the extent that they are accurate and assumption-free descriptions of the fringes and the horizons of their experiences. The symptom, fixed in a concept and forced into a metaphysics, may be labeled, for instance, cervicitis or prostatitis, but the assumption-free description of the first-person given may be more like a kick in the back or a blow below the belt. When, to cite another example, phenomenological analysis cuts through the metaphoric symptomatology of typical middle-age complaints—such as menopause, alcoholism, divorce, and children on drugs—we may in fact uncover guilt over unfulfilled potential, self-contempt for one's weakness, bitterness over the betrayal of possibilities, and rage over the neglect of potency.

Fourth, phenomenology as method recognizes consistently that all experience is first-person experience. It is thus sensitive to the ubiquitous inward and subjective dimension of all experience. Truth, reality, and value are rooted in our inward freedom for ex-nihilo self- and world-definition. Herein lies the ontological foundation for the fact that in psychotherapy insight does not mean cure. On the contrary, healing occurs only after patients take full and personal responsibility for their authenticity.

Occasionally, total carcinoma remissions follow this pattern. Cancer arises in persons who fail to assume total responsibility for their own lives. The spirit, negative and depressed, says no to life. The body does likewise. The subsequent diagnosis of cancer is the patient's first real confrontation with death. The result is to resolutely take charge of the last year of life and make it the best. The ensuing joy and vigor also reverse permanently the spread of the cancer and constitute a cure. This sequence illustrates the therapeutic significance of what in epistemology is the primacy of first-person experience.

Finally, phenomenology—restricted as it is to experiences—is the most radical empiricism possible and is therefore science carried to its logical conclusion.

What, then, are these philosophic facts acquired through phenomenology?

Philosophic Facts and the Phenomenological Model of Being

It is a philosophic fact that reality, being, experience, the life-world, or the universe of ordinary language—however we wish to designate that which is—can best be characterized as a field phenomenon. The world is not, as Democritus and Newton thought, an aggregate of discrete objects within a void, but, as Heraclitus and Einstein saw, discloses itself to be a continuum, a process, a flow, which is also a dialectic, an experience of oscillating wave phenomena. Existence is both the harmony and the living stress of confronting polarities. Typical expressions for this field phenomenon are Husserl's formula "All consciousness is consciousness of something" (sometimes referred to as "the intentionality of consciousness"), Heidegger's formula that "Dasein is a being-in-the-world," and Sartre's notion that the *pour soi* (or nothingness) strives to become the *en soi* (or being).

Reality is thus first and foremost a subject-object field, a consciousness-world and a center-periphery continuity. All acts of consciousness are directed toward objects and, conversely, all objects have a stream of consciousness attached to them—where "object" means not only trees, houses, and protozoa, but also ideas, feelings, my ego, my body, and other minds. It follows that a basic metaphor for being is the magnetic field, where two separate and different poles are what they are precisely because they exist stressfully apart in a nevertheless single and unitary zone.

This first result gives us our basic diagram of being. It is the eye (I) perceiving the world; it is the field model of existence:

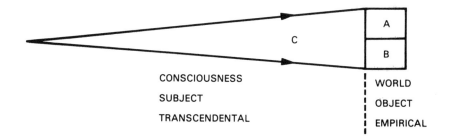

Being is a consciousness (C) - world (A + B) stream, a subject (C) - object (A + B) interface, a transcendental (C) - empirical (A + B) continuum. This paradigm applies equally to world and persons.

Therefore, the first set of philosophic facts is about the field in general, or region A + B + C. The search for these facts is known as the study of the categories—exemplified in the work of Aristotle and Kant and in contemporary naturalism and structuralism. The conclusions of such phenomenological descriptions we call ontological data, world facts, or categoreal facts. An example is "Being is a bipolar field."

There are three additional types of facts, two of which are philosophic:

Facts about region A are precise data or scientific facts. The exploration of region A consists in descriptions of plants and cells, of chemical reactions, of geological strata, and of all those data usually associated with the scientific enterprise. The vast majority of described facts are of this type. They are not philosophic facts.

Region B represents fringe data or poetic facts—such as "a migraine headache feels like a gray rock"—for only in poetry can we seize a feeling. General examples of these amorphous data are moods and emotions, ideas and aesthetic moments. Dreams, fantasies, symbols, and altered states of consciousness are poetic data, required for work in clinical psychology and psychiatry: The practice of psychotherapy is the phenomenological uncovering of recessed elements within these data: We are inclined to say that healing is more art than science. And in legitimizing these data epistemologically, phenomenology has fulfilled Wundt's and Brentano's dreams of psychology as science.

There also are consciousness data or transcendental facts (region C), which represent descriptions of pure inward consciousness, such as "consciousness is experienced as an infinite regress." This region of being is of the utmost therapeutic significance. We shall therefore examine some psychologically relevant results of explorations into transcendental philosophic facts. Later we turn to categoreal facts.

Transcendental Facts

Ordinarily, the field of consciousness exhibits what we call referential thought: the field is an outward moving, future-oriented, and self-transcending vector. However, access to transcendental facts is achieved by reversing this forward look into reflexive thought. Consciousness then becomes self-referential: thought transcends consciousness into self-consciousness. In fact, philosophy itself is to be defined also as a passion for self-reference. The phenomenological description of self-referential material, known as transcendental phenomenology, reveals at least nine transcendental philosophic facts, that is, data about the structure of our inward consciousness. We must remember that, etymologically speaking, psychology is the study or account (*logos*) and psychiatry the healing (*iatreia*) of consciousness, spirit, or breath (*psyche*). Most modern textbooks in psychology, psychiatry, and medicine have been effectively bowdlerized of any real sense of consciousness, thus unloading psychology's ancient task onto transcendental phenomenology and clinical philosophy.

1. Infinite regress. Transcendental consciousness *is* the phenomenon of self-reference. Self-referentiality is an infinite regress. That is, self-reference can be repeated indefinitely, revealing thereby the endless backward moving chain that is the experience of consciousness. The ego sees itself and therewith creates an antecedent ego. That ego in turn can refer to itself and thereby create a third ego. When our experience of this transcendental fact is verbalized, language breaks out in contradictions. And we must be careful not to allow concern for consistency—and thus for a theory of types, metalanguages, or category mistakes—to obscure the infinitely regressive character of experience itself. This regress explains psychopathology, for it is the experience of nihilism, nothingness, foundationlessness, and the death of God.

2. Inner space-time. Transcendental consciousness is inner space-time, conforming thus to the classical view that logic, arithmetic, and geometry are descriptions of thought, time, and space, respectively. There is not only formal logic; there is also descriptive or phenomenological logic. The polar consciousness-world field is an infinite and lived (not conceptual) inner-outer space-time continuum. This was Kant's famous insight in his transcendental aesthetic. It has also been the deeper meaning of the rationalistic tradition in philosophy, where mind and world are so intertwined that one can know the other, innately.

3. Freedom. Because of its total transparency and vacuity, the experience of our pure, inward consciousness is also the experience of total freedom—freedom that ascribes meanings and that organizes givens into things (constitution), and freedom that creates a sense of individual identity or personal *Existenz* by attaching itself to a self-concept (cathexis). Freedom is thus a transcendental fact, and a psychology that does not make room for the transcendental can understand neither the reality nor the structure of freedom and therefore cannot function in a humane clinical setting. The centrality of freedom in the *practice* of psychotherapy is axiomatic. The therapist will always challenge the patient with the statement "You have a choice." We need also freedom's *theoretical* justification available through transcendental phenomenology.

4. Self-deception. Another transcendental philosophic fact is consciousness' polyphony: It operates simultaneously on different levels. This transcendental datum gives rise to consciousness' proclivity for self-deception, which—as Nietzsche was the first to notice—is the therapeutically critical phenomenon of the unconscious. For example, a patient is catatonic for years, until he hears of his wife's death and his orphaned son. He recovers spontaneously in order to leave the hospital and care for his child. He chose his psychosis, and he chose to forget that he chose. But he knew all the time. Likewise, a comatose patient may hear, see, and remember, but may not care enough ever to respond.

5. Reflection. Sanity requires minimally that consciousness actualize its capacity for reduction, reflexivity, and spectatorial non-attachment. Transcendental consciousness is free *either* to be committed to, attached to, or identified with a situation, a person, or an object (the hedonic life-style) *or* to be detached, reflective, aloof, and distanced (the ascetic life-style). To be human means to be able *both* to participate, get involved, and identify with our emotions and our actions (that is, to make commitments and to experience spontaneous joy, but also overwhelming anger) *and* to reflect on them, detach, distance, and disidentify ourselves from them. We freely *choose* to give up the distinctly human capacity for reflection; it does not disappear of its own accord. And when we lose it we lose the right to call ourselves human, for to choose to give up our capacity for reflection is to choose to become psychotic. We must remember that 80 percent of homicides are committed by persons who have temporarily chosen to give up their capacity for reflection. The legal term is temporary insanity. It is a legal defense; but it is neither a psychiatric defense nor is it a philosophic defense. And every loss of impulse control is our decision to choose not to take responsibility for preserving at all times our capacity for reflection, and this includes the use of drugs and intoxicants.

6. Eternity. It is a transcendental fact, discovered through the phenomenological reduction in what should be called a transcendental empiricism, that an infinitely reflexive consciousness and therefore infinitely regressive inner space-time is also indestructible and thus eternal. The non-being of transcendental consciousness—as idea, experience, or phenomenon—is devoid of any possible meaning. If we look closely at the self-referential character of the indwelling witness that is consciousness, we see that its non-being makes no sense. Thinking about the non-being of anything is an action of a conscious inwardness. There must, therefore, always be an inwardness. It follows that the accurate meaning of the thought "I am mortal"—where "I" means "transcendental consciousness"—has never been thought.

Descartes articulated the individualized version of this transcendental fact when he announced his *indubitandum*, "I think, therefore I am." And St. Anselm articulated its universalized version when, in the ontological argument, he prayed "so truly, therefore, do you exist, O Lord, my God, that you cannot be conceived not to exist."

7. Security. Eternity as a transcendental datum—understood, experienced, and integrated into life—is clinically significant in that it is an important grounding device and therefore a source of security. Many who have been severely ill or gravely injured, as well as those who survived death camps and torture chambers, understand the genuinely therapeutic value of the peace of this silent and solitary center.

8. Love. Intimacy, friendship, and intersubjectivity are consciousness-expanding experiences, in which one free conscious center directly touches another free conscious center in a tunnel of inner space-time. It is only by legitimizing transcendental data that we can make a humane and accurate scientific study of the real nature of human communication.

9. Anxiety. Consciousness, when revealed in a transcendental-phenomenological reduction, shows itself to be an infinite regress, inner space-time, freedom, capable of self-deception and of reflection, eternal, secure, and intersubjective. But transcendental consciousness is also intimately connected with anxiety. Separation anxiety—as a symbol for all anxiety—is consciousness severed (as much as possible) from its object—like a child wrenched from its mother. We then understand why the experience of an exposed pure consciousness can also be the experience of ultimate anxiety. Psychology, to understand anxiety, must avail itself of these transcendental philosophic facts.

Self-referential consciousness is like an astronomer's black hole. It is also an abyss as vast as the abyss of physical space itself. And that vision into inner space-time is the combined confrontation with nihilism and freedom: The anxiety of nihilism is the shaking of the foundations; the anxiety of freedom is the realization that we create *ex nihilo* our truth, our values, and our reality. The combined anxieties of nihilism and of freedom are replicated in acrophobia—as when we glance down from the San Francisco Golden Gate Bridge, one of the world's notorious suicide points. Looking into the distant waters below, our vertigo reminds us that we are foundationless and recalls for us our overwhelming freedom to jump or not to jump: We then know that the decision to be or not to be is constant, prerational, and instantaneous. Anxiety neurotics and many schizophrenics are condemned to the permanent perception of these transcendental truths. The so-called healthy person has either learned to tolerate this anxiety or has developed successful defenses against it.

Anxiety is thus a philosophically cognitive and not an emotional state. It is a natural and not a pathological condition, and it is essentially a form of health rather than a type of illness. In many cases, this simple knowledge has therapeutic effect.

The anxiety associated with our knowledge of pure consciousness is mostly existential and symptom-free. Neurotic anxiety results from the repression or distortion of existential anxiety. Since neurotic anxiety thereby denies consciousness, which is transcendental reality, it in fact strictures life itself. And that narrowing of the possibilities of human existence is the meaning of all the symptoms of the classical psychoneuroses.

Coping with Anxiety

We cope with existential anxiety not with phenothiazine or Valium but with philosophy. The key therapeutic step is to learn the constructive uses of anxiety, which is done by understanding the rules of transformation between anxiety and consciousness.

One way to cope with the anxieties of nihilism and freedom is to use naked will-power to establish an identity. That was the way of Sartre and Camus. It is the image of God as the creator of the universe, which is really the powerful and noble vision of a human being forever capable of choosing to say no to any fate and thereby eternally asserting the dignity of the indomitable human spirit. We then realize, with Tillich, that we are the power to resist the threat of non-being. Out of the void we create a sense of individual identity. It is the archetypal decision for finitude, the free choice to be an individual, the act of taking responsibility for being oneself. To freely choose one's finite, dying individuality is thus the ultimate reconciliation with life—and with death. It answers perhaps the most important question in psychotherapy, namely, What is an adult, mature, and individual identity? or, How is individuality constituted or cathected?

An individual is created when consciousness anxiously but freely cuts off forever its sources of support. That act of ontological alienation is the archetypal choice which evolves into a concrete, embodied, and erotic core: a living ego, a body-subject (Merleau-Ponty), an intentional consciousness-world interface. The sense of individual identity is accomplished through the anxious and free courage of saying no to external sources of self-definition: no to parents; no to society, tradition, and ethnicity; no to mate; no to children; no to the child within; and no to God. Given this diagnosis, the treatment is to facilitate, not obstruct, the creation of an authentic individual aloneness. These acts of individuation are the philosophic psychodynamics in teenagers' choices for rebellion against their parents—through smoking, pregnancy, truancy, failure, or acne.

When children yell at their parents, "I hate you!" they are testing their own potency as individual identities. Your proper response as parent is not to moralize but to congratulate: "I'm delighted you're becoming independent!"

Potency, for generations, had been male. The female has therefore been trapped in a vise of guilt. If she denies her potency—an inauthentic act—she feels neurotic guilt: Social and role pressures encrusted in her superego punish her with backaches, menstrual cramps, and menopausal depressions. But beneath it all lurks the authentic resentment of all the oppressed. This sometimes exceedingly subtle fury of the impotent has wrecked many marriages and children.

If she does affirm her potency—an authentic act and a response to existential guilt—she becomes a revolutionary, and the problems of the age must be lived through her. She has been assigned the historical task of redefining the meaning of woman for all mankind.

In short, the creation of the individual is a freely chosen response to anxiety—a decision each of us is making now, continuously. And these crucial therapeutic phenomena can be explained only through the language of transcendental philosophic facts.

A second and contrasting coping device for the existential anxieties of nihilism and of freedom is the surrender to the universal. It is the faith that if we abandon ourselves to ultimate anxiety we will find in it also our security. It is the experience of the skydiver who, when the air resistance equals the force of gravity, transforms his anxiety of falling into the security of resting on a cloud. We surrender to the fall; we trust the chilling emptiness. The phenomenological exploration of the anxiety of nihilism shows us how non-being becomes being and how nothingness is transmuted into ground. This is the image of God as a necessary being and as the foundation.

The fact that surrender to anxiety can transform terror into security and abandonment into home is importantly illustrated in the universal symbol of the sea. The ocean is foreign to us and a threat: it is the abode of monsters; it is dark, deep, cold, suffocating, merciless, enormous. But the ocean is also our home: We come from it ancestrally through biological evolution; it is the most common source of the artist's inspiration for beauty, for calm, for meaning, and for strength. A patient dreamed he was on a small ship in a hurricane. Clutching the wreck, he sank in panic. Now dead, he surrendered to the ocean and became the sea. He awoke with the peace that surpasses understanding.

The first of these solutions—willpower—is humanistic or atheistic. It is Camus' rebel against life and it is expressed in the myth of Prometheus. The second—surrender—is the answer of faith and religion; it is theistic. It is the dimension of trust and of belief, and it is expressed in the myths of salvation.

How do we resolve the contradiction between anxiety and security as philosophic facts about consciousness? Here East and West meet: For the West, consciousness means anxiety. For the East, consciousness means peace. Reconciliation is possible if we consider that anxiety experienced becomes anxiety tolerated. Anxiety and security form part of a continuum, for anxiety can also be the experience of aliveness, of time, of growth: Anxiety justifies love, searches for meaning, and motivates us to creativity.

In sum, the perception of pure, inward, and transcendental consciousness—the philosophic fact revealed by the reduction—is also the experience of anxiety and thus explains a fundamental concept in psychopathology and psychotherapy. We cope with it clinically by either inventing an individual ego (humanism) or by trusting the universal abyss (theism).

Let us now examine how categoreal philosophic facts—which describe the total subject-object field of being—help us in therapy.

Categoreal Facts

Since the total field is a dialectic, the essence of aliveness is opposition, confrontation, alternation, and otherness, all within a unified field of flow.

The dialectic identifies life with optimum stress, and therewith realistically describes mature human relationships. Love is the mirroring of two conscious, free centers. Family transactions are principal symbols for the underlying dialectic of the field of being. Also, in the therapeutic hour, confrontation emphasizes the dual aspect of the dialectic, whereas compassion underscores the unitary aspect of the polar field of being.

One type of psychopathology results from dysfunctions of the unitary continuum of this subject-object field of consciousness, another from the inability to cope with its polar, dual, or contradictory aspect. Let us focus first on the therapeutic significance of dysfunctions of continuity or contact.

DYSFUNCTIONS OF CONTACT

Schizophrenia is the crippled field of consciousness. In some schizophrenics the unified field is cut, or the subject-object flow is blocked, so that the patient's consciousness feels out of touch with his world. Consider these typical quotations from schizophrenics:

> I am like a zombie living behind a glass wall. I can see all that goes on in the world but I can't touch it. I can't reach it. I can't be in contact with it. I am outside. There is nothing there, absolutely nothing.

Or

> There's something wrong with me. I don't seem to feel about my family like others do. I know this mostly when I talk about my wife and children. I talk about them like my neighbors talk about their cars. I certainly like my family. But if they all went away it wouldn't bother me. They are really quite dispensable. I would just get somebody new, just like my neighbors get new cars.

This philosophic diagnosis suggests that one treatment strategy for a blocked or cut field is to force contact, as is now done frequently with autistic children. Another is through the deliberate spiritualization of sports—for example, swimming, jogging, or skiing can become direct experiences of here-there, inner-outer, I-you, subject-object, and consciousness-body connectedness—a technique that is becoming prevalent in the teaching of today's physical education.

Let us then look at dysfunctions of contradiction or conflict.

DYSFUNCTIONS OF CONFLICT

To the authentic individual, the ambiguity of the field is a guarantee of malleability and thus of freedom—with attendant anxiety and opportunity. But the paranoid and the compulsive personalities deny the ambiguities of this field and thus distort reality at its most fundamental. They supplant rigidity for dialectic and therefore cannot cope with life as it really is. As a result, many a schizophrenic is confused about closeness and distance. He yearns for closeness yet rejects it in panic whenever offered.

A typical situation which arises in the consulting room is that the patient brings an insoluble problem. An insoluble problem is not an illness but a symbol for the universal polarity and dialectic of the subject-object field that being is and that we are. Insoluble problems occur in family conflicts, and in disabling, painful, or fatal illnesses, as when leukemic children in pediatric oncology lament, "Mommy, Mommy, why doesn't someone tell me what's happening to me?"

Some insoluble problems are conflicts endemic to human existence itself. Typical endemic conflicts, which may exist exclusively within a single individual, are between the child and the adult, the male and the female, dependence versus independence, the potential versus the actual, and work versus leisure. The most common conflict among healthy and successful professionals is between the values of a highly individualized creative career and the need for deeply devoted, warm, and intense intimate relationships.

The most common conflict among our healthy and intelligent young—sometimes called the generation gap—is between a conventional thing-oriented life-style and an inner life of creative sensuality or spirituality. Their lives—often authentic—are out of step with their environment, which is often mad. They form an unbroken chain of Bohemians, from the beat generation to today's growth movement.

Coping with Categoreal Facts

The philosophic diagnosis that specific conflicts are but manifestations of the general polar structure of the consciousness-world field of being suggests parallel philosophic treatment strategies. Thus, how we cope with dialectic in general determines how we manage its specific instances. Typical and tested philosophic recommendations include the following: noble, exciting, and contagious protest, such as Beethoven rebelling against his deafness in some of his symphonic works; commitment to self-transcending meanings, such as the work of Ghandi and Martin Luther King; pious religious resignation to fate in the prayer "Thy will be done" as illustrated in the life of St. Francis; the mystical denial of the reality of the world of conflict, as with India's erstwhile revolutionary Sri Aurobindo Ghose; finally, the view —sometimes associated with idealist philosophers from Hegel to Josiah Royce—that polarity is self-willed for the sake of feeling real; that polarity itself can be chosen originarily as the best of all possible worlds; that polarity is life—and a mature person understands that an end to polarity is an end to life; that each obstacle turned over is in truth a stepping stone; that the evil in the world builds character; and that an insoluble problem is a privilege, for our examplary response to it is the finest inheritance we can leave to those, like our children, who matter most. Frankl's method of coping with conflict was to point out that the struggle against one's own very special evil gives worth to one's existence. *An underlying incontrovertible philosophic fact remains: we are free to choose that our suffering have precisely these constructive meanings.* The categoreal philosophic fact of freedom-in-meaning-ascriptions comes to the aid of psychotherapy in managing insoluble problems.

Example

Let us summarize with an illustration. Health problems are often symptoms of more basic philosophic conditions. A medical problem, such as fever produced by the influenza virus, or a behavior problem, such as uncontrollable anger due to unresolved Oedipal conflicts, represent concrete, particulate, and metaphoric picture-thinking about what in truth may be abstract, general, ontological, and structural dysfunctions within philosophically described being itself.

For example, a child whose mother wanted to abort her grows up feeling rejected and worthless. Rollo May describes a patient who, as an illegitimate child, was brought up by relatives. Her mother, in periods of anger, often reminded the child of her origin, recounted how she had tried to abort her, and in times of trouble had shouted at the little girl, "If you hadn't been born, we wouldn't have to go through this!" Other relatives had cried at the child, in family quarrels, "Why didn't you kill yourself?" and "You should have been choked the day you were born!"

Conventional psychotherapy believes that the child's sense of worthlessness and the ensuing symptomatology result directly from the rejection and deprivation she suffered during childhood. But, for clinical philosophy, the sense of worth derives ultimately from experiencing one's ontological foundation, *a ground that is always there but is not always perceived.* Mother-love in early childhood may *facilitate* this perception and serves to illustrate to the child this universal fact of existence. But mother-love does not produce or create the sense of security. Security is not a psychological feeling to be learned but a philosophic fact to be known. Security is not a psychological phenomenon, that is, a reality of the world of things and objects, but is a transcendental phenomenon, a metaphysical reality related to the structure of our very own consciousness.

Some people are never taught this insight. Others come to this realization of their own accord. Fortunately, not one but many events in a person's life can teach this truth, and they range from warmly loving parents to a formal program in philosophy, from religion to poetry, from therapy to a harsh life of rejection and adversity.

Two important corollaries follow. If a so-called good parent, a security-facilitating mother, is absent, then the individual can nevertheless make up for it in later life. There is thus always hope. We can discover a foundation, a home, at the core of every human being. And it is there that philosophic therapy must reach. Every person is *worthy, safe, and secure due to his or her nature and not by virtue of the adventitious idiosyncrasies of a particular childhood or environment.*

Conversely, parent-love in childhood does not guarantee authenticity in later life. Some children from so-called good families turn sour, whereas some of the most authentic persons of all time have come from severely deprived childhoods. It is the success of the philosophic educational process—however and whenever that may be accomplished—that helps bring about the authenticity of the individual. The therapeutically useful principle is that the *philosophic facts about a person's essential human nature can be taught at any time.*

Suggestions for New Research Directions

A phenomenological model of being promises to facilitate research in at least three frontiers where data are accumulating exponentially but where lack of adequate conceptualization blocks imminent breakthroughs. One frontier is physics, where the usefulness of a consciousness-world field theory of being began with the work of Faraday and Maxwell in electromagnetism, and culminates in the theories of energy quanta and general relativity, where matter becomes a condensation of space-time (often called the curvature of space).

Another frontier is psychosomatic medicine. The unit in biology is no longer an object—such as an organism, a cell, or a molecule—but a consciousness-body continuum. The old question was, How do consciousness and body interact? The new question is, How can we explain the numerous exceptions to the consciousness-object connection? That is, why are we ill when we do not wish to be?

A concluding example is education. Philosophic facts can be taught early in the schools, with direct influence on the management of death and anxiety, love and health, and on the respect for democracy and ethical behavior.

APPENDIX H • *Simplified Outline of the Practice of Clinical Philosophy*

1. The emphasis is on the person and the personal and not on the technique. The technique helps the therapist to start work and to increase efficiency. The therapist's personal qualities are, in the long run, a higher predictor of effective therapy than training, technique, or orientation.

2. The therapist has conceptual *understanding* and *experiential* support of the *phenomenological model of being*. The therapist also is able to *integrate* this vision into his or her life.

3. Clinical philosophy operates within the following parameters:

   a. The atmosphere is sincerely and profoundly supportive. Even confrontation exists in an atmosphere of support.

   b. The initial complaint is not nearly as significant as the need to explore the undisclosed and originary projects of the patient or client.

   c. Regardless of contrary claims, the *only* problems are (i) the patient's inadequacy in (or resistances against) taking charge of his or her own life, and (ii) lack of contact with the world or not reaching toward the future (self-transcendence).

4. The therapist's tools are limited essentially to his or her empirical ego. Specifically, the therapist has three types of tools:

   a. The power with which the patient or client invests the therapist (the patient's projections).

   b. The structure and intensity of the relationship established between patient and therapist or client and facilitator.

   c. The body and emotions of the therapist.

5. Diagnostic procedures:

   a. Symptoms are essentially ignored. Although they may help to initiate therapy by saying "help," symptoms are mostly *objects* whose function it is to prevent access to the transcendental ego.

   b. Diagnostic measurements can be taken only by the inwardness (or unconscious) of the therapist. Traditional tests and techniques are at best only peripherally relevant.

c. The *foundation* of therapy is the discovery of the reality or *the possibility of a transcendental relationship* between patient and therapist. Such a relationship usually exists in degrees. It is rarely either all present or totally absent. The severity of the personality disturbance is measured by the extent to which a transcendental relationship is absent. If it is present, therapy can proceed. If it is absent, therapy consists solely in attempting to establish a transcendental relationship.

d. The *process* of therapy is the constitution of an *Existenz*, the development of a creative-erotic energy core, the making of an archetypal decision for finitude, and establishing contact with the world. It is thus a matter of the highest diagnostic priority to *ascertain how much of a sense of individual identity the patient or client has*—in short, how real the patient is or feels.

Only the inwardness of the therapist can determine that. The structure of another inwardness (whether it has the capacity for transcendental or intersubjective contact and whether it has created itself into a real and existing individual) can be assessed or reflected only by another inwardness, not by tests.

6. Therapeutic strategies:

The sense of individual identity or *Existenz* and self-transcendence (see 5d above) can be encouraged to grow in the following ways:

a. Identify existing strengths;

b. Repeatedly use an accurate "universality-to-individuality" fantasy;

c. Encourage anger, protest—including anger-at-self—perhaps through confrontation;

d. Be an example of a self-made person.

7. The entire process must possess total integrity and ethicalness, and it must be fully devoted to the real needs of the patient or client. The therapist's neurotic needs and self-deceptions must be totally excluded from the treatment process.

SELECTED BIBLIOGRAPHY

Introductory and Overview Books

Barnes, Wesley. *The Philosophy and Literature of Existentialism*. Woodbury, N.Y.: Barrons, 1968.

Barrett, William. *Irrational Man: A Study in Existential Philosophy*. New York: Doubleday Anchor Books, 1958.

Barrett, William. *What Is Existentialism?* New York: Grove Press, 1964.

Blackham, H. J. *Six Existentialist Thinkers*. London: Routledge & Kegan Paul, 1952.

Breisach, Ernst. *Introduction to Modern Existentialism*. New York: Grove Press, 1962.

Collins, James. *The Existentialists*. Chicago: Henry Regnery, 1952.

Elliston, Frederick, and McCormick, Peter. *Husserl: Exposition and Appraisal*. Notre Dame, Ind.: University of Notre Dame Press, 1976.

Foulquie, Paul. *Existentialism*. Translated by K. Raine. New York: Roy, 1950.

Friedman, Maurice. ed. *The Worlds of Existentialism: A Critical Reader*. New York: Random House, 1964.

Grene, Marjorie. *Dreadful Freedom: A Critique of Existentialism*. Chicago: University of Chicago Press, 1948.

Grene, Marjorie. *Introduction to Existentialism*. Chicago: University of Chicago Press, 1959.

Grimsley, Ronald. *Existentialist Thought*. Cardiff: University of Wales Press, 1955.

Gould, James A., and Truitt, Willis H. *Existentialist Philosophy*. Encino, Calif.: Dickenson Publishing Co., 1973.

Hanna, Thomas. *The Lyrical Existentialist*. New York: Atheneum, 1962.

Häring, Bernard. *The Christian Existentialist*. New York: New York University Press, 1968.

Heinemann, F. H. *Existentialism and the Modern Predicament*. New York: Harper & Bros., 1954.

Herberg, Will, ed. *Four Existentialist Theologians*. Garden City, N.Y.: Doubleday, 1958.

Hubben, William. *Dostoevsky, Kierkegaard, Nietzsche and Kafka: Four Prophets of Our Destiny*. New York: Collier Books, 1972.

Kaufmann, Walter, ed. *Existentialism From Dostoyevky to Sartre*. New York: Meridian Books, 1956.

Kuhn, Helmut. *Encounter with Nothingness*. Chicago: Henry Regnery, 1949.

Langiulli, Nino, ed. *The Existentialist Tradition*. Garden City, N.Y.: Doubleday, 1971.

Lawrence, Nathaniel, and O'Conner, Daniel, eds. *Readings in Existential Phenomenology*. Englewood Cliffs, N.J.: Prentice-Hall, 1967.

Lee, Edward N., and Mandelbaum, Maurice, eds. *Phenomenology and Existentialism*. Baltimore: John Hopkins University Press, 1967.

Luijpen, William A. *Existential Phenomenology*. Translated by Henry J. Koren. Pittsburgh, Pa.: Duquesne University Press, 1960.

MacQuarrie, John. *Existentialism*. Philadelphia: Westminster, 1972.

Martin, Vincent. *Existentialism: Sören Kierkegaard, Jean-Paul Sartre, Albert Camus*. Washington: Thomist Press, 1962.

Molina, Fernando. *Existentialism as Philosophy*. Englewood Cliffs, N.J.: Prentice-Hall, 1962.

Mounier, E. *Existentialist Philosophies: An Introduction*. Translated by E. Blow. London: Rockliff, 1948.

Olson, Robert Goodwin. *An Introduction to Existentialism*. New York: Dover Publications, 1962.

Patka, Frederick, ed. *Existentialist Thinkers and Thought*. New York: Citadel Press, 1962.

Reinhardt, Kurt F. *The Existentialist Revolt*. New York: Ungar Publishing Co., 1952.

Sanborn, Patricia F. *Existentialism*. New York: Pegasus, 1968.

Schrader, George Alfred, ed. *Existential Philosophers: Kierkegaard to Merleau-Ponty*. New York: McGraw-Hill, 1967.

Shinn, Roger. *The Existentialist Posture*. New York: Association Press, 1970.

Solomon, Robert E., ed. *Phenomenology and Existentialism*. New York: Harper & Row, 1972.

Spiegelberg, Herbert. *The Phenomenological Movement: A Historical Introduction*. 2 vols. The Hague: Nijhoff, 1965.

Spiegelberg, Herbert. *Phenomenology in Psychology and Psychiatry: A Historical Introduction*. Evanston, Ill.: Northwestern University Press, 1972.

Vandenberg, Donald. *Being and Education: Essays in Existential Phenomenology*. Englewood Cliffs, N.J.: Prentice-Hall, 1971.

Wahl, Jean. *Philosophies of Existence*. Translated by F. M. Lory. London: Routledge & Kegan Paul, 1969.

Wahl, Jean. *A Short History of Existentialism*. Translated by Forrest Williams and Stanley Maron. New York: Philosophical Library, 1949.

Warnock, Mary. *Existentialism*. London: Oxford University Press, 1970.

Wild, John. *The Challenge of Existentialism*. Bloomington: Indiana University Press, 1966.

Zaner, Richard M., and Ihde, Don, eds. *Phenomenology and Existentialism*. New York: G.P. Putnam's Sons, 1973.

Source Books of Existentialism

Beauvoir, Simone de. *The Ethics of Ambiguity*. Translated by Bernard Frechtman. New York: Citadel Press, 1962.

Berdyaev, Nicolas. *The Destiny of Man*. Translated by Natalie Duddington. London: Geoffrey Bles, 1948.

Berdyaev, Nicolas. *Freedom and the Spirit*. Tanslated by Oliver Clarke. New York: Charles Scribner's Sons, 1935.

Berdyaev, Nicolas. *Slavery and Freedom*. Translated by R. M. French. New York: Charles Scribner's Sons, 1944.

Buber, Martin. *Between Man and Man*. Translated by Ronald Gregor Smith. London: Routledge & Kegan Paul, 1954.

Buber, Martin. *Eclipse of God*. New York: Harper & Row, 1957.

Buber, Martin. *Good and Evil*. Translated by Ronald Gregor Smith. New York: Charles Scribner's Sons, 1953.

Buber, Martin, *I and Thou*. Translated by Ronald G. Smith. New York: Charles Scribner's Sons, 1958.

Bultmann, Rudolph. *Essays: Philosophical and Theological*. Translated by James C. Greig. New York: Macmillan, 1955.

Bultmann, Rudolph. *Kerygma and Myth*. Translated by Reginald Fuller. Edited by Hans Bartsch. London: SPCK, 1954.

Bultmann, Rudolph, *The Presence of Eternity*. New York: Harper & Bros., 1957.

Camus, Albert. *The Fall*. Translated by Justin O'Brien. New York: Alfred A. Knopf, 1956.

Camus, Albert. *The Myth of Sisyphus*. Translated by Justin O'Brien. New York: Alfred A. Knopf, 1955.

Camus, Albert. *The Notebooks: 1935-1942*. Translated by P. Thody. New York: Alfred A. Knopf, 1963.

Camus, Albert. *The Notebooks: 1942-1951*. Translated by P. Thody. New York: Alfred A. Knopf, 1965.

Camus, Albert. *The Plague*. Translated by Stuart Gilbert. New York: Alfred A. Knopf, 1958.

Camus, Albert. *The Rebel*. Translated by A. Bower. New York: Alfred A. Knopf, 1954.

Camus, Albert. *Resistance, Rebellion, and Death*. Translated by Justin O'Brien. New York: Alfred A. Knopf, 1961.

Heidegger, Martin, *Being and Time*. Translated by John MacQuarrie and Edward Robinson. New York: Harper & Row, 1962.

Heidegger, Martin. *Discourse on Thinking*. Translated by John M. Anderson and E. Hans Freund. New York: Harper & Row, 1966.

Heidegger, Martin. *Early Greek Thinking*. Translated by David Farrell Krell and Frank Capuzzi. New York: Harper & Row, 1975.

Heidegger, Martin. *The End of Philosophy*. Translated by Joan Stambaugh. New York: Harper & Row, 1973.

Heidegger, Martin. *The Essence of Reasons*. Translated by Terrence Malick. Evanston, Ill.: Northwestern University Press, 1969.

Heidegger, Martin. *Existence and Being*. Edited by Werner Brock. Chicago: Regnery-Gateway, 1949.

Heidegger, Martin. *Hegel's Concept of Experience*. Edited by J. Glenn Gray. New York: Harper & Row, 1970.

Heidegger, Martin. *Identity and Difference*. Translated by Joan Stambaugh. New York: Harper & Row, 1969.

Heidegger, Martin. *An Introduction to Metaphysics*. Translated by Ralph Manheim.

New Haven, Conn.: Yale University Press, 1959.

Heidegger, Martin. *Kant and the Problem of Metaphysics*. Translated by James S. Churchill. Bloomington: Indiana University Press, 1962.

Heidegger, Martin. *On the Way to Language*. Translated by Peter D. Hertz and Joan Stambaugh. New York: Harper & Row, 1971.

Heidegger, Martin. *On Time and Being*. Translated by Joan Stambaugh. New York: Harper & Row, 1972.

Heidegger, Martin. *The Piety of Thinking*. Translated by James G. Hart and John Maraldo. Bloomington: Indiana University Press, 1976.

Heidegger, Martin. *Poetry, Language, Thought*. Translated by Albert Hofstadter. New York: Harper & Row, 1971.

Heidegger, Martin. *The Question of Being*. Translated by William Kluback and Jean T. Wilde. New York: Twayne, 1958.

Heidegger, Martin. *What is a Thing?* Translated by W. B. Barton and Vera Deutsch. Chicago: Henry Regnery, 1967.

Heidegger, Martin. *What is Called Thinking?* Translated by Fred D. Wieck and J. Glenn Gray. New York: Harper & Row, 1968.

Heidegger, Martin. *What is Philosophy?* Translated by William Kluback and Jean T. Wilde. New York: Twayne, 1958.

Herberg, Will., ed. *The Writings of Martin Buber*. Cleveland: World Publishing Co., 1956.

Jaspers, Karl. *The European Spirit*. Translated by R. G. Smith. New York: Macmillan, 1949.

Jaspers, Karl. *The Future of Mankind*. Translated by E. B. Ashton. Chicago: University of Chicago Press, 1961.

Jaspers, Karl. *General Psychopathology*. Translated by J. Hoening and M. W. Hamilton. Chicago: University of Chicago Press, 1963.

Jaspers, Karl. *The Great Philosophers*. Vols. 1 and 2. Translated by R. Manheim. Edited by H. Arendt. New York: Harcourt, Brace & World, 1962.

Jaspers, Karl. *The Idea of the University*. Translated by H. A. T. Reiche and H. F. Vanderschmidt. Edited by K. W. Deutsch. Boston: Beacon Press, 1959.

Jaspers, Karl. *Man in the Modern Age*. Translated by E. and C. Paul. London: Routledge & Kegan Paul, 1933.

Jaspers, Karl. *Myth and Christianity*. Translated by H. Wolff. New York: Noonday Press, Inc., 1958.

Jaspers, Karl. *Nietzsche and Christianity*. Translated by E. B. Ashton. Chicago: Henry Regnery, 1961.

Jaspers, Karl. *Nietzsche: An Introduction to the Understanding of His Philosophical Activity*. Translated by C.F. Wallraff and F.J. Schmitz. Tucson: University of Arizona Press, 1965.

Jaspers, Karl. *The Origin and Goal of History*. Translated by M. Bullock. New Haven, Conn.: Yale University Press, 1953.

Jaspers, Karl. *The Perennial Scope of Philosophy*. Translated by Ralph Manheim. New York: Philosophical Library, 1949.

Jaspers, Karl. *The Question of German Guilt*. Translated by E. B. Ashton. New York: Dial Press, 1947.

Jaspers, Karl. *Reason and Anti-Reason in Our Time.* Translated by S. Godman. New Haven, Conn.: Yale University Press, 1952.

Jaspers, Karl. *Reason and Existenz.* Translated by William Earle. New York: Noonday Press, Inc., 1955.

Jaspers, Karl. *Tragedy Is Not Enough.* Translated by H. A. T. Reiche, H. T. Moore, and K. W. Deutsch. Boston: Beacon Press, 1952.

Jaspers, Karl. *Truth and Symbol.* Translated by Jean T. Wild, Wm. Kluback and Wm. Kimmel. New York: Twayne, 1959.

Jaspers, Karl. *Way to Wisdom.* Translated by R. Manheim. New Haven, Conn.: Yale University Press, 1954.

Kierkegaard, Sören. *Attack Upon "Christendom."* Translated by Walter Lowrie. Princeton, N.J.: Princeton University Press, 1944.

Kierkegaard, Sören. *The Concept of Dread.* Translated by Walter Lowrie. Princeton, N.J. : Princeton University Press, 1944.

Kierkegaard, Sören. *Concluding Unscientific Postscript to "Philosophical Fragments."* Translated by David F. Swenson; completed and edited by Walter Lowrie. Princeton, N.J.: Princeton University Press, 1941.

Kierkegaard, Sören. *Edifying Discourses.* Translated by David F. Swenson and Lillian Marvin Swenson. Minneapolis: Augsburg Publishing House, 1943-1946.

Kierkegaard, Sören. *Either/Or: A Fragment of Life.* Translated by David F. Swenson, Lillian Marvin Swenson, and Walter Lowrie. Princeton, N.J.: Princeton University Press, 1944.

Kierkegaard, Sören. *Fear and Trembling.* Translated by Walter Lowrie. Princeton, N.J.: Princeton University Press, 1941.

Kierkegaard, Sören. *The Journals of Sören Kierkegaard.* New York: Oxford University Press, 1938.

Kierkegaard, Sören. *Philosophical Fragments.* Translated by David F. Swenson. Princeton, N.J.: Princeton University Press, 1936.

Kierkegaard, Sören. *The Point of View for My Work as an Author.* Translated by Walter Lowrie. New York: Oxford University Press, 1939.

Kierkegaard, Sören. *The Present Age.* Translated by Alexander Dru and Walter Lowrie. New York: Oxford University Press, 1940.

Kierkegaard, Sören. *Repetition.* Translated by Walter Lowrie. Princeton, N.J.: Princeton University Press, 1941.

Kierkegaard, Sören. *The Sickness Unto Death.* Translated by Walter Lowrie. Princeton, N.J.: Princeton University Press, 1941.

Kierkegaard, Sören. *Stages on Life's Way.* Translated by Walter Lowrie. Princeton, N.J.: Princeton University Press, 1940.

Kierkegaard, Sören. *Training in Christianity.* Translated by Walter Lowrie. Princeton, N.J.: Princeton University Press, 1941.

Kierkegaard, Sören. *Works of Love.* Translated by Lillian Marvin Swenson. Princeton, N.J.: Princeton University Press, 1946.

Marcel, Gabriel. *Being and Having.* Translated by Katherine Farrer. Boston: Beacon Press, 1951.

Marcel, Gabriel. *The Existential Background of Human Dignity.* Cambridge, Mass.: Harvard University Press, 1963.

Marcel, Gabriel. *Homo Viator.* Translated by Emma Cranford. Chicago: Henry Regnery, 1951.

Marcel, Gabriel. *Man Against Mass Society.* Translated by G. S. Fraser. Chicago: Henry Regnery, 1962.

Marcel, Gabriel. *Metaphysical Journal.* Translated by Bernard Wall. Chicago: Henry Regnery, 1950.

Marcel, Gabriel. *The Mystery of Being.* Translated by G. S. Fraser (Vol. 1) and Rene Hague (Vol. 2). London: The Harvill Press, Ltd., 1951, 1960.

Marcel, Gabriel. *The Philosophy of Existence.* Translated by Manya Harari. New York: Philosophical Library, 1949.

Marcel, Gabriel. *Royce's Metaphysics.* Translated by Virginia and Gordon Rings. Chicago: Henry Regnery, 1956.

Maritain, Jacques. *Existence and the Existent.* Translated by Lewis Galantiere and Gerald B. Phelan. Garden City, N.Y.: Image Books, 1960.

Merleau-Ponty, Maurice. *Consciousness and the Acquisition of Language.* Translated by Hugh J. Silverman. Evanston, Ill.: Northwestern University Press, 1973.

Merleau-Ponty, Maurice. *Phenomenology of Perception.* Translated by Colin Smith. New York: Humanities Press, 1962.

Merleau-Ponty, Maurice. *The Primacy of Perception: And Other Essays on Phenomenological Psychology, the Philosophy of Art, History, and Politics.* Edited by James M. Edie. Evanston, Ill.: Northwestern University Press, 1964.

Merleau-Ponty, Maurice. *The Prose of the World.* Translated by John O'Neill. Edited by Claude Lefort. Evanston, Ill.: Northwestern University Press, 1973.

Merleau-Ponty, Maurice. *Sense and Non-Sense.* Translated by Hubert L. and Patricia Allen Dreyfus. Evanston, Ill.: Northwestern University Press, 1964.

Merleau-Ponty, Maurice. *Signs.* Translated by Richard C. McCleary. Evanston, Ill.: Northwestern University Press, 1964.

Merleau-Ponty, Maurice. *The Structure of Behavior.* Translated by Alden L. Fisher. Boston: Beacon Press, 1963.

Nietzsche, Friedrich. *The Antichrist.* Translated by Walter Kaufmann in *The Portable Nietzsche,* ed. W. Kaufmann. New York: Viking, 1954.

Nietzsche, Friedrich. *Beyond Good and Evil.* Translated by Walter Kaufmann. New York: Vintage, 1966.

Nietzsche, Friedrich. *The Birth of Tragedy.* Translated by Walter Kaufman in *Basic Writings of Nietzsche.* Edited by W. Kaufmann. New York: Random House, Modern Library, 1968.

Nietzsche, Friedrich. *The Case of Wagner.* Translated by Walter Kaufmann in *Basic Writings of Nietzsche.* Edited by W. Kaufmann. New York: Random House, Modern Library, 1968.

Nietzsche, Friedrich. *Ecce Homo.* Translated by Walter Kaufmann in *Basic Writings of Nietzsche.* Edited by W. Kaufmann. New York: Modern Library, 1968.

Nietzsche, Friedrich. *The Gay Science.* Translated by Walter Kaufmann. New York: Random House, 1974.

Nietzsche, Friedrich. *Nietzsche contra Wagner.* Translated by Walter Kaufmann in *The Portable Nietzsche.* Edited by W. Kaufmann. New York: Viking, 1954.

Nietzsche, Friedrich. *On the Generalogy of Morals.* Translated by Walter Kaufmann in *Basic Writings of Nietzsche*. Edited by W. Kaufmann. New York: Modern Library, 1968.

Nietzsche, Friedrich. *Thus Spoke Zarathustra*. Translated by Walter Kaufmann. New York: Viking, 1966.

Nietzsche, Friedrich. *Twilight of the Idols*. Translated by Walter Kaufmann in *The Portable Nietzsche*. Edited by W. Kaufmann. New York: Viking, 1954.

Nietzsche, Friedrich. *The Will to Power*. Translated by Walter Kaufmann. New York: Random House, 1967.

Ortega y Gasset, José. *Man and People*. Translated by W. Trask. New York: Norton, 1959.

Ortega y Gasset, José. *Man in Crisis*. Translated by M. Adams. New York: Norton, 1959.

Ortega y Gasset, José. *Meditations on Quixote*. Translated by D. Marín. New York: Norton, 1961.

Ortega y Gasset, José. *On Love: Aspects of a Single Theme*. Translated by T. Talbot. New York: Norton, 1957.

Ortega y Gasset, José. *The Origin of Philosophy*. Translated by T. Talbot. New York: Norton, 1967.

Ortega y Gasset, José. *Revolt of the Masses*. New York: Norton, 1932.

Sartre, Jean-Paul. *Anti-Semite and Jew*. Translated by George J. Becker. New York: Schocken Books, 1948.

Sartre, Jean-Paul. *Baudelaire*. Translated by Martin Turnell. Norfolk, Conn.: New Directions, 1950.

Sartre, Jean-Paul. *Being and Nothingness: An Essay on Phenomenological Ontology*. Translated by Hazel E. Barnes. New York: Philosophical Library, 1956.

Sartre, Jean-Paul. *Critique of Dialectical Reason*. London: NLB, 1976.

Sartre, Jean-Paul. *The Emotions: Outline of A Theory*. Translated by Bernard Frechtman. New York: Philosophical Library, 1948.

Sartre, Jean-Paul. *Existentialism and Humanism*. Translated by Philip Mairet. London: Methuen, 1960.

Sartre, Jean-Paul. *Existential Psychoanalysis*. New York: Philosophical Library, 1953.

Sartre, Jean-Paul. *Imagination*. Translated by F. Williams. Ann Arbor: University of Michigan Press, 1962.

Sartre, Jean-Paul. *Literary and Philosophical Essays*. Translated by Annette Michelson. New York: Collier, 1962.

Sartre, Jean-Paul. *Nausea*. Translated by Lloyd Alexander. Norfolk, Conn.: New Directions, 1949.

Sartre, Jean-Paul. *The Problem of Method*. Translated by Hazel Barnes. London: Methuen, 1964.

Sartre, Jean-Paul. *Psychology of Imagination*. Translated by Bernard Frechtman. New York: Philosophical Library, 1948.

Sartre, Jean-Paul. *Saint Genet: Actor and Martyr*. Translated by Bernard Frechtman. New York: George Braziller, Inc., 1969.

Sartre, Jean-Paul. *Situations*. I and III. Translated by B. Eisler. New York: George Braziller, Inc., 1965.

Sartre, Jean-Paul. *The Transcendence of the Ego: An Existentialist Theory of Con-

sciousness. Translated by Forrest Williams and Robert Kirkpatrick. New York: Noonday, 1957.

Scheler, Max. *Man's Place in Nature*. Translated by H. Meyerhoff. Boston: Beacon Press, 1961.

Scheler, Max. *The Nature of Sympathy*. Translated by Peter Heath. New Haven, Conn.: Yale University Press, 1954.

Scheler, Max. *On the Eternal in Man*. Translated by G. Noble. London: SCM, 1958.

Scheler, Max. *Philosophical Perspectives*. Translated by O. Haac. Boston: Beacon Press, 1958.

Scheler, Max. *Ressentiment*. Translated by W. Holdheim. New York: Free Press, 1961.

Shestov, Lev. *Athens and Jerusalem*. Translated by Bernard Martin. New York: Simon and Schuster, 1966.

Shestov, Lev. *Kierkegaard and the Existential Philosophy*. Translated by Elinor Hewitt. Athens: Ohio University Press, 1969.

Tillich, Paul. *Biblical Religion and the Search for Ultimate Reality*. Chicago: University of Chicago Press, 1955.

Tillich, Paul. *The Courage to Be*. New Haven, Conn.: Yale University Press, 1952.

Tillich, Paul. *The Dynamics of Faith*. New York: Harper & Bros., 1958.

Tillich, Paul. *The Interpretation of History*. New York: Charles Scribner's Sons, 1936.

Tillich, Paul. *The Protestant Era*. Translated by James Luther Adams. Chicago: University of Chicago Press, 1948.

Tillich, Paul. *Systematic Theology*. 3 vols. Chicago: University of Chicago Press, 1951-1963.

Unamuno, Miguel de. *The Agony of Christianity*. Translated by Kurt F. Reinhardt. New York: Frederick Ungar Publishing Co., 1960.

Unamuno, Miguel de. *Essays and Soliloquies*. Translated by J. E. Crawford Flitch. New York: Alfred A. Knopf, 1925.

Unamuno, Miguel de. *Perplexities and Paradoxes*. Translated by Stuart Gross. New York: Philosophical Library, 1945.

Unamuno, Miguel de. *The Tragic Sense of Life*. Translated by J. E. C. Flitch. New York: Dover, 1957.

Books About Existentialism and Existentialists

Abbagnano, Nicola. *Critical Existentialism*. Translated by and edited by Nino Langiulli. Garden City, N.Y.: Doubleday, Anchor Books, 1969.

Allen, E.L. *Existentialism From Within*. New York: Macmillan, 1953.

Barnes, Hazel E. *An Existentialist Ethics*. New York: Alfred A. Knopf, 1968.

Barnes, Hazel E. *Humanistic Existentialism: The Literature of Possibility*. Lincoln: University of Nebraska Press, 1959.

Barral, Mary Rose. *Merleau-Ponty: The Role of the Body Subject in Interpersonal Relations*. Pittsburgh, Pa.: Duquesne University Press, 1965.

Bauer, George Howard. *Sartre and the Artist*. Chicago: The University of Chicago Press, 1969.

Boelen, Bernard J. *Existential Thinking: A Philosophical Orientation*. Pittsburgh, Pa.: Duquesne University Press, 1968.

Borowitz, Eugene. *A Layman's Guide to Religious Existentialism*. Philadelphia: Westminster Press, 1965.

Brée, Germaine. ed. *Camus: A Collection of Critical Essays*. Englewood Cliffs, N.J.: Prentice-Hall, 1962.

Brée, Germaine. *Camus and Sartre: Crisis and Commitment*. New York: Dell, 1972.

Collins, James. *The Mind of Kierkegaard*. Chicago: Henry Regnery, 1953.

Copleston, Frederick C. *Contemporary Philosophy: Studies of Logical Positivism and Existentialism*. London: Burns & Oates, 1963.

Croxall, T. H. *Kierkegaard Commentary*. London: James Nisbet & Co. Ltd., 1956.

Croxall, T. H. *Kierkegaard: Johannes Climacus*. London: Adam & Charles Black, 1958.

Dempsey, J. R. Peter. *The Psychology of Sartre*. Westminister, Md.: Newman Press, 1950.

Denton, David E., ed. *Existentialism and Phenomenology in Education: Collected Essays*. New York: Teachers College Press, 1974.

Desan, Wilfred. *The Tragic Finale: An Essay on the Philosophy of Jean-Paul Sartre*. Cambridge, Mass.: Harvard University Press, 1954.

Diem, Hermann. *Kierkegaard's Dialectic of Existence*. Translated by Harold Knight. Edinburgh: Oliver & Boyd, 1959.

Dutt, K. *Existentialism and Indian Thought*. New York: Philosophical Library, 1960.

Edie, James M.; Earle, William; and Wild, John. *Christianity and Existentialism*. Evanston, Ill.: Northwestern University Press, 1963.

Fallico, Arturo B. *Art and Existentialism*. Englewood Cliffs, N.J.: Prentice-Hall, 1962.

Ferrater Mora, José. *Unamuno: A Philosophy of Tragedy*. Translated by Philip Silver. Berkeley: University of California Press, 1962.

Friedman, Maurice S. *Martin Buber: The Life of Dialogue*. New York: Harper & Bros., 1960.

Frings, Manfred S. *Max Scheler*. Pittsburgh, Pa.: Duquesne University Press, 1965.

Gallagher, Kenneth T. *The Philosophy of Gabriel Marcel*. New York: Fordham University Press, 1962.

Greene, Maxine. *Existential Encounter for Teachers*. New York: Random House, 1967.

Greene, Norman Nathaniel. *Jean-Paul Sartre: The Existentialist Ethic*. Ann Arbor: University of Michigan Press, 1960.

Grene, Marjorie. *Martin Heidegger*. New York: Hillary House, 1957.

Harper, Ralph. *Existentialism: A Theory of Man*. Cambridge, Mass.: Harvard University Press, 1949.

Hartmann, Klaus. *Sartre's Ontology: A Study of Being and Nothingness in the Light of Hegel's Logic*. Evanston, Ill.: Northwestern University Press, 1966.

Jolivet, Régis. *Introduction to Kierkegaard*. Translated by W. H. Barber. New York: E. P. Dutton & Co., 1951.

Jolivet, Régis. *Sartre: The Theology of the Absurd.* Translated by Wesley C. Piersol. Westminster, Md.: Newman Press, 1967.

Karl, Frederick R., and Hamalian, Leo, eds. *The Existential Imagination.* Greenwich, Conn.: Fawcett, 1963.

Karl, Frederick R., and Hamalian, Leo, eds. *The Existential Mind: Documents and Fictions.* Greenwich, Conn.: Fawcett, 1974.

Kaufmann, Walter. *Existentialism, Religion and Death.* New York: New American Library, 1976.

Kaufman, Walter. *From Shakespeare to Existentialism.* Garden City, N.Y.: Doubleday, 1960.

Kern, Edith G., ed. *Sartre: A Collection of Critical Essays.* Englewood Cliffs, N.J.: Prentice-Hall, 1962.

Kingston, F. *French Existentialism: A Christian Critique.* Toronto: University of Toronto Press, 1961.

Kwant, Remy C. *The Phenomenological Philosophy of Merleau-Ponty.* Pittsburgh, Pa.: Duquesne University Press, 1963.

Langan, Thomas. *The Meaning of Heidegger.* New York: Columbia University Press, 1959.

Langan, Thomas. *Merleau-Ponty's Critique of Reason.* New Haven, Conn.: Yale University Press, 1966.

Lee, Edward N., and Mandelbaum, Maurice, eds. *Phenomenology and Existentialism.* Baltimore: The Johns Hopkins Press, 1967.

Löwith, Karl. *Nature, History and Existentialism.* Evanston, Ill.: Northwestern University Press, 1966.

Lowrie, Walter. *Kierkegaard.* Vols. 1 and 2. New York: Harper & Bros., 1962.

MacQuarrie, John. *An Existentialist Theology.* London: SCM Press, 1955.

MacQuarrie, John. *Studies in Christian Existentialism.* Philadelphia: Westminster, 1966.

Makkreel, Rudolf A. *Dilthey: Philosopher of the Human Studies.* Princeton, N.J.: Princeton University Press, 1975.

Michalson, Carl, ed. *Christianity and the Existentialists.* New York: Charles Scribner's Sons, 1956.

Mihalich, Joseph C. *Existentialism and Thomism.* New York: Philosophical Library, 1960.

Morris, Van Clere. *Existentialism in Education: What it Means.* New York: Harper & Row, 1966.

Murdoch, Iris. *Sartre, Romantic Rationalist.* Cambridge, Eng.: Bowes & Bowes, 1953.

Natanson, Maurice. *A Critique of Jean-Paul Sartre's Ontology.* Lincoln: University of Nebraska Press, 1951.

Olafson, Frederick A. *Principles and Persons: An Ethical Interpretation of Existentialism.* Baltimore, Md.: Johns Hopkins Press, 1967.

O'Malley, John B. *The Fellowship of Being: An Essay on the Concept of the Person in the Philosophy of Gabriel Marcel.* The Hague: Martinus Nijhoff, 1966.

O'Neill, John. *Perception, Expression, and History: The Social Phenomenology of Maurice Merleau-Ponty.* Evanston, Ill.: Northwestern University Press, 1970.

Poster, Mark. *Existential Marxism in Postwar France: From Sartre to Althusser.* Princeton, N.J.: Princeton University Press, 1975.

Price, G. *The Narrow Pass: A Study of Kierkgaard's Concept of Man.* New York: McGraw-Hill, 1963.

Richardson, W. J. *Heidegger: Through Phenomenology to Thought.* The Hague: Martinus Nijhoff, 1963.

Rintelen, Fritz Joachim von. *Beyond Existentialism.* Translated by Hilda Graef. London: Allen & Unwin, 1962.

Roberts, David Everett. *Existentialism and Religious Belief.* New York: Oxford University Press, 1959.

Roubiczek, Paul. *Existentialism For and Against.* Cambridge, Eng.: Cambridge University Press, 1964.

Ruggiero, Guido de. *Existentialism: The Disintegration of Man's Soul.* New York: Social Science Publishers, 1948.

Sallis, John, ed. *Heidegger and the Path of Thinking.* Pittsburgh, Pa.: Duquesne University Press, 1970.

Schmitt, Richard. *Martin Heidegger on Being Human.* New York: Random House, 1969.

Schrag, Calvin O. *Existence and Freedom: Towards an Ontology of Human Finitude.* Evanston, Ill.: Northwestern University Press, 1961.

Seidel, George Joseph. *Martin Heidegger and the Pre-Socratics.* Lincoln: University of Nebraska Press, 1964.

Slaatte, Howard A. *The Paradox of Existentialist Theology.* New York: Humanities Press, 1971.

Sontag, Frederick. *The Existentialist Prolegomena to a Future Metaphysics.* Chicago: University of Chicago Press, 1969.

Stern, Alfred. *Sartre: His Philosophy and Psychoanalysis.* New York: Liberal Arts Press, 1953.

Thody, Philip. *Albert Camus: A Study of His Work.* New York: Grove Press, 1959.

Troisfontaines, R. *Existentialism and Christian Thought.* Translated by M. Jarret-Kerr. London: A. & C. Black, 1950.

Ussher, A. *Journey Through Dread.* New York: Devin-Adair, 1955.

Versényi, Laszlo. *Heidegger, Being and Truth.* New Haven, Conn.: Yale University Press, 1965.

Vycinas, Vincent. *Earth and Gods: An Introduction to the Philosophy of Martin Heidegger.* The Hague: Martinus Nijhoff, 1961.

Wild, John. *Human Freedom and Social Order.* Durham, N.C.: Duke University Press, 1959.

Wilde, Jean T., and Kimmel, William, eds. *The Search for Being: Essays from Kierkegaard to Sartre on the Problem of Existence.* New York: Twayne, 1962.

Williams, John R. *Contemporary Existentialism and Christian Faith.* Englewood Cliffs, N.J.: Prentice-Hall, 1965.

Wyschogrod, Michael. *Kierkegaard and Heidegger.* London: Routledge & Kegan Paul, 1954.

Books on Phenomenology

Bachelard, Suzanne. *A Study of Husserl's "Formal and Transcendental Logic."* Translated by Lester E. Embree. Evanston, Ill.: Northwestern University Press, 1968.

Berger, Gaston. *The "Cogito" in Husserl's Philosophy.* Translated by Kathleen McLaughlin. Evanston, Ill.: Northwestern University Press, 1972.

Berleant, Arnold. *The Aesthetic Field: A Phenomenology of Aesthetic Experience.* Springfield, Ill.: Thomas, 1969.

Bettes, Joseph Dabney, ed. *Phenomenology of Religion: Eight Modern Descriptions of the Essence of Religion.* New York: Harper & Row, 1969.

Brentano, Franz. *Psychology From An Empirical Standpoint.* Translated by Antos C. Rancurello, D.B. Terrell, and Linda L. McAlister. Edited by Oscar Kraus. New York: Humanities Press, 1973.

Bruzina, Ronald. *Logos and Eidos: The Concept of Phenomenology.* The Hague: Mouton, 1970.

Cairns, Dorion. *Guide for Translating Husserl.* The Hague: Martinus Nijhoff, 1973.

Carlo, William E. *The Ultimate Reducibility of Essence to Existence in Existential Metaphysics.* The Hague: Martinus Nijhoff, 1966.

Carr, David. *Phenomenology and the Problem of History: A Study of Husserl's Transcendental Philosophy.* Evanston, Ill.: Northwestern University Press, 1974.

Carr, David, and Casey, Edward S., eds. *Explorations in Phenomenology.* The Hague: Martinus Nijhoff, 1973.

Casey, Edward S. *Imagining: A Phenomenological Study.* Bloomington: Indiana University Press, 1976.

Chapman, Harmon M. *Sensations and Phenomenology.* Bloomington: Indiana University Press, 1966.

Chisholm, R. M., ed. *Realism and the Background of Phenomenology.* Glencoe, Ill.: The Free Press, 1960.

Cunningham, Suzanne. *Language and the Phenomenological Reductions of Edmund Husserl.* The Hague: Martinus Nijhoff, 1976.

Dagenais, James J. *Models of Man: A Phenomenological Critique of Some Paradigms in the Human Sciences.* The Hague: Martinus Nijhoff, 1974.

Dufrenne, Mikel. *The Phenomenology of Aesthetic Experience.* Translated by Edward S. Casey et al. Evanston, Ill.: Northwestern University Press, 1974.

DeMuralt, André. *The Idea of Phenomenology: Husserlian Exemplarism.* Translated by Garry L. Breckon. Evanston, Ill.: Northwestern University Press, 1974.

Derrida, Jacques. *Speech and Phenomena and Other Essays on Husserl's Theory of Signs.* Translated by David B. Allison. Evanston, Ill.: Northwestern University Press, 1973.

Durfee, Harold A., ed. *Analytic Philosophy and Phenomenology.* 2 vols. The Hague: Martinus Nijhoff, 1976.

Edie, James M., ed. *An Invitation to Phenomenology: Studies in the Philosophy of Experience.* Chicago: Quadrangle, 1965.

Edie, James M., ed. *New Essays in Phenomenology.* Chicago: Quadrangle, 1970.

Edie, James M., ed. *Phenomenology in America: Studies in the Philosophy of Experience.* Chicago: Quadrangle, 1967.

Edie, James M.; Parker, Francis H.; and Schrag, Calvin O., eds. *Patterns of the Life-World: Essays in Honor of John Wild.* Evanston, Ill.: Northwestern University Press, 1970.

Edie, James. *Speaking and Meaning: The Phenomenology of Language.* Bloomington: Indiana University Press, 1976.

Elveton, R. O., ed. *The Phenomenology of Husserl: Selected Critical Readings.*
Chicago: Quadrangle, 1970.

Embree, Lester, E., ed. *Life-World and Consciousness: Essays for Aron Gurwitsch.*
Evanston, Ill.: Northwestern University Press, 1972.

Erickson, Stephen A. *Language and Being: An Analytic Phenomenology.* New
Haven, Conn.: Yale University Press, 1970.

Farber, Marvin. *The Aims of Phenomenology: The Motives, Methods, and Impact
of Husserl's Thought.* New York: Harper & Row, 1966.

Farber, Marvin. *The Foundation of Phenomenology: Edmund Husserl and the
Quest for a Rigorous Science of Philosophy.* Albany, N.Y.: State University
of New York Press, 1967.

Farber, Marvin. *Naturalism and Subjectivism.* Springfield, Ill.: Charles C. Thomas,
1959.

Farber, Marvin. *Phenomenology and Existence: Toward a Philosophy within
Nature.* New York: Harper & Row, 1967.

Farber, Marvin. *Phenomenology as a Method and as a Philosophical Discipline.*
Buffalo, N.Y.: University of Buffalo Press, 1928.

Farber, Marvin., ed. *Philosophical Essays in Memory of Edmund Husserl.* Cambridge, Mass.: Harvard University Press, 1940. Reprint, New York: Greenwood Press, 1968.

Fuchs, Wolfgang Walter. *Phenomenology and the Metaphysics of Presence.* The
Hague: Martinus Nijhoff, 1976.

Garvin, Harry R., ed. *Phenomenology, Structuralism, Semiology.* Lewisburg, Pa.:
Bucknell University Press, 1976.

Gurwitsch, Aron. *The Field of Consciousness.* Pittsburgh, Pa.: Duquesne University
Press, 1964.

Gurwitsch, Aron, et al. *Phenomenological Perspectives: Historical and Systematic
Essays in Honor of Herbert Spiegelberg.* The Hague: Martinus Nijhoff, 1976.

Gurwitsch, Aron. *Phenomenology and the Theory of Science.* Edited by Lester
Embree. Evanston, Ill.: Northwestern University Press, 1974.

Gurwitsch, Aron. *Studies in Phenomenology and Psychology.* Evanston, Ill.:
Northwestern University Press, 1966.

Hanneborg, Kurt. *The Study of Literature: A Contribution to the Phenomenology
of the Humane Sciences.* Oslo: Universitetsforlagert, 1967.

Husserl, Edmund. *Cartesian Meditations: An Introduction to Phenomenology.*
Translated by Dorion Cairns. The Hague: Martinus Nijhoff, 1960.

Husserl, Edmund. *The Crisis of European Sciences and Transcendental Phenomenology: An Introduction to Phenomenological Philosophy.* Translated by
David Carr. Evanston, Ill.: Northwestern University Press, 1970.

Husserl, Edmund. *Experience and Judgment.* Translated by James S. Churchill and
Karl Ameriks. Evanston, Ill.: Northwestern University Press, 1973.

Husserl, Edmund. *Formal and Transcendental Logic.* Translated by Dorion Cairns.
The Hague: Martinus Nijhoff, 1969.

Husserl, Edmund. *The Idea of Phenomenology.* Translated by William P. Alston and George Nakhnikian. The Hague: Martinus Nijhoff, 1964.

Husserl, Edmund. *Ideas: General Introduction to Pure Phenomenology.* Translated by W. R. Boyce Gibson. New York: Macmillan, 1931.

Husserl, Edmund. *Logical Investigations.* Translated by J. N. Findlay. 2 vols. New York: Humanities Press, 1970.

Husserl, Edmund. *The Paris Lectures.* Translated by Peter Koestenbaum. The Hague: Martinus Nijhoff, 1964.

Husserl, ·Edmund. *Phenomenology and the Crisis of Philosophy: Philosophy as Rigorous Science and Philosophy and the Crisis of European Man.* Translated by Quentin Lauer. New York: Harper & Row, 1965.

Husserl, Edmund. *The Phenomenology of Internal Time-Consciousness.* Translated by James S. Churchill. Edited by Martin Heidegger. Bloomington: Indiana University Press, 1964.

Ihde, Don. *Hermeneutic Phenomenology: The Philosophy of Paul Ricoeur.* Evanston, Ill.: Northwestern University Press, 1971.

Ihde, Don. *Listening and Voice: A Phenomenology of Sound.* Athens: Ohio University Press, 1976.

Ihde, Don. *Sense and Significance.* Pittsburgh, Pa.: Duquesne University Press, 1973.

Ihde, Don, and Zaner, Richard M., eds. *Dialogues in Phenomenology.* The Hague: Martinus Nijhoff, 1975.

Ihde, Don, and Zaner, Richard M., eds. *Interdisciplinary Phenomenology.* The Hague: Martinus Nijhoff, 1977.

Ingarden, Roman. *Time and Modes of Being.* Translated by Helen R. Michejda. Springfield, Ill.: Charles C. Thomas, 1964.

James, William. *Psychology: Briefer Course.* New York: Henry Holt & Co., 1910.

James, William. *The Principles of Psychology.* Vols. 1 and 2. New York: Henry Holt & Co., 1890.

Kaelin, Eugene Francis. *Art and Existence: A Phenomenological Aesthetics.* Lewisburg, Pa.: Bucknell University Press, 1970.

Kersten, Frederick I., and Zaner, Richard M., eds. *Phenomenology, Continuation and Criticism: Essays in Memory of Dorion Cairns.* The Hague: Martinus Nijhoff, 1973.

Kockelmans, Joseph J. *Edmund Husserl's Phenomenological Psychology: A Historico-Critical Study.* Translated by Bernd Jager. Revised by the author. Pittsburgh, Pa.: Duquesne University Press, 1967.

Kockelmans, Joseph J. *A First Introduction to Husserl's Phenomenology.* Pittsburgh, Pa.: Duquesne University Press, 1967.

Kockelmans, Joseph J. *Phenomenology and Physical Science.* Pittsburgh, Pa.: Duquesne University Press, 1966.

Kockelmans, Joseph J., ed. *Phenomenology: The Philosophy of Edmund Husserl and Its Interpretation.* Garden City, N.Y.: Doubleday, Anchor Books, 1967.

Kockelmans, Joseph J., and Kisiel, Theodore J., eds. *Phenomenology and the Natural Sciences: Essays and Translations.* Evanston, Ill.: Northwestern University Press, 1970.

Kuenzli, A., ed. *The Phenomenological Problem.* New York: Harper & Row, 1959.

Kwant, Remy C. *Encounter.* Pittsburgh, Pa.: Duquesne University Press, 1965.

Kwant, Remy C. *From Phenomenology to Metaphysics.* Pittsburgh, Pa.: Duquesne University Press, 1966.

Kwant, Remy C. *Phenomenology of Language.* Pittsburgh, Pa.: Duquesne University Press, 1965.

Kwant, Remy C. *Phenomenology of Social Existence.* Pittsburgh, Pa.: Duquesne University Press, 1965.

Lauer, Quentin. *The Triumph of Subjectivity: An Introduction to Transcendental Phenomenology.* New York: Fordham University Press, 1958. Republished as *Phenomenology: Its Genesis and Prospect.* New York: Harper & Row, 1965.

Levin, David Michael. *Reason and Evidence in Husserl's Phenomenology.* Evanston, Ill.: Northwestern University Press, 1970.

Levinas, Emmanuel. *The Theory of Intuition in Husserl's Phenomenology.* Translated by André Orianne. Evanston, Ill.: Northwestern University Press, 1973.

Levinas, Emmanuel. *Totality and Infinity.* Pittsburgh, Pa.: Duquesne University Press, 1969.

Luijpen, William A. *Phenomenology and Atheism.* Pittsburgh, Pa.: Duquesne University Press, 1964.

Luijpen, William A. *Phenomenology and Humanism.* Pittsburgh, Pa.: Duquesne University Press, 1966.

Luijpen, William A. *Phenomenology and Metaphysics.* Pittsburgh, Pa.: Duquesne University Press, 1965.

Mandelbaum, Maurice. *The Phenomenology of Moral Experience.* Baltimore: Johns Hopkins Press, 1969.

Mays, Wolfe, and Brown, S. C., eds. *Linguistic Analysis and Phenomenology.* London: Macmillan, 1972.

Meinong, Alexius. *On Emotional Presentation.* Translated by Marie-Luise Schubert Kalsi. Evanston, Ill.: Northwestern University Press, 1972.

Mohanty, J.N. *Edmund Husserl's Theory of Meaning.* The Hague: Martinus Nijhoff, 1964.

Mohanty, J.N. *Phenomenology and Ontology.* The Hague: Martinus Nijhoff, 1970.

Natanson, Maurice. *Edmund Husserl: Philosopher of Infinite Tasks.* Evanston, Ill.: Northwestern University Press, 1973.

Natanson, Maurice, ed. *Essays in Phenomenology.* The Hague: Martinus Nijhoff, 1966.

Natanson, Maurice. *The Journeying Self: A Study in Philosophy and Social Role.* Reading, Mass.: Addison-Wesley Publishing Co., 1970.

Natanson, Maurice. *Literature, Philosophy, and the Social Sciences: Essays in Existentialism and Phenomenology.* The Hague: Martinus Nijhoff, 1962.

Natanson, Maurice, ed. *Phenomenology and the Social Sciences.* New York: Random House, 1973.

Oden, Thomas C. *The Structure of Awareness.* Nashville, Tenn.: Abingdon Press, 1969.

Osborn, A. D. *Edmund Husserl and His Logical Investigations.* Cambridge, Mass.: Edwards Brothers, 1949.

Owens, Thomas. *Phenomenology and Intersubjectivity: Contemporary Interpretations of the Interpersonal Situation.* The Hague: Martinus Nijhoff, 1970.

Paci, Enzo. *The Function of the Sciences and the Meaning of Man.* Translated by

Paul Piccone and James Hansen. Evanston, Ill.: Northwestern University Press, 1972.

Pettit, Philip. *On the Idea of Phenomenology.* Dublin: Scepter, 1969.

Peursen, Cornelis Anthonie van. *Phenomenology and Analytic Philosophy.* Pittsburgh, Pa.: Duquesne University Press, 1972.

Peursen, Cornelis Anthonie van. *Phenomenology and Reality.* Translated by Henry J. Koren. Pittsburgh, Pa.: Duquesne University Press, 1972.

Pfänder, Alexander. *Phenomenology of Willing and Motivation.* Translated by Herbert Spiegelberg. Evanston, Ill.: Northwestern University Press, 1967.

Pivčević, Edo. *Husserl and Phenomenology.* London: Hutchinson University Library, 1970.

Pivčević, Edo, ed. *Phenomenology and Philosophical Understanding.* New York: Cambridge University Press, 1975.

Ricoeur, Paul. *Fallible Man.* Translated by C. Kelbley. Chicago: Henry Regnery, 1965.

Ricoeur, Paul. *Freud and Philosophy: An Essay on Interpretation.* Translated by Denis Savage. New Haven, Conn.: Yale University, Press, 1970.

Ricoeur, Paul. *Husserl: An Analysis of His Phenomenology.* Translated by Edward G. Ballard and Lester E. Embree. Evanston, Ill.: Northwestern University Press, 1967.

Ricoeur, Paul. *The Symbolism of Evil.* Translated by E. Buchanan. New York: Harper & Row, 1967.

Riepe, Dale, ed. *Phenomenology and Natural Existence: Essays in Honor of Marvin Farber.* Albany: State University of New York, 1973.

Roche, Maurice. *Phenomenology, Language, and the Social Sciences.* London: Routledge & Kegan Paul, 1973.

Sallis, John. *Phenomenology and the Return to Beginnings.* Pittsburgh, Pa.: Duquesne University Press, 1973.

Schrag, Calvin O. *Experience and Being: Prolegomena to a Future Ontology.* Evanston, Ill.: Northwestern University Press, 1969.

Schutz, Alfred. *Collected Papers, Vol. I, The Problem of Social Reality.* Edited by Maurice Natanson. The Hague: Martinus Nijhoff, 1962.

Schutz, Alfred. *Collected Papers, Vol. II, Studies in Social Theory.* Edited by Arvid Brodersen. The Hague: Martinus Nijhoff, 1964.

Schutz, Alfred. *Collected Papers, Vol. III, Studies in Phenomenological Philosophy.* Edited by I. Schutz. The Hague: Martinus Nijhoff, 1966.

Schutz, Alfred. *The Phenomenology of the Social World.* Translated by George Walsh and Frederick Lehnert. Evanston, Ill.: Northwestern University Press, 1967.

Schutz, Alfred, and Luckmann, Thomas, eds. *Structures of the Life-World.* Translated by Richard M. Zaner and H. Tristram Engelhardt, Jr. Evanston, Ill.: Northwestern University Press, 1973.

Sinha, Debabrata. *Studies in Phenomenology.* The Hague: Martinus Nijhoff, 1969.

Smith, F. Joseph, ed. *Phenomenology in Perspective.* The Hague: Martinus Nijhoff, 1970.

Sokolowski, Robert. *Husserlian Meditations: How Words Present Things.* Evanston, Ill.: Northwestern University Press, 1974.

Spiegelberg, Herbert. *Doing Phenomenology: Essays On and In Phenomenology.* The Hague: Martinus Nijhoff, 1976.

Stewart, David, and Algis Mickunas. *Exploring Phenomenology: A Guide to the Field and Its Literature.* Chicago: American Library Association, 1974.

Strasser, Stephan. *The Idea of Dialogal Phenomenology.* Translated by Henry J. Koren. Pittsburgh, Pa.: Duquesne University Press, 1969.

Strasser, Stephan. *Phenomenology and the Human Sciences: A Contribution to a New Scientific Ideal.* Translated by Henry J. Koren. Pittsburgh, Pa.: Duquesne University Press, 1963.

Strasser, Stephan. *The Soul in Metaphysical and Empirical Psychology.* Translated by Henry J. Koren. Pittsburgh, Pa.: Duquesne University Press, 1957.

Straus, Erwin. *The Primary World of Senses.* Translated by Jacob Needleman. Glencoe, Ill.: Free Press, 1963.

Thévenaz, Pierre. *What Is Phenomenology?* Translated by James M. Edie, Charles Courtney, and Paul Brockelman. Edited by James M. Edie. Chicago: Quadrangle, 1962.

Thibault, Herve J. *Creation and Metaphysics: A Genetic Approach to Existential Act.* The Hague: Martinus Nijhoff, 1970.

Tragesser, Robert S. *Phenomenology and Logic.* Ithaca, N.Y.: Cornell University Press, 1977.

Tymieniecka, Anna-Teresa, ed. *For Roman Ingarden: Nine Essays in Phenomenology.* The Hague: Martinus Nijhoff, 1959.

Tymieniecka, Anna-Teresa. *Analecta Husserliana: The Yearbook of Phenomenological Research.* Vols. 1 to 5. Dodrecht, Netherlands: D. Reidel Publishing Co., 1971-1976.

Tymieniecka, Anna-Teresa. *Phenomenology and Science in Contemporary European Thought.* New York: Noonday, 1962.

Tymieniecka, Anna-Teresa. *Why Is There Something Rather Than Nothing?* Assen, Netherlands: Van Gorcum, 1966.

Van Der Leeuw, Gerardus. *Religion in Essence and Manifestation: A Study in Phenomenology.* Translated by J. E. Turner. London: Allen & Unwin, 1938.

Van Peursen, Cornelis A. *Phenomenology and Analytic Philosophy.* Translated by Rex Ambler. Amended by Henry J. Koren. Pittsburgh, Pa.: Duquesne University Press, 1972.

Welch, E. Parl. *The Philosophy of Edmund Husserl: The Origin and Development of His Phenomenology.* New York: Columbia University Press, 1941.

Wilshire, Bruce. *William James and Phenomenology.* Bloomington: Indiana University Press, 1968.

Zaner, Richard M. *The Problem of Embodiment: Some Contributions to a Phenomenology of the Body.* The Hague: Martinus Nijhoff, 1964.

Zaner, Richard M. *The Way of Phenomenology: Criticism as a Philosophical Discipline.* New York: Pegasus, 1970.

Books on Existential Psychology

Allers, R. *Existentialism and Psychiatry.* Springfield, Mass.: Thomas, 1961.

Barton, Anthony. *Three Worlds of Therapy: An Existential-Phenomenological*

Study of the Therapies of Freud, Jung, and Rogers. Palo Alto, Calif.: Mayfield Publishing, 1974.

Binswanger, Ludwig. *Being-in-the-World: Selected Papers of Ludwig Binswanger.* Translated and edited by Jacob Needleman. New York: Basic Books, 1963.

Bogdon, Robert. *Introduction to Qualitative Research Methods: A Phenomenological Approach to the Social Sciences.* New York: Wiley, 1975.

Boss, Medard. *The Analysis of Dreams.* Translated by Arnold J. Pomerans. New York: Philosophical Library, 1958.

Boss, Medard. *Existential Foundations of Medicine and Psychology,* 2nd ed. New York: Aronson, 1977.

Boss, Medard. *Meaning and Content of Sexual Perversions: A Daseinsanalytic Approach to the Psychopathology of the Phenomenon of Love.* Translated by Liese Lewis Abell. New York: Grune & Stratton, 1949.

Boss, Medard. *Psychoanalysis and Daseinsanalysis.* Translated by Ludwig B. Lefebvre. New York: Basic Books, 1963.

Bugental, J. F. T., ed. *Challenges of Humanistic Psychology.* New York: McGraw-Hill, 1967.

Bugental, J. F. T. *The Search For Authenticity.* New York: Holt, Rinehart and Winston, 1965.

Bugental, James F. *The Search For Existential Identity.* San Francisco: Jossey-Bass, 1976.

Burton, A. *Modern Humanistic Psychotherapy.* San Francisco: Jossey-Bass, 1967.

Buytendijk, F. J. J. *Pain: Its Modes and Functions.* Translated by Eda O'Shiel. Chicago: University of Chicago Press, 1962.

Chamberlin, John Gordon. *Toward A Phenomenology of Education.* Philadelphia: Westminster Press, 1969.

Colaizzi, Paul Francis. *Reflection and Research in Psychology: A Phenomenological Study of Learning.* Dubuque, Iowa: Hunt Pub. Co., 1973.

Dempsey, Peter. *The Psychology of Sartre.* Westminster, Md.: Newman Press, 1950.

Denton, David E., ed. *Existentialism and Phenomenology in Education: Collected Essays.* New York: Teachers College Press, 1974.

Farber, Leslie. *The Ways of the Will: Essays Toward A Psychology and Psychopathology of the Will.* New York: Basic Books, 1966.

Feifel, Herman, ed. *The Meaning of Death.* New York: McGraw-Hill, 1959.

Frankl, Viktor. *The Doctor and the Soul.* Translated by Richard and Clara Winston. New York: Alfred A. Knopf, 1965.

Frankl, Viktor. *Man's Search For Meaning: An Introduction to Logotherapy.* Translated by Ilse Lasch. Boston: Beacon Press, 1963.

Frankl, Viktor. *Psychotherapy and Existentialism: Selected Papers on Logotherapy.* New York: Clarion Books, 1968.

Gendlin, Eugene T. *Experiencing and the Creation of Meaning: A Philosophical and Psychological Approach to the Subjective.* New York: The Free Press, 1962.

Giorgi, Amedeo; Fischer, William F.; and Eckartsberg, Rolf von, eds. *Duquesne Studies in Phenomenological Psychology: Volume 1.* Pittsburgh, Pa.: Duquesne University Press, 1971.

Giorgi, Amedeo; Fischer, Constance T.; and Murray, Edward L., eds., *Duquesne*

Studies in Phenomenological Psychology: Volume II. Pittsburgh, Pa.: Duquesne University Press, 1975.

Giorgi, Amedeo. *Psychology as a Human Science: A Phenomenologically Based Approach.* New York: Harper & Row, 1970.

Goldstein, Kurt. *Selected Papers.* Edited by Aron Gurwitsch et al. The Hague: Martinus Nijhoff, 1970.

Gustafson, D. F., ed. *Essays in Philosophical Psychology.* Garden City, N.Y.: Doubleday, 1964.

Johnson, Richard Eaton. *Existential Man: The Challenge of Psychotherapy.* New York: Pergamon Press, 1971.

Jung, Hwa Yol, ed. *Existential Phenomenology and Political Theory: A Reader.* Chicago: Henry Regnery, 1972.

Keen, Earnest. *Primer in Phenomenological Psychology.* New York: Holt, Rinehart & Winston, 1975.

Keen, Earnest. *Psychology and the New Consciousness.* Monterey, Calif.: Brooks/Cole, 1972.

Keen, Earnest. *Three Faces of Being: Toward an Existential Clinical Psychology.* New York: Appleton-Century-Crofts, 1970.

Koestenbaum, Peter. *Existential Sexuality: Choosing To Love.* Englewood Cliffs, N.J.: Prentice-Hall, 1974.

Koestenbaum, Peter. *Is There An Answer To Death?* Englewood Cliffs, N.J.: Prentice-Hall, 1976.

Koestenbaum, Peter. *Managing Anxiety: The Power of Knowing Who You Are.* Englewood Cliffs, N.J.: Prentice-Hall, 1974.

Koestenbaum, Peter. *The Vitality of Death: Essays in Existential Psychology and Philosophy.* Westport, Conn.: Greenwood, 1971.

Kraft, William F. *A Psychology of Nothingness.* Philadelphia: Westminster Press, 1974.

Laing, R. D. *The Divided Self: A Study of Sanity and Madness.* Chicago: Quadrangle Books, 1960.

Laing, R.D. *Interpersonal Perception: A Theory and a Method of Research* (with H. Phillipson and A. R. Lee). New York: Springer, 1960.

Laing, R. D. *The Politics of Experience.* New York: Pantheon, 1967.

Laing, R. D. *Sanity, Madness, and the Family.* New York: Basic Books, 1964.

Laing, R. D. *Self and Others: Further Studies in Sanity and Madness.* Chicago: Quadrangle Books, 1962.

Linschoten, H. *On the Way Toward A Phenomenological Psychology.* Edited by Amedeo Giorgi. Pittsburgh, Pa.: Duquesne University Press, 1968.

Lyons, Joseph. *Psychology and the Measure of Man: A Phenomenological Approach.* New York: Free Press, 1963.

May, Rollo. *The Courage to Create.* New York: Norton, 1975.

May, Rollo, ed. *Existential Psychology.* New York: Random House, 1961.

May, Rollo. *Love and Will.* New York: Norton, 1969.

May, Rollo. *Man's Search For Himself.* New York: Norton, 1953.

May, Rollo. *The Meaning of Anxiety.* New York: Ronald Press, 1950.

May, Rollo. *Power and Innocence: A Search for the Sources of Violence.* New York: Norton, 1972.

May, Rollo. *Psychology and the Human Dilemma*. Princeton, N.J.: Van Nostrand, 1967.

May, Rollo; Angel, Ernest; and Ellenberger, Henri F., eds. *Existence: A New Dimension in Psychiatry and Psychology*. New York: Basic Books, 1958.

Minkowski, Eugene. *Lived Time: Phenomenology and Psychopathological Studies*. Translated by Nancy Metzel. Evanston, Ill.: Northwestern University Press, 1970.

Misiak, H., and Sexton, V. *Phenomenological, Existential, and Humanistic Psychologies: A Historical Survey*. New York: Grone & Stratton, 1973.

Morano, Donald V. *Existential Guilt: A Phenomenological Study*. Assen, Netherlands: Van Gorcum, 1973.

Moustakas, Clark E. *Existentialist Child Therapy*. New York: Basic Books, 1966.

Natanson, Maurice, ed. *Psychiatry and Philosophy*. New York: Springer, 1969.

Ornstein, Robert. *The Psychology of Consciousness*. San Francisco: W. H. Freeman, 1972.

Park, James. *An Existential Understanding of Death: A Phenomenology of Ontological Anxiety*. Minneapolis: Existential Books, 1975.

Park, James. *Authentic Love: An Existential Vision*. Minneapolis: Existential Books, 1976.

Park, James. *Depression, Fragmentation, and the Void*. Minneapolis: Existential Books, 1976.

Park, James. *Obstacles to Existential Freedom*. Minneapolis: Existential Books, 1976.

Plessner, Helmuth. *Laughing and Crying: A Study of the Limits of Human Behavior*. Translated by James S. Churchill and Marjorie Grene. Evanston, Ill.: Northwestern University Press, 1970.

Psathas, George, ed. *Phenomenological Sociology: Issues and Applications*. New York: Wiley, 1973.

Ranly, Earnest W. *Scheler's Phenomenology of Community*. The Hague: Martinus Nijhoff, 1966.

Reeves, Clement. *The Psychology of Rollo May: A Study in Existential Theory and Psychotherapy*. San Francisco: Jossey-Bass, 1977.

Ruitenbeek, Hendrik M., ed. *Psychoanalysis and Existential Philosophy*. New York: E. P. Dutton, 1962.

Sadler, William A. *Existence and Love: A New Approach in Existential Phenomenology*. New York: Charles Scribner's Sons, 1969.

Severin, Frank T. *Discovering Man in Psychology: A Humanistic Approach*. New York: McGraw-Hill, 1973.

Severin, Frank T. *Humanistic Viewpoints in Psychology*. New York: McGraw-Hill, 1965.

Sonnemann, Ulrich. *Existence and Therapy: An Introduction to Phenomenological Psychology and Existential Analysis*. New York: Grune & Stratton, 1954.

Stein, Edith. *On the Problem of Empathy*. Translated by Waltraut Stein. The Hague: Martinus Nijhoff, 1964.

Straus, Erwin, ed. *Language and Language Disturbances. Fifth Lexington Con-

ference on Phenomenology Pure and Applied. Pittsburgh, Pa.: Duquesne University Press, 1974.

Straus, Erwin. *On Obsession: A Clinical and Methodological Study.* New York: Nervous and Mental Disease Monographs, 1948.

Straus, Erwin W. *Phenomenological Psychology: Selected Papers.* Translated by Erling Eng. New York: Basic Books, 1966.

Straus, Erwin W., ed. *Phenomenology, Pure and Applied: The First Lexington Conference.* Pittsburgh, Pa.: Duquesne University Press, 1964.

Straus, Erwin, and Griffith, Richard M., eds., *Phenomenology of Will and Action: The Second Lexington Conference.* Pittsburgh, Pa.: Duquesne University Press, 1967.

Straus, Erwin, and Griffith, Richard, eds. *Phenomenology of Memory: The Third Lexington Conference on Pure and Applied Phenomenology.* Pittsburgh, Pa.: Duquesne University Press, 1970.

Straus, Erwin W., ed. *Aisthesis and Aesthetics: The Fourth Lexington Conference on Phenomenology: Pure and Applied.* Pittsburgh, Pa.: Duquesne University Press, 1972.

Tiryakian, Edward A. *Sociologism and Existentialism: Two Perspectives on the Individual and Society.* Englewood Cliffs, N.J.: Prentice-Hall, 1962.

Ungersma, Aaron J. *The Search For Meaning: A New Approach in Psychotherapy and Pastoral Psychology.* Philadelphia: Westminster Press, 1961.

Van Den Berg, J.H. *The Changing Nature of Man: Introduction to a Historical Psychology, Metabletica.* Translated by H.F. Croes. New York: Norton, 1961.

Van Den Berg, H.J. *A Different Existence: Principles of Phenomenological Psychopathology.* Pittsburgh, Pa.: Duquesne University Press, 1972.

Van Den Berg, J.H. *The Phenomenological Approach to Psychiatry: An Introduction to Recent Phenomenological Psychopathology.* Springfield, Ill.: Charles C. Thomas, 1955.

Van Den Berg, J.H. and Buytendijk, F.J., eds. *Scientific Contributions to a Phenomenological Psychology and Psychopathology.* Springfield, Ill.: Charles C. Thomas, 1955.

Van Kaam, Adrian. *Existential Foundations of Psychology.* Pittsburgh, Pa.: Duquesne University Press, 1966.

Van Kaam, Adrian. *The Art of Existential Counseling.* Wilkes-Barre, Pa.: Dimension Books, 1966.

Van Kaam, Adrian, and Healy, Kathleen. *The Demon and the Dove: Personality Growth Through Literature.* Pittsburgh, Pa.: Duquesne University Press, 1967.

Von Bayer, W., and Griffiths, R., eds. *Conditio Humana: Erwin Straus on His 75th Birthday.* Berlin and New York: Springer, 1966.

Waldman, Roy D. *Humanistic Psychiatry: From Opposition to Choice.* New Brunswick, N.J.: Rutgers University Press, 1971.

Wann, T. W., ed. *Behaviorism and Phenomenology: Contrasting Bases for Modern Psychology.* Chicago: University of Chicago Press, 1965.

Weisman, Avery D. *The Existential Core of Psychoanalysis: Reality, Sense, and Responsibility.* Boston: Little, Brown, 1965.

Wolff, Werner. *Values and Personality: An Existential Psychology of Crisis.* New York: Grune & Stratton, 1950.

Journals

Human Context. Paul A. Senft, ed. The Hague: Martinus Nijhoff, 1968-1975.

Humanitas: Journal of the Institute of Man. Adrian Van Kaam, ed. Pittsburgh, Pa.: Duquesne University Press, 1966-.

Journal of Existentialism. (Formerly *Journal of Existential Psychiatry*). Robert Meister, ed. New York: Libra Publishers, 1959-1975.

Journal of Existential Psychiatry. Jordan Scher, ed. New York: Libra Publishers, 1960-1964.

Journal of Humanistic Psychology. Tom Greening, ed. San Francisco: The Association for Humanistic Psychology, 1961-present.

Journal of Phenomenological Psychology. Amedeo Giorgi, George Thines, and Carl F. Grawmann, eds. New York: Humanities Press, 1970-present.

Philosophy and Phenomenological Research. Marvin Farber, ed. Buffalo: State University of New York at Buffalo, 1940-present.

Research in Phenomenology. John Sallis, ed. Pittsburgh, Pa.: Duquesne University Press, 1971-present.

Review of Existential Psychology and Psychiatry. Adrian Van Kaam, ed. Pittsburgh, Pa.: Duquesne University Press, 1961-1973.

INDEX

ABOUT THE AUTHOR

PETER KOESTENBAUM is professor of philosophy at San Jose State University, California. His books include a translation of Husserl's *Paris Lectures* as well as *Philosophy: A General Introduction*, *The Vitality of Death: Essays in Existential Psychology and Philosophy* (Greenwood Press, 1971), *Managing Anxiety*, *Existential Sexuality*, and *Is There an Answer to Death?*